Virginia Reader

Virginia READER

A Treasury of Writings

From the first voyages to the present

EDITED WITH AN INTRODUCTION
AND NOTES BY
FRANCIS COLEMAN ROSENBERGER

NEW YORK
Published by E. P. Dutton & Company
1948

Contents

5

Contents

6

Contents

Contents

8

Contents

9

Contents

10

Contents

11

Contents

INTRODUCTION

Three and a half centuries and more ago — in the summer of the year 1584 — Captain Arthur Barlowe and his companions, sent out from England by Walter Raleigh, sailed up the coast of North America. On July 13 the little expedition took possession of the land in the name of Queen Elizabeth. On their return to England the Queen named the land *Virginia.* Captain Barlowe's report to Raleigh is the opening selection in this volume. Captain Barlowe did not reach the bounds of the present state of Virginia, but I do not believe that he should be denied his place as the first Virginia writer only because, like Moses, he saw the Promised Land from afar. "We smelt so sweet, and so strong a smel, as if we had bene in the midst of some delicate garden," wrote Captain Barlowe — and what Virginian will say that he was writing about North Carolina?

Virginia writing — and with it American writing — is commonly thought of as beginning with the remarkably literate colony at Jamestown in 1607. In this Reader I have pushed back the date to include, with Barlowe, the authors of two other narratives written before that first permanent English settlement. Ralph Lane, governor of Raleigh's abortive settlement on Roanoke Island in 1585-1586, gave in his *Particularities of the Countrey of Virginia* an account well reckoned to stir the spirit of adventure in others. Lane's Virginia was a land where a native King — Lane was eager to believe the rumors — "had so greate quantitie of Pearle, and doeth so ordinarily take the same, as that not onely his owne skinnes that hee weareth, and the better sort of his gentlemen and followers are full set with the sayd Pearle, but also his beds, and houses are garnished with them." In a land where the houses were garnished with pearls, it could hardly matter that "we had nothing in the world to eate but pottage of Sassafras leaves, the like whereof for a meate was never used before as I thinke."

Virginia Reader

With Lane on Roanoke Island was a more sober observer, the young scientist Thomas Harriot. Harriot made careful notes on the life of the New World, on the plants and animals found there and the manners and customs of the natives. When the expedition returned to England with Sir Francis Drake, Lane took with him a rope of inferior pearls — which he lost in a storm when boarding ship — but Harriot brought back to England such strange new plants as that called *Uppowoc*, or *Tobacco*. Harriot's *A brief and true report of the new found land of Virginia*, which was published in London in 1588, is both a vivid and a trustworthy account of the New World. From Harriot's *Virginia* I have chosen here the note on tobacco, from his descriptive catalogue of plants, and his discerning account of *The Nature and Manners of the People*.

It was twenty years after Lane and Harriot sailed away from Roanoke Island that a permanent settlement was made at Jamestown. Five days before Christmas in the year 1606 an expedition for Virginia sailed down the Thames from London. With the expedition were George Percy and Captain John Smith, who wrote memorable accounts of the settlement. Four long months after leaving London the expedition entered Chesapeake Bay. The colonists sailed up the James River and, as recorded in the excerpt from Percy's account which I have included here, they reached the site of Jamestown "where our shippes doe lie so neere the shoare that they are moored to the Trees in six fathom water." The settlement of Virginia — a vast and unknown area stretching indefinitely to the west — was begun. Of the extensive writings of Captain John Smith, the most forceful figure in the colony, I have included here in full his first account of Virginia (which does not mention the Pocahontas incident) — *A True Relation of such Occurrences and Accidents of Note as hath hapned in Virginia since the first Planting of that Colony* — which was published in London in 1608, just a year after the first settlement was established.

II

From these first accounts of discovery and settlement to the present I have ranged through the rich and varied writing of Virginia to

Introduction

put together this Virginia Reader. I have had no fixed and rigid standards of selection, but have gone forward on the assumption that things which interest me may interest others. The boundaries which I have imposed have been loose ones. In the earliest period, I have limited the selections to the writings of those who actually visited the New World — even when that meant the exclusion of such fine writing as Michael Drayton's poem "To the Virginia Voyage." After the first settlement, most of the authors included here were born in Virginia or lived for a substantial period in Virginia. James Blair, the founder of the College of William and Mary and its president for a half a century, was born in Scotland; but I should hate to meet the ghost of that worthy and disputatious gentleman if I questioned his right to be called a Virginian. A lesser period of residence, a year or two, sufficed for the inclusion of one who left so distinct a picture of life in Virginia as that provided by Philip Vickers Fithian, plantation tutor in Virginia just before the Revolution.

The subject matter of most of the earlier writing is one aspect or another of Virginia, but I have not insisted upon that rule in every case. In the excerpt which I have included from William Strachey's *A True Reportory of the Wracke, and Redemption of Sir Thomas Gates* — a narrative to which Mr. William Shakespeare was considerably indebted in writing *The Tempest* — the storm which Strachey describes was not off the coast of Virginia but off the Bermudas. But the narrative was written in Virginia, where Strachey went on to become secretary of the colony, which seems to me justification aplenty for its inclusion here. And I must admit to a particular fondness for the notion of William Strachey, in the little colony of Jamestown in 1610, writing out his narrative which was to have such an impressive literary influence.

On the other hand, I have not included writing the subject matter of which is so far afield of Virginia as George Sandys' translation of Ovid, even though Sandys worked on his translation at Jamestown and may properly be considered one of Virginia's first men of letters.

The arrangement of the Reader, as will be immediately apparent, is (with a few adjustments) chronological by the date of the birth of the author. This has seemed to me a more practical arrangement

15

than a division by kinds of writing, particularly where there is such a variety of material as I have included here — narratives of exploration and settlement, journals, letters, poems, state papers, public addresses, essays, sketches, short stories and excerpts from novels. And, in fact, the present arrangement provides a certain natural grouping by kinds of writing: the narratives of exploration and settlement inevitably come together in the first portion of the book; the great state papers of the Revolutionary era were written by men who were born within a score of years of each other; the more consciously literary work belongs to the present and the not too distant past.

A biographical note precedes the work of each of the writers included in this Reader. I have been at some pains to make them accurate, but as I have encountered an occasional error even in the *Dictionary of American Biography*, I know that some may be present here. I shall welcome corrections from any reader who may catch me nodding.

A word should be said about the two narratives which, with the full text of Captain John Smith's *A True Relation*, are the longest single selections in this Reader. They are Henry Norwood's *A Voyage to Virginia* (1649) and William Byrd's *A Journey to the Land of Eden in the Year 1733.*

I have read Norwood's *A Voyage to Virginia* with such pleasure that I could not bring myself to offer it to others in an abbreviated version. It is included here in full. Little more is known of Norwood than the bare facts which I have given in the biographical note preceding his narrative, but his personality is revealed so fully in that engaging narrative that he becomes one of the most memorable figures of Virginia's first century. *A Voyage to Virginia* was published in London in 1732 in Awnsham Churchill's *A Collection of Voyages and Travels*. It has been reprinted in full in the United States but once, in Force's *Tracts* in 1844. Some time after I first came upon it, I was pleased to find my enthusiasm for it shared by Howard Mumford Jones, who has written in his recent monograph, *The Literature of Virginia in the Seventeenth Century* (1946): "Why Norwood's *Voyage to Virginia* is not better known to lovers of good narrative must remain a mystery. Almost the first full-blooded adventure story

16

Introduction

in American literature (for Norwood's whole interest is simply in saving his skin and the lives of his associates), the *Voyage to Virginia* is a kind of cross between Daniel Defoe and Samuel Pepys — Defoe-like in its verisimilitude, Pepysian in its exposure, innocent or self-conscious, of the inconsistencies of human nature."

William Byrd's *A Journey to the Land of Eden in the Year 1733*, like Norwood's narrative, reveals as much about the author as about Virginia and provides a double pleasure to the discerning reader. It is printed here in full. I have been generous with space because of its very real interest and for the reason that while Byrd's literary accomplishment has been generally recognized, at least since the publication of Professor John Spencer Bassett's scholarly edition of *The Writings of "Colonel William Byrd, of Westover in Virginia, Esqr."* in 1901, copies of his narratives are not today easy to come by. Selections from Byrd's diaries have recently had a wide circulation, but his more polished writing has remained out of print since the publication of Mark Van Doren's pleasant little volume, *A Journey to the Land of Eden and Other Papers*, in 1928.

III

Virginia's most brilliant era — what Professor Dumas Malone, biographer of Jefferson, has called "The Great Generation" — produced a group of men whose equal it would be difficult to find in any country in any age. I have given them a large portion of this Reader, but nothing proportionate with their importance. Thomas Jefferson, James Madison, George Mason, John Marshall, George Washington, Patrick Henry, James Monroe — their names are a roster of the architects of the Revolution and the Union. Their genius was government, but the lucid prose in which George Mason set forth the Virginia Bill of Rights or Jefferson dealt with the principles of a democratic society are a part of the literary as well as the political heritage of America.

Jefferson published but one book, his *Notes on Virginia*, which was issued in Paris in 1784, but the total amount of his writing is staggering. There are in existence some 18,000 Jefferson letters. The twenty-volume edition of *The Writings of Thomas Jefferson*, edited

17

Virginia Reader

by Andrew A. Lipscomb and Albert Ellery Bergh in 1905, contains but a small part of his work. Now, more than 200 years after Jefferson's birth, the first comprehensive edition of his correspondence and papers is in progress. The projected edition, under the direction of Julian P. Boyd, Librarian of Princeton University, has been made possible by a gift of $200,000 and it is estimated that it will run to some fifty volumes. In the present Reader I have attempted to select a handful of pages from Jefferson's best-known writings which would suggest a little of the mind and heart of this, the greatest of all Virginians.

Second only to the incomparable Jefferson, James Madison was the most brilliant figure in the Revolutionary era in Virginia. Madison's full importance is only beginning to be generally recognized with the publication of Irving Brant's comprehensive biography, two volumes of which, following Madison through the first thirty-six of the eighty-five years of his life, have been published: *James Madison, The Virginia Revolutionist, 1751-1780* and *James Madison, The Nationalist, 1780-1787*. I have chosen here Madison's *A Memorial and Remonstrance to the Virginia General Assembly* of 1785, which opened the way for the passage the following year of Jefferson's Act for Establishing Religious Freedom in Virginia, and which says all that is likely ever to need be said on the separation of church and state.

Standing as the equal of the great papers of Jefferson and Madison is the *Virginia Bill of Rights*, drafted in 1776 by George Mason. "A Declaration of Rights made by the Representatives of the good People of Virginia, assembled in full and Free Convention; which Rights do pertain to them, and their Posterity, as the Basis and Foundation of Government," it is one of the great statements of the rights of man and it was a document of seminal influence on both the American and French Revolutions.

Of the leader of the Revolutionary forces, it is perhaps true that nothing which he himself wrote suggests his character so well as does the admiration which he evoked in others. I have accordingly included here the famous oration on Washington by Henry Lee and the estimate of Washington from the closing pages of the biography

18

Introduction

by John Marshall. Of Washington's own voluminous state papers, I have selected but one, his brief *Reply to Congress on Appointment as Commander-in-Chief*. In addition, I have included the engaging diary written by the sixteen-year-old Washington during a surveying trip in the Shenandoah Valley.

If the limits of this brief Introduction would permit it, it would be a pleasant occupation to provide some commentary upon each of the selections which I have included in this Reader. The main currents, too, in the intellectual development of Virginia in the several periods of its history invite comment: the decline of the "Virginia Dynasty" in national affairs (which came to an end when James Monroe left the Presidency in 1825, and sputtered out in the pyrotechnics of John Randolph); the making of Civil War and its aftermath; the comparatively recent concern with formal literature. But the selections themselves must be the justification for this book. I will add here only a word or two more on the making of the Reader.

IV

If there seems a scarcity of poems in this volume, it is because of somewhat strict standards of admission rather than any lack of verse by Virginia writers. When Professor F. V. N. Painter published his *Poets of Virginia* in 1907 he found, in the 300 years since Jamestown, some 110 Virginia writers who had published a volume, or more than one, of verse — better than a book of verse for every three years. In *Virginian Writers of Fugitive Verse* (1923) Professor Armistead C. Gordon, Jr. made a book — and an interesting book — of the work of still other Virginia poets whose verse had never been collected in volumes of their own. More recently Mary Sinton Leitch assembled a creditable anthology, *Lyric Virginia Today* (1932), from the work of twenty-one contemporary Virginia poets. Perhaps there is not one of Virginia's hundred counties which cannot boast its own poet of the past or present — and often a poet of sensibility. Here I have limited their representation to the dozen or so poets whose work has seemed to me to be of the greatest interest.

The first of these is Richard Rich, "one of the voyage" of 1609, who set down his "Newes from Virginia" in verse. "If thou asks why," he wrote, "It was onely to feede mine owne humour." That has been the most compelling motivation of Virginia poets ever since.

The only other poet before Poe whom I have included is the able — and anonymous — author of "Bacon's Epitaph." Written in 1676 or thereabouts, "Bacon's Epitaph" is a remarkably fine poem and an eloquent expression of man's opposition to tyranny — a theme in Virginia writing which has seldom found as successful expression in verse as in prose.

In the long years between the time of Bacon and the time of Poe, there was verse aplenty in Virginia, but I have found none which seemed to me of such present interest as to demand inclusion here. I have also stopped short of the province of the ballad collector, and will be content with citing a landmark in that field: *Traditional Ballads of Virginia*, edited by Professor Arthur Kyle Davis, Jr. (1929).

Poe was the first man of letters in Virginia — and perhaps in America — who was primarily concerned with problems of aesthetics. He remains Virginia's finest poet — if, indeed, Virginia has any exclusive claim upon him, when, as a later poet has remarked, "Four cities claim him as France recommended."

While they are overshadowed by Poe, there were other nineteenth century poets of interest in Virginia. I have included Philip Pendleton Cooke's "Life in the Autumn Woods," one of James Barron Hope's "Three Summer Studies" and John Banister Tabb's "Poe's Purgatory." And, as a better than average example of the verse of the Civil War, I have included John Reuben Thompson's "Ashby."

In the twentieth century there are a number of Virginia poets of ability, and the problem of selection becomes more difficult. I have chosen the eight whose work has given me the most pleasure. The best of recent writing, it seems to me, has been poetry rather than novels or short stories, so that this Reader closes with three contemporary poets.

V

Finally, this is not quite the anthology which I first assembled. The manuscript which I delivered to the publishers was 150 pages

Introduction

longer than could be included in even this large volume. The required deletion was like saying good-bye to old friends. It was with especial regret that I omitted a fine critical essay, "Ellen Glasgow: Ironic Idealist," by James Southall Wilson, but it seemed better to include as long a selection as possible from Miss Glasgow's own work than to include even the best of writing about her. Professor Wilson's essay will well repay the reader who will seek it out in the Winter, 1939, issue of the *Virginia Quarterly Review*. Selections from three well-known Virginia writers of the preceding generation — Armistead C. Gordon (1855-1931), a Virginia lawyer who was also a novelist, poet, biographer and short-story writer; Amèlie Rives (1863-1945), novelist, poet and playwright; and Mary Johnston (1870-1936), novelist and short-story writer — were reluctantly omitted. Edgar Allan Poe is here represented by a single short story rather than by the several which were originally included, and there are others who are more concisely represented than was the case in the original manuscript of this Reader. But the Virginia Reader in your hands, with its selections from more than sixty authors, is a larger book by far than was anticipated by its publishers.

To the publishers, for their generosity with space as in other matters, I owe a debt of gratitude. And, especially, to Mr. Nicholas Wreden and Miss Louise Townsend Nicholl of the Editorial Department, who have followed the making of this Reader with sympathetic understanding from its beginning, I am permanently indebted.

Francis Coleman Rosenberger

Alexandria, Virginia
Summer, 1948

Virginia Reader

ARTHUR BARLOWE

1550?-1620?

Arthur Barlowe was the captain of one of the two vessels which Walter Raleigh sent out on a voyage of exploration to the New World in 1584. Raleigh, then in his early thirties, had long shared with his half-brother, Sir Humphrey Gilbert, a keen interest in the exploration and colonization of the New World.

Gilbert had obtained a patent from Queen Elizabeth in 1578, good for six years, giving him authority to take possession of new lands, and he set out during the same year on a voyage to the west. Raleigh accompanied him as captain of the *Falcon,* and when Gilbert was forced to return to England Raleigh sailed on to harass Spanish shipping. In 1583 Gilbert set out again with five ships. He reached Newfoundland, but on the return voyage was lost at sea in a storm off the Azores.

Raleigh's rapid rise in favor with Queen Elizabeth made it possible for him to continue the work of exploration. Shortly before the expiration of Gilbert's patent, Raleigh obtained a similar license, good for an additional six years, "to discover, search, find out, and view such remote, heathen and barbarous lands, countreis, and territories, not actually possessed of any Christian prince, nor inhabited by Christian people . . ."

Raleigh immediately fitted out two vessels and dispatched them under the command of Captain Arthur Barlowe and Captain Philip Amandas on a voyage of exploration. They reached North America and explored the coast, but did not sail as far north as the present bounds of the state of Virginia. They took possession of the new land on July 13, 1584. On the return of the expedition to England, Queen Elizabeth conferred a knighthood on Raleigh and named the new land Virginia.

Captain Barlowe, of whom little is known except for his part in the expedition, wrote an enthusiastic account of what they found and addressed it to "sir Walter Ralegh, knight, at whose charge and direction, the said voyage was set forth." Captain Barlowe's account follows.

CAPTAIN ARTHUR BARLOWE'S NARRATIVE
OF THE FIRST VOYAGE TO VIRGINIA: 1584

The first voyage made to the coasts of America, with two barks,
wherein were Captaines M. Philip Amadas, and M. Arthur Barlowe,
who discovered part of the Countrey now called Virginia, Anno 1584.
Written by one of the said Captaines, and sent to sir Walter Ralegh
knight, at whose charge and direction, the said voyage was set forth.

The 27 day of Aprill, in the yeere of our redemption, 1584 we departed the West of England, with two barkes well furnished with
men and victuals, having received our last and perfect directions
by your letters, confirming the former instructions, and commande-
ments delivered by your selfe at our leaving the river Thames. And
I thinke it a matter both unnecessary, for the manifest discoverie of
the Countrey, as also for tediousnesse sake, to remember unto you
the diurnall of our course, sayling thither and returning: onely I
have presumed to present unto you this briefe discourse, by which
you may judge how profitable this land is likely to succeede, as well
to your selfe, (by whose direction and charge, and by whose serv-
antes this our discoverie hath beene performed) as also to her
Highnesse, and the Common wealth, in which we hope your wisedome wilbe satisfied, considering that as much by us hath bene
brought to light, as by those smal meanes, and number of men we
had, could any way have bene expected, or hoped for.

The tenth of May we arrived at the Canaries, and the tenth of
June in this present yeere, we were fallen with the Islands of the
West Indies, keeping a more Southeasterly course then was neede-
full, because wee doubted that the current of the Bay of Mexico, dis-
bogging betweene the Cape of Florida and Havana, had bene of
greater force than afterwardes we found it to bee. At which Islands

26

we found the ayre very unwholsome, and our men grew for the most part ill disposed: so that having refreshed our selves with sweet water and fresh victuall, we departed the twelfth day of our arrivall there. These Islands, with the rest adjoyning, are so well knowen to your selfe, and to many others, as I will not trouble you with the remembrance of them.

The second of July, we found shole water, wher we smelt so sweet, and so strong a smel, as if we had bene in the midst of some delicate garden abounding with all kinde of odoriferous flowers, by which we were assured, that the land could not be farre distant: and keeping good watch, and bearing but slacke saile, the fourth of the same moneth we arrived upon the coast, which we supposed to be a continent and firme lande, and we sayled along the same a hundred and twentie English miles before we could finde any entrance, or river issuing into the Sea. The first that appeared unto us, we entered, though not without some difficultie, and cast anker about three harquebuz-shot within the havens mouth, on the left hand of the same: and after thankes given to God for our safe arrivall thither, we manned our boats, and went to view the land next adjoyning, and to take possession of the same, in the right of the Queenes most excellent Majestie, as rightfull Queene, and Princesse of the same, and after delivered the same over to your use, according to her Majesties grant, and letters patents, under her Highnesse great seale. Which being performed, according to the ceremonies used in such enterprises, we viewed the land about us, being, whereas we first landed, very sandie and low towards the waters side, but so full of grapes, as the very beating and surge of the sea overflowed them, of which we found such plentie, as well there as in all places else, both on the sand and on the greene soile on the hils, as in the plaines, as well on every little shrubbe, as also climing towardes the tops of high Cedars, that I thinke in all the world the like abundance is not to be found: and my selfe having seene those parts of Europe that most abound, find such differences as were incredible to be written.

We passed from the Sea side towardes the toppes of those hilles next adjoyning, being but of meane hight, and from thence wee behelde the Sea on both sides to the North, and to the South, finding no ende any of both wayes. This lande lay stretching it selfe to the

27

West, which after wee found to bee but an Island of twentie miles long, and not above sixe miles broade. Under the banke or hill whereon we stoode, we behelde the vallyes replenished with goodly Cedar trees, and having discharged our harquebuz-shot, such a flocke of Cranes (the most part white) arose under us, with such a cry redoubled by many ecchoes, as if an armie of men had showted all together.

This Island had many goodly woodes full of Deere, Conies, Hares, and Fowle, even in the middest of Summer in incredible abundance. The woodes are not such as you finde in Bohemia, Moscovia, or Hercynia, barren and fruitles, but the highest and reddest Cedars of the world, farre bettering the Ceders of the Açores, of the Indies, or Lybanus, Pynes, Cypres, Sassaphras, the Lentisk, or the tree that beareth the Masticke, the tree that beareth the rine of blacke Sinamon, of which Master Winter brought from the streights of Magellan, and many other of excellent smell and qualitie. We remained by the side of this Island two whole dayes before we saw any people of the Countrey: the third day we espied one small boate rowing towardes us having in it three persons: this boat came to the Island side, foure harquebuz-shot from our shippes, and there two of the people remaining, the third came along the shoreside towards us, and wee being then all within boord, he walked up and downe upon the point of the land next unto us: then the Master and the Pilot of the Admirall, Simon Ferdinando, and the Captaine Philip Amadas, my selfe, and others rowed to the land, whose comming this fellow attended, never making any shewe of feare or doubt. And after he had spoken of many things not understood by us, we brought him with his owne good liking, aboord the ships, and gave him a shirt, a hat and some other things, and made him taste of our wine, and our meat, which he liked very wel: and after having viewed both barks, he departed, and went to his owne boat againe, which hee had left in a little Cove or Creeke adjoyning: assoone as hee was two bow shoot into the water, he fell to fishing, and in lesse then halfe an houre, he had laden his boate as deepe, as it could swimme, with which hee came againe to the point of the lande, and there he divided his fish into two parts, pointing one part to the ship, and the

Arthur Barlowe, 1550?-1620?

other to the pinnesse: which, after he had (as much as he might) requited the former benefites received, departed out of our sight.

The next day there came unto us divers boates, and in one of them the Kings brother, accompanied with fortie or fiftie men, very handsome and goodly people, and in their behaviour as mannerly and civill as any of Europe. His name was Granganimeo, and the king is called Wingina, the countrey Wingandacoa[1] and now by her Majestie Virginia. The manner of his comming was in this sort: hee left his boates altogether as the first man did a little from the shippes by the shore, and came along to the place over against the ships, followed with fortie men. When he came to the place, his servants spread a long matte upon the ground, on which he sate downe, and at the other ende of the matte foure others of his companie did the like, the rest of his men stood round about him, somewhat a farre off: when we came to the shore to him with our weapons, hee never mooved from his place, nor any of the other foure, nor never mistrusted any harme to be offered from us, but sitting still he beckoned us to come and sit by him, which we performed: and being set hee made all signes of joy and welcome, striking on his head and his breast and afterwardes on ours, to shew wee were all one, smiling and making shewe the best he could of all love, and familiaritie. After hee had made a long speech unto us, wee presented him with divers things, which hee received very joyfully, and thankefully. None of the companie durst speake one worde all the time: onely the foure which were at the other ende, spake one in the others eare very softly.

The King is greatly obeyed, and his brothers and children reverenced: the King himselfe in person was at our being there, sore wounded in a fight which hee had with the King of the next countrey, called Wingina, and was shot in two places through the body, and once cleane through the thigh, but yet he recovered: by reason whereof and for that hee lay at the chiefe towne of the countrey, being six dayes journey off, we saw him not at all.

After we had presented this his brother with such things as we

[1]An error in understanding the language of the natives; Wingandacoa means "You wear fine clothes."

thought he liked, wee likewise gave somewhat to the other that sat with him on the matte: but presently he arose and tooke all from them and put it into his owne basket, making signes and tokens, that all things ought to bee delivered unto him, and the rest were but his servants, and followers. A day or two after this, we fell to trading with them, exchanging some things that we had, for Chamoys, Buffe, and Deere skinnes: when we shewed him all our packet of merchandize, of all things that he sawe, a bright tinne dish most pleased him, which hee presently tooke up and clapt it before his breast, and after made a hole in the brimme thereof and hung it about his necke, making signes that it would defende him against his enemies arrowes: for those people maintaine a deadly and terrible warre, with the people and King adjoyning. We exchanged our tinne dish for twentie skinnes, woorth twentie Crownes, or twentie Nobles: and a copper kettle for fiftie skins woorth fiftie Crownes. They offered us good exchange for our hatchets, and axes, and for knives, and would have given anything for swordes: but wee would not depart with any. After two or three dayes the Kings brother came aboord the shippes, and dranke wine, and eat of our meat and of our bread, and liked exceedingly thereof: and after a few dayes overpassed, he brought his wife with him to the ships, his daughter and two or three children: his wife was very well favoured, of meane stature, and very bashfull: shee had on her backe a long cloake of leather, with the furre side next to her body, and before her a piece of the same: about her forehead shee had a bande of white Corall, and so had her husband many times: in her eares shee had bracelets of pearles hanging downe to her middle, (whereof wee delivered your worship a little bracelet) and those were of the bignes of good pease. The rest of her women of the better sort had pendants of copper hanging in either eare, and some of the children of the kings brother and other noble men, have five or sixe in either eare: he himselfe had upon his head a broad plate of golde, or copper, for being unpolished we knew not what mettal it should be, neither would he by any meanes suffer us to take it off his head, but feeling it, it would bow very easily. His apparell was as his wives, onely the women weare their haire long on both sides, and the men but on one. They are of colour yellowish, and their haire black for the most part, and yet we saw children that had very fine aburne and chestnut coloured haire.[2]

After that these women had bene there, there came downe from all parts great store of people, bringing with them leather, corall, divers kindes of dies, very excellent, and exchanged with us: but when Granganimeo the kings brother was present, none durst trade but himselfe: except such as weare red pieces of copper on their heads like himselfe: for that is the difference betweene the noble men, and the governours of countreys, and the meaner sort. And we both noted there, and you have understood since by these men, which we brought home, that no people in the worlde cary more respect to their King, Nobilitie, and Governours, than these do. The Kings brothers wife, when she came to us (as she did many times) was followed with forty or fifty women alwayes: and when she came into the shippe, she left them all on land, saving her two daughters, her nurse and one or two more. The Kings brother alwayes kept this order, as many boates as he would come withall to the shippes, so many fires would hee make on the shore a farre off, to the end we might understand with what strength and company he approched. Their boates are made of one tree, either of Pine or of Pitch trees: a wood not commenly knowen to our people, nor found growing in England. They have no edge-tooles to make them withall: if they have any they are very fewe, and those it seemes they had twentic yeres since, which, as those two men declared, was out of a wrake which happened upon their coast of some Christian ship, being beaten that way by some storme and outragious weather, whereof none of the people were saved, but only the ship, or some part of her being cast upon the sand, out of whose sides they drew the nayles and the spikes, and with those they made their best instruments. The manner of making their boates is thus: they burne downe some great tree, or take such as are winde fallen, and putting gumme and rosen upon one side thereof, they set fire into it, and when it hath burnt it hollow, they cut out the coale with their shels, and ever where they would burne it deeper or wider they lay on gummes, which burne away the timber, and by this meanes they fashion very

[2]Perhaps the descendants of earlier voyagers who, according to the natives, had been wrecked on the coast.

fine boates, and such as will transport twentie men. Their oares are
like scoopes, and many times they set with long poles, as the depth
serveth.

The Kings brother had great liking of our armour, a sword, and
divers other things which we had: and offered to lay a great box of
pearle in gage for them: but we refused it for this time, because we
would not make them knowe, that we esteemed thereof, untill we
had understoode in what places of the countrey the pearle grew:
which now your Worshippe doeth very well understand.

He was very just of his promise: for many times we delivered him
merchandize upon his word, but ever he came within the day and
performed his promise. He sent us every day a brase or two of fat
Bucks, Conies, Hares, Fish the best of the world. He sent us divers
kindes of fruites, Melons, Walnuts, Cucumbers, Gourdes, Pease, and
divers rootes, and fruites very excellent good, and of their Countrey
corne, which is very white, faire and well tasted, and groweth three
times in five moneths: in May they sow, in July they reape, in June
they sow, in August they reape: in July they sow, in September they
reape: onely they cast the corne into the ground, breaking a little of
the soft turfe with a wodden mattock, or pickeaxe: our selves
prooved the soile, and put some of our Pease in the ground, and in
tenne dayes they were of fourteene ynches high: they have also
Beanes very faire of diverse colours and wonderfull plentie: some
growing naturally, and some in their gardens, and so have they both
wheat and oates.

The soile is the most plentifull, sweete, fruitfull and wholsome of
all the worlde: there are above fourteene severall sweete smelling
timber trees, and the most part of their underwoods are Bayes and
such like: they have those Okes that we have, but farre greater and
better. After they had bene divers times aboord our shippes, my
selfe, with seven more went twentie mile into the River, that runneth towarde the Citie of Skicoak,[3] which River they call Occam:
and the evening following, wee came to an Island which they call
Raonoak, distant from the harbour by which we entered, seven
leagues: and at the north end thereof was a village of nine houses,

[3]According to John White's maps, Skicoak was about where Portsmouth,
Virginia, is now.

built of Cedar, and fortified round about with sharpe trees, to keepe out their enemies, and the entrance into it made like a turne pike very artificially: when wee came towardes it, standing neere unto the waters side, the wife of Granganimeo the kings brother came running out to meete us very cheerefully and friendly, her husband was not then in the village: some of her people shee commanded to drawe our boate on shore for the beating of the billoe: others she appointed to cary us on their backes to the dry ground, and others to bring our oares into the house for feare of stealing. When we were come into the utter roome, having five roomes in her house, she caused us to sit downe by a great fire, and after tooke off our clothes and washed them, and dryed them againe: some of the women plucked off our stockings and washed them, some washed our feete in warme water, and shee her selfe tooke great paines to see all things ordered in the best maner shee could, making great haste to dress some meate for us to eate.

After we had thus dryed ourselves, she brought us into the inner roome, where shee set on the boord standing along the house, some wheate like furmentie, sodden Venison, and roasted, fish sodden, boyled and roasted, Melons rawe, and sodden, rootes of divers kindes and divers fruites: their drinke is commonly water, but while the grape lasteth, they drinke wine, and for want of caskes to keepe it, all the yere after they drink water, but it is sodden with Ginger in it, and black Sinamon, and sometimes Sassaphras, and divers other wholesome, and medicinable hearbes and trees. We were entertained with all love and kindnesse, and with as much bountie (after their maner) as they could possibly devise. We found the people most gentle, loving, and faithfull, voide of all guile and treason, and such as live after the maner of the golden age. The people onely care howe to defende them selves from the cold in their short winter, and to feed themselves with such meat as the soile affoordeth: there meate is very well sodden and they make broth very sweet and savorie: their vessels are earthen pots, very large, white and sweete, their dishes are wodden platters of sweet timber: within the place where they feede was their lodging, and within that their Idoll, which they worship, of whome they speake incredible things. While we were at meate, there came in at the gates two or three men with their bowes and arrowes from hunting, whom when wee espied, we beganne to looke one towardes another, and offered to reach our weapons: but assoone as shee espied our mistrust, shee was very much mooved, and caused some of her men to runne out, and take away their bowes and arrowes and breake them, and withall beate the poore fellowes out of the gate againe. When we departed in the evening and would not tary all night she was very sory, and gave us into our boate our supper halfe dressed, pottes and all, and brought us to our boate side, in which wee lay all night, remooving the same a prettie distance from the shoare: she perceiving our jelousie, was much greived, and sent divers men and thirtie women, to sit all night on the banke side by us, and sent us into our boates five mattes to cover us from the raine, using very many wordes to entreate us to rest in their houses: but because wee were fewe men, and if wee had miscaried, the voyage had bene in very great danger, wee durst not adventure any thing, though there was no cause of doubt: for a more kinde and loving people there can not be found in the worlde, as farre as we have hitherto had triall.

Beyond this Island there is the maine lande, and over against this Island falleth into this spacious water, the great river called Occam by the inhabitants on which standeth a towne called Pomeiock, and six dayes journey from the same is situate their greatest citie, called Skicoak, which this people affirme to be very great: but the Savages were never at it, only they speake of it by the report of their fathers and other men, whom they have heard affirme it to bee above one houres journey about.

Into this river falleth another great river, called Cipo, in which there is found great store of Muskles in which there are pearles: likewise there descendeth into this Occam, another river, called Nomopana, on the one side whereof standeth a great towne called Chawanook, and the Lord of that towne and countrey is called Pooneno: this Pooneno is not subject to the king of Wingandacoa, but is a free Lord: beyond this country is there another king, whom they cal Menatonon, and these three kings are in league with each other. Towards the Southwest, foure dayes journey is situate a towne called Sequotan, which is the Southermost towne of Wingandacoa, neere unto which, six and twentie yeres past there was a ship cast away, whereof some of the people were saved, and those were white people, whom the countrey people preserved.

And after ten dayes remaining in an out Island unhabited, called Wocokon, they with the help of some of the dwellers of Sequotan, fastened two boates of the countrey together and made mastes unto them, and sailes of their shirtes, and having taken into them such victuals as the countrey yeelded, they departed after they had remained in this out Island 3 weekes: but shortly after it seemed they were cast away, for the boates were found upon the coast, cast a land in another Island adjoyning: other then these, there was never any people apparelled, or white of colour, either seene or heard of amongst these people, and these aforesaid were seene onely of the inhabitantes of Secotan, which appeared to be very true, for they wondred marvelously when we were amongst them at the whitenes of our skins, ever coveting to touch our breasts, and to view the same. Besides they had our ships in marvelous admiration, and all things els were so strange unto them, as it appeared that none of them had ever seene the like. When we discharged any piece, were it but an harquebuz, they would tremble thereat for very feare, and for the strangenesse of the same: for the weapons which themselves use are bowes and arrowes: the arrowes are but of small canes, headed with a sharpe shell or tooth of a fish sufficient ynough to kill a naked man. Their swordes be of wood hardened: likewise they use wooden breastplates for their defence. They have besides a kinde of club, in the end whereof they fasten the sharpe hornes of a stagge, or other beast. When they goe to warres they cary about with them their idol, of whom they aske counsel, as the Romans were woont of the Oracle of Apollo. They sing songs as they march towardes the battell in stead of drummes and trumpets: their warres are very cruell and bloody, by reason whereof, and of their civill dissentions which have happened of late yeeres amongst them, the people are marvelously wasted, and in some places the countrey left desolate.

Adjoyning to this countrey aforesaid called Secotan beginneth a countrey called Pomovik, belonging to another king whom they call Piemacum, and this king is in league with the next king adjoyning towards the setting of the Sunne, and the countrey Newsiok, situate upon a goodly river called Neus: these kings have mortall warre with Wingina king of Wingandacoa: but about two yeeres past there was a peace made betweene the King Piemacum, and the Lord of Secotan, as these men which we have brought with us to England, have given us to understand: but there remaineth a mortall malice in the Secotanes, for many injuries and slaughters done upon them by this Piemacum. They invited divers men, and thirtie women of the best of his countrey to their towne to a feast: and when they were altogether merry, and praying before their Idol, (which is nothing els but a meer illusion of the devill) the captaine or Lord of the town came suddenly upon them, and slewe them every one, reserving the women and children: and these two have oftentimes since perswaded us to surprize Piemacum his towne, having promised and assured us, that there will be found in it great store of commodities. But whether their perswasion be to the ende they may be revenged of their enemies, or for the love they beare to us, we leave that to the tryall hereafter.

Beyond this Island called Roanoak, are maine Islands very plentifull of fruits and other naturall increases, together with many townes, and villages, along the side of the continent, some bounding upon the Islands, and some stretching up further into the land.

When we first had sight of this countrey, some thought the first land we saw to bee the continent: but after we entred in the Haven, we saw before us another mighty long Sea: for there lyeth along the coast a tracte of Islands, two hundreth miles in length, adjoyning to the Ocean sea, and betweene the Islands, two or three entrances: when you are entred betweene them (these Islands being very narrow for the most part, as in most places sixe miles broad, in some places lesse, in fewe more) then there appeareth another great Sea, containing in bredth in some places, forty, and in some fifty, in some twenty miles over, before you come unto the continent: and in this inclosed Sea there are above an hundreth Islands of divers bignesses, whereof one is sixteene miles long, at which we were, finding it a most pleasant and fertile ground, replenished with goodly Cedars, and divers other sweete woods, full of Corrants, of flaxe, and many other notable commodities, which we at that time had no leasure to view. Besides this Island there are many, as I have sayd, some of two, or three, of foure, of five miles, some more, some lesse, most

36

beautifull and pleasant to behold, replenished with Deere, Conies, Hares, and divers beasts, and about them the goodliest and best fish in the world, and in greatest abundance.

Thus Sir, we have acquainted you with the particulars of our discovery, made this present voyage, as farre foorth as the shortnesse of the time we there continued would affoord us to take viewe of: and so contenting our selves with this service at this time, which wee hope hereafter to inlarge, as occasion and assistance shalbe given, we resolved to leave the countrey, and to apply ourselves to return for England, which we did accordingly, and arrived safely in the West of England about the middest of September.

And whereas wee have above certified you of the countrey taken in possession by us, to her Majesties use, and so to yours by her Majesties grant, wee thought good for the better assurance thereof to record some of the particular Gentlemen, and men of accompt, who then were present, as witnesses of the same, that thereby all occasion of cavill to the title of the countrey, in her Majesties behalfe may be prevented, which otherwise, such as like not the action may use and pretend, whose names are:

> Master Philip Amadas, ⎫ *Captaines.*
> Master Arthur Barlow, ⎭

> William Greenevile,
> John Wood,
> James Browewich,
> Henry Greene,   ⎬ *Of the companie.*
> Benjamin Wood,
> Simon Ferdinando,
> Nicholas Petman,
> John Hewes,

We brought home also two of the Savages being lustie men, whose names were Wanchese and Manteo.[4]

[4]Manteo returned to America with Sir Richard Grenville in 1585; Wanchese also returned, perhaps with Grenville.

RALPH LANE
1530?-1603

Ralph Lane, governor of the first — and impermanent — settlement in Virginia in 1585-1586, held a government post in Ireland when he accepted the offer to go to the New World. Captain Barlowe's enthusiastic account of the expedition of 1584 had encouraged Sir Walter Raleigh's determination to establish a colony in Virginia. Seven vessels sailed from Plymouth on April 9, 1585, under the command of Raleigh's cousin, Sir Richard Grenville (the British naval commander whose later exploits against the Spanish were commemorated in Tennyson's ballad "The Revenge").

Lane and the colonists arrived at Roanoke Island on August 17, 1585. As is evident from Lane's report to Raleigh which follows, they spent much of their time in search of gold and pearls and got along very badly with the Indians. Their food ran out and they began to give up hope for the return of Grenville, who had gone to England for supplies. When the fleet of Sir Francis Drake, on its return from sacking the towns of the Spanish Main, visited the colony the following spring, the colonists obtained supplies and vessels from him; but when these vessels were blown away in a storm and some of the colonists lost, the rest chose to return to England with Drake. They left on June 18, 1586, after ten months in the New World. Grenville arrived with supplies two weeks after the colonists had sailed with Drake. Fifteen men were left by Grenville to hold the country for England.

Lane was later a member of the commission for the defense of England against the Spanish Armada. In 1589 he was a colonel in the expedition which set out under Drake and Sir John Norreys to restore Dom Antonio as king of Portugal. Lane was knighted in 1593.

TEN MONTHS IN VIRGINIA: 1585-1586

An account of the particularities of the imployments of the English men left in Virginia by Richard Greenevill under the charge of Master Ralph Lane Generall of the same, from the 17. of August 1585. until the 18. of June 1586. at which time they departed the Countrey: sent and directed to Sir Walter Ralegh.

That I may proceede with order in this discourse, I thinke it requisite to divide it into two parts.[1] The first shall declare the particularities of such partes of the Countrey within the maine, as our weake number, and supply of things necessarie did inable us to enter into the discovery of.

The second part shall set downe the reasons generally moving us to resolve on our departure at the instant with the Generall Sir Francis Drake, and our common request for passage with him, when the barkes, pinnesses, and boates with the Masters and Mariners meant by him to bee left in the Countrey, for the supply of such, as for a further time meant to have stayed there, were caryed away with tempest and foule weather: In the beginning whereof shall bee declared the conspiracie of Pemisapan, with the Savages of the maine to have cut us off, &c.

THE FIRST PART DECLARING THE PARTICULARITIES OF THE COUNTREY OF VIRGINIA

First therefore touching the particularities of the Countrey, you shall understand that our discoverie of the same hath beene extended from the Iland of Roanoak, (the same having bene the place of our settlement or inhabitation) into the South, into the North, into the Northwest, and into the West.

The uttermost place to the Southward of any discovery was Seco-

[1]The first part is reprinted here.

tan, being by estimation fourescore miles distant from Roanoak. The passage from thence was through a broad sound within the mayne, the same being without kenning of lande, and yet full of flats and shoalds: we had but one boate with foure oares to passe through the same, which boate could not carry above fifteene men with their furniture, baggage, and victuall for seven dayes at the most: and as for our pinnesse, besides that she drew too deep water for that shallow sound, she would not stirre for an oare: for these and other reasons (winter also being at hand) we thought good wholly to leave the discovery of those parts untill our stronger supply.

To the Northward our furthest discovery was to the Chesepians, distant from Roanoak about 130. miles, the passage to it was very shallow and most dangerous, by reason of the bredth of the sound, and the little succour that upon any flawe was there to be had.

But the Territorie and soyle of the Chesepians (being distant fifteene miles from the shoare) was for pleasantnes of seate, for temperature of Climate, for fertilitie of soyle, and for the commoditie of the Sea, besides multitude of Beares (being an excellent good victuall) with great woods of Sassafras, and Wallnut trees, is not to be excelled by any other whatsoever.

There be sundry Kings, whom they call Weroances, and Countreys of great fertility adjoyning to the same, as the Mandoages, Tripanicks, and Opossians, which all came to visite the Colonie of the English, which I had for a time appointed to be resident there.

To the Northwest the farthest place of our discovery was to Chawanook distant from Roanoak about 130. miles. Our passage thither lyeth through a broad sound, but all fresh water, and the chanell of a great depth, navigable for good shipping, but out of the chanell full of shoalds.

The Townes about the waters side situated by the way are these following: Passaquenoke The womans Towne, Chepanoc, Weapomeiok, Muscamunge, and Metackwem: all these being under the jurisdiction of the king of Weapomeiok, called Okisco: from Muscamunge we enter into the River, and jurisdiction of Chawanook: There the River beginneth to straighten untill it come to Chawanook, and then groweth to be as narrow as the Thames betewene Westminster and Lambeth.

Ralph Lane, 1530?-1603

Betwene Muscamunge and Chawanook upon the left hand as wee passe thither, is a goodly high land, and there is a Towne which we called The blinde Towne, but the Savages called it Ohanoak, and hath a very goodly corne field belonging unto it: it is subject to Chawanook.

Chawanook it selfe is the greatest Province and Seigniorie lying upon that River, and the very Towne it selfe is able to put 700. fighting men into the fielde, besides the force of the Province it selfe.

The King of the sayd Province is called Menatonon, a man impotent in his lims, but otherwise for a Savage, a very grave and wise man, and of a very singular good discourse in matters concerning the state, not onely of his owne Countrey, and the disposition of his owne men, but also of his neighbours round about him as well farre as neere, and of the commodities that eache Countrey yeeldeth. When I had him prisoner with me, for two dayes that we were together, he gave mee more understanding and light of the Countrey than I had received by all the searches and Savages that before I or any of my companie had had conference with: it was in March last past 1586. Amongst other things he tolde me, that going three dayes journey in a Canoa up his River of Chawanook, and then descending to the land, you are within foure dayes journey to passe over land Northeast to a certaine Kings countrey, whose Province lyeth upon the Sea, but his place of greatest strength is an Island situate, as hee described unto mee, in a Bay, the water round about the Island very deepe.

Out of this Bay hee signified unto mee, that this King had so greate quantitie of Pearle, and doeth so ordinarily take the same, as that not onely his owne skinnes that hee weareth, and the better sort of his gentlemen and followers are full set with the sayd Pearle, but also his beds, and houses are garnished with them, and that hee hath such quantitie of them, that it is a wonder to see.

He shewed me that the sayd King was with him at Chawanook two yeeres before, and brought him certaine Pearle, but the same of the worst sort, yet was he faine to buy them of him for copper at a deere rate, as he thought. Hee gave mee a rope of the same pearle, but they were blacke, and naught, yet many of them were very great, and a few amongst a number very orient and round, all which I lost

with other things of mine, comming aboord Sir Francis Drake his
Fleete: yet he tolde me that the sayd King had great store of Pearle
that were white, great, and round, and that his blacke Pearle his
men did take out of shallow water, but the white Pearle his men
fished for in very deepe water.

It seemed to me by his speach, that the sayd King had traffique
with white men that had clothes as we have, for these white Pearle,
and that was the reason that hee would not depart with other then
with blacke Pearles, to those of the same countrey.

The King of Chawanook promised to give me guids to go over
land into that kings countrey whensoever I would: but he advised
me to take good store of men with me, and good store of victuall,
for he said, that king would be loth to suffer any strangers to enter
into his Countrey, and especially to meddle with the fishing for any
Pearle there, and that hee was able to make a great many of men
into the field, which he sayd would fight very well.

Hereupon I resolved with my selfe, that if your supplie had come
before the ende of Aprill, and that you had sent any store of boates
or men, to have had them made in any reasonable time, with a sufficient number of men and victuals to have found us untill the newe
corne were come in, I would have sent a small barke with two pinnesses about by Sea to the Northward to have found out the Bay he
spake of, and to have sounded the barre if there were any, which
should have ridden there in sayd Bay about that Iland, while I with
all the small boates I could make, and with two hundred men would
have gone up to the head of the river Chawanook with the guids that
Menatonon would have given me, which I would have bene assured
should have beene of his best men, (for I had his best beloved
sonne prisoner with me) who also should have kept me companie in
an handlocke with the rest, foote by foote, all the voyage over land.

My meaning was further at the head of the River in the place of
my descent where I would have left my boates, to have raised a
sconse with a small trench, and a pallisado upon the top of it, in the
which, and in the guard of my boates I would have left five and
twentie, or thirtie men, with the rest would I have marched with as
much victuall as every man could have caried, with their furniture,
mattocks, spades and axes, two dayes journey. In the ende of my

march upon some convenient plot would I have raised another sconse according to the former, where I would have left fifteene or twentie. And if it would have fallen out conveniently, in the way I would have raised my saide sconse upon some Corne fielde, that my company might have lived upon it.

And so I would have holden this course of insconsing every two dayes march, untill I have bene arrived at the Bay or Port hee spake of: which finding to bee worth the possession, I would there have raised a maine fort, both for the defence of the harborough, and our shipping also, and would have reduced our whole habitation from Roanoak and from the harborough and port there (which by proofe is very naught) unto this other beforementioned, from whence, in the foure dayes march before specified, could I at al times returne with my company back unto my boates riding under my sconse, very neere whereunto directly from the West runneth a most notable River, and in all those parts most famous, called the River of Moratoc. This River openeth into the broad Sound of Weapomeiok. And whereas the River of Chawanook, and all the other Sounds, and Bayes, salt and fresh, shewe no current in the world in calme weather, but are mooved altogether with the winde: This River of Moratoc hath so violent a current from the West and Southwest, that it made me almost of opinion that with oares it would scarse be navigable: it passeth with many creekes and turnings, and for the space of thirtie miles rowing, and more, it is as broad as the Thames betwixt Green-wich and the Isle of dogges, in some place more, and in some lesse: the current runneth as strong, being entred so high into the River, as at London bridge upon a vale water.

And for that not onely Menatonon, but also the Savages of Moratoc themselves doe report strange things of the head of that River, and that from Moratoc it selfe which is a principall Towne upon that River, it is thirtie dayes as some of them say, and some say fourtie dayes voyage to the head thereof, which head they say springeth out of a maine rocke in that abundance, that forthwith it maketh a most violent streame: and further, that this huge rock standeth so neere unto a Sea, that many times in stormes (the wind comming outwardly from the sea) the waves thereof are beaten into the said fresh streame, so that the fresh water for a certaine space, groweth

43

salt and brackish: I tooke a resolution with my selfe, having dismissed Menatonon upon a ransome agreed for, and sent his sonne into the Pinnesse to Roanoak, to enter presently so farre into that River with two double whirries, and fourtie persons one or other, as I could have victuall to cary us, until we could meete with more either of the Moratoks, or of the Mangoaks, which is another kinde of Savages, dwelling more to the Westward of the said River: but the hope of recovering more victuall from the Savages made mee and my company as narrowly to escape starving in that discoverie before our returne, as ever men did, that missed the same.

For Pemisapan, who had changed his name of Wingina upon the death of his brother Granganimo, had given both the Choanists, and Mangoaks worde of my purpose towarde them, I having bene inforced to make him privie to the same, to bee served by him of a guide to the Mangoaks, and yet hee did never rest to solicite continually my going upon them, certifying mee of a generall assembly even at that time made by Menatonon at Chawanook of all his Weroances, and allies to the number of three thousand bowes, preparing to come upon us at Roanoak, and that the Mangoaks also were joyned in the same confederacie, who were able of themselves to bring as many more to the enterprise: And true it was that at that time the assembly was holden at Chawanook about us, as I found at my comming thither, which being unlooked for did so dismay them, as it made us have the better hand at them. But this confederacie against us of the Choanists and Mangoaks was altogether and wholly procured by Pemisapan himselfe, as Menatonon confessed unto me, who sent them continual word, that our purpose was fully bent to destroy them: on the other side he told me, that they had the like meaning towards us.

Hee in like sort having sent worde to the Mangoaks of mine intention to passe up into their River, and to kill them (as he saide) both they and the Moratoks, with whom before wee were entred into a league, and they had ever dealt kindly with us, abandoned their Townes along the River, and retired themselves with their Crenepos,[2] and their Corne within the maine: insomuch as having passed three dayes voyage up the River, wee could not meete a man, nor find a

[2]Women.

graine of Corne in any of their Townes: whereupon considering with my selfe that wee had but two dayes victuall left, and that wee were then 160. miles from home, besides casualtie of contrarie windes or stormes, and suspecting treason of our owne Savages in the discoverie of our voyage intended, though wee had no intention to bee hurtfull to any of them, otherwise then for our copper to have had corne of them: I at night upon the Corps of guard, before the putting foorth of Centinels, advertised the whole company of the case wee stoode in for victuall, and of mine opinion that we were betrayed by our owne Savages, and of purpose drawen foorth by them upon vaine hope to be in the ende starved, seeing all the Countrey fled before us, and therefore while wee had those two dayes victuall left, I thought it good for us to make our returne home-ward, and that it were necessary for us to get the other side of the Sound of Weopomeiok in time, where wee might be relieved upon the weares of Chypanum, and the womens Towne, although the people were fled.

Thus much I signified unto them, as the safest way: neverthelesse I did referre it to the greatest number of voyces, whether wee should adventure the spending of our whole victuall in some further viewe of that most goodly River in hope to meet with some better happe, or otherwise to retire our selves backe againe. And for that they might be the better advised, I willed them to deliberate all night upon the matter, and in the morning at our going aborde to set our course according to the desires of the greatest part. Their resolution fully and wholy was (and not three founde to bee of the contrary opinion) that whiles there was lefte but one halfe pinte of Corne for a man, wee should not leave the search of that River, and that there were in the companie two Mastives, upon the pottage of which with Sassafras leaves (if the worst fell out) the company would make shift to live two dayes, which time would bring them downe the current to the mouth of the River, and to the entrie of the Sound, and in two dayes more at the farthest they hoped to crosse the Sound and to be relieved by the weares, which two dayes they would fast rather then be drawen backe a foote till they had seene the Man-goaks, either as friendes or foes. This resolution of theirs did not a little please mee, since it came of themselves, although for mistrust of that which afterwards did happen, I pretended to have bene rather of the contrary opinion.

And that which made me most desirous to have some doings with the Mangoaks either in friendship or otherwise to have had one or two of them prisoners, was, for that it is a thing most notorious to all the countrey, that there is a Province to the which the said Mangoaks have recourse and trafique up that River of Moratoc, which hath a marveilous and most strange Minerall. This Mine is so notorious amongst them, as not onely to the Savages dwelling up the said river, and also to the Savages of Chawanook, and all them to the Westward, but also to all them of the maine: the Countreis name is of fame, and is called Chaunis Temoatan.

The Minerall they say is Wassador, which is copper, but they call by the name of Wassador every mettall whatsoever: they say it is the colour of our copper, but our copper is better than theirs: and the reason is for that it is redder and harder, whereas that of Chaunis Temoatan is very soft, and pale: they say that they take the saide mettall out of a river that falleth very swift from hie rockes and hils, and they take it in shallow water: the manner is this. They take a great bowle by their description as great as one of our targets, and wrappe a skinne over the hollow parte thereof, leaving one part open to receive in the minerall: that done, they watch the comming downe of the current, and the change of the colour of the water, and then suddenly chop downe the said bowle with the skinne, and receive into the same as much oare as will come in, which is ever as much as their bowle will holde, which presently they cast into a fire, and foorthwith it melteth, and doeth yeelde in five parts at the first melting, two parts of mettall for three partes of oare. Of this mettall the Mangoaks have so great store, by report of all the Savages adjoyning, that they beautify their houses with great plates of the same: and this to be true, I received by report of all the countrey, and particularly by yong Skiko, the King of Chawanooks sonne my prisoner, who also him selfe had bene prisoner with the Mangoaks, and set downe all the particularities to me before mentioned: but hee had not bene at Chawnis Temoatan himselfe: for hee said it was twentie dayes journey overland from the Mangoaks, to the said Mineral Countrey, and that they passed through certaine other territories betweene them and the Mangoaks, before they came to the said Countrey.

Upon report of the premisses, which I was very inquisitive in all places where I came to take very particular information of, by all the Savages that dwelt towardes these parts, and especially of Menatonon himselfe, who in every thing did very particularly informe mee, and promised me guides of his owne men, who should passe over with me, even to the said Country of Chaunis Temoatan (for overland from Chawanook to the Mangoaks is but one dayes journey from Sunne rising to Sunne setting, whereas by water it is seven dayes with the soonest): These things, I say, made me very desirous by all meanes possible to recover the Mangoaks, and to get some of that their copper for an assay, and therefore I willingly yeelded to their resolution: But it fell out very contrary to all expectation, and likelyhood: for after two dayes travell, and our whole victuall spent, lying on shoare all night, wee could never see man, onely fires we might perceive made alongst the shoare where we were to passe, and up into the Countrey, until the very last day. In the evening whereof, about three of the clocke wee heard certaine Savages call as we thought, Manteo, who was also at that time with me in the boat, whereof we all being very glad, hoping of some friendly conference with them, and making him to answere them, they presently began a song, as we thought, in token of our welcome to them: but Manteo presently betooke him to his piece, and tolde mee that they meant to fight with us: which worde was not so soone spoken by him, and the light horseman[3] ready to put to shoare, but there lighted a vollie of their arrowes amongst them in the boat, but did no hurt (God be thanked) to any man. Immediatly, the other boate lying ready with their shot to skoure the place for our hand weapons to lande upon, which was presently done, although the land was very high and steepe, the Savages forthwith quitted the shoare, and betooke themselves to flight: wee landed, and having faire and easily followed for a smal time after them, who had wooded themselves we know not where: the Sunne drawing then towards the setting, and being then assured that the next day if wee would pursue them, though we might happen to meete with them, yet wee should be

[3]A boat.

assured to meete with none of their victuall, which we then had good cause to thinke of: therefore choosing for the company a convenient ground in safetie to lodge in for the night, making a strong Corps of guard, and putting out good Centinels, I determined the next morning before the rising of the Sunne to be going backe againe, if possibly we might recover the mouth of the river, into the broad sound, which at my first motion I found my whole company ready to assent unto: for they were nowe come to their Dogges porredge, that they had bespoken for themselves if that befell them which did, and I before did mistrust we should hardly escape. The ende was, we came the next day by night to the Rivers mouth within foure or five miles of the same, having rowed in one day downe the current, as much as in foure dayes wee had done against the same: we lodged upon an Iland, where we had nothing in the world to eate but pottage of Sassafras leaves, the like whereof for a meate was never used before as I thinke. The broad sound wee had to passe the next day all fresh and fasting: that day the winde blew so strongly and the billow so great, that there was no possibilitie of passage without sinking of our boates. This was upon Easter eve, which was fasted very truely. Upon Easter day in the morning the winde comming very calme, we entred the sound, and by foure of the clocke we were at Chipanum, whence all the Savages that we had left there were fled, but their weares did yeelde us some fish, as God was pleased not utterly to suffer us to be lost: for some of our company of the light horsemen were farre spent. The next morning wee arrived at our home Roanoak.

I have set downe this Voyage somewhat particularly, to the ende it may appeare unto you, (as true it is) that there wanted no great good will from the most to the least amongst us, to have perfited this discoverie of the Mine: for that the discovery of a good Mine, by the goodnesse of God, or a passage to the South-sea, or some way to it, and nothing els can bring this Countrey in request to be inhabited by our nation. And with the discovery of either of the two above shewed, it will bee the most sweete and healthfullest climate, and therewithall the most fertile soyle (being manured) in the world: and then will Sassafras, and many other rootes and gummes there found make good marchandise and lading for shipping, which otherwise of themselves will not be worth the fetching.

Provided also, that there be found out a better harborough then yet there is, which must be to the Northward, if any there bee, which was mine intention to have spent this Summer in the search of, and of the Mine of Chawnis Temoatan: the one I would have done, if the barkes that I should have had of Sir Francis Drake, by his honourable courtesie, had not bene driven away by storme: the other if your supply of more men, and some other necessaries had come to us in any convenient sufficiencie. For this river of Moratico promiseth great things, and by the opinion of M. Hariots the head of it by the description of the Countrey, either riseth from the Bay of Mexico, or els from very neere unto the same, that openeth out into the South sea.

And touching the Minerall, thus doeth M. Youghan affirme, that though it be but copper, seeing the Savages are able to melt it, it is one of the richest Minerals in the world.

Wherefore a good harborough found to the Northward, as before is saide, and from thence foure dayes overland, to the River of Choanoak sconses being raised, from whence againe overland through the province of Choanoak one dayes voyage to the first towne of the Mangoaks up the river of Moratico by the way, as also upon the said River for the defence of our boats like sconses being set, in this course of proceeding you shall cleare your selfe from al those dangers and broad shallow sounds before mentioned, and gaine within foure dayes travell into the heart of the maine 200. miles at the least, and so passe your discovery into that most notable countrey, and to the likeliest parts of the maine, with farre greater felicitie then other wise can bee performed.

Thus Sir, I have though simply, yet truely set downe unto you, what my labour with the rest of the gentlemen, and poore men of our company (not without both paine and perill, which the Lord in his mercy many wayes delivered us from) could yeeld unto you, which might have bene performed in some more perfection, if the Lord had bene pleased that onely that which you had provided for us had at the first bene left with us, or that hee had not in his eternall providence now at the last set some other course in these things, then the wisedome of man coulde looke into, which truely the carying away by a most strange and unlooked for storme of all our provision, with Barks, Master, Mariners, and sundry also of mine owne company, al having bene so courteously supplied by the generall Sir Francis Drake, the same having bene most sufficient to have performed the greatest part of the premisses, must ever make me to thinke the hand of God onely (for some his good purpose to my selfe yet unknowen) to have bene in the matter.

THOMAS HARRIOT
1560-1621

Thomas Harriot, born and educated at Oxford, was a brilliant young scientist who in his early twenties served as tutor to Sir Walter Raleigh, a man eight years his senior. In 1585 Raleigh appointed him geographer to the second expedition to Virginia. Harriot made careful observations of the life and products of the New World, and when he left with Sir Francis Drake in June, 1586, he took with him samples of such strange plants as the *uppowoc,* or *tobacco.* In London, in 1588, he published *A brief and true report of the new found land of Virginia,* which was a precise and accurate account of what he had seen in the New World.

Harriot continued his studies in mathematics and astronomy. He corresponded with Kepler and other leading men of science of his time, employed a telescope contemporaneously with Galileo, and made important contributions to the development of algebra. During Sir Walter Raleigh's long imprisonment in the Tower of London Harriot eased his confinement with news of the intellectual world and gathered material for Raleigh's *History of the World.* Harriot died in 1621. Several of his scientific studies survived, and his *Artis analyticae praxis ad aequationes algebraicas resolvendas* was published in 1631.

THOMAS HARRIOT ON TOBACCO

There is an herbe which is sowed apart by it selfe, and is called by the inhabitants Uppowoc: in the West Indies it hath divers names, according to the severall places and countreys where it groweth and is used: the Spanyards generally call it Tabacco. The leaves thereof being dried and brought into pouder, they use to take the fume or smoake thereof, by sucking it thorow pipes made of clay, into their stomacke and head; from whence it purgeth superfluous fleame and other grosse humours, and openeth all the pores and passages of the body: by which meanes the use thereof not onely preserveth the body from obstructions, but also (if any be, so that they have not bene of too long continuance) in short time breaketh them: whereby their bodies are notably preserved in health, and know not many grievous diseases, wherewithall we in England are often times afflicted.

This Uppowoc is of so precious estimation amongst them, that they thinke their gods are marvellously delighted therewith: whereupon sometime they make hallowed fires, and cast some of the pouder therin for a sacrifice: being in a storme upon the waters, to pacifie their gods, they cast some up into the aire and into the water: so a weare for fish being newly set up, they cast some therein and into the aire: also after an escape of danger, they cast some into the aire likewise: but all done with strange gestures, stamping, sometime dancing, clapping of hands, holding up of hands, and staring up into the heavens, uttering therewithall, and chattering strange words and noises.

We our selves, during the time we were there, used to sucke it after their manner, as also since our returne, and have found many rare and woonderfull experiments of the vertues thereof: of which the relation would require a volume by it selfe: the use of it by so many of late men and women of great calling, as els, and some learned Physicians also, is sufficient witnesse.

THOMAS HARRIOT ON THE NATURE AND MANNERS
OF THE PEOPLE

It resteth I speake a word or two of the naturall inhabitants, their natures and maners, leaving large discourse thereof until time more convenient hereafter: nowe onely so farre foorth, as that you may know, how that they in respect of troubling our inhabiting and planting, are not to be feared, but that they shall have cause both to feare and love us, that shall inhabite with them.

They are a people clothed with loose mantles made of deere skinnes, and aprons of the same round about their middles, all els naked, of such a difference of statures onely as wee in England, having no edge tooles or weapons or yron or steele to offend us withall, neither knowe they how to make any: those weapons that they have, are onely bowes made of Witch-hazle, and arrows of reedes, flat edged truncheons also of wood about a yard long, neither have they any thing to defend themselves but targets made of barkes, and some armours made of sticks wickered together with thread.

Their townes are but small, and neere the Sea coast but fewe, some contayning but teene or twelve houses; some 20. the greatest that we have seene hath bene but of 30. houses: if they bee walled, it is onely done with barkes of trees made fast to stakes, or els with poles onely fixed upright, and close one by another.

Their houses are made of small poles, made fast at the tops in round forme after the maner as is used in many arbories in our gardens of England, in most townes covered with barkes, and in some with artificiall mats made of long rushes, from the tops of the houses downe to the ground. The length of them is commonly double to the breadth, in some places they are but 12. and 16. yards long, and in other some we have seene of four and twentie.

In some places of the Countrey, one onely towne belongeth to the government of a Wiroans or chiefe Lord, in other some two or three, in some sixe, eight, and more: the greatest Wiroans that yet wee had dealing with, had but eighteene townes in his government, and able to make not above seven or eight hundred fighting men at the most. The language of every government is different from any other, and the further they are distant, the greater is the difference.

Their maner of warres amongst themselves is either by sudden surprising one an other most commonly about the dawning of the day, or moone-light, or els by ambushes, or some subtile devises. Set battels are very rare, except it fall out where there are many trees, where either part may have some hope of defence, after the delivery of every arrow, in leaping behind some or other.

If there fall out any warres betweene us and them, what their fight is likely to bee, wee having advantages against them so many maner of wayes, as by our discipline, our strange weapons and devises else, especially Ordinance great and small, it may easily bee imagined: by the experience we have had in some places, the turning up of their heeles against us in running away was their best defence.

In respect of us they are a people poore, and for want of skill and judgement in the knowledge and use of our things, doe esteeme our trifles before things of greater value: Notwithstanding, in their proper maner (considering the want of such means as we have), they seeme very ingenious. For although they have no such tooles, nor any such crafts, Sciences and Artes as wee, yet in those things they doe, they shew excellencie of wit. And by how much they upon due consideration shall finde our maner of knowledges and crafts to exceede theirs in perfection, and speede for doing or execution, by so much the more is it probable that they should desire our friendship and love, and have the greater respect for pleasing and obeying us. Whereby may bee hoped, if meanes of good government be used, that they may in short time bee brought to civilitie, and the imbracing of true Religion.

Some religion they have already, which although it be farre from the trueth, yet being as it is, there is hope it may be the easier and sooner reformed.

They beleeve that there are many gods, which they call Mantoac, but of different sorts & degrees, one onely chiefe and great God, which hath bene from all eternitie. Who, as they affirme, when hee purposed to make the world, made first other gods of a principall order, to be as meanes and instruments to be used in the creation and government to follow, and after the Sunne, moone, and starres as pettie gods, and the instruments of the other order more principal. First (they say) were made waters, out of which by the gods was made all diversitie of creatures that are visible or invisible.

For mankinde they say a woman was made first, which by the working of one of the gods, conceived and brought foorth children: And in such sort they say they had their beginning. But how many yeeres or ages have passed since, they say they can make no relation, having no letters nor other such meanes as we to keepe Records of the particularities of times past, but onely tradition from father to soone.

They thinke that all the gods are of humane shape, and therefore they represent them by images in the formes of men, which they call Kewasowok, one alone is called Kewas: them they place in houses appropriate or temples, which they call Machicomuck, where they worship, pray, sing, and make many times offring unto them. In some Machicomuck we have seene but one Kewas, in some two, and in other some three. The common sort thinke them to be also gods.

They beleeve also the immortalitie of the soule, that after this life as soone as the soule is departed from the body, according to the workes it hath done, it is either carried to heaven the habitacle of gods, there to enjoy perpetuall blisse and happinesse, or els to a great pitte or hole, which they thinke to be in the furthest parts of their part of the world toward the Sunne set, there to burne continually: the place they call Popogusso.

For the confirmation of this opinion, they tolde me two stories of two men that had bene lately dead and revived againe, the one happened but few yeeres before our comming into the Countrey of a wicked man, which having bene dead and buried, the next day the earth of the grave being seene to move, was taken up againe, who made declaration where his soule had bene, that is to say, very neere entring into Popogusso, had not one of the gods saved him, and gave him leave to returne againe, and teach his friends what they should do to avoyd that terrible place of torment. The other happened in the same yeere we were there, but in a towne that was 60. miles from us, and it was told me for strange newes, that one being dead, buried, and taken up againe as the first, shewed that although his body had lien dead in the grave, yet his soule was alive, & had travailed farre in a long broad way, on both sides whereof grew most delicate and pleasant trees, bearing more rare and excellent fruits, then ever hee had seene before, or was able to expresse, and at length came to most brave and faire houses, neere which he met his father that had bene dead before, who gave him great charge to goe backe againe, and shew his friends what good they were to doe to enjoye the pleasures of that place, which when he had done he should after come againe.

What subtiltie soever be in the Wiroances and priestes, this opinion worketh so much in many of the common and simple sort of people, that it maketh them have great respect to their Governours, and also great care what they doe, to avoyd torment after death, and to enjoy blisse, although notwithstanding there is punishment ordeined for malefactours, as stealers, whoremongers, and other sorts of wicked doers, some punished with death, some with forfeitures, some with beating, according to the greatnesse of the facts.

And this is the summe of their Religion, which I learned by having speciall familiaritie with some of their priests. Wherein they were not so sure grounded, nor gave such credite to their traditions and stories, but through conversing with us they were brought into great doubts of their owne, and no small admiration of ours, with earnest desire in many, to learne more than wee had meanes for want of perfect utterance in their language to expresse.

Most things they sawe with us, as Mathematicall instruments, sea Compasses, the vertue of the load-stone in drawing yron, a perspective glasse whereby was shewed many strange sights, burning glasses, wilde firewoorkes, gunnes, hookes, writing and reading, spring-clockes that seeme to goe of themselves and many other things that wee had were so strange unto them, and so farre exceeded their capacities to comprehend the reason and meanes how they should be made and done, that they thought they were rather the workes of gods then of men, or at the leastwise they had bene given and taught us of the gods. Which made many of them to have such opinion of us, as that if they knew not the trueth of God and Religion already, it was rather to bee had from us whom God so specially loved, then from a people that were so simple, as they found themselves to be in comparison of us. Whereupon greater credite was given unto that wee spake of, concerning such matters.

Many times and in every towne where I came, according as I was able, I made declaration of the contents of the Bible, that therein was set foorth the true and onely God, and his mightie workes, that therein was conteined the true doctrine of salvation through Christ, with many particularities of Miracles and chiefe points of Religion, as I was able then to utter, and thought fit for the time. And although I told them the booke materially and of it selfe was not of any such vertue, as I thought they did conceive, but onely the doctrine therein conteined: yet would many be glad to touch it, to embrace it, to kisse it, to holde it to their breastes and heads, and stroke over all their body with it, to shew their hungry desire of that knowledge which was spoken of.

The Wiroans with whom we dwelt called Wingina, and many of his people would bee glad many times to be with us at our Prayers, and many times call upon us both in his owne towne, as also in others whither hee sometimes accompanied us, to pray and sing Psalmes, hoping thereby to be partaker of the same effects which we by that meanes also expected.

Twise this Wiroans was so grievously sicke that he was like to die, and as he lay languishing, doubting of any helpe by his owne priestes, and thinking hee was in such danger for offending us and thereby our God, sent for some of us to pray and bee a meanes to our God that it would please him either that he might live, or after death dwell with him in blisse, so likewise were the requests of many others in the like case.

On a time also when their corne began to wither by reason of a drought which happened extraordinarily, fearing that it had come to passe by reason that in some thing they had displeased us, many would come to us and desire us to pray to our God of England, that he would preserve their Corne, promising that when it was ripe we also should be partakers of the fruit.

There could at no time happen any strange sicknesse, losses, hurts, or any other crosse unto them, but that they would impute to us the cause or meanes thereof, for offending or not pleasing us. One other rare and strange accident, leaving others, wil I mention before I end, which moved the whole Countrey that either knew or heard of us, to have us in wonderfull admiration.

There was no towne where wee had any subtile devise practised against us, wee leaving it unpunished or not revenged (because we sought by all meanes possible to win them by gentlenesse) but that within a few dayes after our departure from every such Towne, the people began to die very fast, and many in short space, in some Townes about twentie, in some fourtie, and in one sixe score, which in trueth was very many in respect of their numbers. This happened in no place that we could learne, but where we had bin, where they used some practise against us, & after such time. The disease also was so strange, that they neither knewe what it was, nor how to cure it, the like by report of the oldest men in the Countrey never happened before, time out of minde. A thing specially observed by us, as also by the naturall inhabitants themselves. Insomuch that when some of the inhabitants which were our friends, and especially the Wiroans Wingina, had observed such effects in foure or five Townes to followe their wicked practises, they were perswaded that it was the worke of our God through our meanes, and that we by him might kill and slay whom we would without weapons, and not come neere them. And thereupon when it had happened that they had understanding that any of their enemies had abused us in our journeys, hearing that we had wrought no revenge with our weapons, and fearing upon some cause the matter should so rest: did come and intreate us that we would be a meanes to our God that they as others that had dealt ill with us might in like sort die, alleadging how much it would bee for our credite and profite, as also theirs, and hoping furthermore that we would doe so much at their requests in respect of the friendship we professed them.

Whose entreaties although wee shewed that they were ungodly, affirming that our God would not subject himselfe to any such prayers and requests of men: that indeede all things have bene and were to be done according to his good pleasure as he had ordeined: and that we to shewe our selves his true servants ought rather to make petition for the contrary, that they with them might live together

with us, be made partakers of his trueth, and serve him in righteous-
nesse, but notwithstanding in such sort, that wee referre that, as
all other things, to bee done according to his divine will and pleasure, and as by his wisedome he had ordeined to be best.

Yet because the effect fell out so suddenly and shortly after according to their desires, they thought nevertheless it came to passe
by our meanes, & that we in using such speeches unto them, did but
dissemble the matter, and therefore came unto us to give us thankes
in their maner, that although we satisfied them not in promise, yet
in deedes and effect we had fulfilled their desires.

This marveilous accident in all the Countrey wrought so strange
opinions of us, that some people could not tell whether to thinke us
gods or men, and the rather because that all the space of their sicknes, there was no man of ours knowen to die, or that was specially
sicke: they noted also that we had no women amongst us, neither
that we did care for any of theirs.

Some therefore were of opinion that we were not borne of women,
and therefore not mortal, but that we were men of an old generation
many yeeres past, then risen againe to immortalitie.

Some would likewise seeme to prophecie that there were more of
our generation yet to come to kill theirs and take their places, as
some thought the purpose was, by that which was already done.
Those that were immediately to come after us they imagined to be in
aire, yet invisible and without bodies, and that they by our intreatie
and for the love of us, did make the people to die in that sort as they
did, by shooting invisible bullets into them.

To confirme this opinion, their Phisitions (to excuse their ignorance in curing the disease) would not be ashamed to say, but earnestly make the simple people beleeve, that the strings of blood that
they sucked out of the sicke bodies, were the strings wherewithall
the invisible bullets were tied and cast. Some also thought that wee
shot them our selves out of our pieces, from the place where wee
dwelt, and killed the people in any Towne that had offended us, as
wee listed, howe farre distant from us soever it were. And other
some said, that it was the speciall worke of God for our sakes, as
we our selves have cause in some sort to thinke no lesse, whatsoever
some doe, or may imagine to the contrary, specially some Astrolo-

gers, knowing of the Eclipse of the Sunne which we saw the same yeere before in our voyage thitherward, which unto them appeared very terrible. And also of a Comet which began to appeare but a fewe dayes before the beginning of the saide sickenesse. But to exclude them from being the speciall causes of so speciall an accident, there are further reasons then I thinke fit at this present to be alleadged. These their opinions I have set downe the more at large, that it may appeare unto you that there is good hope they may be brought through discreete dealing and government to the imbracing of the trueth, and consequently to honour, obey, feare and love us.

And although some of our company towards the end of the yeere, shewed themselves too fierce in slaying some of the people in some Townes, upon causes that on our part might easily ynough have bene borne withall: yet notwithstanding, because it was on their part justly deserved, the alteration of their opinions generally and for the most part concerning us is the lesse to be doubted. And whatsover els they may be, by carefulnesse of our selves neede nothing at all to be feared.

GEORGE PERCY

1580-1632

George Percy was a member of the expedition which sailed for Virginia from London five days before Christmas in the year 1606. He was then twenty-six, and had already had a taste of adventure as a soldier in the Netherlands. A member of the Percy family which had been prominent in English history from the time of William the Conqueror, he was a younger son of Henry, Eighth Earl of Northumberland. His mother was Catherine, daughter of John Neville, Lord Latimer.

The expedition arrived in the West Indies late in March, 1607, and on April 26 sailed into Chesapeake Bay. In the pages which follow Percy describes the exploration up the Appomattox and James rivers in May and June, and the establishment of the first permanent English settlement in America at Jamestown on May 13, 1607.

Percy later served as president of the colony during some of its most difficult times — including the terrible winter of 1609-1610, when all but 60 of the 500 colonists then in Virginia perished. He returned to England, served with distinction as a captain in the Netherlands in the war with Spain, and died in 1632. His account of the exploration in the New World, *Observations gathered out of a Discourse of the Southern Colonie in Virginia by the English,* from which a selection follows, was first printed in 1625.

GEORGE PERCY'S ACCOUNT OF VIRGINIA IN 1607

The eighth day of May we discovered up the River. We landed in the Countrey of Apamatica. At our landing, there came many stout and able Savages to resist us with their Bowes and Arrowes, in the most warlike manner, with the swords at their backes beset with sharpe stones, and pieces of yron able to cleave a man in sunder. Amongst the rest one of the chiefest, standing before them cross-legged, with his Arrow readie in his Bow in one hand, and taking a Pipe of Tobacco in the other, with a bold uttering of his speech, demanded of us our being there, willing us to bee gone. Wee made signes of peace, which they perceived in the end, and let us land in quietnesse.

The twelfth day we went backe to our ships, and discovered a point of Land, called Archers Hope, which was sufficient with a little labour to defend our selves against any Enemy. The soile was good and fruitfull, with excellent good Timber. There are also great store of Vines in bignesse of a mans thigh, running up to the tops of the Trees in great abundance. We also did see many Squirels, Conies, Black Birds with crimson wings, and divers other Fowles and Birds of divers and sundrie collours of crimson, Watchet, Yellow, Greene, Murry, and of divers other hewes naturally without any art using.

We found store of Turkie nests and many Egges. If it had not beene disliked, because the ship could not ride neere the shoare, we had setled there to all the Collonies contentment.

The thirteenth day, we came to our seating place in Paspihas Countrey, some eight miles from the point of Land, which I made mention before: where our shippes doe lie so neere the shoare that they are moored to the Trees in six fathom water.

The fourteenth day, we landed all our men, which were set to worke about the fortification, and others some to watch and ward as it was convenient. The first night of our landing, about midnight, there came some Savages sayling close to our quarter. Presently there was an alarum given; upon that the Savages ran away, and we [were] not troubled any more by them that night. Not long after there came two Savages that seemed to be Commanders, bravely drest, with Crownes of coloured haire upon their heads, which came as Messengers from the Werowance of Paspihae, telling us that their Werowance was comming and would be merry with us with a fat Deare.

The eighteenth day, the Werowance of Paspihae came himselfe to our quarter, with one hundred Savages armed, which garded him in a very warlike manner with Bowes and Arrowes, thinking at that time to execute their villany. Paspihae made great signes to us to lay our Armes away. But we would not trust him so far. He seeing he could not have convenient time to worke his will, at length made signes that he would give us as much land as we would desire to take. As the Savages were in a throng in the Fort, one of them stole a Hatchet from one of our company, which spied him doing the deed: whereupon he tooke it from him by force, and also strooke him over the arme. Presently another Savage seeing that, came fiercely at our man with a wooden sword, thinking to beat out his braines. The Werowance of Paspiha saw us take to our Armes, went suddenly away with all his company in great anger.

The nineteenth day, my selfe and three or foure more walking into the Woods by chance wee espied a pathway like to an Irish pace: wee were desirous to knowe whither it would bring us. Wee traced along some foure miles, all the way as wee went, having the pleasantest Suckles, the ground all flowing over with faire flowers of sundry colours and kindes, as though it had been in any Garden or Orchard in England. There be many Strawberries, and other fruits unknowne. Wee saw the Woods full of Cedar and Cypresse trees, with other trees, which issues out sweet Gummes like to Balsam. Wee kept on our way in this Paradise. At length, wee came to a Savage Towne, where wee found but few people. They told us the rest were gone a hunting with the Werowance of Paspiha. We stayed there a while, and had of them Strawberries and other things. In the meane time one of the Savages came running out of his house with a Bowe and Arrowes and ranne mainly through the Woods.

Then I beganne to mistrust some villanie, that he went to call some companie, and so betray us. Wee made all haste away wee could. One of the Savages brought us on the way to the Wood side, where there was a Garden of Tobacco and other fruits and herbes. He gathered Tobacco, and distributed to every one of us; so wee departed.

The twentieth day the Werowance of Paspiha sent fortie of his men with a Deere, to our quarter: but they came more in villanie than any love they bare us. They faine would have layne in our Fort all night, but wee would not suffer them for feare of their treachery. One of our Gentlemen having a Target which hee trusted in, thinking it would beare out a slight shot, hee set it up against a tree, willing one of the Savages to shoot; who tooke from his backe an Arrow of an elle long, drew it strongly in his Bowe, shoots the Target a foote thorow, or better: which was strange, being that a Pistoll could not pierce it. Wee seeing the force of his Bowe, afterwards set him up a steele Target; he shot again, and burst his arrow all to pieces. He presently pulled out another Arrow, and bit it in his teeth, and seemed to bee in a great rage; so hee went away in great anger. Their Bowes are made of tough Hasell, their strings of Leather, their Arrowes of Canes or Hasell, headed with very sharpe stones, and are made artificially like a broad Arrow: other some of their Arrowes are headed with the ends of Deeres hornes, and are feathered very artificially. Pasphia was as good as his word; for hee sent Venison, but the Sawse came within a few dayes after.

At Port Cotage in our Voyage up the River, we saw a Savage Boy about the age of ten yeeres, which had a head of haire of a perfect yellow and a reasonable white skinne, which is a Miracle amongst all Savages.

This River which wee have discovered is one of the famousest Rivers that ever was found by any Christian. It ebbs and flowes a hundred and three-score miles, where ships of great burthen may harbour in safetie. Wheresoever we landed upon this River, wee saw the goodliest Woods as Beech, Oke, Cedar, Cypresse, Wal-nuts, Sassafras, and Vines in great abundance, which hang in great clusters on many Trees, and other Trees unknowne; and all the grounds bespred with many sweet and delicate flowres of divers colours and

64

kindes. There are also many fruites as Strawberries, Mulberries, Rasberries, and Fruites unknowne. There are many branches of this River, which runne flowing through the Woods with great plentie of fish of all kindes; as for Sturgeon, all the World cannot be compared to it. In this Countrey I have seene many great and large Medowes having excellent good pasture for any Cattle. There is also great store of Deere both Red and Fallow. There are Beares, Foxes, Otters, Bevers, Muskats, and wild beasts unknowne.

The foure and twentieth day wee set up a Crosse at the head of this River, naming it Kings River, where we proclaimed James King of England to have the most right unto it. When wee had finished and set up our Crosse, we shipt our men and made for James Fort. By the way, wee came to Pohatans Towne, where the Captaine went on shore suffering none to goe with him. Hee presented the Commander of this place, with a Hatchet which hee tooke joyfully, and was well pleased.

But yet the Savages murmured at our planting in the Countrie, whereupon this Werowance made answer againe very wisely of a Savage, Why should you bee offended with them as long as they hurt you not, nor take any thing away by force. They take but a little waste ground, which doth you nor any of us any good.

I saw Bread made by their women, which doe all their drugerie. The men take their pleasure in hunting and their warres, which they are in continually, one Kingdome against another. The manner of baking of bread is thus. After they pound their wheat into flowre, with hote water they make it into paste, and worke it into round balls and Cakes, then they put it into a pot of seething water: when it is sod throughly, they lay it on a smooth stone, there they harden it as well as in an Oven.

There is notice to be taken to know married women from Maids. The Maids you shall always see the fore part of their head and sides shaven close, the hinder part very long, which they tie in a pleate hanging downe to their hips. The married women weares their haire all of a length, and is tied of that fashion that the Maids are. The women kinde in this Countrey doth pounce and race their bodies, legges, thighes, armes and faces with a sharpe Iron, which makes a stampe in curious knots, and drawes the proportion of Fowles, Fish, or Beasts; then with paintings of sundry lively colours, they rub it into the stampe which will never be taken away, because it is dried into the flesh where it is sered.

The Savages beare their yeeres well, for when wee were at Pamonkies, wee saw a Savage by their report was above eight score yeeres of age. His eyes were sunke into his head, having never a tooth in his mouth, his haire all gray with a reasonable bigge beard, which was as white as any snow. It is a Miracle to see a Savage have any haire on their faces. I never saw, read, nor heard, any have the like before. This Savage was as lusty and went as fast as any of us, which was strange to behold.

The fifteenth of June we had built and finished our Fort, which was triangle wise, having three Bulwarkes, at every corner, like a halfe Moone, and foure or five pieces of Artillerie mounted in them. We had made our selves sufficiently strong for these Savages. We had also sowne most of our Corne on two Mountains [elevations]. It sprang a mans height from the ground. This Countrey is a fruitfull soile, bearing many goodly and fruitfull Trees, as Mulberries, Cherries, Wal-nuts, Cedars, Cypresse, Sassafras, and Vines in great abundance.

JOHN SMITH

1579-1631

John Smith, one of the most colorful and the best remembered of all the early explorers and settlers of Virginia, was born in Lincolnshire, England, in 1579. In his early teens he began a series of travels and adventures about which he later wrote entertainingly if not always with unimpeachable accuracy. On his return to England in 1605 he became deeply interested in the plans for establishing a colony in the New World. He worked energetically for the London Company and was a member of the band of colonists who set out from England on December 19, 1606.

After more than four months, the colonists reached Virginia on April 26, 1607. Smith was named one of the Council but did not take his place for two months because he had been placed under arrest for conspiracy on the voyage. The colonists landed at Jamestown on May 14, and a week later a party including Smith and Captain Newport explored up the James River as recounted in Smith's *True Relation,* which follows. On June 21 Captain Newport sailed for England, leaving 105 colonists at Jamestown. In the months that followed, Smith emerged as the leader of the colony and the man who most successfully traded with the Indians for provisions to keep the conolists alive. In December he explored up the Chickahominy, where he was taken prisoner by the Indians and — according to his *History of Virginia* written some seventeen years later — was saved from death by Pocahontas. On his return to Jamestown he was charged with responsibility for the death of his companions and was sentenced to be hanged. He was saved by the return of Captain Newport from England on January 9, 1609. When Newport arrived with supplies and additional settlers, he found only 35 of the original 105 colonists alive.

Smith made extensive explorations of the Chesepeake Bay area in 1608. He explored the Rappahannock as far as the present town of Fredericksburg, and the Potomac as far as the present city of Washington. He traveled some 3,000 miles and gathered much material which he used in his later *Map of Virginia.* He was made President of the Council on his return to Jamestown, but soon resumed his explorations. He continued a leading figure in the colony — though often the center of controversy —

until he was forced, by a serious burn from an explosion of gunpowder, to return to England in 1609.

On his return to England, Smith left the service of the London Company but continued his active interest in the colonization of America. In 1614 he explored and mapped the coast of New England, which he named, and he undertook several voyages for the Virginia Company of Bristol. He was given the title of Admiral of New England by the Bristol Company, and his maps and writings did much to promote interest in the New World.

Smith's first account of Virginia, *A True Relation of such Occurrences and Accidents of Note as hath hapned in Virginia since the first planting of that Colony,* was first published in London in 1608, and is reprinted here in full. Smith's later writings were: *A Map of Virginia, with a Description of the Country* (1612); *A Description of New England* (1616); *New England Trials* (1620); *The General History of Virginia, New England, and the Summer Isles* (1624); *An Accidence . . . for all young Seamen* (1626), which was revised the following year as *A Sea Grammar; The True Travels, Adventures, and Observations of Captain John Smith in Europe, Asia, Africa, and America . . .* (1630); and *Advertisement for the Unexperienced Planters* (1631). Smith died in June, 1631, and is buried in London.

CAPTAIN JOHN SMITH'S TRUE RELATION OF VIRGINIA

Kinde Sir, commendations remembred, &c. You shall understand that after many crosses in the downes by tempests, wee arrived safely uppon the Southwest part of the great Canaries: within foure or five daies after we set saile for Dominica, the 26. of Aprill: the first land we made, wee fell with Cape Henry, the verie mouth of the Bay of Chissiapiacke, which at that present we little expected, having by a cruell storme bene put to the Northward. Anchoring in this Bay twentie or thirtie went a shore with the Captain, and in comming aboard, they were assalted with certaine Indians which charged them within Pistoll shot: in which conflict, Captaine Archer and Mathew Morton were shot: whereupon Captaine Newport seconding them, made a shot at them, which the Indians little respected, but having spent their arrowes retyred without harme. And in that place was the Box opened, wherin the Counsell for Virginia was nominated: and arriving at the place where wee are now seated, the Counsel was sworn, and the President elected, which for that yeare was Maister Edm. Maria Wingfield, where was made choice for our scituation, a verie fit place for the erecting of a great cittie, about which some contention passed betwixt Captaine Wingfield and Captaine Gosnold: notwithstanding, all our provision was brought a shore, and with as much speede as might bee wee went about our fortification.

The two and twenty day of Aprill,[1] Captain Newport and my selfe with divers others, to the number of twenty two persons, set forward to discover the River, some fiftie or sixtie miles, finding it in some places broader, and in some narrower, the Countrie (for the moste part) on each side plaine high ground, with many fresh Springes, the people in all places kindely intreating us, daunsing and feasting us with strawberries Mulberies, Bread, Fish, and other their Coun-

[1]An error as to the date. The landing was made on May 14, 1607, and the exploration of the river was started on May 21.

trie provisions wherof we had plenty: for which Captaine Newport kindely requited their least favours with Bels, Pinnes, Needles, beades, or Glasses, which so contented them that his liberallitie made them follow us from place to place, and ever kindely to respect us. In the midway staying to refresh our selves in a little Ile foure or five savages came unto us which described unto us the course of the River, and after in our journey, they often met us, trading with us for such provisions as wee had, and arriving at Arsatecke, hee whom we supposed to bee the chiefe King of all the rest, moste kindely entertained us, giving us in a guide to go with us up the River to Powhatan, of which place their great Emperor taketh his name, where he that they honored for King used us kindely. But to finish this discoverie, we passed on further, where within an ile we were intercepted with great craggy stones in the midst of the river, where the water falleth so rudely, and with such a violence, as not any boat can possibly passe, and so broad disperseth the streame, as there is not past five or sixe Foote at a low water, and to the shore scarce passage with a barge, the water floweth foure foote, and the freshes by reason of the Rockes have left markes of the inundations 8. or 9. foote: The South side is plaine low ground, and the north side is high mountaines the reckes being of a gravelly nature, interlaced with many vains of glistring spangles. That night we returned to Powhatan: the next day (being Whitsunday after dinner) we returned to the fals, leaving a mariner in pawn with the Indians for a guide of theirs; hee that they honoured for King followed us by the river. That afternoone we trifled in looking upon the Rockes and river (further he would not goe) so there we erected a crosse, and that night taking our man at Powhatan, Captaine Newport congratulated his kindenes with a Gown and a Hatchet: returning to Arseteche, and stayed there the next day to observe the height therof, and so with many signes of love we departed. The next day the Queene of Agamatack[2] kindely intreated us, her people being no lesse contented then the rest, and from thence we went to another place (the name whereof I do not remember) where the people shewed us the manner of their diving for Mussels, in which they finde Pearles.

[2]Appomattox.

That night passing by Weanock some twentie miles from our Fort, they according to their former churlish condition, seemed little to affect us, but as wee departed and lodged at the point of Weanocke, the people the next morning seemed kindely to content us, yet we might perceive many signes of a more Jealousie in them then before, and also the Hinde that the King of Arseteck had given us, altered his resolution in going to our Fort, and with many kinde circumstances left us there. This gave us some occasion to doubt some mischiefe at the Fort, yet Capt. Newport intended to have visited Paspahegh and Tappahanocke, but the instant change of the winde being faire for our return we repaired to the fort with all speed where the first we heard was that 400. Indians the day before had assalted the fort, and supprised it, had not God (beyond al their expectations) by meanes of the shippes, at whom they shot with their Ordinances and Muskets, caused them to retire, they had entred the fort with our own men, which were then busied in setting Corne, their Armes beeing then in driefats[3] and few ready but certain Gentlemen of their own, in which conflict, most of the Counsel was hurt, a boy slaine in the Pinnas, and thirteene or fourteene more hurt. With all speede we pallisadoed our Fort: (each other day) for sixe or seaven daies we had alarums by ambuscadoes, and four or five cruelly wounded by being abroad: the Indians losse wee know not, but as they report three were slain and divers hurt.

Captaine Newport having set things in order, set saile for England the 22d of June, leaving provision for 13. or 14 weeks. The day before the Ships departure, the King of Pamaunke sent the Indian that had met us before in our discoverie, to assure us peace; our fort being then palisadoed round, and all our men in good health and comfort, albeit, that throgh some discontented humors, it did not so long continue, for the President and Captaine Gosnold, with the rest of the Counsell, being for the moste part discontented with one another, in so much, that things were neither carried with that discretion nor any busines effected in such good sort as wisdome would, nor our owne good and safetie required, whereby, and through the hard dealing of our President, the rest of the counsell beeing diverslie affected through his audacious commaund; and for Captaine Mar-

[3]Dry-vats.

tin, albeit verie honest, and wishing the best good, yet so sicke and weake; and my selfe so disgrac'd through others mallice: through which disorder God (being angrie with us) plagued us with such famin and sicknes, that the living were scarce able to bury the dead: our want of sufficient and good victualls, with continuall watching, foure or five each night at three Bulwarkes, being the chiefe cause: onely of Sturgion wee had great store, whereon our men would so greedily surfet, as it cost manye their lives: the Sack, Aquavitie, and other preservatives for our health, being kept onely in the Presidents hands, for his owne diet, and his few associates. Shortly after Captaine Gosnold fell sicke, and within three weekes died, Captaine Ratcliffe being then also verie sicke and weake, and my selfe having also tasted of the extremitie thereof, but by Gods assistance being well recovered, Kendall about this time, for divers reasons deposed from being of the Councell: and shortly after it pleased God (in our extremity) to move the Indians to bring us Corne, ere it was halfe ripe, to refresh us, when we rather expected when they would destroy us: about the tenth of September there was about 46. of our men dead, at which time Captaine Wingefield having ordred the affaires in such sort that he was generally hated of all, in which respect with one consent he was deposed from his presidencie, and Captaine Ratcliffe according to his course was elected.

Our provision being now within twentie dayes spent, the Indians brought us great store both of Corne and bread ready made: and also there came such aboundance of Fowles into the Rivers, as greatly refreshed our weake estates, whereuppon many of our weake men were presently able to goe abroad. As yet we had no houses to cover us, our Tents were rotten and our Cabbins worse then nought: our best commoditie was Yron which we made into little chissels. The president and Captaine Martins sicknes, constrayned me to be Cape Marchant, and yet to spare no paines in making houses for the company; who notwithstanding our misery, little ceased their mallice, grudging, and muttering. As at this time were most of our chiefest men either sicke or discontented, the rest being in such dispaire, as they would rather starve and rot with idlenes, then be perswaded to do any thing for their owne reliefe without constraint: our victualles being now within eighteene dayes spent, and the Indians

trade decreasing, I was sent to the mouth of the river, to Kegquouh-
tan an Indian Towne, to trade for Corne, and try the River for Fish,
but our fishing we could not effect by reason of the stormy weather.
The Indians thinking us neare famished, with carelesse kindnes,
offred us little pieces of bread and small handfulls of beanes or
wheat, for a hatchet or a piece of copper: In like maner I entertained their kindnes, and in like scorne offered them like commodities, but the Children, or any that shewed extraordinary kindnes, I
liberally contented with free gifte, such trifles as wel contented
them. Finding this colde comfort, I anchored before the Towne, and
the next day returned to trade, but God (the absolute disposer of
all heartes) altered their conceits, for now they were no lesse desirous of our commodities then we of their Corne: under colour to
fetch fresh water, I sent a man to discover the Towne, their Corne,
and force, to trie their intent, in that they desired me up to their
houses: which well understanding, with foure shot I visited them.
With fish, oysters, bread, and deere, they kindly traded with me and
my men, beeing no lesse in doubt of my intent, then I of theirs; for
well I might with twentie men have fraighted a Shippe with Corne.
The Towne conteineth eighteene houses, pleasantly seated upon
three acres of ground, uppon a plaine, halfe invironed with a great
Bay of the great River, the other parte with a Baye of the other
River falling into the great Baye, with a little Ile fit for a Castle in
the mouth thereof, the Towne adjoyning to the maine by a necke
of Land of sixtie yardes. With sixteene bushells of Corne I returned
towards our Forte: by the way I encountred with two Canowes of
Indians, who came aboord me, being the inhabitants of Warosko-
yack, a kingdome on the south side of the river, which is in breadth
5. miles and 20 mile or neare from the mouth: With these I traded,
who having but their hunting provision, requested me to returne to
their Towne, where I should load my boat with corne: and with near
thirtie bushells I returned to the fort, the very name wherof gave
great comfort to our desparing company.

Time thus passing away, and having not above 14. daies victuals
left, some motions were made about our presidents and Captaine
Archers going for England, to procure a supply: in which meane
time we had reasonably fitted us with houses. And our President

and Captaine Martin being able to walk abroad, with much adoe it was concluded, that the pinnace and barge should goe towards Powhatan, to trade for corne: Lotts were cast who should go in her, the chance was mine; and while she was a rigging, I made a voiage to Topohanack, where arriving, there was but certain women and children who fled from their houses, yet at last I drew them to draw neere; truck they durst not, corne they had plenty, and to spoile I had no commission: In my returne to Paspahegh, I traded with that churlish and trecherous nation: having loaded 10 or 12 bushels of corne, they offred to take our pieces and swords, yet by stelth, but [we] seeming to dislike it, they were ready to assault us: yet standing upon our guard, in coasting the shore, divers out of the woods would meet with us with corn and trade. But least we should be constrained, either to indure overmuch wrong or directly fal to revenge, seeing them dog us from place to place, it being night, and our necessitie not fit for warres, we tooke occasion to returne with 10 bushells of corne: Captaine Martin after made 2 journies to that nation of Paspahegh, but eache time returned with 8. or 10. bushells.

All things being now ready for my journey to Powhatan, for the performance thereof, I had 8. men and my selfe for the barge, as well for discoverie as trading; the Pinnace, 5. Marriners, and 2. landmen to take in our ladings at convenient places. The 9 of November I set forward for the discovery of the country of Chikhamania, leaving the pinnace the next tide to followe, and stay for my comming at Point weanock, 20 miles from our fort: the mouth of this river falleth into the great river at Paspahegh, 8 miles above our fort: That afternoone I stayed the eb in the bay of Paspahegh with the Indians: towards the evening certaine Indians haled me, one of them being of Chikahamania, offred to conduct me to his country. The Paspahegheans grudged thereat: along we went by moonelight: at midnight he brought us before his Towne, desiring one of our men to go up with him, whom he kindely intertained, and returned back to the barge: The next morning I went up to the towne, and shewed them what copper and hatchets they shold have for corne, each family seeking to give me most content: so long they caused me to stay that 100 at least was expecting my comming by the river, with corne. What I liked, I bought; and least they should perceive my too great want, I went higher up the river: This place is called Manosquosick, a quarter of a mile from the river, conteining thirtie or fortie houses, uppon an exceeding high land: at the foote of the hill towards the river, is a plaine wood, watered with many springes which fall twentie yardes right downe into the river. Right against the same is a great marsh, of 4. or 5. miles circuit, divided in 2 Ilands, by the parting of the river, abounding with fish and foule of all sorts. A mile from thence is a Towne called Oraniocke. I further discovered the Townes of Mansa, Apanaock, Werawahone, and Mamanahunt, at eche place kindely used: especially at the last, being the hart of the Country; where were assembled 200. people with such aboundance of corne, as having laded our barge, as also I might have laded a ship.

I returned to Paspahhegh, and considering the want of Corne at our Fort, it being night, with the ebb, by midnight I arived at our fort, where I found our Pinnis run aground: The next morning I unladed seven hogsheds into our store. The next morning I returned againe: the second day I arrived at Mamanahunt, wher the people having heard of my comming, were ready with 3 or 400. baskets litle and great, of which having laded my barge, with many signes of great kindnes I returned: At my departure they requested me to hear our pieces, being in the midst of the river; which in regard of the eccho seemed a peale of ordnance. Many birds and fowles they see us dayly kil that much feared them. So desirous of trade wer they, that they would follow me with their canowes; and for anything, give it me, rather than returne it back. So I unladed again 7 or 8. hogsheads at our fort.

Having thus by Gods assistance gotten good store of corne, notwithstanding some bad spirits not content with Gods providence, still grew mutinous; in so much, that our president having occasion to chide the smith for his misdeamenour, he not only gave him bad language, but also offred to strike him with some of his tooles. For which rebellious act, the smith was by a Jury condemned to be hanged, but being uppon the ladder, continuing very obstinate as hoping upon a rescue, when he saw no other way but death with him, he became penitent, and declared a dangerous conspiracy: for which, Captaine Kendall, as principal, was by a Jury condemned, and shot to death. This conspiracy appeased, I set forward for the discovery of the River Checka Hamania. This third time I discovered the Townes of Matapamient, Morinogh, Ascacap, Moysenock, Righkahauck, Nechanichock, Mattalunt, Attamuspincke, and divers others: their plenty of corne I found decreased, yet lading the barge, I returned to our fort.

Our store being now indifferently wel provided with corne, there was much adoe for to have the pinace goe for England, against which Captain Martin and my selfe stood chiefly against it: and in fine after many debatings *pro et contra*, it was resolved to stay a further resolution: This matter also quieted, I set forward to finish this discovery, which as yet I had neglected in regard of the necessitie we had to take in provision whilst it was to be had. 40. miles I passed up the river, which for the most part is a quarter of a mile broad, and 3. fatham and a half deep, exceeding osey, many great low marshes, and many high lands, especially about the midst at a place called Moysonicke, a Peninsule of 4. miles circuit, betwixt two rivers joyned to the main by a neck of 40. or 50. yards, and 40. or 50 yards from the high water marke: On both sides in the very necke of the maine, are high hills and dales, yet much inhabited, the Ile declining in a plaine fertile corne field, the lower end a low marsh. More plentie of swannes, cranes, geese, duckes, and mallards, and divers sorts of fowles, none would desire: more plaine fertile planted ground, in such great proportions as there, I had not seene; of a light blacke sandy mould, the cliffes commonly red, white, and yellowe coloured sand, and under, red and white clay; fish great plenty, and people aboundance: the most of their inhabitants, in view of the neck of Land, where a better seat for a towne cannot be desired:

At the end of forty miles, this river invironeth many low Ilands at each high water drowned for a mile, where it uniteth it selfe at a place called Apokant, the highest Towne inhabited. 10. miles higher, I discovered with the barge: in the mid way, a greate tree hindered my passage, which I cut in two. Heere the river became narrower, 8. 9 or 10. foote at a high water, and 6. or 7. at a lowe: the streame exceeding swift, and the bottom hard channell: the ground, most part a low plaine, sandy soyle. This occasioned me to suppose it might issue from some lake or some broad ford, for it could not be far to the head, but rather then I would endanger the barge [by exploring further, I decided to take it back to Apocant and use a canoe for the rest of the trip.] Yet to have beene able to resolve this doubt, and to discharge the imputation of malicious tungs, that halfe suspected I durst not, for so long delaying: some of the company as desirous as my self, we resolved to hier a Canow, and returne with the barge to Apocant, there to leave the barge secure, and put our selves upon the adventure: the country onely a vast and wilde wildernes, and but onely that Towne: Within three or foure mile, we hired a Canow, and 2. Indians to row us the next day a fowling. Having made such provision for the barge as was needfull, I left her there to ride, with expresse charge not any to go ashore til my returne.

Though some wise men may condemn this too bould attempt of too much indiscretion, yet if they well consider the friendship of the Indians in conducting me, the desolateness of the country, the probabilitie of some lacke [lake], and the malicious judges of my actions at home [Jamestown], as also to have some matters of worth to incourage our adventurers in england, might well have caused any honest minde to have done the like, as well for his own discharge as for the publike good:

Having 2 Indians for my guide and 2 of our own company, I set forward, leaving 7 in the barge: Having discovered 20 miles further in this desart, the river stil kept his depth and bredth, but much more combred with trees: Here we went ashore (being some 12 miles higher then the barge had bene) to refresh our selves, during the boyling of our vituals: One of the Indians I tooke with me, to see the nature of the soile, and to crosse the boughts of the river: the other Indian I left with Maister Robbinson and Thomas Emry, with their matches light, and order to discharge a peece, for my retreat, at the first sight of any Indian. But within a quarter of an houre I heard a loud cry, and a hollowing of Indians, but no warning peece. Supposing them surprised, and that the Indians had betraid us, presently I seazed him and bound his arme fast to my hand in a garter, with my pistoll ready bent to be revenged on him: he advised me to fly, and seemed ignorant of what was done. But as we went discoursing, I was struck with an arrow on the right thigh, but without harme: upon this occasion I espied 2. Indians drawing their bowes, which I prevented in discharging a french pistoll: By that I had charged againe, 3 or 4 more did the like: for the first fell downe and fled: At my discharge, they did the like. My hinde I made my barricado, who offered not to strive. 20. or 30. arrowes were shot at me but short. 3 or 4 times I had discharged my pistoll ere the king of Pamaunck called Opeckankenough with 200 men, invironed me, eache drawing their bowe: which done they laid them upon the ground, yet without shot: My hinde treated betwixt them and me of conditions of peace; he discovered me to be the Captaine: my request was to retire to the boate: they demaunded my armes, the rest they saide were slaine, onely me they would reserve: The Indian importuned me not to shoot. In retiring being in the midst of a low quagmire, and minding them wore then my steps, I stept fast into the quagmire, and also the Indian in drawing me forth:

Thus surprised, I resolved to trie their mercies: my armes I caste from me, till which none durst approch me. Being ceazed on me, they drew me out and led me to the King. I presented him with a compasse diall, describing by my best meanes the use therof: whereat he so amazedly admired, as he suffered me to proceed in a discourse of the roundnes of the earth, the course of the sunne, moone, starres and plannets. With kinde speeches and bread he requited me, conducting me where the Canow lay and John Robbinson slaine, with 20 or 30. arrowes in him. Emry I saw not.

I perceived by the aboundance of fires all over the woods [that the Indians had been hunting deer]. At each place I expected when they would execute me, yet they used me with what kindnes they could: Approaching their Towne, which was within 6 miles where I was taken, onely made as arbors and covered with mats, which they remove as occasion requires: all the women and children, being advertised of this accident, came foorth to meet them, the King well guarded with 20 bowmen 5 flanck and rear, and each flanck before him a sword and a peece, and after him the like, then a bowman, then I on each hand a boweman, the rest in the reare, which reare led foorth amongst the trees in a bishion, eache his bowe and a handfull of arrowes, a quiver at his back grimly painted: on eache flanck a sargeant, the one running alwaies towards the front, the other towards the reare, each a true pace and in exceeding good order. This being a good time continued, they caste themselves in a ring with a daunce, and so eache man departed to his lodging. The Captain conducting me to his lodging, a quarter of Venison and some ten pound of bread I had for supper: what I left was reserved for me, and sent with me to my lodging: Each morning 3. women presented me three great platters of fine bread, more venison then ten men could devour I had: my gowne, points and garters, my compas and my tablet they gave me again. Though 8 ordinarily guarded me, I wanted not what they could devise to content me: and still our longer acquaintance increased our better affection:

Much they threatned to assault our forte, as they were solicited by the King of Paspahegh: who shewed at our fort great signes of sorrow for this mischance. The King tooke great delight in understanding the manner of our ships, and sayling the seas, the earth and skies, and of our God: what he knew of the dominions he spared not to acquaint me with, as of certaine men cloathed at a place called Ocanahonan, cloathed like me: the course of our river, and that within 4 or 5 daies journey of the falles, was a great turning of salt water: I desired he would send a messenger to Paspahegh [Jamestown in the country of the Paspaheghs], with a letter I would write, by which they shold understand how kindly they used me, and that I was well, least they should revenge my death. This he granted and sent three men, in such weather as in reason were unpossible by any naked to be indured. Their cruell mindes towards the fort I had deverted, in describing the ordinance and the mines in the fields, as also the revenge Captain Newport would take of them at his returne. Their intent, I incerted the fort, the people of Ocanahonum and the back sea: this report they after found divers Indians that confirmed:

The next day after my letter, came a salvage to my lodging, with his sword, to have slaine me: but being by my guard intercepted, with a bowe and arrow he offred to have effected his purpose: the cause I knew not, till the King understanding thereof came and told me of a man a dying, wounded with my pistoll: he tould me also of another I had slayne, yet the most concealed they had any hurte: This was the father of him I had slayne, whose fury to prevent, the

King presently conducted me to another Kingdome, upon the top of the next northerly river, called Youghtanan. Having feasted me, he further led me to another branch of the river, called Mattapament, to two other hunting townes they led me: and to each of these Countries, a house of the great Emperour of Pewhakan, whom as yet I supposed to bee at the Fals; to him I tolde him I must goe, and so returne to Paspahegh. After this foure or five days march, we returned to Rasawrack, the first towne they brought me too: where binding the Mats in bundels, they marched two dayes journey, and crossed the River of Youghtanan, where it was as broad as Thames: so conducting me to a place called Menapacute in Pamaunke, where the King inhabited.

The next day another King of that nation called Kekataugh, having received some kindnes of me at the Fort, kindly invited me to feast at his house, the people from all places flocked to see me, each shewing to content me. By this, the great King hath foure or five houses, each containing foure score or an hundred foote in length, pleasantly seated upon an high sandy hill, from whence you may see westerly a goodly low Country, the river before the which his crooked course causeth many great Marshes of exceeding good ground. An hundred houses, and many large plaines are here togither inhabited. More abundance of fish and fowle, and a pleasanter seat cannot be imagined. The King with fortie Bowmen to guard me, intreated me to discharge my Pistoll, which they there presented me, with a mark at six score [yards] to strike therwith: but to spoil the practise, I broke the cocke, whereat they were much discontented, though a chaunce supposed.

From hence, this kind King conducted mee to a place called Topahanocke, a kingdome upon another River northward: The cause of this was, that the yeare before, a shippe had beene in the River of Pamaunke, who having beene kindly entertained by Powhatan their Emperour, they returned thence, and discovered the River of Topahanocke: where being received with like kindnesse, yet he slue the King, and tooke of his people, and they supposed I were hee. But the people reported him a great [tall] man that was Captaine, and using mee kindly, the next day we departed.

This River of Topahanock seemeth in breadth not much lesse then that we dwell upon. At the mouth of the River is a Countrey called Cuttata women: upwards is Marraugh tacum, Tapohanock, Appamatuck, and Nantaugs tacum: at top, Manahocks, the head issuing from many Mountaines. The next night I lodged at a hunting town of Powhatans, and the next day arrived at Waranacomoco upon the river of Pamauncke, where the great king is resident. By the way we passed by the top of another little river, which is betwixt the two, called Payankatank. The most of this Country though Desert, yet exceeding fertil; good timber, most hils and dales, in each valley a cristall spring.

Arriving at Weramocomoco, their Emperour proudly lying uppon a Bedstead a foote high, upon tenne or twelve Mattes, richly hung with manie Chaynes of great Pearles about his necke, and covered with a great Covering of Rahaughcums [raccoon skins]. At heade sat a woman, at his feete another; on each side sitting uppon a Matte uppon the ground, were raunged his chiefe men on each side of the fire, tenne in a ranke, and behinde them as many yong women, each a great Chaine of white Beades over their shoulders, their heades painted in redde: and with such a grave and Majesticall countenance, as drave me into admiration to see such state in a naked Salvage, hee kindly welcomed me with good wordes, and great Platters of sundrie Victuals, assuring mee his friendship, and my libertie within foure days. Hee much delighted in Opechan Conoughs relation of what I had described to him, and oft examined me upon the same. Hee asked mee the cause of our comming. I tolde him being in fight with the Spaniards our enemie, beeing overpowred, neare put to retreat, and by extreame weather put to this shore: where landing at Chesipiack, the people shot us, but at Kequoughtan they kindly used us: we by signes demaunded fresh water, they described us up the River was all fresh water: at Paspahegh also they kindly used us: our Pinnasse being leake, we were inforced to stay to mend her, till Captaine Newport my father came to conduct us away. He demaunded why we went further with our Boate. I tolde him, in that I would have occasion to talke of the backe Sea, that on the other side the maine, where was salt water. My father had a childe slaine, whiche wee supposed Monocan his enemie: whose death we intended to revenge.

After good deliberation, hee began to describe mee the Countreys beyonde the Falles, with many of the rest; confirming what not onely Opechancanoyes, and an Indian which had beene prisoner to Pewhatan had before tolde mee: but some called it five dayes, some sixe, some eight, where the sayde water dashed amongest many stones and rockes, each storm; which caused oft tymes the heade of the River to bee brackish: Anchanachuck he described to bee the people that had slaine my brother: whose death hee would revenge. Hee described also upon the same Sea, a mighty Nation called Pocoughtronack, a fierce Nation that did eate men, and warred with the people of Moyaoncer and Pataromerke [Patawomecke, i. e. Potomac], Nations upon the toppe of the heade of the Bay, under his territories: where the yeare before they had slain an hundred. He signified their crownes were shaven, long haire in the necke, tied on a knot, Swords like Pollaxes.

Beyond them, he described people with short Coates, and Sleeves to the Elbowes, that passed that way in Shippes like ours. Many Kingdomes hee described mee, to the heade of the Bay, which seemed to bee a mightie River issuing from mightie Mountaines betwixt the two Seas: The people cloathed at Ocamahowan, he also confirmed; and the Southerly Countries also, as the rest that reported us to be within a day and a halfe of Mangoge, two dayes of Chawwonock, 6. from Roonock [Roanoke], to the south part of the backe sea: He described a countrie called Anone, where they have abundance of Brasse, and houses walled as ours.

I requited his discourse (seeing what pride hee had in his great and spacious Dominions, seeing that all hee knewe were under his Territories) in describing to him the territories of Europe, which was subject to our great King whose subject I was, the innumerable multitude of his ships, I gave him to understand the noyse of Trumpets, and terrible manner of fighting were under captain Newport my father: whom I intituled the Meworames, which they call the King of all the waters. At his greatnesse, he admired: and not a little feared. He desired mee to forsake Paspahegh, and to live with him upon his River, a Countrie called Capa Howasicke. Hee promised to give me Corne, Venison, or what I wanted to feede us: Hatchets and Copper wee should make him, and none should disturbe us. This request I promised to performe: and thus, having with all the kindnes hee could devise, sought to content me, hee sent me home, with 4. men: one that usually carried my Gowne and Knapsacke after me, two other loded with bread, and one to accompanie me.

This River of Pamaunke is not past twelve mile from that we dwell on, his course northwest and westerly as the other. Weraocomoco is upon salt water in bredth two myles, and so keepeth his course without any tarrying some twenty miles; where at the parting of the fresh water and the salt, it divideth it selfe into two partes, the one part to Goughland as broad as Thames, and navigable with a Boate threescore or fourescore miles, and with a Shippe fiftie: exceeding crooked, and manie low grounds and marishes, but inhabited with aboundance of warlike and tall people. The Countrey of Youghtomam, of no lesse worth, onely it is lower; but all the soyle, a fatte, fertill, sandie ground. Above Manapacumter, many high sandie mountaines. By the River is many Rockes, seeming, if not, of severall Mines. The other branch a little lesse in breadth, yet extendeth not neare so farre, nor so well inhabited, somewhat lower, and a white sandie, and a white clay soyle: here is their best *Terra Sigillata*. The mouth of the River, as I see in the discoverie therof with captain Newport, is halfe a mile broad, and within foure miles not above a Musket shot: the channell exceeding good and deepe, the River straight to the devisions. Kiskirk the nearest Nation to the entrances.

Their religion and Ceremonie I observed was thus: Three or foure dayes after my taking, seven of them in the house where I lay, each with a rattle, began at ten a clocke in the morning to sing about the fire, which they invironed with a Circle of meale, and after a foote or two from that, at the end of each song, layde downe two or three graines of wheate: continuing this order till they have included sixe or seven hundred in a halfe Circle; and after that, two or three more Circles in like maner, a hand bredth from other. That done, at each song, they put betwixt everie three, two, or five graines, a little sticke; so counting as an old woman her *Pater noster*.

One disguised with a great Skinne, his head hung round with little Skinnes of Weasels and other vermine, with a Crownet of feathers on his head, painted as ugly as the divell, at the end of each song will make many signes and demonstrations, with strange and vehement actions, great cakes of Deere suet, Deare, and Tobacco he casteth in the fire: till sixe a clocke in the Evening, their howling would continue ere they would depart. Each morning in the coldest frost, the principall, to the number of twentie or thirtie, assembled themselves in a round circle, a good distance from the towne: where they told me they there consulted where to hunt the next day: So fat they fed mee, that I much doubted they intended to have sacrificed mee to the Quiyoughquosicke, which is a superiour power they worship: a more uglier thing cannot be described. One they have for chief sacrifices, which also they call Quiyoughquosick. To cure the sick, a man, with a Rattle, and extreame howling, showting, singing, and such violent gestures and Anticke actions over the patient, will sucke out blood and flegme from the patient, out of their unable stomacke, or any diseased place, as no labour will more tire them. Tobacco, they offer the water in passing in fowle weather. The death of any they lament with great sorrow and weeping. Their Kings they burie betwixt two mattes within their houses, with all his beads, jewels, hatchets, and copper: the other in graves like ours. They acknowledge no resurrection.

Powhatan hath three brethren, and two sisters, each of his brethren succeeded [succeedeth] other. For the Crowne, their heyres inherite not, but the first heyres of the Sisters, and so successively the weomens heires. For the Kings have as many weomen as they will, his Subjects two, and most but one.

From Weramocomoco is but 12. miles, yet the Indians trifled away that day,[4] and would not goe to our Forte by any perswasions: but in certaine olde hunting houses of Paspahegh we lodged all night. The next morning ere Sunne rise, we set forward for our Fort, where we arrived within an houre: where each man with the truest signes of joy they could expresse welcommed me, except M. Archer, and some 2. or 3. of his, who was then in my absence, sworne Counsellour, though not with the consent of Captaine Martin: Great blame and imputation was laide upon mee by them, for the losse of our two men which the Indians slew: insomuch that they pur-

[4]January 1, 1608.

posed to depose me. But in the midst of my miseries, it pleased God to send Captaine Nuport: who arriving there the same night, so tripled our joy as for a while these plots against me, which were deferred; though with much malice against me, which captain Newport in short time did plainly see. Now was maister Scrivener, captaine Martin, and my selfe, called Counsellers.

Within five or sixe dayes after the arrivall of the Ship, by a mischaunce our Fort was burned, and the most of our apparell, lodging and private provision. Many of our old men diseased, and of our new for want of lodging perished. The Empereur Powhatan, each weeke once or twice, sent me many presents of Deare, bread, Raugroughcuns; halfe alwayes for my father [Captain Newport] whom he much desired to see, and halfe for me: and so continually importuned by messengers and presents, that I would come to fetch the corne, and take the Countrie their King had given me, as at last Captaine Newport resolved to go see him. Such acquaintance I had amongst the Indians, and such confidence they had in me, as neare the Fort they would not come till I came to them; every of them calling me by my name, would not sell any thing till I had first received their presents, and what they had that I liked, they deferred to my discretion: but after acquaintance, they usually came into the Fort at their pleasure: The President and the rest of the Councell, they knewe not; but Captaine Newports greatnesse I had so described, as they conceyved him the chiefe, the rest his children, Officers, and servants.

We had agreed with the king of Paspahegh, to conduct two of our men to a place called Panawicke beyond Roonok, where he reported many men to be apparelled. Wee landed him at Warraskoyack, where playing the villaine, and deluding us for rewards, returned within three or foure dayes after, without going further. Captaine Newport, maister Scrivener, and my selfe, found the mouth of Pamauncks river, some 25. or 30. miles north ward from Cape Henricke, the chanell good as before expressed.

Arriving at Weramocomoca, being jealous of the intent of this politick salvage; to discover his intent the better, I with 20. shot armed in Jacks, went a shore. The Bay where he dwelleth hath in it 3. cricks, and a mile and a halfe from the chanel all os [ooze, i. e., marsh]. Being conducted to the towne, I found my selfe mistaken in the creeke, for they al there were within lesse then a mile: the Emperors sonne called Naukaquawis, the captaine that tooke me, and diverse others of his chiefe men, conducted me to their kings habitation. But in the mid way I was intercepted by a great creek over which they had made a bridge of grained stakes and railes. The king of Kiskieck, and Namontack, who all the journey, the king had sent to guide us, had conducted us this passage, which caused me to suspect some mischiefe: the barge I had sent to meet me at the right landing, when I found my selfe first deceyved. And knowing by experience the most of their courages to proceede from others feare, though fewe lyked the passage, I intermingled the Kings sonne, our conductors, and his chiefe men amongst ours, and led forward, leaving halfe at the one ende to make a guard for the passage of the Front. The Indians seeing the weakenesse of the Bridge, came with a Canow, and tooke me in of the middest, with foure or five more: being landed, wee made a guard for the rest till all were passed. Two in a ranke we marched to the Emperors house. Before his house stood fortie or fiftie great Platters of fine bread. Being entred the house, with loude tunes they all made signes of great joy. This proude salvage, having his finest women, and the principall of his chiefe men assembled, sate in rankes as before is expressed: himself as upon a Throne at the upper ende of the house, with such a Majestie as I cannot expresse, nor yet have often seene, either in Pagan or Christian. With a kinde countenance hee bad mee welcome, and caused a place to bee made by himselfe to sit. I presented him a sute of red cloath, a white Greyhound, and a Hatte: as Jewels he esteemed them, and with a great Oration made by three of his Nobles, if there be any amongst Salvages, kindly accepted them, with a publike confirmation of a perpetuall league and friendship.

After that, he commanded the Queene of Apamatuc, a comely yong Salvage, to give me water, a Turkie cocke, and breade to eate: Being thus feasted, hee began his discourse to this purpose. Your kinde visitation doth much content mee, but where is your father [Captain Newport] whom I much desire to see, is he not with you. I told him, he remained aboord, but the next day he would come unto him. With a merrie countenance he asked me for certaine peeces [guns] which I promised him, when I went to Paspahegh. I told according to my promise, that I proferred the man that went with me foure Demy Culverings [small cannon], in that he so desired a great Gunne: but they refused to take them. Whereat with a lowde laughter, he desired to give him some of lesse burden: as for the other I gave him them, being sure that none could carrie them. But where are these men you promised to come with you. I told him, without. Who thereupon gave order to have them brought in, two after two, ever maintaining the guard without. And as they presented themselves, ever with thankes he would salute me: and caused each of them to have foure or five pound of bread given them. This done, I asked him for the corne and ground he promised me. He told me I should have it: but he expected to have all these men lay their armes at his feet, as did his subjects. I tolde him that was a ceremonie our enemies desired, but never our Friends, as we presented ourselves unto him; yet that he should not doubt of our friendship. The next day my Father would give him a child of his, in full assurance of our loves, and not only that, but when he should thinke it convenient, wee would deliver under his subjection the Country of Manacam and Pocoughtaonack his enemies.

This so contented him, as immediately with attentive silence, with a lowd oration he proclaimed me Awerowanes [a chief] of Powhaton, and that all his subjects should so esteeme us, and no man account us strangers nor Paspaheghans, but Powhatans, and that the Corne, weomen and Country, should be to us as to his owne people. This proffered kindnes for many reasons we contemned not, but with the best Languages and signes of thankes I could expresse, I tooke my leave.

The King rising from his seat, conducted me foorth, and caused each of my men to have as much more bread as hee could beare: giving me some in a basket, and as much he sent a board for a present to my Father. Victuals you must know is all there wealth, and the greatest kindnes they could shew us.

Arriving at the River, the Barge was fallen so low with the ebbe, though I had given order and oft sent to prevent the same, yet the messengers deceived mee. The Skies being very thick and rainie, the

King understanding this mischance, sent his Sonne and Mamontacke, to conduct mee to a great house sufficient to lodge mee: where entring I saw it hung round with bowes and arrowes. The Indians used all diligence to make us fires, and give us content: the kings Orators presently entertained us with a kinde oration, with expresse charge that not any should steale, or take our bowes or arrowes, or offer any injury. Presently after he sent me a quarter of Venizon to stay my stomacke: In the evening hee sent for mee to come onely with two shot with me. The company I gave order to stand upon their guard, and to maintaine two sentries at the ports all night. To my supper he set before me meate for twenty men, and seeing I could not eate, hee caused it to be given to my men: for this is a generall custome, that what they give, not to take againe, but you must either eate it, give it away, or carry it with you. Two or three houres we spent in our auncient discourses; which done, I was with a fire stick lighted to my lodging.

The next day the King conducting mee to the River, shewed me his Canowes, and described unto me how hee sent them over the Baye, for tribute Beades: and also what Countries paid him Beads, Copper, or Skins. But seeing Captaine Nuport, and Maister Scrivener, comming a shore, the King returned to his house, and I went to meete him. With a trumpet before him, wee marched to the King: who after his old manner kindly received him, especially a Boy of thirteen yeares old, called Thomas Salvage, whom he gave him as his Sonne. He requited this kindnes with each of us a great basket of Beanes. And entertaining him with the former discourse, we passed away that day, and agreed to bargaine the next day and so returned to our Pinnis.

The next day comming a shore in like order, the King having kindly entertained us with a breakfast, questioned us in this manner: Why we came armed in that sort, seeing hee was our friend, and had neither bowes nor arrowes; what did wee doubt? I told him it was the custome of our Country, not doubting of his kindnes any waies: wherewith though hee seemed satisfied, yet Captaine Nuport caused all our men to retire to the water side, which was some thirtie score [yards] from thence.

But to prevent the worst, Maister Scrivener or I were either the one or other by the Barge: experience had well taught me to beleeve his friendship till convenient opportunity suffred him to betray us. But quickly this polititian had perceived my absence, and cunningly sent for me; I sent for Maister Scrivener to supply my place: the King would demand for him, I would againe releeve him. And they sought to satisfie our suspition with kind Language: and not being agreed to trade for corne, hee desired to see all our Hatchets and Copper together, for which he would give us corne. With that auncient tricke the Chickahamaniens had oft acquainted me: his offer I refused, offering first to see what hee would give for one piece. Hee seeming to despise the nature of a Merchant, did scorn to sell: but we freely should give him, and he liberally would requite us.

Captaine Nuport would not with lesse then twelve great Coppers try his kindnes, which he liberally requited with as much corne as at Chickahamania I had for one of lesse proportion. Our Hatchets hee would also have at his owne rate: for which kindnes hee much seemed to affect Captaine Nuport. Some few bunches of blew Beades I had, which he much desired, and seeing so few, he offred me a basket of two pecks, and that I drew to be three pecks at the least, and yet [he] seemed contented and desired more. I agreed with him, the next day, for two bushells: for the ebbe now constrained us to returne to our Boate, although he earnestly desired us to stay dinner which was a providing; and being ready he sent abroad after us, which was bread and venizon sufficient for fiftie or sixtie persons.

The next day hee sent his Sonne in the morning, not to bring a shore with us any pieces, least his weomen and children should feare. Captaine Nuports good beliefe would have satisfied that request. Yet twentie or twentie five shot we got ashore: the King importuning mee to leave my armes a board, much misliking my sword pistol and target. I told him the men that slew my Brother with the like tearmes had perswaded me, and being unarmed shot at us, and so betraide us.

He oft entreated Captaine Nuport that his men might leave their armes: which still hee [Captain Newport] commanded to the water side. This day we spent in trading for blew Beads: and having neare fraighted our Barge, Captaine Nuport returned with them that came abord, leaving me and Maister Scrivener a shore, to follow in Canowes. Into one I got with six of our men, which beeing launched, a stones cast from the shore stuck fast in the Ose [ooze]. Master Scrivener seeing this example, with seven or eight more passed the dreadfull bridge, thinking to have found deeper water on the other creeke: but they were inforced to stay, with such entertainment as a salvage. Being forced ashore with wind and raine, having in his Canow as commonly they have, his house and houshold, instantly set up a house of mats, which succoured them from the storme.

The Indians seeing me pestred in the Ose, called to me: six or seven of the Kings chiefe men threw off their skins, and to the middle in Ose, came to bear me out on their heads. Their importunacie caused me better to like the Canow than their curtesie, excusing my deniall for feare to fall into the Ose: desiring them to bring me some wood, fire, and mats to cover me, and I would content them. Each presently gave his helpe to satisfie my request, which paines a horse would scarce have indured: yet a couple of bells richly contented them.

The Emperor sent his Seaman Mantivas in the evening with bread and victuall for me and my men: he no more scrupulous then the rest seemed to take a pride in shewing how litle he regarded that miserable cold and durty passage, though a dogge would scarce have indured it. This kindnes I found, when I litle expected lesse then a mischiefe: but the blacke night parting our companies, ere midnight the flood served to carry us aboard.

The next day we came ashore, the King with a solemne discourse, causing all to depart but his principall men: and this was the effect. When as hee perceived that we had a desire to invade Monacum, against whom he was no professed enemy: yet thus farre he would assist us in his enterprise. First hee would send his spies, perfectly to understand their strength and ability to fight, with which he would acquaint us himselfe. Captaine Nuport would not be seene in it himselfe, being great Werowances. They [Powhatan and Newport] would stay at home: but I, Maister Scrivener, and two of his [Powhatan's] Sonnes, and Opechankanough the King of Pamaunke should have 100. of his men to goe before as though they were hunting; they giving us notise where was the advantage, we should kill them: the weomen and young children he wished we should spare, and bring them to him. Only 100. or 150. of our men he held sufficient for this exploit. Our boats should stay at the falls, where we might hew timber, which we might convey, each man a piece, till we were past the stones; and there joyne them to passe our men by water. If any were shot, his men should bring them backe to our boats. This faire tale had almost made Captaine Nuport undertake by this meanes to discover the South sea: which will not be without trecherie, if wee ground our intent upon his constancie.

This day we spent in trading, dancing, and much mirth. The King of Pamaunke sent his messenger (as yet not knowing Captaine Nuport) to come unto him: who had long expected mee, desiring also my Father to visite him. The messenger stayed to conduct us: but Powhatan understanding that we had Hatchets lately come from Paspahegh, desired the next day to trade with us, and not to go further. This new tricke he cunningly put upon him, but onely to have what he listed, and to try whether we would go or stay. Opechankenoughs messenger returned [answered], that wee would not come. The next day his Daughter came to entreat me, shewing her Father had hurt his legge, and much sorrowed he could not see me.

Captaine Nuport being not to bee perswaded to goe, in that Powhatan had desired us to stay: sent her away with the like answer. Yet the next day, upon better consideration, intreatie prevailed; and wee anchored at Cinquoateck, the first twaine [town] above the parting of the river, where dwelled two Kings of Pamaunke, Brothers to Powhatan; the one called Opitchapam, the other Katatough. To these I went a shore, who kindly intreated mee and Maister Scrivener, sending some presents aboard to Captaine Nuport. Whilst we were trucking with these Kings, Opechankanough his wife, weomen, and children came to meete me: with a naturall kind affection hee seemed to rejoyce to see me.

Captaine Nuport came a shore, with many kind discourses wee passed that forenoone: and after dinner, Captaine Nuport went about with the Pinnis to Menapacant, which is twenty miles by water, and not one by land. Opechankanough conducted me and Maister Scrivener by land: where having built a feasting house a purpose to entertaine us, with a kind Oration, after their manner, and his best provision, kindly welcomed us. That day he would not trucke, but did his best to delight us with content: Captaine Nuport arrived towards evening; whom the King presented with six great platters of fine bread, and Pansarowmana. The next day till noone wee traded: the King feasted all the company; and the afternoone was spent in playing, dauncing, and delight. By no meanes hee would have us depart till, the next day, he had feasted us with venizon; for which he had sent, having spent his first and second provision in expecting our comming: The next day, he performed his promise, giving more to us three, then would have sufficed 30. and in that we carried not away what we left, hee sent it after us to the Pinnis. With what words or signes of love he could expresse, we departed.

Captaine Nuport in the Pinnis, leaving mee in the Barge to digge a rocke, where wee supposed a Mine, at Cinquaoteck: which done, ere midnight, I arrived at Weracomoco, where our Pinnis anchored, being 20. miles from Cinquaotecke. The next day, we tooke leave of Powhatan: who, in regard of his kindness, gave him an Indian. He well affected to goe with him for England in steed of his Sonne: the cause, I assure me, was to know our strength and Countries condition: The next day we arrived at Kiskiack. The people so scornefully entertained us, as with what signes of scorne and discontent we could, we departed: and returned to our Fort with 250. bushells of Corne.[5] Our president, being not wholy recovered of his sicknes, in discharging his Piece, brake and split his hand off, which he is not yet [6] well recovered. At Captaine Nuports arrivall,[7] wee were victualled for twelve weeks: and having furnished him of what hee thought good, hee set saile for England the tenth of April. Master Scrivener and my selfe, with our shallop, accompanied him to Cape Hendrick: Powhatan having for a farrewell, sent him five or six mens loadings, with Turkeys for swords which hee sent him. In our return to the fort, we discovered the river of Nausamd, a proud warlike Nation, as well we may testifie, at our first arrivall at Chesiapiack: but that injury Captaine Nuport well revenged at his re-

[5]March 9, 1608.
[6]June 2, 1608.
[7]March 9, 1608.

turne. Where some of them intising him to their Ambuscadoes by a daunce, hee perceiving their intent, with a volly of musket shot, slew one, and shot one or two more, as themselves confesse.

The King at our arivall sent for me to come unto him. I sent him word what commodities I had to exchange for wheat [Indian corn], and if he would, as had the rest of his Neighbours, conclude a Peace, we were contented. At last he came downe before the Boate which rid at anchor some fortie yards from the shore. He signified to me to come a shore, and sent a Canow with foure or five of his men: two whereof I desired to come aboard and to stay, and I would send two to talke with their King a shore. To this hee agreed. The King wee presented with a piece of Copper, which he kindly excepted [accepted], and sent for victualls to entertaine the messengers. Maister Scrivener and my selfe also, after that, went a shore. The King kindly feasted us, requesting us to stay to trade till the next day. Which having done, we returned to the Fort.

This river is a musket shot broad, each side being should [shoal] bayes; a narrow channel, but three fadom: his course for eighteene miles, almost directly South, and by West where beginneth the first inhabitants: for a mile it turneth directly East; towards the West, a great bay, and a white chaukie Iland convenient for a Fort: his next course South, where within a quarter of a mile, the river divideth in two, the neck a plaine high Corne field, the wester bought [bend] a highe plaine likewise, the Northeast answerable in all respects. In these plaines are planted aboundance of houses and people; they may containe 1000. Acres of most excellent fertill ground: so sweete, so pleasant, so beautifull, and so strong a prospect, for an invincible strong City, with so many commodities, that I know as yet I have not seene. This is within one daies journey of Chawwonocke, the river falleth into the Kings river, within twelve miles of Cape-hendicke.

At our Fort, the tooles we had, were so ordinarily stolen by the Indians, as necessity inforced us to correct their braving theeverie: for he that stole to day, durst come againe the next day. One amongst the rest, having stolen two swords, I got the Counsels consent to set in the bilboes.[8] The next day, with three more, he came, with their

[8]Stocks for confining prisoners.

woodden swordes, in the midst of our men to steale. Their custome
is to take any thing they can ceaze off: onely the people of Pamaunke wee have not found stealing, but what others can steale,
their King receiveth. I bad them depart, but flourishing their swords,
they seemed to defend what they could catch but out of our hands:
his pride urged me to turne him from amongst us, whereat he offred
to strike me with his sword; which I prevented, striking him first.
The rest offring to revenge the blow, received such an incounter,
and fled. The better to affright them, I pursued them with five or sixe
shot, and so chased them out of the Iland [peninsula].

The beginner of this broyle, litle expecting by his carriage, we
durst have resisted, having, even till that present, not beene contra-
dicted, especially them of Paspahegh: these Indians within one
houre, having by other Salvages then in the Fort, understood that
I threatened to be revenged, came presently of themselves, and fell
to working upon our wears which were then in hand by other Salvages: who seeing their pride so incountred, were so submissive,
and willing to doe any thing as might be. And with trembling feare
desired to be friends, within three daies after. From Nawsamond,
which is 30. miles from us, the King sent us a Hatchet which they
had stollen from us at our being there: the messenger, as is the custome, also wee well rewarded and contented.

The twenty of Aprill, being at worke, in hewing downe Trees, and
setting Corne, an alarum caused us with all speede to take our
armes, each expecting a new assault of the Salvages: but understanding it a Boate under saile, our doubts were presently satisfied
with the happy sight of Maister Nelson, his many perrills of extreame stormes and tempests [passed], his ship well as his company
could testifie, his care in sparing our provision was well: but the
providence thereof, as also of our stones, Hatchets and other tooles
(onely ours excepted) which of all the rest was most necessary:
which might inforce us to thinke either a seditious traitor to our
action, or a most unconscionable deceiver of our treasurs.

This happy arrivall of Maister Nelson in the *Phenix*, having beene
then about three monethes missing after Captaine Nuports arrivall,
being to all our expectations lost: albeit that now at the last, having
beene long crossed with tempestuous weather and contrary winds,

his so unexpected comming did so ravish us with exceeding joy, that now we thought our selves as well fitted as our harts could wish, both with a competent number of men, as also for all other needfull provisions, till a further supply should come unto us. Whereupon the first thing that was concluded was that my selfe and Maister Scrivener, should with 70. men goe with the best meanes we could provide, to discover beyong the Falls, as in our judgements conveniently we might. Six or seaven daies we spent only in trayning our men to march, fight, and scirmish in the woods. Their willing minds to this action so quickned their understanding in this exercise as, in all judgements, wee were better able to fight with Powhatans whole force, in our order of battle amongst the Trees (for Thicks there is few) then the Fort was to repulse 400. at the first assault, with some tenne or twenty shot not knowing what to doe, nor how to use a Piece.

Our warrant being sealed, Maister Nelson refused to assiste us with the voluntary Marriners and himself, as he promised, unlesse we would stand bound to pay the hire for shippe and Marriners, for the time they stayed. And further there was some controversie, through the diversitie of Contrary opinions: some alleadging that how profitable, and to what good purpose soever our journey should portend, yet our commission commanding no certaine designe, we should be taxed for the most indiscreete men in the world, besides the wrong we should doe to Captaine Nuport, to whom only all discoveries did belong, and to no other:

The meanes for guides, besides the uncertaine courses of the river from which we could not erre much, each night would fortifie us in two houres better then that they first called the Fort. Their Townes upon the river each within one dayes journey of other, besides our ordinary provision, might well be supposed to adde reliefe: for truck and dealing only, but in love and peace, as with the rest. If they assalted us, their Townes they cannot defend, nor their luggage so convey that we should not share: but admit the worst, 16. daies provision we had of Cheese Oatmeale and bisket; besides our randevous we could, and might, have hid in the ground. With six men, Captaine Martin would have undertaken it himselfe, leaving the rest to defend the Fort and plant our Corne. Yet no reason could be reason to proceede forward, though we were going aboard to set saile. These discontents caused so many doubts to some, and discouragements to others, as our journey ended. Yet some of us procured petitions to set us forward, only with hope of our owne confusions.

Our next course was to turne husbandmen, to fell Trees and set Corne. Fiftie of our men we imployed in this service; the rest kept the Fort, to doe the command of the president and Captaine Martin. 30. dayes[9] the ship lay expecting the triall of certain matters which for some cause I keepe private.[10]

The next exploit was an Indian having stolen an Axe, was so pursued by Maister Scrivener and them next him, as he threw it downe: and flying, drew his bow at any that durst incounter him. Within foure or five dayes after, Maister Scrivener and I, being a litle from the Fort, among the Corne, two Indians, each with a cudgell, and all newly painted with *Terrasigillata,* came circling about me as though they would have clubed me like a hare. I knew their faining love is towards me not without a deadly hatred: but to prevent the worst, I calling maister Scrivener retired to the Fort. The Indians seeing me suspect them, with good tearmes, asked me for some of their men whom they would beate; and went with me into our Fort. Finding one that lay ordinarily with us, only for a spie; they offered to beat him. I in perswading them to forbeare, they offered to beginne with me; being now foure: for two other arrayed in like manner, came in on the other side the Fort. Whereupon I caused to shut the Ports, and apprehend them. The president and Counsell, being presently acquainted, remembring at the first assault, they came in like manner, and never else but against some villanie, concluded to commit them to prison, and expect the event. Eight more we ceazed at that present. An houre after came three or foure other strangers extraordinarily fitted with arrowes, skinnes, and shooting gloves: their jealousie and feare bewrayed their bad intent, as also their suspitious departure.

The next day, came first an Indian, then another, as Embassadors

---

[9]May 4, 1608 to June 2, 1608.

[10]A disagreement between Smith and Captain Martin as to the cargo which the *Phoenix* should take back to England.

John Smith, 1579-1631

for their men. They desired to speake with me. Our discourse was, that what Spades, Shovells, swords, or tooles they had stolne to bring home: if not, the next day, they should hang. The next newes was, they had taken two of our men ranging in the woods (which mischiefe no punishment will prevent but hanging): and these they would, should redeeme their owne 16. or 18.; thus braving us to our doores.

We desired the president, and Captaine Martin, that afternoone to sally upon them, that they might but know what we durst do: and at night, mand our Barge, and burnt their Townes, and spoiled and destroyed what we could. But they brought our men, and freely delivered them. The President released one. The rest we brought well guarded, to Morning and Evening prayers. Our men all in armes, their trembling feare then caused them to [too] much sorrow, which till then scoffed and scorned at what we durst doe. The Counsell concluded, that I should terrifie them with some torture, to know if I could know their intent. The next day, I bound one in hold to the maine Mast: and presenting sixe Muskets with match in the cockes, forced him to desire life. To answer my demaunds he could not: but one of his Comovodos was of the counsell of Paspahegh, that could satisfie me: I releasing him out of sight, I affrighted the other, first with the rack, then with Muskets; which seeing, he desired me to stay, and hee would confesse. To this execution Maister Scrivener came, his discourse was to this effect. That Paspehegh, the Chickahamaniar, Youghtanum, Pamaunka, Mattapanient, and Kiskiack: these Nations were al together a hunting that tooke me. Paspahegh and Chicahamanya had entended to surprise us at worke, to have had our tools. Powhatan and al his would seeme friends, till Captaine Nuports returne, that he had againe his man, which he called Namontack: where, with a great feast, hee would so enamor Captain Nuport and his men, as they should ceaze on him. And the like traps would be laied for the rest.

This trap for our tooles we suspected. The chiefe occasion was foure daies before, Powhatan had sent the boy he had to us, with many Turkies to Maister Scrivener and me: understanding I would go up unto his Countries to destroy them; and he doubted [suspected] it the more, in that I so ofte practised my men, whose shoot-

97

ing he heard to his owne lodging, that much feared his wives and children. We sent him word, we entended no such thing, but only to goe to Powhatan, to seeke stones to make Hatchets; except his men shot at us, as Paspahegh had told us they would: which if they did shoote but one arrowe, we would destroy them. And, least this mischiefe might happen, sent the boy to acquaint him thus much; and request him to send us Weanock, one of his subjects for a guide.

The boy he returned backe with his Chest and apparell, which then we had given him: desiring another for him. The cause was, he was practising with the Chikahamanias, as the boy suspected some villanie, by their extraordinary resort and secret conference, from whence they would send him. The boy we keepe. Now we would send him many messengers and presents, the guide we desired he sent us: and withall requested us to returne him, either the boy or some other. But none he could have. And that day these Indians were apprehended, his sonne with others that had loaded at our Fort, returned, and being out of the Fort, rayled on me, to divers of our men, to be enemies to him, and to the Chikamanias. Not long after, Weanock that had bin with us for our guide, whom wee kept to have conducted us in another journey, with a false excuse returned: and secretly after him, Amocis the Paspaheyan, who alwaies they kept amongst us for a spie, whom, the better to avoide suspition, presently after they came to beate away: These presumptions induced me to take any occasion, not onely to try the honesty of Amocis the spie, but also the meaning of these cunning trickes of their Emperour of Powhatan; whose true meaning Captaine Martin most confidently pleaded.

The confession of Macanoe, which was the counseller of Paspahegh, first I, then Maister Scrivener, upon their severall examinations, found by them all confirmed, that Paspahegh and Chickahammania did hate us, and intended some mischiefe: and who they were that tooke me, the names of them that stole our tooles and swords, and that Powhatan received them they all agreed. Certaine vollies of shot we caused to be discharged, which caused each other to think that their fellowes had beene slaine.

Powhatan understanding we detained certaine Salvages, sent his Daughter, a child of tenne yeares old: which, not only for feature, countenance, and proportion, much exceedeth any of the rest of his people: but for wit and spirit, the only Nonpariel of his Country. This hee sent by his most trustie messenger, called Rawhunt, as much exceeding in deformitie of person; but of a subtill wit and crafty understanding. He, with a long circumstance, told mee, how well Powhatan loved and respected mee; and in that I should not doubt any way of his kindnesse, he had sent his child, which he most esteemed, to see me; a Deare and bread besides, for a present: desiring me that the Boy might come againe, which he loved exceedingly. His litle Daughter hee had taught this lesson also, not taking notice at all of the Indeans that had beene prisoners three daies, till that morning that she saw their fathers and friends come quietly, and in good tearmes to entreate their libertie.

Opechankanough sent also unto us, that for his sake, we would release two that were his friends: and for a token, sent me his shooting Glove and Bracer, which [he used] the day our men was taken upon, separating himselfe from the rest a long time, [the messenger] intreated to speake with me, where in token of peace, he had preferred me the same. Now all of them having found their peremptorie conditions but to increase our malice; which they seeing us begin to threaten to destroy them, as familiarly as before, without suspition or feare, came amongst us, to begge libertie for their men. In the afternoone, they being gone, we guarded them as before to the Church; and after prayer, gave them to Pocahuntas, the Kings Daughter, in regard of her fathers kindnesse in sending her. After having well fed them, as all the time of their imprisonment, we gave them their bowes, arrowes, or what else they had; and with much content, sent them packing. Pocahuntas also we requited with such trifles as contented her, to tel that we had used the Paspaheyans very kindly in so releasing them.

The next day, we had suspition of some other practise for an Ambuscado; but perfectly wee could not discover it. Two daies after, a Paspaheyan came to shew us a glistering Minerall stone, and with signes demonstrating it to be in great aboundance like unto Rockes: with some dozen more, I was sent to seeke to digge some quantitie, and the Indean to conduct me. But suspecting this some trick to delude us, for to get some Copper of us; or with some ambuscado

99

to betray us, seeing his falter in his tale, being two miles on our way, led him ashore: where abusing us from place to place, and so seeking either to have drawne us with him into the woods, or to have given us the slippe, I shewed him Copper, which I promised to have given him, if he had performed his promise. But for his scoffing and abusing us, I gave him twentie lashes with a Rope; and his bowes and arrowes, bidding him shoote if he durst: and so let him goe.

In all this time, our men being all or the most part well recovered, and we not willing to trifle away more time then necessitie enforced us unto: we thought good, for the better content of the adventurers, in some reasonable sort to fraight home Maister Nelson, with Cedar wood. About which, our men going with willing minds, was in very good time effected, and the ship sent for England. Wee now remaining being in good health, all our men wel contented, free from mutinies, in love one with another, and as we hope in a continuall peace with the Indians: where we doubt not but by Gods gracious assistance, and the adventurers willing minds and speedie furtherance to so honorable an action, in after times to see our Nation to enjoy a Country, not onely exceeding pleasant for habitation, but also very profitable for comerce in generall; no doubt pleasing to almightie God, honourable to our gracious Soveraigne, and commodious generally to the whole Kingdome.

WILLIAM STRACHEY
fl. 1610

William Strachey, first secretary of the colony at Jamestown, sailed on the *Sea Adventure* from England on June 2, 1609. In July the ship, which also carried Sir Thomas Gates, the new governor of the colony, and Sir George Somers, admiral of the expedition, was blown away from the other ships and was wrecked on the Bermudas. There the party built two small vessels, and they finally reached Jamestown on May 23, 1610.

Strachey, a man of literary interests who wrote poetry and was a friend of John Donne, was appointed secretary of the colony by Lord De La Warr. When Gates left for England in July, 1610, he took with him a long letter written by Strachey vividly describing the tempest at sea and the experiences of the colonists. This manuscript, written in Virginia, came to the attention of Shakespeare, who made use of it in writing his play, *The Tempest*. An interesting examination of the extent of Shakespeare's indebtedness to Strachey's first-hand account of the storm off the Bermudas has been made by R. R. Cawley ("Shakspere's Use of the Voyages in The Tempest," in the Publications of the Modern Language Association of America, September, 1926). Strachey's manuscript was first printed under the title, *A True Reportory of the Wracke, and Redemption of Sir Thomas Gates . . .* by Samuel Purchas in *Purchas His Pilgrimes* in 1625. A selection from it follows.

Strachey returned to England in 1611, where he edited the first code of laws for the colony in Virginia. He undertook a comprehensive work, *The Historie of Travaile into Virginia Britannia, Expressing the Cosmographie and Comodities of the Country, Togither with the Manners and Customes of the People,* and completed two parts; but finding little encouragement for its publication, he left it unfinished. This manuscript was published by the Hakluyt Society in 1849.

THE TEMPEST

We had followed this course so long, as now we were within seven or eight dayes at the most, by Cap. Newports reckoning of making Cape Henry upon the coast of Virginia: When on S. James his day, July 24. being Monday (preparing for no lesse all the blacke night before) the cloudes gathering thicke upon us, and the windes singing, and whistling most unusually, which made us to cast off our Pinnace towing the same untill then asterne, a dreadfull storme and hideous began to blow from out the North-east, which swelling, and roaring as it were by fits, some houres with more violence then others, at length did beate all light from heaven; which like an hell of darkenesse turned blacke upon us, so much the more fuller of horror, as in such cases horror and feare use to overrunne the troubled, and overmastered sences of all, which (taken up with amazement) the eares lay so sensible to the terrible cries, and murmurs of the windes, and distraction of our Company, as who was most armed, and best prepared, was not a little shaken. For surely (Noble Lady) as death comes not so sodaine nor apparant, so he comes not so elvish and painfull (to men especially even then in health and perfect habitudes of body) as at Sea; who comes at no time so welcome, but our frailty (so weake is the hold of hope in miserable demonstrations of danger) it makes guilty of many contrary changes, and conflicts: For indeede death is accompanied at no time, nor place with circumstances every way so uncapable of particularities of goodnesse and inward comforts, as at Sea. For it is most true, there ariseth commonly no such unmercifull tempest, compound of so many contrary and divers Nations, but that it worketh upon the whole frame of the body, and most loathsomely affecteth all the powers thereof: and the manner of the sicknesse it laies upon the body, being so unsufferable, gives not the minde any free and quiet time, to use her judgement and Empire: which made the Poet say:

102

William Strachey, fl. 1610

Hostium uxores, puerique caecos
Sentiant motus orientis Haedi, &
Aequoris nigri fremitum, & trementes
Verbere ripas.

For foure and twenty houres the storme in a restlesse tumult, had
blowne so exceedingly, as we could not apprehend in our imagina-
tions any possibility of greater violence, yet did wee still finde it,
not onely more terrible but more constant, fury added to fury, and
one storme urging a second more outragious then the former;
whether it so wrought upon our feares, or indeede met with new
forces: Sometimes strikes in our Ship amongst women, and passengers, not used to such hurly and discomforts, made us looke one
upon the other with troubled hearts, and panting bosomes: our
clamours dround in the windes, and the windes in thunder. Prayers might well be in the heart and lips, but drowned in the outcries
of the Officers: nothing heard that could give comfort, nothing seene
that might incourage hope. It is impossible for me, but I the voyce
of Stentor, and expression of as many tongues, as his throate of
voyces, to expresse the outcries and miseries, not languishing, but
wasting his spirits, and art constant to his owne principles, but not
prevailing. Our sailes wound up lay without their use, and if at any
time wee bore but a Hollocke, or halfe forecourse, to guide her before the Sea, six and sometimes eight men were not inough to hold
the whipstaffe in the steerage, and the tiller below in the Gunner
roome, by which may be imagined the strength of the storme: In
which, the Sea swelled above the Clouds, and gave battell unto
Heaven. It could not be said to raine, the waters like whole Rivers
did flood in the ayre. And this I did still observe, that whereas upon
the Land, when a storme hath powred it selfe forth once in drifts
of raine, the winde as beaten downe, and vanquished therewith, not
long after indureth: here the glut of water (as if throatling the winde
ere while) was no sooner a little emptied and qualified, but instantly
the windes (as having gotten their mouthes now free, and at liberty)
spake more loud, and grew more tumultuous, and malignant. What
shall I say? Windes and Seas were as mad, as fury and rage could
make them; for mine owne part, I had bin in some stormes before, as

103

well upon the coast of Barbary and Algeere, in the Levant, and once more distressfull in the Adriatique gulfe, in a bottome of Candy, so as I may well say. Ego quid sit ater Adriae novi sinus, & quid albus Peccet Iapex. Yet all that I had ever suffered gathered together, might not hold comparison with this: there was not a moment in which the sodaine splitting, or instant over-setting of the Shippe was not expected.

Howbeit this was not all; It pleased God to bring a greater affliction yet upon us; for in the beginning of the storme we had received likewise a mighty leake. And the Ship in every joynt almost, having spued out her Okam, before we were aware (a casualty more desperate then any other that a Voyage by Sea draweth with it) was growne five foote suddenly deepe with water above her ballast, and we almost drowned within, whilest we sat looking when to perish from above. This imparing no lesse terrour then danger, ranne through the whole Ship with much fright and amazement, startled and turned the bloud, and tooke downe the braves of the most hardy Marriner of them all, insomuch as he that before happily felt not the sorrow of others, now began to sorrow for himselfe, when he saw such a pond of water so suddenly broken in, and which he knew could not (without present avoiding) but instantly sinke him. So as joyning (onely for his owne sake, not yet worth the saving) in the publique safety; there might be seene Master, Masters Mate, Boateswaine, Quarter Master, Coopers, Carpenters, and who not, with candels in their hands, creeping along the ribs viewing the sides, searching every corner, and listening in every place, if they could heare the water runne. Many a weeping leake was this way found, and hastily stopt, and at length one in the Gunner roome made up with I know not how many pieces of Beefe: but all was to no purpose, the Leake (if it were but one) which drunke in our greatest Seas, and tooke in our destruction fastest, could not then be found, nor ever was, by any labour, counsell, or search. The waters still increasing, and the Pumpes going, which at length choaked with bringing up whole and continuall Bisket (and indeede all we had, tenne thousand weight) it was conceived, as most likely, that the Leake might be sprung in the Bread-roome, whereupon the Car-

penter went downe, and ript up all the roome, but could not finde
it so.

I am not able to give unto your Ladiship every mans thought in
this perplexity, to which we were now brought; but to me, this Leak-
age appeared as a wound given to men that were before dead. The
Lord knoweth, I had as little hope, as desire of life in the storme,
& in this, it went beyond my will; because beyond my reason, why
we should labour to preserve life; yet we did, either because so deare
are a few lingring houres of life in all mankinde, or that our Christian knowledge taught us, how much we owed to the rites of Nature, as bound, not to be false to our selves, or to neglect the meanes
of our owne preservation; the most despairefull things amongst
men, being matters of no wonder nor moment with him, who is the
rich Fountaine and admirable Essence of all mercy.

Our Governour, upon the tuesday morning (at what time, by such
who had bin below in the hold, the Leake was first discovered) had
caused the whole Company, about one hundred and forty, besides
women, to be equally divided into three parts, and opening the Ship
in three places (under the forecastle, in the waste, and hard by the
Bitacke) appointed each man where to attend; and thereunto every
man came duely upon his watch, tooke the Bucket, or Pumpe for
one houre, and rested another. Then men might be seene to labour,
I may well say, for life, and the better sort, even our Governour,
and Admirall themselves, not refusing their turne, and to spell each
the other, to give example to other. The common sort stripped naked,
as men in Gallies, the easier both to hold out, and to shrinke from
under the salt water, which continually leapt in among them, kept
their eyes waking, and their thoughts and hands working, with tyred
bodies, and wasted spirits, three dayes and foure nights destitute of
outward comfort, and desperate of any deliverance, testifying how
mutually willing they were, yet by labour to keepe each other from
drowning, albeit each one drowned whilest he laboured.

Once, so huge a Sea brake upon the poope and quarter, upon us,
as it covered our Shippe from stearne to stemme, like a garment or
a vast cloude, it filled her brimme full for a while within, from the
hatches up to the sparre decke. This source or confluence of water

was so violent, as it rusht and carried the Helm-man from the Helme, and wrested the Whip-staffe out of his hand, which so flew from side to side, that when he would have ceased the same againe, it so tossed him from Star-boord to Lar-boord, as it was Gods mercy it had not split him: It so beat him from his hold, and so bruised him, as a fresh man hazarding in by chance fell faire with it, and by maine strength bearing somewhat up, made good his place, and with much clamour incouraged and called upon others; who gave her now up, rent in pieces and absolutely lost. Our Governour was at this time below at the Capstone, both by his speech and authoritie heartening every man unto his labour. It strooke him from the place where hee sate, and groveled him, and all us about him on our faces, beating together with our breaths all thoughts from our bosomes, else, then that wee were now sinking. For my part, I thought her alreadie in the bottome of the Sea; and I have heard him say, wading out of the floud thereof, all his ambition was but to climbe up above hatches to dye in Aperto coelo, and in the company of his old friends. It so stun'd the ship in her full pace, that shee stirred no more, then if shee had beene caught in a net, or then, as if the fabulous Remora had stucke to her fore-castle. Yet without bearing one inch of saile, even then shee was making her way nine or ten leagues in a watch. One thing, it is not without his wonder (whether it were the feare of death in so great a storme, or that it pleased God to be gracious unto us) there was not a passenger, gentleman, or other, after hee beganne to stirre and labour, but was able to relieve his fellow, and make good his course: And it is most true, such as in all their life times had never done houres worke before (their mindes now helping their bodies) were able twice fortie eight houres together to toile with the best.

During all this time, the heavens look'd so blacke upon us, that it was not possible the elevation of the Pole might be observed: nor a Starre by night, not Sunne beame by day was to be seene. Onely upon the thursday night Sir George Summers being upon the watch, had an apparition of a little round light, like a faint Starre, trembling, and streaming along with a sparkeling blaze, halfe the height upon the Maine Mast, and shooting sometimes from Shroud to Shroud, tempting to settle as it were upon any of the foure Shrouds: and for

106

three or foure houres together, or rather more, halfe the night it kept with us; running sometimes along the Maine-yard to the very end, and then returning. At which, Sir George Summers called divers about him, and shewed them the same, who observed it with much wonder, and carefulnesse: but upon a sodaine, towards the morning watch, they lost the sight of it, and knew not what way it made. The superstitious Sea-men make many constructions of this Sez-fire, which neverthelesse is usuall in stormes: the same (it may be) which the Graecians were wont in the Mediterranean to call Castor and Pollux, of which, if one onely appeared without the other, they tooke it for an evill signe of great tempest. The Italians, and such, who lye open to the Adriatique and Tyrrene Sea, call it (a sacred Body) Corpo sancto: the Spaniards call it Saint Elmo, and have an authentique and miraculous Legend for it. Be it what it will, we laid other foundations of safety or ruine, then in the rising or falling of it, could it have served us now miraculously to have taken our height by, it might have strucken amazement, and a reverence in our devotions, according to the due of a miracle. But it did not light us any whit the more to our knowne way, who ran now (as doe hoodwinked men) at all adventures, sometimes North, and North-east, then North and by West, and in an instant againe varying two or three points, and sometimes halfe the Compasse. East and by South we steered away as much as we could to beare upright, which was no small carefulnesse nor paine to doe, albeit, we much unrigged our Ship, threw over-boord much luggage, many a Trunke and Chest (in which I suffered no meane losse) and staved many a Butt of Beere, Hogsheads of Oyle, Syder, Wine, and Vinegar, and heaved away all our Ordnance on the Starboord side, and had now purposed to have cut downe the Maine Mast, the more to lighten her, for we were much spent, and our men so weary, as their strengths together failed them, with their hearts, having travailed now from Tuesday till Friday morning, day and night, without either sleepe or foode; for the leakeage taking up all the hold, wee could neither come by Beere nor fresh water; fire we could keepe none in the Cooke-roome to dresse any meate, and carefulnesse, grief and our turne at the Pumpe or Bucket, were sufficient to hold sleepe from our eyes.

And surely Madam, it is most true, there was not any houre (a matter of admiration) all these dayes, in which we freed not twelve hundred Barricos of water, the least whereof contained six gallons, and some eight, besides three deepe Pumpes continually going, two beneath at the Capstone, and the other above in the halfe Decke, and at each Pumpe foure thousand stroakes at the least in a watch; so as I may well say, every foure houres, we quitted one hundred tunnes of water: and from tuesday noone till friday noone, we bailed and pumped two thousand tunne, and yet doe what we could, when our Ship held least in her, (after tuesday night second watch) shee bore ten foote deepe, at which stay our extreame working kept her one eight glasses, forbearance whereof had instantly sunke us, and it being now Friday, the fourth morning, it wanted little, but that there had bin a generall determination, to have shut up hatches, and commending our sinfull soules to God, committed the Shippe to the mercy of the Sea: surely, that night we must have done it, and that night had we then perished: but see the goodnesse and sweet introduction of better hope, by our mercifull God given unto us. Sir George Summers, when no man dreamed of such happinesse, had discovered, and cried Land. Indeede the morning now three quarters spent, had wonne a little cleerenesse from the dayes before, and it being better surveyed, the very trees were seene to move with the winde upon the shoare side: whereupon our Governour commanded the Helme-man to beare up, the Boateswaine sounding at the first, found it thirteene fathome, & when we stood a little in seven fatham; and presently heaving his lead the third time, had ground at foure fathome, and by this, we had got her within a mile under the South-east point of the land, where we had somewhat smooth water. But having no hope to save her by comming to an anker in the same, we were inforced to runne her ashoare, as neere the land as we could, which brought us within three quarters of a mile of shoare, and by the mercy of God unto us, making out our Boates, we had ere night brought all our men, women, and children, about the number of one hundred and fifty, safe into the Iland.

RICHARD RICH

fl. 1610

Richard Rich, author of the first indigenous Virginia poem, sailed for the New World with the expedition which left England on June 2, 1609. On his return to England, he published *News from Virginia* in London in 1610, in which he described the expedition in verse.

His was "no idle fabulous tale," he began, "For Truth herselfe is heere arriv'd." His verses tell how for "Eleaven monthes and more" the expedition was "depriv'd Virginia's sight," how their ship was wrecked off Bermuda ("Bermoothawes"), how they killed hogs for food and built two ships and made their way on to Virginia. He gives an enthusiastic account of the resources of Virginia, of corn, fish, "Great store of Fowle, of Venison, of Grapes, and Mulberries," and declares the determination of the expedition:

> *Wee hope to plant a Nation, where none before hath stood.*

Little is known of Rich. There is a question even that his name was Richard; he signed his verse tract only as "R. Rich, Gent. one of the Voyage." In a note to the reader he describes himself: "I am a soldier, blunt and plaine." He adds of his account of the expedition: "If thou aske why I put it in Verse? It was onely to feede mine owne humour."

Several reprints of *News from Virginia* have been published. The most recent was a facsimile edition, with an introduction by Wesley F. Craven, issued by Scholars' Facsimiles and Reprints in 1937 and now out of print.

It is no idle fabulous tale, nor is it fayned newes:
For Truth herselfe is heere arriv'd, because you should not
    muse.
With her both Gates and Newport come, to tell Report doth
    lye,
Which did divulge unto the world that they at sea did dye.

Tis true that eleaven monthes and more, these gallant worthy
    wights
Were in the shippe (*Sea-venture* nam'd) depriv'd Virginia's
    sight.
And bravely did they glyde the maine, till Neptune gan to
    frowne,
As if a courser prowdly backt would throwe his ryder
    downe.

The seas did rage, the windes did blowe, distressed were
    they then
Their ship did leake, her tacklings breake, in danger were
    her men.
But heaven was pylotte in this storme, and to an Iland
    nere,
Bermoothawes call'd, conducted them, which did abate their
    feare.

But yet these worthies forcèd were, opprest with weather
    againe,
To runne their ship betweene two rockes, where she doth
    still remaine.
And then on shore the Iland came, inhabited by hogges:

110

Some foule and tortoyses there were, they only had one
dogge.

To kill these swyne, to yield them foode that little had to
eate,
Their store was spent, and all things scant, alas! they
wanted meate.
A thousand hogges that dogge did kill, their hunger to sus-
taine,
And with such foode did in that Ile two and forty weekes
remaine.

And there two gallant Pynases did build of seader-tree;
The brave *Deliverance* one was call'd, of seaventy tonne was
shee.
The other *Patience* had to name, her burthen thirty tonne;
Two only of their men which there pale death did overcome.

And for the losse of those two soules, which were accounted
deere,
A sonne and daughter then were borne, and were baptizèd
there.
The two and forty weekes being past, they hoyst sayle and
away;
Their ships with hogges well freighted were, their hearts
with mickle joy.

And so unto Virginia came, where these brave soldiers finde
The English-men opprest with griefe and discontent in
minde.
They seem'd distracted and forlorne, for those two worthyes
losse,
Yet at their home returne they joyd, among'st them some
were crosse.

And in the midst of discontent came noble Delaware;
He heard the griefes on either part, and sett them free from
care.

111

He comforts them and cheres their hearts, that they abound
    with joy;
He feedes them full and feedes their soules with God's word
    every day.

A discreet counsell he creates of men of worthy fame,
That noble Gates leiftenant was the admirall had to name.
The worthy Sir George Somers knight, and others of com-
    maund;
Maister George Pearcy, which is brother unto Northumber-
    land.

Sir Fardinando Wayneman knight, and others of good fame,
That noble lord his company, which to Virginia came,
And landed there; his number was one hundred seaventy;
    then
Ad to the rest, and they make full foure hundred able men.

Where they unto their labour fall, as men that meane to
    thrive;
Let's pray that heaven may blesse them all, and keep them
    long alive.
Those men that vagrants liv'd with us, have there deservèd
    well;
Their governour writes in their praise, as divers letters tel.

And to th' adventurers thus he writes, be not dismayed at all,
For scandall cannot doe us wrong, God will not let us fall.
Let England knowe our willingnesse, for that our worke is
    goode,
Wee hope to plant a Nation, where none before hath stood.

To glorifie the Lord tis done, and to no other end;
He that would crosse so good a worke, to God can be no
    friend.

Richard Rich, fl. 1610

There is no feare of hunger here for corne much store here
  growes,
Much fish the gallant rivers yield, tis truth without suppose.

Great store of Fowle, of Venison, of Grapes and Mullberries,
Of Chestnuts, Walnuts, and such like, of fruits and Straw-
  berries,
There is indeed no want at all, but some, condicioned ill,
That wish the worke should not goe on, with words doe
  seeme to kill.

And for an instance of their store, the noble Delaware
Hath for a present hither sent, to testifie his care
In managing so good a worke, to gallant ships, by name
The *Blessing* and the *Hercules*, well fraught, and in the same

Two ships, are these commodities, Furres, Sturgeon, Caviare,
Blacke walnut-tree, and some deale boords, with such they
  laden are;
Some Pearle, some Wainscot and clapbords, with some Sas-
  safras wood,
And Iron promist, for tis true their Mynes are very good.

Then, maugre scandall, false report, or any opposition,
Th' adventurers doe thus devulge to men of good condition,
That he that wants shall have reliefe, be he of honest minde
Apparel, coyne, or any thing, to such they will be kinde.

To such as to Virginia do purpose to repaire;
And when that they shall thither come, each man shall have
  his share.
Day wages for the laborer, and for his more content,
A house and garden plot shall have; besides, tis further
  ment

That every man shall have a part, and not thereof denaid,
Of general profit, as if that he twelve pounds ten shillings
  paid;

And he that in Virginia shall copper coyne receive,
For hyer or commodities, and will the country leave

Upon delivery of such coyne unto the Governour,
Shall by exchange at his returne be by their treasurer
Paid him in London at first sight, no man shall cause to
grieve,
For tis their generall will and wish that every man should
live.

The number of adventurers, that are for this plantation,
Are full eight hundred worthy men, some noble, all of
fashion.
Good, discreete, their worke is good, and as they have begun,
May Heaven assist them in their worke, and thus our newes
is done.

HENRY NORWOOD

fl. 1650

Henry Norwood, a kinsman of Governor Berkeley, set sail for Virginia about the middle of September in the year 1649 on the ship *The Virginia Merchant*, which carried some 330 colonists bound for Jamestown. The account that Norwood wrote of that eventful voyage, which is one of the most vivid records of the period that have come down to us, is printed here in its entirety.

In 1650 Norwood went back across the Atlantic. He visited Charles II in Scotland and was appointed treasurer of Virginia. In 1654 he was imprisoned in the Tower of London, no doubt for political reasons, but with the restoration of Charles II to the English throne Norwood became a man of position. He was given the Virginia quit-rents for his private use, and in 1661 he received an appointment for life as captain of Sandown Castle, Kent. He seems, however, to have continued to lead a life of considerable adventure. In 1664 he was one of the officers who were present at the surrender of the Dutch at Manhattan, and in 1667 he was Lieutenant Governor of Tangier.

Norwood's *A Voyage to Virginia* was published in London in 1732 in Awnsham Churchill's *A Collection of Voyages and Travels*. It has been reprinted in the United States but once, in Force's *Tracts* in 1844.

A VOYAGE TO VIRGINIA

The month of *August, Anno* 1649, being the time I ingag'd to
meet my two comrades, Major *Francis Morrison,* and Major *Richard
Fox,* at *London,* in order to a full accomplishment of our purpose
to seek our fortunes in *Virginia,* (pursuant to our agreement the year
before in *Holland)* all parties very punctually appear'd at the time
and place assign'd, and were all still in the same mind, fully bent
to put in practice what we had so solemnly agreed upon, our inclinations that way being nothing abated, but were rather quicken'd,
by the new changes that we saw in the state of things, and that
very much for the worse: For if our spirits were somewhat depress'd in contemplation of a barbarous restraint upon the person
of our king in the *Isle of Wight;* to what horrors and despairs must
our minds be reduc'd at the bloody and bitter stroke of his assassina-
tion, at his palace of *Whitehall?*

This unparallel'd butchery made the rebels cast away the scab-
bards of their swords with both their hands, in full resolution never
to let them meet again, either by submission or capitulation; so that
the sad prospect of affairs in this juncture, gave such a damp to all
the royal party who had resolved to persevere in the principle which
ingag'd them in the war, that a very considerable number of no-
bility, clergy, and gentry, so circumstanc'd, did fly from their native
country, as from a place infected with the plague, and did betake
themselves to travel any where to shun so hot a contagion, there
being no point on the compass that would not suit with some of
our tempers and circumstances, for transportation into foreign lands.

Of the number who chose to steer their course for *America,* such
of them as inclin'd to try their fortunes at *Surinam, Barbados, An-
tigua,* and the *Leeward Islands,* were to be men of the first rate,
who wanted not money or credit to balance the expence necessary
to the carrying on the sugar-works: And this consideration alone was

116

enough to determine our choice for *Virginia*, had we wanted other arguments to ingage us in the voyage. The honour I had of being nearly related to Sir *William Barkeley*, the governor, was no small incitation to encourage me with a little stock to this adventure: Major *Morrison* had the king's commission to be captain of the fort; and Mr. *Fox* was to share in our good or bad success: But my best cargaroon was his majesty's gracious letter in my favour, which took effect beyond my expectation, because it recommended me (above whatever I had or could deserve) to the governor's particular care.

To proceed then, without any further *exordium,* to the subject of this narrative: It fell out to be about the first day of *September, Anno* 1649, that we grew acquainted on the *Royal-Exchange* with Capt. *John Locker,* whose bills upon the posts made us know he was master of a good ship, (untruly so call'd) *The Virginia Merchant,* burden three hundred tons, of force thirty guns, or more: We were not long in treaty with the captain, but agreed with him for ourselves and servants at six pounds a head, to be transported into *James River;* our goods to be paid for at the current price.

About the fifteenth day, we were ordered to meet the ship at *Gravesend,* where the captain was to clear with his merchants, and we to make our several payments; which when we had performed, we staid not for the ship, but took post for the *Downs,* where, with some impatience, we expected her coming there. About the sixteenth *ditto,* we could see the whole fleet under sail, with a southwest wind; which having brought them to that road, kept them there at anchor, until our money was almost spent at *Deal.*

SCARCITY OF WATER

September 23. the wind veered to the east, and we were summoned by signs and guns to repair on board. We had a fresh large gale three days, which cleared us of the channel, and put us out of soundings. With this propitious beginning we pursued our course for about twenty days, desiring to make the western islands; at which time the cooper began to complain, that our water-cask was almost empty, alledging, that there was not enough in hold, for our great family (about three hundred and thirty souls) to serve a month.

Virginia Reader

Our early want of water gave the master an alarm, and an occasion to consult with his officers for a remedy to so important an evil as that might be, if not timely helped. We were now, by all accounts, very near the western islands: *Fyall* was that we were likely first to see, and our captain resolved to touch there to supply this defect, as the most commodious port for our purpose; and this was good news to the passangers, who are always glad at sight of land.

The day-break of *October* 14th, shewed us the peek of that island, the highest and most conspicuous land of any I have heard the seamen mention for land-marks, except that of *Teneriff.* We stood directly for the harbour, which is also a good road, land-lock'd by the peak, which stands easterly about a mile distant from the town.

Assoon as we had saluted the castle, and returned thanks for being civilly answered, captain *John Tatam,* our countryman, did the same from aboard his goodly ship the *John.* He was newly returned from *Brasil,* in the kingdom of *Portugal's* service, and now bound for *Lisbon,* with a rich freight, and some lady of great note, who with her family took passage with him.

The *English* merchants from the town came soon on board our ship, and gave us a very civil welcome. Of them, one Mr. *Andrews* invited me, with my two comrades, to refresh our selves with fruit and meat such as the island produced. Our captain dined with us at his house, and so did captain *Tatam,* who in like courteous manner engaged us all to dine on board his ship the next day. We visited the peach-trees for our desert, of which I took at least a double share, and did not fail to visit and revisit them in the dead of night, to satisfy a ravenous appetite nature has too prodigally given me for that species.

The next morning we surveyed the island, and thought the castle well fortified, especially on the sea-barr'd parts. The governor very civilly declared, he had lately received command from his majesty the king of *Portugal,* to treat all ships that belonged and were faithful to the king of *Great Britain,* with more than common courtesy, as he, for his part, did in all we could desire.

A little before the time of dinner captain *Tatam* had sent his boats to bring us on board his ship; and it was well for us he did so, our ship's long boat having been staved in pieces the night before, by

118

the seamen's neglect, who had all tasted so liberally of new wine, by the commodiousness of the vintage, that they lay up and down dead drunk in all quarters, in a sad pickle.

The loss of our long-boat, as it was likely to make our watering tedious, and chargeable to the owners, so did it expose us to the hazard of many inconveniences and perils in the whole course of our voyage, wherein frequent occasions occur that render that boat necessary to preserve the whole fabrick and lives of the ship and company; but to this breach no other reparation was applicable, but by recourse to that great stock of patience we were to be furnished withal for our support in the mighty straights we must encounter before we come to safe port.

Our captain, disabled hereby to take the best course for our dispatch, made choice of the next best way to effect it, by the island boats; and having ordered his officers to use all diligence, and greater care than before, he led the van into *Tatam's* boat, which brought us safe on board the *John*.

At our arrival we were welcomed with a whole tyre of guns, and with a very kind aspect in the captain. He gave us excellent wines to drink before dinner, and at our meat as good of other sorts for concoction. There was a handsome plenty of fish and fowl, several ways cooked, to relish the *Portuguese's* and the *English* palates; and, which made our entertainment more complete, he had prevailed with that great lady, with her pretty son of about twelve years old (tho' contrary to the custom even of the meaner sort at land) to sit at the table with us. She was taller than the ordinary stature of that nation, finely shap'd, had a very clear skin; her eyes and hair vying for the blackness and beauty of the jet; her modesty served, without any other art, to put a tincture of red upon her face; for when she saw herself environed with a company of strange faces, that had or might have had beards upon them, her blushes raised in her face a delicate complexion of red and white.

The captain was our interpreter to tell her how much we esteemed our selves honoured with her presence, which (for her better justification) she was in a manner forced to grant us, the ship affording her no other place fit for her retreat whilst we were there. Her young son sat by her, on whom all our eyes were fix'd; and our minds united with one opinion, that the air and lineaments of his face, full of sweetness, made him so like our king when he was of that age, that, every one whispering his thoughts to his neighbour, we all broke out at length in an open admiration of so great resemblance.

The health of the two kings were passing about with thundering peals of cannon; the youth was permitted by his mother to kiss the cup, and drink a small portion to that of our king; and she was in so pleasant an humour at this honour done to her son, that, to close our feast, she ordered the table to be covered anew, and a handsome banquet placed upon it, which we must partake of before we parted. To conclude this rare treat, she repeated the health of our king in a sort of choice rich wine that they make in *Brasil*, and drank the proportion she would take, without the allay of water, which till then she drank with little or no wine.

The approaching night made us take leave sooner than our inclinations would have led us ashore, the merchants having told us, there was no safe walking the streets in the night, for fear the *Pycaroes* (a sort of land-pyrates) should snatch away our hats and looser garments, as they use to treat strangers.

When we had paid our thanks to the captain, we desired his best language to make our compliments to the lady and her son, which she returned with her wishes for our happy voyage.

Whilst we were caress'd in this manner on shipboard, the seamen on shore continued in their debauchery, with very little advance of our dispatch; the getting water was so tedious in itself for lack of our boat, and so full of delays by drunken contests of ours with the islanders, and with themselves, that, after some days stay upon the island, when our captain resolved to sail away, he found the ship in worse condition for liquors, than when we came on shore; for if we got a new supply of water, the proportion was hardly enough to balance the expence of beer that was spent in the time we got it.

Some days before we parted, we saw the *John* under sail, bound for *Lisbon;* where the captain no sooner arrived and discharged his ship, but he listed himself as a man of war in a squadron of ships then there, under command of the prince *Rupert:* which I mention for his honour, because I have heard the prince acknowledge in his favour, that he did his duty very well when there was like to be an occasion of trying his valour.

OCTOBER 22

It was about the 22d of *October* that we took leave of our landlord and *Fyal.* We had store of black pigs for fresh meat, and I carry'd peaches without number. We parted with an easterly wind a topsail gate, which soon brought us into a trade-wind that favoured us at fifty or sixty leagues in twenty-four hours, till we came to the height of Bermudas. In that latitude it is the general observation of seamen, that the seas are rough, and the weather stormy. It was my fortune to have a curiosity to look out, when the officer on the watch shewed me a more than ordinary agitation of the sea in one particular place above the rest; which was the effect of what they call a spout, a raging in the bowels of the sea (like a violent birth) striving to break out, and at last springs up like a mine at land, with weight and force enough to have hoised our ship out of her proper element, into the air (had the helm been for it) and to have made her do the supersalt; but God's providence secured us from that danger.

The sight of the island was welcome to all: the mariners learned thereby our true distance from cape *Hatteras;* and the passengers were relieved with hopes to be soon at shore from a hungry pester'd ship and company.

Nov. 8

The gale continued fair till *November* 8: then we observed the water changed; and having the lead, we had thirty-five fathom of water, which was joyful news; our want of all things necessary for human life, made it so.

Towards break of day, weary of my lodging, I visited mate *Putts* on the watch, and would have treated him with brandy, but he refused that offer, unless I could also give him tobacco, which I had not. He said, it was near break of day, and he would look out to see what change there was in the water. No sooner were his feet upon the deck, but with stamps and noise he calls up the seamen, crying out, *All hands aloft! Breaches, breaches on both sides! All hands aloft!*

The seamen were soon on deck with this dismal alarm, and saw the cause thereof; but instead of applying their hands for their preservation (through a general despondency) they fell on their knees, commending their souls as at the last gasp. The captain came out at the noise to rectify what was amiss; but seeing how the case stood, his courage failed. Mate *Putts* (a stout seaman) took heart again, and cryed out, Is there no good fellow that will stand to the helm, and loose a sail? But of all the ship's crew there were but two foremast men that would be perswaded to obey commands, namely, *Thomas Reafin* and *John Smith*, men of innate courage, who, for their good resolution on that and divers other occasions in the various traverses of this voyage, deserve to have their names kept in lasting remembrance.

One of them got up and loosed the fore top-sail, to put the ship (if possible) in steerage way, and under command; the other stood to the helm, and he shifted it in a nick of time; for the ship was at the point of dashing on the starboard breach: and altho', in the rest of the voyage, she was wont to be blamed for the ill quality of not feeling the helm, she did, in this instance, redeem her credit, and fell round off for our rescue from that danger. But the sense of this escape lasted but a moment; for no sooner was she fallen from that breach, but another on the larboard-bow was ready to receive her. The ship's crew, by this time (reproached by the courage of *Reafin* and *Smith*) were all at work; and the helm shifting opportunely, she fell off again as before. The light of the day (which now broke forth) did discover our condition to be altogether as perillous as possible; for we now saw our selves surrounded with breaches; scarce any water like a channel appeared for a way to shun them. In this sad condition the ship struck ground, and raised such a war of water and sand together, which fell on the main-chains, that now all hopes of safety were laid aside; but the ship being still afloat, and the seamen all of them now under command, nothing was omitted for our preservation that was in their power.

Tom Reafin, seeing the ship go a-head in the likeliest water for a channel, and ordering the helm accordingly, heaved the lead; and after a little further advance into that new channel, wholly against his hopes, he had a good deal of water more than the ship drew, which soon mended upon us, the next cast of the lead affording eighteen or twenty foot. We stood to this channel, and the light of the morning enabling the quartermasters to con the ship, we were by this miraculous mercy of God, soon clear of the breaches at cape *Hatteras*, and got out to sea.

No sooner was the ship freed of this danger, and gotten a little into the offing, but the seamen (like so many spirits) surveyed each other, as if they doubted the reality of the thing, and shook hands like strangers, or men risen from the other world, and did scarce believe they were, what they seemed to be, men of flesh and blood. As they recovered force, they made what sail they could to stand to sea-ward.

A Storm

The gale came fresh at north-west, and this fresh gale did soon grow up to a violent storm, which increased to so great a rigour, separating us from the land at the rate of eight leagues a watch, merely with our fore-courses, insomuch that the master thought it necessary to stop that career; and, in order thereunto, he did advise with his officers to bring the ship about, to furl all sails, and to try with the mizzen.

The mountainous towring north-west seas that this storm made, were so unruly, that the seamen knew not how to work the ship about. We were already at a great distance from land, and something must be done to hinder our running off at that excessive rate. The first thing they did, was to lower the main-yard, to give some ease to that mast, by laying it on the ship's waste. Our great difficulty was, how to deal so with the fore-sails, that the ship might work about with safety, or at least with as little hazard as possible. All hands were too little to hale the sheet close, in order to bring the ship about. Many great seas were shipp'd as she came to work thro' the trough of the sea: amongst the rest one chanc'd to break upon the poop (where we were quartered) and that with so sad a weight, that we guess'd a tun of water (at the least) did enter the tarpaulin, and set us all on float who were in the round-house. The noise it made by discharging itself in that manner, was like the report of a great gun, and did put us all into a horrible fright, which we could not soon shake off. This shock being past, the ship about, and our fore-sail handled, we now lay trying with our mizzen.

GREAT NUMBER OF PORPOISES

I cannot forget the prodigious number of porpoises that did that evening appear about the ship, to the astonishment of the oldest seamen in her. They seemed to cover the surface of the sea as far as our eyes could discern; insomuch that a musket bullet, shot at random, could hardly fail to do execution on some of them. This the seamen would look upon as of bad portent, predicting ill weather; but in our case, who were in present possession of a storm, they appeared too late to gain the credit of foretelling what should come upon us in that kind.

The seas thus enraged, and all in foam, the gale still increasing upon us, the officers on the watch made frequent visits to the round-house, to prepare the captain for some evil encounter which this mighty tempest must bring forth: and their fears proved reasonable; for, about the hour of ten or eleven, our new disasters did begin with a crash from aloft. All hands were summon'd up with loud cries, that the fore-topmast was come by the board, not alone, but in conjunction with the fore-mast head broken short off, just under the cap.

This was a sore business, and put all to their wits end to recover to any competent condition; what could be done was done to prevent further mischiefs; but the whole trim and rigging of a ship depending much upon stays and tackle fixed to that mast, we had reason to expect greater ruins to follow, than what had already befallen us. Mate *Putts* was then on the watch, and did not want his apprehension of what did soon ensue, which in all likelihood was to end in our utter perdition; for about the hours of twelve or one at night, we heard and felt a mighty sea break on our fore-ship, which made such an inundation on the deck where the mate was walking, that he retired back with all diligence up to his knees in water, with short ejaculations of prayers in his mouth, supposing the ship was foundering, and at the last gasp. This looked like a stroke of death in every seaman's opinion: the ship stood stock still, with her head under water, seeming to bore her way into the sea. My two comrades and myself lay on our platform, sharing liberally in the general consternation. We took a short leave of each other, men, women, and children. All assaulted with the fresh terror of death, made a most dolorous outcry throughout the ship, whilst mate *Putts* perceiving the deck almost freed of water, called out aloud for hands to pump. This we thought a lightning before death, but gave me occasion (as having the best sea legs) to look out and learn the subject of this astonishing alarm, which proved to arise from no less cause than the loss of our forecastle, with six guns, and our anchors (all but one that was fastened to a cable) together with our two cooks, whereof one was recovered by a strange providence.

This great gap, made by want of our forecastle, did open a passage into the hold for other seas that should break there before a remedy was found out to carry them off, and this made our danger almost insuperable; but it fell out propitiously, that there were divers land-carpenter passengers, who were very helpful in this distress; and, in a little time, a slight platform of deal was tack'd to the timbers, to carry off any ordinary sea in the present straight we were in; every moment of this growing tempest cutting out new work to employ all hands to labour.

The bowsprit, too top-heavy in itself, having lost all stays and rigging that should keep it steady, sway'd to and fro with such bangs on the bows, that at no less rate than the cutting it close off, could the ship subsist.

All things were in miserable disorder; and it was evident our danger increas'd upon us: the stays of all the masts were gone, the shrouds that remained were loose and useless, and it was easy to foretel, our main-topmast would soon come by the board. *Tom Reafin* (who was always ready to expose himself) with an ax in his hand, ran up with speed to prevent that evil, hoping thereby to ease the main-mast, and preserve it; but the danger of his person in the enterprize, was so manifest, that he was called down amain; and no sooner was his foot upon the deck, but what was feared came to pass with a witness, both main and topmast all came down together, and, in one shock, fell all to the windward clear into the sea, without hurt to any man's person.

Our main-mast thus fallen to the broadside, was like to incommode us more in the sea, than in her proper station; for the shrouds and rigging not losing the hold they had of the ship, every surge did so check the mast (whose but-end lay charg'd to fall perpendicular on the ship's side) that it became a ram to batter and force the plank, and was doing the last execution upon us, if not prevented in time by edge-tools, which freed the ship from that unexpected assault and battery.

Abandon'd in this manner to the fury of the raging sea, tossed up and down without any rigging to keep the ship steady, our seamen frequently fell overboard, without any one regarding the loss of another, every man expecting the same fate, tho' in a different manner. The ceilings of this hulk (for it was no better) were for the same cause so uneasy, that, in many tumbles, the deck would touch the sea, and there stand still as if she would never make another. Our mizzen mast only remained, by which we hoped to bring the ship about in proper season, which now lay stemming to the east.

In this posture did we pass the tenth and eleventh days of *November;* the twelfth in the morning we saw an *English* merchant, who shewed his ensign, but would not speak with us, tho' the storm was abated, and the season more fit for communication. We imagined the reason was, because he would not be compelled to be civil to us: he thought our condition desperate, and we had more guns than he could resist, which might enable us to take what he would not sell or give. He shot a gun to leeward, stood his course, and turn'd his poop upon us.

Before we attempted to bring the ship about, it was necessary to refresh the seamen, who were almost worn out with toil and want of rest, having had no leisure of eating set meals for many days. The passengers, overcharged with excessive fears, had no appetite to eat; and (which was worst of all) both seamen and passengers were in a deplorable state as to the remaining victuals, all like to fall under extreme want; for the storm, by taking away the forecastle, having thrown much water into the hold, our stock of bread (the staff of life) was greatly damnified; and there remained no way to dress our meat, now that the cook-room was gone: the incessant tumbling of the ship (as has been observ'd) made all such cookery wholly impracticable. The only expedient to make fire betwixt decks, was, by sawing a cask in the middle, and filling it with ballast, which made a hearth to parch pease, and broil salt beef; nor could this be done but with great attendance, which was many times frustrated by being thrown topsy-turvy in spite of all circumspection, to the great defeat of empty stomachs.

Nov. 13

The seas were much appeas'd the thirteenth day, and divers *English* ships saw, and were seen by us, but would not speak with us; only one, who kept the pump always going, for having tasted too liberally of the storm, he was so kind as to accost us. He lay by till our wherry (the only surviving boat that was left us) made him a visit. The master shewed our men his leaks, and proposed, that ours would spare him hands to pump in lieu of any thing he could spare for our relief. He promised however to keep us company, and give us a tow to help to weather the cape, if occasion offered; but that was only a copy of his countenance; for in the night we lost each other, and we never heard more of him, tho' he was bound to our port.

The weather now invited us to get the ship about with our mizzen; and having done so, the next consideration was, how to make sail. The fore mast, all this while (as much as was of it) stood its ground: and as it was without dispute, that a yard must in the first place be fixed to it, so was it a matter of no small difficulty how to advance to the top of that greatly slippery stump, since he that would attempt it, could take no hold himself, nor receive any help for his rise, by other hands. This was a case that put all the ship's crew to a nonplus; but *Tom Reafin* (a constant friend at need, that would not be baffled by any difficulty) shewed by his countenance, he had a mind to try his skill to bring us out of this unhappy crisis. To encourage him the more, all passengers did promise and subscribe to reward his service, in *Virginia*, by tobacco, when God should enable us so to do. The proportions being set down, many were the more generous, because they never thought to see the place of payment, but expected to anticipate that by the payment of a greater debt to nature, which was like to be exacted every hour by an arrest of the merciless sea, which made small shew of taking bail for our appearance in *Virginia.*

The manner of *Tom Reafin's* ascent to this important work, was thus. Among the scatter'd parcels of the ship's stores he had the luck to find about half a dozen iron spikes fit for his purpose. His first onset was to drive one of them into the mast, almost to the head, as high as he could reach; which being done, he took a rope of about ten foot long, and having threaded the same in a block or pulley, so as to divide it in the middle, he made both ends meet in a knot upon the spike, on both sides of the mast; so that the block falling on the contrary side, became a stirrup to mount upon for driving another spike in the same manner: and thus from step to step, observing the best advantage of striking with his hammer in the smoothest sea, he got aloft, drove cleats for shrouds, to rest upon, and was soon in a posture of receiving help from his comrades, who got a yard and sails (with other accomodation) such as could be had, and thus we were enabled, in a few hours time, to make some sail for our port.

The main-yard, that in the storm had been lowered to the wast to lie out of harm's way, was now preferred to the place of the main mast, and was accordingly fitted and accoutred, and grafted into the stump of what was left in the storm, some eight or ten foot from the deck. It was a hard matter to find out rigging answerable to that new-fashioned mast and yard; top-gallant sails and yards were most agreeable to this equipage, and was the best part of our remaining stores. The seas grew every moment smoother, and the weather more comfortable; so that for a while we began to shake off the visage of utter despair, as hoping ere long to see our selves in some capacity to fetch the cape. We discovered another ship bound to *Virginia,* who as frankly promised to stand by us, the wind at N. N. W. We did what could be done by a ship so mangled, to get the weather-gage of the cape *Henry,* conceiving our selves to the southward of cape *Hatteras:* but by taking an observation of a sunshine day, we found our selves carried by a current we knew not of, to the windward, much beyond all our dead reckonings and allowances for failing, insomuch that when we thought we had been to the southward of the cape, we found our selves considerably shot to the north of *Achomat,* and that in the opinion of mate *Putts,* who was as our north star.

We passed this night with greater alacrity than we had done any other since we had left *Fyall;* for mate *Putts,* our trusty pilot, did confidently affirm, that, if the gale stood, there would be no question of our dining the next day within the capes. This was seasonable news, our water being long since spent, our meat spoiled (or useless) no kind of victuals remaining to sustain life, but a bisket cake a day for a man; at which allowance there was not a quantity to hold out many days. In the dark time of the night, in tacking about, we lost our new comrade, and with much impatience we expected the approaching day; the wind N. W.

The morning appeared foggy, as the wind veered to the east, and that did cover and conceal the land from our clearer sight; howbeit we concluded by mate *Putts's* computation, we were well to the northward of the capes. Many times he would mount the mizzen top for discovery, as the weather seemed to clear up, and would espy and point at certain hum-works of trees that used to be his several land-marks in most of the twenty-two voyages he had made to that plantation. Under this confidence he made more sail, the day-light confirming him in what he thought was right.

All the forenoon we lost the sight of land and marks by trees, by reason of the dark fogs and mists that were not yet dispelled; but assoon as the sun, with a north-west gale, had cleared all the coast (which was about the hours of two or three o'clock) mate *Putts* perceived his error from the deck, and was convinced, that the humworks of trees he had seen and relied on for sure land-marks, had counter points to the south cape, which had misguided him; and that it was the opening of the bay which made the land at distance out of sight.

This fatal disappointment (which was now past human help) might have met an easy remedy, had our sails and rigging been in any tolerable condition to keep the windward gage (for we had both the capes in our sight) but under our circumstances it was vain to endeavour such a thing; all our equipage, from stem to stern, being no better than that of a western barge, and we could not lie within eleven or twelve points of the wind.

Defeated thus of lively hopes we had the night before entertain'd to sleep in warm beds with our friends in *Virginia*, it was a heavy spectacle to see our selves running at a round rate from it, notwithstanding all that could be done to the contrary. Nothing was now to be heard but sighs and groans thro' all that wretched family, which must be soon reduced to so short allowance, as would just keep life and soul together. Half a bisket cake a day to each (of which five whole ones made a pound) was all we had to trust to. Of liquors there remained none to quench thirst: *Malaga* sack was given plentifully to every one, which served rather to inflame and increase thirst, than to extinguish it.

The gale blew fresh (as it uses to do) towards night, and made a western sea that carry'd us off at a great rate. Mate *Putts*, extremely abash'd to see his confidence so miserably deluded, grew sad and contemplative, even to the moving compassion in those whom his unhappy mistake had reduc'd to this misery. We cherish'd him the best we could, and would not have him so profoundly sad, for what was rather his misfortune than his fault.

The wind continued many days and nights to send us out into the ocean, insomuch that until we thought our selves at least an hundred leagues from the capes, the north-west gale gave us no truce to consider what was the best to do. All little helps were used by topgallant sails, and masts placed where they could be fixed, to keep the windward gage; but, for lack of borbolins and other tackle to keep them stiff to draw, every great head-sea would check them in the wind, and rend and tear them in pieces; so that it was an ordinary exercise with us to lie tumbling in the sea a watch or two together, driving to leeward, whilst the broken sails were in hand to be repaired.

It would be too great a trial of the reader's patience to be entertain'd with every circumstance of our sufferings in the remaining part of this voyage, which continued in great extremity for at least forty days from the time we left the land, our miseries increasing every hour: I shall therefore omit the greatest number of our ill encounters, which were frequently repeated on us, and remember only what has in my thoughts been most remarkable, and have made the deepest impression in my memory.

Nov. 19

To give us a little breathing, about the nineteenth day the wind shifted to the east, but so little to our avail (the gale so gentle, and the seas made against us like a strong current) that, with the sail we were able to make, we could hardly reckon the ship shortened the way, but that she rather lost ground. In less than two watches the gale faced about; and if we saved our own by the change, it was all we could pretend unto.

Our mortal enemy, the north-west gale, began afresh to send us out to sea, and to raise our terrors to a higher pitch. One of our pumps grew so unfix'd, that it could not be repair'd; the other was kept in perpetual motion; no man was excus'd to take his turn that had strength to perform it. Amongst the manifold perils that threatened every hour to be our last, we were in mortal apprehension, that the guns which were all aloft, would shew us a slippery trick, and some of them break loose, the tackle that held them being grown very rotten: and it was another providence they held so long, considering how immoderately the ship rolled, especially when the sails were mending that should keep them steady, which was very near a third part of our time, whilst we plyed to the windward with a contrary gale.

To prevent this danger which must befal when any one gun should get loose, mate *Putts* found an expedient by a more than ordinary smooth water; and by placing timber on the hatch-way, to supply the place of shrouds, he got them safe in hold; which tended much to our good, not only in removing the present danger, but by making the ship (as seamen say) more wholesome, by having so great weight removed from her upper works into her centre, where ballast was much wanted.

But the intolerable want of all provisions, both of meat and drink, jostled the sense of this happiness soon out of our minds. And to aggravate our misery yet the more, it was now our interest to pray, that the contrary gale might stand; for whilst the westerly wind held, we had rain water to drink, whereas at east the wind blew dry.

131

In this miserable posture of ship and provision, we reckoned our selves driven to the east, in less than a week's time, at least two hundred leagues, which we despaired ever to recover without a miracle of divine mercy. The storm continued so fresh against us, that it confounded the most knowing of our ship's company in advising what course to take. Some reckoned the ship had made her way most southerly, and therefore counselled we should put our selves in quest of the *Bermudas* islands, as to the nearest land we could hope to make: but that motion had great opposition in regard of the winter season, which would daily produce insuperable difficulties, and give greater puzzle in the discovery of it, than our circumstances would admit. Others would say, The furthest way about, in our case, would prove the nearest way home; and judged it best to take advantage of the westerly winds, and impetuous seas made to our hands, to attempt returning back to the western islands, as a thing more likely to succeed (tho' at a great distance) than thus to strive against the stream without any hopeful prospect of gaining the capes. But that motion met with a more general aversion, because the run was so long, that, tho' the gale had been in our own power to continue it, we could not have subsisted. Backwards we could not go, nor forwards we could not go in the course we desired: it followed then of consequence, that we must take the middle way; and it was resolved, that, without further persisting in endeavouring to gain our port by a close hale, we should raise our tackle, and sail tardy for the first *American* land we could fetch, tho' we ran to the leeward as far as the coast of *New England*.

A FAMINE

Whilst this determination was agreed and put in practice, the famine grew sharp upon us. Women and children made dismal cries and grievous complaints. The infinite number of rats that all the voyage had been our plague, we now were glad to make our prey to feed on; and as they were insnared and taken, a well grown rat was sold for sixteen shillings as a market rate. Nay, before the voyage did end (as I was credibly inform'd) a woman great with child offered twenty shillings for a rat, which the proprietor refusing, the woman died.

132

Henry Norwood, fl. 1650

Many sorrowful days and nights we spun out in this manner, till the blessed feast of *Christmas* came upon us, which we began with a very melancholy solemnity; and yet, to make some distinction of times, the scrapings of the meal-tubs were all amassed together to compose a pudding. *Malaga* sack, sea water, with fruit and spice, all well fryed in oyl, were the ingredients of this regale, which raised some envy in the spectators; but allowing some privilege to the captain's mess, we met no obstruction, but did peaceably enjoy our *Christmas* pudding.

My greatest impatience was of thirst, and my dreams were all of cellars, and taps running down my throat, which made my waking much the worse by that tantalizing fancy. Some relief I found very real by the captain's favour in allowing me a share of some butts of small claret he had concealed in a private cellar for a dead list. It wanted a mixture of water for qualifying it to quench thirst; however, it was a present remedy, and a great refreshment to me.

I cannot forget another instance of the captain's kindness to me, of a like obligation. He singled me out one day to go with him into the hold to seek fresh water in the bottoms of the empty casks. With much ado we got a quantity to satisfy our longing, tho' for the thickness thereof it was not palatable. We were now each of us astride on a butt of *Malaga,* which gave the captain occasion to taste of their contents. We tasted and tasted it again; and tho' the total we drank was not considerable, yet it had an effect on our heads that made us suspend (tho' we could not forget) our wants of water. The operation this little debauch had upon the captain, was very different from what it wrought on me, who felt myself refresh'd as with a cordial; but the poor captain fell to contemplate (as it better became him) our sad condition; and being troubled in mind for having brought so many wretched souls into misery, by a false confidence he gave them of his having a good ship, which he now thought would prove their ruin; and being conscious, that their loss would lie all at his door, it was no easy matter to appease his troubled thoughts. He made me a particular compliment for having engaged me and my friends in the same bottom, and upon that burst into tears. I comforted him the best I could, and told him, We must all submit to the hand of God, and rely on his goodness, hoping, that the same providence which had hitherto so miraculously preserved us, would still be continued in our favour till we were in safety. We retired obscurely to our friends, who had been wondering at our absence.

The westerly wind continued to shorten our way to the shore, tho' very distant from our port; but this did not at all incline us to change our resolution of sailing large for the first land; it did rather animate and support us in our present disasters of hunger and thirst, toil and fatigue. The hopes of touching land was food and raiment to us.

JAN. 3

In this wearisome expectation we pass'd our time for eight or nine days and nights, and then we saw the water change colour, and had soundings. We approach'd the shore the night of *January* 3d. with little sail; and, as the morning of the fourth day gave us light, we saw the land; but in what latitude we could not tell, for that the officers, whose duty it was to keep the reckoning of the ship, had for many days past totally omitted that part; nor had we seen the sun a great while, to take observations, which (tho' a lame excuse) was all they had to say for that omission. But in truth it was evident, that the desperate estate of the ship, and hourly jeopardy of life did make them careless of keeping either log or journal; the thoughts of another account they feared to be at hand, did make them neglect that of the ship as inconsiderable.

About the hours of three or four in the afternoon of the twelfth eve, we were shot in fair to the shore. The evening was clear and calm, the water smooth; the land we saw nearest was some six or seven *English* miles distant from us, our soundings twenty-five fathoms in good ground for anchor-hold.

These invitations were all attractive to encourage the generality (especially the passengers) to execute what we had resolved on for the shore: but one old officer who was husband for the ship's stores whilst there were any, would not consent on any terms to trust the only anchor that was left us for preservation, out of his sight at sea. His arguments to back his opinion were plausible; as, *first,* The hazard of losing that only anchor by any sudden storm, bringing with it

a necessity to cut or slip, on which every life depended. *2dly*. The
shortness of the cable, very unfit for anchorage in the ocean: And
3dly. The weakness of the ship's crew, many dead and fallen over
board, and the passengers weakened by hunger, dying every day on
the decks, or at the pump, which with great difficulty was kept going, but must not rest.

Against the old man's reasonings was urged the very small remains of bisket, at our short allowance, which would hardly hold a
week; the assurance of our loss by famine if we should be forced to
sea again by a north-west storm, and the great possibility of finding a harbour to save our ship, with our lives and goods, in some
creek on the coast. These last reasons prevailed upon the majority
against all negatives: and when the anchor was let loose, mate *Putts*
was ordered to make the first discovery of what we might expect
from the nearest land. He took with him twelve sickly passengers,
who fancied the shore would cure them; and he carry'd *Morrison*
on shore with him in pursuit of such adventures as are next in course
to be related; for according to the intelligence that could be got
from land, we were to take our measures at sea, either to proceed
on in our voyage in that sad condition that has been in some proportion set forth, or to land our selves, and unload the ship, and try
our fortunes amongst the Indians.

In four or five hours time we could discover the boat returning
with mate *Putts* alone for a setter, which we look'd upon as a signal
of happy success. When he came on board his mouth was full of
good tidings, as namely, That he discovered a creek that would harbour our ship, and that there was a depth of water on the bar, sufficient for her draught when she was light. That there was excellent
fresh water, (a taste whereof major *Morrison* had sent me in a bottle.) That the shore swarm'd with fowl, and that major *Morrison*
stayed behind in expectation of the whole ship's company to follow.

I opened mine ears wide to the motion, and promoted the design
of our landing there with all the rhetorick and interest I had. The
captain was no less forward for it, hoping thereby to save the lives
of the passengers that remained: and that he might not wholly rely
on mate *Putts's* judgment in a matter wherein he was most concern'd, he embark'd with me in the wherry, with a kinsman of his,

135

and some others; and the seamen were glad of my help to put the boat to shore, my hands having been very well season'd at the pump, by taking my turn for many weeks at the rate of three hours in twenty four. My passionate desire to be on shore at the fountain head to drink without stint, did not a little quicken me, insomuch that the six or seven miles I rowed on this occasion, were no more than the breadth of the *Thames* at *London,* at another time, would have been toilsome to me.

In our passage to the shore, the darkness of the evening made us glad to see the fires of our friends at land, which were not only our beacons to direct us to their company, but were also a comfortable relief to our chill bodies when we came near them, the weather being very cold (as it ever is) the wind northwest on that coast.

LAND

Assoon as I had set my foot on land and had rendred thanks to almighty God for opening this door of deliverance to us, after so many rescues even from the jaws of death at sea, major *Morrison* was pleased to oblige me beyond all requital, in conducting me to the running stream of water, where, without any limitation of short allowance, I might drink my fill. I was glad of so great liberty, and made use of it accordingly, by prostrating myself on my belly, and setting my mouth against the stream, that it might run into my thirsty stomach without stop. The rest of the company were at liberty to use their own methods to quench their thirst; but this I thought the greatest pleasure I ever enjoyed on earth.

After this sweet refreshment, the captain, myself, and his kinsman crossed the creek in our wherry, invited thither by the cackling of wild-fowl. The captain had a gun charged, and the moon shining bright in his favour, he killed one duck of the flock that flew over us, which was roasted on a stick out of hand by the seamen, whilst we walk'd on the shore of the creek for further discovery.

In passing a small gullet we trod on an oyster bank that did happily furnish us with a good addition to our duck. When the cooks had done their parts, we were not long about ours, but fell on without using the ceremony of calling the rest of our company, which would have been no entertainment to so many, the proverb telling us, *The fewer the better chear.* The bones, head, legs, and inwards were agreed to be the cook's fees; so we gave God thanks, and returned to our friends, without making boast of our good fortunes.

Fortify'd with this repast, we inform'd our selves of the depth of water at the bar of the creek, in which the captain seem'd satisfy'd, and made shews in all his deportment, of his resolution to discharge the ship there in order to our safety. Towards break of day he ask'd me in my ear, If I would go back with him on board the ship? I told him, No, because it would be labour lost, in case he would persist in his resolution to do what he pretended, which he ratify'd again by protestations, and so went off with his kinsman, who had a large coarse cloth gown I borrow'd of him to shelter me from the sharpest cold I ever felt. That which had sometimes been a paradox to me, was by this experience made demonstrable, (*viz.*) That the land on the continent is much colder than that of islands, tho' in the same latitude; and the reason is evident to any who shall consider the many accidents on the continent that cool the air by winds that come from the land; as in those parts of *America,* the mighty towring mountains to the northwest, covered all the year with snow, which does refrigerate the air even in the heat of summer; whereas winds coming from the sea are generally warm: and this hath proved a fatal truth to the inhabitants of *Virginia,* who, in the southeast winds, have gone to bed in sultry heat and sweat, without any covering, and have awaked in the night stiff and benumb'd with cold, without the use of their limbs, occasion'd by a shifting of the wind in the night from sea to land.

No sooner had the captain cleared himself of the shore but the day-break made me see my error in not closing with his motion in my ear. The first object we saw at sea was the ship under sail, standing for the capes with what canvass could be made to serve the turn. It was a very heavy prospect to us who remained (we knew not where) on shore, to see our selves thus abandon'd by the ship, and more, to be forsaken by the boat, so contrary to our mutual agreement. Many hours of hard labour and toil were spent before the boat could fetch the ship: and the seamen (whose act it was to set sail without the captain's order, as we were told after) car'd not for the boat whilst the wind was large to carry them to the capes. But mate

Putts, who was more sober and better natur'd, discovering the boat from the mizzen-top, lay by till she came with the captain on board.

In this amazement and confusion of mind that no words can express, did our miserable distress'd party condole with each other our being so cruelly abandon'd and left to the last despairs of human help, or indeed of ever seeing more the face of man. We entred into a sad consultation what course to take; and having, in the first place, by united prayers, implored the protection of Almighty God, and recommended our miserable estate to the same providence which, in so many instances of mercy, had been propitious to us at sea; the whole party desired me to be as it were the father of this distressed family, to advise and conduct them in all things I thought might most tend to our preservation. This way of government we agreed must necessarily reside in one, to avoid disputes, and variety of contradictory humours, which would render our deliverance the more impracticable; and it was thought most reasonable to be placed in me, for the health and strength it had pleased God to preserve unto me above my fellows, more than for any other qualification.

At the time I quitted the ship my servant *Thomas Harman,* a *Dutchman,* did, at parting, advertise me (for I left him on board to look to my goods) that, in the bundle I ordered to be carry'd with me on shore, I should find about thirty bisket cakes which he, by unparallel'd frugality, had saved out of his own belly in the great dearth and scarcity we lived in. The thoughts of these biskets entring upon me at the time I was press'd to accept this charge, I thought myself obliged, in christian equity, to let every one partake of what I had; and so dividing the bread into nineteen parts (which was our number) perhaps I added the fraction to my own share.

JAN. 5

It was, to the best of my remembrance, upon the fifth day of *January* that we entred into this method of life, or rather into an orderly way unto our graves, since nothing but the image of death was represented to us: but that we might use our utmost endeavours to extract all the good we could out of those evil symptoms that did every way seem to confound us, I made a muster of the most able bodies for arms and labour; and, in the first place, I put a fowling-piece into every man's hand that could tell how to use it. Amongst the rest, a young gentleman, Mr. *Francis Cary* by name, was very helpful to me in the fatigue and active part of this undertaking. He was strong and healthy, and was very ready for any employment I could put upon him. He came recommended to me by Sir *Edward Thurlan,* his genius leading him rather to a planter's life abroad, than to any course his friends could propose to him in *England;* and this rough entrance was like to let him know the worst at first.

All our woodmen and fowlers had powder and shot given them, and some geese were killed for supper. Evening came on apace, and our resolution being taken to stay one night more in these quarters, I sent my cousin *Cary* to head the creek, and make what discovery he could as he passed along the shore, whether of *Indians* or any other living creatures that were likely to relieve our wants, or end our days. To prepare like men for the latter, we resolved to die fighting, if that should be the case; or if, on the contrary, the *Indians* should accost us in a mein of amity, then to meet them with all imaginable courtesy, and please them with such trivial presents as they love to deal in, and so engage them into a friendship with us.

My cousin *Cary* was not absent much above an hour, when we saw him return in a contrary point to that he sallied out upon. His face was clouded with ill news he had to tell us, namely, that we were now residing on an island without any inhabitant, and that he had seen its whole extent, surrounded (as he believed) with water deeper than his head; that he had not seen any native, or any thing in human shape, in all his round, nor any other creature besides the fowls of the air, which he would, but could not bring unto us.

This dismal success of so unexpected a nature, did startle us more than any single misfortune that had befallen us, and was like to plunge us into utter despair. We beheld each other as miserable wretches sentenc'd to a lingering death, no man knowing what to propose for prolonging life any longer than he was able to fast. My cousin *Cary* was gone from us without notice, and we had reason (for what followed) to believe he was under the conduct of an angel; for we soon saw him return with a chearful look, his hands carrying something we could not distinguish by any name at a distance; but by nearer approach we were able to descry they were a parcel of oysters, which, in crossing the island, as he stept over a small current of water, he trod upon to his hurt; but laying hands on what he felt with his feet, and pulling it with all his force, he found himself possessed of this booty of oysters, which grew in clusters, and were contiguous to a large bank of the same species, that was our staple subsistance whilst we remained there.

While this very cold season continued, great flights of fowl frequented the island, geese, ducks, curlieus, and some of every sort we killed and roasted on sticks, eating all but the feathers. It was the only perquisite belonging to my place of preference to the rest, that the right of carving was annexed to it, wherein, if I was partial to my own interest, it was in cutting the wing as large and full of meat as possible; whereas the rest was measured out as it were with scale and compass.

But as the wind veered to the southward, we had greater warmth and fewer fowl, for they would then be gone to colder climates. In their absence we were confined to the oyster bank, and a sort of weed some four inches long, as thick as houseleek, and the only green (except pines) that the island afforded. It was very insipid on the palate; but being boiled with a little pepper (of which one had brought a pound on shore) and helped with five or six oysters, it became a regale for every one in turn.

In quartering our family we did observe the decency of distinguishing the sexes: we made a small hut for the poor weak women to be by themselves; our cabbin for men was of the same fashion, but much more spacious, as our numbers were. One morning, in walking on the shore by the sea side, with a long gun in my hand loaden with small shot, I fired at a great flight of small birds called *Ox-eyes*, and made great slaughter among them, which gave refreshment to all our company.

But this harvest had a short end; and as the weather by its warmth, chafed the fowl to the north, our hunger grew sharper upon us. And in fine, all the strength that remained unto us was employed in a heartless struggling to spin out life a little longer; for we still deemed our selves doom'd to die by famine, from whose sharpest and most immediate darts tho' we seemed to be rescued for a small

140

time, by meeting these contingent helps on shore, yet still we apprehended (and that on too great probability) they only served to reprieve us for a little longer day of execution, with all the dreadful circumstances of a lingering death.

For the south-west winds that had carry'd away the fowl, brought store of rain; which meeting with a spring-tide, our chief magazine, the oyster bank, was overflown; and as they became more accessible, our bodies also decayed so sensibly, that we could hardly pull them out of their muddy beds they grew on. And from this time forward we rarely saw the fowl; they now grew shy and kept aloof when they saw us contriving against their lives.

Add to this, our guns most of them unfix'd and out of order, and our powder much decayed, insomuch that nothing did now remain to prolong life, but what is counted rather sauce to whet, than substance to satisfy the appetite; I mean the oysters, which were not easily gotten by our crazy bodies after the quantity was spent that lay most commodious to be reach'd, and which had fed us for the first six days we had been on the island. And thus we wish'd every day to be the last of our lives (if God had so pleased) so hopeless and desperate was our condition, all expectation of human succour being vanished and gone.

They Feed on Their Dead Companions

Of the three weak women before-mentioned, one had the envied happiness to die about this time; and it was my advice to the survivors, who were following her apace, to endeavour their own preservation by converting her dead carcase into food, as they did to good effect. The same counsel was embrac'd by those of our sex: the living fed upon the dead; four of our company having the happiness to end their miserable lives on *Sunday* night the — day of *January*. Their chief distemper, 'tis true, was hunger; but it pleased God to hasten their *exit* by an immoderate access of cold, caused by a most terrible storm of hail and snow at north-west, on the *Sunday* aforesaid, which did not only dispatch those four to their long homes, but did sorely threaten all that remained alive, to perish by the same fate.

Great was the toil that lay on my hands (as the strongest to labour) to get fuel together sufficient for our preservation. In the first place I divested myself of my great gown, which I spread at large, and extended against the wind in nature of a screen, having first shifted our quarters to the most calm commodious place that could be found to keep us, as much as possible, from the inclemency of that prodigious storm.

Under the shelter of this traverse I took as many of my comrades as could be comprehended in so small a space; whereas those who could not partake of that accommodation, and were enabled to make provision for themselves, were forced to suffer for it. And it was remarkable, that nothwithstanding all the provision that could possibly be made against the sharpness of this cold, either by a well-burning fire consisting of two or three loads of wood, or shelter of this great gown to the windward, we could not be warm. That side of our wearing cloaths was singed and burnt which lay towards the flames, whilst the other side that was from the fire, became frozen and congeal'd. Those who lay to the leeward of the flame, could not stay long to enjoy the warmth so necessary to life, but were forced to quit and be gone to avoid suffocation by the smoke and flame.

When the day appeared, and the sun got up to dissipate the clouds, with downcast looks and dejected, the survivors of us entred into a final deliberation of what remained to be done on our parts (besides our prayers to Almighty God) to spin out a little longer time of life, and wait a further providence from heaven for our better relief. There were still some hands that retained vigour, tho' not in proportion to those difficulties we were to encounter, which humanly did seem insuperable. The unhappy circumstance of our being coop'd up in an island, was that which took from us all probable hopes of escaping this terrible death that did threaten us every hour. Major *Morrison,* on whose counsel I had reason to rely most, was extremely decayed in his strength, his legs not being able to support him. It was a wonderful mercy that mine remained in competent strength, for our common good, which I resolved, by God's help, to employ for that end to the last gasp.

In this last resolution we had to make, I could not think on any thing worthy my proposal, but by an attempt to cross the creek, and swim to the main (which was not above an hundred yards over)

142

and being there to coast along the woods to the south-west (which was the bearing of *Virginia*) until I should meet *Indians,* who would either relieve or destroy us. I fancied the former would be our lot when they should see our conditions, and that no hurt was intended to them; or if they should prove inhuman, and of a bloody nature, and would not give us quarter, why even in that case it would be worth this labour of mine to procure a sudden period to all our miseries.

I open'd my thoughts to this purpose to the company, who were sadly surprized at the motion; but being fully convinc'd in their judgment, that this was the only course that could be depended on (humanly speaking) for our relief, they all agreed it must be done.

To fortify me for this expedition, it was necessary that some provision should be made for a daily support to me in this my peregrination. Our choice was small; our only friend the oyster bank was all we had to rely on; which being well stew'd in their own liquor, and put up into bottles, I made no doubt, by God's blessing, but that two of them well filled, would suffice to prolong my life in moderate strength, until I had obtain'd my end. To accomplish this design, my cousin *Cary* laboured hard for oysters, hoping to make one in the adventure.

About the ninth day of our being in the island, I fell to my oyster-cookery, and made a good progress that very day; when in the heat of my labour my cousin *Cary* brought me word, That he had just in that instant seen *Indians* walking on the main. I suspended my cookery out of hand, and hastened with all possible speed to be an eye-witness of that happy intelligence; but with all the haste I could make I could see no such thing, but judg'd it a chimera that proceeded from some operation of my cousin's fancy, who was more than ordinary of a sanguine nature, which made him see (as it were by inchantment) things that were not, having many times been deluded (as I judg'd) by the same deception.

Defeated in this manner of my hopes to see *Indians* without the pains of seeking them, I returned to my work, and continued at it till one bottle was full, and myself tired: wherefore, that I might be a little recreated, I took a gun in my hand, and hearing the noise of geese on our shore, I approached them privately, and had the good hap to be the death of one. This goose, now in my possession without witnesses, I resolved to eat alone (deducting the head, bones, guts, &c. which were the cook's fees) hoping thereby to be much the better enabled to swim the creek, and perform the work I had upon my hand. I hung my goose upon the twist of a tree in a shrubby part of the wood, whilst I went to call aside our cook with his broach, and a coal of fire to begin the roast. But when we came to the place of execution, my goose was gone all but the head, the body stollen by wolves, which the *Indians* told us after, do abound greatly in that island.

The loss of this goose, which my empty stomach look'd for with no small hopes of satisfaction, did vex me heartily. I wish'd I could have taken the thief of my goose to have serv'd him in the same kind, and to have taken my revenge in the law of retaliation. But that which troubled me more, was an apprehension that came into my mind, that this loss had been the effect of divine justice on me, for designing to deal unequally with the rest of my fellow-sufferers; which I thought, at first blush, look'd like a breach of trust: but then again when I consider'd the equity of the thing, that I did it merely to enable myself to attain their preservation, and which otherwise I could not have done, I found I could absolve myself from any guilt of that kind. Whatever I suffer'd in this disappointment, the cook lost not all his fees; the head and neck remained for him on the tree.

Being thus over-reach'd by the wolf, it was time to return to my cookery, in order to my sally out of the island; for I had little confidence in the notice frequently brought me of more and more *Indians* seen on the other side, since my own eyes could never bear witness of their being there.

RELIEVED BY INDIANS

The next morning, being the ninth or tenth of our being there, I fell to work afresh, hoping to be ready to begin my journey that day; and being very busy, intelligence was brought, that a canoe was seen to lie on the broken ground to the south of our island, which was not discovered till now, since our being there: but this I thought might be a mistake cast in the same mould of many others that had deceived those discoverers, who fancy'd all things real according to their own wishes. But when it was told me, That *Indians* had been at the poor womens cabbin in the night, and had given them shell-fish to eat, that was a demonstration of reality beyond all suspicion. I went immediately to be inform'd from themselves, and they both avowed it for truth, shewing the shells (the like whereof I ne'er had seen) and this I took for proof of what they said.

The further account these women gave of the *Indians*, was, that they pointed to the south-east with their hands, which they knew not how to interpret, but did imagine by their several gestures, they would be with them again to morrow. Their pointing to the south-east was like to be the time they would come, meaning nine o'clock to be their hour, where the sun will be at that time. Had the women understood their language, they could not have learned the time of the day by any other computation than pointing at the sun. It is all the clock they have for the day, as the coming and going of the *Cahuncks* (the geese) is their almanack or prognostick for the winter and summer seasons.

This news gave us all new life, almost working miracles amongst us, by making those who desponded, and totally yielded themselves up to the weight of despair, and lay down with an intent never more to rise again, to take up their beds and walk. This friendly charitable visit of the *Indians* did also put a stop to my preparations to seek them, who had so humanely prevented me, by their seeking ways to preserve and save our lives.

Instead of those preparations for my march which had cost me so much pains, I passed my time now in contriving the fittest posture our present condition would allow us to put on when these angels of light should appear again with the glad tidings of our relief; and the result was, that every able man should have his gun lying by his side, laden with shot, and as fit for use as possible, but not to be handled unless the *Indians* came to us like enemies (which was very unlikely, the premises considered) and then to sell our lives at as dear a rate as we could; but if they came in an amicable posture, then would we meet them unarm'd, chearfully, which the *Indians* like, and hate to see a melancholy face.

In these joyful hopes of unexpected deliverance by these *Indians*, did we pass the interval of their absence. Every eye look'd sharply out when the sun was at south-east, to peep thro' the avenues of the wood to discover the approaches of our new friends. When the sun came to the south we thought our selves forgotten by them, and began to doubt the worst, as losing gamesters, at play for their last estate, suspect some stabcast to defeat the hopes of the fairest game. We feared some miscarriage, either from their inconstancy by change of their mind, or that some unlook'd-for misfortune that our evil fates reserved for us, had interposed for our ruin.

Scouts were sent out to the right and left hands, without discovery of any body all the forenoon: and then, considering our case admitted no delay, I began to resume my former resolution of swiming to them that would not come to us. But how wholesome soever this counsel might seem in itself, it was most difficult to be put in practice, in regard of the cold time.

The northerly wind that in these climates does blow very cold in the heat of summer, does much more distemper the air in the winter season (as our poor comrades felt that *Sunday* night to their cost) and did send so cold a gale upon the surface of the water in the creek I was to pass, that, in the general opinion of all the concern'd, it was not a thing to be attempted; and that if I did, I must surely perish in the act. I was easily perswaded to forbear an action so dangerous, and the rather, because I verily believed the *Indians* would bring us off, if our patience would hold out.

About the hours of two or three o'clock it pleased God to change the face of our condition for the best; for whilst I was busy at the fire in preparation to wait on them, the *Indians,* who had placed themselves behind a very great tree, discovered their faces with most cheerful smiles, without any kind of arms, or appearance of evil design; the whole number of them (perhaps twenty or thirty in all) consisting of men, women and children; all that could speak accosting us with joyful countenances, shaking hands with every one they met. The words *Ny Top,* often repeated by them, made us believe they bore a friendly signification, as they were soon interpreted to signify my friend.

After many salutations and *Ny Tops* interchang'd, the night approaching, we fell to parley with each other; but perform'd it in

146

signs more confounded and unintelligible than any other conversation I ever met withal; as hard to be interpreted as if they had express'd their thoughts in the *Hebrew* or *Chaldean* tongues.

They did me the honour to make all applications to me, as being of largest dimensions, and equip'd in a camlet coat glittering with galoon lace of gold and silver, it being generally true, that where knowledge informs not, the habit qualifies.

The ears of *Indian* corn they gave us for present sustenance, needed no other interpreter to let them know how much more acceptable it was to us than the sight of dead and living corpses, which raised great compassion in them, especially in the women, who are observed to be of a soft tender nature.

One of them made me a present of the leg of a swan, which I eat as privately as it was given me, and thought it so much the more excellent, by how much it was larger than the greatest limb of any fowl I ever saw.

The *Indians* stayed with us about two hours, and parted not without a new appointment to see us again the next day: and the hour we were to expect them by their pointing to the sun, was to be at two o'clock in the afternoon. I made the chief of them presents of ribbon and other slight trade, which they lov'd, designing by mutual endearment, to let them see, it would gratify their interest as well as their charity, to treat us well. *Ha-na Haw* was their parting word, which is farewell, pointing again at the place where the sun would be at our next meeting. We took leave in their own words, *Ha-na Haw.*

The going away of the *Indians,* and leaving us behind, was a separation hard to be born by our hungry company, who nevertheless had received a competent quantity of corn and bread to keep us till they returned to do better things for our relief; we did not fail to give glory to God for our approaching deliverance, and the joy we conceiv'd in our minds in the sense of so great a mercy, kept us awake all the night, and was a cordial to the sick and weak to recover their health and strength.

The delay of the *Indians* coming next day, beyond their set time, we thought an age of tedious years: At two o'clock we had no news of them, but by attending their own time with a little patience, we might see a considerable number of them, men, women, and children, all about our huts, with recruits of bread and corn to stop every mouth. Many of them desir'd beads and little truck they use to deal in, as exchange for what they gave us; and we as freely gave them what we had brought on shore; but to such of us as gave them nothing, the *Indians* failed not however to give them bread for nothing.

One old man of their company, who seem'd, by the preference they gave him, to be the most considerable of the party, apply'd himself to me by gestures and signs, to learn something (if possible) of our country, and occasion of the sad posture he saw us in, to the end that he might inform his master, the king of *Kickotank,* (on whose territories we stood) and dispose him to succour us, as we had need.

I made return to him in many vain words, and in as many insignificant signs as himself had made to me, and neither of us one jot the wiser. The several nonplus's we both were at in striving to be better understood, afforded so little of edification to either party, that our time was almost spent in vain. It came at last into my head, that I had long since read Mr. *Smith's* travels thro' these parts of *America,* and that the word *Werowance* (a word frequently pronounced by the old man) was in *English* the king. That word, spoken by me, with strong emphasis, together with the motions of my body, speaking my desire of going to him, was very pleasing to the old man, who thereupon embrac'd me with more than common kindness, and by all demonstrations of satisfaction, did shew that he understood my meaning. This one word was all the *Indian* I could speak, which (like a little armour well plac'd) contributed to the saving of our lives.

In order to what was next to be done, he took me by the hand and led me to the sea side, where I embark'd with himself and one more *Indian* in a canoe, that had brought him there, which the third man rowed over to that broken ground, where, not long before, we made discovery of a canoe newly laid there, and (as they told us) was lodg'd there on purpose to be ready for our transport, at such time as they thought fit to fetch us off; and the reason of their taking me with them was to help launch this weighty embarkation, which was very heavy for its proportion, as being made of the body of an oak or pine, some twenty-two foot in length, hollowed like a pig-trough, which is the true description of a canoe. The manner of its being put into motion is very particular; the labourers with long booms place their feet on the starboard and larboard sides of the boat, and with this fickle footing do they heave it forward.

I cannot omit a passage of one major *Stephens,* who had been an officer in the late civil war, under Sir *William Waller,* and was now one of our fellow-sufferers. He could not be persuaded by any means to give his vote for prosecuting the way we were in for our relief, but differ'd as much in judgment with us, in this our design of going to the king of this country, as he had done in *England,* by engaging against his natural sovereign; he cry'd out these rogues would draw us into their power, and take away our lives, advising, rather than to put our trust in this king, we should put ourselves into one of these canoes, and taking advantage of the calm time, we should try to get the north cape.

His fears and objections were so unreasonable, that they were not worth an answer, and his project of our going thus by sea was so ridiculous, that it did exceed all chimera's of knight-errantry, and his apprehending the king would ensnare us, we all esteemed vain, as nothing could be more childish: We had been in the king's power (though we knew it not) ever since we set foot on that ground, so that had his mind been that way bent, he need use no other stratagem to end our lives, than to have forborn the sending us relief; every one dissented to the main project, and I did unfeignedly profess, for my own part, that I would much rather expose my life to the honour of a king (tho' never so mean) than to the billows of the sea, in such a bottom; which would be to tempt God to destroy us, and punish our presumption by his justice, at the same time that he was saving us by a miracle of his mercy.

I should not have remembered this passage of major *Stephens,* had he only shew'd his antipathy in this single instance, but because he repeated the rancor of his mind, in two other very small occasions, which will follow, 'tis just that the malignity of so ill an humour should suffer some reprimand.

The canoes being fitted to take us in and waft us to the main, I made a fair muster of the remnant we had to carry off, and found we wanted six of the number we brought on shore (*viz.*) four men and two women: five of those six we knew were dead, but missing one of our living women, we made the *Indians* understand the same, who as readily made us know that she was in their thoughts, and should be cared for assoon as we were settled in our quarters.

In passing the creek that was to lead us to an honest fisherman's house, we entred a branch of it to the southward, that was the roadway to it. The tide was going out, and the water very shoal, which gave occasion to any one that had a knife, to treat himself with oysters all the way. At the head of that branch we were able in a short time to discover that heaven of happiness where our most courteous host did, with a chearful countenance, receive and entertain us. Several fires were kindled out of hand, our arms and powder were laid up in safety, and divers earthen pipkins were put to boil with such varieties as the season would afford. Every body had something or other to defend and save them from the cold; and my obligation to him, by a peculiar care that he had of me, exceeded all the rest. I had one intire side of the fire, with a large platform to repose on, to myself; furrs and deer skins to cover my body, and support my head, with a priority of respect and friendly usage, which, to my great trouble, I was not able to deserve at his hands, by any requital then in my power to return.

Our kind entertainment in the house of this poor fisherman, had so many circumstances of hearty compassion and tenderness in every part of it, that as it ought to be a perpetual motive to engage all of us who enjoyed the benefit of it, to a daily acknowledgement of the Almighty's goodness for conducting us in this manner by his immediate hand, out of our afflictions, so may it ever be look'd upon as a just approach to christians, who, on all our sea-coasts, are so far from affording succour to those who, by shipwreck and misfortunes of the sea, do fall into their power, that they treat with all inhuman savage barbarity, those unhappy souls whom God hath thus afflicted, seizing on their goods as their proper perquisites, which the waves of the sea (by divine providence) would cast upon the shore for the true proprietors; and many times dispatching them out of the world to silence complaints, and to prevent all after-reckonings. And the better to intitle themselves to what they get in this way of rapine, they wickedly call such devilish acquests by the sacred name of God's good, prophaning and blaspheming at the same time that holy name, as they violate all the laws of hospitality and human society: whereas, on the contrary, our charitable host, influenced only by natural law, without the least shew of coveting any thing we had, or prospect of requital in the future, did not only treat in this manner our persons, but did also, with as much honesty, secure for us our small stores of guns, powder, &c. as if he had read and understood the duty of the gospel, or had given his only child as a hostage to secure his dealing justly with us; so that I can never sufficiently applaud the humanity of this *Indian,* nor express the high contentment that I enjoyed in this poor man's cottage, which was made of nothing but mat and reeds, and bark of trees fix'd to poles. It had a loveliness and symmetry in the air of it, so pleasing to the eye, and refreshing to the mind, that neither the splendor of the *Escurial,* nor the glorious appearance of *Versailles* were able to stand in competition with it. We had a boiled swan for supper, which gave plentiful repasts to all our upper mess.

Our bodies thus refresh'd with meat and sleep, comforted with fires, and secured from all the changes and inclemencies of that sharp piercing cold season, we thought the morning (tho' clad in sunshine) did come too fast upon us. Breakfast was liberally provided and set before us, our arms faithfully delivered up to my order for carriage; and thus in readiness to set forward, we put our selves in a posture to proceed to the place where the king resided. The woman left behind at the island, had been well look'd to, and was now brought off to the care of her comrade that came with us; neither of them in a condition to take a journey, but they were carefully attended and nourished in this poor man's house, till such time as boats came to fetch them to *Virginia,* where they did soon arrive in perfect health, and lived (one or both of them) to be well married, and to bear children, and to subsist in as plentiful a condition as they could wish.

In beginning our journey thro' the woods, we had not advanced half a mile till we heard a great noise of mens voices, directed to meet and stop our further passage. These were several *Indians* sent by the king to order us back to our quarters. Major *Stephens* (not cured of his jealous humour by the experience of what he felt the night before) took this alarm in a very bad sense, and as much different from the rest of the company as in his former fit. He was again deluded with a strong fancy, that these violent motions in the *Indians* who approach'd us, were the effect of some sudden change in their counsels to our detriment, and that nothing less than our perdition could be the consequence thereof, which he feared would immediately be put in practice by the clamorous men that made such haste to meet us, and (as he would apprehend) to kill and destroy us.

This passion of major *Stephens*, cast in the same mould with that other he discovered in the island, had not (as we all thought and told him) whereon to raise the least foundation of terror to affright a child; for besides the earnest we had received of their good intentions the night before, these men who came so fast upon us, were all unarm'd; nor was it likely, that king would now possibly imbrew his hands in our blood, and provoke he knew not how powerful a nation to destroy him, after such kind caresses, and voluntary expressions of a temper very contrary to such cruelty. In fine, we saw no cause in all the carriage of the *Indians* on which I could ground any fear, and therefore I long'd with all impatience to see this king, and to enjoy the plenty of his table, as we quickly did.

When these *Indians* came up to us, this doubt was soon cleared. The good-natur'd king being inform'd of our bodily weakness, and inability to walk thro' the woods to his house, on foot (which might be about four miles distant from our setting out) had a real tenderness for us, and sent canoes to carry us to the place nearest his house, by the favour of another branch of the same creek; and to the end we might take no vain steps (as we were going to do) and exhaust our strength to no purpose, these *Indians* made this noise to stop us.

We entred the canoes that were mann'd, and lay ready to receive us. We had a pleasant passage in the shallow water, eat oysters all the way: for altho' the breakfast we had newly made, might well excuse a longer abstinence than we were like to be put to, our arrear to our stomachs was so great, that all we swallowed was soon concocted, and our appetite still fresh and craving more.

Henry Norwood, fl. 1650

QUEEN OF THE COUNTRY DESCRIBED

Having pass'd this new course for some three *English* miles in another branch of the creek, our landing place was contriv'd to be near the house of the queen then in waiting. She was a very plain lady to see to, not young, nor yet ill-favour'd. Her complexion was of a sad white: but the measure of beauty in those parts where they are exposed to the scorching sun from their infancy, are not taken from red and white, but from colours that will better lie upon their tawny skins, as hereafter will be seen.

The beauty of this queen's mind (which is more permanent than that of colour) was conspicuous in her charity and generosity to us poor starved weather-beaten creatures, who were the object of it. A mat was spread without the house, upon the ground, furnish'd with *Pone, Homini,* oysters, and other things. The queen made us sit down and eat, with gestures that shewed more of courtesy than majesty, but did speak as hearty welcome as could in silence be expected: and these were the graces that, in our opinion, transcended all other beauties in the world, and did abundantly supply all defects of outward appearance in the person and garb of the queen. The southerly wind made the season tolerable; but that lasted but little, the north-west gale coming violently on us again.

THE KING'S PALACE

When this collation of the queen was at an end, we took leave of her majesty with all the shews of gratitude that silence knew how to utter. We were now within half an hour's walk of the king's mansion, which we soon discovered by the smoak, and saw it was made of the same stuff with the other houses from which we had newly parted, namely, of mat and reed. Locust posts sunk in the ground at corners and partitions, was the strength of the whole fabrick. The roof was tied fast to the body with a sort of strong rushes that grew there, which supply'd the place of nails and pins, mortises and tenants.

The breadth of this palace was about eighteen or twenty foot, the length about twenty yards. The only furniture was several platforms for lodging, each about two yards long and more, plac'd on both

153

sides of the house, distant from each other about five foot; the space in the middle was the chimney, which had a hole in the roof over it, to receive as much of the smoak as would naturally repair to it; the rest we shared amongst us, which was the greatest part; and the sitters divided to each side, as our soldiers do in their *corps de guarde*.

Fourteen great fires, thus situated, were burning all at once. The king's apartment had a distinction from the rest; it was twice as long, and the bank he sat on was adorn'd with deer skins finely dress'd, and the best furrs of otter and beaver that the country did produce.

KING'S DAUGHTER

The fire assign'd to us was suitable to our number, to which we were conducted, without intermixture of any *Indian* but such as came to do us offices of friendship. There we were permitted to take our rest until the king pleased to enter into communication with us. Previous to which he sent his daughter, a well-favour'd young girl of about ten or twelve years old, with a great wooden bowl full of homini (which is the corn of that country, beat and boiled to mash). She did in a most obliging manner give me the first taste of it, which I would have handed to my next neighbour after I had eaten, but the young princess interposed her hand, and taking the bowl out of mine, delivered it to the same party I aimed to give it, and so to all the rest in order. Instead of a spoon there was a well-shap'd muscle-shell that accompanied the bowl.

The linen of that country grows ready made on the branches of oak trees (or pine) the *English* call it *moss*. It is like the threads of unwhited cotton-yarn ravelled, and hangs in parcels on the lower boughs, divine providence having so ordered it for the conveniency and sustenance of the deer, which is all the food they can get in times of snow. It is very soft, sweet and cleanly, and fit for the purpose of wiping clean the hands, and doing the duty of napkins.

AUDIENCE OF THE KING

About three hours after this meal was ended, the king sent to have me come to him. He called me *Ny a Mutt*, which is to say, My brother, and compelled me to sit down on the same bank with him-

154

self, which I had reason to look upon as a mighty favour. After I had sat there about half an hour, and had taken notice of many earnest discourses and repartees betwixt the king and his *crotemen* (so the *Indians* call the king's council) I could plainly discover, that the debate they held was concerning our adventure and coming there. To make it more clear, the king address'd himself to me with many gestures of his body, his arms display'd in various postures, to explain what he had in his mind to utter for my better understanding. By all which motions I was not edify'd in the least, nor could imagine what return to make by voice or sign, to satisfy the king's demands in any thing that related to the present straights of our condition. In fine, I admir'd their patient sufferance of my dulness to comprehend what they meant, and shew'd myself to be troubled at it; which being perceiv'd by the king, he turn'd all into mirth and jollity, and never left till he made me laugh with him, tho' I knew not why.

I took that occasion to present the king with a sword and long shoulder-belt, which he received very kindly; and to witness his gracious acceptance, he threw off his *Mach coat* (or upper covering of skin) stood upright on his bank, and, with my aid, did accoutre his naked body with his new harness, which had no other apparel to adorn it, besides a few skins about his loyns to cover his nakedness. In this dress he seem'd to be much delighted; but to me he appear'd a figure of such extraordinary shape, with sword and belt to set it off, that he needed no other art to stir me up to laughter and mirth, than the sight of his own proper person.

Having made this short acquaintance with the king, I took leave, and returned to my comrades. In passing the spaces betwixt fire and fire, one space amongst the rest was blinded with a traverse of mat; and by the noise I heard from thence, like the beating of hemp, I took it to be some kind of elaboratory. To satisfy a curiosity I had to be more particularly inform'd, I edg'd close to the mat; and, by standing on tiptoe for a full discovery, I saw a sight that gave me no small trouble. The same specifical queen (whose courtesy for our kind usage the other day, can never be enough applauded) was now employed in the hard servile labour of beating corn for the king's dinner, which raised the noise that made me thus inquisitive. I wish'd myself in her place for her ease: but the queens of that country do esteem it a privilege to serve their husbands in all kind of cookery, which they would be as loth to lose, as any christian queen would be to take it from them.

Several *Indians* of the first rank followed me to our quarters, and used their best endeavours to sift something from us that might give them light into knowing what we were. They sought many ways to make their thoughts intelligible to us, but still we parted without knowing what to fix upon, or how to steer our course in advance of our way to *Virginia*.

In this doubtful condition we thought it reasonable to fall upon a speedy resolution what was next to be done on our parts, in order to the accomplishment of our voyage by land, which we hop'd (by the divine aid) we might be able to effect after a little more refreshment by the plenty of victuals allowed us by the king, who was no less indulgent and careful to feed and caress us, than if we had been his children.

Towards morning we were treated with a new regale brought to us by the same fair hand again. It was a sort of spoon-meat, in colour and taste not unlike to almond-milk temper'd and mix'd with boiled rice. The ground still was *Indian* corn boiled to a pap, which they call *Homini*, but the ingredient which performed the milky part, was nothing but dry pokickery nuts, beaten shells and all to powder, and they are like our walnuts, but thicker shell'd, and the kernel sweeter; but being beaten in a mortar, and put into a tray, hollow'd in the middle to make place for fair water, no sooner is the water poured into the powder, but it rises again white and creamish; and after a little ferment it does partake so much of the delicate taste of the kernel of that nut, that it becomes a rarity to a miracle.

Major *Morrison*, who had been almost at death's door, found himself abundantly refreshed and comforted with this delicacy; he wished the bowl had been a fathom deep, and would say, when his stomach called on him for fresh supplies, that if this princess royal would give him his fill of that food, he should soon recover his strength.

Our bodies growing vigorous with this plenty, we took new courage, and resolv'd (as many as were able) to attempt the finding out of *Virginia*. We guess'd the distance could not be great, and that it bore from us S. by W. to S. W. Our ignorance of the latitude we were in, was some discouragement to us; but we were confident, from what the seamen discoursed, we were to the southward of the *Menados*, then a *Dutch* plantation, now *New York:* Fair weather and full stomachs made us willing to be gone. To that end we laid out for a quantity of pone; and for our surer conduct we resolved to procure an *Indian* to be our pilot through the wilderness, for we were to expect many remora's in our way, by swamps and creeks, with which all those sea-coasts do abound.

The king remarking our more than ordinary care to procure more bread than amounted to our usual expence, gathered thence our design to leave him, and shift for ourselves. To prevent the rashness and folly of such attempt, he made use of all his silent rhetorick to put us out of conceit of such design, and made us understand the peril and difficulty of it by many obstacles we must meet with. He shew'd us the danger we should expose ourselves unto, by rain and cold, swamps and darkness, unless we were conducted by other skill than we could pretend to: He pointed to his fires and shocks of corn, of which he had enough, and made it legible to us in his countenance, that we were welcome to it. All the signs the king made upon this occasion, we were content to understand in the best sense; and taking for granted our sojourning there was renewed to another day, we retired to our quarters.

About midnight following, the king sent to invite me to his fire. He placed me near him as before, and in the first place shewing me quarters of a lean doe, new brought in. He gave me a knife to cut what part of it I pleased, and then pointing to the fire, I inferr'd I was left to my own discretion for the dressing of it. I could not readily tell how to shew my skill in the cookery of it, with no better ingredients than appear'd in sight; and so did no more but cut a collop and cast it on the coals. His majesty laugh'd at my ignorance, and to instruct me better, he broach'd the collop on a long scewer, thrust the sharp end into the ground (for there was no hearth but what nature made) and turning sometimes one side, sometimes the other, to the fire, it became fit in short time to be served up, had there been a dining-room of state such as that excellent king deserved.

I made tender of it first to the king, and then to his nobles, but all refused, and left all to me, who gave God and the king thanks for that great meal. The rest of the doe was cut in pieces, stewed in a pipkin, and then put'into my hands to dispose of amongst my company.

Assoon as I had dispatch'd this midnight venison feast, and sent the rest to my comrades, the king was greatly desirous to make me comprehend, by our common dialect of signs and motions, the ingenious stratagem by which they use to take their deer in the winter season, especially when the surface of the earth is cover'd with snow. He shewed me in the first place a small leather thong, in which (said he) any kind of deer should be invited to hamper himself and lie fast ty'd on his back, until the engineer (or some body else for him) should take quiet possession of him. I could not conceive the particular structure of this machine, so as to direct the making of it elsewhere; but thus much in the general I did understand; they would fasten a pine green branch at the end of a pole (such as hops grow upon) which should lie athwart an oak, like the pole of a turner's lath, and the green hanging dingle-dangle at the pole end, fastened by a string; it should be set at a height for a deer to reach, but not without mounting and resting on his hinder legs, that so in pulling the branch, as at a trigger, the machine discharging, his heels are struck up to fly in the air, and there he remains on his back so straitly hamper'd, that the least child may approach to touch and take him.

Before I parted, the king attack'd me again, with reiterated attempts to be understood, and I thought by these three or four days conversation, I had the air of his expression much more clear and intelligible than at first. His chief drift for the first essay seemed to be a desire to know which way we were bound, whether north or south; to which I pointed to the south. This gave him much satisfaction, and thereupon steps in the little grotman before described, who by the motion of his hand seemed to crave my regard to what he was going about. He took up a stick, with which he made divers circles by the fireside, and then holding up his finger to procure my attention, he gave to every hole a name; and it was not hard to conceive that the several holes were to supply the place of a sea-chart, shewing the situation of all the most noted *Indian* territories that lay to the southward of *Kickotank.*

That circle that was most southerly, he called *Achomack,* which, tho' he pronounc'd with a different accent from us, I laid hold on that word with all demonstrations of satisfaction I could express, giving them to understand, that was the place to which I had a desire to be conducted.

The poor king was in a strange transport of joy to see me receive satisfaction, and did forthwith cause a lusty young man to be called to him, to whom, by the earnestness of his motions, he seemed to give ample instructions to do something for our service, but what it was we were not yet able to resolve. In two or three days time, seeing no effect of what he had so seriously said, we began again to despond, and did therefore resume our former thoughts of putting ourselves in posture to be gone; but the king seeing us thus ready at every turn to leave him, shewed in his looks a more than ordinary resentment; still describing (as he could) the care he had taken for us, and impossibility of accomplishing our ends by ourselves, and that we should surely faint in the way and die without help, if we would not be ruled by him.

He shewed me again his stores of corn, and made such reiterated signs, by the chearfulness of his countenance, that we should not want, whilst he had such a plenty, as made us lay aside all thoughts of stirring till he said the word. But as oft as he look'd or pointed to the coast of *Achomack,* he would shake his head, with abundance of grimaces, in dislike of our design to go that way till he saw it good we should do so. I was abundantly convinced of our folly in the resolution we were ready to take of going away without better information of the distance from *Achomack,* and way that led to it; and having so frank a welcome where we were, we resolved to stay till the king should approve of our departure, which he was not able to determine till the messenger came back, that he had sent to *Achomack,* who, it now seemed more plainly, was dispatch'd upon my owning that place to be our home, tho' we knew it not from any cause we could rely upon, before we saw the effect.

While we liv'd in this suspense, the king had a great mind to see our fire-arms, and to be acquainted with the use and nature of them. That which best did please his eye I presented to him, and shew'd him how to load and discharge it. He was very shy at first essay, fearing it might hurt him, but I made him stand upon his lodging place, and putting him in a posture to give fire, he presented the mouth of his gun to the chimney hole, and so let fly. The combustible nature of the king's palace not well consider'd, the fabrick was endangered by the king's own hand, for the flashing of the powder having taken hold of the roof at the smoke-hole, all was in a flame; but a nimble lad or two ran up to quench it, and did soon extinguish it without considerable damage to the building, which was of mat and boughs of oak as aforesaid.

The king's eldest son, of about eighteen years of age, was hugely enamour'd with our guns, and look'd so wistfully on me, when he saw what wonders they would do, that I could not forbear presenting him with a birding-piece. Some of our company, who knew that by the laws of *Virginia,* it was criminal to furnish the *Indians* with fire-arms, gave me caution in this case, but I resolved, for once, to borrow a point of that law; for tho' it might be of excellent use in the general, yet as our condition was, I esteemed it a much greater crime to deny those *Indians* any thing that was in our power, than the penalty of that law could amount to.

Father and son abundantly gratify'd in this manner, the king thought himself largely requited for the cost we put him to in our entertainment. I taught his son to shoot at fowls, to charge his gun and clean it, insomuch that in a few minutes, he went among the flocks of geese, and firing at random he did execution on one of them to his great joy, and returned to his father with the game in his hand, with such celerity, as if he had borrowed wings of the wind.

JAN. 24

About three o'clock this afternoon, the king was pleased in great condescension to honour me with a visit, a favour which I may (without vanity) assume to myself, and my better habit, from the many particular applications that he made to me, exclusive of the rest of the company. He thought I was too melancholy, (for the *Indians,* as has been observ'd, are great enemies to that temper) and

Henry Norwood, fl. 1650

shew'd me by his own chearful looks, what humour he would have me put on; he would not have me in the least apprehensive of wanting any thing his country afforded, as his mien and gesture witnessed; and for the higher proof of his reality, he found me out a divertisement, that was very extraordinary. He came at this time attended by his young daughter, who had done us the good offices before-mention'd, and having first by kind words and pleasant gestures given us renewed assurance of hearty welcome, he singled me out, and pointed with his hand to a way he would have me take, but whither, or to what end, I was at liberty to guess; upon that he produced his little daughter for my conductrix to the place to which I should go, and shewed his desire that I should follow her whereever she should lead me.

Major *Stephens,* not yet enough convinc'd of the *Indians* fidelity, would have discouraged me from leaving the company in that manner, unreasonably fancying that this was a contrivance in the king to take away my life in a private way; but this I thought did so much out-strip all his other senseless jealousies, that after I had acknowledg'd the obligation I had to his care of my person, his needless caution had no other effect on me than to turn it into ridicule. These inordinate fears of this major in three foregoing instances, might (I confess) have been very well omitted, as not worthy the mention, and so they should have been, had his humour and constitution in prosperous times been any way suitable to this wary temper; but because his habits on shore were scandalously vicious his mouth always belching oaths, and his tongue proving him the vainest hector I had seen, I thought it was pity to lose such a strong confirmation of that known truth, (*viz.*) That true innate courage does seldom reside in the heart of a quarrelling and talking hector.

The weather (as I have said) was excessive cold, with frost, and the winds blowing very fresh upon my face, it almost stopt my breath. The late condition I had been in, under a roof, with great fires, and much smoke, did conduce to make me the more sensible of the cold air: but in less than half an hour that pain was over; we were now in sight of the house whereto we were bound, and the lady of the place was ready to receive us, (who proved to be the

161

mother of my conductrix) and to shew me my apartment in the middle of the house, which had the same accommodation to sit and rest upon, as before has been described in other instances.

The lusty rousing fire, prepared to warm me, would have been noble entertainment of itself, but attended (as it was quickly) with good food for the belly, made it to be that compleat good chear, I only aimed at; a wild turkey boiled, with oysters, was preparing for my supper, which, when it was ready, was served up in the same pot that boiled it. It was a very savoury mess, stew'd with muscles, and I believe would have passed for a delicacy at any great table in England, by palates more competent to make a judgment than mine, which was now more gratify'd with the quantity than the quality of what was before me.

This queen was also of the same mould of her majesty whom we first met at our landing place, somewhat ancient (in proportion to the king's age) but so gentle and compassionate, as did very bountifully requite all defects of nature; she passed some hours at my fire, and was very desirous to know the occasion that brought us there (as her motion and the emphasis of her words did shew) but I had small hopes to satisfy her curiosity therein, after so many vain attempts to inform the king in that manner. In fine, I grew sleepy, and about nine o'clock every one retired to their quarters, separated from each other by traverses of mat, which (besides their proper virtue) kept the ladies from any immodest attempts, as secure as if they had been bars of iron.

As soon as the day peeped in, I went out and felt the same cold as yesterday, with the same wind, N. W. I was not forward to quit a warm quarter, and a frank entertainment, but my young governess, who had her father's orders for direction, knew better than myself what I was to do: she put herself in a posture to lead the way back from whence we came, after a very good repast of stew'd muscles, together with a very hearty welcome plainly appearing in the queen's looks.

My nimble pilot led me away with great swiftness, and it was necessary so to do; the weather still continuing in that violent sharpness, nothing but a violent motion could make our limbs useful. No sooner had I set my foot in the king's house to visit my comrades, but a wonderful surprize appeared to me in the change of every countenance, and as every face did plainly speak a general satisfaction, so did they with one voice explain the cause thereof, in telling me the messengers of our delivery were arriv'd, and now with the king.

I hastened to see those angels, and addressing myself to one of them in *English* habit, ask'd him the occasion of his coming there? He told me his business was to trade for furs, and no more; but assoon as I had told him my name, and the accidents of our being there, he acknowledg'd he came under the guidance of the *Kickotank Indian* (which I imagin'd, but was not sure the king had sent) in quest of me and those that were left on shore, sent by the governor's order of *Virginia* to enquire after us, but knew not where to find us till that *Indian* came to his house; he gave me a large account of the ship's arrival, and the many dangers and difficulties she encountred before she could come into *James* river, where she ran ashore, resolving there to lay her bones. His name was *Jenkin Price,* he had brought an *Indian* of his neighbourhood with him that was very well acquainted in those parts, for our conduct back to *Achomack,* which *Indian* was called *Jack.*

The king was very glad of this happy success to us, and was impatient to learn something more of our history than hitherto he had been able to extract from signs and grimaces. *Jenkin Price,* with his broken *Indian,* could make a shift to instruct *Jack* to say any thing he pleased, and *Jack* was the more capable to understand his meaning by some sprinklings of *English,* that he had learnt at our plantations. Betwixt them both they were able to satisfy the king in what he pleased to know. *Jack* told them of himself what a mighty nation we were in that country, and gave them caution not to imbezzle any goods we had brought with us, for fear of an after-reckoning. I wondered, upon this serious discourse he had with the king, to see guns and stockings, and whatever trifles we had given, offer'd to be return'd, and being told the reason of it by *Jenkin Price,* I was very much ashamed of *Jack's* too great zeal in our service, which, tho' it did proceed from a principle of honesty, and good morality in him, we were to consider that our dearest lives, and all we could enjoy in this world, was (next to divine providence) owing to the virtue and charity of this king, and therefore not only what they had in possession, but whatever else he should desire that was in my power, would be too mean an acknowledgment for so high obligations. I took care to let them know that I· had no hand in the menace by which *Jack* brought them to refund what they had got of us; the right understanding whereof increased our good intelligence, and became a new endearment of affection betwixt us.

By better acquaintance with these our deliverers, we learn'd that we were about fifty *English* miles from *Virginia:* That part of it where *Jenkin* did govern, was call'd *Littleton's Plantation,* and was the first *English* ground we did expect to see. He gave me great encouragement to endure the length of the way, by assuring me I should not find either stone or shrub to hurt my feet thorow my thinsoaled boots, for the whole colony had neither stone nor underwood; and having thus satisfy'd my curiosity in the knowledge of what *Jenkin Price* could communicate, we deferred no longer to resolve how and when to begin our journey to *Achomack.*

The *Indian* he brought with him (who afterwards lived and died my servant) was very expert, and a most incomparable guide in the woods we were to pass, being a native of those parts, so that he was as our sheet-anchor in this peregrination. The king was loth to let us go till the weather was better-temper'd for our bodies; but when he saw we were fully resolved, and had pitch'd upon the next morning to begin our journey, he found himself much defeated in a purpose he had taken to call together all the flower of his kingdom to entertain us with a dance, to the end that nothing might be omitted on his part for our divertisement, as well as our nourishment, which his small territory could produce. Most of our company would gladly have deferred our march a day longer, to see this masquerade, but I was wholly bent for *Achomack,* to which place I was to dance almost on my bare feet, the thoughts of which took off the edge I might otherwise have had to novelties of that kind.

When the good old king saw we were fully determined to be gone the next day, he desired as a pledge of my affection to him, that I would give him my camblet coat, which he vowed to wear whilst he lived for my sake; I shook hands to shew my willingness to please him in that or in any other thing he would command, and was the more willing to do myself the honor of compliance in this particular, because he was the first king I could call to mind that had ever shew'd any inclinations to wear my old cloaths.

To the young princess, that had so signally obliged me, I presented a piece of two-penny scarlet ribbon, and a *French* tweezer, that I had in my pocket, which made her skip for joy, and to shew how little she fancy'd our way of carrying them concealed, she retired apart for some time, and taking out every individual piece of which it was furnish'd, she tied a snip of ribbon to each, and so came back with scissars, knives and bodkins hanging at her ears, neck and hair. The case itself was not excus'd, but bore a part in this new dress: and to the end we might not part without leaving deep impressions of her beauty in our minds, she had prepared on her forefingers, a lick of paint on each, the colours (to my best remembrance) green and yellow, which at one motion she discharg'd on her face, beginning upon her temples, and continuing it in an oval line downwards as far as it would hold out. I could have wish'd this young princess would have contented herself with what nature had done for her, without this addition of paint (which, I thought, made her more fulsome than handsome); but I had reason to imagine the royal family were only to use this ornament exclusive of all others, for that I saw none other of her sex so set off; and this conceit made it turn again, and appear lovely, as all things should do that are honour'd with the royal stamp.

I was not furnish'd with any thing upon the place, fit to make a return to the two queens for the great charity they used to feed and warm me; but when I came into a place where I could be supply'd, I was not wanting that way, according to my power.

Early next morning we put our selves in posture to be gone, (*viz.*) major *Stephens*, myself, and three or four more, whose names are worn out of my mind. Major *Morrison* was so far recovered as to be heart-whole, but he wanted strength to go thro' so great a labour as this was like to prove. We left him with some others to be brought in boats that the governor had order'd for their accommodation; and with them the two weak women, who were much recover'd by the good care and nourishment they receiv'd in the poor fisherman's house.

Breakfast being done, and our pilot *Jack* ready to set out, we took a solemn leave of the good king. He inclosed me in his arms with kind embraces, not without expressions of sorrow to part, beyond the common rate of new acquaintance. I made *Jack* pump up his best compliments, which at present was all I was capable to return to the king's kindness; and so, after many *Hana haes,* we parted.

Their Departure

We were not gone far till the fatigue and tediousness of the journey discovered itself in the many creeks we were forc'd to head, and swamps to pass (like *Irish* bogs) which made the way at least double to what it would have amounted to in a strait line: and it was our wonder to see our guide *Jack* lead on the way with the same confidence of going right, as if he had had a *London* road to keep him from straying. Howbeit he would many times stand still and look about for landmarks; and when on one hand and the other his marks bore right for his direction, he would shew himself greatly satisfied. As to the purpose, an old deform'd tree that lay north-west, opposite to a small hammock of pines to the south-east, would evidence his going right in all weathers. It is true, they know not the compass by the loadstone, but, which is equivalent, they never are ignorant of the north-west point, which gives them the rest; and that they know by weather-beaten moss that grows on that side of every oak, different from the rest of the tree, which is their compass. Towards evening we saw smoak (an infallible sign of an *Indian* town) which *Jack* knew to arise from *Gingo Teague.* We went boldly into the king's house (by advice of his brother of *Kickotank*) who was also a very humane prince. What the place and season produced was set before us with all convenient speed, which was enough to satisfy hunger, and to fit us for repose.

I was extremely tir'd with this tedious journey; and it was the more irksome to me, because I perform'd it in boots (my shoes being worn out) which at that time were commonly worn to walk in; so that I was much more sleepy than I had been hungry. The alliance I had newly made at *Kickotank* did already stand me in some stead, for that it qualified me to a lodging apart, and gave me a first taste of all we had to eat, tho' the variety was not so great as I had seen in other courts.

And yet (as we see in all worldly honours) this grandeur of mine was not without its allay; for as it gave me accommodation of eating and sleeping in preference to my comrades, so did it raise the hopes of the royal progeny of gifts and presents, beyond what I was either able or willing to afford them: for when I would have taken my rest, I was troubled beyond measure with their visits, and saw by their carriage what they would be at; wherefore, to free myself of further disturbance, and to put myself out of the pain of denials, I resolv'd to comply with the necessities of nature, which press'd me hard to sleep; and to that end I took the freedom by *Jack*, to desire they would all withdraw until I found myself refresh'd.

I pass'd the night till almost day-break in one intire sleep; and when I did awake (not suddenly able to collect who, or where I was) I found myself strangely confounded, to see a damsel plac'd close to my side, of no meaner extract than the king's eldest daughter, who had completely finish'd the rape of all the gold and silver buttons that adorn'd the king of *Kickotank's* coat, yet on my back. When I was broad awake, and saw this was no enchantment (like those trances knights-errant use to be in) but that I was really despoiled of what was not in my power to dispense withal, I called for *Jack*, and made him declare my resentment and much dislike of this princess's too great liberty upon so small acquaintance, which made me have a mean opinion of her. *Jack* shew'd more anger than myself to see such usage by any of his country, and much more was he scandaliz'd, that one of the blood royal should purloin.

But the king, upon notice of the fact and party concerned in it, immediately caused the buttons to be found out and returned, with no slight reprimand to his daughter, and then all was well, and so much the better by the gift of such small presents as I was able to make to the king and princess. Breakfast was given us, and we hasten'd to proceed in our journey to *Achomack*.

The uneasiness of boots to travel in, made me by much the more weary of the former day's journey, and caus'd me to enter very unwillingly upon this second day's work. We reckon'd our selves about twenty-five miles distant from *Jenkin's* house. It pleased God to send us dry weather, and not excessive cold. We had made provision of *Pone* to bait on by the way, and we found good water to refresh us; but all this did not hinder my being tir'd and spent almost to the last degree. *Jack* very kindly offer'd his service to carry me on his shoulders (for I was brought to a moderate weight by the strict diet I had been in) but that would have been more uneasy to me, in contemplation of his more than double pains, and so I resolved to try my utmost strength, without placing so great a weight on his shoulders.

The hopes of seeing *English* ground in *America,* and that in so short a time as they made us expect, did animate my spirits to the utmost point. *Jack* fearing the worst, was of opinion, that we should call at his aunt's town, the queen of *Pomumkin,* not far out of the way: but *Jenkin Price* opposed that motion, and did assure me our journey's end was at hand. His words and my own inclination carried the question, and I resolved, by God's help, that night to sleep at *Jenkin's* house.

But the distance proving yet greater than had been described, and my boots trashing me almost beyond all sufferance, I became desperate, and ready to sink and lie down. *Jenkin* lull'd me on still with words that spurr'd me to the quick; and would demonstrate the little distance betwixt us and his plantation, by the sight of hogs and cattle, of which species the *Indians* were not masters. I was fully convinc'd of what he said, but would however have consented to a motion of lying without doors on the ground, within two or three flights shot of the place, to save the labour of so small a remainder.

The close of the evening, and a little more patience (thro' the infinite goodness of the Almighty) did put a happy period to our cross adventure. A large bed of sweet straw was spread ready in *Jenkin's* house for our reception, upon which I did hasten to extend and stretch my wearied limbs. And being thus brought into safe harbour by the many miracles of divine mercy, from all the storms and fatigues, perils and necessities to which we had been exposed by sea and land for almost the space of four months, I cannot conclude this voyage in more proper terms, than the words that are the burthen of that psalm of providence, *O that men would therefore praise the*

Henry Norwood, fl. 1650

Lord for his goodness, and for his wondrous works unto the children of men!

Our landlord *Jenkin Price,* and conductor *Jack* took great care to provide meat for us; and there being a dairy and hens, we could not want. As for our stomachs, they were open at all hours to eat what-e'er was set before us, assoon as our wearied bodies were refresh'd with sleep. It was on *Saturday* the — day of January, that we ended this our wearisome pilgrimage, and entred into our king's dominions at *Achomat,* call by the *English, Northampton* county, which is the only county on that side of the bay belonging to the colony of *Virginia,* and is the best of the whole for all sorts of necessaries for human life.

Having been thus refresh'd in *Jenkin's* house this night with all our hearts could wish, on the next morning, being *Sunday,* we would have been glad to have found a church for the performance of our duty to God, and to have rendred our hearty thanks to him in the publick assembly, for his unspeakable mercies vouchsafed to us; but we were not yet arrived to the heart of the country where there were churches, and ministry perform'd as our laws direct, but were glad to continue our own chaplains, as formerly. As we advanced into the plantations that lay thicker together, we had our choice of hosts for our entertainment, without money or its value; in which we did not begin any novelty, for there are no inns in the colony; nor do they take other payment for what they furnish to coasters, but by requital of such courtesies in the same way, as occasions offer.

When I came to the house of one *Stephen Charlton,* he did not only outdo all that I had visited before him, in variety of dishes at his table, which was very well order'd in the kitchen, but would also oblige me to put on a good farmer-like suit of his own wearing cloaths, for exchange of my dirty habit; and this gave me opportunity to deliver my camlet coat to *Jack,* for the use of my brother of *Kickotank,* with other things to make it worth his acceptance.

Having been thus frankly entertain'd at Mr. *Charlton's,* our company were in condition to take care for themselves. We took leave of each other, and my next stage was to esquire *Yardly,* a gentleman of good name, whose father had sometimes been governor of *Virginia.* There I was received and treated as if I had in truth and real-

169

ity been than man of honour my brother of *Kickotank* had created me. It fell out very luckily for my better welcome, that he had not long before brought over a wife from *Rotterdam,* that I had known almost from a child. Her father (*Custis* by name) kept a victualling house in that town, liv'd in good repute, and was the general host of our nation there. The esquire knowing I had the honour to be the governor's kinsman, and his wife knowing my conversation in *Holland,* I was receiv'd and caress'd more like a domestick and near relation, than a man in misery, and a stranger. I stay'd there for a passage over the bay, about ten days, welcomed and feasted not only by the esquire and his wife, but by many neighbours that were not too remote.

FEB. 13

About the midst of *February* I had an opportunity to cross the bay in a sloop, and with much ado landed in *York* river, at esquire *Ludlow's* plantation, a most pleasant situation. I was civilly receiv'd by him, who presently order'd an accommodation for me in a most obliging manner. But it fell out at that time, that captain *Wormly* (of his majesty's council) had guests in his house (not a furlong distant from Mr. *Ludlow's*) feasting and carousing, that were lately come from *England,* and most of them my intimate acquaintance. I took a sudden leave of Mr. *Ludlow,* thank'd him for his kind intentions to me, and using the common freedom of the country, I thrust myself amongst captain *Wormly's* guests in crossing the creek, and had a kind reception from them all, which answered (if not exceeded) my expectation.

Sir *Thomas Lundsford,* Sir *Henry Chickly,* Sir *Philip Honywood,* and colonel *Hammond* were the persons I met there, and enjoy'd that night with very good chear, but left them early the next morning, out of a passionate desire I had to see the governor, whose care for my preservation had been so full of kindness.

Captain *Wormly* mounted me for *James Town,* where the governor was pleased to receive and take me to his house at *Greenspring,* and there I pass'd my hours (as at mine own house) until *May* following; at which time he sent me for *Holland* to find out the king, and to sollicite his majesty for the treasurer's place of *Virginia,* which the governor took to be void by the delinquency of *Clay-bourne*, who had long enjoy'd it. He furnish'd me with a sum of money to bear the charge of this sollicitation; which took effect, tho' the king was then in *Scotland*. He was not only thus kind to me (who had a more than ordinary pretence to his favour by our near affinity in blood) but, on many occasions, he shew'd great respect to all the royal party, who made that colony their refuge. His house and purse were open to all that were so qualify'd. To one of my comrades (major *Fox*) who had no friend at all to subsist on, he shew'd a generosity that was like himself; and to my other (major *Morrison*) he was more kind, for he did not only place him in the command of the fort, which was profitable to him whilst it held under the king, but did advance him after to the government of the country, wherein he got a competent estate.

And thus (by the good providence of a gracious God, who helpeth us in our low estate, and causeth his angels to pitch tents round about them that trust in him) have I given as faithful an account of this signal instance of his goodness to the miserable objects of his mercy in this voyage, as I have been able to call to a clear remembrance.

"BACON'S MAN"

fl. 1676

In 1676 there flared the first revolt against royal authority in Virginia. Its leader was Nathaniel Bacon, a young man still in his twenties, who had come to Virginia in 1674 and acquired a large estate in the colony. He was a man of means, well educated and well traveled. A graduate of Cambridge, he had visited the Netherlands, Germany, France and Italy, and had studied at the Inns of Court. He made many friends in Virginia and was appointed a member of the Governor's Council.

Feeling was running high in Virginia against the autocratic rule which had been imposed by Governor Berkeley. It was he who had declared some years before: "I thank God there are no free schools nor printing, and I hope we shall not have these hundred years; for learning has brought disobedience, and heresy and sects into the world, and printing has divulged them, and libels against the government. God keep us from both." The biennial election of the House of Burgesses had been abolished and no election had been held for a decade and a half. Matters came to a head when Berkeley refused to defend the Virginia frontier against Indian raids.

Bacon defied the governor and led a party of colonists against the Indians. Berkeley retaliated by declaring Bacon a rebel. "Bacon's Rebellion" had begun. Its purpose became not only to provide protection against the Indians but to institute economic and political reforms. The prospect of success ended suddenly with Bacon's death from fever on October 1, 1676. Berkeley then speedily and mercilessly hunted down and executed Bacon's followers. Berkeley was recalled to England by Charles II, who is said to have exclaimed: "That old fool! He has taken more lives in that naked country than I in all England for the murder of my father."

The following elegy was found in the contemporary "Burwell Papers," which were first printed in 1814. The only hint as to its authorship is the note "After he was dead he was bemoaned in these following lines, drawn by the man that waited upon his person (as it is said), and who attended his corpse to their burial place." Whoever was the author, he was a person of very real literary abilities. The "Epitaph" is an eloquent poem, perhaps the finest in colonial American writing.

172

BACON'S EPITAPH, MADE BY HIS MAN

Death, why so cruel? What! no other way
To manifest thy spleen, but thus to slay
Our hopes of safety, liberty, our all,
Which, through thy tyranny, with him must fall
To its late chaos? Had thy rigid force
Been dealt in retail, and not thus in gross,
Grief had been silent. Now, we must complain,
Since thou in him hast more than thousands slain,
Whose lives and safeties did so much depend
On him their life, with him their lives must end.
If't be a sin to think Death bribed can be,
We must be guilty; say't was bribery
Guided the fatal shaft. Virginia's foes
To whom for secret crimes just vengeance owes
Deserved plagues, dreading their just desert,
Corrupted Death by Paracelsian art
Him to destroy; whose well-tried courage such,
Their heartless hearts, nor arms, nor strength could touch.
Who now must heal those wounds, or stop that blood
The heathen made, and drew into a flood?
Who is't must plead our cause? Nor trump, nor drum,
Nor deputations; these, alas, are dumb,
And cannot speak. Our arms—though ne'er so strong—
Will want the aid of his commanding tongue,
Which conquered more than Caesar: he o'erthrew
Only the outward frame; this could subdue
The rugged works of nature. Souls replete
With dull chill cold, he'd animate with heat
Drawn forth of reason's lymbic. In a word
Mars and Minerva both in him concurred

173

For arts, for arms, whose pen and sword alike,
As Cato's did, may admiration strike
Into his foes; while they confess withal,
It was their guilt styled him a criminal.
Only this difference doth from truth proceed,
They in the guilt, he in the name must bleed;
While none shall dare his obsequies to sing
In deserved measures, until Time shall bring
Truth crowned with freedom, and from danger free;
To sound his praises to posterity.

Here let him rest; while we this truth report,
He's gone from hence unto a higher court,
To plead his cause, where he by this doth know
Whether to Caesar he was friend, or foe.

JAMES BLAIR

1655-1743

James Blair was one of the most influential men of colonial Virginia. He was the founder of the College of William and Mary at Williamsburg — the second institution of higher learning in America — and served for half a century as its president. He was also an active member of the Governor's Council, the minister of a Virginia parish, and the representative, or Commissary, of the Bishop of London for Virginia.

Blair was a native of Scotland and was educated at the University of Edinburgh. He came to Virginia in 1685, and rapidly assumed the position of importance in the colony which he maintained throughout his long career.

In 1697 Blair joined with Henry Hartwell and Edward Chilton in the preparation of a report for the London Board of Trade on conditions in Virginia. It is from this report, *The Present State of Virginia, and the College,* that the following account, "Concerning the Church and Religion," by Blair is taken.

The report was first published in London in 1727. It was republished in 1940, with a scholarly introduction by the late Hunter Dickinson Farish, as the first volume of the Williamsburg Restoration Historical Studies.

CONCERNING THE CHURCH AND RELIGION

The Inhabitants do generally profess to be of the Church of *England*, which accordingly is the Religion and Church by Law establish'd. The Number of Dissenters in that Country are very inconsiderable, there not being so many of any Sort as to set up a Meeting-House, except three or four Meetings of *Quakers*, and one of *Presbyterians*.

The Country is divided into Fifty Parishes, in most of which there are two, sometimes three Churches and Chappels, yet some of these Parishes are exceeding small, in Proportion to the rest, so that they are not able to maintain a Minister: The Reason whereof was, that these Parishes were in the most fertile and lovely Spots of Ground, where the first *English* Inhabitants did chiefly settle; and it is very likely, when the Division of the Parishes was made, it was thought Towns would be built in those Places, and therefore they assign'd them but a small Compass of Country. But this Design miscarrying, it is great Pity that there is not a more convenient Division of the Parishes order'd.

As to the Government of the Church, from the first Settlement that whole Matter, as all Things else, was put into the Hands of the Governor. By the Laws of the Country, the Ministers were oblig'd to produce their Orders to him, and to shew that they had Episcopal Ordination.

In every Parish, by the Law of that Country, there is a Vestry consisting of twelve Men, chosen at first by all the Masters of Families in the Parish. They have a Power to continue themselves, for as one dyes or removes out of the Parish, the remaining Vestry-men chuse another in his room. Those Vestry-men lay the Parish Levy, and manage all other parochial Matters. The Power of presenting Ministers is in them by the Law of that Country; But the Law in this Point is little taken Notice of, by reason of a contrary Custom of making annual Agreements with the Ministers, which they call by a Name coarse enough, *viz.* Hiring of the Ministers; so that they seldom present any Ministers, that they may by that Means keep them in more Subjection and Dependence. This Custom has had a great many bad Consequences. No good Ministers that were inform'd of it would come into the Country, and if they came, ignorant of any such Custom, they quickly felt the Effects of it in the high Hand wherewith most Vestries manag'd their Power, and got out of the Country again as soon as they could. The Mansion-Houses, if there were any, went to Decay, the Minister holding the Living so precariously, that it could not be expected he would bestow much on Reparation; and very often the Glebe was not in his Hand. He stood likewise on so precarious Terms, that he must have a special Care how he preach'd against the Vices that any great Man of the Vestry was guilty of; for if he did, he might expect a Faction would be made in the Vestry, to be against renewing the Agreement with him for another Year. In short, several Ministers were turn'd out by the Vestries, without any Crime proved, or so much as alledg'd against them. And this is their Case at this Day: They are only in the nature of Chaplains, and hold their Livings by annual Agreements with the Vestries; at the Expiration of which Agreement, the Minister is dismiss'd or retain'd again at the Vestries Pleasure. By reason of these their precarious Circumstances, it comes to pass that the Country is very badly provided with Ministers, there not being at present above half so many Ministers as there are Parishes. The Governor connives at this, and tho' he is Ordinary, yet never presents *jure devoluto;* so that really many Parishes chuse to be without a Minister, for by that Means they save all the Minister's Dues in their own Pockets.

The yearly Salary of the Ministers, establish'd by Law, is 16000 Pounds of Tobacco, without Cask. This Tobacco is levy'd by the Vestry on the Parish, according to the Number of Tythables, and collected by the Church-Wardens with the rest of the Parish Levy: They have 5 *per Cent.* for their Pains.

King *Charles* II. gave the Bishop of *London* Jurisdiction over all the Churches in the *English* Plantations, except as to three Things, *viz.* Licenses of Marriages, Probates of Wills, and Inductions of Ministers, which he reserved to the several Governors.

In *Virginia* the Lord Bishop of London deputes a Commissary for this Part of his Jurisdiction, whose Business is to make Visitations of Churches, and to take the Inspection of the Clergy. The present Commissary is Mr. *James Blair,* he hath no Salary nor Perquisites, but the King makes it up by his Royal Bounty, having been graciously pleas'd, for two Years, to order him 100 *l.* a Year, out of the Quit-Rents of *Virginia,* which we suppose his Majesty intends to continue.

HUGH JONES
1670?-1760

Hugh Jones, minister, historian, and professor of mathematics at the College of William and Mary, came to Virginia in 1716. He served as chaplain to the Virginia House of Burgesses and was a minister at Jamestown and Williamsburg, in addition to his post at William and Mary. He was the author of a lively account of Virginia, the full title of which was: *The Present State of Virginia. Giving a particular and short account of the Indian, English, and negroe inhabitants of that colony. Shewing their religion, manners, government, trade, way of living, &c., with a description of the country.* He was the author also of the first English grammar written in America. Jones went to London in 1721 and both books were published there in 1724. He returned to Virginia, but shortly afterward moved to Maryland, where for many years he was the influential rector of St. Stephen's Parish. He died on September 8, 1760. A reprint of *The Present State of Virginia* was published in New York in 1865.

OF THE HABITS, CUSTOMS, PARTS, IMPLOYMENTS, TRADE &c. OF THE VIRGINIANS; AND OF THE WEATHER, COIN, SICKNESS, LIQUORS, SERVANTS, POOR, PITCH, TAR, OAR, &c.

The *Habits, Life, Customs, Computations,* &c. of the *Virginians* are much the same as about *London,* which they esteem their *Home;* and for the most Part have contemptible Notions of *England,* and wrong Sentiments of *Bristol,* and the other *Out-Ports,* which they entertain from seeing and hearing the common Dealers, Sailors, and Servants that come from those Towns, and the Country Places in *England* and *Scotland,* whose Language and Manners are strange to them; for the *Planters,* and even the *Native Negroes* generally talk good *English* without *Idiom* or *Tone,* and can discourse handsomly upon *most* common Subjects; and conversing with Persons belonging to Trade and Navigation from *London,* for the most Part they are much civilized, and wear the best of Cloaths according to their Station; nay, sometimes too good for their Circumstances, being for the Generality comely handsom Persons, of good Features and fine Complexions (if they take Care) of good Manners and Address. The Climate makes them bright, and of excellent Sense, and sharp in Trade, an Ideot, or deformed Native being almost a Miracle.

Thus they have good natural Notions, and will soon learn Arts and Sciences; but are generally diverted by Business or Inclination from profound Study, and prying into the Depth of Things; being ripe for Management of their Affairs, before they have laid so good a Foundation of Learning, and had such Instructions, and acquired such Accomplishments, as might be instilled into such good natural Capacities. Nevertheless thro' their quick Apprehension, they have a Sufficiency of Knowledge, and Fluency of Tongue, tho' their Learning for the most Part be but superficial.

They are more inclinable to read Men by Business and Conver-

180

sation, than to dive into Books, and are for the most Part only desirous of learning what is absolutely necessary, in the shortest and best Method.

Having this Knowledge of their Capacities and Inclination from sufficient Experience, I have composed on Purpose some short Treatises adapted with my best Judgment to a Course of Education for the Gentlemen of the Plantations; consisting in a short *English Grammar;* and *Accidence to Christianity;* and *Accidence to the Mathematicks,* especially to Arithmetick in all its parts and Applications, *Algebra, Geometry, Surveying of Land,* and *Navigation.*

These are the most useful Branches of Learning for *them,* and such as they willingly and readily master, if taught in a plain and short Method, truly applicable to their *Genius;* which I have endeavoured to do, for the Use of *them,* and *all others* of their Temper and Parts.

They are not very easily persuaded to the Improvement of useful Inventions (except a few, such as Sawing Mills) neither are they great Encouragers of Manufactures, because of the Trouble and certain Expence in Attempts of this kind, with uncertain Prospect of Gain; whereas by their staple Commodity, Tobacco, they are certain to get a plentiful Provision; nay, often very great Estates.

Upon this Account they think it Folly to take off their *Hands* (or Negroes) and employ their Care and Time about any thing, that may make them lessen their Crop of Tobacco.

So that though they are apt to learn, yet they are fond of, and will follow their own Ways, Humours, and Notions, being not easily brought to new Projects and Schemes; so that I question, if they would have been imposed upon by the *Missisippi* or *South-Sea,* or any other such monstrous Bubbles.

In their Computations of Time, Weights and Measures both of Length, Superficies, and Solidity, they strictly adhere to what is legal; not running into precarious Customs, as they do in *England.* Thus their Quart is the true *Winchester,* their Hundred is 100, not 112, and they survey Land by Statute Measure.

Indeed, what *English* Coin is there, is advanced in Value; so that a Shilling passes for 14 *d.* and a Guinea goes by Tale for 26 *s.* but the Current Money is the *Spanish;* which in Reality is about 15 *l.*

per Cent. inferior to our *English* Coin, as settled by Law; but frequently the Value of this varies in Respect of Sterling Bills according to the Circumstances of Trade; Currency and Sterling being sometimes at a *Par;* but for the Generality 10 *per Cent.* Discount is allowed for Sterling Bills.

As for Education several are sent to *England* for it; though the *Virginians* being naturally of good Parts, (as I have already hinted) neither require nor admire as much Learning, as we do in *Britain;* yet more would be sent over, were they not afraid of the Small-Pox, which most commonly proves fatal to them.

But indeed when they come to *England* they are generally put to learn to Persons that know little of their Temper, who keep them drudging on in what is of least Use to them, in pedantic Methods, too tedious for their volatile Genius.

For *Grammar* Learning taught after the common round-about Way is not much beneficial nor delightful to them; so that they are noted to be more apt to spoil their School-Fellows than improve themselves; because they are imprisoned and enslaved to what they hate, and think useless, and have not peculiar Management proper for their Humour and Occasion.

A civil Treatment with some Liberty, if permitted with Discretion is most proper for them, and they have most Need of, and readily take polite and mathematical Learning; and in *English* may be conveyed to them (without going directly to *Rome* and *Athens*) all the Arts, Sciences, and learned Accomplishments of the Antients and Moderns, without the Fatigue and Expence of another Language, for which few of them have little Use or Necessity, since (without another) they may understand their own Speech; and all other Things requisite to be learn'd by them sooner and better.

Thus the Youth might as well be instructed there as here by proper Methods, without the Expence and Danger of coming hither; especially if they make Use of the great Advantage of the *College* at *Williamsburgh,* where they may (and many do) imbibe the Principles of all human and divine Literature, both in *English* and in the learned Languages.

By the happy Opportunity of this College may they be advanced to religious and learned Education, according to the Discipline and

Hugh Jones, 1670?-1760

Doctrine of the established *Church of England;* in which Respect this College may prove of singular Service, and be an advantageous and laudable Nursery and strong Bulwark against the contagious dissentions in *Virginia;* which is the most antient and loyal, the most plentiful and flourishing, the most extensive and beneficial Colony belonging to the Crown of *Great Britain,* upon which it is most directly dependent; wherein is establish'd the Church of *England* free from Faction and Sects, being ruled by the Laws, Customs, and Constitutions of *Great Britain,* which it strictly observes, only where the Circumstances and Occasion of the Country by an absolute Necessity require some small Alterations; which nevertheless must not be contrary (though different from and subservient) to the laws of *England.*

Though the Violence of neither *Whig* nor *Tory* reigns there, yet have they Parties; for the very best Administration must expect to meet with some Opposition in all Places; especially where there is a Mixture of People of different Countries concerned, whose Education and Interest may propose to them Notions and Views different from each other.

Most other Plantations, especially they that are granted away to Proprietors, are inferior to *Virginia:* where the seeming Interest and Humour of the Owners often divert them from Pursuit of the most proper Methods; besides, they cannot have such a right Claim to the Favour of the Crown, nor demand its best Protection, since they may often interfere with its Interest: whereas *Virginia* is esteemed one of the most valuable Gems in the Crown of *Great Britain.*

Thus *Virginia* having to itself (with *Maryland*) the staple Commodity of Tobacco, has a great Advantage of all other Plantations on the Continent for the Encouragement of the Crown; whereas others belonging to Gentlemen, or having no peculiar Trade, cannot expect such Power to advance and promote their Interest.

To this add, that *Virginia* equals, if not exceeds, all others in Goodness of Climate, Soil, Health, Rivers, Plenty, and all Necessaries, and Conveniencies of Life: Besides she has, among others, these particular Advantages of her younger Sister *Maryland, viz.* Freedom from Popery, and the Direction of Proprietors; not but that Part of *Virginia,* which is between the Rivers *Potowmack* and *Rappahan-*

nock belongs to Proprietors, as to the Quit-Rent; yet the Government of these Counties (called the *Northern Neck*) is under the same Regulation with the other Parts of the Country.

If *New England* be called a Receptacle of Dissenters, and an *Amsterdam* of Religion, *Pennsylvania* the Nursery of Quakers, *Maryland* the Retirement of Roman Catholicks, *North Carolina* the Refuge of Run-aways, and *South Carolina* the Delight of Buccaneers and Pyrates, *Virginia* may be justly esteemed the happy Retreat of *true Britons* and *true Churchmen* for the most Part; neither soaring too high nor drooping too low, consequently should merit the greater Esteem and Encouragement.

The Common Planters leading easy Lives don't much admire Labour, or any manly Exercise, except Horse-Racing, nor Diversion, except Cock-Fighting, in which some greatly delight. This easy Way of Living, and the Heat of the Summer makes some very lazy, who are then said to be Climate-struck.

The Saddle Horses, though not very large, are hardy, strong, and fleet; and will pace naturally and pleasantly at a prodigious Rate.

They are such Lovers of Riding, that almost every ordinary Person keeps a Horse; and I have known some spend the Morning in ranging several Miles in the Woods to find and catch their Horses only to ride two or three Miles to Church, to the Court-House, or to a Horse-Race, where they generally appoint to meet upon Business; and are more certain of finding those that they want to speak or deal with, than at their Home.

No People can entertain their Friends with better Cheer and Welcome; and Strangers and Travellers are here treated in the most free, plentiful, and hospitable Manner; so that a few Inns or Ordinaries on the Road are sufficient.

As to the Weather, the Spring and Fall are not unlike those Seasons in *England,* only the Air is never long foggy, nor very cloudy; but clear, sometimes of a bluish Colour, occasioned by the thin Smoak, dispersed in the Air, from the Flames of the Woods and Leaves, which are fired in Hunting, to drive the Beasts from their lurking Places; or in the Spring to burn the old Leaves and Grass, that there may be the better Pasture the next Summer.

The Months of *December, January* and *February* are generally much colder, and *June, July* and *August* are much hotter than in England; tho' sometimes 'tis on a sudden very cool in Summer, and pretty warm in Winter, the Weather being govern'd by the Wind; which with sudden Storms from the *North-West,* and sometimes from the *West* and *South-West* bring violent Gusts or Tempests, with Thunder, Lightning, and Rain very terrible, but soon over.

The *North West* Winds are exquisitely sharp and cold, preceding from Clouds arising from the vast Lakes and prodigious snowy Mountains that lie to that Quarter; but the Southerly Winds and others are very warm.

The Days and Nights are there always much nearer the Equality of twelve Hours, than in the Latitude of *England.*

At the sudden Changes of the Weather, from Heat to Cold, People are apt to take Cold, often neglecting to shift their Cloaths with the Weather; which with Abundance of Damps and Mists from the Water, and by eating too plentifully of some delicious Fruits, makes the People subject to Feavers and Agues, which is the Country Distemper, a severe Fit of which (called a *Seasoning*) most expect, some time after their Arrival in that Climate; but the Goodness of God has furnished us with a perfect *Catholicon* for that Sickness, *viz.* the *Bark;* which being taken and repeated in a right Manner, seldom fails of a Cure, unless the morbisick Matter comes to a Head again from fresh Causes, and so returns with Mastery; upon which Recourse must be had to the same specifick Remedy; besides which there are several Ways of Cure, but none so universal and sure as that.

Some for Want of timely Care, through Ignorance or Obstinacy, will permit the Distemper to lurk about them so long, till at last it has reduced them to an irrecoverable, lingering, ill Habit of Body; especially if they live meanly, drinking too much Water, and eating too much salt Meat; and this *Cachexy* generally ends their Lives with a Dropsy, Consumption, the Jaundice, or some such illness.

Besides this, some are troubled with the dry Gripes, proceeding from Colds (I suppose) which take away for a long Time the Use of the Limbs of some, especially hard Drinkers of Rum; some that have lain out in mighty cold Weather have been Frost-bitten, and lost their Fingers or Toes.

There is no Danger of wild Beasts in traveling; for the Wolves and Bears, which are up the Country, never attack any, unless they be first assaulted and hurt; and the Wolves of late are much destroyed by Virtue of a Law, which allows good Rewards for their Heads with the Ears on, to prevent Imposition and cheating the Public; for the Ears are crop'd when a Head is produced.

The Bears are also much destroyed by the Out-Planters, &c. for the Sake of their Flesh and Skins.

As for Rattle-Snakes, &c. they make off from you, unless you by Carelesness chance to tread on them; and then their Bite is found now not to be mortal, if Remedies can be applied in Time.

The worst Inconveniency in travelling a-cross the Country, is the Circuit that must be taken to head Creeks, &c. for the main Roads wind along the rising Ground between the Rivers, tho' now they much shorten their Passage by mending the Swamps and building of Bridges in several Places; and there are established Ferries at convenient Places, over the great Rivers; but in them is often much Danger from sudden Storms, bad Boats, or unskilful or wilful Ferrymen; especially if one passes in a Boat with Horses, of which I have great Reason to be most sensible by the Loss of a dear *Brother* at *Chickohomony Ferry*, in *Feb.* 172 3/4.

As for their Drink, good Springs of excellent Water abound every where almost, which is very cooling and pleasant in Summer, and the general Drink of abundance; not so much out of Necessity, as Choice.

Some Planters, &c. make good small Drink with Cakes of *Parsimmons* a kind of Plumbs, which grow there in great Plenty; but the comon small Beer is made of *Molossus,* which makes extraordinary brisk good tasted Liquor at a cheap Rate, with little Trouble in brewing; so that they have it fresh and fresh, as they want it in Winter and Summer.

And as they brew, so do they bake daily, Bread or Cakes, eating too much hot and new Bread, which cannot be wholsom, tho' it be pleasanter than what has been baked a Day or two.

Some raise Barely and make Malt there, and others have Malt from *England,* with which those that understand it, brew as good Beer as in *England,* at proper Seasons of the Year; but the common strong

186

Malt-Drink mostly used, is *Bristol* Beer; of which is consumed vast Quantities there yearly; which being well brew'd and improv'd by crossing the Sea, drinks exceedingly fine and smooth; but Malt Liquor is not so much regarded as Wine, Rack, Brandy, and Rum, Punch, with Drams of Rum or Brandy for the common Sort, when they drink in a Hurry.

The common Wine comes from *Madera* or *Phial,* which moderately drank is fittest to cheer the fainting Spirits in the Heat of Summer, and to warm the chilled Blood in the bitter Colds of Winter, and seems most peculiarly adapted for this Climate: Besides this, are plentifully drank with the better Sort, of late Years, all Kinds of *French,* and other *European* Wine, especially Claret and Port.

Here is likewise used a great deal of Chocolate, Tea and Coffee, which, with several Sorts of Apparel, they have as cheap, or cheaper than in *England,* because of the Debenture of such Goods upon their Exportation thither: Besides, they are allowed to have Wines directly from *Madera,* and other Commodities are brought from the *West-Indies,* and the Continent, which cannot be brought to *England* without spoiling.

As for grinding Corn, &c. they have good Mills upon the Runs and Creeks; besides Hand-Mills, Wind-Mills, and the *Indian* Invention of pounding Hommony in Mortars burnt in the Stump of a Tree, with a Log for a Pestle hanging at the End of a Pole, fix'd like the Pole of a Lave.

Though they are permitted to trade to no Parts but *Great Britain,* except these Places; yet have they in many Respects better and cheaper Comodities than we in *England,* especially of late Years; for the Country may be said to be altered and improved in Wealth and polite Living within these few Years, since the Beginning of *Col. Spotswood's* Government, more than in all the Scores of Years before that, from its first Discovery. The Country is yearly supplied with vast Quantities of Goods from *Great Britain,* chiefly from *London, Bristol, Liverpool, Whitehaven,* and from *Scotland.*

The Ships that transport these Things often call at *Ireland* to victual, and bring over frequently white Servants, which are of three Kinds. 1. Such as come upon certain Wages by Agreement for a certain Time. 2. Such as come bound by Indenture, commonly call'd

Kids, who are usually to serve four or five Years; and 3. those Convicts or Felons that are transported, whose Room they had much rather have than their Company; for abundance of them do great Mischiefs, commit Robbery and Murder, and spoil Servants, that were before very good: But they frequently there meet with the End they deserved at Home, though indeed some of them prove indifferent good. Their being sent thither to work as Slaves for Punishment, is but a mere Notion, for few of them ever lived so well and so easy before, especially if they are good for any thing. These are to serve seven, and sometimes fourteen Years, and they and Servants by Indentures have an Allowance of Corn and Cloaths, when they are out of their Time, that they may be therewith supported, till they can be provided with Services, or otherwise settled. With these three Sorts of Servants are they supplied from *England, Wales, Scotland,* and *Ireland,* among which they that have a Mind to it, may serve their Time with Ease and Satisfaction to themselves and their Masters, especially if they fall into good Hands.

Except the last Sort, for the most Part who are loose Villains, made tame by *Wild,* and then enslaved by his *Forward Namesake:* To prevent too great a Stock of which Servants and Negroes many Attempts and Laws have been in vain made.

These if they forsake their Roguery together with the other Kids of the later *Jonathan,* when they are free, may work Day-Labour, or else rent a small Plantation for a Trifle almost; or else turn Overseers, if they are expert, industrious, and careful, or follow their Trade, if they have been brought up to any; especially Smiths, Carpenters, Taylors, Sawyers, Coopers, Bricklayers, &c. The Plenty of the Country, and the good Wages given to Work-Folks occasion very few Poor, who are supported by the Parish, being such as are lame, sick, or decrepit through Age, Distempers, Accidents, or some Infirmities; for where there is a numerous Family of poor Children the Vestry takes Care to bind them out Apprentices, till they are able to maintain themselves by their own Labour; by which Means they are never tormented with Vagrant, and Vagabond Beggars, there being a Reward for taking up Runaways, that are at a small Distance from their Home; if they are not known, or are without a Pass from their

Hugh Jones, 1670?-1760

Master, and can give no good Account of themselves, especially Negroes.

In all convenient Places are kept Stores or Ware-Houses of all Sorts of Goods, managed by Store-Keepers or Factors, either for themselves or others in the Country, or in *Great Britain*.

This Trade is carried on in the fairest and genteelest Way of Merchandize, by a great Number of Gentlemen of Worth and Fortune; who with the Commanders of their Ships, and several *Virginians* (who come over through Business or Curiosity, or often to take Possession of Estates, which every Year fall here to some or other of them) make as considerable and handsom a Figure, and drive as great and advantageous a Trade for the Advancement of the Publick Good, as most Merchants upon the *Royal-Exchange*.

At the Stores in *Virginia*, the Planters, *&c.* may be supplied with what *English* Commodities they want.

The Merchants, Factors, or Store-Keepers in *Virginia* buy up the Tobacco of the Planters, either for Goods or current *Spanish* Money, or with *Sterling* Bills payable in *Great Britain*.

The Tobacco is rolled, drawn by Horses, or carted to convenient Rolling Houses, whence it is conveyed on Board the Ships in Flats or Sloops, *&c.*

Some Years ago there was made an Act to oblige all Tobacco to be sent to convenient Ware-Houses, to the Custody and Management of proper Officers, who were by Oath to refuse all bad Tobacco, and gave printed Bills as Receipts for each Parcel or Hogshead; which Quantity was to be delivered according to Order upon Return of those Bills; and for their Trouble and Care in viewing, weighing, and stamping, the Officers were allowed 5 *s. per* Hogshead.

The Intent of this Law was to improve the Commodity, prevent Frauds in publick Payments; and for Ease of the common Planters, and Expedition and Conveniency of Shipping.

But though the first Design was for publick Tobacco only, yet the private Crops of Gentlemen being included in the Law, was esteemed a great Grievance; and occasioned Complaints, which destroyed a Law, that with small Amendments might have proved most advantageous.

189

The Abrogation of this Law reduced the Sailors to their old Slavery of rolling the Tobacco in some Places; where they draw it for some Miles, as Gardeners draw a Roller, which makes them frequently curse the Country, and thro' Prejudice give it a very vile Character.

The Tobacco purchased by the Factors or Store-Keepers, is sent Home to their Employers, or consign'd to their correspondent Merchants in *Great Britain.*

But most Gentlemen, and such as are beforehand in the World, lodge Money in their Merchants's Hands here, to whom they send their Crop of Tobacco, or the greatest Part of it.

This Money is employed according to the Planter's Orders; chiefly in sending over yearly such Goods, Apparel, Liquors, &c. as they write for, for the Use of themselves, their Families, Slaves and Plantation; by which Means they have every Thing at the best Hand, and the best of its Kind.

Besides *English* Goods, several Merchants in *Virginia* import from the *West-Indies* great Quantities of Rum, Sugar, Molossus, &c. and Salt very cheap from the *Salt Islands;* which Things they purchase with Money, or generally with Pork, Beef, Wheat, *Indian-Corn,* and the like.

In some of the poorer Parts of the Country abounding in Pine, do they gather up the *Light-wood,* or Knots of the old Trees, which will not decay, being piled up (as a Pit of Wood to be burnt to Charcoal) and encompassed with a Trench, and covered with Earth, is set on Fire; whereby the Tar is melted out, and running into the Trench is taken up, and filled into Barrels; and being boiled to a greater Consistency becomes Pitch.

Of Pitch and Tar they send Home great Quantities, though not near so much as *North Carolina,* which formerly was the *South* Part of *Virginia;* but has long since been given away to Proprietors, tho' the Bounds between the Colony of *Virginia,* and the Government of *North Carolina* are disputed; so that there is a very long *List* of Land fifteen Miles broad between both Colonies (called the *disputed Bounds*) in due Subjection to neither; which is an *Asylum* for the Runagates of both Countries.

The greatest Part of *Virginia* is uneven; and near the Water they are free from great Stones, Rocks, and high Hills; but far in the

Country they have vast Rocks, Stones, and Mountains; and though in the Salts there is no Stone for Lime nor Building; (but with *Oyster-Shells* they make good Lime and enough) yet up the Freshes, and above the Falls of the Rivers are discovered free and common Stone of several Sorts, among which may be expected Lime-Stone.

Here are also vast Quantities of *Iron Oar,* and various Kinds of *Minerals,* whose Nature and Vertues are as yet undiscovered.

Moses's Words of Exhortation to the *Israelites* for Obedience to God's Laws, *Deut. viii.* 6, 7, 8, 9, may be applied to the *Virginians;* and particularly when he saith that God had brought them into a Land whose Stones are Iron; and for what we know the following Words may also be applied to them, when he saith out of the Hills of that Land might be digged Brass, for which there is no small Prospect and Expectation; and in all Probability there may be found the nobler Metals of *Gold* and *Silver,* if we did but search for them in the Bowels of the Earth, if we would but be at the Expence and Trouble to seek for them.

Why may not our Mountains in *America,* for what we know, be as rich as those of *Mexico* and *Peru* in the same Country? Since the little Hills so plentifully abound with the best of Iron; for the digging, melting, working, and Exportation whereof Providence has furnish'd us with all wonderful Conveniences; if we would add but a little Expence, Art and Industry.

This Iron has been proved to be good, and 'tis thought, will come at as cheap a Rate as any imported from other Places; so that 'tis to be hoped *Col. Spotswood's Works* will in a small Time prove very advantageous to *Great Britain,* which undoubtedly will be carried to great Perfection and universal Benefit, by his skilful Management and indefatigable Application to such noble Undertakings and glorious Projects.

ROBERT BEVERLEY

1673?-1722

Robert Beverley was born at his father's plantation in Middlesex County, Virginia. His father, who had come to Virginia some ten years before from Yorkshire, became known as a partisan of Governor Berkeley during Bacon's Rebellion. Young Beverley was sent to England for schooling, but returned to Virginia after his father's death in 1687. He served as clerk of the Virginia Council, held other posts in the government of the colony, and in 1697 married the sister of William Byrd of Westover.

In 1703 he went to England on a matter in litigation before the Privy Council, and there he was invited by a London bookseller to examine the manuscript of a book on the colonies. Beverley felt that the manuscript was so full of error that he undertook to write his own book on Virginia. The result was *The History and Present State of Virginia,* published in London in 1705. It was a lively account of the colony and enjoyed an immediate success. A French edition was published in Amsterdam in 1707, and another the same year in Paris. New editions in French were brought out in 1712 and 1718. Beverley returned to Virginia, where he speculated in frontier lands and built an estate, "Blandfield," on the Rappahannock. In 1722 he published in London *The Abridgement of The Public Laws of Virginia* and a revised edition of his *History.* He died the same year.

The *History* was first published in the United States in 1855. A new edition, with a scholarly introduction by Louis B. Wright, was published by the University of North Carolina Press for the Institute of Early American History and Culture at Williamsburg, Virginia, in 1947.

OF THE RECREATIONS, AND PASTIMES USED
IN VIRGINIA

For their Recreation, the Plantations, Orchards, and Gardens constantly afford 'em fragrant and delightful Walks. In their Woods and Fields, they have an unknown variety of Vegetables, and other rarities of Nature to discover and observe. They have Hunting, Fishing, and Fowling, with which they entertain themselves an hundred ways. Here is the most Good-nature, and Hospitality practis'd in the World, both towards Friends and Strangers: but the worst of it is, this Generosity is attended now and then, with a little too much Intemperance. The Neighbourhood is at much the same distance, as in the Country in *England:* but with this Advantage, that all the better sort of People have been abroad, and seen the World, by which means they are free from that stiffness and formality, which discover more Civility, than Kindness: And besides, the goodness of the Roads, and the fairness of the Weather, bring People oftener together.

The *Indians,* as I have already observ'd, had in their Hunting, a way of concealing themselves, and coming up to the Deer, under the blind of a Stalking-Head, in imitation of which, many People have taught their Horses to stalk it, that is, to walk gently by the Huntsman's side, to cover him from the sight of the Deer. Others cut down Trees for the Deer to browze upon, and lie in wait behind them. Others again set Stakes, at a certain distance within their Fences, where the Deer have been used to leap over into a Field of Peas, which they love extreamly; these Stakes they so place, as to run into the Body of the Deer, when he Pitches, by which means they Impale him.

They Hunt their Hares, (which are very numerous) a Foot, with Mungrils or swift Dogs, which either catch them quickly, or force them to hole in a hollow Tree, whither all their Hares generally tend, when they are closely pursued. As soon as they are thus holed, and have crawl'd up into the Body of the Tree, the business is to kindle a Fire, and smother them with Smoak, till they let go their hold, and fall to the bottom stifled; from whence they take them. If they have a mind to spare their Lives, upon turning them loose, they will be as fit as ever to hunt at another time; for the mischief done them by the Smoak, immediately wears off again.

They have another sort of Hunting, which is very diverting, and that they call Vermine Hunting; It is perform'd a Foot, with small Dogs in the Night, by the Light of the Moon or Stars. Thus in Summertime they find abundance of Raccoons, Opossums, and Foxes in the Corn-Fields, and about their Plantations: but at other times, they must go into the Woods for them. The Method is to go out with three or four Dogs, and as soon as they come to the place, they bid the Dogs seek out, and all the Company follow immediately. Where-ever a Dog barks, you may depend upon finding the Game; and this Alarm, draws both Men and Dogs that way. If this Sport be in the Woods, the Game by that time you come near it, is perhaps mounted to the top of an high Tree, and then they detach a nimble Fellow up after it, who must have a scuffle with the Beast, before he can throw it down to the Dogs; and then the sport increases, to see the Vermine encounter those little Currs. In this sort of Hunting, they also carry their great Dogs out with them, because Wolves, Bears, Panthers, Wild-Cats, and all other Beasts of Prey, are abroad in the Night.

For Wolves they make Traps, and set Guns bated in the Woods, so that when he offers to seize the Bate, he pulls the Trigger, and the Gun discharges upon him. What Elian and Pliny write, of the Horses being benummed in their Legs, if they tread in the Track of a Wolf, does not hold good here; for I my self, and many others, have rid full Speed after Wolves in the Woods and have seen live ones taken out of a Trap, and drag'd at a Horse's Tail; and yet those that follow'd on Horseback, have not perceived any of their Horses to falter in their pace.

They have many pretty devices besides the Gun, to take wild Turkeys; And among others, a Friend of mine invented a great Trap, wherein he at times caught many Turkeys, and particularly seventeen at one time, but he could not contrive it so, as to let

194

others in after he had entrapped the first flock, until they were taken out.

The *Indian* Invention of Weirs in Fishing, is mightily improved by the English besides which, they make use of Seins, Trolls, Casting-Netts, Setting-Netts, Hand-fishing, and Angling, and in each find abundance of Diversion. I have set in the shade, at the Heads of the Rivers Angling, and spent as much time in taking the Fish off the Hook, as in waiting for their taking it. Like those of the *Euxine* Sea, they also Fish with Spilyards, which is a long Line staked out in the River, and hung with a great many Hooks on short strings, fasten'd to the main Line, about three or four Foot asunder. The only difference is, our Line is supported by Stakes, and theirs is buoyed up with Gourds.

Their Fowling is answerable to their Fishing for plenty of Game, in its proper Season, no Plantation being so ill stored, as to be without a great deal. They have a vast variety of it, several sorts of which, I have not yet mention'd, as Beaver, Otter, Squirrels, Partridges, Pigeons, and an infinite number of small Birds, &c.

The admirable Economy of the Beavers, deserves to be particularly remember'd. They cohabit in one House, are incorparated in a regular Form of Government, something like Monarchy, and have over them a Superintendent, which the *Indians* call *Pericu*. He leads them out to their several Imployments, which consist in Felling of Trees, biting off the Branches, and cutting them into certain lengths, suitable to the business they design them for, all which they perform with their Teeth. When this is done, the Governor orders several of his Subjects to joyn together, and take up one of those Logs, which they must carry to their House or Damm, as occasion requires. He walks in State by them all the while, and sees that every one bear his equal share of the burden; while he bites with his Teeth, and lashes with his Tail, those that lag behind, and do not lend all their Strength. They commonly build their Houses in Swamps, and then to raise the Water to a convenient height, they make a Damm with Logs, and a binding sort of Clay, so firm, that though the Water runs continually over, it cannot wash it away. Within these Damms, they'll inclose Water enough to make a Pool, like a Mill-pond; and if a Mill happen to be built upon the same Stream, below their

Damm, the Miller in a dry Season, finds it worth his while to cut it, to supply his Mill with Water. Upon which Disaster, the Beavers are so expert at their Work, that in one or two Nights time, they will repair the breach, and make it perfectly whole again. Sometimes they build their Houses in a broad Marsh, where the Tide ebbs and flows, and then they make no Damm at all. The Doors into their Houses are under Water. I have been at the Demolishing of one of these Houses, that was found in a Marsh, and was surpriz'd to find it fortify'd with Logs, that were six Foot long, and ten inches through, and had been carried at least one hundred and fifty yards. This House was three Stories high, and contain'd five Rooms, that is to say, two in the lower, and middle Stories, and but one at the top. These Creatures have a great deal of Policy, and know how to defeat all the Subtilty and Strategems of the Hunter, who seldom can meet with them, tho' they are in great numbers all over the Country.

There is yet another kind of Sport, which the young People take great Delight in, and that is, the Hunting of wild Horses; which they pursue sometimes with Dogs, and sometimes without. You must know they have many Horses foaled in the Woods of the Uplands, that never were in hand, and are as shy as any Savage Creature. These having no mark upon them, belong to him, that first takes them. However, the Captor commonly purchases these Horses very dear, by spoiling better in the pursuit; in which case, he has little to make himself amends, besides the pleasure of the Chace. And very often this is all he has for it, for the wild Horses are so swift, that 'tis difficult to catch them; and when they are taken, 'tis odds but their Grease is melted, or else being old, they are so sullen, that they can't be tam'd.

The Inhabitants are very Courteous to Travellers, who need no other Recommendation, but the being Human Creatures. A Stranger has no more to do, but to inquire upon the Road, where any Gentleman, or good House-keeper Lives, and there he may depend upon being received with Hospitality. This good Nature is so general among their People, that the Gentry when they go abroad, order their Principal Servant to entertain all Visitors, with every thing the Plantation affords. And the poor Planters, who have but one Bed, will very often sit up, or lie upon a Form or Couch all Night, to make room for a weary Traveller, to repose himself after his Journey.

If there happen to be a Churl, that either out of Covetousness, or Ill-nature, won't comply with this generous Custom, he has a mark of Infamy set upon him, and is abhorr'd by all. But I must confess, (and am heartily sorry for the occasion) that this good Neighbour-hood has of late been much depraved by the present Governor, who practices, the detestable Politicks of governing by Parties; by which, Feuds and Heart-burnings have been kindled in the Minds of the People; and Friendship, Hospitality, and Good-Neighbour-hood, have been extreamly discouraged.

OF THE MARRIAGES AMONGST THE INDIANS, AND MANAGEMENT OF THEIR CHILDREN

The *Indians* have their solemnities of Marriage, and esteem the Vows made at that time, as most sacred and inviolable. Notwith-standing they allow both the Man and the Wife to part upon dis-agreement; yet so great is the disreputation of a Divorce, that Marry'd people, to avoid the Character of Inconstant and Ungener-ous, very rarely let their Quarrels proceed to a Separation. However, when it does so happen, they reckon all the ties of Matrimony dis-solv'd, and each hath the liberty of marrying another. But Infidelity is accounted the most unpardonable of all Crimes in either of the Parties, as long as the Contract continues.

In these Separations, the Children go, according to the affection of the Parent, with the one or the other; for Children are not reck-on'd a Charge among them, but rather Riches, according to the blessing of the Old Testament; and if they happen to differ about dividing their Children, their method is then, to part them equally, allowing the Man the first choice.

Tho the young *Indian* Women are said to prostitute their bodies for *Wampom* Peak, Runtees, Beads, and other such like fineries; yet I never could find any ground for the accusation, and believe it only to be an unjust scandal upon them. This I know, that if ever they have a Child while they are single, it is such a disgrace to them, that they never after get Husbands. Besides, I must do 'em the jus-tice to say, I never heard of a Child any of them had before Mar-

197

riage, and the *Indians* themselves disown any such custom; tho they acknowledge at the same time, that the Maidens are entirely at their own disposal, and may manage their persons as they think fit.

Indeed I believe this Story to be an aspersion cast on those innocent Creatures, by reason of the freedom they take in Conversation, which uncharitable Christians interpret as Criminal, upon no other ground, than the guilt of their own Consciences.

The *Indian* Damsels are full of spirit, and from thence are always inspir'd with Mirth and good Humour. They are extremely given to laugh, which they do with a Grace not to be resisted. The excess of Life and Fire, which they never fail to have, makes them frolicksom, but without any real imputation to their Innocence. However, this is ground enough for the *English,* who are not very nice in distinguishing betwixt guilt, and harmless freedom, to think them Incontinent: Tho it be with as little justice, as the jealous *Spaniards* condemn the liberty us'd by the Women of *France,* which are much more chast than their own Ladies, which they keep under the strictest confinement.

The manner of the *Indians* treating their young Children is very strange, for instead of keeping them warm, at their first entry into the World, and wrapping them up, with I don't know how many Cloaths, according to our fond custom; the first thing they do, is to dip the Child over Head and Ears in cold Water, and then to bind it naked to a convenient Board, having a hole fitly plac'd for evacuation, but they always put Cotton, Wool, Furr, or other soft thing, for the Body to rest easy on, between the Child and the Board. In this posture they keep it several months, till the Bones begin to harden, the Joynts to knit, and the Limbs to grow strong; and then they let it loose from the Board, suffering it to crawl about, except when they are feeding, or playing with it.

While the Child is thus at the Board, they either lay it flat on its back, or set it leaning on one end, or else hang it up by a string fasten'd to the upper end of the Board for that purpose. The Child and Board being all this while carry'd about together. As our Women undress their Children to clean them and shift their Linnen, so they do theirs to wash and grease them.

The method the Women have of carrying their Children after

they are suffer'd to crawl about, is very particular; they carry them at their backs in Summer, taking one Leg of the Child under their Arm, and the Counter-Arm of the Child in their Hand over their Shoulder; the other Leg hanging down, and the Child all the while holding fast with its other Hand; but in Winter they carry them in the hollow of their Match-coat at their back, leaving nothing but the Child's Head out.

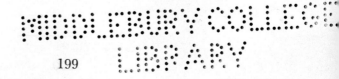

JOHN FONTAINE

1693-17—

John Fontaine was a member of a French Huguenot family which was well known in Virginia. The son of the Rev. James Fontaine, he came to Virginia in 1714 as a young man of twenty-one after service in Spain as an ensign in the British army. In 1716 he accompanied Governor Alexander Spotswood on the expedition into the Shenandoah Valley. The journal which he kept of that expedition follows. He subsequently returned to England. His brother, the Rev. Peter Fontaine, was chaplain to the Commission which ran the boundary line between Virginia and North Carolina in 1728-1729. A younger brother, the Rev. Francis Fontaine, was minister of the French settlement at Manakintown, Virginia, in 1720-1722, professor of Oriental languages at the College of William and Mary in 1729, and rector of Yorkhampton Parish, Virginia, from 1722 until his death in 1749. John Fontaine's journal was published by Ann Maury in 1853 in the volume, *Memoirs of a Huguenot Family: Translated and compiled from the original autobiography of the Rev. James Fontaine, and other family manuscripts; comprising an original journal of travels in Virginia, New York, etc., in 1715 and 1716.*

JOURNAL OF JOHN FONTAINE

Williamsburg, 20th August, 1716. — In the morning got my horses ready, and what baggage was necessary, and I waited on the Governor, who was in readiness for an expedition over the Appalachian mountains. We breakfasted, and about ten got on horseback, and at four came to the Brick-house, upon York River, where we crossed the ferry, and at six we came to Mr. Austin Moor's house, upon Mattapony River, in King William County; here we lay all night and were well entertained.

21st. — Fair weather. At ten we set out from Mr. Moor's, and crossed the river of Mattapony, and continued on the road, and were on horseback till nine of the clock at night, before we came to Mr. Robert Beverley's house, where we were well entertained, and remained this night.

22d. — At nine in the morning, we set out from Mr. Beverley's. The Governor left his chaise here, and mounted his horse. The weather fair, we continued on our journey until we came to Mr. Woodford's, where we lay, and were well entertained. This house lies on Rappahannoc River, ten miles below the falls.

23d. — Here we remained all this day, and diverted ourselves and rested our horses.

24th. — In the morning, at seven, we mounted our horses, and came to Austin Smith's house about ten, where we dined, and remained till about one of the clock, then we set out, and about nine of the clock we came to the German-town, where we rested that night — bad beds and indifferent entertainment.

German-town, 25th. — After dinner we went to see the mines, but I could not observe that there was any good mine. The Germans pretend that it is a silver mine; we took some of the ore and endeavored

201

to run it, but could get nothing out of it, and I am of opinion it will not come to any thing, no, not as much as lead. Many of the gentlemen of the county are concerned in this work. We returned, and to our hard beds.

26th. — At seven we got up, and several gentlemen of the country, that were to meet the Governor at this place for the expedition, arrived here, as also two companies of Rangers, consisting each of six men, and an officer. Four Meherrin Indians also came.

In the morning I diverted myself with other gentlemen shooting at a mark. At twelve we dined, and after dinner we mounted our horses and crossed Rappahannoc River, that runs by this place, and went to find out some convenient place for our horses to feed in, and to view the land hereabouts. Our guide left us, and we went so far in the woods that we did not know the way back again; so we hallooed and fired our guns. Half an hour after sunset the guide came to us, and we went to cross the river by another ford higher up. The descent to the river being steep, and the night dark, we were obliged to dismount and lead our horses down to the river side, which was very troublesome. The bank being very steep, the greatest part of our company went into the water to mount their horses, where they were up to the crotch in the water. After we had forded the river and came to the other side, where the bank was steep also, in going up, the horse of one of our company slipped and fell back into the river on the top of his rider, but he received no other damage than being heartily wet, which made sport for the rest. A hornet stung one of the gentlemen in the face, which swelled prodigiously. About ten we came to the town, where we supped, and to bed.

27th. — Got our tents in order, and our horses shod. About twelve, I was taken with a violent headache and pains in all my bones, so that I was obliged to lie down, and was very bad that day.

28th. — About one in the morning, I was taken with a violent fever, which abated about six at night, and I began to take the bark, and had one ounce divided into eight doses, and took two of them by ten of the clock that night. The fever abated, but I had great pains in my head and bones.

29th. — In the morning we got all things in readiness, and about one we left the German-town to set out on our intended journey.

John Fontaine, 1693-17—

At five in the afternoon, the Governor gave orders to encamp near a small river, three miles from Germanna, which we called Expedition Run, and here we lay all night. This first encampment was called Beverley Camp in honor of one of the gentlemen of our party. We made great fires, and supped, and drank good punch. By ten of the clock I had taken all of my ounce of Jesuit's Bark, but my head was much out of order.

30th. — In the morning about seven of the clock, the trumpet sounded to awake all the company, and we got up. One Austin Smith, one of the gentlemen with us, having a fever, returned home. We had lain upon the ground under cover of our tents, and we found by the pains in our bones that we had not had good beds to lie upon. At nine in the morning, we sent our servants and baggage forward, and we remained, because two of the Governor's horses had strayed. At half past two we got the horses, at three we mounted, and at half an hour after four, we came up with our baggage at a small river, three miles on the way, which we called Mine River, because there was an appearance of a silver mine by it. We made about three miles more, and came to another small river, which is at the foot of a small mountain, so we encamped here and called it Mountain Run, and our camp we called Todd's Camp. We had good pasturage for our horses, and venison in abundance for ourselves, which we roasted before the fire upon wooden forks, and so we went to bed in our tents. Made 6 miles this day.

31st. — At eight in the morning, we set out from Mountain Run, and after going five miles we came upon the upper part of Rappahannoc River. One of the gentlemen and I, we kept out on one side of the company about a mile, to have the better hunting. I saw a deer, and shot him from my horse, but the horse threw me a terrible fall and ran away; we ran after, and with a great deal of difficulty got him again; but we could not find the deer I had shot, and we lost ourselves, and it was two hours before we could come upon the track of our company. About five miles further we crossed the same river again, and two miles further we met with a large bear, which one of our company shot, and I got the skin. We killed several deer, and about two miles from the place where we killed the bear, we encamped upon Rappahannoc River. From our encampment we could see the Appalachian Hills very plain. We made large fires, pitched our tents, and cut boughs to lie upon, had good liquor, and at ten we went to sleep. We always kept a sentry at the Governor's door. We called this Smith's Camp. Made this day fourteen miles.

1st. September. — At eight we mounted our horses, and made the first five miles of our way through a very pleasant plain, which lies where Rappahannoc River forks. I saw there the largest timber, the finest and deepest mould, and the best grass that I ever did see. We had some of our baggage put out of order, and our company dismounted, by hornets stinging the horses. This was some hindrance, and did a little damage, but afforded a great deal of diversion. We killed three bears this day, which exercised the horses as well as the men. We saw two foxes but did not pursue them; we killed several deer. About five of the clock, we came to a run of water at the foot of a hill, where we pitched our tents. We called the encampment Dr. Robinson's Camp, and the river, Blind Run. We had good pasturage for our horses, and every one was cook for himself. We made our beds with bushes as before. On this day we made 13 miles.

2d. — At nine we were all on horseback, and after riding about five miles we crossed Rappahannoc River, almost at the head, where it is very small. We had a rugged way; we passed over a great many small runs of water, some of which were very deep, and others very miry. Several of our company were dismounted, some were down with their horses, others under their horses, and some thrown off. We saw a bear running down a tree, but it being Sunday, we did not endeavor to kill any thing. We encamped at five by a small river we called White Oak River, and called our camp Taylor's Camp.

3d. — About eight we were on horseback, and about ten we came to a thicket, so tightly laced together, that we had a great deal of trouble to get through; our baggage was injured, our clothes torn all to rags, and the saddles and holsters also torn. About five of the clock we encamped almost at the head of James River, just below the great mountains. We called this camp Colonel Robertson's Camp. We made all this day but eight miles.

4th. — We had two of our men sick with the measles, and one of our horses poisoned with a rattlesnake. We took the heaviest of our baggage, our tired horses, and the sick men, and made as convenient a lodge for them as we could, and left people to guard them, and hunt for them. We had finished this work by twelve, and so we set out. The sides of the mountains were so full of vines and briers, that we were forced to clear most of the way before us. We crossed one of the small mountains this side the Appalachian, and from the top of it we had a fine view of the plains below. We were obliged to walk up the most of the way, there being abundance of loose stones on the side of the hill. I killed a large rattlesnake here, and the other people killed three more. We made about four miles, and so came to the side of James River, where a man may jump over it, and there we pitched our tents. As the people were lighting the fire, there came out of a large log of wood a prodigious snake, which they killed; so this camp was called Rattlesnake Camp, but it was otherwise called Brooks' Camp.

5th. — A fair day. At nine we were mounted; we were obliged to have axe-men to clear the way in some places. We followed the windings of James River, observing that it came from the very top of the mountains. We killed two rattle snakes during our ascent. In some places it was very steep, in others, it was so that we could ride up. About one of the clock we got to the top of the mountain; about four miles and a half, and we came to the very head spring of James River, where it runs no bigger than a man's arm, from under a large stone. We drank King George's health, and all the Royal Family's, at the very top of the Appalachian mountains. About a musket-shot from the spring there is another, which rises and runs down on the other side; it goes westward, and we thought we could go down that way, but we met with such prodigious precipices, that we were obliged to return to the top again. We found some trees which had been formerly marked, I suppose, by the Northern Indians, and following these trees, we found a good, safe, descent. Several of the company were for returning; but the Governor persuaded them to continue on. About five, we were down on the other side, and continued our way for about seven miles further, until we came to a large river, by the side of which we encamped. We made this day fourteen miles. I, being somewhat more curious than the rest, went on a high rock on the top of the mountain, to see fine prospects, and I lost my gun. We saw, when we were over the mountains, the footing of elks and buffaloes, and their beds. We saw a vine which bore a sort of wild cucumber, and a shrub with a fruit like unto a current. We ate very good wild grapes. We called this place Spotswood Camp, after our Governor.

6th. — We crossed the river, which we called Euphrates. It is very deep; the main course of the water is north; it is fourscore yards wide in the narrowest part. We drank some healths on the other side, and returned; after which I went a swimming in it. We could not find any fordable place, except the one by which we crossed, and it was deep in several places. I got some grasshoppers and fished; and another and I, we catched a dish of fish, some perch, and a fish they call chub. The others went a hunting, and killed deer and turkeys. The Governor had graving irons, but could not grave any thing, the stones were so hard. I graved my name on a tree by the river side; and the Governor buried a bottle with a paper inclosed, on which he writ that he took possession of this place in the name and for King George the First of England. We had a good dinner, and after it we got the men together, and loaded all their arms, and we drank the King's Health in Champagne, and fired a volley — the Princess's health in Burgundy, and fired a volley, and all the rest of the Royal Family in claret, and fired a volley. We drank the Governor's health and fired another volley. We had several sorts of liquors, viz., Virginia red wine and white wine, Irish usquebaugh, brandy, shrub, two sorts of rum, champagne, canary, cherry, punch, water, cider, &c.

I sent two of the rangers to look for my gun, which I dropped in the mountains; they found it, and brought it to me at night, and I gave them a pistole for their trouble. We called the highest mountain Mount George, and the one we crossed over Mount Spotswood.

7th. — At seven in the morning we mounted our horses, and parted with the rangers, who were to go farther on, and we returned homewards; we repassed the mountains, and at five in the afternoon we came to Hospital Camp, where we left our sick men, and heavy baggage, and we found all things well and safe. We encamped here, and called it Captain Clouder's Camp.

8th. — At nine we were all on horseback. We saw several bears and deer, and killed some wild turkeys. We encamped at the side of a run, and called the place Mason's Camp. We had good forage for our horses, and we lay as usual. Made twenty miles this day.

9th. — We set out at nine of the clock, and before twelve we saw several bears, and killed three. One of them attacked one of our men that was riding after him, and narrowly missed him; he tore his things that he had behind him from off the horse, and would have destroyed him, had he not had immediate help from the other men and our dogs. Some of the dogs suffered severly in this engagement. At two we crossed one of the branches of the Rappahannoc River, and at five we encamped on the side of the Rapid Ann, on a tract of land that Mr. Beverley hath design to take up. We made, this day, twenty-three miles, and called this Captain Stith's Camp. We ate part of one of the bears, which tasted very well, and would be good, and might pass for veal, if one did not know what it was. We were very merry, and diverted ourselves with our adventure.

10th. — At eight we were on horseback, and about ten, as we were going up a small hill, Mr. Beverley and his horse fell down, and they both rolled to the bottom; but there were no bones broken on either side. At twelve, as we were crossing a run of water, Mr. Clouder fell in, so we called this place Clouder's Run. At one we arrived at a large spring, where we dined and drank a bowl of punch. We called this Fontaine's Spring. About two we got on horseback, and at four we reached Germanna. The Governor thanked the gentlemen for their assistance in the expedition. Mr. Mason left us here. I went at five to swim in the Rappahannoc River, and returned to the town.

11th. — After breakfast all our company left us, excepting Dr. Robinson and Mr. Clouder. We walked all about the town, and the Governor settled his business with the Germans here, and accommodated the minister and the people, and then to bed.

12th. — After breakfast went a fishing in the Rappahannoc, and took seven fish, which we had for dinner; after which Mr. Robinson and I, we endeavored to melt some ore in the smith's forge, but could get nothing out of it. Dr. Robinson's and Mr. Clouder's boys were taken violently ill with fever. Mr. Robinson and Mr. Clouder left us, and the boys remained behind.

13th. — About eight of the clock we mounted our horses, and went to the mine, where we took several pieces of ore; and at nine we set out from the mine, our servants having gone before; and about three we overtook them in the woods, and there the Governor and I dined. We mounted afterwards, and continued on our road. I killed a black snake about five feet long. We arrived at Mr. Woodford's, on Rappahannoc River, about six, and remained there all night.

14th. — At seven we sent our horses and baggage before us; and at ten we mounted our horses; we killed another snake, four feet nine inches long. At twelve we came to the church, where we met with Mr. Buckner, and remained till two, to settle some county business; then we mounted our horses, and saw several wild turkeys on the road; and at seven we reached Mr. Beverley's house, which is upon the head of Mattapony River, where we were well entertained. My boy was taken with a violent fever, and very sick.

15th. — At seven my servant was somewhat better, and I sent him away with my horses, and about ten o'clock the Governor took his chaise, and I with him, and at twelve we came to a mill-dam, which we had great difficulty to get the chaise over. We got into it again, and continued on our way, and about five we arrived at Mr. Baylor's, where we remained all night.

16th. — My servant was so sick, that I was obliged to leave him, and the Governor's servants took care of my horses. At ten we sent the chaise over Mattapony River, and it being Sunday, we went to the church in King William County where we heard a sermon from Mr. Monroe. After sermon we continued our journey until we came to Mr. West's plantation, where Colonel Basset waited for the Governor with his pinnace, and other boats for his servants. We arrived at his house by five of the clock, and were nobly entertained.

17th. — At ten we left Colonel Basset's, and at three we arrived at Williamsburg, where we dined together, and I went to my lodgings, and to bed, being well tired, as well as my horses.

I reckon that from Williamsburg to the Euphrates River is in all 219 miles, so that our journey, going and coming, has been in all 438 miles.

WILLIAM BYRD

1674-1744

William Byrd was born in Virginia on March 28, 1674. His father, William Byrd (1652-1704), son of a London goldsmith, had come to Virginia four years before at the age of eighteen upon the invitation of his uncle, Thomas Stegg, a merchant who had achieved a place of influence in the colony. When Stegg died a year later, he left his nephew a plantation of some 1800 acres along the James River. It was here that young Byrd was born. When he was ten years old he was sent to school in England. "Doubtless," writes his biographer, R. C. Beatty, his father reflected "that the amenities of London, which he had seen only externally, on holiday occasions, could be enjoyed by his son as a matter of course." There he grew up as the son of an affluent colonial planter, enrolled as a law student in the Middle Temple, and was called to the bar. He returned to Virginia in 1796 and through the influence of his father was promptly elected to the Virginia Assembly.

Upon the death of his father, he succeeded him as a leading figure in the colony. For thirty-five years he was a member of the King's Council in Virginia and made numerous trips to London as a representative of the colony. He enlarged the holdings of land which he had inherited and lived in baronial style at "Westover." There he built up a library of more than 3000 volumes, the largest in the colonies. In 1841, nearly two hundred years after his death at Westover on August 26, 1744, a group of Byrd's own writings were first published as *The Westover Manuscripts*. A more carefully edited volume appeared a quarter of a century later, and in 1901 J. S. Basset brought out a comprehensive collection, *The Writings of "Colonel William Byrd, of Westover in Virginia, Esqr.",* accompanied by a biographical memoir. A popular edition, *A Journey to the Land of Eden and Other Papers,* edited by Mark Van Doren, was published in 1928.

Byrd's principal literary work consisted of three papers, marked by a vigorous style and an urbane temper. *The History of the Dividing Line* was an account of his experiences as one of the commissioners who established the boundary line between Virginia and North Carolina in 1727-28. A *Progress to the Mines* was based upon a journey made in 1732 to iron mines on the frontier. The third was *A Journey to the Land of Eden,* which follows. Byrd also kept an extensive diary, the first selection from which, *The Secret Diary of William Byrd of Westover, 1709-1712* (622 pages), edited by Louis B. Wright and Marion Tinling, was published in 1941. A second volume, *Another Secret Diary of William Byrd of Westover, 1739-1741* (490 pages), appeared in 1942. Several other miscellaneous items have been published. A biography, *William Byrd of Westover,* by R. C. Beatty, was published in 1932.

A JOURNEY TO THE LAND OF EDEN
IN THE YEAR 1733

September 11th. Having recommended my family to the protection of the Almighty, I crossed the river with two servants and four horses, and rode to Col. Mumford's. There I met my friend, Mr. Banister, who was to be the kind companion of my travels. I stayed dinner with the good colonel, while Mr. Banister made the best of his way home, to get his equipage ready, in order to join me the next day. After dining plentifully, and wishing all that was good to the household, I proceeded to major Mumford's, who had also appointed to go along with me. I was the more obliged to him, because he made me the compliment to leave the arms of a pretty wife, to lie on the cold ground for my sake. She seemed to chide me with her eyes, for coming to take her bedfellow from her, now the cold weather came on, and to make my peace, I was forced to promise to take an abundance of care of him, in order to restore him safe and sound to her embraces.

12th. After the major had cleared his pipes, in calling with much authority about him, he made a shift to truss up his baggage about nine o'clock. Near the same hour my old friend and fellow traveler, Peter Jones, came to us completely accoutered. Then we fortified ourselves with a beef-steak, kissed our landlady for good luck, and mounted about ten. The major took one Robin Bolling with him, as squire of his body, as well as conductor of his baggage. Tom Short had promised to attend me, but had married a wife and could not come. We crossed Hatcher's run, Gravelly run, Stony creek, and in the distance of about twenty miles reached Sapponi chapel, where Mr. Banister joined us. Thus agreeably reënforced we proceeded ten miles further, to major Embry's, on the south side of Nottoway river. The major was ill of a purging and vomiting, attended with a fever which had brought him low; but I prescribed him a gallon or

211

two of chicken broth, which washed him as clean as a gun, and quenched his fever. Here major Mayo met us, well equipped for a march into the woods, bringing a surveyor's tent, that would shelter a small troop. Young Tom Jones also repaired hither to make his excuse; but old Tom Jones, by the privilege of his age, neither came nor sent, so that we were not so strong as we intended, being disappointed of three of our ablest foresters. The entertainment we met with was the less sumptuous by reason of our landlord's indisposition. On this occasion we were as little troublesome as possible, by sending part of our company to Richard Birch's, who lives just by the bridge over the river. We sent for an old Indian called Shacco- Will, living about seven miles off, who reckoned himself seventy-eight years old. This fellow pretended he could conduct us to a silver mine, that lies either upon Eno river, or a creek of it, not far from where the Tuscaroras once lived. But by some circumstances in his story, it seemed to be rather a lead than a silver mine. However, such as it is, he promised to go and show it to me whenever I pleased. To comfort his heart, I gave him a bottle of rum, with which he made himself very happy, and all the family very miserable by the horrible noise he made all night.

13th. Our landlord had great relief from my remedy, and found himself easy this morning. On this account we took our departure with more satisfaction, about nine, and having picked up our friends at Mr. Birch's, pursued our journey over Quoique creek, and Sturgeon run, as far as Brunswick courthouse, about twelve miles beyond Nottoway. By the way, I sent a runner half a mile out of the road to Col. Drury Stith's, who was so good as to come to us. We cheered our hearts with three bottles of pretty good Madeira, which made Drury talk very hopefully of his copper mine. We easily prevailed with him to let us have his company, upon condition we would take the mine in our way. From thence we proceeded to Meherrin river, which lies eight miles beyond the courthouse, and in our way forded Great creek. For fear of being belated, we called not at my quarter, where Don Pedro is overseer, and lives in good repute amongst his neighbors. In compliment to the little major we went out of our way, to lie at a settlement of his upon Cock's creek, four miles short of Roanoke. Our fare here was pretty coarse, but Mr.

William Byrd, 1674-1744

Banister and I took possession of the bed, while the rest of the company lay in bulk upon the floor. This night the little major made the first discovery of an impatient and peevish temper, equally unfit both for a traveler and a husband.

14th. In the morning my friend Tom Wilson made me a visit, and gave me his parole that he would meet us at Blue Stone Castle. We took horse about nine, and in the distance of ten miles reached a quarter of Col. Stith's, under the management of John Tomasin. This plantation lies on the west side of Stith's creek, which was so full of water, by reason of a fresh in the river, that we could not ford it, but we and our baggage were paddled over in a canoe, and our horses swam by our sides. After staying here an hour, with some of Diana's maids of honor, we crossed Miles' creek a small distance off, and at the end of eight miles were met by a tall, meager figure, which I took at first for an apparition, but it proved to be Col. Stith's miner. I concluded that the unwholesome vapors arising from the copper mine had made this operator such a skeleton, but upon inquiry understood it was sheer famine had brought him so low. He told us his stomach had not been blessed with one morsel of meat for more than three weeks, and that too he had been obliged to short allowance of bread, by reason corn was scarce and to be fetched from Tomasin's, which was ten long miles from the mine where he lived. However, in spite of this spare diet, the man was cheerful, and uttered no complaint. Being conducted by him, we reached the mines about five o'clock, and pitched our tents, for the first time, there being yet no building erected but a log-house, to shelter the miner and his two negroes. We examined the mine and found it dipped from east to west, and showed but a slender vein, embodied in a hard rock of white spar. The shaft they had opened was about twelve feet deep, and six over. I saw no more than one peck of good ore above ground, and that promised to be very rich. The engineer seemed very sanguine, and had not the least doubt but his employer's fortune was made. He made us the compliment of three blasts, and we filled his belly with good beef in return, which in his hungry circumstances was the most agreeable present we could make him.

15th. It rained in the morning, which made us decamp later than

213

we intended, but the clouds clearing away about ten, we wished good luck to the mine and departed. We left Col. Stith there to keep fast with his miner, and directed our course through the woods to Boucher's creek, which hath its name from an honest fellow that lives upon it. This place is about six miles from Col. Stith's works, and can also boast of a very fair show of copper ore. It is dug out of the side of a hill, that rises gradually from the creek to the house. The good man was from home himself; but his wife, who was as old as one of the Sibyls, refreshed us with an ocean of milk. By the strength of that entertainment, we proceeded to Mr. Mumford's quarter, about five miles off, where Joseph Colson is overseer. Here our thirsty companions raised their drooping spirits with a cheerful dram, and having wet both eyes, we rode on seven miles farther to Blue Stone Castle, five whereof were through my own land, that is to say, all above Sandy creek. My land there in all extends ten miles upon the river; and three charming islands, namely, Sapponi, Occaneeche, and Totero, run along the whole length of it. The lowest of these islands is three miles long, the next four, and the uppermost three, divided from each other by only a narrow strait. The soil is rich in all of them, the timber large, and a kind of pea, very grateful to cattle and horses, holds green all the winter. Roanoke river is divided by these islands; that part which runs on the north side is about eighty yards, and that on the south more than one hundred. A large fresh will overflow the lower part of these islands, but never covers all, so that the cattle may always recover a place of security. The middlemost island, called Occaneeche island, has several fields in it where Occaneeche Indians formerly lived, and there are still some remains of the peach trees they planted. Here grow likewise excellent wild hops without any cultivation. My overseer, Harry Morris, did his utmost to entertain me and my company; the worst of it was, we were obliged all to be littered down in one room, in company with my landlady and four children, one of which was very sick, and consequently very fretful.

16th. This being Sunday, and the place where we were quite out of Christendom, very little devotion went forward. I thought it no harm to take a Sabbath day's journey, and rode with my overseer to a new entry I had made upon Blue Stone creek, about three miles from the castle, and found the land very fertile and convenient. It consists of low grounds and meadows on both sides the creek. After taking a view of this, we rode two miles farther to a stony place, where there were some tokens of a copper mine, but not hopeful enough to lay me under any temptation. Then we returned to the company, and found Tom Wilson was come according to his promise, in order to proceed into the woods along with us. Jo. Colson likewise entered into pay, having cautiously made his bargain for a pistole. There were three Tuscaruda Indians, (which I understood had been kept on my plantation to hunt for Harry Morris,) that with much ado were also persuaded to be of the party. My landlady could not forbear discovering some broad signs of the fury, by breaking out into insolent and passionate expressions against the poor negroes. And if my presence could not awe her, I concluded she could be very outrageous when I was a hundred miles off. This inference I came afterwards to understand was but too true, for, between the husband and the wife, the negroes had a hard time of it.

17th. We set off about nine from Blue Stone Castle, and rode up the river six miles (one-half of which distance was on my own land,) as far as major Mumford's quarter, where master Hogen was tenant upon halves. Here were no great marks of industry, the weeds being near as high as the corn. My islands run up within a little way of this place, which will expose them to the inroad of the major's creatures. That called Totero island lies too convenient not to receive damage that way; but we must guard against it as well as we can. After the major had convinced himself of the idleness of his tenant, he returned back to Blue Stone, and Harry Morris and I went in quest of a fine copper mine, which he had secured for me in the fork. For which purpose, about a quarter of a mile higher than Hogen's, we crossed a narrow branch of the river into a small island, not yet taken up, and after traversing that, forded a much wider branch into the fork of Roanoke river. Where we landed was near three miles higher up than the point of the fork. We first directed our course easterly towards that point, which was very sharp, and each branch of the river where it divided first seemed not to exceed eighty yards in breadth. The land was broken and barren off from the river, till we came within half a mile of the point where the low-grounds began. The same sort of low ground ran up each branch of the river. That on the Staunton (being the northern branch) was but narrow, but that on the south, which is called the Dan, seemed to carry a width of at least half a mile. After discovering this place, for which I intended to enter, we rode up the midland five miles to view the mine, which in my opinion hardly answered the trouble of riding so far out of our way. We returned downwards again about four miles, and a mile from the point found a good ford over the north branch, into the upper end of Totero island. We crossed the river there, and near the head of the island saw a large quantity of wild hops growing, that smelt fragrantly, and seemed to be in great perfection. At our first landing we were so hampered with brambles, vines and poke bushes, that our horses could hardly force their way through them. However, this difficulty held only about twenty-five yards at each end of the island, all the rest being very level and free from underwood. We met with old fields where the Indians had formerly lived, and the grass grew as high as a horse and his rider. In one of these fields were large duck ponds, very firm at the bottom, to which wild fowl resort in the winter. In the woody part of the island grows a vetch, that is green all the winter, and a great support for horses and cattle, though it is to be feared the hogs will root it all up. There is a cave in this island, in which the last Totero king, with only two of his men, defended himself against a great host of northern Indians, and at last obliged them to retire. We forded the strait out of this into Occaneeche island, which was full of large trees, and rich land, and the south part of it is too high for any flood less than Noah's to drown, we rode about two miles down this island, (being half the length of it,) where finding ourselves opposite to Blue Stone Castle, we passed the river in a canoe, which had been ordered thither for that purpose, and joined our friends, very much tired, not so much with the length of the journey, as with the heat of the weather.

18th. We lay by till the return of the messenger that we sent for the ammunition, and other things left at the courthouse. Nor had the Indians yet joined us according to their promise, which made us begin to doubt of their veracity. I took a solitary walk to the first ford of Blue Stone creek, about a quarter of a mile from the house. This creek had its name from the color of the stones, which paved the bottom of it, and are so smooth that it is probable they will burn into lime. I took care to return to my company by dinner time, that I might not trespass upon their stomachs. In the afternoon I was paddled by the overseer and one of my servants up the creek, but could proceed little farther than a mile because of the shoal water. All the way we perceived the bottom of the creek full of the blue stones above mentioned, sufficient in quantity to build a large castle. At our return we went into the middle of the river, and stood upon a large blue rock to angle, but without any success. We broke off a fragment of the rock, and found it as heavy as so much lead. Discouraged by our ill luck, we repaired to the company, who had procured some pieces of copper ore from Cargil's mine, which seemed full of metal. This mine lies about twelve miles higher than major Mumford's plantation, and has a better show than any yet discovered. There are so many appearances of copper in these parts, that the inhabitants seem to be all mine-mad, and neglect making of corn for their present necessities, in hopes of growing very rich hereafter.

19th. The heavens lowered a little upon us in the morning, but, like a damsel ruffled by too bold an address, it soon cleared up again. Because I detested idleness, I caused my overseer to paddle me up the river so far as the strait that divides Occaneeche from Totero island, which is about twenty yards wide. There runs a swift stream continually out of the south part of the river into the north, and is in some places very deep. We crossed the south part to the opposite shore, to view another entry I had made, beginning at Buffalo creek and running up the river to guard my islands, and keep off bad neighbors on that side. The land seems good enough for corn along the river, but a quarter of a mile back it is broken, and full of stones. After satisfying my curiosity, I returned the way that I came, and shot the same strait back again, and paddled down the river in to the company. When we got home, we laid the foundation of two large cities. One at Shacco's, to be called Richmond, and the other at the point of Appomattox river, to be named Petersburg. These major Mayo offered to lay out into lots without fee or reward.

The truth of it is, these two places being the uppermost landing of James and Appomattox rivers, are naturally intended for marts, where the traffic of the outer inhabitants must center. Thus we did not build castles only, but also cities in the air. In the evening our ammunition arrived safe, and the Indians came to us, resolved to make part of our company, upon condition of their being supplied with powder and shot, and having the skins of all the deer they killed to their own proper use.

20th. Everything being ready for a march, we left Blue Stone Castle about ten. My company consisted of four gentlemen (namely, major Mayo, major Mumford, Mr. Banister and Mr. Jones,) and five woodsmen, Thomas Wilson, Henry Morris, Joseph Colson, Robert Bolling and Thomas Hooper, four negroes and three Tuscaruda Indians. With this small troop we proceeded up the river as far as Hogen's, above which, about a quarter of a mile, we forded into the little island, and from thence into the fork of the river. The water was risen so high, that it ran into the top of my boots, but without giving me any cold, although I rode in my wet stockings. We landed three miles above the point of the fork, and after marching three miles farther, reached the tenement of Peter Mitchell, the highest inhabitant on Roanoke river. Two miles above that we forded a water, which we named Birche's creek, not far from the mouth, where it discharges itself into the Dan. From thence we rode through charming low grounds, for six miles together, to a larger stream, which we agreed to call Banister river. We were puzzled to find a ford by reason the water was very high, but at last got safe over, about one and a half miles from the banks of the Dan. In our way we killed two very large rattlesnakes, one of fifteen and the other of twelve rattles. They were both fat, but nobody would be persuaded to carry them to our quarters, although they would have added much to the luxury of our supper. We pitched our tents upon Banister river, where we feasted on a young buck which had the ill luck to cross our way. It rained great part of the night, with very loud thunder, which rumbled frightfully amongst the tall trees that surrounded us in that low ground, but, thank God! without any damage. Our Indians killed three deer, but were so lazy they brought them not to the camp, pretending for their excuse that they were too lean.

William Byrd, 1674-1744

21st. The necessity of drying our baggage prevented us from marching till eleven o'clock. Then we proceeded through low-grounds which were tolerably wide for three miles together, as far as a small creek, named by us Morris' creek. This tract of land I persuaded Mr. Banister to enter for, that he might not be a loser by the expedition. The low grounds held good a mile beyond the creek, and then the highland came quite to the river, and made our traveling more difficult. All the way we went we perceived there had been tall canes lately growing on the bank of the river, but were universally killed; and inquiring into the reason of this destruction, we were told that the nature of those canes was, to shed their seed but once in seven years, and the succeeding winter to die, and make room for young ones to grow up in their places. Thus much was certain, that four years before we saw canes grow and flourish in several places, where they now lay dead and dry upon the ground. The whole distance we traveled in this day by computation was fifteen miles, and then the appearance of a black cloud, which threatened a gust, obliged us to take up our quarters. We had no sooner got our tents over our heads, but it began to rain and thunder furiously, and one clap succeeded the lightning the same instant, and made all tremble before it. But, blessed be God! it spent its fury upon a tall oak just by our camp. Our Indians were so fearful of falling into the hands of the Catawbas, that they durst not lose sight of us all day; so they killed nothing, and we were forced to make a temperate supper upon bread and cheese. It was strange we met with no wild turkeys, this being the season in which great numbers of them used to be seen towards the mountains. They commonly perched on the high trees near the rivers and creeks. But this voyage, to our great misfortune, there were none to be found. So that we could not commit that abomination, in the sight of all Indians, of mixing the flesh of deer and turkeys in our broth.

22d. We were again obliged to dry our baggage, which had been thoroughly soaked with the heavy rain that fell in the night. While we stayed for that, our hunters knocked down a brace of bucks, wherewith we made ourselves amends for our scanty supper the aforegoing night. All these matters being duly performed made it near noon before we sounded to horse. We marched about two miles over fine low-grounds to a most pleasant stream, which we named the Medway, and by the way discovered a rich neck of highland that lay on the south side of the Dan, and looked very tempting. Two miles beyond the Medway, we forded another creek, which we called Maosty creek. The whole distance between these two streams lay exceeding rich lands, and the same continued two miles higher. This body of low-grounds tempted me to enter for it, to serve as a stage between my land at the fork, and the Land of Eden. The heavens looked so menacing that we resolved to take up our quarters two miles above Maosty creek, where we intrenched ourselves on a rising ground. We had no sooner taken these precautions, but it began to rain unmercifully, and to put out our fire as fast as we could kindle it; nor was it only a hasty shower, but continued with great impetuosity most part of the night. We preferred a dry fast to a wet feast, being unwilling to expose the people to the weather, to gratify an unreasonable appetite. However it was some comfort, in the midst of our abstinence, to dream of the delicious breakfast we intended to make next morning, upon a fat doe and two-year-old bear our hunters had killed the evening before. Notwithstanding all the care we could take, several of the men were dripping wet, and, among the rest, Harry Morris dabbled so long in the rain, that he was seized with a violent fit of an ague that shook him almost out of all his patience.

23d. It was no loss of time to rest in our camp according to the duty of the day, because our baggage was so wet it needed a whole day to dry it. For this purpose we kindled four several fires, in the absence of the sun, which vouchsafed us not one kind look the whole day. My servant had dropped his great-coat yesterday, and two of the men were so good-natured as to ride back and look for it to-day, and were so lucky as to find it. Our Indians having no notion of the sabbath, went out to hunt for something for dinner, and brought a young doe back along with them. They laughed at the English for losing one day in seven; though the joke may be turned upon them for losing the whole seven, if idleness and doing nothing to the purpose may be called loss of time. I looked out narrowly for ginseng, this being the season when it wears its scarlet fruit, but neither now nor any other time during the whole journey could I find one single plant of it. This made me conclude that it delighted not in quite so southerly a climate; and in truth I never heard of its growing on this side of thirty-eight degrees of latitude. But to make amends we saw abundance of sugar trees in all these low-grounds, which the whole summer long the woodpeckers tap, for the sweet juice that flows out of them. Towards the evening a strong northwester was so kind as to sweep all the clouds away, that had blackened our sky, and moistened our skins, for some time past.

24th. The rest the sabbath had given us made everybody alert this morning, so that we mounted before nine o'clock. This diligence happened to be the more necessary, by reason the woods we encountered this day were exceedingly bushy and uneven. At the distance of four miles we forded both branches of Forked creek, which lay within one thousand paces from each other. My horse fell twice under me, but, thank God! without any damage either to himself or his rider; and major Mayo's baggage horse rolled down a steep hill, and ground all his biscuits to rocahominy. My greatest disaster was that, in mounting one of the precipices, my steed made a short turn and gave my knee an unmerciful bang against a tree, and I felt the effects of it several days after. However, this was no interruption of our journey, but we went merrily on, and two miles farther crossed Peter's creek, and two miles after that Jones' creek. Between these creeks was a good breadth of low-grounds, with which Mr. Jones was tempted, though he shook his head at the distance. A little above Jones' creek, we met with a pleasant situation, where the herbage appeared more inviting than usual. The horses were so fond of it that we determined to camp there, although the sun had not near finished his course. This gave some of our company leisure to go out and search for the place where our line first crossed the Dan, and by good luck they found it within half a mile of the camp. But the place was so altered by the desolation which had happened to the canes, (which had formerly fringed the banks of the river a full furlong deep,) that we hardly knew it again. Pleased with this discovery, I forgot the pain in my knee, and the whole company ate their venison without any other sauce than keen appetite.

25th. The weather now befriending us, we despatched our little affairs in good time, and marched in a body to the line. It was already grown very dim, by reason many of the marked trees were burnt or blown down. However, we made shift, after riding little more than half mile, to find it, and having once found it, stuck as close to it as we could. After a march of two miles, we got upon Cane creek, where we saw the same havoc amongst the old canes that we had observed in other places, and a whole forest of young ones springing up in their stead. We pursued our journey over hills and dales till we arrived at the second ford of the Dan, which we passed with no other damage than sopping a little of our bread and shipping some water at the tops of our boots. The late rains having been a little immoderate, had raised the water and made a current in the river. We drove on four miles farther to a plentiful run of very clear water, and quartered on a rising ground a bow-shot from it. We had no sooner pitched the tents, but one of our woodsmen alarmed us with the news that he had followed the track of a great body of Indians to the place where they had lately encamped. That there he had found no less than ten huts, the poles whereof had green leaves still fresh upon them. That each of these huts had sheltered at least ten Indians, who, by some infallible marks, must have been northern Indians. That they must need have taken their departure from thence no longer ago than the day before, having erected those huts to protect themselves from the late heavy rains. These tidings I could perceive were a little shocking to some of the company, and particularly the little major, whose tongue had never lain still, was taken speechless for sixteen hours. I put as good a countenance upon the matter as I could, assuring my fellow travelers, that the northern Indians were at peace with us, and although one or two of them may now and then commit a robbery or a murder, (as other rogues do,) yet nationally and avowedly they would not venture to hurt us. And in case they were Catawbas, the danger would be as little from them, because they are too fond of our trade to lose it for the pleasure of shedding a little English blood. But supposing the worst, that they might break through all the rules of self-interest, and attack us, yet we ought to stand bravely on our defense, and sell our lives as dear as we could. That we should have no more fear of this occasion, than just to make us more watchful and better provided to receive the enemy, if they had the spirit to venture upon us. This rea-

soning of mine, though it could not remove the panic, yet it abated
something of the palpitation, and made us double our guard. However, I found it took off the edge of most of our appetites, for everything but the rum bottle, which was more in favor than ever, because of its cordial quality. I hurt my other knee this afternoon, but
not enough to spoil either my dancing or my stomach.

26th. We liked the place so little that we were glad to leave it this
morning as soon as we could. For that reason we were all on horseback before nine, and after riding four miles arrived at the mouth of
Sable creek. On the eastern bank of that creek, six paces from the
mouth, and just at the brink of the river Dan, stands a sugar tree,
which is the beginning of my fine tract of land in Carolina, called
the Land of Eden. I caused the initial letters of my name to be cut
on a large poplar and beech near my corner, for the more easy finding it another time. We then made a beginning of my survey, direct-
ing our course due south from the sugar tree above-mentioned. In a
little way we perceived the creek forked, and the western branch was
wide enough to merit the name of a river. That to the east was much
less, which we intersected with this course. We ran southerly a mile,
and found the land good all the way, only towards the end of it we
saw the trees destroyed in such a manner that there were hardly any
left to mark my bounds. Having finished this course, we encamped
in a charming peninsula, formed by the western branch of the creek.
It contained about forty acres of very rich land, gradually descending to the creek, and is a delightful situation for the manor house.
My servant had fed so intemperately upon bear, that it gave him a
scouring, and that was followed by the piles, which made riding
worse to him than purgatory. But anointing with the fat of the same
bear, he soon grew easy again.

27th. We were stirring early from this enchanting place, and ran
eight miles of my back line, which tended south eighty-four and a
half westerly. We found the land uneven, but tolerably good, though
very thin of trees, and those that were standing fit for little but fuel
and fence-rails. Some conflagration had effectually opened the country, and made room for the air to circulate. We crossed both the
branches of Lowland creek, and sundry other rills of fine water.
From every eminence we discovered the mountains to the north-

west of us, though they seemed to be a long way off. Here the air felt very refreshing and agreeable to the lungs, having no swamps or marshes to taint it. Nor was this the only good effect it had, but it likewise made us very hungry, so that we were forced to halt and pacify our appetites with a frugal repast out of our pockets, which we washed down with water from a purling stream just by. My knees pained me very much, though I broke not the laws of traveling by uttering the least complaint. Measuring and marking spent so much of our time, that we could advance no further than eight miles, and the chain carriers thought that a great way. In the evening we took up our quarters in the low-grounds of the river, which our scouts informed us was but two hundred yards ahead of us. This was no small surprise, because we had flattered ourselves that this back line would not have intersected the Dan at all; but we found ourselves mistaken, and plainly perceived that it ran more southerly than we imagined, and in all likelihood pierces the mountains where they form an amphitheater. The venison here was lean; and the misfortune was we met no bear in so open a country, to grease the way and make it slip down. In the night our sentinel alarmed us with an idle suspicion that he heard the Indian whistle (which amongst them is a signal for attacking their enemies). This made every one stand manfully to his arms in a moment, and I found nobody more undismayed in this surprise, than Mr. Banister; but after we had put ourselves in battle array, we discovered this whistle to be nothing but the nocturnal note of a little harmless bird, that inhabits those woods. We were glad to find the mistake, and commending the sentinel for his great vigilance, composed our noble spirits again to rest till the morning. However, some of the company dreamed of nothing but scalping all the rest of the night.

28th. We snapped up our breakfast as fast as we could, that we might have the more leisure to pick our way over a very bad ford across the river. Though, bad as it was, we all got safe on the other side. We were no sooner landed, but we found ourselves like to encounter a very rough and almost impassable thicket. However, we scuffled through it without any dismay or complaint. This was a copse of young saplings, consisting of oak, hickory and sassafras, which are the growth of a fertile soil. We gained no more than two miles in three hours in this perplexed place, and after that had the pleasure to issue out into opener woods. The land was generally good, though pretty bare of timber, and particularly we traversed a rich level of at least two miles. Our whole day's journey amounted not quite to five miles, by reason we had been so hampered at our first setting out. We were glad to take up our quarters early in a piece of fine low-ground, lying about a mile north of the river. Thus we perceived the river edged away gently towards the south, and never likely to come in the way of our course again. Nevertheless, the last time we saw it, it kept much the same breadth and depth that it had where it divided its waters from the Staunton, and in all likelihood holds its own quite as high as the mountains.

29th. In measuring a mile and a half farther we reached the lower ford of the Irvin, which branches from the Dan about two miles to the south, southeast of this place. This river was very near threescore yards over, and in many places pretty deep. From thence, in little more than a mile, we came to the end of this course, being in length fifteen miles and eighty-eight poles. And so far the land held reasonably good; but when we came to run our northern course of three miles, to the place where the country line intersects the same Irvin higher up, we passed over nothing but stony hills, and barren grounds, clothed with little timber, and refreshed with less water. All my hopes were in the riches that might lie underground, there being many goodly tokens of mines. The stones which paved the river, both by their weight and color, promised abundance of metal; but whether it be silver, lead or copper, is beyond our skill to discern. We also discovered many shows of marble, of a white ground, with streaks of red and purple. So that it is possible the treasure in the bowels of the earth may make ample amends for the poverty of its surface. We encamped on the bank of this river, a little below the dividing line, and near the lower end of an island half a mile long, which, for the metallic appearances, we dignified with the name of Potosi. In our way to this place we treed a bear, of so mighty a bulk that when we fetched her down she almost made an earthquake. But neither the shot nor the fall disabled her so much, but she had like to have hugged one of our dogs to death in the violence of her embrace. We exercised the discipline of the woods, by tossing a very careless servant in a blanket, for losing one of our axes.

30th. This being Sunday, we were glad to rest from our labors; and, to help restore our vigor, several of us plunged into the river, notwithstanding it was a frosty morning. One of our Indians went in along with us, and taught us their way of swimming. They strike not out both hands together, but alternately one after another, whereby they are able to swim both farther and faster than we do. Near the camp grew several large chestnut trees very full of chestnuts. Our men were too lazy to climb the trees for the sake of the fruit, but, like the Indians, chose rather to cut them down, regardless of those that were to come after. Nor did they esteem such kind of work any breach of the sabbath, so long as it helped to fill their bellies. One of the Indians shot a bear, which he lugged about half a mile for the good of the company. These gentiles have no distinction of days, but make every day a sabbath, except when they go out to war or a hunting, and then they will undergo incredible fatigues. Of other work the men do none, thinking it below the dignity of their sex, but make the poor women do all the drudgery. They have a blind tradition amongst them, that work was first laid upon mankind by the fault of the female, and therefore it is but just that sex should do the greatest part of it. This they plead in their excuse; but the true reason is, that the weakest must always go to the wall, and superiority has from the beginning ungenerously imposed slavery on those who are not able to resist it.

October 1. I plunged once more into the river Irvin this morning, for a small cold I had caught, and was entirely cured by it. We ran the three-mile course from a white oak standing on my corner upon the western bank of the river, and intersected the place, where we ended the back line exactly, and fixed that corner at a hickory. We steered south from thence about a mile, and then came upon the Dan, which thereabouts makes but narrow low-grounds. We forded it about a mile and a half to the westward of the place where the Irvin runs into it. When we were over, we determined to ride down the river on that side, and for three miles found the high-land come close down to it, pretty barren and uneven. But then on a sudden the scene changed, and we were surprised with an opening of large extent, where the Sauro Indians once lived, who had been a considerable nation. But the frequent inroads of the Senecas annoyed them incessantly, and obliged them to remove from this fine situation about thirty years ago. They then retired more southerly, as far as Pee Dee river, and incorporated with the Kewawees, where a remnant of them is still surviving. It must have been a great misfortune to them to be obliged to abandon so beautiful a dwelling, where the air is wholesome, and the soil equal in fertility to any in the world. The river is about eighty yards wide, always confined within its lofty banks, and rolling down its waters, as sweet as milk, and as clear as crystal. There runs a charming level, of more than a mile square, that will bring forth like the lands of Egypt, without being overflowed once a year. There is scarce a shrub in view to intercept your prospect, but grass as high as a man on horseback. Towards the woods there is a gentle ascent, till your sight is intercepted by an eminence, that overlooks the whole landscape. This sweet place is bounded to the east by a fine stream, called Sauro creek, which running out of the Dan, and tending westerly, makes the whole a peninsula. I could not quit this pleasant situation without regret, but often faced about to take a parting look at it as far as I could see, and so indeed did all the rest of the company. But at last we left it quite out of sight, and continued our course down the river, till where it intersects my back line, which was about five miles below Sauro town. We took up our quarters at the same camp where we had a little before been alarmed with the supposed Indian whistle, which we could hardly get out of our heads. However, it did not spoil our rest; but we dreamed all night of the delights of Tempe and the Elysian fields.

2d. We awoke early from these innocent dreams, and took our way along my back line till we came to the corner of it. From thence we slanted to the country line, and kept down that as far as the next fording place of the river, making in the whole eighteen miles. We breathed all the way in pure air, which seemed friendly to the lungs, and circulated the blood and spirits very briskly. Happy will be the people destined for so wholesome a situation, where they may live to fullness of days, and which is much better still, with much content and gayety of heart. On every rising ground we faced about to take our leave of the mountains, which still showed their towering heads. The ground was uneven, rising into hills, and sinking into valleys great part of the way, but the soil was good, abounding in most places with a greasy black mold. We took up our quarters on the western bank of the river, where we had forded it at our coming up. One of our men, Joseph Colson by name, a timorous, lazy fellow, had squandered away his bread, and grew very uneasy when his own ravening had reduced him to short allowance. He was one of those drones who love to do little and eat much, and are never in humor unless their bellies are full. According to this wrong turn of constitution, when he found he could no longer revel in plenty, he began to break the rules by complaining and threatening to desert. This had like to have brought him to the blanket, but his submission reprieved him. Though bread grew a little scanty with us, we had venison in abundance, which a true woodsman can eat contentedly without any bread at all. But bears' flesh needs something of the farinaceous to make it pass easily off the stomach. In the night we heard a dog bark at some distance, as we thought, when we saw all our own dogs lying about the fire. This was another alarm; but we soon discovered it to be a wolf, which will sometimes bark very like a dog, but something shriller.

3d. The fine season continuing, we made the most of it by leaving our quarters as soon as possible. We began to measure and mark the bounds of major Mayo's land on the south of the country line. In order to do this we marched round the bend of the river, but he being obliged to make a traverse, we could reach no farther than four miles. In the distance of about a mile from where we lay, we crossed Cliff creek, which confined its stream within such high banks that it was difficult to find a passage over. We kept close to the river, and two miles farther came to Hixe's creek, where abundance of canes lay dry and prostrate on the ground, having suffered in the late septennial slaughter of that vegetable. A mile after that we forded another stream, which we called Hatcher's creek, from two Indian traders of that name, who used formerly to carry goods to the Sauro Indians. Near the banks of this creek I found a large beech tree, with the following inscription cut upon the bark of it, "J.H., H.H.,

William Byrd, 1674-1744

B.B., lay here the 24th of May, 1673." It was not difficult to fill up those initials with the following names, Joseph Hatcher, Henry Hatcher and Benjamin Bullington, three Indian traders, who had lodged near that place sixty years before, in their way to the Sauro town. But the strangest part of the story was this, that these letters, cut in the bark, should remain perfectly legible so long. Nay, if no accident befalls the tree, which appears to be still in a flourishing condition, I doubt not but this piece of antiquity may be read many years hence. We may also learn from it, that the beech is a very long-lived tree, of which there are many exceedingly large in these woods. The major took in a pretty deal of rich low-ground into his survey, but unhappily left a greater quantity out, which proves the weakness of making entries by guess. We found the Dan fordable hereabouts in most places. One of the Indians shot a wild goose, that was very lousy, which nevertheless was good meat, and proved those contemptible tasters to be no bad tasters. However, for those stomachs that were so unhappy as to be squeamish, there was plenty of fat bear, we having killed two in this day's march.

4th. I caused the men to use double diligence to assist major Mayo in fixing the bounds of his land, because he had taken a great deal of pains about mine. We therefore mounted our horses as soon as we had swallowed our breakfast. Till that is duly performed a woodsman makes a conscience of exposing himself to any fatigue. We proceeded then in this survey, and made an end before night, though most of the company were of opinion the land was hardly worth the trouble. It seemed most of it was below the character the discoverers had given him of it. We fixed his eastern corner on Cocquade creek, and then continued our march, over the hills and far away, along the country line two miles farther. Nor had we stopped there, unless a likelihood of rain had obliged us to encamp on an eminence where we were in no danger of being over-flowed. Peter Jones had a smart fit of ague, which shook him severely, though he bore it like a man; but the small major had a small fever, and bore it like a child. He groaned as if he had been in labor, and thought verily it would be his fate to die like a mutinous Israelite in the wilderness, and be buried under a heap of stones. The rain was so kind as to give us leisure to secure ourselves against it, but came how-

229

ever in time enough to interrupt our cookery, so that we supped as temperately as so many philosophers, and kept ourselves snug within our tents. The worst part of the story was, that the sentinels could hardly keep our fires from being extinguished by the heaviness of the shower.

5th. Our invalids found themselves in traveling condition this morning, and began to conceive hopes of returning home and dying in their own beds. We pursued our journey through uneven and perplexed woods, and in the thickest of them had the fortune to knock down a young buffalo, two years old. Providence threw this vast animal in our way very seasonably, just as our provisions began to fail us. And it was the more welcome too, because it was change of diet, which of all varieties, next to that of bedfellows, is the most agreeable. We had lived upon venison and bear until our stomachs loathed them almost as much as the Hebrews of old did their quails. Our butchers were so unhandy at their business that we grew very lank before we could get our dinner. But when it came, we found it equal in goodness to the best beef. They made it the longer because they kept sucking the water out of the guts, in imitation of the Catawba Indians, upon the belief that it is a great cordial, and will even make them drunk, or at least very gay. We encamped upon Hico river, pretty high up, and had much ado to get our house in order, before a heavy shower descended upon us. I was in pain lest our sick men might suffer by the rain, but might have spared myself the concern, because it had the effect of a cold bath upon them, and drove away their distemper, or rather changed it into a canine appetite, that devoured all before it. It rained smartly all night long, which made our situation on the low-ground more fit for otters than men.

6th. We had abundance of drying work this morning after the clouds broke away and showed the sun to the happy earth. It was impossible for us to strike the tents till the afternoon, and then we took our departure, and made an easy march of four miles to another branch of Hico river, which we called Jesuit's creek, because it misled us. We lugged as many of the dainty pieces of the buffalo along with us as our poor horses could carry, envying the wolves the pleasure of such luxurious diet. Our quarters were taken upon a delightful eminence, that scornfully overlooked the creek, and afforded us a dry habitation. We made our supper on the tongue and udder of the buffalo, which were so good, that a cardinal legate might have made a comfortable meal upon them during the carnival. Nor was this all, but we had still a rarer morsel, the bunch rising up between the shoulders of this animal, which is very tender and very fat. The primings of a young doe, which one of the men brought to the camp, were slighted amidst these dainties, nor would even our servants be fobbed off with cates so common. The low-ground of this creek are wide in many places, and rich, but seem to lie within reach of every inundation; and this is commonly the case with most low-grounds, that lie either on the rivers or on the creeks that run into them. So great an inconvenience lessens their value very much, and makes highland, that is just tolerable, of greater advantage to the owner. There he will be more likely to reap the fruits of his industry every year, and not run the risk, after all his toil, to see the sweat of his brow carried down the stream, and perhaps many of his cattle drowned into the bargain. Perhaps in times to come people may bank their low-grounds as they do in Europe, to confine the water within its natural bounds to prevent these inconveniences.

7th. The scarcity of bread, joined to the impatience of some of our company, laid us under a kind of necessity to hasten our return home. For that reason we thought we might be excused for making a sabbath day's journey of about five miles, as far as our old camp upon Sugar Tree creek. On our way we forded Buffalo creek, which also empties its waters into Hico river. The woods we rode through were open, and the soil very promising, great part thereof being low-grounds, full of tall and large trees. A she bear had the ill luck to cross our way, which was large enough to afford us several luxuri-our meals. I paid for violating the sabbath by losing a pair of gold buttons. I pitched my tent on the very spot I had done when we ran the dividing line between Virginia and Carolina. The beech whose bark recorded the names of the Carolina commissioners was still standing, and we did them the justice to add to their names a sketch of their characters. We got our house in order time enough to walk about and make some slight observations. There were sugar trees in-numerable growing in the low-grounds of this creek, from which it received its name. They were many of them as tall as large hickories, with trunks from fifteen to twenty inches through. The woodpeckers, for the pleasure of the sweet juice which these trees yield, pierce the bark in many places, and do great damage, though the trees live a great while under all these wounds. There grows an infinite quantity of maidenhair, which seems to delight most in rich grounds. The sorrel tree is frequent there, whose leaves, brewed in beer, are good in dropsies, green-sickness, and cachexies. We also saw in this place abundance of papaw trees, the wood whereof the Indians make very dry on purpose to rub fire out of it. Their method of doing it is this: they hold one of these dry sticks in each hand, and by rubbing them hard and quick together, rarify the air in such a manner as to fetch fire in ten minutes. Whenever they offer any sacrifice to their God, they look upon it as a profanation to make use of fire already kindled, but produce fresh virgin fire for that purpose, by rubbing two of these sticks together that never had been used before on any occasion.

8th. After fortifying ourself with a bear breakfast, major Mayo took what help he thought necessary, and began to survey the land, with which the commissioners of Carolina had presented him upon this creek. After running the bounds, the major was a little disappointed in the goodness of the land, but as it had cost him nothing it could be no bad pennyworth, as his upper tract really was. While that business was carrying on, I took my old friend and fellow traveler, Tom Wilson, and went to view the land I had entered for upon this creek, on the north of the country line. We rode down the stream about six miles, crossing it sundry times, and found very wide low grounds on both sides of it, only we observed, wherever the low-grounds were broad on one side the creek, they were narrow on the other. The highlands we were obliged to pass over were very good, and in some places descended so gradually to the edge of the low-grounds, that they formed very agreeable prospects and pleasant situations for building. About four miles from the line, Sugar Tree creek emptied itself into the Hico, which with that addition swelled into a fine river. In this space we saw the most, and most promising good land we had met with in all our travels. In our way we shot a doe, but she not falling immediately, we had lost our game had not

232

William Byrd, 1674-1744

the ravens, by their croaking, conducted us to the thicket where she fell. We plunged the carcass of the deer into the water, to secure it from these ominous birds till we returned, but an hour afterwards were surprised with the sight of a wolf which had been fishing for it, and devoured one side. We knocked down an ancient she bear that had no flesh upon her bones, so we left it to the free-booters of the forest. In coming back to the camp we discovered a solitary bull buffalo, which boldly stood his ground, contrary to the custom of that shy animal, we spared his life, from a principle of never slaughtering an innocent creature to no purpose. However, we made ourselves some diversion, by trying if he would face our dogs. He was so far from retreating at their approach, that he ran at them with great fierceness, cocking up his ridiculous little tail, and grunting like a hog. The dogs in the meantime only played about him, not venturing within reach of his horns, and by their nimbleness came off with a whole skin. All these adventures we related at our return to the camp, and what was more to the purpose, we carried to them the side of venison which the wolf had vouchsafed to leave us. After we had composed ourselves to rest, our horses ran up to our camp as fast as their hobbles would let them. This was to some of us a certain argument that Indians were near, whose scent the horses can no more endure than they can their figures; though it was more likely they had been scared by a panther or some other wild beast, the glaring of whose eyes are very terrifying to them in a dark night.

9th. Major Mayo's survey being no more than half done, we were obliged to amuse ourselves another day in this place. And that the time might not be quite lost, we put our garments and baggage into good repair. I for my part never spent a day so well during the whole voyage. I had an impertinent tooth in my upper jaw, that had been loose for some time, and made me chew with great caution. Particularly I could not grind a biscuit but with much deliberation and presence of mind. Tooth-drawers we had none amongst us, nor any of the instruments they make use of. However, invention supplied this want very happily, and I contrived to get rid of this troublesome companion by cutting a caper. I caused a twine to be fastened round the root of my tooth, about a fathom in length, and then tied the other end to the snag of a log that lay upon the ground, in such a

233

manner that I could just stand upright. Having adjusted my string in this manner, I bent my knees enough to enable me to spring vigorously off the ground, as perpendicularly as I could. The force of the leap drew out the tooth with so much ease that I felt nothing of it, nor should have believed it was come away, unless I had seen it dangling at the end of the string. An under tooth may be fetched out by standing off the ground and fastening your string at due distance above you. And having so fixed your gear, jump off your standing, and the weight of your body, added to the force of the spring, will prize out your tooth with less pain than any operator upon earth could draw it. This new way of tooth-drawing, being so silently and deliberately performed, both surprised and delighted all that were present, who could not guess what I was going about. I immediately found the benefit of getting rid of this troublesome companion, by eating my supper with more comfort than I had done during the whole expedition.

10th. In the morning we made an end of our bread, and all the rest of our provisions, so that now we began to travel pretty light. All the company were witnesses how good the land was upon Sugar Tree creek, because we rode down it four miles, till it fell into Hico river. Then we directed our course over the highland, thinking to shorten our way to Tom Wilson's quarter. Nevertheless, it was our fortune to fall upon the Hico again, and then kept within sight of it several miles together, till we came near the mouth. Its banks were high and full of precipices on the east side, but it afforded some low-grounds on the west. Within two miles of the mouth are good shows of copper mines, as Harry Morris told me, but we saw nothing of them. It runs into the Dan just below a large fall, but the chain of rocks does not reach quite across the river, to intercept the navigation. About a mile below lives Aaron Pinston, at a quarter belonging to Thomas Wilson, upon Tewahominy creek. This man is the highest inhabitant on the south side of the Dan, and yet reckons himself perfectly safe from danger. And if the bears, wolves, and panthers were as harmless as the Indians, his stock might be so too. Tom Wilson offered to knock down a steer for us, but I would by no means accept of his generosity. However, we were glad of a few of his peas and potatoes, and some rashers of his bacon, upon which we made

234

good cheer. This plantation lies about a mile from the mouth of Tewahominy, and about the same distance from the mouth of Hico river, and contains a good piece of land. The edifice was only a log house, affording a very free passage for the air through every part of it, nor was the cleanliness of it any temptation to lie out of our tents, so we encamped once more, for the last time, in the open field.

11th. I tipped our landlady with what I imagined a full reward for the trouble we had given her, and then mounted our horses, which pricked up their ears after the two meals they had eaten of corn. In the distance of about a mile we reached the Dan, which we forded with some difficulty into the fork. The water was pretty high in the river, and the current something rapid, nevertheless all the company got over safe, with only a little water in their boots. After traversing the fork, which was there at least two good miles across, we forded the Staunton into a little island, and then the narrow branch of the same to the mainland. We took major Mumford's tenant in our way, where we moistened our throats with a little milk, and then proceeded in good order to Blue Stone Castle. My landlady received us with a grim sort of a welcome, which I did not expect, since I brought her husband back in good health, though perhaps that might be the reason. It is sure something or other did tease her, and she was a female of too strong passions to know how to dissemble. However, she was so civil as to get us a good dinner, which I was the better pleased with because Col. Cock and Mr. Mumford came time enough to partake of it. The colonel had been surveying land in these parts, and particularly that on which Mr. Stith's copper mine lies, as likewise a tract on which Cornelius Cargill has fine appearances. He had but a poor opinion of Mr. Stith's mine, foretelling it would be all labor in vain, but thought something better of Mr. Cargill's. After dinner these gentlemen took their leaves, and at the same time I discharged two of my fellow travelers, Thomas Wilson and Joseph Colson, after having made their hearts merry, and giving each of them a piece of gold to rub their eyes with. We now returned to that evil custom of lying in a house, and an evil one it is, when ten or a dozen people are forced to pig together in a room, as we did, and were troubled with the squalling of peevish dirty children into the bargain.

12th. We ate our fill of potatoes and milk, which seems delicious fare to those who have made a campaign in the woods. I then took my first minister, Harry Morris, up the hill, and marked out the place where Blue Stone Castle was to stand, and overlook the adjacent country. After that I put my friend in mind of many things he had done amiss, which he promised faithfully to reform. I was so much an infidel to his fair speeches, (having been many times deceived by them,) that I was forced to threaten him with my highest displeasure, unless he mended his conduct very much. I also let him know, that he was not only to correct his own errors, but likewise those of his wife, since the power certainly belonged to him, in virtue of his conjugal authority. He scratched his head at this last admonition, from whence I inferred that the gray mare was the better horse. We gave our heavy baggage two hours' start, and about noon followed them, and in twelve miles reached John Butcher's, calling by the way for master Mumford, in order to take him along with us. Mr. Butcher received us kindly, and we had a true Roanoke entertainment of pork upon pork, and pork again upon that. He told us he had been one of the first seated in that remote part of the country, and in the beginning had been forced, like the great Nebuchadnezzar, to live a considerable time upon grass. This honest man set a mighty value on the mine he fancied he had in his pasture, and showed us some of the ore, which he was made to believe was a gray copper, and would certainly make his fortune. But there is a bad distemper rages in those parts, that grows very epidemical. The people are all mine mad, and neglecting to make corn, starve their families in hopes to live in great plenty hereafter. Mr. Stith was the first that was seized with the frenzy, and has spread the contagion far and near. As you ride along the woods, you see all the large stones knocked to pieces, nor can a poor marcasite rest quietly in its bed for these curious inquirers. Our conversation ran altogether upon this darling subject, until the hour came for our lying in bulk together.

13th. After breaking our fast with a sea of milk and potatoes, we took our leave, and I crossed my landlady's hand with a piece of money. She refused the offer at first, but, like a true woman, accepted of it when it was put home to her. She told me the utmost she was able to do for me was a trifle in comparison of some favor I had formerly done her; but what that favor was, neither I could recollect, nor did she think proper to explain. Though it threatened rain, we proceeded on our journey, and jogged on in the new road for twenty miles, that is as far as it was cleared at that time, and found it would soon come to be a very good one after it was well grubbed. About nine miles from John Butcher's, we crossed Allen's creek, four miles above Mr. Stith's mine. Near the mouth of this creek is a good body of rich land, whereof Occaneeche neck is a part. It was entered for many years ago by Col. Harrison and Col. Allen, but to this day is held without patent or improvement. And they say Mr. Bolling does the same, with a thousand acres lying below John Butcher's. After beating the new road for twenty miles, we struck off towards Meherrin, which we reached in eight miles farther, and then came to the plantation of Joshua Nicholson, where Daniel Taylor lives for halves. There was a poor dirty house, with hardly anything in it but children, that wallowed about like so many pigs. It is a common case in this part of the country, that people live worse upon good land; and the more they are befriended by the soil and the climate, the less they will do for themselves. This man was an instance of it, although his plantation would make plentiful returns for a little industry, yet he wanting that, wanted everything. The woman did all that was done in the family, and the few garments they had to cover their dirty hides were owing to her industry. We could have no supplies from such neighbors as these, but depended on our own knapsacks, in which we had some remnants of cold fowls that we brought from Blue Stone Castle. When my house was in order, the whole family came and admired it, as much as if it had been the grand vizier's tent in the Turkish army.

14th. The sabbath was now come round again, and although our horses would have been glad to take the benefit of it, yet we determined to make a Sunday's journey to Brunswick church, which lay about eight miles off. Though our landlord could do little for us, nevertheless, we did him all the good we were able, by bleeding his sick negro, and giving him a dose of Indian physic. We got to church in decent time, and Mr. Betty, the parson of the parish, entertained us with a good honest sermon, but whether he bought it, or borrowed it, would have been uncivil in us to inquire. Be that as it will, he is a decent man, with a double chin that sits gracefully over his band, and his parish, especially the female part of it, like him well. We were not crowded at church, though it was a new thing in that remote part of the country. What women happened to be there, were very gim and tidy in the work of their own hands, which made them look tempting in the eyes of us foresters. When church was done, we refreshed our teacher with a glass of wine, and then receiving his blessing, took horse and directed our course to major Embry's. The distance thither was reputed fifteen miles, but appeared less by the company of a nymph of those woods, whom innocence, and wholesome flesh and blood made very alluring. In our way we crossed Sturgeon creek and Queocky creek, but at our journey's end were so unlucky as not to find either master or mistress at home. However, after two hours of hungry expectation, the good woman luckily found her way home, and provided very hospitably for us. As for the major, he had profited so much by my prescription, as to make a journey to Williamsburg, which required pretty good health, the distance being little short of one hundred miles.

15th. After our bounteous landlady had cherished us with roast beef and chicken-pie we thankfully took leave. At the same time we separated from our good friend and fellow traveler, major Mayo, who steered directly home. He is certainly a very useful, as well as an agreeable companion in the woods, being ever cheerful and good-humored, under all the little crosses, disasters, and disappointments of that rambling life. As many of us as remained jogged on together to Sapponi chapel, where I thanked major Mumford and Peter Jones for the trouble that they had taken in this long journey. That ceremony being duly performed, I filed off with my honest friend, Mr. Banister, to his habitation on Hatcher's run, which lay about fourteen miles from the chapel above-mentioned. His good-humored little wife was glad to see her runaway spouse returned in safety, and treated us kindly. It was no small pleasure to me, that my worthy friend found his family in good health, and his affairs in good order. He came into this ramble so frankly, that I should have been sorry if he had been a sufferer by it. In the gayety of our hearts we drank our bottle a little too freely, which had an unusual effect on persons so long accustomed to simple element. We were both of us raised out of our beds in the same manner, and near the same time, which was a fair proof that people who breathe the same air, and are engaged in the same way of living, will be very apt to fall into the same indispositions. And this may explain why distempers sometimes go round a family, without any reason to believe they are infectious, according to the superstition of the vulgar.

16th. After pouring down a basin of chocolate, I wished peace to that house, and departed. As long as Mr. Banister had been absent from his family, he was yet so kind as to conduct me to major Mumford's, and which was more, his wife very obligingly consented to it. The major seemed overjoyed at his being returned safe and sound from the perils of the woods, though his satisfaction had some check from the change his pretty wife had suffered in her complexion. The vermillion of her cheeks had given place a little to the saffron, by means of a small tincture of the yellow jaundice. I was sorry to see so fair a flower thus faded, and recommended the best remedy I could think of. After a refreshment of about an hour, we went on to Col. Bolling's, who was so gracious as to send us an invitation. As much in haste as I was to return to my family, I spent an hour or two at that place, but could by no means be persuaded to stay dinner, nor could even madam de Graffenriedt's smiles on one side of her face shake my resolution. From thence we proceeded to Col. Mumford's, who seemed to have taken a new lease, were any dependence to be upon looks, or any indulgence allowed to the wishes of his friends. An honester a man, a fairer trader, or a kinder friend, this country never produced: God send any of his sons may have the grace to take after him. We took a running repast with this good man, and then bidding adieu both to him and Mr. Banister, I mounted once more, and obstinately pursued my journey home, though the clouds threatened, and the heavens looked very lowering. I had not passed the courthouse before it began to pour down like a spout upon me. Nevertheless, I pushed forward with vigor, and got dripping wet before I could reach Merchant's Hope Point. My boat was there luckily waiting for me, and wafted me safe over. And the joy of meeting my family in health made me in a moment forget all the fatigues of the journey, as much as if I had been husquenawed. However, the good Providence that attended me, and my whole company, will I hope stick fast in my memory, and make me everlastingly thankful.

JOHN LOGAN

1725?-1780

John Logan was an American Indian leader of mixed Indian and white ancestry. His father was a white man who had been captured as a child by the Indians and had grown up among them to become a chief of the Cayuga tribe. Logan, who was known also as Tahgah-jute, was born about the year 1725. He married into the Shawnee tribe and became a leader among them. He maintained good relations with the white settlers on the western frontier of Virginia until the time of "Lord Dunmore's war" in 1774. This conflict was precipitated by the death of a group of Indians, including Logan's sister and other relatives, at the hands of a band of white frontiersmen. Lord Dunmore, the royal governor of Virginia, led a force against the Indians and defeated them at the battle of Point Pleasant. Logan refused to take part in the council of peace after the battle and sent to Lord Dunmore the address which follows. Jefferson quoted the address in his *Notes on Virginia*, and it became famous as an example of Indian eloquence. Logan died in 1780.

LOGAN'S ADDRESS TO LORD DUNMORE

I appeal to any white man to say, if ever he entered Logan's cabin hungry, and he gave him not meat; if ever he came cold and naked, and he clothed him not. During the course of the last long and bloody war Logan remained idle in his cabin, an advocate for peace. Such was my love for the whites, that my countrymen pointed as they passed, and said, "Logan is the friend of white men." I had even thought to have lived with you, but for the injuries of one man. Colonel Cresap, the last spring, in cold blood, and unprovoked, murdered all the relations of Logan, not even sparing my women and children. There runs not a drop of my blood in the veins of any living creature. This called on me for revenge. I have sought it: I have killed many: I have fully glutted my vengeance: for my country I rejoice at the beams of peace. But do not harbor a thought that mine is the joy of fear. Logan never felt fear. He will not turn on his heel to save his life. Who is there to mourn for Logan?—Not one.

241

GEORGE MASON

1725-1792

George Mason, one of the great shapers of the American democratic tradition, was born in Fairfax County, Virginia, of a family which had been prominent in Virginia affairs for several generations. He grew up in Virginia and was educated privately. He read widely and was a man of unusual intellectual attainments. Jefferson said of him that "he is one of those strong, very rare intellects which are created only by a special effort of nature."

When he came of age he inherited some 5,000 acres of land along the Potomac below Alexandria, where he was a life-long friend and neighbor of Washington. He was a successful planter and exerted an important influence in colonial affairs. He early identified himself with the anti-Royalist forces in Virginia, and in 1769 wrote a series of non-importation resolutions which were presented by Washington to the Virginia House of Burgesses and adopted. In July, 1774, he wrote the famous "Fairfax Resolutions," proposing a colonial congress and the breaking off of intercourse with Great Britain, which helped to shape the policy of Virginia and of the Continental Congress.

He was a member of the Virginia Committee of Safety in 1775, and of the Virginia Convention in 1775 and 1776. There he drew up the Virginia Bill of Rights, one of the great democratic documents of all time, which was adopted by the Virginia Convention on June 12, 1776. In it he set forth brilliantly and succinctly the fundamental rights of man.

Mason served in the Virginia House of Delegates from 1776 to 1788, where he joined with Jefferson in the fight for religious freedom and the separation of church and state. He was a prominent member of the Constitutional Convention in Philadelphia in 1787, where he vigorously opposed slavery and the slave trade. The Constitution, as drafted, seemed to him to give too many and vague powers to the Congress, and he opposed its ratification by Virginia. When it was ratified, he proposed a number of amendments. His proposals were of seminal influence in the drafting of the first ten amendments to the Constitution, the Bill of Rights of today.

He refused an appointment as United States Senator from Virginia, and retired to his home, "Gunstan Hall," in Fairfax County. There he died on October 7, 1792.

VIRGINIA BILL OF RIGHTS

*Drawn originally by George Mason and adopted by
the Convention of Delegates June 12, 1776*

A Declaration of Rights made by the Representatives of the good People of Virginia, assembled in full and free Convention; which Rights do pertain to them, and their Posterity, as the Basis and Foundation of Government.

I.

That all Men are by Nature equally free and independent, and have certain inherent Rights, of which, when they enter into a State of Society, they cannot, by any Compact, deprive or divest their Posterity; namely, the Enjoyment of Life and Liberty, with the Means of acquiring and possessing Property, and pursuing and obtaining Happiness and Safety.

II.

That all Power is vested in, and consequently derived from, the People; that Magistrates are their Trustees and Servants, and at all Times amenable to them.

III.

That Government is, or ought to be, instituted for the common Benefit, Protection, and Security, of the People, Nation, or Community; of all the various Modes and Forms of Government that is best, which is capable of producing the greatest Degree of Happiness and Safety, and is most effectually secured against the Danger of Mal-administration; and that, whenever any Government shall be found inadequate or contrary to these Purposes, a Majority of the Community hath an indubitable, unalienable, and indefeasible Right, to reform, alter, or abolish it, in such Manner as shall be judged most conducive to the public Weal.

243

IV.

That no Man, or Set of Men, are entitled to exclusive or separate Emoluments or Privileges from the Community, but in Consideration of public Services; which, not being descendible, neither ought the Magistrate, Legislator, or Judge, to be hereditary.

V.

That the legislative and executive Powers of the State should be separate and distinct from the Judicative; and, that the Members of the two first may be restrained from Oppression, by feeling and participating the Burthens of the People, they should, at fixed Periods, be reduced to a private Station, return into that Body from which they were originally taken, and the Vacancies be supplied by frequent, certain, and regular Elections, in which all, or any Part of the former Members, to be again eligible, or ineligible, as the Laws shall direct.

VI.

That Elections of Members to serve as Representatives of the People, in Assembly, ought to be free; and that all Men, having sufficient Evidence of permanent common Interest with, and Attachment to, the Community, have the Right of Suffrage, and cannot be taxed or deprived of their Property for public Uses without their own Consent or that of their Representatives so elected, nor bound by any Law to which they have not, in like Manner, assented, for the public Good.

VII.

That all Power of suspending Laws, or the Execution of Laws, by any Authority without Consent of the Representatives of the People, is injurious to their Rights, and ought not to be exercised.

VIII.

That in all capital or criminal Prosecutions a Man hath a Right to demand the Cause and Nature of his Accusation, to be confronted with the Accusers and Witnesses, to call for Evidence in his Favour, and to a speedy Trial by an impartial Jury of his Vicinage, without whose unanimous Consent he cannot be found guilty, nor can he be compelled to give Evidence against himself; that no Man be deprived of his Liberty except by the Law of the Land, or the Judgment of his Peers.

IX.

That excessive Bail ought not to be required, nor excessive Fines imposed; nor cruel and unusual Punishments inflicted.

X.

That general Warrants, whereby any Officer or Messenger may be commanded to search suspected Places without Evidence of a Fact committed, or to seize any Person or Persons not named, or whose Offence is not particularly described and supported by Evidence, are grievous and oppressive, and ought not to be granted.

XI.

That in Controversies respecting Property, and in Suits between Man and Man, the ancient Trial by Jury is preferable to any other, and ought to be held sacred.

XII.

That the Freedom of the Press is one of the greatest Bulwarks of Liberty, and can never be restrained but by despotic Governments.

XIII.

That a well regulated Militia, composed of the Body of the People, trained to Arms, is the proper, natural, and safe Defence of a free State; that standing Armies, in Time of Peace, should be avoided, as dangerous to Liberty; and that, in all Cases, the Military should be under strict Subordination to, and governed by, the civil Power.

XIV.

That the People have a Right to uniform Government; and therefore, that no Government separate from, or independent of, the Government of *Virginia,* ought to be erected or established within the Limits thereof.

XV.

That no free Government, or the Blessing of Liberty, can be preserved to any people but by a firm Adherence to Justice, Moderation, Temperance, Frugality, and Virtue, and by frequent Recurrence to fundamental Principles.

XVI.

That Religion, or the Duty which we owe to our Creator, and the Manner of discharging it, can be directed only by Reason and Conviction, not by Force or Violence; and therefore, all Men are equally entitled to the free Exercise of Religion, according to the Dictates of Conscience; and that it is the mutual Duty of all to practice Christian Forbearance, Love, and Charity, towards each other.

RICHARD HENRY LEE

1732-1794

Richard Henry Lee, Revolutionary patriot and member of the prominent Lee family of Virginia, was born at the family estate, "Stratford," in Westmoreland County, Virginia, on January 20, 1732. He was educated in Virginia and in England. He became a member of the Virginia House of Burgesses in 1758 and served until 1775. One of his first addresses there was the speech against slavery which follows.

Lee became a leader of the growing opposition in Virginia to royal authority. He worked closely in the Virginia House of Burgesses with Patrick Henry and, after Jefferson's election in 1769, with the future author of the Declaration of Independence. They were the chief movers of the Committees of Correspondence in 1773. The following year Lee was a delegate from Virginia to the Continental Congress in Philadelphia, where he immediately won the admiration of such men as Samuel Adams.

On June 7, 1776, Lee introduced the famous resolution "that these united Colonies are, and of right ought to be, free and independent States . . ." and he was a signer of the Declaration of Independence. He opposed the adoption of the Constitution on grounds similar to those of George Mason, that it lacked a bill of rights and opened the door to despotism; and after its adoption he offered the Tenth Amendment.

He served as Senator and Member of the House of Representatives from Virginia in the new government, and returned to Virginia as a member of the House of Delegates. He died on June 19, 1794.

ADDRESS TO THE VIRGINIA HOUSE OF BURGESSES

On the motion "to lay so heavy a duty on the importation of slaves as effectually to put an end to that iniquitous and disgraceful traffic within the colony of Virginia."

Sir, as the consequences of the determination we must make in the subject of this day's debate will greatly affect posterity, as well as ourselves, it surely merits our most serious attention. And well am I persuaded, sir, that if it be so considered, it will appear, both from reason and experience, that the importation of slaves into this colony has been, and will be attended with effects, dangerous, both to our political and moral interests. When it is observed that some of our neighbouring colonies, though much later than ourselves in point of settlement, are now far before us in improvement, to what, sir, can we attribute this strange, this unhappy truth? The reason seems to be this: *that with their whites they import arts and agriculture, whilst we, with our blacks, exclude both.* Nature has not partially favoured them with superiour fertility of soil, nor do they enjoy more of the sun's cheering and enlivening influence; yet greatly have they outstript us.

Were not this sufficient, sir, let us reflect on our dangerous vicinity to a powerful neighbour, and that slaves, from the nature of their situation, can never feel an interest in our cause, because they see us enjoying every privilege and luxury, and find security established, not for them, but for others, and because they observe their masters possessed of liberty which is denied to them, whilst they and their posterity are subjected for ever to the most abject and mortifying slavery. Such a people must be natural enemies to society, and their increase consequently dangerous.

This reasoning we find verified in the Grecian and Roman histories, where some of the greatest convulsions recorded, were occasioned by the insurrections of their slaves; insomuch, says a Roman

248

historian, that Sicily was more cruelly laid waste by the war with the slaves, than by that with the Carthagenians. This slavish policy still continuing at Rome, at length increased their slaves to such a prodigious number, as obliged the Romans to make laws for their government so severe, that the bare relation of them is shocking to human nature.

Nor, sir, are these the only reasons to be urged against the importation. In my opinion, not the cruelties practised in the conquest of Spanish America, not the savage barbarity of a Saracen, can be more big with atrocity, than our cruel trade to Africa. There we encourage those poor, ignorant people, to wage eternal war against each other; not nation against nation, but father against son, children against parents, and brothers against brothers, whereby parental, filial, and fraternal duty is terribly violated; that by war, stealth, or surprise, we *Christians* may be furnished with our *fellow-creatures*, who are no longer to be considered as created in the image of God as well as ourselves, and equally entitled to liberty and freedom by the great law of nature, but they are to be deprived, for ever deprived, of all the comforts of life, and to be made the most wretched of the human kind. I have seen it observed by a great writer, that Christianity, by introducing into Europe the truest principles of humanity, universal benevolence, and brotherly love, had happily abolished civil slavery. Let us, who profess the same religion, practise its precepts; and by agreeing to this duty, convince the world that we know and practise our true interests, and that we pay a proper regard to the dictates of justice and humanity!

GEORGE WASHINGTON

1732-1799

George Washington left an enormous body of writing — letters, state papers, orders, addresses — for one who is not customarily regarded as an author. The comprehensive collection of his writing edited by John C. Fitzpatrick for the Washington Bicentennial Commission (U. S. Government Printing Office, 1931-1947) is a library of nearly forty volumes.

One of the most human items in that monumental collection is the diary which the sixteen-year-old Washington kept on a surveying trip in the Shenandoah Valley of Virginia in 1748. Of the writing of the mature Washington there is perhaps no better single example than the brief "Reply to Congress on Appointment as Commander-in-Chief."

Washington was born on February 22, 1732, in Westmoreland County, Virginia, on his father's estate which later became known as "Wakefield." He received little formal education and in his youth became a surveyor. He took an active part in the French and Indian War, and was elected to the Virginia House of Burgesses in 1758. The following year he married and settled at "Mount Vernon" on the Potomac, where in the years before the Revolution he became one of the wealthiest planters of Virginia. He early became prominently identified with the anti-Royalist movement in Virginia. He was a member of the first Continental Congress, and in 1775 he became Commander in Chief of the American forces. More than any other one man, he was responsible for the military success of the Revolution. He presided over the Constitutional Convention of 1787, and was elected first President of the United States in 1789. At the end of his second term in 1797 he retired to "Mount Vernon," and there he died on December 14, 1799.

JOURNEY OVER THE MOUNTAINS, 1748

Fryday March 11th 1747-8. Began my Journey in Company with George Fairfax, Esqr., we travell'd this day 40 Miles to Mr. George Neavels in Prince William County

Saturday March 12th This Morning Mr. James Genn the surveyer came to us we travell'd over the Blue Ridge to Capt. Ashby's on Shenandoah River, Nothing remarkable happen'd

Sunday March 13 Rode to his Lordships Quarter about 4 Miles higher up y. River we went through most beautiful Groves of Sugar Trees and spent the best part of the Day in admiring the Trees and richness of the Land

Monday 14th We sent our Baggage to Capt. Hites (near Frederick Town) went ourselves down the River about 16 Miles to Capt. Isaac Penningtons (the Land exceeding Rich and Fertile all the way produces abundance of Grain Hemp Tobacco &ca.) in order to lay of some Lands on Cates Marsh and Long Marsh

Tuesday 15th We set out early with Intent to Run round the sd. Land but being taken in a Rain and it Increasing very fast obliged us to return it clearing about one oClock and our time being too Precious to Loose we a second time ventur'd out and Worked hard till Night and then return'd to Penningtons we got our Supper and was lighted into a Room and I not being so good a Woodsman as the rest of my Company striped myself very orderly and went into the Bed as they called it when to my Surprize I found it to be nothing but a Little Straw-Matted together without Sheets or any thing else but only one thread Bear blanket with double its Weight of Vermin such as Lice Fleas &c. I was glad to get up (as soon as the Light was carried from us) I put on my Cloths and Lay as my Companions. Had we not been very tired I am sure we should not have slep'd much that night I made a Promise not to Sleep so from that time forward chusing rather to sleep in the open Air before a fire as will appear hereafter.

251

March the 15th. Survey'd for George Fairfax Esqr. a Tract of Land
lying on Gates Marsh and Long Marsh. . . .

Wednesday 16th We set out early and finish'd about one oClock
and then Travell'd up to Frederick Town where our Baggage came
to us we cleaned ourselves (to get Rid of the Game we had catched
the Night before) and took a Review of the Town and thence return'd to our Lodgings where we had a good Dinner prepar'd for us
Wine and Rum Punch in Plenty and a good Feather Bed with clean
Sheets which was a very agreeable regale.

Thursday 17th Rain'd till Ten oClock and then clearing we reached
as far as Major Campbells one of these Burgesses about 25 Miles
from Town nothing Remarkable this day nor Night but that we had
a Tolerable good Bed [to] lay on.

Fryday 18th We Travell'd up about 35 Miles to Thomas Barwicks
on Potomack where we found the River so excessively high by Reason of the Great Rains that had fallen up about the Allegany Mountains they told us which was then bringing down the melted Snow
and that it would not be fordable for several Days it was then above
Sixx foot Higher than usual and was rising we agreed to stay till
Monday we this day call'd to see the Fam'd Warm Springs we
camped out in the field this Night Nothing Remarkable happen'd
till Sunday the 20th.

Sunday 20th finding the River not much abated we in the Evening
Swam our horses over and carried them to Charles Polks in Maryland for Pasturage till the next Morning

Monday 21st We went over in a Canoe and travell'd up Maryland
side all the Day in a Continued Rain to Collo Cresaps right against
the Mouth of the South Branch about 40 Miles from Polks I believe
the worst Road that ever was trod by Man or Beast.

Tuesday 22d Continued Rain and the Freshes kept us at Cresaps.

Wednesday 23d Rain'd till about two oClock and Clear'd when
we were agreeably surpris'd at the sight of thirty odd indians coming from War with only one Scalp. We had some Liquor with us of
which we gave them Part it elevating there Spirits put them in the
Humour of Dancing of whom we had a War Dance there manner of
Dancing is as follows Viz They clear a Large Circle and make a
Great Fire in the middle then seats themselves around it the Speaker

makes a grand speech telling them in what Manner they are to Daunce after he has finished the best Dauncer jumps up as one awaked out of a Sleep and runs and Jumps about the Ring in a most comical Manner he is followed by the Rest then begins there Musicians to Play the Musick is a Pot half [full] of Water with a Deerskin Stretched over it as tight as it can and a goard with some Shott in it to Rattle and a Piece of an horses Tail tied to it to make it look fine the one keeps Rattling and the other Drumming all the while the others is Dauncing

Fryday 25th Nothing Remarkable on thursday but only being with the Indians all day so shall slip it this day left Cresaps and went up to the mouth of Patersons Creek and there swam our Horses over got over ourselves in a Canoe and traveld up the following Part of the Day to Abram Johnstones 15 Miles from the Mouth where we camped.

Saturday 26 Travelld up the Creek to Solomon Hedges Esqr one of his Majestys Justices of the Peace for the County of Frederick where we camped when we came to Supper there was neither a Cloth upon the Table nor a knife to eat with but as good luck would have it we had knives of [our] own.

Sunday 27th Travell'd over to the South Branch attended with the Esqr to Henry Vanmetriss in order to go about Intended Work of Lots.

Monday 28th Travell'd up the Branch about 30 Miles to Mr. James Rutlidges Horse Jockey and about 70 Miles from the Mouth

Tuesday 29th This Morning went out and Survey'd five Hundred Acres of Land and went down to one Michael Stumps on the So. Fork of the Branch on our way Shot two Wild Turkies.

Thursday 31st Early this Morning one of our Men went out with the Gun and soon Returned with two Wild Turkies we then went to our Business run of three lots and returned to our Camping place at Stumps

March 31st Lot 4th. this Lot survey'd myself Beginning at a Pine by a Rock . . .

April

Fryday April the 1st This Morning Shot twice at Wild Turkies but kill'd none run of three Lots and returned to Camp.

Virginia Reader

Saterday 2d Last Night was a blowing and Rainy night Our Straw catch'd a Fire yt. we were laying upon and was luckily Preserv'd by one of our Mens awaking when it was in a [blaze] we run of four Lots this Day which Reached below Stumps. . . .

Sunday 3d Last Night was a much more blostering night than the former we had our Tent carried Quite of with the Wind and was obliged to Lie the Latter part of the night without covering there came several Persons to see us this day one of our Men Shot a Wild Turkie

Monday 4th this morning Mr. Fairfax left us with Intent to go down to the Mouth of the Branch we did two Lots and was attended by a great Company of People Men Women and Children that attended us through the Woods as we went showing there Antick tricks I really think they seemed to be as Ignorant a Set of People as the Indians they would never speak English but when spoken to they speak all Dutch this day our Tent was blown down by the Violentness of the Wind

*   *   *   *   *

Wednesday 6th Last Night was so Intolerable smoky that we were obliged all hands to leave the Tent to the Mercy of the Wind and Fire this day was attended by our afored Company until about 12 oClock when we finish'd we travell'd down the Branch to Henry Vanmetris's on our Journey was catched in a very heavy Rain we got under a Straw House until the Worst of it was over and then continued our Journey

Thursday 7th Rain'd Successively all Last Night this Morning one of our men Killed a Wild Turkie that weight 20 Pounds we went and Survey'd 15 Hundred Acres of Land and Return'd to Vanmetris's about 1 oClock about two I heard that Mr Fairfax was come up and at 1 Peter Casseys about 2 Miles of in the same Old Field I then took my Horse and went up to see him we eat our Dinners and Walked down to Vanmetris's we stayed about two Hours and Walked back again and slept in Casseys House which was the first Night I had slept in a House since I came to the Branch.

Fryday 8th we breakfasted at Casseys and Rode down to Vanmetris's to get all our Company together which when we had accomplished we Rode down below the Trough in order to Lay of Lots there we laid of one this day The Trough is [a] couple of Ledges of Mountain Impassable running side and side together for above 7 or 8 Miles and the River down between them you must Ride Round the back of the Mountain for to get below them we Camped this Night in the Woods near a Wild Meadow where was a Large Stack of Hay after we had Pitched our Tent and made a very Large Fire we pull'd out our Knapsack in order to Recruit ourselves every [one] was his own Cook our Spits was Forked Sticks our Plates was a Large Chip as for Dishes we had none.

Saterday 9th Set the Surveyor to work whilst Mr Fairfax and myself stayed at the Tent our Provisions being all exhausted and the Person that was to bring us a Recruit disappointing us we were obliged to go without untill we could get some from the Neighbours which was not till about 4 or 5 oClock in the Evening we then took our Leaves of the Rest of our Company Road Down to John Colins in order to set off next Day homewards.

Sunday 10th We took our farewell of the Branch and travell'd over Hills and Mountains to 1 Coddys on Great Cacapehon about 40 Miles.

Monday 11th We Travell'd from Coddys down to Frederick Town where we Reached about 12 oClock we dined in Town and then went to Capt. Hites and Lodged

Tuesday 12th We set of from Capt. Hites in order to go over Wms. Gap about 20 Miles and after Riding about 20 Miles we had 20 to go for we had lost ourselves and got up as High as Ashbys Bent we did get over Wms. Gap that Night and as low as Wm. Wests in Fairfax County 18 Miles from the Top of the Ridge This day [we] see a Rattle Snake the first we had seen in all our Journey.

Wednesday the 13th of April 1748 Mr. Fairfax got safe home and I myself safe to my Brothers which concludes my Journal.

REPLY TO CONGRESS ON APPOINTMENT AS COMMANDER-IN-CHIEF, 1775

In Congress, 16 June, 1775

Mr. President,

Though I am truly sensible of the high honor done me, in this appointment, yet I feel great distress, from a consciousness that my abilities and military experience may not be equal to the extensive and important trust. However, as the Congress desire it, I will enter upon the momentous duty, and exert every power I possess in their service, and for the support of the glorious cause. I beg they will accept my cordial thanks for this distinguished testimony of their approbation.

But, lest some unlucky event should happen, unfavorable to my reputation, I beg it may be remembered by every gentleman in the room, that I, this day, declare with the utmost sincerity, I do not think myself equal to the command I am honored with.

As to pay, Sir, I beg leave to assure the Congress, that, as no pecuniary consideration could have tempted me to accept this arduous employment, at the expense of my domestic ease and happiness, I do not wish to make any profit from it. I will keep an exact account of my expenses. Those, I doubt not, they will discharge; and that is all I desire.

PHILIP VICKERS FITHIAN

1747-1776

Philip Vickers Fithian, author of a diary which is the most interesting first-hand account that has survived of plantation life in Virginia just before the Revolution, was a graduate of Princeton who served as tutor to the children of Robert Carter at "Nomini Hall" in Westmoreland County, Virginia, in 1773-1774. Fithian was born in Greenwich, New Jersey, on December 29, 1747. He entered Princeton in 1770 – in a class which included James Madison and Henry Lee – studied theology for a year after his graduation, and came to Virginia as a tutor in 1773. Excerpts from the diary which he kept in Virginia and one of his letters from Virginia follow.

After his year as a tutor, Fithian was licensed in New Jersey as a Presbyterian minister. He returned to Virginia on a mission tour and traveled through the Shenandoah Valley. He was married to Elizabeth Beatty on October 23, 1775, in New Jersey, and shortly afterwards set out on a second mission tour in Virginia. On these tours also he kept an interesting diary. The following year he was appointed a chaplain in a New Jersey regiment in the Revolutionary army. He died in camp of dysentery on October 8, 1776, before his twenty-ninth birthday.

Three large volumes of Fithian's writings have been published. A collection of his earlier diaries and letters, including those written while he was a tutor in Virginia, was edited by John Rogers Williams and published in 1900 by the Princeton Historical Society under the title, *Philip Vickers Fithian: Journal and Letters, 1767-1774*. A second volume was edited by Robert Greenhalgh Albion and Leonidas Dodson and published in 1934 by the Princeton University Press under the title, *Philip Vickers Fithian: Journal, 1775-1776, Written on the Virginia-Pennsylvania Frontier and in the Army around New York*. A new edition of the earlier Virginia material was edited by Hunter Dickinson Farish and published in 1943 by Colonial Williamsburg, Inc. under the title, *Journal and Letters of Philip Vickers Fithian, 1773-1774: A Plantation Tutor of the Old Dominion*.

EXCERPTS FROM THE JOURNAL OF
PHILIP VICKERS FITHIAN

Monday 13. [December 13, 1773]

Mr Carter is preparing for a Voyage in his Schooner, the Hariot, to the Eastern Shore in Maryland, for Oysters: there are of the party, Mr *Carter*, Captain *Walker* Colonel *Richd Lee*, & Mr *Lancelot Lee*. With Sailors to work the vessel — I observe it is a general custom on Sundays here, with Gentlemen to invite one another home to dine, after Church; and to consult about, determine their common business, either before or after Service — It is not the Custom for Gentlemen to go into Church til Service is beginning, when they enter in a Body, in the same manner as they come out; I have known the Clerk to come out and call them in to prayers. — They stay also after the Service is over, usually as long, sometimes longer, than the Parson was preaching — Almost every Lady wears a red Cloak; and when they ride out they tye a white handkerchief over their Head and face, so that when I first came into Virginia, I was distress'd whenever I saw a Lady, for I thought She had the Tooth-Ach! — The People are extremely hospitable, and very polite both of which are most certainly universal Characteristics of the Gentlemen in Virginia — some swear bitterly, but the practise seems to be generally disapproved — I have heard that this Country is notorious for Gaming, however this be, I have not seen a Pack of *Cards*, nor a *Die*, since I left home, nor gaming nor Betting of any kind except at the Richmond-Race. Almost every Gentleman of Condition, keeps a Chariot and *Four;* many drive with six Horses — I observe that all the Merchants & shopkeepers in the Sphere of my acquaintance and I am told it is the Case through the Province, are young Scotch-Men; Several of whom I know, as *Cunningham, Jennings, Hamilton, Blain;* — And it has been the custom heretofore to have all their Tutors, and Schoolmasters from Scotland, tho' they begin to be willing to

258

Philip Vickers Fithian, 1747-1776

employ their own Countrymen — Evening Ben Carter and myself had a long dispute on the practice of fighting — He thinks it best for two persons who have any dispute to go out in good-humor & fight manfully, & says they will be sooner and longer friends than to brood and harbour malice — Mr *Carter* is practising this Evening on the *Guittar* He begins with the *Trumpet Minuet*. He has a good Ear for Music; a vastly delicate Taste: and keeps good Instruments, he has here at Home a *Harpsichord, Forte-Piano, Harmonica, Guittar, Violin, & German Flutes*, & at Williamsburg, has a good *Organ*, he himself also is indefatigable in the Practice.

Teusday 18. [January 18, 1774]

Mrs *Carter*, & the young Ladies came Home last Night from the Ball, & brought with them Mrs *Lane*, they tell us there were upwards of Seventy at the Ball; forty one Ladies; that the company was genteel; & that Colonel *Harry Lee*, from *Dumfries*, & his Son *Harrey* who was with me at College, were also there; Mrs *Carter* made this an argument, and it was a strong one indeed, that to-day I must dress & go with her to the Ball — She added also that She Desired my Company in the Evening when she should come Home as it would be late — After considering a while I consented to go, & was dressed — we set away from Mr Carters at two; Mrs *Carter* & the young Ladies in the Chariot, Mrs Lane in a Chair, & myself on Horseback — As soon as I had handed the Ladies out, I was saluted by Parson *Smith;* I was introduced into a small Room where a number of Gentlemen were playing Cards, (the first game I have seen since I left Home) to lay off my Boots Riding-Coat &c — Next I was directed into the Dining-Room to see Young Mr *Lee;* He introduced me to his Father — With them I conversed til Dinner, which came in at half after four. The Ladies dined first, when some Good order was preserved; when they rose, each nimblest Fellow dined first — The Dinner was as elegant as could be well expected when so great an Assembly were to be kept for so long a time. — For Drink, there was several sorts of Wine, good Lemon Punch, Toddy, Cyder, Porter &c. — About Seven the Ladies & Gentlemen begun to dance in the Ball-Room — first Minuets one Round; Second Giggs; third Reels; And last of All Country-Dances; tho' they struck several Marches oc-

259

casionally — The Music was a French-Horn and two Violins — The Ladies were Dressed Gay, and splendid, & when dancing, their Silks & Brocades rustled and trailed behind them! — But all did not join in the Dance for there were parties in Rooms made up, some at Cards; some drinking for Pleasure; some toasting the Sons of america; some singing "Liberty Songs" as they call'd them, in which six, eight, ten or more would put their Heads near together and roar, & for the most part as unharmonious as an affronted — Among the first of these Vociferators was a young Scotch-Man, Mr *Jack Cunningham;* he was nimis bibendo appotus; noisy, droll, waggish, yet civil in his way & wholly inoffensive — I was solicited to dance by several, Captain Chelton, Colonel Lee, Harry Lee, and others; But George Lee, with great Rudeness as tho' half drunk, asked me why I would come to the Ball & neither dance nor play Cards? I answered him shortly, (for his Impudence moved my resentment) that my Invitation to the Ball would Justify my Presence; & that he was ill qualified to direct my Behaviour who made so indifferent a Figure himself — Parson Smiths, & Parson Gibberns Wives danced, but I saw neither of the Clergymen either dance or game — At Eleven Mrs Carter call'd upon me to go, I listned with gladness to the summons & with Mrs Lane in the Chariot we rode Home, the Evening sharp and cold! — I handed the Ladies out, waited on them to a warm Fire, then ran over to my own Room, which was warm and had a good Fire; oh how welcome! Better this than to be at the Ball in some corner nodding, and awaked now & then with a midnight Yell! — In my Room by half after twelve; & exceeding happy that I could break away with Reputation. —

Saturday 11. [June 11, 1774]

I was sitting in the Colonels Library I took a Catalogue of the whole of His Books — & he tells me he has left behind him at Williamsburg, with many other things 458 Volumes besides Music & Pamphlets.

It is with considerable Difficulty that I keep the Children in School til twelve o Clock as they used to go out all the last winter at Breakfast — *Bob* especially is vastly vociferous on the Occasion — Our Bells for School & play-Hours are at present under good Regulations.

Philip Vickers Fithian, 1747-1776

The Children come in as soon as they rise and are Drest which is usually about seven — The Bell rings at eight for Breakfast — At nine it Rings for two purposes; for the Children to enter School, & for the Gardiners, Carpenters, & other workmen to come into Breakfast — At ten it Rings them to work. At twelve it rings for the School play hours — At two it rings for us to Dine, & the workmen — And the las[t] bell is at three for School & for the workmen to go to Labour — I dismiss them by my watch at half after Five. — After Dinner I rode alone to Mr Blains Store; bought a pen-knife, nine Jacket-Buttons, & a primmer for Miss *Harriot* 3/. It is alarming to observe how hard, & dusty the Country is; towards evening some clouds arose & looked promising in the West, but they bring no rain — No rain has fell here since the 24th of May, & then but a Scanty Shower, & most of the time since windy.

Sunday 3. [July 3, 1774]

We were all to go to Church to day, but we were prevented by a storm of thunder & Rain; the Ground is now sufficiently wetted — I have not heard a Sermon on Sunday since the fifteenth of May; a longer Vacancy from publick worship than I have ever had since my first remembrance. About ten an old Negro Man came with a complaint to Mr Carter of the Overseer that he does not allow him his Peck of corn a Week — The humble posture in which the old Fellow placed himself before he began moved me. We were sitting in the passage, he sat himself down on the Floor clasp'd his Hands together, with his face directly to Mr *Carter*, & then began his Narration — He seem'd healthy, but very old, he was well dress'd but complained bitterly — I cannot like this thing of allowing them no meat, & only a Peck of Corn & a Pint of Salt a Week, & yet requiring of them hard & constant Service. We have several Rains this day so that the Ground is sufficiently wetted — I spent the greater part of the day writing at my Sermon.

Thursday 25. [August 25, 1774]

Still stormy. The Gentlemen who are sailing up the Bay to the Congress have a disagreeable time — This is a true August Northeaster, as we call it in Cohansie — *Ben* is in a wonderful *Fluster* lest

261

he shall have no company to-morrow at the Dance — But blow high, blow low, he need not be afraid; *Virginians* are of genuine Blood — They will dance or die! — I wrote some at my Letter for Mr *Peck* — The people here pronounce Shower "Sho-er" — And what in New-Jersey we call a Vendue here they a "Sale" — All Taverns they call "Ordinary's" — When a Horse is frolicsome & brisk, they, say at once he is "gayly" — she is mischievous, they call him, "vicious." — At five, with *Ben*. I rode out for exercise — After a while we arrived at *George-Lee's* — He gave us some excellent Peaches — He returned with us to Mr Turberville's — We met here with Miss *Betsy Lee*, Mr *Grubb, Lancelot Lee* & here we spent the evening — *Fish-Feasts, & Fillies,* Loud disputes concerning the Excellence of each others Colts — Concerning their Fathers, Mothers (for so they call the Dams) Brothers, Sisters, Uncles, Aunts, Nephews, Nieces, & Cousins to the fourth Degree! — All the Evening Toddy constantly circulating — Supper came in, & at Supper I had a full, broad, satisfying View of Miss *Sally Panton* — I wanted to hear her converse, but poor Girl any thing She attempted to say was drowned in the more polite & useful Jargon about Dogs & Horses! — For my Part, as I was unwilling to be singular, if I attempted to push in a word, I was seldom heard, & never regarded, & yet they were constantly refering their Cases to me, as to a supposed honest fellow, I suppose because I wear a black Coat, & am generally silent; at Home I am thought to be noisy enough; here I am thought to be silent & circumspect as a *Spy* — How different the Manners of the People! I try to be as cheerful as I can. & yet I am blamed for being stupid as a Nun —

Sunday 18. [September 18, 1774]

The Colonel gave me, at Breakfast the offer of a Seat in his Boat to Church. The Morning was fine, & Nomini-River alive with Boats Canoes &c some going to Church, some fishing, & some Sporting — Mr *Smith* gave us a very practical Sermon against the common vices here, in particular against the practise of abusing Slaves — The report concerning Boston is much talked off & still confirmed! — We dined all at Mr Tuberville's; Miss *Corbin* looks *fresh & plump* as ever. Towards evening arose a pretty furious Thunder-Gust, which we hardly escaped on our way home I observed that several, but in special Mr *Carter* is not pleased with Mr. Smith's Sentiments of Slavery.

ADVISE FOR A VIRGINIA PLANTATION TUTOR

Letter from Philip Vickers Fithian to his Successor John Peck

Nomini Hall August 12th 1774.

"SI BENE MONEO, ATTENDE." —

Sir.

I never reflect, but with secret, and peculiar pleasure, on the time when I studied in *Deerfield* with you, & several other pleasant Companions, under our common, & much respected instructor, Mr *Green*. And I acknowledge now, with a thankful heart, the many favours, which I received from your family while I was a member of it. This sense of obligation to your Family, And personal friendship for you, have excited me, when it was in my power, to introduce you to the business which I now occupy; into a family, where, if you be prudent and industrious, I am confident you will speedily acquire to yourself both Honour & Profit — But inasmuch as you are wholly a stranger to this Province; & have had little or no Experience in the business which you are shortly to enter upon; & lest, from common Fame, which is often erroneous, you shall have entertained other notions of the manners of the People here, & of your business as a Tutor, than you will find, when you come, to be actually true; I hope you will not think it *vain* or *untimely*, if I venture to lay before you some Rules for your direction which I have collected from a year's observation. I shall class what I have to say in the following order. First. I shall attempt to give you some direction for the plan of your Conduct among your neighbors, & the People in General here, so long as you sustain the character of a Tutor. Then I shall advise you concerning the rules which I think will be most profitable & convenient in the management of your little lovely charge, the School. Last of all. I choose to proceed in the order I have laid down, as well that you may more fully & speedily receive my mind, as that you may also the more readily select out and apply what you shall find to be most necessary.

First. When you have thought of removing, for a Time, out of the Colony in which you were born, & in which you have hitherto constantly resided, I make no doubt but you have at the same time expected to find a very considerable alteration of manners, among your new acquaintances, & some peculiarities *toto Caelo* different, from any you have before been accustomed to. Such a thought is natural; And you will if you come into Virginia, in much shorter time than a year, be convinced that it is just. In New-Jersey Government throughout, but especially in the Counties where you have any personal acquaintance, Gentlemen in the first rank of Dignity & Quality, of the Council, general Assembly, inferior Magistrates, Clergy-men, or independent Gentlemen, without the smallest fear of bringing any manner of reproach either on their office, or their high-born, long recorded Families associate freely & commonly with Farmers & Mechanicks tho' they be poor & industrious. Ingenuity & industry are the Strongest, & most approved recommendations to a Man in that Colony. The manners of the People seem to me, (probably I am overborn by the force of prejudice in favour of my native Soil), to bear some considerable resemblance of the manners in the ancient Spartan Common-Wealth — The Valour of its Inhabitants — was the best, & only security of that State against the enemy; & the wise laws of its renowned Legislator were the powerful Cement which kept them firm & invincible — In our Government, the laborious part of Men, who are commonly ranked in the midling or lower Class, are accounted the strength & Honour of the Colony; & the encouragement they receive from Gentlemen in the highest stations in the spring of Industry, next to their private advantage. The Level which is admired in New-Jersey Government, among People of every rank, arises, no doubt, from the very great division of the lands in that Province, & consequently from the near approach to an equality of Wealth amongst the Inhabitants, since it is not famous for trade. You know very well that the Lands in a small township are divided, & then again subdivided into two & three Hundred Separate, proper, creditable estates; for example *Deerfield* & *Fairfield* two

Townships, or Precincts, in which you & I are tolerably well acquainted, in the former of which, are the Seats of two Judges of the Sessions; & in the latter resides one of the representatives in General Assembly for the County; But if 16000 £ would purchase the whole landed estates of these three Gentlemen, who are supposed to be the most wealthy in the County, if we rate their Land at the Low Consideration of 4 £ p acre, with all conveniences, each would have 4000 Acres. Now you may suppose how small a quantity many must have when two or three hundred Landholders reside in each of these small Precincts; Hence we see Gentlemen, when they are not actually engaged in the publick Service, on their farms, setting a laborious example to their Domesticks, & on the other hand we see labourers at the Tables & in the Parlours of their Betters enjoying the advantage, & honour of their society and Conversation — I do not call it an objection to this, that some few, who have no substance but work like Slaves as necessity drives them for a few Months in the year; with the price of this Labour they visit Philadelphia; & having there acquired a fashionable Coat, & a Stock of Impudence, return home to spend the remainder of the year, in idleness & disgrace! — But you will find the tables turned the moment you enter this Colony. The very Slaves, in some families here, could not be bought under 30000 £. Such amazing property, no matter how deep it is involved, blows up the owners to an imagination, which is visible in all, but in various degrees according to their respective virtue, that they are exalted as much above other Men in worth & precedency; excepting always the value they put upon posts of honour, & mental acquirements — For example, if you should travel through this Colony, with a well-confirmed testimonial of your having finished with Credit a Course of studies at Nassau-Hall; you would be rated, without any more questions asked, either about your family, your Estate, your business, or your intention, at 10,-000 £; and you might come, & go, & converse, & keep company, according to this value; & you would be dispised & slighted if yo[u] rated yourself a farthing cheaper. But when I am giving directions to you, from an expectation that you will be shortly a resident here, altho you have gone through a College Course, & for any thing I know, have never written a Libel, nor stolen a Turkey, yet I think myself in duty bound to advise you, lest some powdered Coxcomb should reproach your education, to cheapen your price about 5000 £; because any young Gentleman travelling through the Colony, as I said before, is presum'd to be acquainted with Dancing, Boxing, playing the Fiddle, & Small-Sword, & Cards. Several of which you was only entering upon, when I left New-Jersey; towards the Close of last year; and if you stay here any time your Barrenness in these must be detected. I will however allow, that in the Family where you act as tutor you place yourself, according to your most accute Calculation, at a perfect equi-distance between the father & the eldest Son. Or let the same distance be observed in every article of behaviour between you & the eldest Son, as there ought to be, by the latest & most approved precepts of Moral-Philosophy, between the eldest Son, & his next youngest Brother. But whenever you go from Home, where you are to act on your own footing, either to a Ball; or to a *Horse-Race,* or to a *Cock-Fight,* or to a *Fish-Feast,* I advise that you rate yourself very low, & if you bett at all, remember that 10,000 £ in Reputation & learning does not amount to a handfull of Shillings in ready Cash! — One considerable advantage which you promise yourself by coming to this Colony is to extend the Limits of your acquaintance; this is laudable, & if you have enough of pru- dence & firmness, it will be of singular advantage — Yet attempt slowly & with the most Jealous Circumspection — If you fix your familiarity wrong in a single instance, you are in danger of total, if not immediate ruin — You come here, it is true, with an intention to teach, but you ought likewise to have an inclination to learn. At any rate I solemnly injoin it upon you, that you never suffer the spirit of a Pedagogue to attend you without the walls of your little Seminary. In all promiscuous Company be as silent & attentive as Decency will allow you, for you have nothing to communicate, which such company, will hear with pleasure, but you may learn many things which, in after life, will do you singular service. — In regard to Company in general, if you think it worth the while to at- tend to my example, I can easily instruct you in the manner of my Conduct in this respect. I commonly attend Church; and often, at the request of Gentlemen, after Service according to the custom, dine abroad on Sunday — I seldom fail, when invited by Mr or Mrs

Carter, of going out with them; but I make it a point, however strongly solicited to the contrary, to return home with them too — Except in one of these cases, I seldom go out, but with a valuable variety of books I live according to Horace's direction, & love *"Secretum Iter et fallentis Semita Vitae."* Close retirement and a life by Stealth. The last direction I shall venture to mention on this head, is, that you abstain totally from Women. What I would have you understand from this, is, that by a train of faultless conduct in the whole course of your tutorship, you make every Lady within the Sphere of your acquaintance, who is between twelve & forty years of age, so much pleased with your person, & so fully satisfied as to your abilities in the capacity of — a Teacher; & in short, fully convinced, that, from a principle of Duty, you have, both by night & by day endeavoured to acquit yourself honourably, in the Character of a Tutor; & that, on this account, you have their free & hearty consent, without making any manner of demand upon you, either to stay longer in the County with them, which they would choose, or whenever your business calls you away, that they may not have it in their Power either by charms or Justice to detain you, & when you must leave them, have their sincere wishes & constant prayrs for Length of days & much prosperity, I therefore beg that you will attend litterally to this advice, & abstain totally from Women. But this last precaution, which I have been at some pains to dress in the plainest language, I am much inclined to think, will be wholly useless in regard to you, notwithstanding it is founded in that *Honour* and *Equity* which is on all hands allow'd to be due from one Sex to the other, & to many of your *age,* & *Standing* no doubt would be entirely salutary. Because the necessary connections which you have had with the Fair, from your Puberty upwards have been so unfavourable & ill-fated, that instead of apprehending any danger on the score of over fondness, I am fearful your rancour has grown so inveterate at length, as, not only to preserve you, in thought & practice, pure of every Fleshly foible, but has carried you so far towards the other extream, as that you will need many persuasions, when your circumstances shall seem to require it, to bring you back to a rational & manly habit of thinking & acting with respect to the Sex; which yet, after all (& eternally will continue to

267

be, tho it is so much courted & whined after) if considered in the fullest manner, & set forth to the best advantage, never rises above its divine definition Viz "The weaker Vessel." But without detaining you any longer with a matter merely depending on accident or Circumstance I pass on to the second General Head; in which *"Ludis atque Jocis amotis"* I shall offer to your consideration & recommend for your practice several Rules concerning the management of the School.

2. You will act wisely, if, from the begining, you convince all your Scholars which you may easily do, of your abilities in the several branches, which you shall profess to teach; you are not to tell them, *totidem Verbis*, "that you understand, perhaps as well as any man on the Continent both the Latin & Greek Classicks": "& have gone through the usual Course in the noted College of New-Jersey, under Dr Witherspoon, so universally known & admired, where you have studied Criticism, Oratory, History, not to mention Mathematical & philosophical Studies, & dipt a good way into the French-Language, & that you have learn'd a smattering of Dancing, Cards &c. &c. &c." For Dun–p or Hack—n or the most profound dunce in your College or School would have too much sense to pass such impudence by, & not despise and reproach it; but you may speedily & certainly make them think you a "Clever Fellow" (which is a phrase in use here for a good Scholar) if you never mention any thing before them, only what you seem to be wholly master of — This will teach them never to dispute your determination, & always to rely upon your Judgment; two things which are most essential for your peace, & their advantage. That you may avoid yourself of this with certainty I shall recommend for your practice the following method, as useful at least, if not intirely necessary. Read over carefully, the lessons in Latin & Greek, in your leisure hours, that the story & Language be fresh in your memory, when you are hearing the respective lessons; for your memory is treacherous, & I am pretty certain it would confound you if you should be accosted by a pert School-Boy, in the midst of a blunder, with "Physician heal thyself"! — You ought likewise to do this with those who are working Figures; probably you may think that because the highest Cypherer is only in decimal arithmetic, it is not therefore worth your

critical attention to be looking previously into the several Sums. But you are to consider that a sum in the Square-Root, or even in the Single Rule of three direct, is to your Pupils of as great importance, as the most abstruse problem in the Mathematicks to an able artist; & you may lay this down for a Maxim, that they will reckon upon your abilities, according as they find you acquainted & expert in what they themselves are studying. If therefore you have resolution (as I do not question your ability) to carry this plan which I have laid down into execution; you will thereby convince them of the propriety of their Subordination to you, & obedience to your instructions, so that you may lead them, without any resistance, and fix them to the Study of whatever Science you think proper, in which they will rise according to their respective Capacities. I have said that you ought to strive "from the beginning" in fixing this very material article in the minds of your Scholars, Viz a Sense of your authority; for one error of Judgment, or false determination will diminish your Ability with them more than doing forty things with truth would increase your authority — They act in this case as you would do in the company of a number of Strangers — A whole evenings conversation, if it was tolerable good Sense, would perhaps make little or no impression on you; But if through hast in speaking, or inattention, any one should let fall a sentence either remarkably foolish, or grossly wicked, it would be difficult if not impossible to persuade you presently that the author was not either a *thick-Scull*, or a *Villain!* — The education of children requires constant unremitting attention. The meanest qualification you can mention in a useful teacher is *diligence* And without diligence no possible abilities or qualifications can bring children on either with speed or profit. There must be a Combination of qualifications which must all operate strongly & uniformly. In short, give this said Pedagogizing the softest name you will, it is still a "difficult Task." You will meet with numberless difficulties, in your new employment, which you never dreamt had yet existence. All these you must endeavour to resist & Subdue. This I have seen compared to a Man swimming against a current of Water. But I am mistaken if you will agree, after having six months practice, that the comparison be strong as the truth: You will add to the figure, I am certain, & throw into the Current sharp fragments of *Ice,* & *Blocks,* which would make swimming not only difficult but dangerous! I am not urging these things to discourage you; they are hints for your direction, which, if you will attend to, tho' at first the practice seem rough & unpleasant, shall yet make the remainder of your task pleasing, & the whole of it useful, I will mention several of these Obstacles that you may the more easily guard against them. You will, in the first place, be often solicited, probably oftner than you would wish, to ride abroad; this, however, if you do it moderately, & in seasonable time, & go to proper company, I recommend as conducive to health to one in your sedentary manner of living. But if you go much into company, you will find it extremely difficult to break away with any manner of credit till very late at night or in most cases for several days, & if you are wanting to your School, you do manifest injury to your Imployer. In this case, I advise you to copy Mr *Carter.* Whenever he invites you, ride. You may *stay,* and talk, & drink, & ride to as great excess as he; & may with safety associate yourself with those whom you find to be his intimates. In all other Cases, except when you ride to Church, at least till you are very intimate in the Colony, you had better ride to a certain Stump, or to some noted plantation, or pretty landscape; you will have in this every advantage of exercise, the additional advantage of undisturbed Meditation, & you will be under no Jealous apprehension in point of behaviour, nor any restraint as to the time of your return.

Another current difficulty will be petitions for holidays. You must have good deal of steadiness if you are able to evade cleverly this practice which has grown so habitual to your little charge from a false method in their early education that they absolutely claim it as a necessary right.

You must also as much as you can, avoid visible partiality. At least you must never suffer your fondness for one Scholar to grow so manifest, as that all your School shall see you look over a fault in him or her which same fault, if commited by another, you severely chastise. This will certainly produce in the others hatred & contempt. A fourth difficulty, and the last I shall mention, consists in knowing when, & in what measure to give the Boys Liberty to go from Home. The two younger Boys are wholly under your inspection; so that not

270

only the progress they make in learning, but their moral Conduct (for both of these are critically observed & examined) either justifies or condemns your management to the World. If you keep them much at home, & close to business, they themselves will call you unfeeling and cruel; & refuse to be industrious; if you suffer them to go much abroad they are certainly out of the way of improvement by Study, probably, by discovering their gross Ignorance, they will expose to ridicule both themselves & all their former instructors, & possibly they may commit actual Crimes so as very much to injure themselves; & scandalize their family; but in each of these you will have a large share of blame, perhaps more than the parents, or even the Boys themselves — It will be said that the parents gave them no license relying wholly on your Judgment & prudence, this will in good measure Justify them to the world. And as to the Boys they are full of youthful impetuosity & vigour, & these compel them, when they are free of restraint, to commit actions which with proper management they had surely avoided. I say, when you lay these things together, & view them on every side you will find so many perplexities arising in your mind, from a sense of ignorance of your duty, that you will proceed with caution & moderation, & will be careful to examine with some precision into the circumstances of *time, company,* & *Business* when you license them to go out entirely at the risk of your Reputation — But the practice of three or four Weeks will give you a more full notion of these & many other incidents than I am able now either to recollect or express; I shall have gained my End if these hints prevent you from setting off wrong, & doing inadvertantly at first what your Scholars will assert to be precedents for your after conduct. I go on, therefore, in the third place as I proposed,

3. To mention several Rules for your personal conduct. The happy Education which you have had in point of religion, you ought to consider as an important and distinguishing Blessing of Heaven. That train of useful *Instruction, Advice* & *Example* to which you have been accustomed from your infancy is a more perfect, & will be a safer guide in your future walk, than any directions I am able to give you. You have taken notice of a method for Assistance in Composition, which Longinus recommends.

Place, says he, in imagination, several eminent ancient Authors before your Eyes, & suppose that they inspect your Work, a Sense of inferiority would make you diligent, & your composition accurate. Perhaps the same advice when transferr'd to Morality, would be equally salutary. Unless it be objected that a Belief of Gods presence at all times in every place is the strongest possible restraint against committing Sin. This I constantly admit; but when I consider how easily our minds are put in motion, & how strongly they are sometimes agitated merely by the senses, & that the senses are affected most by things which fall under their immediate notice, I am fully convinced that if some such plans as I have just mentioned should be fallen upon, & practiced, it would make a visible and useful change in our behaviour — In this place I think it needful to caution you against hasty & ill founded prejudices. When you enter among a people, & find that their manner of living, their *Eating, Drinking, Diversions, Exercise* &c, are in many respects different from any thing you have been accustomed to, you will be apt to fix your opinion in an instant, & (as some divines deal with poor Sinners) you will condemn all before you without any meaning or distinction what seems in your Judgment disagreeable at first view, when you are smitten with the novelty. You will be making ten thousand Comparisons. The face of the Country, The *Soil*, the *Buildings*, the *Slaves*, the *Tobacco*, the method of spending *Sunday* among Christians; *Ditto* among the Negroes; the three grand divisions of time at the Church on Sundays, Viz. before Service giving and receiving letters of business, reading Advertisements, consulting about the price of Tobacco, Grain &c, & settling either the lineage, Age, or qualities of favourite Horses 2. In the Church at Service, prayrs read over in haste, a Sermon seldom under & never over twenty minutes, but always made up of sound morality, or deep studied Metaphysicks. 3. After Service is over three quarters of an hour spent in strolling round the Church among the Crowd, in which time you will be invited by several different Gentlemen home with them to dinner. The Balls, the Fish-Feasts, the Dancing-Schools, the Christnings, the Cock fights, the Horse-Races, the Chariots, the Ladies Masked, for it is a custom among the Westmorland Ladies whenever they go from home, to muffle up their heads, & Necks, leaving only a narrow passage for the Eyes, in Cotton or silk handkerchiefs; I was in distress for them when I first came into the Colony, for every Woman that I saw abroad, I looked upon as ill either with the *Mumps* or Tooth-Ach! — I say, you will be often observing & comparing these things which I have enumerated, & many more that now escape me, with the manner of spending Money time & credit at Cohansie: You are young, &, (you will allow me the Expression) in the morning of Life. But I hope you have plann'd off, and entered upon the work which is necessary to be performed in the course of your Day; if not, I think it my duty to acquaint you, that a combination of the amusements which I have just now mentioned, being always before your Eyes, & inviting your Compliance will have a strong tendency to keep you doubtful & unsettled, in your notions of Morality & Religion, or else will fix you in a false & dangerous habit of *thinking* & *acting*, which must terminate at length in Sorrow & despair. You are therefore, if you count any thing upon the value of my advice, to fix the plan in which you would spend your life; let this be done with deliberation, Candour, & precision, looking to him for direction, by fervent Prayr, who is the "Wonderful Counsellor"; & when you have done this, let no importunity of whatever kind prevail over you, & cause you to transgress your own Limitations. I have already exceeded the usual bounds of an Epistle. But you will easily pardon a little prolixity, when I assure you it flows from a heart deeply impressed with a sense of the many difficulties which you must encounter, & the dangers which will surround you when you come first out from the peaceful recess of Contemplation, & enter, young and unexperienced, into the tumultuous undiscerning World. I submit these hints to your consideration, & have nothing more than sincere & ardent wishes for your present & perpetual Felicity.

I am, Sir,

yours.

PHILIP V. FITHIAN.

To Mr John Peck.

On going to Virginia in Character of a Tutor.

PATRICK HENRY

1736-1799

Patrick Henry, Revolutionary patriot and governor of Virginia, was born at Studley, Hanover County, Virginia, on March 29, 1736. His father was a Virginia County judge. Young Henry was admitted to the bar at the age of twenty-four and rapidly built up a large practice. When he was twenty-seven he argued the "Parson's Case," which made him one of the best known and most popular lawyers in Virginia.

He was elected to the Virginia House of Burgesses and there, still in his twenties, he was the author of the "Virginia Resolutions," which were an important step toward American independence. In support of the resolutions, he delivered the address containing the famous words: "Caesar had his Brutus, Charles the First his Cromwell, and George the Third —" here were cries of "Treason! Treason!"—"and George the Third may profit by their example. If this be treason, make the most of it."

He was a leading member of the revolutionary Committee of Correspondence and was a delegate from Virginia to the Continental Congress. In 1775 he urged the arming of Virginia, eloquently supporting his proposal in the address which follows (as printed in William Wirt's *Sketches of the Life and Character of Patrick Henry*).

His proposal was carried, and for a time he served as the chief commander of the Virginia forces. In 1776 he counseled postponement of the Declaration of Independence until the colonies had won foreign support. He helped draw up the first Constitution of Virginia in 1776, and was elected governor of Virginia in that year and in 1777 and 1778, serving the maximum continuous period permitted by the Constitution. He was active in the Virginia legislature and served again as governor in 1784, 1785 and 1786. With George Mason and Richard Henry Lee, he opposed the adoption of the Federal Constitution on the grounds that it did not provide sufficient protection against despotism.

During the last five years of his life he declined an impressive series of public offices: Senator from Virginia, Secretary of State under President Washington, Chief Justice of the Supreme Court, Governor of Virginia and Envoy to France. He died in Virginia on June 6, 1799.

TO THE VIRGINIA CONVENTION

Mr. President, it is natural to man to indulge in the illusions of hope. We are apt to shut our eyes against a painful truth — and listen to the song of that siren, till she transforms us into beasts. Is this the part of wise men, engaged in a great and arduous struggle for liberty? Are we disposed to be of the number of those who, having eyes, see not, and having ears, hear not, the things which so nearly concern their temporal salvation? For my part, whatever anguish of spirit it may cost, I am willing to know the whole truth; to know the worst, and to provide for it.

I have but one lamp by which my feet are guided, and that is the lamp of experience. I know of no way of judging the future but by the past. And judging by the past, I wish to know what there has been in the conduct of the British ministry for the last ten years to justify those hopes with which gentlemen have been pleased to solace themselves and the house? Is it that insidious smile with which our petition has been lately received? Trust it not, sir; it will prove a snare to your feet. Suffer not yourself to be betrayed with a kiss. Ask yourself how this gracious reception of our petition comports with those warlike preparations which cover our waters and darken our land. Are fleets and armies necessary to a work of love and reconciliation? Have we shown ourselves so unwilling to be reconciled that force must be called in to win back our love? Let us not deceive ourselves, sir. These are the implements of war and subjugation — the last arguments to which kings resort. I ask gentlemen, sir, what means this martial array if its purpose be not to force us to submission? Can gentlemen assign any other possible motive to it? Has Great Britain any enemy in this quarter of the world, to call for this accumulation of navies and armies? No, sir, she has none. They are meant for us: they can be meant for no other. They are sent over to bind and rivet upon us those chains which the British ministry have been so long forging. And what have we to oppose

275

to them? Shall we try arguments? Sir, we have been trying that for the last ten years. Have we anything new to offer upon the subject? Nothing. We have the subject up in every light of which it is capable; but it has been all in vain. Shall we resort to entreaty and humble supplication? What terms shall we find which have not been already exhausted? Let us not, I beseech you, sir, deceive ourselves longer. Sir, we have done everything that could be done to avert the storm which is now coming on. We have petitioned — we have remonstrated — we have supplicated — we have prostrated ourselves before the throne, and we have implored its interposition to arrest the tyrannical hands of the ministry and Parliament. Our petitions have been slighted; our remonstrances have produced additional violence and insult; our supplications have been disregarded; and we have been spurned with contempt from the foot of the throne. In vain, after these things, may we indulge the fond hope of peace and reconciliation. There is no longer any room for hope. If we wish to be free — if we mean to preserve inviolate those inestimable privileges for which we have been so long contending — if we mean not basely to abandon the noble struggle in which we have been so long engaged, and which we have pledged ourselves never to abandon until the glorious object of our contest shall be obtained — we must fight! — I repeat it, sir, we must fight; an appeal to arms and to the God of Hosts is all that is left us!

They tell us, sir, that we are weak — unable to cope with so formidable an adversary. But when shall we be stronger? Will it be the next week or the next year? Will it be when we are totally disarmed, and when a British guard shall be stationed in every house? Shall we gather strength by irresolution and inaction? Shall we acquire the means of effectual resistance by lying supinely on our backs and hugging the delusive phantom of hope, until our enemy shall have bound us hand and foot? Sir, we are not weak, if we make a proper use of those forces which the God of nature hath placed in our power. Three millions of people armed in the holy cause of liberty, and in such a country as that which we possess, are invincible by any force which our enemy can send against us. Besides, sir, we shall not fight our battles alone. There is a just God who presides over the destinies of nations, and who will raise up friends to fight our battles for us. The battle, sir, is not to the strong alone; it is to the vigilant, the active, the brave. Besides, sir, we have no election. If we were base enough to desire it, it is now too late to retire from the contest. There is no retreat but in submission and slavery! Our chains are forged. Their clanking may be heard on the plains of Boston! The war is inevitable — and let it come! ! I repeat it, sir, let it come! ! !

It is vain, sir, to extenuate the matter. Gentlemen may cry, Peace, peace — but there is no peace. The war is actually begun! The next gale that sweeps from the north will bring to our ears the clash of resounding arms! Our brethren are already in the field! Why stand we here idle? What is it that gentlemen wish? What would they have? Is life so dear, or peace so sweet, as to be purchased at the price of chains and slavery? Forbid it, Almighty God! I know not what course others may take; but as for me, give me liberty, or give me death!

THOMAS JEFFERSON
1743-1826

Thomas Jefferson, America's most brilliant apostle of democracy, was born at Shadwell, in Albermarle County, Virginia, on April 13, 1743. His father, Peter Jefferson, was a substantial landowner of the Virginia upcountry. His mother, Jane Randolph, was a member of one of the most prominent families of the tidewater aristocracy. "They trace their pedigree far back in England and Scotland," Jefferson wrote pithily, "to which let every one ascribe the faith and merit he chooses."

As a youth Jefferson enjoyed the advantages of social position but grew up in the democratic-minded Virginia frontier. He received an excellent education, was graduated from the College of William and Mary when he was twenty, further pursued his studies in science and languages independently (he had a good knowledge of Greek, Latin, French, Anglo-Saxon, Spanish and Italian) and studied law under George Wythe, the leader of the Virginia bar.

He was admitted to the bar in 1767 and rapidly built up a successful practice, but when at the beginning of the Revolution he turned his back on the profession he left it with few regrets and no very high opinion of lawyers. He was elected to the Virginia House of Burgesses in 1769 and was reelected to every assembly until the Revolution. He became a figure of conspicuous influence, and with Patrick Henry and others vigorously championed the cause of American liberty. In 1774 he prepared A Summary View of the Rights of British America, which considered the basic issues of allegiance and natural rights. It was considered too radical a document for adoption by the Virginia Convention, but was widely distributed as a pamphlet and on both sides of the Atlantic it attracted attention to its author as a foremost intellectual leader of the revolutionary movement.

Jefferson was elected to the Continental Congress in 1775 and there he drew up the reply of the Congress to Lord North's proposals to the colonies. The following year he had the responsibility of drafting the most important document in American history, the Declaration of Independence. Benjamin Franklin, John Adams and others made some changes in Jefferson's draft, but the language of that momentous document is his. Had he died at the age of thirty-three his place in the history of America

278

Thomas Jefferson, 1743-1826

— and in the history of man's struggle for freedom the world over — would have been secure.

With the adoption of the Declaration of Independence, Jefferson returned to Virginia. As a member of the House of Delegates and as Governor, he devoted himself to the achievement in his native state of the "inherent and inalienable rights" of man which he had championed before the world in the Declaration of Independence. He succeeded in abolishing the laws of primogeniture and entails, which were the foundation of the old order of great landed estates. He fought for public education as a bulwark of democracy, and with Madison he led the struggle for freedom of conscience and the separation of church and state. It was his purpose to form "a system by which every trace would be eradicated of ancient or future aristocracy, and a foundation laid for a government truly republican." The text of his Act for Religious Freedom in Virginia, which he ranked with the authorship of the Declaration of Independence and the founding of the University of Virginia as one of the three accomplishments for which he cared to be remembered, is included in the brief selection of his writings which follows.

Upon his retirement from the Governorship of Virginia, a post in which he served during one of the darkest periods of the Revolution, Jefferson returned to "Monticello" and sincerely hoped to remain a private citizen the rest of his life. He devoted himself to his increasingly large correspondence, to the many activities of his estate, and prepared his *Notes on Virginia* in reply to a series of inquiries by the Marquis de Barbé-Marbois. The *Notes on Virginia* was later published by Jefferson in Paris in 1784, where its humanitarian liberalism made a deep impression, and it was reprinted in French, German, English and American editions.

Jefferson, however, was not to remain a private citizen. The democracy of which he was the ablest champion was to be achieved only by a continuing struggle — one which is still continuing — and he reluctantly left his beloved "Monticello" for the public arena. As Minister to France, Secretary of State under President Washington, Vice-President and President of the United States, he devoted his strength during the next thirty years to the "hated occupation" of politics. He became the symbol of republican government, in opposition to the "Anglican, monarchical, aristocratical party" which grew up around Alexander Hamilton. It was not until the end of his second term as President that he at last returned to "Monticello," to devote himself to his intellectual pursuits, to his plans for the University of Virginia, to his friends and correspondents, to his books and gardens and fields. There he died on July 4, 1826.

AN ACT FOR ESTABLISHING RELIGIOUS FREEDOM IN VIRGINIA

Proposed in 1779 and Enacted by the General Assembly in 1786

Well aware that Almighty God hath created the mind free; that all attempts to influence it by temporal punishments or burdens, or by civil incapacitations, tend only to beget habits of hypocrisy and meanness, and are a departure from the plan of the Holy Author of our religion, who being Lord both of body and mind, yet chose not to propagate it by coercion on either, as was in his Almighty power to do; that the impious presumption of legislators and rulers, civil as well as ecclesiastical, who, being themselves but fallible and uninspired men have assumed dominion over the faith of others, setting up their own opinions and modes of thinking as the only true and infallible, and as such endeavoring to impose them on others, hath established and maintained false religions over the greatest part of the world, and through all time; that to compel a man to furnish contributions of money for the propagation of opinions which he disbelieves, is sinful and tyrannical; that even the forcing him to support this or that teacher of his own religious persuasion, is depriving him of the comfortable liberty of giving his contributions to the particular pastor whose morals he would make his pattern, and whose powers he feels most persuasive to righteousness, and is withdrawing from the ministry those temporal rewards, which proceeding from an approbation of their personal conduct, are an additional incitement to earnest and unremitting labors for the instruction of mankind; that our civil rights have no dependence on our religious opinions, more than our opinions in physics or geometry; that, therefore, the proscribing any citizen as unworthy the public confidence by laying upon him an incapacity of being called to the offices of trust and emolument, unless he profess or renounce this or that religious opinion, is depriving him injuriously of those privileges and advantages to which in common with his fellow citizens he has a natural

280

right; that it tends also to corrupt the principles of that very religion it is meant to encourage, by bribing, with a monopoly of worldly honors and emoluments, those who will externally profess and conform to it; that though indeed these are criminal who do not withstand such temptation, yet neither are those innocent who lay the bait in their way; that to suffer the civil magistrate to intrude his powers into the field of opinion and to restrain the profession or propagation of principles, on the supposition of their ill tendency, is a dangerous fallacy, which at once destroys all religious liberty, because he being of course judge of that tendency, will make his opinions the rule of judgment, and approve or condemn the sentiments of others only as they shall square with or differ from his own; that it is time enough for the rightful purposes of civil government, for its offices to interfere when principles break out into overt acts against peace and good order; and finally, that truth is great and will prevail if left to herself, that she is the proper and sufficient antagonist to error, and has nothing to fear from the conflict, unless by human interposition disarmed by her natural weapons, free argument and debate, errors ceasing to be dangerous when it is permitted freely to contradict them.

Be it therefore enacted by the General Assembly, That no man shall be compelled to frequent or support any religious worship, place or ministry whatsoever, nor shall be enforced, restrained, molested, or burthened in his body or goods, nor shall otherwise suffer on account of his religious opinions or belief; but that all men shall be free to profess, and by argument to maintain, their opinions in matters of religion, and that the same shall in nowise diminish, enlarge, or affect their civil capacities.

And though we well know this Assembly, elected by the people for the ordinary purposes of legislation only, have no power to restrain the acts of succeeding assemblies, constituted with the powers equal to our own, and that therefore to declare this act irrevocable, would be of no effect in law, yet we are free to declare, and do declare, that the rights hereby asserted are of the natural rights of mankind, and that if any act shall be hereafter passed to repeal the present or to narrow its operation, such act will be an infringement of natural right.

Virginia Reader

"IT IS ERROR ALONE WHICH NEEDS THE SUPPORT OF GOVERNMENT . . ."

From *Notes On Virginia,* Query xvii, The different
religions received into that State?

. . . This is a summary view of that religious slavery under which
a people have been willing to remain, who have lavished their lives
and fortunes for the establishment of their civil freedom. The error
seems not sufficiently eradicated, that the operations of the mind,
as well as the acts of the body, are subject to the coercion of the
laws. But our rulers can have no authority over such natural rights,
only as we have submitted to them. The rights of conscience we
never submitted, we could not submit. We are answerable for them
to our God. The legitimate powers of government extend to such
acts only as are injurious to others. But it does me no injury for my
neighbor to say there are twenty gods, or no God. It neither picks my
pocket nor breaks my leg. If it be said, his testimony in a court of
justice cannot be relied on, reject it then, and be the stigma on him.
Constraint may make him worse by making him a hypocrite, but
it will never make him a truer man. It may fix him obstinately in his
errors, but will not cure them. Reason and free inquiry are the only
effectual agents against error. Give a loose to them, they will support the true religion by bringing every false one to their tribunal,
to the test of their investigation. They are the natural enemies of
error, and of error only. Had not the Roman government permitted
free inquiry, Christianity could never have been introduced. Had
not free inquiry been indulged at the era of the Reformation, the
corruptions of Christianity could not have been purged away. If it
be restrained now, the present corruptions will be protected, and
new ones encouraged. Was the government to prescribe to us our
medicine and diet, our bodies would be in such keeping as our souls
are now. Thus in France the emetic was once forbidden as a medicine, and the potato as an article of food. Government is just as infallible, too, when it fixes systems in physics. Galileo was sent to the

Thomas Jefferson, 1743-1826

Inquisition for affirming that the earth was a sphere; the government had declared it to be as flat as a trencher, and Galileo was obliged to abjure his error. This error, however, at length prevailed, the earth became a globe, and Descartes declared it was whirled round its axis by a vortex. The government in which he lived was wise enough to see that this was no question of civil jurisdiction, or we should all have been involved by authority in vortices. In fact, the vortices have been exploded, and the Newtonian principle of gravitation is now more firmly established, on the basis of reason, than it would be were the government to step in, and to make it an article of necessary faith. Reason and experiment have been indulged, and error has fled before them. It is error alone which needs the support of government. Truth can stand by itself. Subject opinion to coercion: whom will you make your inquisitors? Fallible men; men governed by bad passions, by private as well as public reasons. And why subject it to coercion? To produce uniformity. But is uniformity of opinion desirable? No more than of face and stature. Introduce the bed of Procrustes then, and as there is danger that the large men may beat the small, make us all of a size, by lopping the former and stretching the latter. Difference of opinion is advantageous in religion. The several sects perform the office of a *censor morum* over such other. Is uniformity attainable? Millions of innocent men, women, and children, since the introduction of Christianity, have been burnt, tortured, fined, imprisoned; yet we have not advanced one inch toward uniformity. What has been the effect of coercion? To make one half the world fools, and the other half hypocrites. To support roguery and error all over the earth. Let us reflect that it is inhabited by a thousand millions of people. That these profess probably a thousand different systems of religion. That ours is but one of that thousand. That if there be but one right, and ours that one, we should wish to see the nine hundred and ninety-nine wandering sects gathered into the fold of truth. But against such a majority we cannot effect this by force. Reason and persuasion are the only practicable instruments. To make way for these, free inquiry must be indulged; and how can we wish others to indulge it while we refuse it ourselves. But every State, says an inquisitor, has established some religion. No two, say I, have established the

283

same. Is this proof of the infallibility of establishments? Our sister States of Pennsylvania and New York, however, have long subsisted without any establishment at all. The experiment was new and doubtful when they made it. It has answered beyond conception. They flourish infinitely. Religion is well supported; of various kinds, indeed, but all good enough; all sufficient to preserve peace and order; or if a sect arises, whose tenets would subvert morals, good sense has fair play, and reasons and laughs it out of doors, without suffering the State to be troubled with it. They do not hang more malefactors than we do. They are not more disturbed with religious dissensions. On the contrary, their harmony is unparalleled, and can be ascribed to nothing but their unbounded tolerance, because there is no other circumstance in which they differ from every nation on earth. They have made the happy discovery, that the way to silence religious disputes, is to take no notice of them. Let us too give this experiment fair play, and get rid, while we may, of those tyrannical laws. It is true, we are as yet secured against them by the spirit of the times. I doubt whether the people of this country would suffer an execution for heresy, or a three years' imprisonment for not comprehending the mysteries of the Trinity. But is the spirit of the people an infallible, a permanent reliance? Is it government? Is this the kind of protection we receive in return for the rights we give up? Besides, the spirit of the times may alter, will alter. Our rulers will become corrupt, our people careless. A single zealot may commence persecutor, and better men be his victims. It can never be too often repeated, that the time for fixing every essential right on a legal basis is while our rulers are honest, and ourselves united. From the conclusion of this war we shall be going down hill. It will not then be necessary to resort every moment to the people for support. They will be forgotten, therefore, and their rights disregarded. They will forget themselves, but in the sole faculty of making money, and will never think of uniting to effect a due respect for their rights. The shackels, therefore, which shall not be knocked off at the conclusion of this war, will remain on us long, will be made heavier and heavier, till our rights shall revive or expire in a convulsion.

Thomas Jefferson, 1743-1826

"AN UNHAPPY INFLUENCE ON THE MANNERS OF OUR PEOPLE . . ."

From *Notes On Virginia*, Query xviii, The particular customs and manners that may happen to be received in that State?

It is difficult to determine on the standard by which the manners of a nation may be tried, whether *catholic* or *particular*. It is more difficult for a native to bring to that standard the manners of his own nation, familiarized to him by habit. There must doubtless be an unhappy influence on the manners of our people produced by the existence of slavery among us. The whole commerce between master and slave is a perpetual exercise of the most boisterous passions, the most unremitting despotism on the one part, and degrading submissions on the other. Our children see this, and learn to imitate it; for man is an imitative animal. This quality is the germ of all education in him. From his cradle to his grave he is learning to do what he sees others do. If a parent could find no motive either in his philanthropy or his self-love, for restraining the intemperance of passion towards his slave, it should always be a sufficient one that his child is present. But generally it is not sufficient. The parent storms, the child looks on, catches the lineaments of wrath, puts on the same airs in the circle of smaller slaves, gives a loose to the worst of passions, and thus nursed, educated, and daily exercised in tyranny, cannot but be stamped by it with odious peculiarities. The man must be a prodigy who can retain his manners and morals undepraved by such circumstances. And with what execration should the statesman be loaded, who, permitting one half the citizens thus to trample on the rights of the other, transforms those into despots, and these into enemies, destroys the morals of the one part, and the *amor patriae* of the other. For if a slave can have a country in this world, it must be any other in preference to that in which he is born to live and labor for another; in which he must lock up the faculties of his nature, contribute as far as depends on his individual endeavors to the evanishment of the human race, to entail his own mis-

285

erable condition on the endless generations proceeding from him. With the morals of the people, their industry also is destroyed. For in a warm climate, no man will labor for himself who can make another labor for him. This is so true, that of the proprietors of slaves a very small proportion indeed are ever seen to labor. And can the liberties of a nation be thought secure when we have removed their only firm basis, a conviction in the minds of the people that these liberties are of the gift of God? That they are not to be violated but with his wrath? Indeed I tremble for my country when I reflect that God is just; that his justice cannot sleep forever; that considering numbers, nature and natural means only, a revolution of the wheel of fortune, an exchange of situation is among possible events; that it may become probable by supernatural interference! The Almighty has no attribute which can take side with us in such a contest. But it is impossible to be temperate and to pursue this subject through the various considerations of policy, of morals, of history natural and civil. We must be contented to hope they will force their way into every one's mind. I think a change already perceptible, since the origin of the present revolution. The spirit of the master is abating, that of the slave rising from the dust, his condition mollifying, the way I hope preparing, under the auspices of heaven, for a total emancipation, and that this is disposed, in the order of events, to be with the consent of the masters, rather than by their extirpation.

"A LITTLE REBELLION, NOW AND THEN, IS A GOOD THING . . ."

From a Letter to James Madison, January 30, 1787

My last to you was of the 16th of December; since which, I have received yours of November the 25th, and December the 4th, which afforded me, as your letters always do, a treat on matters public, individual and economical. I am impatient to learn your sentiments on the late troubles in the Eastern States.[1] So far as I have yet seen,

[1]Shays' Rebellion.

Thomas Jefferson, 1743-1826

they do not appear to threaten serious consequences. Those States have suffered by the stoppage of the channels of their commerce, which have not yet found other issues. This must render money scarce, and make the people uneasy. This uneasiness has produced acts absolutely unjustifiable; but I hope they will provoke no severities from their governments. A consciousness of those in power that their administration of the public affairs has been honest, may, perhaps, produce too great a degree of indignation; and those characters, wherein fear predominates over hope, may apprehend too much from these instances of irregularity. They may conclude too hastily, that nature has formed man insusceptible of any other government than that of force, a conclusion not founded in truth nor experience. Societies exist under three forms, sufficiently distinguishable. 1. Without government, as among our Indians. 2. Under governments, wherein the will of every one has a just influence; as is the case in England, in a slight degree, and in our States, in a great one. 3. Under governments of force; as is the case in all other monarchies, and in most of the other republics. To have an idea of the curse of existence under these last, they must be seen. It is a government of wolves over sheep. It is a problem, not clear in my mind, that the first condition is not the best. But I believe it to be inconsistent with any great degree of population. The second state has a great deal of good in it. The mass of mankind under that, enjoys a precious degree of liberty and happiness. It has its evils, too; the principal of which is the turbulence to which it is subject. But weigh this against the oppressions of monarchy, and it becomes nothing. *Malo periculosam libertatem quam quietam servitutem.*[2] Even this evil is productive of good. It prevents the degeneracy of government, and nourishes a general attention to the public affairs. I hold it, that a little rebellion, now and then, is a good thing, and as necessary in the political world as storms in the physical. Unsuccessful rebellions, indeed, generally establish the encroachments on the rights of the people, which have produced them. An observation of this truth should render honest republican governors so mild in their punishment of rebellions, as not to discourage them too much. It is a medicine necessary for the sound health of government.

[2] I prefer freedom with danger to slavery with ease.

Virginia Reader

"THE TREE OF LIBERTY MUST BE REFRESHED WITH THE BLOOD OF TYRANTS . . ."

From a Letter to William S. Smith, November 13, 1787

. . . The British ministry have so long hired their gazetteers to repeat, and model into every form, lies about our being in anarchy, that the world has at length believed them, the English nation has believed them, the ministers themselves have come to believe them, and what is more wonderful, we have believed them ourselves. Yet where does this anarchy exist? Where did it ever exist, except in the single instance of Massachusetts? And can history produce an instance of rebellion so honorably conducted? I say nothing of its motives. They were founded in ignorance, not wickedness. God forbid we should ever be twenty years without such a rebellion. The people cannot be all, and always, well informed. The part which is wrong will be discontented, in proportion to the importance of the facts they misconceive. If they remain quiet under such misconceptions, it is a lethargy, the forerunner of death to the public liberty. We have had thirteen States independent for eleven years. There has been one rebellion. That comes to one rebellion in a century and a half, for each State. What country before, ever existed a century and a half without rebellion? And what country can preserve its liberties, if its rulers are not warned from time to time, that this people preserve the spirit of resistance? Let them take arms. The remedy is to set them right as to facts, pardon and pacify them. What signify a few lives lost in a century or two? The tree of liberty must be refreshed from time to time, with the blood of patriots and tyrants. It is its natural manure. Our convention has been too much impressed by the insurrection of Massachusetts . . .

Thomas Jefferson, 1743-1826

"RETURNING TO THE SCENES OF MY EARLY LIFE . . ."

Address to the People of Albemarle County, Virginia, April 3, 1809

Returning to the scenes of my birth and early life, to the society of those with whom I was raised, and who have been ever dear to me, I receive, fellow-citizens and neighbors, with inexpressible pleasure, the cordial welcome you were so good as to give me. Long absent on duties which the history of a wonderful era made incumbent on those called to them, the pomp, the turmoil, the bustle and splendor of office; have drawn but deeper sighs for the tranquil and irresponsible occupations of private life, for the enjoyment of an affectionate intercourse with you, my neighbors and friends, and the endearments of family love, which nature has given us all, as the sweetner of every hour. For these I gladly lay down the distressing burthen of power, and seek, with my fellow-citizens, repose and safety under the watchful cares, the labors and perplexities of younger and abler minds. The anxieties you express to administer to my happiness, do, of themselves, confer that happiness; and the measure will be complete, if any endeavors to fulfil my duties in the several public stations to which I have been called, have obtained for me the approbation of my country. The part which I have acted on the theatre of public life, has been before them; and to their sentence I submit it; but the testimony of my native county, of the individuals who have known me in private life, to my conduct in its various duties and relations, is the more grateful, as proceeding from eye-witnesses and observers, from triers of the vicinage. Of you, then, my neighbors, I may ask, in the face of the world, "Whose ox have I taken, or whom have I defrauded? Whom have I oppressed, or of whose hand have I received a bribe to blind mine eyes therewith?" On your verdict I rest with conscious security. Your wishes for my happiness are received with just sensibility, and I offer sincere prayers for your own welfare and prosperity.

"THERE IS AN ARTIFICIAL ARISTOCRACY, FOUNDED ON WEALTH AND BIRTH . . ."

From a Letter to John Adams, October 28, 1813

. . . For I agree with you that there is a natural aristocracy among men. The grounds of this are virtue and talents. Formerly, bodily powers gave place among the aristoi. But since the invention of gunpowder has armed the weak as well as the strong with missile death, bodily strength, like beauty, good humor, politeness and other accomplishments, has become but an auxiliary ground of distinction. There is also an artificial aristocracy, founded on wealth and birth, without either virtue or talents; for with these it would belong to the first class. The natural aristocracy I consider as the most precious gift of nature, for the instruction, the trusts, and government of society. And indeed, it would have been inconsistent in creation to have formed man for the social state, and not to have provided virtue and wisdom enough to manage the concerns of the society. May we not even say, that that form of government is the best, which provides the most effectually for a pure selection of these natural aristoi into the offices of government? The artificial aristocracy is a mischievous ingredient in government, and provision should be made to prevent its ascendency. On the question, what is the best provision, you and I differ; but we differ as rational friends, using the free exercise of our own reason, and mutually indulging its errors. You think it best to put the pseudo-aristoi into a separate chamber of legislation, where they may be hindered from doing mischief by their coordinate branches, and where, also, they may be a protection to wealth against the agrarian and plundering enterprises of the majority of the people. I think that to give them power in order to prevent them from doing mischief, is arming them for it, and increasing instead of remedying the evil. For if the co-ordinate branches can arrest their action, so may that of the co-ordinates. Mischief may be done negatively as well as positively. Of this, a cabal in the Senate of the United States has furnished many proofs.

Thomas Jefferson, 1743-1826

Nor do I believe them necessary to protect the wealthy; because enough of these will find their way into every branch of the legislation, to protect themselves. From fifteen to twenty legislatures of our own, in action for thirty years past, have proved that no fears of an equalization of property are to be apprehended from them. I think the best remedy is exactly that provided by all our constitutions, to leave to the citizens the free election and separation of the aristoi from the pseudo-aristoi, of the wheat from the chaff. In general they will elect the really good and wise. In some instances, wealth may corrupt, and birth may blind them; but not in sufficient degree to endanger the society.

It is probable that our difference of opinion may, in some measure, be produced by a difference of character in those among whom we live. From what I have seen of Massachusetts and Connecticut myself, and still more from what I have heard, and the character given of the former by yourself, who know them so much better, there seems to be in those two States a traditionary reverence for certain families, which has rendered the offices of the government nearly hereditary in those families. I presume that from an early period of your history, members of those families happening to possess virtue and talents, have honestly exercised them for the good of the people, and by their services have endeared their names to them. In coupling Connecticut with you, I mean it politically only, not morally. For having made the Bible the common law of their land, they seem to have modeled their morality on the story of Jacob and Laban. But although this hereditary succession to office with you, may, in some degree, be founded in real family merit, yet in a much higher degree, it has proceeded from your strict alliance of Church and State. These families are canonized in the eyes of the people on common principles, "you tickle me, and I will tickle you." In Virginia we have nothing of this. Our clergy, before the revolution, having been secured against rivalship by fixed salaries, did not give themselves the trouble of acquiring influence over the people. Of wealth, there were great accumulations in particular families, handed down from generation to generation, under the English law of entails. But the only object of ambition for the wealthy was a seat in the King's Council. All their court then was paid to the crown and its creatures; and they Philipized in all collisions between the King and the people. Hence they were unpopular; and that unpopularity continues attached to their names. A Randolph, a Carter, or a Burwell must have great personal superiority over a common competitor to be elected by the people even at this day. At the first session of our legislature after the Declaration of Independence, we passed a law abolishing entails. And this was followed by one abolishing the privilege of primogeniture, and dividing the lands of intestates equally among all their children, or other representatives. These laws, drawn by myself, laid the axe to the foot of pseudoaristocracy. And had another which I prepared been adopted by the legislature, our work would have been complete. It was a bill for the more general diffusion of learning. This proposed to divide every county into wards of five or six miles square, like your townships; to establish in each ward a free school for reading, writing and common arithmetic; to provide for the annual selection of the best subjects from these schools, who might receive, at the public expense, a higher degree of education at a district school; and from these district schools to select a certain number of the most promising subjects, to be completed at an university, where all the useful sciences should be taught. Worth and genius would thus have been sought out from every condition of life, and completely prepared by education for defeating the competition of wealth and birth for public trusts. My proposition had, for a further object, to impart to these wards those portions of self-government for which they are best qualified, by confiding to them the care of their poor, their roads, police, elections, the nomination of jurors, administration of justice in small cases, elementary exercises of militia; in short, to have made them little republics, with a warden at the head of each, for all those concerns which, being under their eye, they would better manage than the larger republics of the county or State. A general call of ward meetings by their wardens on the same day through the State, would at any time produce the genuine sense of the people on any required point, and would enable the State to act in mass, as your people have so often done, and with so much effect by their town meetings. The law for religious freedom, which made a part of this system, having put down the aristocracy of the clergy, and

restored to the citizen the freedom of the mind, and those of entails
and descents nurturing an equality of condition among them, this
on education would have raised the mass of the people to the high
ground of moral respectability necessary to their own safety, and
to orderly government; and would have completed the great object
of qualifying them to select the veritable aristoi, for the trusts of
government . . .

"NOTHING IS UNCHANGEABLE BUT THE UNALIENABLE RIGHTS OF MAN . . ."

From a Letter to John Cartwright, June 5, 1824

. . . You will perceive by these details, that we have not yet so far
perfected our constitutions as to venture to make them unchangeable. But still, in their present state, we consider them not otherwise
changeable than by the authority of the people, on a special election of representatives for that purpose expressly: they are until
then the *lex legum.*

But can they be made unchangeable? Can one generation bind another, and all others, in succession forever? I think not. The Creator
has made the earth for the living, not the dead. Rights and powers
can only belong to persons, not to things, not to mere matter, un-
endowed with will. The dead are not even things. The particles of
matter which composed their bodies, make part now of the bodies of
other animals, vegetables, or minerals, of a thousand forms. To what
then are attached the rights and powers they held while in the form
of men? A generation may bind itself as long as its majority continues in life; when that has disappeared, another majority is in
place, holds all the rights and powers their predecessors once held,
and may change their laws and institutions to suit themselves. Nothing then is unchangeable but the inherent and unalienable rights
of man.

Virginia Reader

"THE MASS OF MANKIND HAS NOT BEEN BORN WITH SADDLES ON THEIR BACKS . . ."

Jefferson's Last Letter, to Roger C. Weightman, June 24, 1826

Respected Sir, — The kind invitation I received from you, on the part of the citizens of the city of Washington, to be present with them at their celebration on the fiftieth anniversary of American Independence, as one of the surviving signers of an instrument pregnant with our own, and the fate of the world, is most flattering to myself, and heightened by the honorable accompaniment proposed for the comfort of such a journey. It adds sensibly to the sufferings of sickness, to be deprived by it of a personal participation in the rejoicings of that day. But acquiescence is a duty, under circumstances not placed among those we are permitted to control. I should, indeed, with peculiar delight, have met and exchanged there congratulations personally with the small band, the remnant of that host of worthies, who joined with us on that day, in the bold and doubtful election we were to make for our country, between submission or the sword; and to have enjoyed with them the consolatory fact, that our fellow citizens, after half a century of experience and prosperity, continue to approve the choice we made. May it be to the world, what I believe it will be, (to some parts sooner, to others later, but finally to all,) the signal of arousing men to burst the chains under which monkish ignorance and superstition had persuaded them to bind themselves, and to assume the blessings and security of self-government. That form which we have substituted, restores the free right to the unbounded exercise of reason and freedom of opinion. All eyes are opened, or opening, to the rights of man. The general spread of the light of science has already laid open to every view the palpable truth, that the mass of mankind has not been born with saddles on their backs, nor a favored few booted and spurred, ready to ride them legitimately, by the grace of God. These are grounds of hope for others. For ourselves, let the annual return of this day forever refresh our recollections of these rights, and an undiminished devotion to them.

I will ask permission here to express the pleasure with which I should have met my ancient neighbors of the city of Washington and its vicinities, with whom I passed so many years of a pleasing social intercourse; an intercourse which so much relieved the anxieties of the public cares, and left impressions so deeply engraved in my affections, as never to be forgotten. With my regret that ill health forbids me the gratification of an acceptance, be pleased to receive for yourself and those for whom you write, the assurance of my highest respect and friendly attachments.

JEFFERSON'S SUMMARY OF HIS OWN ACHIEVEMENTS

I have sometimes asked myself, whether my country is the better for my having lived at all? I do not know that it is. I have been the instrument of doing the following things; but they would have been done by others; some of them, perhaps, a little better.

The Rivanna had never been used for navigation; scarcely an empty canoe had ever passed down it. Soon after I came of age, I examined its obstructions, set on foot a subscription for removing them, got an Act of Assembly passed, and the thing effected, so as to be used completely and fully for carrying down all our produce.

The Declaration of Independence.

I proposed the demolition of the church establishment, and the freedom of religion. It could only be done by degrees; to wit, the Act of 1776, c. 2. exempted dissenters from contributions to the Church, and left the Church clergy to be supported by voluntary contributions of their own sect; was continued from year to year, and made perpetual 1779, c. 36. I prepared the act for religious freedom in 1777, as part of the revisal, which was not reported to the Assembly till 1779, and that particular law not passed till 1785, and then by the efforts of Mr. Madison.

The act putting an end to entails.

The act prohibiting the importation of slaves.

Virginia Reader

The act concerning citizens, and establishing the natural right of man to expatriate himself, at will.

The act changing the course of descents, and giving the inheritance to all the children, &c., equally, I drew as part of the revisal.

The act for apportioning crimes and punishments, part of the same work, I drew. When proposed to the legislature, by Mr. Madison, in 1785, it failed by a single vote. G. K. Taylor afterwards, in 1796, proposed the same subject; avoiding the adoption of any part of the diction of mine, the text of which had been studiously drawn in the technical terms of the law, so as to give no occasion for new questions by new expressions. When I drew mine, public labor was thought the best punishment to be substituted for death. But, while I was in France, I heard of a society in England, who had successfully introduced solitary confinement, and saw the drawing of a prison at Lyons, in France, formed on the idea of solitary confinement. And, being applied to by the Governor of Virginia for the plan of a Capitol and Prison, I sent him the Lyons plan, accompanying it with a drawing on a smaller scale, better adapted to our use. This was in June, 1786. Mr. Taylor very judiciously adopted this idea, (which had now been acted on in Philadelphia, probably from the English model) and substituted labor in confinement, to the public labor proposed by the Committee of revisal; which themselves would have done, had they been to act on the subject again. The public mind was ripe for this in 1796, when Mr. Taylor proposed it, and ripened chiefly by the experiment in Philadelphia; whereas, in 1785, when it had been proposed to our Assembly, they were not quite ripe for it.

In 1789 and 1790, I had a great number of olive plants, of the best kind, sent from Marseilles to Charleston, for South Carolina and Georgia. They were planted, and are flourishing; and, though not yet multiplied, they will be the germ of that cultivation in those States.

In 1790, I got a cask of heavy upland rice, from the river Denbigh, in Africa, about lat. 9°30′ North, which I sent to Charleston, in hopes it might supersede the culture of the wet rice, which renders South Carolina and Georgia so pestilential through the summer. It was divided, and a part sent to Georgia. I know not whether it has been attended to in South Carolina; but it has spread in the upper parts of Georgia, so as to have become almost general, and is highly prized. Perhaps it may answer in Tennessee and Kentucky. The greatest service which can be rendered any country is, to add an useful plant to its culture; especially, a bread grain; next in value to bread is oil.

Whether the act for the more general diffusion of knowledge will ever be carried into complete effect, I know not. It was received by the legislature with great enthusiasm at first; and a small effort was made in 1796, by the act to establish public schools, to carry a part of it into effect, viz., that for the establishment of free English schools; but the option given to the courts has defeated the intention of the act.

JAMES MADISON

1751-1836

James Madison, next to Jefferson himself, the most able political figure produced by Virginia in the Revolutionary era, was born at Port Conway, in King George County, Virginia, on March 16, 1751. His forebears were among the early settlers of the colony. He grew up in Virginia and entered Princeton (then the College of New Jersey) in 1769. He was an indefatigable student and after his graduation in 1771 he remained at Princeton another year studying ethics and Hebrew under the direction of John Witherspoon, the president of the college.

On his return to Virginia he continued his reading and study and acted as tutor for his younger brothers and sisters. He became deeply interested in the question of religious freedom in Virginia and in the political struggle with England. In 1775, when he was twenty-four, he became chairman of the Committee of Safety for Orange County, and the following year he was a member of the Virginia Convention. There he proposed an amendment to the new Virginia constitution declaring that "all men are equally entitled to the full and free exercise" of religion. If adopted, the amendment would have brought about the immediate disestablishment of the Anglican Church in Virginia.

During the next forty years Madison devoted himself to the affairs of the new nation, as a member of the Continental Congress, the House of Delegates of Virginia, the Congress of the United States, as Secretary of State in Jefferson's administration and as the fourth President of the United States. His prodigious labors in the Constitutional Convention won for him the popular title of "father of the Constitution." Joining with Alexander Hamilton and John Jay to write *The Federalist* papers, he had an important part in a work, designed to persuade the people of the new nation to ratify the Constitution, which remains a major classic of political literature.

On his retirement from the presidency on March 4, 1817, Madison lived at his estate, "Montpelier," in Orange County, Virginia. He aided Jefferson in founding the University of Virginia and after the death of Jefferson in 1826 he served as rector of the University. He died at "Montpelier" on June 28, 1836.

James Madison, 1751-1836

"A Memorial and Remonstrance to the Virginia General Assembly," which follows, was prepared in 1785 in reply to a proposal to provide state support in Virginia for the teaching of religion. Madison's masterful remonstrance secured the defeat of the proposal and marshaled for future generations the arguments for the separation of church and state.

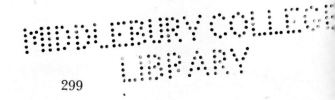

A MEMORIAL AND REMONSTRANCE TO THE
VIRGINIA GENERAL ASSEMBLY

To the Honorable the General Assembly of the Commonwealth of
Virginia:

We, the subscribers, citizens of the said commonwealth, having
taken into serious consideration a bill printed by order of the last
session of General Assembly, entitled "A Bill establishing a provision
for Teachers of the Christian Religion," and conceiving that the
same, if finally armed with the sanctions of a law, will be a dangerous
abuse of power, are bound as faithful members of a free state to
remonstrate against it, and to declare the reasons by which we are
determined. We remonstrate against the said bill —

1. Because we hold it for a fundamental and undeniable truth
"that religion, or the duty which we owe to our Creator, and the
manner of discharging it, can be directed only by reason and conviction, not by force or violence." The religion, then, of every man
must be left to the conviction and conscience of every man; and it
is the right of every man to exercise it as these may dictate. The
right is in its nature an unalienable right. It is unalienable because
the opinions of men, depending only on the evidence contemplated
by their own minds, cannot follow the dictates of other men. It is
unalienable, also, because what is here a right toward men is a duty
towards the Creator. It is the duty of every man to render to the
Creator such homage, and such only, as he believes to be acceptable
to him. The duty is precedent, both in order of time and in degree
of obligation, to the claims of civil society. Before any man can be
considered as a member of civil society, he must be considered as a
subject of the Governor of the universe; and if a member of civil
society who enters into any subordinate association must always do
it with a reservation of his duty to the general authority, much more
must every man, who becomes a member of any particular civil
society, do it with a saving of his allegiance to the Universal Sover-

300

eign. We maintain, therefore, that in matters of religion no man's right is abridged by the institution of civil society, and that religion is wholly exempt from its cognizance. True it is that no other rule exists by which any question which may divide a society can be ultimately determined than the will of the majority; but it is also true that the majority may trespass on the rights of the minority.

2. Because, if religion be exempt from the authority of the society at large, still less can it be subject to that of the legislative body. The latter are but the creatures and vicegerents of the former. Their jurisdiction is both derivative and limited. It is limited with regard to the co-ordinate departments; more necessarily is it limited with regard to the constituents. The preservation of a free government requires, not merely that the metes and bounds which separate each department of power be invariably maintained, but more especially that neither of them be suffered to overleap the great barrier which defends the rights of the people. The rulers who are guilty of such an encroachment exceed the commission from which they derive their authority, and are tyrants. The people who submit to it are governed by laws made neither by themselves nor by an authority derived from them, and are slaves.

3. Because it is proper to take alarm at the first experiment on our liberties. We hold this prudent jealousy to be the first duty of citizens, and one of the noblest characteristics of the late Revolution. The freedom of America did not wait till usurped power had strengthened itself by exercise and entangled the question in precedents. They saw all the consequences in the principle, and they avoided the consequences by denying the principle. We revere this lesson too much soon to forget it. Who does not see that the same authority which can establish Christianity in exclusion of all other religions may establish, with the same ease, any particular sect of Christians in exclusion of all other sects? that the same authority which can force a citizen to contribute threepence only of his property for the support of any one establishment may force him to conform to any other establishment in all cases whatsoever?

4. Because the bill violates that equality which ought to be the basis of every law, and which is more indispensable in proportion as the validity or expediency of any law is more liable to be im-

peached. "If all men are by nature equally free and independent," all men are to be considered as entering into society on equal conditions; as relinquishing no more, and therefore retaining no less, one than another, of their natural rights. Above all, are they to be considered as retaining an "*equal* title to the free exercise of religion according to the dictates of conscience." Whilst we assert for ourselves a freedom to embrace, to profess, and to observe the religion which we believe to be of divine origin, we cannot deny an equal freedom to them whose minds have not yet yielded to the evidence which has convinced us. If this freedom is abused, it is an offense against God, not against man. To God, therefore, not to man, must an account of it be rendered. As the bill violates equality by subjecting some peculiar burdens, so it violates the same principle by granting to others peculiar exemptions. Are the Quakers and Menonists the only sects who think a compulsive support of their religions unnecessary and unwarrantable? Can their piety alone be entrusted with the care of public worship? Ought their religions to be endowed above all others with extraordinary privileges, by which proselytes may be enticed from all others? We think too favorably of the justice and good sense of these denominations to believe that they either covet pre-eminences over their fellow citizens or that they will be seduced by them from the common opposition to the measure.

5. Because the bill implies either that the civil magistrate is a competent judge of religious truths or that he may employ religion as an engine of civil policy. The first is an arrogant pretension, falsified by the contradictory opinions of rulers in all ages and throughout the world; the second, an unhallowed perversion of the means of salvation.

6. Because the establishment proposed by the bill is not requisite for the support of the Christian religion. To say that it is is a contradiction to the Christian religion itself, for every page of it disavows a dependence on the powers of this world. It is a contradiction to fact, for it is known that this religion both existed and flourished, not only without the support of human laws, but in spite of every opposition from them; and not only during the period of miraculous aid, but long after it had been left to its own evidence

and the ordinary care of providence. Nay, it is a contradiction in terms; for a religion not invented by human policy must have pre-existed and been supported before it was established by human policy. It is, moreover, to weaken in those who profess this religion a pious confidence in its innate excellence and the patronage of its Author; and to foster in those who still reject it a suspicion that its friends are too conscious of its fallacies to trust it to its own merits.

7. Because experience witnesseth that ecclesiastical establishments, instead of maintaining the purity and efficacy of religion, have had a contrary operation. During almost fifteen centuries has the legal establishment of Christianity been on trial. What have been its fruits? More or less, in all places, pride and indolence in the clergy; ignorance and servility in the laity; in both, superstition, bigotry, and persecution. Inquire of the teachers of Christianity for the ages in which it appeared in its greatest luster; those of every sect point to the ages prior to its incorporation with civil policy. Propose a restoration of this primitive state in which its teachers depended on the voluntary rewards of their flocks, many of them predict its downfall. On which side ought their testimony to have greatest weight, when for or when against their interest?

8. Because the establishment in question is not necessary for the support of civil government. If it be urged as necessary for the support of civil government only as it is a means of supporting religion, and it be not necessary for the latter purpose, it cannot be necessary for the former. If religion be not within the cognizance of civil government, how can its legal establishment be necessary to civil government? What influence, in fact, have ecclesiastical establishments had on civil society? In some instances they have been seen to erect a spiritual tyranny on the ruins of the civil authority; in many instances they have been seen upholding the thrones of political tyranny; in no instance have they been seen the guardians of the liberties of the people. Rulers who wished to subvert the public liberty may have found an established clergy convenient auxiliaries. A just government, instituted to secure and perpetuate it, needs them not. Such a government will be best supported by protecting every citizen in the enjoyment of his religion with the same equal hand

which protects his person and his property; by neither invading the equal rights of any sect, nor suffering any sect to invade those of another.

9. Because the proposed establishment is a departure from that generous policy which, offering an asylum to the persecuted and oppressed of every nation and religion, promised a luster to our country, and an accession to the number of its citizens. What a melancholy mark is the bill of sudden degeneracy! Instead of holding forth an asylum to the persecuted, it is itself a signal of persecution. It degrades from the equal rank of citizens all those whose opinions in religion do not bend to those of the legislative authority. Distant as it may be in its present form from the Inquisition, it differs from it only in degree. The one is the first step, the other the last, in the career of intolerance. The magnanimous sufferer under this cruel scourge in foreign regions must view the bill as a beacon on our coast warning him to seek some other haven, where liberty and philanthropy, in their due extent, may offer a more certain repose from his troubles.

10. Because it will have a like tendency to banish our citizens. The allurements presented by other situations are every day thinning their number. To superadd a fresh motive to emigration by revoking the liberty which they now enjoy would be the same species of folly which has dishonored and depopulated flourishing kingdoms.

11. Because it will destroy that moderation and harmony which the forbearance of our laws to intermeddle with religion has produced among its several sects. Torrents of blood have been spilt in the Old World in consequence of vain attempts of the secular arm to extinguish religious discord by proscribing all differences in religious opinion. Time has at length revealed the true remedy. Every relaxation of narrow and rigorous policy, wherever it has been tried, has been found to assuage the disease. The American theater has exhibited proofs that equal and complete liberty, if it does not wholly eradicate it, sufficiently destroys its malignant influence on the health and prosperity of the state. If, with the salutary effects of this system under our own eyes, we begin to contract the bounds of religious freedom, we know no name which will too severely reproach our folly. At least, let warning be taken at the first fruits of

the threatened innovation. The very appearance of the bill has transformed "that Christian forbearance, love, and charity" which of late mutually prevailed, into animosities and jealousies which may not soon be appeased. What mischiefs may not be dreaded, should this enemy to the public quiet be armed with the force of law?

12. Because the policy of the bill is adverse to the diffusion of the light of Christianity. The first wish of those who enjoy this precious gift ought to be that it may be imparted to the whole race of mankind. Compare the number of those who have as yet received it with the number still remaining under the dominion of false religions, and how small is the former! Does the policy of the bill tend to lessen the disproportion? No; it at once discourages those who are strangers to the light of revelation from coming into the region of it, and countenances by example the nations who continue in darkness in shutting out those who might convey it to them. Instead of leveling, as far as possible, every obstacle to the victorious progress of truth, the bill, with an ignoble and unchristian timidity, would circumscribe it with a wall of defense against the encroachments of error.

13. Because attempts to enforce, by legal sanctions, acts obnoxious to so great a proportion of citizens tend to enervate the laws in general, and to slacken the bands of society. If it be difficult to execute any law which is not generally deemed necessary or salutary, what must be the case where it is deemed invalid and dangerous? And what may be the effect of so striking an example of impotency in the government on its general authority?

14. Because a measure of such singular magnitude and delicacy ought not to be imposed without the clearest evidence that it is called for by a majority of citizens; and no satisfactory method is yet proposed by which the voice of the majority in this case may be determined, or its influence secured. "The people of the respective counties are, indeed, requested to signify their opinion respecting the adoption of the bill to the next session of the Assembly." But the representation must be made equal before the voice of either of the representatives or of the counties will be that of the people. Our hope is that neither of the former will, after due consideration, espouse the dangerous principle of the bill. Should the event disappoint us,

it will still leave us in full confidence that a fair appeal to the latter will reverse the sentence against our liberties.

15. Because, finally, "the equal right of every citizen to the free exercise of his religion, according to the dictates of conscience," is held by the same tenure with all our other rights. If we recur to its origin, it is equally the gift of nature; if we weigh its importance, it cannot be less dear to us; if we consult the Declaration of those rights "which pertain to the good people of Virginia as the basis and foundation of government," it is enumerated with equal solemnity, or rather with studied emphasis. Either, then, we must say that the will of the legislature is the only measure of their authority, and that in the plenitude of that authority they may sweep away all our fundamental rights, or that they are bound to leave this particular right untouched and sacred. Either we must say that they may control the freedom of the press, may abolish the trial by jury, may swallow up the executive and judiciary powers of the state; nay, that they may despoil us of our very right of suffrage, and erect themselves into an independent and hereditary Assembly; or we must say that they have no authority to enact into a law the bill under consideration.

We, the subscribers, say that the General Assembly of this commonwealth have no such authority. And in order that no effort may be omitted on our part against so dangerous an usurpation, we oppose to it this remonstrance; earnestly praying, as we are in duty bound, that the Supreme Lawgiver of the Universe, by illuminating those to whom it is addressed, may, on the one hand, turn their councils from every act which would affront his holy prerogative or violate the trust committed to them; and, on the other, guide them into every measure which may be worthy of his blessing, redound to their own praise, and establish more firmly the liberties, the prosperity, and the happiness of the commonwealth.

ST. GEORGE TUCKER

1752-1828

St. George Tucker was an officer in the Revolution, a distinguished and influential jurist, and — as is evident from the selection of his writing which follows — a man with a firm belief in democracy and a deep sense of justice and of human dignity.

He was born in Bermuda on July 10, 1752, and came to Virginia when he was nineteen to continue his education at the College of William and Mary in Williamsburg. He spent a year in study there, was admitted to the bar, and began the practice of law. He returned to Bermuda but came back to Virginia at the beginning of the war for independence and entered the revolutionary struggle. He fought with skill as a colonel of militia at the battle of Guilford Court House and, as a lieutenant colonel, was wounded in the siege of Yorktown.

He married the widow Frances Bland Randolph in 1778, becoming the stepfather of her young son, later famous as John Randolph of Roanoke. Frances Bland died in 1788, and in 1791 St. George Tucker married Lelia Skipwith Carter, daughter of Sir Peyton Skipwith.

Tucker was an occasional poet of talent and he maintained an active interest in literature throughout his life. He tried his hand at drama, published a volume of political satires, and his poem *Resignation* ("Days of my youth") has been included in a number of anthologies.

At the close of the Revolution, Tucker resumed the practice of law in Virginia. He was a delegate to the Annapolis convention of 1786, and served with growing reputation as judge of the general court of Virginia in 1788-1804. While a member of the court, he became professor of law at William and Mary in 1790, and in 1803 he published his annotated edition of Blackstone's *Commentaries* in five volumes, with an appendix on the principles of government and the Federal Constitution, which became one of the most influential legal works of the period.

He was elected to the supreme court of appeals of Virginia in 1803 and served for eight years. In 1813 he was appointed by President Madison as judge of the Federal district court of Virginia, a post which he held until 1827, when he resigned because of ill health. He died on November 10, 1828.

Virginia Reader

In 1796, when he was professor of law at William and Mary and a member of the general court of Virginia, he published *A Dissertation On Slavery: With A Proposal For The Gradual Abolition Of It, In The State Of Virginia*, addressed to the general assembly. It was widely read in its day and was republished in 1861. "If we do not set about the abolition of slavery," he asked, "will not our posterity . . . execrate the memory of those ancestors, who, having it in their power to avert evil, have, like their first parents, entailed a curse upon all future generations?"

The *Dissertation* is an effective document, presented in lucid and vigorous prose. "We know," he wrote prophetically, "that the rigour of the law respecting slaves unavoidably must increase with their numbers: What a blood-stained code must that be which is calculated for the restraint of *millions* in bondage! Such must our unhappy country exhibit within a century, unless we are both wise and just enough to avert from posterity the calamity and reproach, which are otherwise unavoidable."

A selection from the *Dissertation*, which describes the condition of slaves in Virginia, follows.

THE CONDITION OF SLAVES IN VIRGINIA

We are next to consider the condition of slaves in Virginia, or the legal consequences attendant on a state of slavery in this commonwealth; and here it is not my intention to notice those laws which consider slaves merely as *property*, and have from time to time been enacted to regulate the disposition of them *as such;* for these will be more properly considered elsewhere: my intention at present is therefore to take a view of such laws only as regard slaves as a distinct class of *persons*, whose rights, if indeed they possess any, are reduced to a much narrower compass than those of which we have been speaking before.

Civil rights, we may remember, are reducible to three primary heads; the right of personal security; the right of personal liberty; and the right of private property. In a state of slavery the two last are wholly abolished, the person of the slave being at the absolute disposal of his master; and property, what he is incapable in that state either of acquiring or holding in his own use. Hence it will appear how perfectly irreconcilable a state of slavery is to the principles of a democracy, which form the *basis* and *foundation* of our government. For our bill of rights declares, "that all men are by nature *equally free* and independent, and have certain rights of which they cannot deprive or divest their posterity, namely the enjoyment of life and *liberty*, with the means of *acquiring* and *possessing property."* This is indeed no more than a recognition of the first principles of the law of nature, which teaches us this equality and enjoins every man, whatever advantages he may possess over another as to the various qualities or endowments of body or mind, to practice the precepts of the law of nature to those who are in these respects his *inferiors*, no less than it enjoins his *inferiors* to practice them toward *him*. Since he has no more right to insult *them*, than they have to injure him. Nor does the *bare unkindness*

309

of nature or of fortune condemn a man to a *worse* condition than others as to the enjoyment of common privileges. It would be hard to reconcile reducing the Negroes to a state of slavery to these principles, unless we first degrade them below the rank of human beings, not only politically but also physically and morally. The Roman lawyers look upon those only properly as *persons* who are *free* — putting *slaves* into the rank of *goods* and *chattels;* and the policy of our legislature, as well as the practice of slave-holders in America in general, seems conformable to that idea: but surely it is time we should admit the evidence of moral truth, and learn to regard them as our fellow men, and equals, except in those particulars where accident, or perhaps nature, may have given us some advantage; a recompense for which they perhaps enjoy in other respects.

Slavery, says Hargrave, always imports an obligation of perpetual service, which only the consent of the master can dissolve: it also generally gives to the master an arbitrary power of administering every sort of correction, however inhuman, not immediately affecting life or limb, and even these in some countries, as formerly in Rome and at this day among the Asiatics and Africans, are left exposed to the arbitrary will of a master or protected only by fines or other slight punishments. The property of the slave also is absolutely the property of his master, the slave himself being the subject of property, and as such saleable or transmissible at the will of his master. — A slavery, so malignant as that described, does not leave to its wretched victims the least vestige of any civil right, and even divests them of all their natural rights. It does not, however, appear that the rigours of slavery in this country were ever as great as those above described: yet it must be confessed that, at times, they have fallen very little short of them.

The first severe law respecting slaves now to be met with in our code is that of 1669, already mentioned, which declared that the death of a slave *resisting* his master, or other person correcting him by his order, *happening by extremity of the correction,* should not be accounted felony. The alterations which this law underwent in three successive acts were by no means calculated effectually to mitigate its severity; it seems rather to have been augmented by the act of 1723, which declared that a person indicted for the murder of a slave, and found guilty of *manslaughter,* should not incur any punishment for the same.

All these acts were at length repealed in 1788. So that homicide of a slave stands now upon the same footing as in the case of any other person. In 1672 it was declared lawful for any person pursuing any runaway Negroe, mulattoe, Indian slave, or *servant for life,* by virtue of an *hue and cry,* to kill them in case of resistance without being questioned for the same. A few years afterwards this act was extended to persons *employed to apprehend* runaways. In 1705 these acts underwent some small alteration; two justices being authorized by proclamation to *outlaw* runaways, who might thereafter be *killed* and destroyed by any person whatsoever, by *such ways and means* as he may think fit, without accusation or impeachment of any crime for so doing: And if any such slave were apprehended, he might be punished at the discretion of the county court, either by *dismembering,* or in any other manner *not touching life.* The inhuman rigour of this act was afterwards extended to the venial offence of going abroad by night, if the slave were *notoriously* guilty of it. — Such are the cruelties to which a state of slavery gives birth; such the horrors to which the human mind is capable of being reconciled by its adoption. The dawn of humanity at length appeared in the year 1769, when the power of dismembering, even under the authority of a county court, was restricted to the single offence of *attempting* to ravish a white woman, in which case perhaps the punishment is perhaps not more than commensurate to the crime. In 1772 some restraints were laid upon the practice of outlawing slaves, requiring that it should appear to the *satisfaction* of the justices that the slaves were outlying, and *doing mischief.* These loose expressions of the act left too much in the discretion of men not much addicted to weighing their import. — In 1792 every thing relative to the outlawry of slaves was *expunged* from our code, and I trust will never again find a place in it. By the act of 1680, a Negroe, a mulattoe, or Indian, bond or *free,* presuming to lift his hand in opposition to any Christian should receive thirty lashes on his bare back for every offence. The same act prohibited slaves from carrying any club, staff, gun, sword, or other weapon, offensive or defensive. This was afterwards extended to all Negroes, mulattoes, and Indians

311

whatsoever, with a few exceptions in favour of housekeepers, residents on a frontier plantation, and such as were enlisted in the militia. Slaves, by these and other acts, are prohibited from going abroad without leave in writing from their masters, and if they do may be whipped: any person suffering a slave to remain on his plantation for four hours together, or dealing with him without leave in writing from his master, is subject to a fine. A runaway slave may be apprehended and committed to jail, and if not claimed within three months (being first advertised) he shall be hired out, having an iron collar first put about his neck: and if not claimed within a year, shall be sold. These provisions were in general re-enacted in 1792, but the punishment to be inflicted on a Negroe or mulattoe, for lifting his hand against a white person, is restricted to those cases where the former is not wantonly assaulted. In this act the word Indian appears to have been designedly omitted: the small number of these people, or their descendants remaining among us, concurring with a more liberal way of thinking probably gave occasion to this circumstance. The act of 1748, c. 31, made it felony, without benefit of clergy, for a slave to prepare, exhibit, or administer any medicine whatever, without the order or consent of the master; but *allowed clergy* if it appeared that the medicine was not administered with an *ill intent;* the act of 1792, with more justice, directs that in such case he shall be acquitted. To consult, advise, or conspire, to rebel, or to plot, or conspire the death of any person whatsoever, is still felony, without benefit of clergy, in a slave. Riots, routs, unlawful assemblies, trespasses and seditious speeches by slaves are punishable with stripes at the discretion of a justice of the peace. — The master of a slave permitting him to go at large and trade as a freeman is subject to a fine; and if he suffers the slave to hire himself out the latter may be sold and twenty-five per cent of the price be applied to the use of the county. — Negroes and mulattoes, whether slaves or not, are incapable of being witnesses, but against, or between Negroes and mulattoes; they are not permitted to intermarry with any white person; yet no punishment is annexed to the offence in the slave; nor is the marriage void; but the white person contracting the marriage, and the clergyman by whom it is celebrated are liable to fine and imprisonment; and this is probably the only in-

stance in which our laws will be found more favorable to a Negroe than a white person. These provisions though introduced into our code at different periods were all re-enacted in 1792.

From this melancholy review it will appear that not only the right of property, and the right of personal liberty, but even the right of personal security, has been, at times, either wholly annihilated, or reduced to a shadow: and even in these days the protection of the latter seems to be confined to very few cases. Many actions, indifferent in themselves, being permitted by the law of nature to all mankind, and by the laws of society to all free persons, are either rendered highly criminal in a slave, or subject him to some kind of punishment or restraint. Nor is it in this respect only that his condition is rendered thus deplorable by law. The measure of punishment for the same offence is often, and the manner of trial and conviction is always, different in the case of a slave and a free-man. If the latter be accused of any crime, he is entitled to an examination before the court of the county where the offence is alleged to have been committed; whose decision, if in his favor, is held to be a legal and final acquittal, but it is not final if against him; for after this, both a grand jury, and a petit jury of the county, must successively pronounce him guilty; the former by the concurrent voices of twelve at least of their body, and the latter by their unanimous verdict upon oath. He may take exception to the proceedings against him by a motion in arrest of judgment; and in this case, or if there be a special verdict, the same unanimity between his judges, as between his jurors, is necessary to his condemnation. Lastly, though the punishment which the law pronounces for his offence amount to death itself, he shall in many cases have the benefit of clergy, unless he has before received it. But in the case of a slave, the mode was formerly and still remains essentially different. How early this distinction was adopted I have not been able to discover. The title of an act occurs which passed in the year 1705 for the *speedy* and *easy* prosecution of slaves committing capital crimes. In 1723 the governor was authorized, whenever any slave was committed for any capital offence, to issue a special commission of oyer and terminer, to *such persons as he should think fit*, the number being left to his discretion, who should thereupon proceed to the trial of such slave, taking for evidence the confession of the defendant, the oath of one or more credible witnesses, or such testimony of Negroes, mulattoes, or Indians, bond or free, with pregnant circumstances, as to them should seem convincing, without the solemnity of a jury. No exception, formerly, could be taken to the proceedings, on the trial of a slave, but that proviso is omitted in the act of 1792, and the justices moreover seem bound to allow him counsel for his defence, whose fee shall be paid by his master. In case of conviction, execution of the sentence was probably very speedily performed, since the act of 1748 provides that, thereafter, it should not be performed in less than ten days, except in cases of insurrection or rebellion; and further, that if the court be divided in opinion the accused should be acquitted. In 1764 an act passed authorizing general, instead of special, commissioners of oyer and terminer, constituting all the justices of any county judges for the trial of slaves committing capital offences within their respective counties; any four of whom, one being of the quorum, should constitute a court for that purpose. In 1772 one step further was made in favour of humanity by an act declaring that no slave should thereafter be condemned to die unless four of the court should concur in opinion of his guilt. The act of 1786, c. 58, confirmed by that of 1792, constitutes the justices of every county and corporation justices of oyer and terminer for the trial of slaves; requires *five* justices, at least, to constitute a court, and *unanimity* in the court for his condemnation; allows him counsel for his defence, to be paid by his owner, and, I apprehend, admits him to object to the proceedings against him; and finally enlarges the time of execution to *thirty* days, instead of ten (except in cases of conspiracy, insurrection, or rebellion), and extends the benefit of clergy to him in all cases, where any other person should have the benefit thereof, except in the cases before mentioned.

To an attentive observer these gradual and almost imperceptible amendments in our jurisprudence respecting slaves will be found, upon the whole, of infinite importance to that unhappy race. The mode of trial in criminal cases, especially, is rendered infinitely more beneficial to them than formerly, though perhaps still liable to exception for want of the aid of a jury: the solemnity of an oath administered the moment the trial commences may be considered as operating more forcibly on the mind than a general oath of office taken, perhaps, twenty years before. Unanimity may also be more readily expected to take place among *five* men than among *twelve*. These objections to the want of a jury are not without weight: on the other hand it may be observed that if the number of triers be not equal to a full jury, they may yet be considered as more select; a circumstance of infinitely greater importance to the slave. The unanimity requisite in the court in order to conviction, is a more happy acquisition to the accused, than may at first appear; the opinions of the court must be delivered openly, immediately, and seriatim, beginning with the youngest judge. A single voice in favor of the accused is an acquittal, for unanimity is not necessary, as with a jury, to acquit, as well as to condemn: there is less danger in this mode of trial, where the suffrages are to be openly delivered, that a few will be brought over to the opinion of the majority as may too often happen among jurors, whose deliberations are in *private*, and whose impatience of confinement may go further than real conviction to produce the requisite unanimity. That this happens not unfrequently in civil cases there is too much reason to believe; that it may also happen in criminal cases, especially where the party accused is not one of their equals, might not unreasonably be apprehended. In New York, before the revolution, a slave accused of a capital crime should have been tried by a jury if his master required it. That is, perhaps, still the law of that state. Such a provision might not be amiss in this; but considering the ordinary run of juries in the county courts, I should presume the privilege would be rarely insisted upon.

Slaves, we have seen, are now entitled to the benefit of clergy in all cases where it is allowed to any other offenders, except in cases of consulting, advising, or conspiring to rebel, or make insurrection; or plotting or conspiring to murder any person; or preparing, exhibiting, or administering medicine with an *ill* intent. The same lenity was not extended to them formerly. The act of 1748, c. 31, denied it to a slave in case of manslaughter; or the felonious breaking and entering *any* house, in the night time: or breaking and entering *any* house in the day time, and taking therefrom goods to the value of twenty shillings. The act of 1764, c. 9, extended the benefit

315

of clergy to a slave convicted of the manslaughter of a slave; and the act of 1772, c. 9, extended it further to a slave convicted of housebreaking in the night time, unless such breaking be burglary; in the latter case, other offenders would be equally deprived of it. But wherever the benefit of clergy is allowed to a slave, the court, besides burning him in the hand (the usual punishment inflicted on free persons) may inflict such further corporal punishment as they may think fit; this also seems to be the law in the case of free Negroes and mulattoes. By the act of 1723, c. 4, it was enacted that when *any Negroe*, or *mulattoe* shall be found, upon due proof made, or *pregnant circumstances*, to have given false testimony, every such offender shall, *without further trial*, have his ears successively nailed to the pillory for the space of an hour, and then cut off, and moreover receive thirty-nine lashes on his bare back, or such other punishment as the court shall think proper, not extending to life or limb. This act, with the exception of the words *pregnant circumstances*, was re-enacted in 1792. The punishment of perjury, in a *white* person, is only a fine and imprisonment. A slave convicted of hog stealing shall, for the first offence, receive thirty-nine lashes: any other person twenty-five: but the latter is also subject to a fine of thirty dollars, besides paying eight dollars to the owner of the hog. The punishment for the second and third offence of this kind is the same in the case of a free person as of a slave; namely, by the pillory and loss of ears, for the second offence; the third is declared felony, to which clergy is, however, allowed. The preceding are the only positive distinctions which now remain between the punishment of a slave and a white person in those cases where the latter is liable to a determinate corporal punishment. But we must not forget that many actions which are either not punishable at all when perpetrated by a white person, or at most, by fine and imprisonment only, are liable to severe corporal punishment when done by a slave; nay, even to death itself in some cases. To go abroad without a written permission; to keep or carry a gun or other weapon; to utter any seditious speech; to be present at any unlawful assembly of slaves; to lift the hand in opposition to a white person unless wantonly assaulted, are all offences punishable by whipping. To attempt the chastity of a white woman forcibly is punishable by dismemberment: such an attempt would be a high misdemeanor in a white free man, but the punishment would be far short of that of a slave. To administer medicine without the order or consent of the master, unless it *appear not to have been done with an ill intent;* to *consult,* advise, or conspire, to rebel or make insurrection; or to *conspire* or *plot* to *murder* any person, we have seen, are all capital offences, from which the benefit of clergy is utterly excluded. But a *bare intention* to commit a felony is not punishable in the case of a free white man; and even the attempt, if not attended with an actual breach of the peace, or prevented by such circumstances, only, as do not tend to lessen the guilt of the offender, is at most a misdemeanor by the common law: and in statutable offences in general, to consult advise, and even to procure any person to commit a felony, does not constitute the crime of felony in the adviser or procurer, unless the felony be actually perpetrated.

From this view of our jurisprudence respecting slaves, we are unavoidably led to remark how frequently the laws of nature have been set aside in favour of institutions the pure result of prejudice, usurpation, and tyranny. We have found actions, innocent or indifferent, punishable with a rigour scarcely due to any but the most atrocious offences against civil society; justice distributed by an unequal measure to the master and slave; and even the hand of mercy arrested, where mercy might have been extended to the wretched culprit had his complexion been the same with that of his judges: for the short period of ten days between his condemnation and execution was often insufficient to obtain a pardon for a slave, convicted in a remote part of the country, whilst a free man, condemned at the seat of government and tried before the governor himself, in whom the power of pardoning was vested, had a respite of thirty days to implore the clemency of the executive authority. — It may be urged, and I believe with truth, that these rigours do not proceed from a sanguinary temper in the people of Virginia, but from those political considerations indispensably necessary where slavery prevails to any great extent: I am moreover happy to observe that our police respecting this unhappy class of people is not only less rigorous than formerly, but perhaps milder than in any other country where there are so many slaves, or so large a proportion of them in respect to the free inhabitants: it is also, I trust, unjust to censure the present generation for the existence of slavery in Virginia: for I think it unquestionably true that a very large proportion of our fellow citizens lament that as a misfortune which is imputed to them as a reproach; it being evident from what has been already shown upon the subject that, *antecedent to the revolution,* no exertion to abolish, or even check the progress of slavery in Virginia, could have received the smallest countenance from the crown, without whose assent the united wishes and exertions of every individual here would have been wholly fruitless and ineffectual: it is, perhaps, also demonstrable that at no period since the revolution could the abolition of slavery in this state have been safely undertaken until the foundations of our newly established governments had been found capable of supporting the fabric itself, under any shock, which so arduous an attempt might have produced. But these obstacles being now happily removed, considerations of policy, as well as justice and humanity, must evince the necessity of eradicating the evil before it becomes impossible to do it without tearing up the roots of civil society with it.

JOHN TAYLOR

1753-1824

John Taylor, spokesman for agrarian liberalism, was born in Virginia on December 19, 1753. He grew up in Virginia, attended William and Mary College, was admitted to the bar in 1774, and served in the Revolutionary army. After the war he was a member of the Virginia House of Delegates and was later three times United States Senator from Virginia.

He was an original and intellectually vigorous opponent of Hamiltonian philosophy, and saw in a healthy agrarianism a bulwark against the exploitation of the mass of the people. He was the author of a number of penetrating economic and political studies. A collection of his agricultural papers were brought together in book form in 1813 under the title, *Arator*. The following year he published his most important political work, *An Inquiry into the Principles and Policy of the Government of the United States*. Shortly before his death he published *New Views of the Constitution of the United States*. He died on August 21, 1824.

Thomas Hart Benton wrote of Taylor: "He belonged to that constellation of great men which shone so brightly in Virginia in his day, and the light of which was not limited to Virginia, or our America, but spread through the bounds of the civilized world."

THE PLEASURES OF AGRICULTURE*

The pleasures of agriculture, in free countries, are more, and in enslaved, fewer, than the pleasures of most other employments. The reason of it is, that agriculture both from its nature, and also as being generally the employment of a great portion of a nation, cannot be united with power, considered as an exclusive interest. It must of course be enslaved, wherever despotism exists, and its masters will enjoy more pleasures in that case, than it can ever reach. On the contrary, where power is not an exclusive, but a general interest, agriculture can employ its own energies for the attainment of its own happiness.

Under a free government it has before it, the inexhaustible sources of human pleasure, of fitting ideas to substances, and substances to ideas; and of a constant rotation of hope and fruition.

The novelty, frequency and exactness of accommodations between our ideas and operations, constitutes the most exquisite source of mental pleasure. Agriculture feeds it with endless supplies in the natures of soils, plants, climates, manures, instruments of culture and domestic animals. Their combinations are inexhaustible, the novelty of results is endless, discrimination and adaption are never idle, and an unsatiated interest receives gratifications in quick succession.

Benevolence is so closely associated with this interest that its exertion in numberless instances, is necessary to foster it. Liberality in supplying its labourers with the comforts of life, is the best sponsor for the prosperity of agriculture, and the practice of almost every moral virtue is amply remunerated in this world, whilst it is also the best surety for attaining the blessings of the next. Poetry, in allowing more virtue to agriculture, than to any other profession,

*From *Arator,* by John Taylor. Sixth edition, 1818. For the use of a copy of this rare volume, the editor is indebted to the Library of the United States Department of Agriculture.

has abandoned her privilege of fiction, and yielded to the natural moral effect of the absence of temptation. The same fact is commemorated by religion, upon an occasion the most solemn, within the scope of the human imagination. At the awful day of judgment, the discrimination of the good from the wicked, is not made by the criterion of sects or of dogmas, but by one which constitutes the daily employment and the great end of agriculture. The judge upon this occasion has by anticipation pronounced, that to feed the hungry, clothe the naked, and give drink to the thirsty, are the passports to future happiness; and the divine intelligence which selected an agricultural state as a paradise for its first favourites, has here again prescribed the agricultural virtues as the means for the admission of their posterity into heaven.

With the pleasures of religion, agriculture unites those of patriotism, and among the worthy competitors for pre-eminence in the practice of this cardinal virtue, a profound author assigns a high station to him who has made two blades of grass grow instead of one; an idea capable of a signal amplification, by a comparison between a system of agriculture which doubles the fertility of a country, and a successful war which doubles its territory. By the first the territory itself is also substantially doubled, without wasting the lives, the wealth, or the liberty of the nation which has thus subdued sterility, and drawn prosperity from a willing source. By the second, the blood pretended to be enriched, is spilt; the wealth pretended to be increased, is wasted; the liberty said to be secured, is immolated to the patriotism of a victorious army; and desolation in every form is made to stalk in the glittering garb of false glory, throughout some neighbouring country. Moral law decides the preference with undeviating consistency, in assigning to the nation, which elects true patriotism, the recompense of truth, and to the electors of the false, the expiation of error. To the respective agents, the same law assigns the remorses of a conqueror, and the quiet conscience of the agriculturist.

The capacity of agriculture for affording luxuries to the body, is not less conspicuous than its capacity for affording luxuries to the mind; it being a science singularly possessing the double qualities of feeding with unbounded liberality, both the moral appetites of

321

the one, and the physical wants of the other. It can even feed a morbid love for money, whilst it is habituating us to the practice of virtue; and whilst it provides for the wants of the philosopher, it affords him ample room for the most curious and yet useful researches. In short, by the exercise it gives both to the body and to the mind, it secures health and vigour to both; and by combining a thorough knowledge of the real affairs of life, with a necessity for investigating the arcana of nature, and the strongest invitations to the practice of morality, it becomes the best architect of a complete man.

If this eulogy should succeed in awaking the attention of men of science to a skilful practice of agriculture they will become models for individuals, and guardians for national happiness. The discoveries of the learned will be practised by the ignorant; and a system which sheds happiness, plenty and virtue all around will be gradually substituted for one, which fosters vice, breeds want, and begets misery.

Politicians (who ought to know the most, and generally know the least, of a science in which the United States are more deeply interested than in any other) will appear, of more practical knowledge, or at least of better theoretical instruction; and the hopeless habit of confiding our greatest interest to people most ignorant of it, will be abandoned.

The errors of politicians ignorant of agriculture, or their projects designed to oppress it, can only rob it of its pleasures, and consign it to contempt and misery. This revolution of its natural state, is invariably effected by war, armies, heavy taxes, or exclusive privileges. In two cases alone, have nations ever gained any thing by war. Those of repelling invasion and emigrating into a more fruitful territory. In every other case, the industrious of all professions suffer by war, the effects of which in its modern form, are precisely the same to the victorious and the vanquished nation. The least evil to be apprehended from victorious armies, is a permanent system of heavy taxation, than which, nothing can more vitally wound or kill the pleasures of agriculture. Of the same stamp, are exclusive privileges in every form; and to pillage or steal under the sanction of the statute books, is no less fatal to the happiness of agriculture, than the hierarchical tyranny over the soul, under the pretended sanction of

John Taylor, 1753-1824

God, or the feudal tyranny over the body, under the equally fraudulent pretence of defending the nation. In a climate and soil, where good culture never fails to beget plenty, where bad cannot produce famine, begirt by nature against the risque of invasion, and favoured by accident with the power of self government, agriculture can only lose its happiness by the folly or fraud of statesmen, or by its own ignorance.

JOHN MARSHALL

1755-1835

John Marshall was born in a log cabin near Germantown on the Virginia frontier (later Fauquier County) on September 24, 1755. He was the son of Thomas Marshall, a member of the Virginia House of Burgesses, and through his mother he was related to the well-known Randolph family and was a kinsman of Thomas Jefferson. He grew up in the newly settled area where he was born. At the outbreak of the Revolution he joined the army, and became a captain in his early twenties. After the war he began the practice of law in Fauquier County, was elected to the House of Delegates, and moved to Richmond. There he built up a successful law practice, and in 1786 was counsel in the important case which settled the title to a large area in the Shenandoah Valley as between the Pennsylvania-German settlers and the original grant to Lord Fairfax. The next year he was a member of the Virginia Convention which ratified the Constitution, and he rapidly became a leader of the Federalist party in Virginia. He declined the positions of Attorney General and Minister to France in President Washington's administration, but he later served as a special commissioner in France and in 1799 was elected to Congress from Virginia. He served briefly as Secretary of State under President John Adams and in 1801 was appointed by Adams as Chief Justice of the United States. He served as Chief Justice during the next thirty-four years, until his death on July 6, 1835, and, through his decisions in a great series of cases of fundamental importance, he became the principal architect of the American system of Constitutional law.

During his early years as Chief Justice he published *The Life of George Washington* (5 volumes, 1804-1807), from which the following selection is taken. There have been a number of editions of the biography; most recently it has been republished in five volumes in Fredericksburg, Virginia, in 1926, and in two volumes in New York in 1930.

AN ESTIMATE OF WASHINGTON

General Washington was rather above the common size, his frame was robust, and his constitution vigorous — capable of enduring great fatigue, and requiring a considerable degree of exercise for the preservation of his health. His exterior created in the beholder the idea of strength, united with manly gracefulness.

His manners were rather reserved than free, though they partook nothing of that dryness, and sternness, which accompany reserve when carried to an extreme; and on all proper occasions, he could relax sufficiently to show how highly he was gratified by the charms of conversation, and the pleasures of society. His person and whole deportment exhibited an unaffected and indescribable dignity, unmingled with haughtiness of which all who approached him were sensible; and the attachment of those who possessed his friendship, and enjoyed his intimacy, was ardent, but always respectful.

His temper was humane, benevolent, and conciliatory; but there was a quickness in his sensibility to any thing apparently offensive, which experience had taught him to watch, and to correct.

In the management of his private affairs he exhibited an exact yet liberal economy. His funds were not prodigally wasted on capricious and ill examined schemes, nor refused to beneficial though costly improvements. They remained therefore competent to that expensive establishment which his reputation, added to a hospitable temper, had in some measure imposed upon him; and to those donations which real distress has a right to claim from opulence.

He made no pretensions to that vivacity which fascinates, or to that wit which dazzles, and frequently imposes on the understanding. More solid than brilliant, judgment, rather than genius, constituted the most prominent feature of his character.

Without making ostentatious professions of religion, he was a sincere believer in the Christian faith, and a truly devout man.

325

As a military man, he was brave, enterprising, and cautious. That malignity which was sought to strip him of all the higher qualities of a General, has conceded to him personal courage, and a firmness of resolution which neither dangers nor difficulties could shake. But candour will allow him other great and valuable endowments. If his military course does not abound with splendid achievements, it exhibits a series of judicious measures adapted to circumstances, which probably saved his country.

Placed, without having studied the theory, or been taught in the school of experience the practice of war, at the head of an undisciplined, ill organized multitude, which was impatient of the restraints, and unacquainted with the ordinary duties of a camp, without the aid of officers possessing those lights which the Commander-in-chief was yet to acquire, it would have been a miracle indeed had his conduct been absolutely faultless. But, possessing an energetic and distinguishing mind, on which the lessons of experience were never lost, his errors, if he committed any, were quickly repaired; and those measures which the state of things rendered most adviseable, were seldom, if ever, neglected. Inferior to his adversary in the numbers, in the equipment, and in the discipline of his troops, it is evidence of real merit that no great and decisive advantages were ever obtained over him, and that the opportunity to strike an important blow never passed away unused. He has been termed the American Fabius; but those who compare his actions with his means, will perceive at least as much of Marcellus as of Fabius, in his character. He could not have been more enterprising, without endangering the cause he defended, nor have put more to hazard, without incurring justly the imputation of rashness. Not relying upon those chances which sometimes give a favourable issue to attempts apparently desperate, his conduct was regulated by calculations made upon the capacities of his army, and the real situation of his country. When called a second time to command the armies of the United States, a change of circumstances had taken place, and he meditated a corresponding change of conduct. In modelling the army of 1798, he sought for men distinguished for their boldness of execution, not less than for their prudence in counsel, and contemplated a system of continued attack. "The enemy," said the General in his private letters, "must never be permitted to gain a foothold on our shores."

In his civil administration, as in his military career, ample and repeated proofs were exhibited of that practical good sense, of that sound judgment, which is perhaps the most rare, and is certainly the most valuable quality of the human mind. Devoting himself to the duties of his station, and pursuing no object distinct from the public good, he was accustomed to contemplate at a distance those critical situations in which the United States might probably be placed; and to digest, before the occasion required action, the line of conduct which it would be proper to observe. Taught to distrust first impressions, he sought to acquire all the information which was attainable, and to hear, without prejudice, all the reasons which could be urged for or against a particular measure. His own judgment was suspended until it became necessary to determine; and his decisions, thus maturely made, were seldom if ever to be shaken. His conduct therefore was systematic, and the great objects of his administration were steadily pursued.

Respecting, as the first magistrate in a free government must ever do, the real and deliberate sentiments of the people, their gusts of passion passed over, without ruffling the smooth surface of his mind. Trusting to the reflecting good sense of the nation for approbation and support, he had the magnanimity to pursue its real interests, in opposition to its temporary prejudices; and, though far from being regardless of popular favour, he could never stoop to retain, by deserving to lose it. In more instances than one, we find him committing his whole popularity to hazard, and pursuing steadily, in opposition to a torrent which would have overwhelmed a man of ordinary firmness, that course which had been dictated by a sense of duty.

In speculation, he was a real republican, devoted to the constitution of his country, and to that system of equal political rights on which it is founded. But between a balanced republic and a democracy, the difference is like that between order and chaos. Real liberty, he thought, was to be preserved, only by preserving the authority of the laws, and maintaining the energy of government. Scarcely did society present two characters which, in his opinion, less resembled each other, than a patriot and a demagogue.

No man has ever appeared upon the theatre of public action, whose integrity was more incorruptible, or whose principles were more perfectly free from the contamination of those selfish and unworthy passions, which find their nourishment in the conflicts of party. Having no views which required concealment, his real and avowed motives were the same; and his whole correspondence does not furnish a single case, from which even an enemy would infer that he was capable, under any circumstances, of stooping to the employment of duplicity. No truth can be uttered with more confidence than that his ends were always upright, and his means always pure. He exhibits the rare example of a politician to whom wiles were absolutely unknown, and whose professions to foreign governments and to his own countrymen, were always sincere. In him was fully exemplified the real distinction, which forever exists, between wisdom and cunning, and the importance as well as truth of the maxim that "honesty is the best policy."

If Washington possessed ambition, that passion was, in nis bosom, so regulated by principles, or controlled by circumstances, that it was neither vicious, nor turbulent. Intrigue was never employed as the means of its gratification, nor was personal aggrandizement its object. The various high and important stations to which he was called by the public voice, were unsought by himself; and, in consenting to fill them, he seems rather to have yielded to a general conviction that the interests of his country would be thereby promoted, than to an avidity for power.

Neither the extraordinary partiality of the American people, the extravagant praises which were bestowed upon him, nor the inveterate opposition and malignant calumnies which he encountered, had any visible influence upon his conduct. The cause is to be looked for in the texture of his mind.

In him, that innate and unassuming modesty which adulation would have offended, which the voluntary plaudits of millions could not betray into indiscretion, and which never obtruded upon others his claims to superior consideration, was happily blended with a high and correct sense of personal dignity, and with a just consciousness of that respect which is due to station. Without exertion, he could maintain the happy medium between that arrogance which wounds, and that facility which allows the office to be degraded in the person who fills it.

It is impossible to contemplate the great events which have occurred in the United States under the auspices of Washington, without ascribing them, in some measure, to him. If we ask the causes of the prosperous issue of a war, against the successful termination of which there were so many probabilities? of the good which was produced, and the ill which was avoided, during an administration fated to contend with the strongest prejudices, that a combination of circumstances and of passions, could produce? of the constant favour of the great mass of his fellow citizens, and of the confidence which, to the last moment of his life, they reposed in him? the answer, so far as these causes may be found in his character, will furnish a lesson well meriting the attention of those who are candidates for political fame.

Endowed by nature with a sound judgment, and an accurate discriminating mind, he feared not that laborious attention which made him perfectly master of those subjects, in all their relations, on which he was to decide: and this essential quality was guided by an unvarying sense of moral right, which would tolerate the employment, only, of those means that would bear the most rigid examination; by a fairness of intention which neither sought nor required disguise: and by a purity of virtue which was not only untainted, but unsuspected.

HENRY LEE

1756-1818

Henry Lee, known as "Light Horse Harry" Lee, Revolutionary soldier, governor of Virginia, and father of Robert E. Lee, was born at "Leesylvania" in Prince William County, Virginia, on January 29, 1756. He attended Princeton and at the outbreak of the Revolution joined the army as a cavalry captain. He served with distinction under Washington, became a major at the age of twenty-two, and won the popular name of "Light Horse Harry." He took an important part in the battle of Paulus Hook and was promoted to lieutenant colonel. In 1780 and 1781 he had a leading role in the Southern campaign and was present at the surrender of Cornwallis at Yorktown.

After the war he was elected to the Virginia House of Delegates, was a member of the Continental Congress, took an active part in the Virginia Convention of 1788 which ratified the Federal Constitution, and was governor of Virginia. He was sent by Washington in 1794 to suppress the "Whiskey Rebellion" in Pennsylvania and was elected to Congress in 1799. On the death of Washington, he delivered the address which follows, containing the famous lines, "first in war, first in peace and first in the hearts of his countrymen."

The last two decades of his life were a difficult time. He made his home at "Stratford" in Westmoreland County, the Lee estate inherited by his wife, his cousin Matilda Lee, but lived there in straitened circumstances. Shortly after the birth of Robert E. Lee in 1807, the fifth child of his second marriage, he was imprisoned for a time for debt. During his imprisonment he devoted himself to writing his *Memoirs of the War in the Southern Department*. In 1812, in Baltimore, he attempted to aid his friend A. C. Hanson, editor of the *Federal Republican*, in defending his press against mob violence, and in the ensuing riot received injuries from which he never recovered. He died on March 25, 1818.

TRIBUTE TO WASHINGTON

In obedience to your will, I rise, your humble organ, with the hope of executing a part of the system of public mourning which you have pleased to adopt, commemorative of the death of the most illustrious and most beloved personage this country has ever produced; and which, while it transmits to posterity your sense of the awful event, faintly represents your knowledge of the consummate excellence you so cordially honor.

Desperate, indeed, is any attempt on earth to meet correspondently this dispensation of Heaven; for while with pious resignation we submit to the will of an all-gracious Providence, we can never cease lamenting, in our finite view of Omnipotent wisdom, the heartrending privation for which our nation weeps. When the civilized world shakes to its center; when every moment gives birth to strange and momentous changes; when our peaceful quarter of the globe, of the human race, may yet be compelled to abandon her pacific policy and to risk the doleful casualties of war, what limit is there to the extent of our loss? None within the reach of my words to express; none which your feeling will not disavow.

The founder of our federate Republic—our bulwark in war, our guide in peace, is no more! O that this were but questionable! Hope, the comforter of the wretched, would pour into our agonizing hearts its balmy dew. But alas! there is no hope for us; Washington is removed forever! Possessing the stoutest frame and purest mind, he had passed nearly to his sixty-eighth year in the enjoyment of high health, when, habituated by his care of us to neglect himself, a slight cold, disregarded, became inconvenient on Friday, oppressive on Saturday, and, defying every medical interposition, before the morning of Sunday put an end to the best of men. An end, did I say? — his fame survives, bounded only by the limits of the earth and by the extent of the human mind. He survives in our hearts, in the growing knowledge of our children, in the affection of the good throughout the world: and when our monuments shall be done away; when nations now existing shall be no more; when even our young and far-spreading empire shall have perished, still will our Washington's glory unfaded shine, and die not until love of virtue cease on earth, or earth itself sinks into chaos.

How, my fellow citizens, shall I signal to your grateful hearts his preeminent worth? Where shall I begin in opening to your view a character throughout sublime? Shall I speak of his warlike achievements, all springing from obedience to his country's will—all directed to his country's good?

Will you go with me to the banks of the Monongahela, to see your youthful Washington supporting, in the dismal hour of Indian victory, the ill-fated Braddock, and saving, by his judgment and by his valor, the remains of a defeated army, pressed by the conquering savage foe; or, when oppressed America nobly resolved to risk her all in defense of her violated rights, he was elevated by the unanimous voice of Congress to the command of her armies? Will you follow him to the high grounds of Boston, where to an undisciplined, courageous, and virtuous yeomanry his presence gave the stability of system and infused the invincibility of love of country; or shall I carry you to the painful scenes of Long Island, York Island, and New Jersey, when combating superior and gallant armies, aided by powerful fleets and led by chiefs high in the roll of fame, he stood the bulwark of our safety, undismayed by disaster, unchanged by change of fortune? Or will you view him in the precarious fields of Trenton, where deep gloom, unnerving every arm, reigned triumphant through our thinned, worn-down, unaided ranks, himself unmoved? Dreadful was the night. It was about this time of winter; the storm raged, the Delaware, rolling furiously with floating ice, forbade the approach of man. Washington, self-collected, viewed the tremendous scene; his country called; unappalled by surrounding dangers, he passed to the hostile shore; he fought; he conquered. The morning sun cheered the American world. Our country rose on the event; and her dauntless chief, pursuing his blow, completed in the lawns of Princeton what his vast soul had conceived on the shores of the Delaware.

Thence to the strong grounds of Morristown he led his small but gallant band, and through an eventful winter, by the high efforts of his genius, whose matchless force was measurable only by the growth of difficulties, he held in check formidable hostile legions, conducted by a chief experienced in the art of war and famed for his valor on the ever memorable heights of Abraham, where fell Wolfe, Montcalm, and, since, our much lamented Montgomery, all covered with glory. In this fortunate interval, produced by his masterly conduct, our fathers, ourselves, animated by his resistless example, rallied around our country's standard and continued to follow her beloved chief through the various and trying scenes to which the destinies of our Union led.

Who is there that has forgotten the vales of Brandywine, the fields of Germantown, or the plains of Monmouth? Everywhere present, wants of every kind obstructing, numerous and valiant armies encountering, himself a host, he assuaged our sufferings, limited our privations, and upheld our tottering Republic. Shall I display to you the spread of the fire of his soul by rehearsing the praises of the hero of Saratoga and his much-loved compeer of the Carolinas? No; our Washington wears not borrowed glory. To Gates, to Greene, he gave without reserve the applause due to their eminent merit; and long may the chiefs of Saratoga and of Eutaw receive the grateful respect of a grateful people.

Moving in his own orbit, he imparted heart and light to his most distant satellites; and, combining the physical and moral force of all within his sphere, with irresistible weight he took his course, commiserating folly, disdaining vice, dismaying treason, and invigorating despondency, until the auspicious hour arrived when, united with the intrepid forces of a potent and magnanimous ally, he brought to submission the since conqueror of India; thus finishing his long career of military glory with a luster corresponding to his great name, and in this, his last act of war, affixing the seal of fate to our nation's birth.

To the horrid din of battle, sweet peace succeeded; and our virtuous chief, mindful only of the common good in a moment tempting personal aggrandizement, hushed the discontents of growing sedition; and surrendering his power into the hands from which he had received it, converted his sword into a ploughshare, teaching an admiring world that to be truly great you must be truly good.

Virginia Reader

Were I to stop here, the picture would be incomplete and the task imposed unfinished. Great as was our Washington in war, and much as did that greatness contribute to produce the American Republic, it is not in war alone his preeminence stands conspicuous. His various talents, combining all the capacities of a statesman with those of a soldier, fitted him alike to guide the councils and the armies of martial toils, while his invaluable parental advice was still sounding in our ears, when he, who had been our shield and our sword, was called forth to act a less splendid but more important part.

Possessing a clear and penetrating mind, a strong and sound judgment, calmness and temper for deliberation, with invincible firmness and perseverance in resolutions maturely formed; drawing information from all; acting from himself, with incorruptible integrity and unvarying patriotism; his own superiority and the public confidence alike marked him as the man designed by Heaven to lead in the great political as well as military events which have distinguished the era of his life.

The finger of an overruling Providence, pointing at Washington, was neither mistaken nor unobserved when, to realize the vast hopes to which our revolution had given birth, a change of political system became indispensable.

How novel, how grand the spectacle! Independent states, stretched over an immense territory, and known only by common difficulty, clinging to their union as the rock of their safety, deciding by frank comparison of their relative condition to rear on that rock, under the guidance of reason, a common government through whose commanding protection liberty and order, with their long train of blessings, should be safe to themselves and the sure inheritance of their posterity.

This arduous task devolved on citizens selected by the people from knowledge of their wisdom and confidence in their virtue. In this august assembly of sages and of patriots Washington of course was found; and, as if acknowledged to be most wise where all were wise, with one voice he was declared their chief. How well he merited this rare distinction, how faithful were the labors of himself and his compatriots, the work of their hands and our union, strength, and prosperity, the fruits of that work, best attest.

Henry Lee, 1756-1818

But to have essentially aided in presenting to this country this consummation of her hopes neither satisfied the claims of his fellow citizens on his talents nor those duties which the possession of those talents imposed. Heaven had not infused into his mind such an uncommon share of its ethereal spirit to remain unemployed, nor bestowed on him his genius unaccompanied with the corresponding duty of devoting it to the common good. To have framed a constitution was showing only, without realizing, the general happiness. This great work remained to be done; and America, steadfast in her preference, with one voice summoned her beloved Washington, unpracticed as he was in the duties of civil administration, to execute this last act in the completion of the national felicity. Obedient to her call, he assumed the high office with that self-distrust peculiar to his innate modesty, the constant attendant of preeminent virtue. What was the burst of joy through our anxious land on this exhilarating event is known to us all. The aged, the young, the brave, the fair, rivalled each other in demonstrations of their gratitude; and this high-wrought, delightful scene was heightened in its effect by the singular contest between the zeal of the bestower and the avoidance of the receiver of the honors bestowed. Commencing his administration, what heart is not charmed with the recollection of the pure and wise principles announced by himself as the basis of his political life! He best understood the indissoluble union between virtue and happiness, between duty and advantage, between the genuine maxims of an honest and magnanimous policy and the solid rewards of public prosperity and individual felicity; watching, with an equal and comprehensive eye, over this great assemblage of communities and interests, he laid the foundations of our national policy in the unerring, immutable principles of morality, based on religion, exemplifying the preeminence of a free government, by all the attributes which won the affections of its citizens, or commanded the respect of the world.

"O fortunatos nimium, sua si bona norint!"

Leading through the complicated difficulties produced by previous obligations and conflicting interests, seconded by succeeding houses of congress, enlightened and patriotic, he surmounted all original obstruction and brightened the path of our national felicity.

The presidential term expiring, his solicitude to exchange exaltation for humility returned with a force increased with increase of age; and he had prepared his farewell address to his countrymen, proclaiming his intention, when the united interposition of all around him, enforced by the eventful prospects of the epoch, produced a further sacrifice of inclination to duty. The election of president followed; and Washington, by the unanimous vote of the nation, was called to resume the chief magistracy. What a wonderful fixture of confidence! Which attracts most our admiration, a people so correct, or a citizen combining an assemblage of talents forbidding rivalry and stifling even envy itself? Such a nation ought to be happy, such a chief must be forever revered.

War, long menaced by the Indian tribes, now broke out; and the terrible conflict deluging Europe with blood began to shed its baneful influence over our happy land. To the first, outstretching his invincible arm, under the orders of the gallant Wayne, the American Eagle soared triumphant through distant forests. Peace followed victory; and the melioration of the condition of the enemy followed peace. Godlike virtue, which uplifts even the subdued savage!

To the second he opposed himself. New and delicate was the conjecture, and great was the stake. Soon did his penetrating mind discern and seize the only course continuing to us all the felicity enjoyed. He issued his proclamation of neutrality. This index to his whole subsequent conduct was sanctioned by the approbation of both Houses of Congress and by the approving voice of the people.

To this sublime policy he inviolably adhered, unmoved by foreign intrusion, unshaken by domestic turbulence.

> "Justum et tenacem propositi virum,
> Non civium ardor prava jubentium,
> Non vultus instantis tyranni,
> Mente quatit solida."

Maintaining his pacific system at the expense of no duty, America, faithful to herself and unstained in her honor, continued to enjoy

Henry Lee, 1756-1818

the delights of peace, while afflicted Europe mourns in every quarter under the accumulated miseries of an unexampled war — miseries in which our happy country must have shared, had not our preeminent Washington been as firm in council as he was brave in the field.

Pursuing steadfastly his course, he held safe the public happiness, preventing foreign war and quelling internal discord, till the revolving of a third election approached, when he executed his interrupted but inextinguishable desire of returning to the humble walks of private life.

The promulgation of his fixed resolution stopped the anxious wishes of an affectionate people from adding a third unanimous testimonial of their unabated confidence in the man so long enthroned in their hearts. When before was affection like this exhibited on earth? Turn over the records of ancient Greece; review the annals of mighty Rome; examine the volumes of modern Europe: you search in vain. America and her Washington only afford the dignified exemplification.

The illustrious personage called by the general voice in succession to the arduous office of guiding a free people had new difficulties to encounter. The amicable effort of settling our difficulties with France, begun by Washington and pursued by his successor in virtue as in station, proving abortive, America took measures of self-defense. No sooner was the public mind roused by a prospect of danger than every eye was turned to the friend of all, though secluded from public view and gray in public service. The virtuous veteran, following his plough, received the unexpected summons with mingled emotions of indignation at the unmerited ill-treatment of his country and of a determination once more to risk his all in her defense.

The annunciation of these feelings, in his affecting letter to the President accepting the command of the army, concludes his official conduct.

First in war, first in peace, and first in the hearts of his countrymen, he was second to none in the humble and endearing scenes of private life. Pious, just, humane, temperate, and sincere; uniform, dignified, and commanding, his example was as edifying to all around him as were the effects of that example lasting.

337

To his equals he was kind; to his inferiors condescending; and to the dear object of his affections, exemplarily tender. Correct throughout, vice shuddered in his presence and virtue always felt his fostering hand; the purity of his private character gave effulgence to his public virtues.

His last scene comported with the whole tenor of his life; although in extreme pain, not a sigh, not a groan escaped him; and with undisturbed serenity he closed his well-spent life. Such was the man America has lost! Such was the man for whom our nation mourns!

Methinks I see his august image, and hear, falling from his venerable lips, these deep-sinking words:

"Cease, sons of America, lamenting our separation; go on, and confirm by your wisdom the fruits of our joint counsels, joint efforts, and common dangers. Reverence religion; diffuse knowledge throughout your land; patronize the arts and sciences; let liberty and order be inseparable companions; control party spirit, the bane of free government; observe good faith to, and cultivate peace with, all nations; shut up every avenue of foreign influence; contract rather than extend national connection; rely on yourselves only; be American in thought and deed. Thus will you give immortality to that Union which was the constant object of my terrestrial labors. Thus will you preserve, undisturbed to the latest posterity, the felicity of a people to me most dear; and thus will you supply (if my happiness is now aught to you) the only vacancy in the round of pure bliss Heaven bestows."

JAMES MONROE

1758-1831

James Monroe, disciple of Jeffersonian democracy and fifth President of the United States, was born in Westmoreland County, Virginia, on April 28, 1758. He entered the College of William and Mary at the age of sixteen but left at the outbreak of the Revolution to enlist as a lieutenant in a Virginia regiment of the Continental line. He fought in half a dozen battles, was wounded, and became a major. A veteran at twenty-two, he began the study of law under Jefferson, whose example and principles influenced him all his life.

He was elected to the Virginia House of Delegates when he was twenty-four, and until his retirement from the presidency more than forty years later he devoted himself unstintingly to the affairs of the new nation. A member of the House of Representatives and of the Senate, minister to France under President Washington, governor of Virginia, negotiator of the Louisiana Purchase under President Jefferson, Secretary of State and Secretary of War under President Madison, and President of the United States, he was the "last of the cocked hats" of the Revolutionary "Virginia dynasty" on the national scene.

At the end of his second term as President, Monroe retired to his home, "Oak Hill," in Loudoun County, Virginia. He became a member of the board of visitors of the University of Virginia in 1826, and served as the presiding officer of the Virginia Constitutional Convention of 1829. He died on July 4, 1831.

The address to the National Convention of France which follows was delivered on August 15, 1794, when Monroe was President Washington's minister to France.

"REPUBLICS SHOULD APPROACH NEAR TO EACH OTHER . . ."

Address to the National Convention of France, August 15, 1794

Citizens, President and Representatives of the French People:

My admission into this Assembly, in the presence of the French Nation (for all the citizens of France are represented here) to be recognized as the Representative of the American Republic impresses me with a degree of sensibility which I cannot express. I consider it as a new proof of that friendship and regard which the French Nation has always shown to their ally, the United States of America.

Republics should approach near to each other. In many respects they all have the same interest. But this is more especially the case with the American and French Republics:—their governments are similar; they both cherish the same principles and rest on the same basis, the equal and unalienable rights of men. The recollection too of common dangers and difficulties will increase their harmony, and cement their union. America had her day of oppression, difficulty and war, but her sons were virtuous and brave and the storm which long clouded her political horizon has passed and left them in the enjoyment of peace, liberty, and independence. France, our ally and our friend and who aided in the contest, has now embarked in the same noble career; and I am happy to add that whilst the fortitude, magnanimity, and heroic valor of her troops, command the admiration and applause of the astonished world, the wisdom and firmness of her councils unite equally in securing the happiest result.

America is not an unfeeling spectator of your affairs in the present crisis. I lay before you in the declarations of every department of our Government, declarations which are founded in the affection of the citizens at large, the most decided proof of her sincere attachment to the liberty, prosperity, and happiness of the French Republic. Each branch of Congress according to the course of proceedings

340

there has requested the President to make this known to you in its behalf; and in fulfilling the desires of those branches I am instructed to declare to you that he has expressed his own.

In discharging the duties of the office which I am now called on to execute, I promise myself the highest satisfaction; because I well know that whilst I pursue the dictates of my own heart in wishing the liberty and happiness of the French Nation, and which I most sincerely do, I speak the sentiments of my own Country; and that by doing everything in my power to preserve and perpetuate the harmony so happily subsisting at present between the two Republics, I shall promote the interest of both. To this great object therefore all my efforts will be directed. If I shall be so fortunate as to succeed in such manner as to merit the approbation of both Republics I shall deem it the happiest event of my life and return hereafter with a consolation, which those who mean well and have served the cause of liberty alone can feel.

WILLIAM WIRT

1772-1834

William Wirt began the practice of law in Culpeper County, Virginia, at the age of twenty, starting a career which took him to the top of the American bar and brought him considerable literary acclaim in his day. In his early twenties he married Mildred Gilmer, sister of Francis Walker Gilmer, and moved to the Gilmer estate, "Pen Park," in Albemarle County, Virginia. There he made lasting friendships with many of the leading men of the time, including Jefferson, Madison and Monroe. After the early death of his wife he moved to Richmond, practiced law there and in Norfolk, and remarried. He first attracted wide attention as a lawyer in a test of the Alien and Sedition laws. He gained still more prominence for his part in the prosecution of the treason case against Aaron Burr. In 1817 President Monroe appointed Wirt Attorney General of the United States. He held the post during the next twelve years, under Monroe and John Quincy Adams, and did much to establish the office as an important part of the Federal government. He continued his practice of law and appeared before the Supreme Court in such important cases as McCulloch vs. Maryland, the Dartmouth College case, and Gibbons vs. Ogden.

Despite his eminence at the bar, Wirt was never entirely happy as a lawyer. Jefferson wrote to him with much insight in 1808: "I suspected, from your desire to go into the army, that you disliked your profession, notwithstanding that your prospects in it were inferior to none in the State." Jefferson suggested that he run for Congress. But to change the life of a lawyer for that of a politician was not what Wirt wanted. What he yearned for was a career as a man of letters. He never devoted himself whole-heartedly to writing, but he maintained an active interest in literature all his life and wrote in the intervals of his busy practice of law.

Wirt's best known work, *The Letters of a British Spy*, was written when he was thirty. Cast in the form of the letters of a visiting Englishman, the essays were published anonymously in the Richmond *Argus* and were immediately collected in book form. The book enjoyed a wide popularity and its authorship was an open secret. The following year he collaborated with several friends in Richmond with literary interests in writing a series

342

William Wirt, 1772-1834

of essays published as *The Rainbow*. A second series of *The Rainbow* essays were published in the Richmond *Enquirer* but were not issued in book form. In 1810-1813 Wirt and his literary circle wrote some thirty-three essays, which were published as *The Old Bachelor*. In 1817 Wirt published his most ambitious work, *Sketches of the Life and Character of Patrick Henry*. This biography of Henry, which has gone through many editions, is the chief source of the popular conception of that Revolutionary figure, and it is the source of the text of his famous speech to the Virginia Convention in March 1775.

Of German and Swiss ancestry, Wirt was born on November 8, 1772, in Bladensburg, Maryland, where his father was a tavern keeper. His parents died when he was a child. He was fortunate in early having access to several private libraries, in which he cultivated a taste for good reading, a taste which remained with him all his life. He died in Washington, D. C., on February 18, 1834.

MEDITATION AT JAMESTOWN*

I have taken a pleasant ride of sixty miles down the river, in order, my dear S...., to see the remains of the first English settlement in Virginia.

The site is a very handsome one. The river is three miles broad; and, on the opposite shore, the country presents a fine range of bold and beautiful hills. But I find no vestiges of the ancient town, except the ruins of a church steeple, and a disordered group of old tombstones. On one of these, shaded by the boughs of a tree, whose trunk has embraced and grown over the edge of the stone, and seated on the head-stone of another grave, I now address you.

What a moment for a lugubrious meditation among the tombs! but fear not; I have neither the temper nor the genius of a Hervey; and, as much as I revere his pious memory, I cannot envy him the possession of such a genius and such a temper. For my own part, I would not have suffered the mournful pleasure of writing his book, and Doctor Young's Night Thoughts, for all the just fame which they have both gained by those celebrated productions. Much rather would I have danced and sung, and played the fiddle with Yorick, through the whimsical pages of Tristram Shandy: that book which everybody justly censures and admires alternately; and which will continue to be read, abused and devoured, with ever fresh delight, as long as the world shall relish a joyous laugh, or a tear of the most delicious feeling.

By the by, here on one side is an inscription on a gravestone, which would constitute no bad theme for an occasional meditation from Yorick himself. The stone, it seems, covers the grave of a man who was born in the neighbourhood of London; and his epitaph concludes the short and rudely executed account of his birth and death, by declaring him to have been "a great sinner, in hopes of a joyful resur-

*Title supplied. Letter VI of *The Letters of a British Spy*, by William Wirt. First published 1803. Tenth edition, revised and corrected, 1832.

344

rection;" as if he had sinned with no other intention, than to give himself a fair title to these exulting hopes. But awkwardly and ludicrously as the sentiment is expressed, it is in its meaning most just and beautiful; as it acknowledges the boundless mercy of Heaven, and glances at that divinely consoling proclamation, "come unto me all ye who are weary and heavy laden, and I will give you rest."

The ruin of the steeple is about thirty feet high, and mantled, to its very summit, with ivy. It is difficult to look at this venerable object, surrounded as it is with these awful proofs of the mortality of man, without exclaiming in the pathetic solemnity of our Shakespeare,

> "The cloud-capt towers, the gorgeous palaces,
> The solemn temples, the great globe itself,
> Yea, all which it inherits, shall dissolve;
> And, like this insubstantial pageant faded,
> Leave not a wreck behind."

Whence, my dear S...., arises the irrepressible reverence and tender affection with which I look at this broken steeple? Is it that my soul, by a secret, subtile process, invests the mouldering ruin with her own powers; imagines it a fellow being; a venerable old man, a Nestor, or an Ossian, who has witnessed and survived the ravages of successive generations, the companions of his youth, and of his maturity, and now mourns his own solitary and desolate condition, and hails their spirits in every passing cloud? Whatever may be the cause, as I look at it, I feel my soul drawn forward, as by the cords of gentlest sympathy, and involuntarily open my lips to offer consolation to the drooping pile.

Where, my S...., is the busy, bustling crowd which landed here two hundred years ago? Where is Smith, that pink of gallantry, that flower of chivalry? I fancy that I can see their first, slow and cautious approach to the shore; their keen and vigilant eyes piercing the forest in every direction, to detect the lurking Indian, with his tomahawk, bow and arrow. Good Heavens! what an enterprise! how full of the most fearful perils! and yet how entirely profitless to the daring men who personally undertook and achieved it! Through what a series of the most spirit-chilling hardships, had they to toil! How often did they cast their eyes to England in vain! and with what delusive hopes, day after day, did the little, famished crew strain their sight to catch the white sail of comfort and relief! But day after day, the sun set, and darkness covered the earth; but no sail of comfort or relief came. How often in the pangs of hunger, sickness, solitude and disconsolation, did they think of London; her shops, her markets groaning under the weight of plenty; her streets swarming with gilded coaches, bustling hacks, with crowds of lords, dukes and commons, with healthy, busy, contented faces of every description; and among them none more healthy or more contented, than those of their ungrateful and improvident directors! But now — where are they all? the little, famished colony which landed here, and the many-coloured crowd of London — where are they, my dear S ... .? Gone, where there is no distinction; consigned to the common earth. Another generation succeeded them: which, just as busy and as bustling as that which fell before it has sunk down into the same nothingness. Another and yet another billow has rolled on, each emulating its predecessor in height; towering for its moment, and curling its foaming honours to the clouds; then roaring, breaking, and perishing on the same shore.

It is not strange, that, familiarly and universally as these things are known, yet each generation is as eager in the pursuit of its earthly objects, projects its plans on a scale as extensive as and laborious in their execution, with a spirit as ardent and unrelaxing, as if this life and this world were to last for ever? It is, indeed, a most benevolent interposition of Providence, that these palpable and just views of the vanity of human life are not permitted entirely to crush the spirits, and unnerve the arm of industry. But at the same time, methinks, it would be wise in man to permit them to have, at least, so much weight with him, as to prevent his total absorption by the things of this earth, and to point some of his thoughts and his exertions, to a system of being, far more permanent, exalted and happy. Think not this reflection too solemn. It is irresistibly inspired by the objects around me; and, as rarely as it occurs, (much too rarely,) it is most certainly and solemnly true, my S ... .

It is curious to reflect, what a nation, in the course of two hundred years, has sprung up and flourished from the feeble, sickly germ which was planted here! Little did our short-sighted court suspect the conflict which she was preparing for herself; the convulsive throe by which her infant colony would in a few years burst from her, and start into political importance that would astonish the earth.

But Virginia, my dear S . . . ., as rapidly as her population and her wealth must continue to advance, wants one more important source of solid grandeur; and that, too, the animating soul of a republic. I mean, public spirit; that sacred *amor patriae* which filled Greece and Rome with patriots, heroes and scholars.

There seems to me to be but one object throughout the state; *to grow rich:* a passion which is visible, not only in the walks of private life, but which has crept into and poisoned every public body in the state. Indeed, from the very genius of the government, by which all the public characters are, at short periodical elections, evolved from the body of the people, it cannot but happen, that the councils of the state must take the impulse of the private propensities of the country. Hence, Virginia exhibits no great public improvements; hence, in spite of her wealth, every part of the country manifests her sufferings, either from the penury of her guardians, or their want of that attention and noble pride, wherewith it is their duty to consult her appearance. Her roads and highways are frequently impassable, sometimes frightful; the very few public works which have been set on foot, instead of being carried on with spirit, are permitted to languish and pine and creep feebly along, in such a manner, that the first part of an edifice grows grey with age, and almost tumbles in ruins, before the last part is lifted from the dust; highest officers are sustained with so avaricious, so niggardly a hand, that if they are not driven to subsist on roots, and drink ditch-water, with old Fabricius, it is not for the want of republican economy in the projectors of the salaries; and, above all, the general culture of the human mind, that best cure for the aristocratic distinctions which they profess to hate, that best basis of the social and political equality, which they profess to love: this culture, instead of becoming a national care, is intrusted merely to such individuals, as hazard, indigence, misfortunes or crimes, have forced from their native Europe to seek an asylum and bread in the wilds of America.

They have only one public seminary of learning: a college in Williamsburg, about seven miles from this place, which was erected in the reign of our William and Mary, derives its principal support from their munificence, and therefore very properly bears their names. This college, in the fastidious folly and affectation of republicanism, or what is worse, in the niggardly spirit of parsimony which they dignify with the name of economy, these democrats have endowed with a few despicable fragments of surveyors' fees, &c., thus converting their national academy into a mere *lazaretto,* and feeding its polite, scientific, and highly respectable professors, like a band of beggars, on the scraps and crumbs that fall from the financial table. And, then, instead of aiding and energizing the police of the college, by a few civil regulations, they permit their youth to run riot in all the wildness of dissipation; while the venerable professors are forced to look on, in the deep mortification of conscious impotence, and see their care and zeal requited, by the ruin of their pupils and the destruction of their seminary.

These are points which, at present, I can barely touch; when I have an easier seat and writing desk, than a grave and a tombstone, it will give me pleasure to dilate on them; for, it will afford an opportunity of exulting in the superiority of our own energetic monarchy, over this republican body without a soul.[2]

For the present, my dear S . . . ., I bid you adieu.

[2]British insolence! Yet it cannot be denied, however painful the admission, that there is some foundation for his censures. [Wirt's footnote.]

JOHN RANDOLPH

1773-1833

John Randolph, known as "John Randolph of Roanoke," a designation which he adopted to distinguish himself from a kinsman of the same name whom he disliked, was born at "Cawsons" in Prince George County, Virginia, on June 2, 1773. He was brought up by his stepfather, St. George Tucker. His formal education was desultory, but he studied briefly at Princeton, Columbia and William and Mary.

At the age of twenty-six he was elected to Congress from Virginia and won an immediate reputation in that body for brilliance and eloquence. With Jefferson's election as President, Randolph, not yet thirty, became the acknowledged leader of his party in Congress.

Randolph soon parted company with Jefferson and during much of his thirty years in Congress he was a lonely figure, contentious, eccentric, devastating in debate, but without real influence. Twice, however, he again won a dominant position in Congress: in 1820, when he led the opposition to the Missouri Compromise; and a decade later, when he solidified the opposition to the administration of John Quincy Adams.

He served briefly as Senator from Virginia, took an important part in the Virginia Constitutional Convention of 1829, and was sent to Russia on a special mission by President Jackson. His mind was disordered from time to time during his later years, and throughout his life his brilliance was often close to the border line of insanity. He died on May 24, 1833.

The following examples of Randolph's wit are from the monumental biography, *John Randolph of Roanoke 1773-1833*, by the Virginia-born Senator from Maryland, William Cabell Bruce. The final quip is one of the finest epigrams in American politics: "Denouncing me! That is strange. I never did him a favor."

EPIGRAMS OF JOHN RANDOLPH*

Never did a man have a cleverer gift of minting phrases that passed into general circulation.

Benjamin Hardin, of Kentucky, a vigorous but unpolished speaker, was "a carving knife whetted on a brickbat."

The wavering Edmund Randolph was "the chameleon on the aspen, always trembling, always changing."

Of Robert Wright and John Rea (Ray) he said that the House exhibited two anomalies: "A Wright always wrong; and a Ray without light."

The politic and secretive Van Buren, Randolph said, "rowed to his object with muffled oars."

Of a cautious statesman, he said that, under his direction, the Ship of State might never take a prize, but it would probably never become one.

Benton's four-day speech, he observed, consumed one day more than the French Revolution (of 1830).

Yes, Thomas Ritchie (the distinguished editor of the Richmond *Enquirer*) did have seven principles, but they were the 5 loaves and the two fishes.

"Clay's eye is on the Presidency; and my eye is on him."

Turning away from a lady who had been pouring her sympathy with the struggling Greeks into his ear, Randolph pointed to a group of ragged little Negroes near the steps of her home and exclaimed: "Madam, the Greeks are at your door!"— words that soon winged their way to every part of the United States.

Referring to the naval strength of England, and to Madison's pamphlet on neutral rights, he said: "Against 800 ships in commission we enter the lists with a three-shilling pamphlet."

*From "General Observations on Randolph as an Orator," Chapter VII, Volume 2, *John Randolph of Roanoke 1773-1833*, by William Cabell Bruce. G. P. Putnam's Sons. Copyright 1922. Reprinted by permission.

John Randolph, 1773-1833

Other epigrams of his were these: "The bad blood *will* show in some part of the four-mile heat."

"An English noble has but one son, all the rest are bastards."

"England is Elysium for the rich; Tartarus for the poor."

"I am an aristocrat; I love liberty, I hate equality."

"Asking one of the states to surrender part of her sovereignty is like asking a lady to surrender part of her chastity."

"New Orleans is the key to our strong-box."

"The three degrees of comparison — begging, borrowing, and stealing."

"A rat hole will let in the ocean."

"It is a turnstyle; it is in everybody's way but it stops no one."

"Poverty, that nurse of genius, though she sometimes overlays it."

"Stick to a friend a *little* in the wrong."

"That most delicious of privileges — spending other people's money."

"Denouncing me! That is strange. I never did him a favor."

NATHANIEL BEVERLEY TUCKER
1784-1851

Nathaniel Beverley Tucker was the author of a book, *The Partisan Leader*, which was a sensation in its day. Issued under the pseudonym Edward William Sidney in 1836 (by a publisher who hoped to influence the presidential election against Van Buren), it carried the fictitious date 1856 and the legend, *A Tale of the Future*, on the title page, and recounted the "history" of a dictatorship established by Van Buren, the secession of the South from the Union, and civil war.

Tucker was the son of St. George Tucker, but differed in temperament and politics from his democratic-minded father. He was born at "Matoax," Chesterfield County, Virginia, on September 6, 1784, the half-brother of John Randolph, and the younger brother of Henry St. George Tucker. He apparently felt keenly all his life his position as a younger and less well-known brother.

He attended William and Mary College and began the practice of law in Virginia. He was a lieutenant in the War of 1812, returned to the practice of law, and in 1815 went to the Territory of Missouri. There he spent the next fifteen years; he was appointed a territorial judge and for a year or two after Missouri became a state he held a Federal judgeship. He opposed the Missouri Compromise, was violent on the subject of "Yankees" and proposed that all Northerners be excluded from Missouri.

He returned to Virginia and was appointed to the professorship at William and Mary which his father had held a generation earlier. He was three times married. He remained a teacher until his death on August 26, 1851, and expounded his views in letters and articles and public speeches. Tucker felt that he was a member of a small aristocracy surrounded by the "peasantry" of Virginia, and he became the self-appointed spokesman for the *élite*. He was vigorously anti-democratic, opposed the administration of Jackson, was one of the earliest proponents of secession, defended slavery as energetically as his father had opposed it, and broke with his brother, Henry St. George Tucker, a member of Congress from Virginia, on the issue of nullification. In *The Partisan Leader* he projected a history of the years ahead to justify his views. He was the author of two other novels, *George Balcombe* (1836) and *Gertrude*, published in the *Southern*

352

Nathaniel Beverley Tucker, 1784-1851

Literary Messenger (1844-45). He was also a contributor to William Gilmore Simms' *Southern Quarterly Review* and other periodicals.

The Partisan Leader was reprinted as propaganda by both the North and the South at the beginning of the Civil War: in 1861 in New York as evidence that secession had been planned for a quarter of a century; and in Richmond in 1862 as evidence that secession had been justified for a quarter of a century. A new edition, with a scholarly introduction by Carl Bridenbaugh, was published by Alfred A. Knopf, Inc. in the "Americana Deserta" series in 1933.

THE PARTISANS MEET THE ENEMY*

A Preview of the Civil War, 1836

While these arrangements were in progress scouts were hourly arriving. The country being altogether friendly, they were readily provided with fresh horses; and, before the enemy were half way from Lynchburg, we were fully apprised of their number, equipments, and order of march. First came a squadron of dragoons; then a light company; then Trevor's regiment, about five hundred strong; then a company of artillery; then one battalion of Mason's regiment, consisting of something more than two hundred men; the whole followed by a few light troops, by way of rear-guard. The whole might amount to a thousand men, well appointed and prepared at all points for efficient action.

On the morning of the fifth of November, the men were ordered to betake themselves to their allotted posts; and Douglas, having visited each, and seen that all was right, and rightly understood, addressed himself to his particular command. Where every man is an officer, each must be told individually beforehand what is expected from him. Panic apart, they will be apt to fulfil such instructions, and will fight with the terrible efficiency of individual animosity. Hence the formidable character of partisan warfare.

At length the enemy made their appearance. Clinging to the idea of surprising Douglas, Col. Trevor sent forward no advance, but determined to bring the whole strength of his corps to bear upon him at once. If he employed any scouts, they were either unfaithful, or were not permitted to approach near enough to learn any thing of the position or movements of Douglas. The consequence was, that Col. Trevor received the first intimation of his presence from a sharp

*Title supplied. From *The Partisan Leader*, by Nathaniel Beverley Tucker, 1836. Chapter XXXVIII.

354

firing in front, which sent his horse to the right-about and back to the rear. Pressing forward, he immediately ordered his sharp-shooters to disperse and take positions to gall us, while he pushed on his solid column of heavy infantry. The reception prepared for them was such as he had not dreamed of. His men fell like leaves in autumn; and, as fast as one platoon of the mountaineers discharged their pieces, another was on the same ground to pour in again that terrible fire, of which the martinets of the regular service have so inadequate an idea. Instead of the deep-mouthed peal of muskets, discharged simultaneously, there is the sharp, short crack of rifle after rifle, fired by men no one of whom touches the trigger until he sees precisely where his ball is to go. The effect was suitable to the cause; but yet the steady infantry pressed on,

"Each stepping where his comrade stood,"

to form an unbroken front, in order to charge with the bayonet.

Suddenly the firing ceased, and, behold, their enemy seemed to have fled from the expected charge. The fact was, that my last platoon, having fired, had withdrawn like their predecessors, and were running at full speed after their companions, down the hill and across the river. At the water's edge, I stopped and joined Schwartz in his ambush. It had been arranged that I should do this; because, in case we should be so fortunate as to seize the cannon, my skill as an artillerist might be of great use. Meantime, my men having crossed over, dispersed themselves along the bank, the face of the hills, and across the road, to cover the retreat of those who remained.

The regulars had necessarily spent a few moments in repairing the wreck of their shattered column before they advanced. They then moved forward; but, before they turned the angle of the road, most of my men were across the river. At the same time, the column under the immediate command of Douglas was seen drawn up in the road, near the foot of the hill, with the rear resting on the water's edge. As the enemy advanced the front platoon fired, faced to the right, and filing along the flank of the column, entered the river and crossed just below the ford. They next filed to the left in the same way, and crossed above the ford. In this manner the whole column disappeared, one platoon after another, while their fire was answered by a roar of musketry, which, being discharged from the higher ground, did more harm to those on the farther bank of the river than to the nearer enemy. At length the last platoon was withdrawn, and the regulars rushed down toward the river for the purpose of annoying them in crossing. In this attempt they were again checked and driven back by the terrible fire of my men, who, having already crossed, were drawn up, as I have said, on the other bank.

Col. Trevor now saw the necessity of advancing his artillery, which was accordingly hurried down to the water's edge to clear a passage for the infantry. By the time the cannon were untimbered, not a man of the mountaineers was to be seen. As soon as their companions had crossed, they dispersed with every appearance of confusion and alarm; some scampering along the road, and some clambering up the hills on both sides of it.

The way was now open, and the infantry advanced to cross the river. At this moment Colonel Mason, riding up to Colonel Trevor, pointed out the advantageous position of the artillery as a cover to his rear, if he should be forced to retreat. "Give me leave to suggest," said he, "that it may be well to leave the cannon where they are. The cavalry, too, cannot act with effect among those hills, and the two together, should the fortune of the day be unpropitious, may be of more use here than on the other side."

"You say true," said Trevor. "It shall be as you advise, and you, Colonel, will remain in command of this reserve."

"I earnestly beg, sir," said Mason, "that you will not deny me a share in the work of the day. The Captains of artillery and dragoons are all-sufficient to the command of their respective corps."

"Pardon me, sir," said Trevor. "None can be so proper to execute your prudent and cautious device as you, its author. You will be pleased, therefore, to repair to the rear, rally the dragoons, and bring them down to the water's edge. Let them be ready to cross at a moment's warning, to assist in the pursuit as soon as I have driven the enemy into the plain."

Saying this, Colonel Trevor turned off, and giving the word to march, dashed into the river. Poor Mason, insulted and mortified, nevertheless patiently addressed himself to the duty assigned him. Thus was this able and brave man denied all participation in an affair which his arrogant and sanguine commander believed to be an abounding source of honor to all who might be engaged in it.

I have omitted to mention that, as soon as the plan of endeavoring to surprise the artillery had been adopted, Schwartz had requested me to draw the outline of a piece of mounted ordinance in the sand, and to mark the proper positions of the artillerists employed about it. While I did this, some ten or fifteen of our best marksmen stood by, looking on attentively. When my sketch was done, he turned to one of them, and pointing to one of the marks made to stand for an artillerist, said coolly: "Now, this is your man;" and to another, "this is yours." Thus he went on till he had doomed every victim.

While we are supplying this omission in our narrative, the reader will please to suppose that Col. Trevor's regiment have forded the river, and have passed up the road and out of sight. It will be remembered that the hills on both sides of the defile had been lined with concealed marksmen, and that the greater part of the advance had, on recrossing the river, thrown themselves into the same places of concealment. But the idea that they had done so for any purpose but that of safety, entered not into Col. Trevor's mind. Indeed, if he had had any doubt, it must have been removed when he found, that as his column wound through the deep defile, not a shot molested their march. At the first angle of the road he halted and let the column march past him. He could see, from this point, both the head of it, as it advanced, and the rear as it came up. As the latter passed the spot where he stood, the leading platoon was in the act of turning the next angle of the road. At that moment he heard the startling report of a volley of rifles. He set spurs to his horse to gallop to the front, when every rock and every tree of the surrounding hills burst into flame, and the deep ravine echoed to the report of a hundred rifles. A shot struck his horse, and another piercing his hat, grazed the top of his head deep enough to lay bare the skull, and stun him, as he fell under his slaughtered horse. He was thus placed *hors de combat*, owing the preservation of his life to the insignia of his rank which had endangered it.

The sound of this firing was the signal for us. Each of the selected

marksmen fixed his aim on his appropriate victim; and, at a word
from Schwartz, the artillerymen at the guns fell as if swept away
by the breath of a tempest. Rushing from our hiding-place, the
cannon were instantly in our possession. The company of artillery
were not slow to disappear behind the angle of the rock, and one
or two who peeped out, being instantly picked off, we saw no more
of them.

Presently we heard the heavy tramp of the squadron slowly descending the hill, accompanied with the peculiar sound of dragoons,
dressing the front in preparation for a sudden and overwhelming
charge. While this was passing, our guns were all reloaded. "Mind,
boys," said Schwartz; "all of number one." The word was understood, and every alternate man stood ready, with rifle cocked and
trigger set, to receive the enemy. The charge was sounded, and the
leading horsemen, wheeling around the rock, were rushing on at full
speed, when horses and riders were seen to go down in one promiscuous heap. The greater number of the squadron were still out of
sight; and, had the way been open, might have followed to share
the fate of their companions, and finally to ride us down when our
guns should have been all discharged. But the work had been done
too effectually. The dead and wounded (both horse and rider)
nearly filled the road; and for dragoons to pick their way among such
appalling obstacles, in the face of fifty loaded rifles, at a distance of
twenty paces, was out of the question. A few who made the attempt
found this to their cost. The charge was not renewed, and some of
our men advancing to the angle of the rock, and occupying inaccessible but commanding points on the hills, soon made them draw
off to a safe distance.

While this was doing, I, with the few men selected for the service of the artillery, gave my attention to that. Glancing my eye along
both pieces, I saw that both had been accurately pointed into the
road on the other side. I had nothing, therefore, to do but to apply
the port-fire, which was still burning in the clenched hand of a dead
artillerist. By this time the column had fallen back, and the road
below the first angle was fast filling with the retreating mass. I had
never before witnessed the effusion of blood; and, heated as mine
now was, it ran cold as I applied the match. As the smoke cleared

off, I saw the enemy throwing away their arms, and stretching out their hands, some toward me, and some aloft to the unseen foe that galled them from the hills. The fire instantly slackened, and cravats and handkerchiefs being raised on the points of swords and bayonets, it ceased altogether. The mountaineers now poured down from the hills into the ravine, securing the arms of the enemy, mixing among them and hemming them in on every side. Douglas, whose place, since he had recrossed the river, had been among these concealed marksmen, was one of the first to approach the enemy. Advancing to those whose rank was most conspicuous, he made known his authority, and received their swords.

Meantime Col. Trevor had recovered his senses, and found himself fastened to the ground by the weight of his horse, which lay upon his leg. He was presently discovered, relieved, and helped to rise. At this moment he caught the eye of Douglas, who hastened to him, less from impatience to demand his sword, than to offer assistance to one who seemed to be an officer of high rank, and badly wounded. In the figure before him, all smeared with blood and dirt, he saw nothing by which he could recognize his brother. To the Colonel, the disguise of Douglas was hardly less complete. He had seen him receiving the surrender of others, and stood prepared to go through the same humiliating ceremony. He felt that his own disgrace was complete, and the form of surrender was thought of with indifference. He had already reached the lowest depth of abasement.

"But in that lowest depth a lower deep," seemed to open, when, as he extended his hand to deliver his sword to the victor, he discovered that the hand put forth to receive it was that of Douglas. He flung down his sword, stamping with rage, and immediately after called to his men to resume their arms. The voice struck the ear of Douglas, though dissonant with passion. The figure, too, confirmed his suspicion of the truth; and he immediately rushed to screen his brother with his own body from the rifles pointed against him. Calling for aid to those around, he presently succeeded in securing the Colonel, and after one or two fruitless attempts to soothe him, ordered him away to the house of Mr. Gordon. To that gentleman he spoke aside, and explaining in confidence the strange scene that he had just witnessed, besought him to take command of the escort, and to pay all imaginable attention to the health, comfort, and feelings of the Colonel. He was accordingly led away, raging and foaming at the mouth like a spoiled child who has been deprived of his toy, or baulked in his amusement. The mortification of Douglas was extreme; but he had the satisfaction to find that Arthur was not present; and to no other person but Schwartz and myself did the name of Colonel Trevor afford a hint of the connexion.

JOHN TYLER
1790-1862

John Tyler, member of the Virginia House of Delegates, Governor of Virginia, Representative and Senator from Virginia, Vice-President and President of the United States, was born at Greenway, Charles City county, Virginia, on March 29, 1790. He died in Richmond, Virginia, on January 18, 1862. He was the son of John Tyler (1747-1813), friend of Jefferson and governor of Virginia in 1808-1811. He was educated at the College of William and Mary and was admitted to the Virginia bar in 1809. He began his public career with his election to the Virginia House of Delegates at the age of twenty-one as a supporter of Jeffersonian principles. When Jefferson died in 1826 Tyler was serving as governor of Virginia, and he delivered the funeral oration from which the following selection is taken.

From the governorship of Virginia, Tyler went to the United States Senate, defeating John Randolph in 1827. He was reelected to the Senate in 1833 although he had exhibited considerable independence of party. He resigned his seat in the Senate in 1836 when he reached an impasse with his party leaders in Virginia over his opposition to President Jackson. In the Presidential election of that year he received 44 electoral votes, none of them from Virginia, for the Vice-Presidency on an independent Democratic ticket in opposition to Van Buren, who was supported by Jackson. He returned to the Virginia House of Delegates in 1838 and the following year was an unsuccessful candidate for the Senate. The next year he was nominated for the Vice-Presidency on the Whig ticket with William Henry Harrison. The Whigs won an overwhelming victory. On April 4, 1841, just a month after the inauguration, Harrison died and Tyler became the tenth President of the United States.

TRIBUTE TO JEFFERSON

Excerpts from the Funeral Oration by Governor Tyler

. . . But not to the future millions of these happy States shall his fame be confined. That celebrated state paper [the Declaration of Independence] will be found wherever is found the abode of civilized man. Sounded in the ears of tyrants, they shall tremble on their thrones, while man, so long the victim of oppression, awakes from the sleep of ages and bursts his chains. The day is rapidly approaching, a prophetic tongue has pronounced it "to some nations sooner, to others later, but finally to all," when it will be made manifest "that the mass of mankind have not been born with saddles on their backs, nor a favored few booted and spurred ready to ride them legitimately, by the grace of God." Already has this truth aroused the one-half of this continent from the lethargy in which it has so long reposed. Already are the paeans of liberty chanted from the Gulf of Mexico to the Rio de la Plata, and its altars are erecting on the ruins of a superstitious idolatry. A mighty spirit walks abroad upon the earth, which shall, in its onward march, overturn principalities and powers, and trample thrones in the dust. . . .

. . . He had to encounter prejudices become venerable by age, to assail error in its strong places, and to expel it even from its fastnesses. He advanced to the charge with a bold and reckless intrepidity, but with a calculating coolness. The Declaration, of which I have just spoken, had announced the great truth that man was capable of self-government, but it still remained for him to achieve a conquest over an error which was sanctified by age and fortified by the prejudices of mankind. He dared to proclaim the important truths, — "that Almighty God hath created the mind free . . ."

This is the language of the bill establishing religious freedom, and it is to be found on our statute-book. How solemn and sublime,

362

and how transcendently important are the truths which it announces to the world. What but his great and powerful genius could have contemplated the breaking asunder those bonds in which the conscience had been bound for centuries? Who but the ardent and devoted friend of man would have exposed himself to the thunders and denunciations of the church throughout all Christendom, by breaking into its very sanctuary, and dissolving its connection with government? . . .

. . . He had not yet finished his memorable efforts in the cause of human liberty. The temple had been reared, but it was exposed to violent assaults from without. Those principles which in former ages had defeated the hopes of man, and had overthrown republics, remained to be hunted out, exposed, and guarded against. The most powerful of these was the concentration and perpetuation of wealth in the hands of particular families, and the creation thereby of an overweening aristocracy. The fatal influence of this principle had been felt in all ages and in all countries. The feeling of pride and haughtiness which wealth is so well calculated to engender, and the homage which mankind are unhappily so much disposed to render it, cause the perpetuation of large fortunes in the hands of families, the most fearful antagonist of human liberty. Marcus Crassus has said, that the man who aspires to rule a republic should not be content until he has mastered wealth sufficient to maintain an army; and Julius Caesar paved the way to the overthrow of Roman liberty by the unsparing distribution, from his inexhaustible stores, of largesses to the people. Mr. Jefferson saw, therefore, the great necessity for reformation in our municipal code, and the act abolishing entails, and that regulating descents, are, in all their essential features, the offsprings of his well-constituted intellect. He has acted throughout on the great principle of the equality of mankind, and his every effort has been directed to the preservation of that equality among his countrymen. . . .

FRANCIS WALKER GILMER
1790-1826

Francis Walker Gilmer was born in Albemarle County, Virginia, on October 9, 1790. He attended William and Mary College, where he won a reputation for brilliance, and studied law under his brother-in-law, William Wirt. He began the practice of law in Virginia and enjoyed the admiration of a number of eminent men. In 1815 Jefferson wrote to Governor Milledge of Georgia that the twenty-five-year-old Gilmer "will be in future whatever he pleases in either State, or General Government." In 1816 Gilmer published anonymously the small volume, *Sketches of American Orators,* from which the following sketch of John Randolph is taken. He achieved success as a lawyer but maintained an active interest in literature. In 1824, at the request of Jefferson, he went abroad to obtain European scholars for the faculty of the new University of Virginia, and it was largely through his efforts that the first faculty was chosen. He accepted Jefferson's invitation to become professor of law, but his death on February 25, 1826, occurred before he could undertake his duties as a teacher. A posthumous collection of his *Sketches, Essays and Translations* was published in 1828. Richard Beale Davis is the author of a recent comprehensive biography, *Francis Walker Gilmer: Life and Learning in Jefferson's Virginia* (1939).

SKETCHES OF AMERICAN ORATORS: JOHN RANDOLPH*

The first time that I ever felt the spell of eloquence was when standing in the gallery of the capitol in the year 1808. It was on the floor of that house I saw rise a gentleman, who in every quality of his person, his voice, his mind, his character, is a phenomenon amongst men. His figure is tall, spare, and somewhat emaciated: his limbs long, delicate, slow and graceful in all their motions; his countenance with the lineaments of boyhood, but the wrinkles, the faded complexion, the occasional sadness of old age and even of decrepitude: possessing however vast compass and force of expression. His voice is small, but of the clearest tone and most flexible modulation I ever heard. In his speech not a breath of air is lost; it is all compressed into round, smooth, liquid sound; and its inflections are so sweet, its emphasis so appropriate and varied, that there is a positive pleasure in hearing him speak any words whatever. His manner of thinking is as peculiar as his person and voice. He has so long spoken parables, that he now thinks in them. Antithesis, jests, beautiful conceits, with a striking turn and point of expression, flow from his lips with the same natural ease, and often with singular felicity of application, as regular series of arguments follow each other in the deductions of logical thinkers. His invective, which is always *piquant*, is frequently adorned with the beautiful metaphors of Burke, and animated by bursts of passion worthy of Chatham. Popular opinion has ordained Mr. Randolph the most eloquent speaker now in America.

On analysing his pretensions to true oratory by another test, he will be found wanting in some of the great essentials of his art. It is the part of an orator, says the only one whose faculties were capacious enough to comprehend and amplify all his duties, 'to inform,

*From Francis Walker Gilmer's *Sketches of American Orators,* published in 1816. A revised and less critical sketch of Randolph appears in Gilmore's *Sketches, Essays and Translations,* published in 1828.

to delight, and to inflame,' *docere, delectare, permovere*. Mr. Randolph is always too deficient in matter. He does not make us understand all the parts of his subject in their several relations. He amuses by his striking and graceful delivery, and by the most original combinations of thought, and ludicrous imagery. Of this, his attack upon Mr. Madison's answer to 'War in Disguise,' may be cited as an example, which perhaps has never been surpassed — "against six hundred ships in commission, (said he,) we enter the lists with a three shilling pamphlet." Could the copious and splendid imagination of Burke have placed in a stronger light the unequal contest? *Delectat, sed non docet*. Does he then inflame?

His powers of exciting passions are very limited. Indignation, hatred, contempt and laughter obey the magic of his genius, but he never awakens pity, and rarely kindles admiration. The style of his eloquence is not favorable to the excitement of any deep or permanent passion; such effects can only be produced by successive impulses. It is not the momentary violence, but the continued impetus of the tempest, which lifts the billows in aspiration to the heavens. We must too be persuaded, and not commanded to sympathise. Whereas, every thing in the manner, the mind, the voice of Mr. Randolph, is imperious. His genius too is fickle, and continues but a short time under the influence of any one emotion. The epithets applicable to his style of speaking are 'striking and brilliant.' His deliberate, graceful, and commanding delivery cannot be too much praised, his total want of method cannot be too much condemned.

The original texture of his mind was exquisite, and as he has never done more than obey its impulse, the early effusions of his genius possess a freshness and brilliancy in their impressions which his recent efforts want. I am sorry there should be any one who can view with pleasure, the fading splendour of such an intellect: I have seen and heard it a volcano, terrible for its flames, and whose thunders were awful, instead of that exhausted crater covered with scoria and smoke, to which a listener in the gallery lately compared it.

WILLIAM ALEXANDER CARUTHERS

1802-1846

William Alexander Caruthers was an able writer and a Virginian of broad sympathies and cultivated taste. He was born in Virginia in 1802, and attended Washington College (now Washington and Lee University). He studied medicine at the University of Pennsylvania, became a practicing physician, and traveled widely in both the North and the South. His first book was published when he was thirty-two. It was the two-volume work *The Kentuckian in New-York, or the Adventures of Three Southerns*. Its observations of contemporary society, in the form of the impressions of three open-minded young Southerners, still makes interesting reading. His second book, a two-volume novel of the time of Bacon's Rebellion, *The Cavaliers of Virginia, or the Recluse of Jamestown. An Historical Romance of the Old Dominion*, was published the following year, and is a fast-moving story of Indian fights and colonial life. His third book, and the one for which he is best remembered, *The Knights of the Horse-Shoe; a Traditionary Tale of the Cocked Hat Gentry in the Old Dominion*, appeared in 1845, a year before his death. It found many readers and new editions of it appeared in 1882, 1909 and 1928. Caruthers died in Georgia on August 29, 1846. An interesting note on his life is given in "Chronicler of the Cavaliers" (*Virginia Magazine of History and Biography*, July 1947) by Curtis Carroll Davis, who is also the author of a forthcoming full-length biography of Caruthers.

THE DAY OF DEPARTURE*

The eventful day at length dawned upon the thronged capital of Virginia — that day pregnant with so many bright hopes — so long looked for, and so ardently desired, in particular by the chivalrouse governor of the colony.

At the first peep of day the drums and trumpets were in requisition, and the young gentry were seen marshaling their little bands of followers in separate squads over the common and in the by-lanes and streets. Any one who has ever seen a militia training, or a "general muster," in Old Virginia, may form a pretty accurate idea of these raw troops and their maneuvers.

The Rangers, or regular troops, as they may be called, presented quite a different aspect. They were paraded in Gloucester Street, in full uniform, well equipped and mounted. They had long been under the supervision of the old veteran their commander, and presented an array never before seen in Virginia, for they had never before paraded at the capital in one body.

In addition to this solid column of soldierly-looking men, there was drawn up on the other side of the street a long line of sumpter mules, loaded with every kind of dried provisions, clothing, cooking utensils, tools and iron. Many carts and wagons were also in requisition with the heavier baggage and provender. These were intended to go no farther than the frontier, when the tents and baggage would be transferred to the backs of the mules and the wagons would return.

Even thus early in the morning General Spotswood was mounted upon his horse, and was busily superintending the delivery of arms from the round tower to the militia, of whom we have already spoken. The old hero could scarce preserve his gravity as he, one

*From *The Knights of the Horse-Shoe; a Traditionary Tale of the Cocked Hat Gentry in the Old Dominion*, by William Alexander Caruthers. First published in 1845.

368

after the other, ordered up the militia in review before him. He had yet to learn, in actual service in the field, the worth of these hardy tatterdemalions. They were mostly dressed in hunting shirts and foraging-caps, rudely put together from the fur of every sort of wild animal — many of them still flourishing the tail which belonged to the animal. To any but the stern military eye of their camp-drilled commander their appearance would have been quite picturesque.

Such a parade, it may be readily believed, was not without interest to those who were not to be of the expedition — the ladies filled every window, balcony, or cupola, and gayly fluttered their white handkerchiefs in the wind as some well known cavalier rode by with his troops.

Frank Lee and young Nathaniel Dandridge had been appointed aides to the governor, and their occupations on this busy morning were arduous indeed. They were kept constantly on the gallop — bringing up one troop, and marching off another. Both, doubtless, though glorying in their appointments, would have far preferred another occupation on this particular occasion. There remained a hundred unsaid things to their lady-loves which they now recalled for the first time; but they did not yet despair of saying at least farewell once again. Often they caught the beam of a bright eye upon them as they rode through the streets. The governor's two daughters already had their horses saddled at the court of the palace, intending to accompany the expedition for some miles on the journey.

There was yet one solemn public ceremony which remained to be performed, after the distribution of arms and ammunition was completed. A platform had been erected in front of the new church, on Gloucester Street, and here, it was understood, the reverend commissary would dismiss the little army, with an exhortation and solemn benediction.

After the morning meal was completed, the troops were set in motion toward this point. The open space enclosed for a cemetery was already filled with a crowd of spectators, and the troops, now closely packed in front of the church and along the square in front of the palace, formed quite an imposing array. The bell had ceased its summons, and a solemn silence pervaded the assembly when the reverend commissary, accompanied by the Rev. Hugh Jones, appeared in front of the church.

Instantly every hat was doffed, and the clear voice of the good old prelate was heard in earnest exhortation. He approved decidedly of the enterprise, and urged them to go forward in the great march of civilization, and told them that thousands yet unborn would bless the hardy pioneers then about to set out upon the exploration of a new and unknown country. He told them that it was no idle military conquest, barren of all useful results — no pageant, to result in unmeaning and fruitless trophies, but emphatically an enterprise in behalf of their country — of the age — of the world. He trusted, he said, that their conquests would be bloodless ones, and their message to the benighted inhabitants of the regions to which they were bound one of peace, and mercy, and good-will — that the past conduct of his excellent friend, their commander, in behalf of the aborigines, was a sure guarantee of his future conduct toward them.

He said that his chief aid in the ministry, the reverend gentleman then present, would accompany them, and he trusted that they would continue to render homage to that Being in whose hands was the success or defeat of their enterprise.

Every knee was then bowed to supplicate the divine favor for the undertaking in which they were all about to engage with so much enthusiasm. It was a solemn sight to behold these gay young cavaliers and their rude followers, and the more disciplined Rangers, all kneeling beside their horses, and every tongue hushed to a solemn stillness, while the venerable prelate poured forth his honest and eloquent appeals in their behalf.

Then followed a scene of indescribable confusion — the leave-taking — wives rushing in among soldiers and horses, to have one more shake of the hand, or one more parting word; lassies taking a parting good-bye of their lovers, and fathers of their sons. Few old men joined the enterprise — the governor himself was, perhaps, the oldest man of the little army. After a grand flourish of drums, something like order was once more resumed, and the troops began to deploy into line, preparatory to their final departure.

The old veteran rode along the line with real pride and a martial glow mantling his cheeks, which had long lain dormant for want of proper occasion for its display. Like most successful military leaders, he felt as confident of success on that day as he did on the day of his return, for he knew that he possessed the energy and the knowledge to insure it. To us, at this distant day, with all the results before us, this does not seem strange or improbable; but it was by no means so then.

His grand hobby, as it was called by the elderly gentry, met with far more ridicule than support and countenance. As we have before said, many over-prudent fathers opposed their sons accompanying him at all; and wiseacres were not wanting in abundance who predicted its total failure, and that the final catastrophe would be an Indian massacre in some mountain defile.

This last surmise had gained not a little ground since the daring inroad of a band of the Indians during the night into the very heart of the capital, garrisoned as it was by their whole army. And they reasoned — not very unjustly — that if such things could be done with impunity there, what might not be done among their own mountain fastnesses, whose intricate defiles were known only to themselves?

A white guide had been provided hastily in Chunoluskee's stead. He was a hunter, and had penetrated farther toward the mountains than any one known in the colonies. He was of tried metal, too, for he had fought the Indians in his day. His name was Jarvis — son of the old fisherman whom we introduced to the reader in the early part of our narrative. Joe Jarvis — commonly called Red Jarvis — was of a class which is fast gliding from notice in the older settlements of the States. They were called in that day, and indeed long afterward, *scouts.*

The troops were now in motion, and the front lines were already passing the College Square, the long line of sumpter-mules and wagons bringing up the rear. The governor and his suite had not yet left the city. They waited for the scout, who had gone on a farewell visit the night before to his father at Temple Farm.

While the governor and his aides, with many of the young gentry, sat on their horses near the round tower in the market square, and while they were beginning to express doubts and misgivings of their second guide, the very man himself glided into their midst;

and such a man — so remarkable, and he performs such an important part in the grand expedition — that we must describe him.

He was a tall specimen in every sense of the word — six feet and more in his stockings (if he ever wore any). On the present occasion his feet and legs were clad in buckskin leggings and moccasins fitting close to the members. His breeches were of homespun, and his hunting-shirt of the same material, held together by a broad leather strap, into which were stuck various utensils of the woodman's craft, with others of a more warlike character, among which was a knife, cased in a leather sheath, which, in a single-handed encounter, would be a most deadly weapon.

His face expressed anything but daring and decided character. Its principal characteristic was fun and frolic, but of a quiet and subdued sort. There was a constant inclination of the head to one side, with one eye partially closed at the same time, and a quiet smile about the mouth. His excessive self-confidence would have given him the appearance of boldness and presumption had it not been for the sly peculiarities we are attempting to describe.

He had large red whiskers, extending under his throat, the only protection it had, and these were burnt and faded to a sandy or yellow shade at their extremities, by long exposure to sun and rain. Hence his *soubriquet* of Red Jarvis.

Upon his shoulder he carried a long gun — much longer than the pony upon which he was mounted. Thus accoutred, he rode into the midst of the gentry who awaited so impatiently his arrival, followed by a large dog, which was just about as much used to such company as his master. There was this great difference between them, however — the dog slunk about the horse's legs, quite confounded and abashed; while Joe rode into their midst, one eye cocked, with as quiet a leer as if he had rode to the front of his father's cabin.

As he glanced around, his eye naturally fell upon the short carbines slung across the backs of the young gentlemen who sat on horseback around him, and then wandered along the huge thing which he carried himself. The result of the mental comparison was a sly inward chuckle, which, however, he subdued into his habitual cock of one eye as it rested upon the governor, who was surveying

372

him, from the coonskin cap on his head to his feet, which almost touched the ground.

The result of the governor's examination was pretty much like Joe's survey of the young men's armaments — a laugh; he could not resist Joe's *outré* appearance. "Well, Jarvis," said he, "how far do you expect to carry that pony?"

"Jist as far as he'll carry me, your honor."

"Well said; but I fear that will not be far."

"*Hosses* is like men, governor: it is not always the smoothest coats has the bravest hearts inside on 'em;" and his half-closed eye ranged again over the gaudy attire and gold-lace around him, which gradually grew into an unsuppressed chuckle, the cause of which the governor was induced to inquire.

"Why, I was thinkin', sir, how all this gold and flummery would look the day we marched in again."

"True, true, Joe; these lads will be glad to have your hunting-shirt and moccasins before they return, and so I have been telling them."

"There won't be a whole shirt, sir, in the army when we come back; and for that reason I left mine behind;" and here he gave another quiet laugh, as he surveyed the magnificent lace ruffles and collars flowing about him.

Some of the young cavaliers had a curiosity to know what substitute *he* had in place of a shirt.

"Why, here," said Joe, handling the red hair under his throat, as if he was bearding a lion, "is my ruffles;" and pulling open his hunting-shirt, he displayed a buckskin, tanned with the hair on, and corresponding so near in color to the ruffles of which he had just boasted that it looked like part and parcel of the same animal. He enjoyed highly the stare of astonishment with which his garments were examined by the ball-room soldiers, as he called them.

"But, Jarvis," said the governor, "how comes it that you are so dilatory this first morning of the march? We thought you were the very soul of punctuality and promptitude."

Joe looked a little confused for a moment, and tugged at his coonskin cap, so as to place the tail exactly behind, and coughed and hemmed several times ere he answered, "You see, your worship, as I was comin' to town this mornin' 'fore day I heard the news of the *rupture* of the savages last night, and I jist tuck a turn or two through the woods on my own hook, to see if I could find the trail."

Here one of the young gentlemen, bending over, whispered to the governor that Joe had formerly been an admirer of Wingina.

"Ay, ay," said the old veteran, "I see. Well, did you fall upon their trail?"

"Yes, sir, I rather think I did. It would take a cunning Indian, and more 'specially a dozen of 'em, to march through these pines and leave no trail that I couldn't find. I *blazed* a couple of miles or so, and then turned back, for fear you mought be a-waitin' on me."

Blazing was performed in those days by the scouts, or pioneer, taking the lead in a new or untried route, by striking a chip off one side of a tree. They may be seen at night, if not very dark. New roads were laid off in the same primitive manner. Joe carried his tomahawk in his belt, ready for such service — not a little of which he was about to perform; for, the army once beyond the ruins of Germana, every foot of the route had to be marked out by him after the manner described.

The governor, after some consultation with his aides and the scout, came to the conclusion that it was useless to follow the trail marked out by Joe at present, as he assured them that they would fall upon it again before night, at such a distance from the settlement as would render pursuit more likely to result in success.

The last sumpter-mules were now passing the suburbs of the city, and the little party round the military tower separated to bid a last farewell with those near and dear to them. . . .

EDGAR ALLAN POE

1809-1849

Edgar Allan Poe was the first American writer to be primarily concerned with the esthetics of literature. If there is a good deal of truth in James Russell Lowell's estimate of Poe: "Three fifths of him genius and two fifths sheer fudge," still genius in any measure is rare enough that the dozen or so poems and stories by Poe which display it have a secure place in the small body of American literature of indisputable excellence. The "sheer fudge" is all too obvious, the "corpses and expensive junk" and the "data false as a waxwork" which a later poet has remarked in a perceptive poem (Karl Shapiro's *Israfel* in this anthology). But the genius was there, and a hundred years after his death "Four cities claim him as France recommended."

Richmond, where he grew up and where he later made the *Southern Literary Messenger* a journal of brilliant criticism, has as good a claim as any. Elizabeth Arnold Poe, an itinerant actress, died in Richmond in December, 1811, at the age of twenty-four, leaving three children. Her husband, David Poe, was already dead. Her three-year-old son, Edgar Poe, who was born in Boston on January 19, 1809, was taken in by Mrs. John Allan, the wife of a Richmond merchant who reluctantly acquiesced but refused legally to adopt the child. Poe grew up in the Allan household, was taken to England with them, attended school there and in Richmond, and at the age of seventeen entered the University of Virginia.

He was an able student and began seriously to write poetry, but his lot was an unhappy one. At a time when heavy drinking was common, he found that a little was too much for him. His foster father did not provide him even with the full university fee, and from his arrival at the university he was in debt. He attempted to make money at cards and only increased his debts. He returned to Richmond at the end of the year to be met with Mr. Allan's refusal to pay his debts or to assist him in finding employment. In desperation, Poe left Richmond and made his way to Boston. There, at the age of eighteen, he published his first collection of poetry, *Tamerlane and Other Poems,* in an edition of half a hundred copies.

Without any means of support, the youth enlisted in the army. He had a good record and was promoted to the highest non-commissioned post, regimental sergeant major. On the death of his foster mother in 1829, Poe visited Richmond and Mr. Allan undertook to arrange his appointment to West Point. In December, 1829, shortly before his twentieth birthday, Poe published his second collection of poetry, *Al Aaraaf, Tamerlane, and Minor Poems.* In 1830 he entered West Point and remained there until the following year, when he deliberately provoked his dismissal and determined to devote himself to writing. Early in 1831 Poe published his third volume, *Poems,* which in addition to revisions of his earlier work contained *To Helen, Israfel, The Valley of Unrest, The City in the Sea, The Sleeper* and *Lenore.* At twenty-two he had made a powerful bid for literary immortality.

The rest of his life he struggled against poverty, illness, the indifference of America and the disabilities of his own personality, to perform the work of the serious creative artist. Often starvation itself was warded off only by the ministry of Mrs. Maria Clemm, his father's sister, whose young daughter Virginia became Poe's bride when he was twenty-seven.

Following the publication of his volume of *Poems* in 1831, Poe devoted himself energetically to the writing of prose. The next year, when he was twenty-four, five of his stories appeared in the *Philadelphia Saturday Courier.* In 1833 he won a story prize offered by the *Baltimore Saturday Visitor,* to which he had submitted a whole manuscript volume of tales, and attracted the favorable attention of the influential John Pendleton Kennedy who smoothed the way to a position on the new *Southern Literary Messenger.* Poe contributed prodigiously to the *Messenger,* writing scores of critical essays as well as publishing poems and stories, making its reputation as he later made the reputation of several other periodicals. In all, Poe wrote some seventy stories. He died in Baltimore on October 7, 1849.

Poe's prose works published in book form in his own lifetime were: *The Narrative of Arthur Gordon Pym* (1838), *Tales of the Grotesque and Arabesque* (2 volumes, 1840), *The Murders in the Rue Morgue and The Man That Was Used Up* (1843, the first and only number of a projected series of *The Prose Romances of Edgar A. Poe*), *Tales* (1845) and *Eureka: A Prose Poem* (1848). *The Raven and Other Poems* was published in 1845. Of the many editions of his work published after his death, the Virginia Edition prepared by J. A. Harrison in 17 volumes (1902) is the most complete. Of the many biographies of Poe, *Israfel* by Hervey Allen (1926, revised 1934) is the most comprehensive.

A TALE OF THE RAGGED MOUNTAINS*

During the fall of the year 1827, while residing near Charlottesville, Virginia, I casually made the acquaintance of Mr. Augustus Bedloe. This young gentleman was remarkable in every respect, and excited in me a profound interest and curiosity. I found it impossible to comprehend him either in his moral or his physical relations. Of his family I could obtain no satisfactory account. Whence he came, I never ascertained. Even about his age — although I call him a young gentleman — there was something which perplexed me in no little degree. He certainly *seemed* young — and he made a point of speaking about his youth — yet there were moments when I should have had little trouble in imagining him a hundred years of age. But in no regard was he more peculiar than in his personal appearance. He was singularly tall and thin. He stooped much. His limbs were exceedingly long and emaciated. His forehead was broad and low. His complexion was absolutely bloodless. His mouth was large and flexible, and his teeth were more wildly uneven, although sound, than I had ever before seen teeth in a human head. The expression of his smile, however, was by no means unpleasing, as might be supposed; but it had no variation whatever. It was one of profound melancholy — of a phaseless and unceasing gloom. His eyes were abnormally large, and round like those of a cat. The pupils, too, upon any accession or diminution of light, underwent contraction or dilation, just such as is observed in the feline tribe. In moments of excitement the orbs grew bright to a degree almost inconceivable; seeming to emit luminous rays, not of a reflected, but of an intrinsic lustre, as does a candle or the sun; yet their ordinary condition was so totally vapid, filmy, and dull, as to convey the idea of the eyes of a long-interred corpse.

These peculiarities of person appeared to cause him much an-

*First published in *Goedy's Lady's Book* for April, 1844.

noyance, and he was continually alluding to them in a sort of half explanatory, half apologetic strain, which, when I first heard it, impressed me very painfully. I soon, however, grew accustomed to it, and my uneasiness wore off. It seemed to be his design rather to insinuate than directly to assert that, physically, he had not always been what he was — that a long series of neuralgic attacks had reduced him from a condition of more than usual personal beauty, to that which I saw. For many years past he had been attended by a physician, named Templeton — an old gentleman, perhaps seventy years of age — whom he had first encountered at Saratoga, and from whose attention, while there, he either received, or fancied that he received, great benefit. The result was that Bedloe, who was wealthy, had made an arrangement with Doctor Templeton, by which the latter, in consideration of a liberal annual allowance, had consented to devote his time and medical experience exclusively to the care of the invalid.

Doctor Templeton had been a traveller in his younger days, and, at Paris, had become a convert, in great measure, to the doctrines of Mesmer. It was altogether by means of magnetic remedies that he had succeeded in alleviating the acute pains of his patient; and this success had very naturally inspired the latter with a certain degree of confidence in the opinions from which the remedies had been educed. The Doctor, however, like all enthusiasts, had struggled hard to make a thorough convert of his pupil, and finally so far gained his point as to induce the sufferer to submit to numerous experiments. — By a frequent repetition of these, a result had arisen, which of late days has become so common as to attract little or no attention, but which, at the period of which I write, had very rarely been known in America. I mean to say, that between Doctor Templeton and Bedloe there had grown up, little by little, a very distinct and strongly marked rapport, or magnetic relation. I am not prepared to assert, however, that this rapport extended beyond the limits of the simple sleep-producing power; but this power itself had attained great intensity. At the first attempt to induce the magnetic somnolency, the mesmerist entirely failed. In the fifth or sixth he succeeded very partially, and after long continued effort. Only at the twelfth was the triumph complete. After this the will of the

Edgar Allan Poe, 1809-1849

patient succumbed rapidly to that of the physician, so that, when I first became acquainted with the two, sleep was brought about almost instantaneously, by the mere volition of the operator, even when the invalid was unaware of his presence. It is only now, in the year 1845, when similar miracles are witnessed daily by thousands, that I dare venture to record this apparent impossibility as a matter of serious fact.

The temperament of Bedloe was, in the highest degree, sensitive, excitable, enthusiastic. His imagination was singularly vigorous and creative; and no doubt it derived additional force from the habitual use of morphine, which he swallowed in great quantity, and without which he would have found it impossible to exist. It was his practice to take a very large dose of it immediately after breakfast each morning — or rather immediately after a cup of strong coffee, for he ate nothing in the forenoon — and then set forth alone, or attended only by a dog, upon a long ramble among the chain of wild and dreary hills that lie westward and southward of Charlottesville, and are there dignified by the title of the Ragged Mountains.

Upon a dim, warm, misty day, towards the close of November, and during the strange interregnum of the seasons which in America is termed the Indian Summer, Mr. Bedloe departed as usual, for the hills. The day passed, and still he did not return.

About eight o'clock at night, having become seriously alarmed at his protracted absence, we were about setting out in search of him, when he unexpectedly made his appearance, in health no worse than usual, and in rather more than ordinary spirits. The account which he gave of his expedition, and of the events which had detained him, was a singular one indeed.

'You will remember,' said he, 'that it was about nine in the morning when I left Charlottesville. I bent my steps immediately to the mountains, and, about ten, entered a gorge which was entirely new to me. I followed the windings of this pass with much interest. — The scenery which presented itself on all sides, although scarcely entitled to be called grand, had about it an indescribable, and to me, a delicious aspect of dreary desolation. The solitude seemed absolutely virgin. I could not help believing that the green sods and the gray rocks upon which I trod, had been trodden never before by

379

the foot of a human being. So entirely secluded, and in fact inaccessible, except through a series of accidents, is the entrance of the ravine, that it is by no means impossible that I was indeed the first adventurer — the very first and sole adventurer who had ever penetrated its recesses.

'The thick and peculiar mist, or smoke, which distinguishes the Indian Summer, and which now hung heavily over all objects, served, no doubt, to deepen the vague impressions which these objects created. So dense was this pleasant fog, that I could at no time see more than a dozen yards of the path before me. This path was excessively sinuous, and as the sun could not be seen, I soon lost all idea of the direction in which I journeyed. In the meantime the morphine had its customary effect — that of enduing all the external world with an intensity of interest. In the quivering of a leaf — in the hue of a blade of grass — in the shape of a trefoil — in the humming of a bee — in the gleaming of a dew-drop — in the breathing of the wind — in the faint odours that came from the forest — there came a whole universe of suggestion — a gay and motley train of rhapsodical and immethodical thought.

'Busied in this, I walked on for several hours, during which the mist deepened around me to so great an extent, that at length I was reduced to an absolute groping of the way. And now an indescribable uneasiness possessed me — a species of nervous hesitation and tremor. — I feared to tread, lest I should be precipitated into some abyss. I remembered, too, strange stories told about these Ragged Hills, and of the uncouth and fierce races of men who tenanted their groves and caverns. A thousand vague fancies oppressed and disconcerted me — fancies the more distressing because vague. Very suddenly my attention was arrested by the loud beating of a drum.

'My amazement was, of course, extreme. A drum in these hills was a thing unknown. I could not have been more surprised at the sound of the trump of the Archangel. But a new and still more astounding source of interest and perplexity arose. There came a wild rattling or jingling sound, as if of a bunch of large keys — and upon the instant a dusky-visaged and half-naked man rushed past me with a shriek. He came so close to my person that I felt his hot breath upon my face. He bore in one hand an instrument composed of an assemblage of steel rings, and shook them vigorously as he ran. Scarcely had he disappeared in the mist, before, panting after him, with open mouth and glaring eyes, there darted a huge beast. I could not be mistaken in its character. It was a hyena.

'The sight of this monster rather relieved than heightened my terrors — for I now made sure that I dreamed, and endeavoured to arouse myself to waking consciousness. I stepped boldly and briskly forward. I rubbed my eyes. I called aloud. I pinched my limbs. A small spring of water presented itself to my view, and here, stooping, I bathed my hands and my head and neck. This seemed to dissipate the equivocal sensations which had hitherto annoyed me. I arose, as I thought, a new man, and proceeded steadily and complacently on my unknown way.

'At length, quite overcome by exertion, and by a certain oppressive closeness of the atmosphere, I seated myself beneath a tree. Presently there came a feeble gleam of sunshine and the shadow of the leaves of the tree fell faintly but definitely upon the grass. At this shadow I gazed wonderingly for many minutes. Its character stupefied me with astonishment. I looked upward. The tree was a palm.

'I now arose hurriedly, and in a state of fearful agitation — for the fancy that I dreamed would serve me no longer. I saw — I felt that I had perfect command of my senses — and these senses now brought to my soul a world of novel and singular sensation. The heat became all at once intolerable. A strange odour loaded the breeze. — A low continuous murmur, like that arising from a full, but gently flowing river, came to my ears, intermingled with the peculiar hum of multitudinous human voices.

'While I listened in an extremity of astonishment which I need not attempt to describe, a strong and brief gust of wind bore off the incumbent fog as if by the wand of an enchanter.

'I found myself at the foot of a high mountain, and looking down into a vast plain, through which wound a majestic river. On the margin of this river stood an Eastern-looking city, such as we read of in the Arabian Tales, but of a character even more singular than any there described. From my position, which was far above the level of the town, I could perceive its every nook and corner, as if delineated on a map. The streets seemed innumerable, and crossed each other irregularly in all directions, but were rather long winding alleys than streets, and absolutely swarmed with inhabitants. The houses were wildly picturesque. On every hand was a wilderness of balconies, of verandas, of minarets, of shrines, and fantastically carved oriels. Bazaars abounded; and in these were displayed rich wares in infinite variety and profusion — silks, muslins, the most dazzling cutlery, the most magnificent jewels and gems. Besides these things, were seen, on all sides, banners and palanquins, litters with stately dames close veiled, elephants gorgeously caparisoned, idols grotesquely hewn, drums, banners and gongs, spears, silver and gilded maces. And amid the crowd, and the clamour, and the general intricacy and confusion — amid the million of black and yellow men, turbaned and robed, and of flowing beard, there roamed a countless multitude of holy filleted bulls, while vast legions of the filthy but sacred ape clambered, chattering and shrieking about the cornices of the mosques, or clung to the minarets and oriels. From the swarming streets to the banks of the river, there descended innumerable flights of steps leading to bathing places, while the river itself seemed to force a passage with difficulty through the vast fleets of deeply-burdened ships that far and wide encountered its surface. Beyond the limits of the city arose, in frequent majestic groups, the palm and the cocoa, with other gigantic and weird trees of vast age; and here and there might be seen a field of rice, the thatched hut of a peasant, a tank, a stray temple, a gypsy camp, or a solitary graceful maiden taking her way, with a pitcher upon her head, to the banks of the magnificent river.

'You will say now, of course, that I dreamed; but not so. What I saw — what I heard — what I felt — what I thought — had about it nothing of the unmistakable idiosyncrasy of the dream. All was rigorously self-consistent. At first, doubting that I was really awake, I entered into a series of tests, which soon convinced me that I really was. Now, when one dreams, and, in the dream, suspects that he dreams, the suspicion *never fails to confirm itself,* and the sleeper is almost immediately aroused. Thus Novalis errs not in saying that "we are near waking when we dream that we dream." Had the vision occurred to me as I describe it, without my suspecting it as a dream, then a dream it might absolutely have been, but, occurring as it did, and suspected and tested as it was, I am forced to class it among other phenomena.'

'In this I am not sure that you are wrong,' observed Dr. Templeton, 'but proceed. You arose and descended into the city.'

'I arose,' continued Bedloe, regarding the Doctor with an air of profound astonishment, 'I arose, as you say, and descended into the city. On my way, I fell in with an immense populace, crowding through every avenue, all in the same direction, and exhibiting in every action the wildest excitement. Very suddenly, and by some inconceivable impulse, I became intensely imbued with personal interest in what was going on. I seemed to feel that I had an important part to play, without exactly understanding what it was. Against the crowd which environed me, however, I experienced a deep sentiment of animosity. I shrank from amid them, and, swiftly, by a circuitous path, reached and entered the city. Here all was the wildest tumult and contention. A small party of men, clad in garments half Indian, half European, and officered by gentlemen in a uniform partly British, were engaged, at great odds, with the swarming rabble of the alleys. I joined the weaker party, arming myself with the weapons of a fallen officer, and fighting I knew not whom with the nervous ferocity of despair. We were soon overpowered by numbers, and driven to seek refuge in a species of kiosk. Here we barricaded ourselves, and, for the present, were secure. From a loophole near the summit of the kiosk, I perceived a vast crowd, in furious agitation, surrounding and assaulting a gay palace that overhung the river. Presently, from an upper window of this palace, there descended an effeminate-looking person, by means of a string made of the turbans of his attendants. A boat was at hand, in which he escaped to the opposite bank of the river.

'And now a new object took possession of my soul. I spoke a few hurried but energetic words to my companions, and, having succeeded in gaining over a few of them to my purpose, made a frantic sally from the kiosk. We rushed amid the crowd that surrounded it. They retreated, at first, before us. They rallied, fought madly, and retreated again. In the meantime we were borne far from the kiosk, and became bewildered and entangled among the narrow streets of tall overhanging houses, into the recesses of which the sun had never been able to shine. The rabble pressed impetuously upon us, harrassing us with their spears, and overwhelming us with flights of arrows. These latter were very remarkable, and resembled in some respects the writhing creese of the Malay. They were made to imitate the body of a creeping serpent, and were long and black, with a poisoned barb. One of them struck me upon the right temple. I reeled and fell. An instantaneous and dreadful sickness seized me. I struggled — I gasped — I died.

'You will hardly persist now,' said I, smiling, 'that the whole of your adventure was not a dream. You are not prepared to maintain that you are dead?'

When I said these words, I of course expected some lively sally from Bedloe in reply; but, to my astonishment, he hesitated, trembled, became fearfully pallid, and remained silent. I looked towards Templeton. He sat erect and rigid in his chair — his teeth chattered, and his eyes were starting from their sockets. 'Proceed!' he at length said hoarsely to Bedloe.

'For many minutes,' continued the latter, 'my sole sentiment — my sole feeling — was that of darkness and nonentity, with the consciousness of death. At length, there seemed to pass a violent and sudden shock through my soul, as if of electricity. With it came the sense of elasticity and of light. This latter I felt — not saw. In an instant I seemed to rise from the ground. But I had no bodily, no visible, audible, or palpable presence. The crowd had departed. The tumult had ceased. The city was in comparative repose. Beneath me lay my corpse, with the arrow in my temple, the whole head greatly swollen and disfigured. But all these things I felt — not saw. I took interest in nothing. Even the corpse seemed a matter in which I had no concern. Volition I had none, but appeared to be impelled into motion, and flitted buoyantly out of the city, retracing the circuitous path by which I had entered it. When I had attained that point of the ravine in the mountains, at which I had encountered the hyena, I again experienced a shock as of a galvanic battery; the sense of weight, of volition, of substance, returned. I became my original self, and bent my steps eagerly homewards — but the past had not lost the vividness of the real — and not now, even for an instant, can I compel my understanding to regard it as a dream.'

'Nor was it,' said Templeton, with an air of deep solemnity, 'yet it would be difficult to say how otherwise it should be termed. Let us

384

suppose only, that the soul of the man of today is upon the verge of some stupendous psychical discoveries. Let us content ourselves with this supposition. For the rest I have some explanation to make. Here is a water-colour drawing, which I should have shown you before, but which an unaccountable sentiment of horror has hitherto prevented me from showing.'

We looked at the picture which he presented. I saw nothing in it of an extraordinary character; but its effect upon Bedloe was prodigious. He nearly fainted as he gazed. And yet it was but a miniature portrait — a miraculously accurate one, to be sure — of his own very remarkable features. At least this was my thought as I regarded it.

'You will perceive,' said Templeton, 'the date of this picture — it is here, scarcely visible, in this corner — 1780. In this year was the portrait taken. It is the likeness of a dead friend — a Mr. Oldeb — to whom I became much attached at Calucutta, during the administration of Warren Hastings. I was then only twenty years old. When I first saw you, Mr. Bedloe, at Saratoga, it was the miraculous similarity which existed between yourself and the painting which induced me to accost you, to seek your friendship, and to bring about those arrangements which resulted in my becoming your constant companion. In accomplishing this point, I was urged partly, and perhaps principally, by a regretful memory of the deceased, but also, in part, by an uneasy, and not altogether horrorless curiosity respecting yourself.

'In your detail of the vision which presented itself to you amid the hills, you have described, with the minutest accuracy, the Indian city of Benares, upon the Holy River. The riots, the combats, the massacre, were the actual events of the insurrection of Cheyte Sing, which took place in 1780, when Hastings was put in imminent peril of his life. The man escaping by the string of turbans, was Cheyte Sing himself. The party in the kiosk were sepoys and British officers, headed by Hastings. Of this party I was one, and did all I could to prevent the rash and fatal sally of the officer who fell, in the crowded alleys, by the poisoned arrow of a Bengalee. That officer was my dearest friend. It was Oldeb. You will perceive by these manuscripts' (here the speaker produced a note-book in which several pages appeared to have been freshly written) 'that at the very period in which you fancied these things amid the hills, I was engaged in detailing them upon paper here at home.'

'In about a week after this conversation, the following paragraphs appeared in a Charlottesville paper:

'We have the painful duty of announcing the death of MR. AU-GUSTUS BEDLO, a gentleman whose amiable manners and many virtues have long endeared him to the citizens of Charlottesville.

'Mr. B., for some years past, has been subject to neuralgia, which has often threatened to terminate fatally; but this can be regarded only as the mediate cause of his decease. The proximate cause was one of especial singularity. In an excursion to the Ragged Mountains, a few days since, a slight cold and fever were contracted, attended with great determination of blood to the head. To relieve this, Dr. Templeton resorted to topical bleeding. Leeches were applied to the temples. In a fearfully brief period the patient died, when it appeared that, in the jar containing the leeches, had been introduced, by accident, one of the venomous vermicular sangsues which are now and then found in the neighboring ponds. This creature fastened itself upon a small artery in the right temple. Its close resemblance to the medicinal leech caused the mistake to be overlooked until too late.

'N. B. The poisonous sangsue of Charlottesville may always be distinguished from the medicinal leech by its blackness, and especially by its writhing or vermicular motions, which very nearly resemble those of a snake.'

I was speaking with the editor of the paper in question, upon the topic of this remarkable accident, when it occurred to me to ask how it happened that the name of the deceased had been given as Bedlo.

'I presume,' said I, 'you have authority for this spelling, but I have always supposed the name to be written with an *e* at the end.'

'Authority? — no,' he replied. 'It is a mere typographical error. The name is Bedlo with an *e*, all the world over, and I never knew it to be spelt otherwise in my life.'

'Then,' said I mutteringly, as I turned upon my heel, 'then indeed has it come to pass that one truth is stranger than any fiction — for Bedlo, without the *e*, what is it but Oldeb conversed? And this man tells me it is a typographical error.'

TO HELEN

Helen, thy beauty is to me
  Like those Nicean barks of yore,
That gently, o'er a perfumed sea,
  The weary, wayworn wanderer bore
  To his own native shore.

On desperate seas long wont to roam,
  Thy hyacinth hair, thy classic face,
Thy Naiad airs have brought me home
  To the glory that was Greece
And the grandeur that was Rome.

Lo! in yon brilliant window-niche
  How statue-like I see thee stand,
  The agate lamp within thy hand!
Ah, Psyche, from the regions which
  Are Holy Land!

THE SLEEPER

At midnight, in the month of June,
I stand beneath the mystic moon.
An opiate vapor, dewy, dim,
Exhales from out her golden rim,
And, softly dripping, drop by drop,
Upon the quiet mountain top,
Steals drowsily and musically
Into the universal valley.
The rosemary nods upon the grave;
The lily lolls upon the wave;
Wrapping the fog about its breast,
The ruin molders into rest;
Looking like Lethe, see! the lake
A conscious slumber seems to take,
And would not, for the world, awake.
All Beauty sleeps! — and lo! where lies
Irene, with her Destinies!

O, lady bright! can it be right —
This window open to the night?
The wanton airs, from the tree-top,
Laughingly through the lattice drop —
The bodiless airs, a wizard rout,
Flit through thy chamber in and out,
And wave the curtain canopy
So fitfully — so fearfully —
Above the closed and fringèd lid
'Neath which thy slumb'ring soul lies hid,
That, o'er the floor and down the wall,
Like ghosts the shadows rise and fall!
Oh, lady dear, hast thou no fear?

Edgar Allan Poe, 1809-1849

Why and what art thou dreaming here?
Sure thou art come o'er far-off seas,
A wonder to these garden trees!
Strange is thy pallor! strange thy dress,
Strange, above all, thy length of tress,
And this all solemn silentness!

The lady sleeps! Oh, may her sleep,
Which is enduring, so be deep!
Heaven have her in its sacred keep!
This chamber changed for one more holy,
This bed for one more melancholy,
I pray to God that she may lie
For ever with unopened eye,
While the pale sheeted ghosts go by!
My love, she sleeps! Oh, may her sleep
As it is lasting, so be deep!
Soft may the worms about her creep!
For in the forest, dim and old,
For her may some tall vault unfold —
Some vault that oft has flung its black
And wingèd panels fluttering back,
Triumphant, o'er the crested palls,
Of her grand family funerals —
Some sepulchre, remote, alone,
Against whose portal she hath thrown,
In childhood, many an idle stone —
Some tomb from out whose sounding door
She ne'er shall force an echo more,
Thrilling to think, poor child of sin!
It was the dead who groaned within.

TO ONE IN PARADISE

Thou wast all that to me, love,
   For which my soul did pine —
A green isle in the sea, love,
   A fountain and a shrine,
All wreathed with fairy fruits and flowers,
   And all the flowers were mine.

Ah, dream too bright to last!
   Ah, starry Hope! that didst arise
But to be overcast!
   A voice from out the Future cries,
"On! on!" — but o'er the Past
   (Dim gulf!) my spirit hovering lies
Mute, motionless, aghast!

For, alas! alas! with me
   The light of Life is o'er!
   "No more — no more — no more —"
(Such language holds the solemn sea
   To the sands upon the shore)
Shall bloom the thunder-blasted tree
   Or the stricken eagle soar!

And all my days are trances,
   And all my nightly dreams
Are where thy grey eye glances,
   And where thy footstep gleams —
In what ethereal dances,
   By what eternal streams.

PHILIP PENDLETON COOKE

1816-1850

Philip Pendleton Cooke was born at Martinsburg, Virginia (now West Virginia), on October 26, 1816. He was the son of John Rogers Cooke, a well-known Virginia lawyer, and was the older brother of the novelist John Esten Cooke. At the age of fifteen he entered Princeton, where he found the reading and writing of poetry far more exciting than the prescribed curriculum. Chaucer and Spencer were his masters, and his own work appeared in the *Knickerbocker Magazine* as early as 1833. After his graduation he returned to Virginia, studied law under his father, was married, and was admitted to the Virginia bar. He began the practice of law before his twenty-first birthday, but divided much of his time between writing and hunting. In 1835, when he was nineteen, he contributed a series of articles on English poetry to the *Southern Literary Messenger*, and he continued to write poetry, fiction and literary articles until his death. "Florence Vane," a poem which has found its way into many anthologies, was published in *Burton's Gentleman's Magazine* in 1840 and attracted considerable attention. A collection of verse, *Froissart Ballads and Other Poems*, was published in 1847, at the suggestion of his kinsman, John Pendleton Kennedy. Several prose romances — *The Crime of Andrew Blair, John Carper, the Hunter of Lost River,* and *The Two Country Houses* among them — appeared in the *Southern Literary Messenger*, and an unfinished novel, which won the praise of Poe, was being serialized there at the time of his death. He died on January 20, 1850, at the age of thirty-three, from pneumonia contracted while swimming in the icy Shenandoah River during a hunting expedition.

LIFE IN THE AUTUMN WOODS*

Summer has gone,
And fruitful autumn has advanced so far
That there is warmth, not heat, in the broad sun,
And you may look, with naked eye, upon
    The ardors of his car;
The stealthy frosts, whom his spent looks embolden,
    Are making the green leaves golden.

What a brave splendor
Is in the October air! How rich and clear,
And bracing, and all-joyous! we must render
Love to the spring-time, with its sproutings tender,
    As to a child quite dear;
But autumn is a thing of perfect glory,
    A manhood not yet hoary.

I love the woods,
In this good season of the liberal year;
I love to seek their leafy solitudes,
And give myself to melancholy moods,
    With no intruder near,
And find strange lessons, as I sit and ponder,
    In every natural wonder.

But not alone,
As Shakespeare's melancholy courtier loved Ardennes,
Love I the browning forest; and I own
I would not oft have mused, as he, but flown
    To hunt with Amiens —

*First published in the *Southern Literary Messenger*, December, 1843. A
revised version was included in Cooke's volume, *Froissart Ballads and Other
Poems* (Carey and Hart, Philadelphia, 1847). The earlier text is used here.

Philip Pendleton Cooke, 1816-1850

And little thought, as up the bold deer bounded,
   Of the sad creature wounded.

   A brave and good,
But world-worn knight — soul wearied with the part
Is this vexed life — gave man for solitude,
And built a lodge and lived in Wantley wood,
   To hear the belling Hart.
It was a gentle taste, but its sweet sadness
   Yields to the Hunter's madness.

   What passionate
And keen delight is in the proud swift chase!
Go out what time the lark at heaven's red gate
Soars joyously singing — quite infuriate
   With the high pride of his place;
What time the unrisen sun arrays the morning
   In its first bright adorning.

   Hark! the quick horn —
As sweet to hear as any clarion —
Piercing with silver call the ear of morn;
And mark the steeds, stout Curtal and Topthorne,
   And Greysteil and the Don —
Each one of them his fiery mood displaying
   With pawing and with neighing.

   Urge your swift horse,
After the crying hounds in this fresh hour,
Vanquish high hills — stem perilous streams perforce,
On the free plain give free wings to your course,
   And you will know the power
Of the brave chase — and how of griefs the sorest
   A cure is in the forest.

   Or stalk the deer;
The same red lip of dawn has kissed the hills,

The gladdest sounds are crowding on your ear,
There is a life in all the atmosphere: —
  Your very nature fills
With the fresh hour, as up the hills aspiring
  You climb with limbs untiring.

  It is a fair
And goodly sight to see the antlered stag,
With the long sweep of his swift walk, repair
To join his brothers; or the plethoric Bear
  Lying on some high crag,
With pinky eyes half closed, but broad head shaking,
  As gad-flies keep him waking.

  And these you see,
And seeing them, you travel to their death
With a slow, stealthy step, from tree to tree,
Noting the wind however faint it be.
  The hunter draws a breath
In times like these, which, he will say, repays him
  For all care that waylays him.

  A strong joy fills
(A joy beyond the tongue's expressive power)
My heart in Autumn weather — fills and thrills!
And I would rather stalk the breezy hills,
  Descending to my bower
Nightly, by the sweet spirit of Peace attended,
  Than pine where life is splendid.

MATTHEW FONTAINE MAURY

1806-1873

Matthew Fontaine Maury, Virginia's best-known man of science, was born near Fredericksburg on January 14, 1806, of a family which had been prominent in Virginia for several generations. He spent his boyhood in Tennessee. He became a midshipman in 1825 and spent much of the next decade at sea, including a trip around the world. In 1841, following an accident which left him lame and unfit for active service, he was given charge of the Navy's hydrographic records. In this post he began his monumental work of mapping the winds and currents of the sea, which won him world-wide recognition. He was the chief mover of an international conference in Brussels in 1853. He held the rank of Commander at the outbreak of the Civil War, when he left the United States Navy to help organize the coast defenses of the Confederacy. His letter in reply to an attractive Russian offer follows. After the war he went to Mexico and served as immigration commissioner for Emperor Maximilian. When his hope of establishing a Virginia colony in Mexico failed, he went to England. He returned to the United States in 1868 and became professor of meteorology at the Virginia Military Institute. He died there on February 1, 1873. Maury was the author of *Physical Geography of the Sea* (1855) and a number of other scientific publications.

"THE STATE OF VIRGINIA GAVE ME BIRTH . . ."

A Letter to the Grand Admiral of Russia

Richmond, Va., October 29th, 1861

Admiral: — Your letter reached me only a few days ago; it filled me with emotion. In it I am offered the hospitalities of a great and powerful Empire, with the Grand Admiral of its fleets for patron and friend. Inducements are held out such as none but the most magnanimous of princes could offer, and such as nothing but a stern sense of duty may withstand.

A home in the bosom of my family on the banks of the Neva, where, in the midst of books and surrounded by friends, I am without care for the morrow, to have the most princely means and facilities for prosecuting those studies, and continuing those philosophical labours in which I take most delight: all the advantages that I enjoyed in Washington are, with a larger discretion, to be offered me in Russia.

Surely a more flattering invitation could not be uttered! Certainly it could not reach a more grateful heart. I have slept upon it. It is becoming that I should be candid, and in a few words frankly state the circumstances by which I find myself surrounded.

The State of Virginia gave me birth; within her borders, among many kind friends, the nearest of kin, and troops of excellent neighbours, my children are planting their vine and fig-tree. In her green bosom are the graves of my fathers; the political whirlpool from which your kind forethought sought to rescue me has already plunged her into a fierce and bloody war.

In 1788, when this State accepted the Federal Constitution and entered the American Union, she did so with the formal declaration that she reserved to herself the right to withdraw from it for cause, and resume those powers and attributes of sovereignty which she

396

had never ceded away, but only delegated for certain definite and specified purposes.

When the President-elect commenced to set at naught the very objects of the Constitution, and without authority of law proceeded to issue his proclamation of 15th April last[1], Virginia, in the exercise of that reserved right, decided that the time had come when her safety, her dignity, and honour required her to resume those "delegated" powers and withdraw from the Union. She did so; she then straightway called upon her sons in the Federal Service to retire therefrom and come to her aid.

This call found me in the midst of those quiet physical researches at the Observatory in Washington which I am now, with so much delicacy of thought and goodness of heart, invited to resume in Russia. Having been brought up in the School of States-rights, where we had for masters the greatest statesmen of America, and among them Mr. Madison, the wisest of them all, I could not, and did not hesitate; I recognized this call, considered it mandatory, and, formally renouncing all allegiance to the broken Union, hastened over to the South side of the Potomac, there to renew to Fatherland those vows of fealty, service, and devotion which the State of Virginia had permitted me to pledge to the Federal Union so long only as by serving it, I might serve her.

Thus my sword has been tendered to her cause, and the tender has been accepted. Her soil is invaded, the enemy is actually at her gates; and here I am contending, as the fathers of the Republic did, for the right of self-government, and those very principles for the maintenance of which Washington fought when this, his native State, was a colony of Great Britain. The path of duty and of honour is therefore plain.

By following it with the devotion and loyalty of a true sailor, I shall, I am persuaded, have the glorious and proud recompense that is contained in the "well done" of the Grand Admiral of Russia and his noble companions-in-arms.

When the invader is expelled, and as soon thereafter as the State will grant me leave, I promise myself the pleasure of a trip across

[1]A call for troops from Virginia.

the Atlantic, and shall hasten to Russia, that I may there in person, on the banks of the Neva, have the honour and the pleasure of expressing to her Grand Admiral the sentiments of respect and esteem with which his oft-repeated acts of kindness, and the generous encouragement that he has afforded me in the pursuits of science, have inspired his

Obedient servant,
M. F. Maury, *Commander C. S. Navy.*

To H.I.H. The Grand Duke Constantine,
Grand Admiral of Russia,
St. Petersburg.

ROBERT E. LEE

1807-1870

Robert E. Lee, leader of the Confederate forces in the Civil War —
and the symbol of the Southern cause — was born at "Stratford" in
Westmoreland County, Virginia, on January 19, 1807. His father was
the Revolutionary soldier Henry ("Light Horse Harry") Lee. Lee attended
West Point, where he graduated with distinction in 1829, and was com-
missioned in the Corps of Engineers. At twenty-four he married Mary
Custis, great-granddaughter of Martha Washington, and made his home
at "Arlington," overlooking the Potomac. During the war with Mexico he
was a captain on the staff of General Winfield Scott and won a reputation
as an able soldier. He served as superintendent of West Point and as a
colonel of cavalry in the Comanche Indian country. At the time of John
Brown's raid on Harper's Ferry, Lee was dispatched to capture Brown and
his followers.

As Civil War moved closer, Lee wrote: "I can anticipate no greater calamity for the country than the dissolution of the Union. . . . Still a union
that can only be maintained by swords and bayonets, and in which strife
and civil war are to take the place of brotherly love and kindness, has no
charms for me. If the Union is dissolved and the Government dispersed, I
shall return to my native State and share the miseries of my people and,
save in defense, will draw my sword no more." His reputation as a soldier
was such that overtures were made to him to take command of the Federal army that was to be brought into the field. He declined on April 18,
1861, resigned from the army, and accepted command of the Virginia
forces on April 23. His letter of acceptance follows, as do his farewell
letter to the army at the close of the war and his letter accepting the
presidency of Washington College in 1865.

After the war Lee remained above the controversies around him and
even refused to write his memoirs of the struggle in which he had taken
a leading part. He devoted himself to Washington College, and died on
October 12, 1870.

TO THE VIRGINIA CONVENTION

Accepting Command of the Virginia Forces, April 23, 1861

Mr. President and Gentlemen of the Convention: Deeply impressed with the solemnity of the occasion on which I appear before you, and profoundly grateful for the honor conferred upon me, I accept the position your partiality has assigned me, though I would greatly have preferred your choice should have fallen on one more capable.

Trusting to Almighty God, an approving conscience, and the aid of my fellow-citizens, I will devote myself to the defense and service of my native State, in whose behalf alone would I have ever drawn my sword.

FAREWELL ORDER TO THE ARMY

Headquarters, Army of Northern Virginia,
April 10, 1865.

After four years' of arduous service, marked by unsurpassed courage and fortitude, the Army of Northern Virginia has been compelled to yield to overwhelming numbers and resources. I need not tell the survivors of so many hard-fought battles, who have remained steadfast to the last, that I have consented to this result from no distrust of them; but, feeling that valour and devotion could accomplish nothing that could compensate for the loss that would have attended the continuation of the contest, I have determined to avoid the useless sacrifice of those whose past service have endeared them to their countrymen. By the terms of the agreement, officers and men can return to their homes and remain there until exchanged. You will take with you the satisfaction that proceeds from the consciousness of duty faithfully performed; and I earnestly pray that a merciful God will extend to you His blessing and protection. With an increasing admiration of your constancy and devotion to your country, and a grateful remembrance of your kind and generous consideration of myself, I bid you an effectionate farewell.

R. E. Lee, General.

ACCEPTING THE PRESIDENCY OF
WASHINGTON COLLEGE

Powhatan County, August 24, 1865.

Gentlemen: — I have delayed for some days replying to your letter of the 5th inst., informing me of my election by the board of trustees to the presidency of Washington College, from a desire to give the subject due consideration. Fully impressed with the responsibilities of the office, I have feared that I should be unable to discharge its duties to the satisfaction of the trustees or to the benefit of the country. The proper education of youth requires not only great ability, but I fear more strength than I now possess, for I do not feel able to undergo the labour of conducting classes in regular courses of instruction. I could not, therefore, undertake more than the general administration and supervision of the institution. There is another subject which has caused me serious reflection, and is, I think, worthy of the consideration of the board. Being excluded from the terms of amnesty in the proclamation of the President of the United States of the 29th of May last, and an object of censure to a portion of the country, I have thought it probable that my occupation of the position of president might draw upon the college a feeling of hostility; and I should, therefore, cause injury to an institution which it would be my highest desire to advance. I think it the duty of every citizen, in the present condition of the country, to do all in his power to aid in the restoration of peace and harmony, and in no way to oppose the policy of the State or general government directed to that object. It is particularly incumbent on those charged with the instruction of the young to set them an example of submission to authority, and I could not consent to be the cause of animadversion upon the college. Should you, however, take a different view, and think that my services in the position tendered to me by the board will be advantageous to the college and country, I will yield to your judgment and accept it; otherwise I must most respectfully decline the office. Begging you to express to the trustees of the college my heartfelt gratitude for the honour conferred upon me, and requesting you to accept my cordial thanks for the kind manner in which you have communicated their decision, I am, gentlemen, with great respect, your most obedient servant,

R. E. Lee.

JUDITH W. McGUIRE

1812-1896

Judith W. McGuire was born in Richmond, Virginia, on March 19, 1812, the daughter of William Brockenbrough, a Judge of the Virginia Supreme Court, and was christened Judith White Brockenbrough. She was married to the Reverend John P. McGuire, principal of the Episcopal High School, near Alexandria, Virginia. At the beginning of the Civil War she became a refugee before the approaching Federal troops and left her home in northern Virginia for Richmond. There she worked in the War Department and as a nurse, and her husband was chaplain of the Officers Hospital. During the period she kept a diary "for the members of the family who are too young to remember these days." It is a highly interesting day-by-day record of life in wartime Virginia. Although it was not written with the idea of publication, she yielded to the suggestion of friends that it be made public. The *Diary of a Southern Refugee, During the War, by a Lady of Virginia,* covering the years May, 1861, to May, 1865, was published in New York in 1867. A second edition appeared the next year. Following the war she and her husband opened a school for girls at Tappahannock, Virginia, and after her husband's death in 1869 she continued the school until 1875. She was also the author of a short biography of Lee, *General Robert E. Lee, the Christian Soldier* (1873), and a third edition of the *Diary of a Southern Refugee* was published in Richmond in 1889. Mrs. McGuire died in Richmond on March 21, 1896.

Saturday Night, May 9. — So much has happened since I last wrote in my diary, that I can scarcely collect my thoughts to give a plain detail of facts as they occurred. Ten days ago, Mr. —— and myself went in to spend two days with our children who are living in Richmond. It soon became apparent that we could not return, as the Government had taken the cars for the purpose of transporting soldiers to Fredericksburg. Hooker was making immense demonstrations, and was crossing 159,000 men. They fought on Saturday, Sunday, and Monday, at different points, principally at Chancellorsville, and the enemy was repulsed at all points. Hooker and his host retired to the Rappahannock, and recrossed, I think, on Wednesday. It is said that General Lee would have followed him, but for the dreadful storm of Monday night and Tuesday. General Lee in his official report speaks of it as a "signal victory." Our army was smaller than usual, as Longstreet was still near Suffolk, and could not get up in time. It is pretty certain that Hooker — fighting Joe!! — had two to Lee's one, and was defeated. The great Stonewall is lost to us for a time; his left arm has been amputated, and there is a severe wound in his right hand. Oh, I pray that God may raise him up to be a continued blessing to the country. His wife has gone to him. The best surgical skill of the army, the sympathy and anxiety of the whole South, and the prayers of the country, are his. General Paxton, of the Stonewall Brigade, was killed, and many, ah, how many, valuable lives were lost! it is impossible for us yet to know, as the telegraphic wires are cut, and mail communication very uncertain. From my own family boys we have not heard, and we are willing to believe that "no news is good news." Two more of the dear ones over whose youth we so anxiously watched have fallen — Hill Carter, of Shirley, and Benjamin White, of Charlestown, Jefferson County. Thank God, they were both Christians! My heart aches for their parents. The

405

last was an only son, and justly the pride and joy of his household. His parents are in the enemy's lines. O Lord, uphold that tender mother when the withering stroke is known to her! Major Channing Price and Colonel Thomas Garnett are gone! God help our country! We can't afford to lose such men.

While our army was busily engaged last Sunday, the Yankees took occasion to send out a raiding party of their superfluous numbers. A party of several hundred came here about three o'clock in the afternoon. They knew that the cars containing the wounded from the battle-field would be here. The cars arrived, and were immediately surrounded and the soldiers paroled. The ladies all the while were here in the cars administering comfort to the wounded. They remained about three hours, took off every horse they could find, and every servant that they could induce to go, which was very few, and then rode off without burning the houses or offering other injury to the villagers. They belonged to Stoneman's command. They went over this country, Goochland, Louisa, and a part of Fluvanna, without molestation. They became alarmed, however, and cut their career short. They went to Columbia for the purpose of destroying the canal, but in their haste did it very little injury. The injury to the railroads was slight, and easily repaired. To individuals they did some mischief; at W. they fed four hundred horses at my brother's barn, took his buggy horse, and rode off. His neighbours, and others in their route, fared very much in the same way. In Richmond the excitement was terrible. The alarm-bell pealed out its startling notes; citizens were armed, and sent out to man the batteries; extemporaneous cavalry companies were formed and sent out; women were seen crying and wringing their hands on the streets; wild rumours were afloat; but it all ended in the raiders not attempting to get to the Richmond batteries, and the city in a few hours became perfectly quiet.

Sunday, May 10. — Sad, sad tidings were brought to our cottage this morning! Washington, the youngest and darling son of our dear friend, Mrs. Stuart, has fallen. The mother and sisters are overwhelmed, while our whole household is shrouded in sorrow. He was young, brave, and a Christian. He fell while nobly fighting with his company, the famous Rockbridge Battery, on Marye's Hill. We have heard no other particulars. The brave boy had scarcely recovered from a most severe wound received last summer near Winchester. To God we commend his afflicted, though quietly submissive, mother. He alone can soothe the sorrow which He has seen fit to permit.

Tuesday Evening, May 12th. — How can I record the sorrow which has befallen our country! General T. J. Jackson is no more. The good, the great, the glorious Stonewall Jackson is numbered with the dead! Humanly speaking, we cannot do without him; but the same God who raised him up, took him from us, and He who has so miraculously prospered our cause, can lead us on without him. Perhaps we have trusted too much to an arm of flesh; for he was the nation's idol. His soldiers almost worshipped him, and it may be that God has therefore removed him. We bow in meek submission to the great Ruler of events. May his blessed example be followed by officers and men, even to the gates of heaven! He died on Sunday the 10th, at a quarter past three, P. M. His body was carried by yesterday, in a car, to Richmond. Almost every lady in Ashland visited the car, with a wreath or a cross of the most beautiful flowers, as a tribute to the illustrious dead. An immense concourse had assembled in Richmond, as the solitary car containing the body of the great soldier, accompanied by a suitable escort, slowly and solemnly approached the depot. The body lies in state to-day at the Capitol, wrapped in the Confederate flag, and literally covered with lilies of the valley and other beautiful Spring flowers. To-morrow the sad *cortege* will wend its way to Lexington, where he will be buried, according to his dying request, in the "Valley of Virginia." As a warrior, we may appropriately quote from Byron:

> "His spirit wraps the dusky mountain,
> His memory sparkles o'er the fountain,
> The meanest rill, the mightiest river,
> Rolls mingling with his fame forever."

As a Christian, in the words of St. Paul, I thank God to be able to say, "He has fought the good fight, he has finished his course, he has kept the faith. Henceforth there is laid up for him a crown of righteousness, which the Lord, the righteous Judge, shall give him at the last day."

Wednesday, 13th. — I have just heard that my dear nephew, Will'by N., was wounded at Chancellorsville, and that his left leg has been amputated. He is at Mr. Marye's near Hamilton's Crossings, receiving the warm-hearted hospitality of that house, now so widely known. His mother has reached him, and he is doing well. I pray that God may have mercy upon him, and raise him up speedily, for the Saviour's sake.

May 16th. — We were aroused this morning before daylight, by reports that the Yankees were making a raid, and were very near this place. We all dressed hastily, and the gentlemen went out to devise means to stop the trains which were to pass through. Though within five miles of us, they became aware that notice had been given of their purpose, and they immediately turned their steps to some more private place, where they might rob and plunder without molestation. The miserable poltroons, when on one of their raids, will become frightened by the sudden rising of a covey of partridges, and be diverted from their course; then they will ride bravely to a house, where they know they will only find women and children; order meals to be prepared; search the house; take the valuables; feed their horses at the barns; take off the horses from the stables; shoot the pigs, sheep, and other stock, and leave them dead in the fields; rob the poultry-yards; then, after regaling themselves on the meals which have been prepared by force, with the threats of bayonets and pistols, they ride off, having pocketed the silver spoons and forks, which may have unwittingly been left in their way.

I have been in Richmond for two days past, nursing the wounded of our little hospital. Some of them are very severely injured, yet they are the most cheerful invalids I ever saw. It is remarked in all the hospitals that the cheerfulness of the wounded in proportion to their suffering is much greater than that of the sick. Under my care, yesterday, was one poor fellow, with a ball embedded in his neck; another with an amputated leg; one with a hole in his breast, through which a bullet had passed; another with a shattered arm; and others with slighter wounds; yet all showed indomitable spirit; evinced a readiness to be amused or interested in every thing around them;

asked that the morning papers might be read to them, and gloried in their late victory; and expressed an anxiety to get well, that they may have another *"chance at them fellows."* The Yankees are said to have landed at West Point, and are thence sending out raiding parties over the country. Colonel Davis, who led the party here on the third, has been severly wounded by a scouting party, sent out by General Wise towards Tunstall's Station. It is said he has lost his leg. So may it be!

Monday, May 18th. — This morning we had the gratification of a short visit from General Lee. He called and breakfasted with us, while the other passengers in the cars breakfasted at the hotel. We were very glad to see that great and good man look so well and so cheerful. His beard is very long, and painfully gray, which makes him appear much older than he really is. One of the ladies at table, with whom he is closely connected, rallied him on allowing his beard to grow, saying, "Cousin R., it makes you look too venerable for your years." He was amused, and pleaded as his excuse the inconvenience of shaving in camp. "Well," she replied, "if I were in Cousin Mary's place (Mrs. L's) I would allow it to remain now, but I would take it off as soon as the war is over." He answered, while a shade passed over his bright countenance, "When the war is over, my dear L., she may take my beard off, and my head with it, if she chooses." This he said as the whistle summoned him to his seat in the cars, not meaning to depress us, or imagining for an instant that we would think of it again; but it proved to us that he *knew* that the end was not yet, and disappointed us, for after every great victory we cannot help hoping that the Federal Government may be tired of war and bloodshed, rapine and murder, and withdraw its myriads to more innocent pursuits.

Yesterday evening we were agreeably surprised by a call from W. B. C., just recovered from his dreadful wound, received at Fredericksburg last winter. He is an infantry captain of the Stonewall Brigade, and is just returning to his company. Alas! alas! his great Captain has passed away during his absence, which makes his return very sad. He thinks that Generall Ewell is the man of all others to put in his place, though no man can fill it. General Ewell, he says, is one of General Jackson's most enthusiastic admirers, be-

lieving him to have been almost an inspired man. General E. re-
lates an incident of him, when on their victorious march through
the Valley last summer, which is beautifully characteristic of General J. One night, when it was evident that there must be a battle
next day, he (General E) went to General Jackson for his plans.
General J. replied that he would give them to him next morning,
as they had not yet been formed. General E. felt uneasy and restless, and could not sleep. About midnight he arose, and, passing
through the sleeping multitudes, he reached General Jackson's tent,
and was about to raise the curtain to enter it, when his attention was
arrested by the voice of prayer. General Jackson was praying fervently for guidance through the coming day. General E. remarked
to a friend that he had never before heard a prayer so devout and
beautiful; he then, for the first time, felt the desire to be a Christian.
He retired to his tent quietly, without disturbing General J., feeling
assured that all would be well. The next morning a fight came off,
replete with victory. General Ewell was subsequently wounded at
the second battle of Manassas, and it is said that he has since become
a Christian. God grant that it may be so!

May 20th. — I feel depressed to-night. Army news from the South
bad. General Pemberton has been repulsed between Jackson and
Vicksburg. General Johnston is there; I hope, by the mercy of God,
he may be able to keep the enemy out of Vicksburg. Besides the
depressing news, the day has been distressing in the hospital — so
much suffering among the wounded. One fine young man has the
appearance and manner of imbecility, from having been struck on
the head by a piece of shell. No relief can be given him, and the
surgeons say that he must die.

Mr. —— staid in town to attend the Church "Council," as it is
now called. This new name may be more appropriate to an ecclesiastical meeting, yet "Virginia Convention" has a sweet, hallowed sound to me.

23d — We tremble for Vicksburg; an immense army has been sent
against it; we await its fate with breathless anxiety.

25th — The enemy repulsed at Vicksburg, though it is still in a
state of siege. General Johnston is there, and we hope that the best

means will be used to save that heroic little city; and we pray that God may bless the means used.

A friend called this morning and told us of the fall of another of those dear youths, over whose boyish sojourn with us memory loves to linger. Kennedy Groghan of Baltimore, who, in the very beginning of the war, came over to help us, fell in a skirmish in the Valley, a short time ago. The only account given us is, that the men were forced to retreat hastily, and were only able to place his loved body under the spreading branches of a tree. Oh! I trust that some kindly hand has put him beneath God's own earth, free from the din of war, from the strife of man, and from the curse of sin forever. I remember so well when, during our stay in Winchester, the first summer of the war, while General Johnston's army was stationed near there, how he, and so many others, would come in to see us, with their yet unfaded suits of gray — already sunburnt and soldier-like, but bright and cheerful. Alas! alas! how many now fill the graves of heroes — their young lives crushed out by the unscrupulous hand of an invading foe!

27th. — The news from Vicksburg by the morning's papers is very delightful, if authentic. We pause for confirmation of it. The young people among the villagers and refugees have been amusing themselves, during the past two evenings, with tableaux. I am too old to enjoy such things in these troubled times, but one picture I regretted not seeing. It represented the young Confederacy. The whole bright galaxy was there — South Carolina in scarlet, restive and fiery; Virginia, grave and dignified, yet bright with hope, seemed to be beckoning Kentucky on, who stood beyond the threshold, her eyes cast down with shame and suffering; Maryland was at the threshold, but held back by a strong hand; all the rest of the fair sisters were there in their appropriate places, forming a beautiful picture.

I am amused to see how the Democrats of the North are speechifying and exciting themselves about the arrest of Vallandigham, and how Lincoln will soon make them *back down.*

May 28. — Hospital day. The wounded cheerful and doing well. I read, distributed books, and talked with them. They are always ready to be amused, or to be instructed. I have never but in one instance had an unpleasant word or look from any whom I endeavoured to treat with kindness in any way. Bible reading is always kindly received. J. J. has returned home, as usual much interested in hospital work.

June 1 — L. and B. went up to Mr. Marye's near Fredericksburg to-day, to visit their brother's grave. They took flowers with which to adorn it. It is a sweet, though sad office, to plant flowers on a Christian's grave. They saw my sister, who is there, nursing her wounded son.

News from Vicksburg cheering.

5th. — Our household circle has been broken to-day by Mrs. S. and her daughter B. leaving it for South Carolina. We are grieved to give them up.

6th. — We have been interested lately by a visit to this village of our old friend, Mrs. T., of Rappahannock County. She gives most graphic description of her sojourn of seven weeks among the Yankees last summer. Sixty thousand surrounded her house, under command of General Siegel. On one occasion, he and his staff rode up and announced that they would *take tea with her.* Entirely alone, that elegant old lady retained her composure, and with unruffled countenance rang her bell; when the servant appeared, she said to him, "John, tea for fourteen." She quietly retained her seat, conversing with them with dignified politeness, and submitting as best she could to the General's very free manner of walking about her beautiful establishment, pronouncing it "baronial," and regretting, in her presence, that he had not known of its elegancies and comforts in time, that he might have brought Mrs. Siegel, and have made it his head-quarters. Tea being announced, Mrs. T., before proceeding to the dining-room, requested the servant to call a soldier in, who had been guarding her house for weeks, and who had sought occasion to do her many kindnesses. When the man entered, the General demurred: "No, no, madam, he will not go to table with us." Mrs. T. replied, "General, I must beg that you will allow this *gentleman* to come to *my table,* for he has been a friend to me when I have sadly wanted one." The General objected no farther; the *man* took tea with the master. After tea, the General proposed music, asking Mrs. T. if she had ever played; she replied that "such was still her habit." The piano being opened, she said if she sang at all she must sing the songs of her own land, and then, with her uncommonly fine voice, she sang, "The Bonnie Blue Flag," "Dixie", and other Southern songs, with great spirit. They listened with apparent pleasure. One of the staff then suggested that the General was a musician. Upon her vacating the seat he took it, and played in grand style; with so much beauty and *accuracy*, she added, with a twinkle of her eye, that I strongly suspected him of having been a music-master. Since that time she has heard that he was once master of that beautiful art in Mobile. Well, he was at least a more innocent man then than now. Almost every woman of the South, or at least of Virginia, will have her tale to tell when this "cruel war is over." The life of too many will be, alas! as a "tale that is told;" its interest, its charm even its hope, as far as this world is concerned, having passed away. Their crown of rejoicing will be in the public weal, which their loved and lost have fought, bled, and died to establish; but their own hearts will be withered, their hearths deserted.

Mrs. G. D. of Fredericksburg, has been giving some amusing incidents of her sudden departure from her home. She had determined to remain, but when, on the night of the bombardment, a shell burst very near her house, her husband aroused her to say that she must go. They had no means of conveyance, and her two children were both under three years of age, and but one servant, (the others having gone to the Yankees,) a girl twelve years old. It so happened that they had access to three straw carriages, used by her own children and those of her neighbours. They quickly determined to put a child in each of two carriages, and to bundle up as many clothes as would fill the third. The father drew the carriage containing one child, the mother the other child, and the little girl drew the bundle of clothes. They thus set out, to go they knew not whither, only to get out of the way of danger. It was about midnight, a dark, cold night. They went on and on, to the outskirts of the town, encountering a confused multitude rushing pell-mell, with ever and anon a shell bursting at no great distance, sent as a threat of what they might expect on the morrow. They were presently overtaken by a respectable shoemaker whom they knew, rolling a wheelbarrow containing a large bundle of clothes, and *the baby*. They were attracted by the poor little child rolling off from its elevated place on the bundle, and as Mrs. D. stopped, with motherly solicitude for the child, the poor man told his story. In the darkness and confusion he had become separated from his wife and other children, and knew not where to find them; he thought he might find them but for anxiety about the baby. Mrs. D. then proposed that he should take her bundle of clothes with his in the wheelbarrow, and put his child into the third straw carriage. This being agreed to, the party passed on. When they came to our encampment, a soldier ran out to offer to draw one carriage and thus rest the mother; having gone as far as he dared from his regiment, then another soldier took his place to the end of his line, and so on from one soldier to another until our encampment was passed. Then she drew on her little charge about two miles farther, to the house of an acquaintance, which was wide open to the homeless. Until late the next day the shoemaker's baby was under their care, but he at last came, bringing the bundle in safety. As the day progressed the cannon roared and the shells whistled, and it was thought advisable for them to go on to Chancellorsville. The journey of several miles was performed on foot, still with the straw carriages, for no horse nor vehicle could be found in that desolated country. They remained at Chancellorsville until the 2d or 3d of May, when that house became within range of cannon. Again she gathered up her little flock, and came on to Ashland. Her little three-years old boy explored the boarding-house as soon as he got to it, and finding no cellar he became alarmed, and running to his mother, exclaimed, "This house won't do, mother; we all have no cellar to go into when they shell it!" Thus our children are born and reared amid war and bloodshed! It seemed so sad to me to see a bright little girl, a few days ago, of four years old, stop in the midst of her play, when she heard distant thunder, exclaiming, "Let me run home, they are firing!" Poor little child, her father had been a sacrifice; no wonder that she wanted to run to her mother when she thought she heard firing. Tales far more sad than that of Mrs. D. are told, of the poor assembled by hundreds on the roadside in groups, having no shelter to cover them, and often nothing to eat, on that dark winter's night.

Judith W. McGuire, 1812-1896

June 7. — We are living in fear of a Yankee raid. They have a large force on York River, and are continually sending parties up the Pamunky and Mattapony Rivers, to devastate the country and annoy the inhabitants. Not long ago a party rode to the house of a gentleman on Mattapony; meeting him on the lawn, the commander accosted him: "Mr. R., I understand you have the finest horses in King William County?" "Perhaps, sir, I have," replied Mr. R. "Well, sir," said the officer, "I want those horses immediately." "They are not yours," replied Mr. R, "and you can't get them." The officer began to curse, and said he would burn every house on the place if the horses were not produced. Suiting the action to the word, he handed a box of matches to a subordinate, saying, "Burn!" In half an hour Mr. R. saw fourteen of his houses in a light blaze, including the dwelling, the kitchen, corn-houses and barn filled with grain, meat-house filled with meat, and servants' houses. Scarcely any thing was saved, not even the family clothes. But he did not get the horses, which were the objects of his peculiar wishes; the faithful servants had carried them away to a place of safety. How strange it is that we can be so calm, surrounded as we are by danger!

8th. — We have had a cavalry fight near Culpeper Courthouse. We drove the enemy back, but I am afraid that our men won no laurels, for we were certainly surprised most shamefully.

16th. — The morning papers gave a telegram from General Lee, announcing that General Early's Brigade had taken Winchester by storm. So again Winchester and all that beautiful country, Clarke, etc. are disenthralled.

It is said that our army will go to Pennsylvania. This I dread; but it is in God's hands, I believe, for good and not for evil.

21st. — We hear of fights and rumours of fights. It is said that Ewell's Division captured 6,000 prisoners at Winchester, and that General Edward Johnson went to Berryville and captured 2,000 that were on their way to reinforce Millroy. They have driven the enemy out of the Valley, so that now we have possession of it once more. Our cavalry has been as far as Chambersburg, Pennsylvania, but I do not know what they have accomplished.

26th. — While in the midst of preparation to visit my sisters at W. and S. H., we have been startled by the account of Yankees approaching. They have landed in considerable force at the White House, and are riding over the country to burn and destroy. They have burned the South Anna Bridge on the Central Railroad, and this evening were advancing on the bridge over the South Anna, on this railroad, which is but four miles above us. We have a small force there, and a North Carolina regiment has gone up to-night to reinforce them. We are, of course, in considerable excitement. I am afraid they are ruining the splendid wheat harvests which are now being gathered on the Pamunky. Trusting in the Lord, who hath hitherto been our help, we are going quietly to bed, though we believe that they are very near us. From our army we can hear nothing. No one can go farther than Culpeper Court-House in that direction. Why this has been ordered I know not, but for some good military reason, I have no doubt. It is said that Stuart's cavalry have been fighting along the line of the Manassas Gap Railroad with great success. We can hear no particulars.

Saturday Evening — Just heard from W. and S. H.; both terribly robbed by the raiders in the last three days. All of my brother's horses and mules taken. Some of the servants were forced off, who staid so faithfully by them and resisted all the Yankee entreaties twice before. They attempted to burn the wheat, which is shocked in the field, but an opportune rain made it too wet to burn. The raiders came up the river, destroying crops, carriages, etc., stealing horses and cattle, and carrying off the servants from every plantation, until they got to Hickory Hill, (Mr. W. F. Wickham's,) where they found a prize in the person of General W. F. Lee, who was wounded at the cavalry fight of Beverley's Ford, and was at Mr. W's, unable to move. Notwithstanding the remonstrances of his wife and mother, they took him out of his bed, placed him in Mr. Wickham's carriage, and drove off with him. I can't conceive greater hardness of heart than it required to resist the entreaties of that beautiful young wife and infirm mother. F. has just received a note from the former, written in sorrow and loneliness. She fears that the wound may suffer greatly by locomotion; beyond that, she has much to dread, but she scarcely knows what.

Wednesday. — Many exciting rumours to-day about the Yankees being at Hanover Court-House, within a few miles of us. They can be

416

traced everywhere by the devastation which marks their track. There are also rumours that our army is in Pennsylvania. So may it be! We are harassed to death with their ruinous raids, and why should not the North feel it in its homes? Nothing but their personal suffering will shorten the war. I don't want their women and children to suffer; nor that our men should follow their example, and break through and steal. I want our warfare carried on in a more honorable way; but I do want our men and horses to be fed on the good things of Pennsylvania; I want the fine dairies, pantries, granaries, meadows, and orchards belonging to the rich farmers of Pennsylvania, to be laid open to our army; and I want it all paid for with our *Confederate money, which will be good at some future day.* I want their horses taken for our cavalry and wagons, in return for the hundreds of thousands that they have taken from us; and I want their fat cattle driven into Virginia to feed our army. It amuses me to think how the Dutch farmers' wives will be concealing the golden products of their dairies, to say nothing of their apple-butter, peach-butter, and their wealth of apple pies.

ROBERT LEWIS DABNEY

1820-1898

Robert Lewis Dabney was born in Louisa County, Virginia, where his father had a small estate, on March 5, 1820. He grew up in Virginia, attended Hampden-Sydney College, taught school, and continued his education at the University of Virginia and the Virginia Union Theological Seminary. He served for a time as a Presbyterian minister, and for thirty years he taught at the Union Theological Seminary and occasionally at near-by Hampden-Sydney. He became well known as a writer in Presbyterian publications and just before the Civil War was offered positions, neither of which he accepted, as professor at Princeton and as minister of the New York Fifth Avenue Presbyterian Church. He opposed secession, but in 1861 became a Confederate army chaplain. The following year he became a major on the staff of Stonewall Jackson. He was the author of a number of books and essays on theology and related subjects, but is now remembered as the author of the first important biography of Stonewall Jackson. His *Life and Campaigns of Lieutenant-General Thomas J. Jackson,* a selection from which follows, was first published in London in 1865 and in New York in 1866. In his later years Dabney taught at the University of Texas. He died on January 3, 1898.

STONEWALL JACKSON AND THE SECOND BATTLE OF MANASSAS*

The narrative must return to the lines of General Jackson. Anxiously did that General watch the distant road which led from Thoroughfare Gap down to the Warrenton turnpike, on the morning of the 29th [August 29, 1862]. His little army was now manifestly confronted by the whole Federal host, which, concentrating itself more toward his left, was preparing to force him back from Bull Run, and to crush him before his supports could arrive. His lines, exhausted by their almost superhuman exertions, thinned by battle, and pallid with hunger, stood grimly at bay; but the stoutest hearts were anxious, in view of the more terrible struggle before them. In the early morning, clouds of dust arising along the Thoroughfare road had mocked their hopes; but they were raised by the Federalists, who, having occupied that pass the day before to obstruct the march of Longstreet, were now retiring upon their masses toward Bristoe Station. As the day verged toward the meridian, other and denser clouds again arose, along the same highway; and soon the couriers of Stuart came, with the welcome news, that it was the *corps* of Longstreet, advancing to connect with the right of Jackson. Already the Federalists, warned of the shortness of their time, had begun the attack by a heavy cannonade upon that part of his position, at ten o'clock. The batteries of Taliaferro's division now commanded by the brave General Starke, replied. But the head of General Longstreet's column was now at hand, and threatened to insinuate itself behind the Federal left. They therefore shifted their demonstration to Jackson's left, opening upon that part of his position with a furious cannonade, and preparing vast masses of infantry to force it. While Longstreet deployed his line across the Warrenton turnpike, and fronting toward the east, Jack-

---

*Title supplied. From *Life and Campaigns of Lieut.-Gen. Thomas J. Jackson (Stonewall Jackson)*, by R. L. Dabney. New York, 1866.

son's *corps* was now disposed at right angles to it, along the excavations and embankments of an unfinished railroad, which, crossing Bull Run a half mile below Sudley, ran westward, parallel to the Warrenton turnpike. This work had been begun to connect the city of Alexandria directly with the Manassas Gap road near Thoroughfare. Running across the hills and vales of an undulating country, and presenting now an elevated embankment and anon a cut, it offered to the Confederates almost the advantages of a regular field-work. Here General Jackson had arranged his infantry in two lines of battle, with the artillery chiefly posted upon eminences in the rear. A. P. Hill formed his left, Ewell his centre, and Starke his right. An interval between his right and the left of Longstreet was occupied by a large collection of the artillery of the latter, posted upon a large hill, whence they assisted, by their fire, in the repulse of the enemy on either hand. Pope, now contenting himself with showing a front against Longstreet, began, at two o'clock, P. M., to hurl his infantry with fury and determination against the lines of Jackson. Especially did the storm of battle rage in front of the left, occupied by the division of A. P. Hill. In defiance of his deadly fire, delivered from the shelter of the railroad embankments, line after line was advanced to close quarters, only to be mowed down, and to recoil in confusion. Soon the second line of Hill was advanced to the support of the first. Six times the Federalists rushed forward in separate and obstinate assaults, and as many times were repulsed. At an interval between the brigade of Gregg, on the extreme left, and that of Thomas, the enemy broke across in great numbers, and threatened to separate the former from his friends, and surround him. But two regiments of the reserve, advancing within ten paces of the triumphant foe, poured such volleys into their dense masses that they were hurled back before this murderous fire, and the lines reestablished. The brigade of Hays from the division of Ewell, now commanded by General Lawton, was first brought to the support of Gregg. The struggle raged until the cartridges of the infantry were in many places exhausted. When Hill sent to the gallant Gregg to ask if he could hold his own, he answered, "Tell him I have no ammunition, but I will hold my position with the bayonet." In several places, the Confederate lines, without a single round of cartridges, lay in the railroad cuts, within a few yards of their enemies, sternly defying their nearer approach with the cold steel, while the staff-officers from the rear sent in a scanty supply of ammunition, by the hand of some daring volunteer, who ventured to run the gauntlet of a deadly fire to reach them. In other parts the men, laying aside their empty muskets, seized the stones which lay near, and with them beat back the foe. When the bloody field was reviewed, not a few were found whose skulls were broken with these primitive weapons. But the strength of the extreme left was now exhausted by seven hours of strife; nature could do no more; and General Jackson ordered Early, with his brigade and the 8th Louisiana and 13th Georgia, to relieve Gregg and Hays. The enemy had by this time occupied a considerable tract of the railroad, and the woods in front of it. Early advanced upon them, drove them out of the thickets and across the excavation with fearful slaughter, and pursued them for a distance beyond it, when he was recalled to the original line. With this magnificent charge, the struggle of the day closed. It had raged in similar manner along the centre, where that sturdy veteran, Brigadier-General Trimble, was severely wounded. But the carnage upon the left was most ghastly. Here might be seen upon the fields, the black lines of corpses, clearly defining the positions where the Federal lines of battle had stood and received the deadly volleys of the Confederates; while the woods and railroad cuts were thickly strewn for a mile with killed and wounded. In the division of Hill the loss was also serious; and among the severely wounded were two brigade commanders, Field and Forno. During the heat of the battle, a detachment of Federal troops had penetrated to Jackson's rear, near Sudley Church, and captured a few wounded men and ambulances. The horse artillery of Pelham, with a battalion of cavalry, under Major Patrick, speedily brushed the annoyance away, and recovered the captures. But this incident cost the army the loss of one of its most enlightened and efficient officers, the chivalrous Patrick, who was mortally wounded while pursuing the fugitives.

While this struggle was raging along Jackson's lines, the *corps* of Longstreet continued to confront the observing force of Federalists before them, and the batteries of his left engaged those of the enemy in a severe cannonade. As the afternoon advanced, Stuart reported to him the approach of a heavy column of the enemy upon his right and rear, from the direction of Bristoe. This was indeed a *corps* of the army of McClellan from the Peninsula, which, landing on the Potomac, had been pushed forward to support Pope. Against this new enemy Longstreet showed a front, while Stuart raising a mighty dust along the road near Gainsville, by causing a number of his troopers to drag bundles of brushwood along the highway, persuaded him that some heavy mass of fresh Confederate troops was advancing from Thoroughfare to meet his assault upon Longstreet's right. The Federal commander therefore recoiled, after a feeble demonstration; and, passing by a circuit to the eastward, sought to unite himself with the forces in front of Jackson. Longstreet now advanced several brigades to the attack, with those of Hood in the van, and until nine o'clock at night, drove back the enemy before him with great vigor, capturing a number of prisoners, a cannon, and three colors. Darkness then closed the bloody day, and the Confederates on every side withdrew to lie upon their arms upon their selected lines of combat. From this respite, the boastful Pope took the pretext to despatch to his masters a pompous bulletin of victory, claiming that the Confederates were repulsed on all hands! With a stupidity equal to his impudence, he concealed from himself the fact that this lull in the tempest was but the prelude to its final and resistless burst. The mighty huntsman now had the brutal game secure in his toils, and only awaited the moment of his exhaustion to despatch him.

As Jackson gathered his officers around him in the darkness, at the close of this second act of the tragedy, and prepared to lie down for a short repose under the open sky, their triumph wore a solemn hue. A week of marching and fighting without any regular supply for their wants, had worn down their energies to a grade where nothing but a determined will could sustain them. Many of the bravest and best had fallen, and the sufferers and the dead were all around them. The Medical Director, Doctor McGuire, recounting the many casualties which he had witnessed, said, "General, this day has been won by nothing but stark and stern fighting." "No," said Jackson, "It has been won by nothing but the blessing and protection of Providence." It was strong evidence of the devout spirit of the patriot troops, that amidst all these fatigues and horrors, they yet found time for acts of devotion. The Chaplains, after spending the day in attentions to the wounded, at nightfall returned to their regiments, and gathered such groups in the woods as could be spared from the watches, where they spent a season in prayer and praise. Many were the brave men who joined in these strange and solemn prayer-meetings, whose next worship was offered in the upper sanctuary.

The advance of Longstreet at nightfall, upon the Confederate right had disclosed the fact that the Federalists were posted, in heavy masses, upon a position of great natural strength. The choice offered to General Lee now was, to leave the favorable ground which he had chosen, and taking the aggressive, to dislodge them at a great cost; or else to await their attack with the prospect of turning their retreat into a disaster, if they attempted to cross Bull Run in his immediate front and retire without fighting. He well knew that Pope would scarcely be so rash as to attempt the latter expedient; for the two armies were now at such close quarters, that there was no room for either to turn away without a deadly side blow from the other; and the Federal commander had been so obliging as to manoeuvre himself into a position which had the stream immediately in its rear, with two practicable crossings for artillery, of which one was a stone arch which a few well directed round shot might have dismantled. General Lee, therefore, calmly awaited the final struggle, standing on the defensive, in his previous lines. These formed a vast, obtuse *fourchette*, presenting its concavity toward the enemy. The left of Longstreet did not touch the right of Jackson at the angle; but a space of half a mile between the two was occupied by an elevated ridge, which commanded the fronts of both wings. This hill was now crowned with the artillery battalions of Shumaker of Jackson's *corps*, and S. D. Lee of Longstreet's making an aggregate of thirty-six pieces. From this arrangement it resulted, first, that the troops of Pope, operating within the jaws of the Confederate army, would naturally become more densely massed than their opponents, and would thus afford a more certain mark for their accurate fire; which no force on earth could ever face in close order, without murderous loss. The second result was, that the superior *momentum* of the Federal masses must yet result only in a bloody failure, when hurled against either wing of the Confederates, because they would be enfiladed from the other wing. By these dispositions, the battle was decided before it was fought. The only gleam of good sense which the ill starred Federal leader showed, was in delaying the decisive hour until the late afternoon; so that the friendly darkness might speedily supervene upon the disaster which was destined to follow, and save him from utter destruction. The forenoon of Saturday, August 30th, was therefore spent in a desultory cannonade, addressed first to one, and then to another part of the Confederate lines, with irregular skirmishes interspersed. He was employed in disposing his infantry, under cover of the woods and valleys, chiefly in Jackson's front; for against him he again destined his main attack. The infantry of the latter was still posted along the unfinished railroad, in two lines, the first sheltered, where the ground was favorable, by the excavations and embankments, and the second massed upon the wooded hills above. At half past three o'clock, the enemy made a show of attack along the lines of Longstreet. But scarcely had this begun when they advanced, without preliminary skirmishing, in enormous masses, against Jackson. Three lines of battle surged forward like mighty waves, and rolled up to the Confederate position. As one recoiled before their fire, another took its place, with a dogged resolution, as though determined to break through by sheer weight of numbers. The Federal flags were planted sometimes within twenty paces of the excavations which contained the opposing line; and again the Confederates after exhausting their ammunition, resorted to the stones of the field to beat back their assailants. When this furious struggle had raged for half an hour, and the wearied lines of Jackson were yielding at some points, he sent word to Longstreet to move for his relief. But his desire was already anticipated; the artillery in the centre was advanced, and wherever the attacking lines of Federalists exposed themselves before Jackson's front, it showered a crushing and enfilading fire upon them. The third and second lines were first broken, and the woods in which they attempted to rally searched with shells. Meantime, the artillery of Ewell's and Hill's divisions, from Jackson's rear and left, joined in the melee as position offered. Before this fire in front and flank, the Federal lines wavered, broke, and resolved themselves into huge hordes of men, without order or guidance. General Jackson now ordered the advance of his whole line of infantry; and the Commander-in-Chief, seeing that the moment for the final blow had come, sent a similar order to his right wing. But its energetic leader had divined his wishes, and had already begun the movement. Over several miles of hill and dale, of field and forest, the two lines now swept forward, with a terrible grandeur, closing upon the disordered masses of the enemy like the jaws of a leviathan; while Jackson upon the left and Stuart upon the right, urged forward battery after battery at a gallop, to seize every commanding hill whence they could fire between the gaps, or over the heads of the infantry, and plough up the huddled crowds of fugitives. But at many points, these did not yield without stubborn resistance. The brigades of Jackson dashed at them with fierce enthusiasm, and such scenes of close encounter and murderous strife were witnessed, as are not often seen on fields of battle. The supreme hour of vengeance had now come; in the expressive phrase of Cromwell, the victors "had their will upon their enemies." As they drove them for two miles toward Bull Run, they strewed the ground with slaughter, until fury itself was sated and fatigued with the carnival of blood. And now, night again closed upon the third act of the tragedy, black with a double gloom of the battle smoke and a gathering storm; but still the pursuers plied their work with cannon shot and fierce volleys, fired into the populous darkness before them. At ten o'clock they ceased their pursuit, for they found that amidst the confusion of the field, and the obscurity, friend could no longer be distinguished from foe. The army then lay down to rest upon the ground they had won; while all night long, the broken fragments of the Federalists were stealing across the stream, and retreating to the heights of Centreville.

In this three days' battle, the Confederate loss was heavy, but that of their enemies was frightful. Compared to it, the carnage of the Chickahominy was child's play. The bloody field told the story of the disproportion for itself, and when the Federal surgeons came upon it under a flag of truce such was the multitude of the wounded lying helpless upon it, that days were exhausted in collecting them, while many wretches perished miserably of neglect during the delay. This disproportionate carnage was due to the masterly handling of the Confederate troops, to their advantageous position, to the density of the enemy's masses, and especially to the terrible moment of the rout, when the work of destruction was pursued, for a time, without resistance. The Sabbath morning dawned upon a scene in most fearful contrast with its peace and sanctity. The storm which had gathered during the night was descending in a comfortless rain, drenching the ghastly dead, the miserable wounded, and the weary victors. The soldiers of Jackson arose from the ground stiffened with the cold, and after devoting a few hours to refreshment, resumed the march, while those of Longstreet remained to bury the dead and collect the spoils. Stuart had reported that he found the enemy rallied upon the heights of Centreville, commanding the Warrenton turnpike, where General Joseph E. Johnston had constructed a powerful line of works, the first winter of the war, which were capable of defence either in front or rear. Here the fragments of Pope, supported by large reinforcements from the army of McClellan, again showed a front against the pursuers. Jackson was therefore directed to turn this position, and compel the retreat of the enemy from it without a battle. To effect this, he crossed the Bull Run at Sudley, and marching northward by a country road, came the next day into the Little River turnpike, which leads eastward, and intersects the Warrenton road at Fairfax Court House, far in the rear of Centreville. No sooner was this movement perceived by the enemy, than they resumed a hasty retreat. But as their crowded column approached Fairfax Court House, they found Jackson at hand, prepared to strike their line of march from the side. They therefore detached a strong force to make head against him, and posted it upon a ridge near the little hamlet of Germantown. As soon as Jackson ascertained the position of this force, he threw his infantry into line of battle, Hill on the right, Ewell in the centre, and his old division on the left, and advanced to the assault. The enemy, knowing that the salvation of their army depended upon them, made a desperate resistance, and the combat assumed a sudden fury in the front of Hill, equal to that of any previous struggle. The enemy were encouraged by a momentary success in breaking Hayes' brigade, but his lines were immediately reinstated by the reserves, and after a short but bloody strife, the battle died away as suddenly as it had begun, and the enemy retired in the darkness. This affair, which was known as the battle of Ox Hill, closed the evening of September 1st. Its thunders were aggravated by those of a tempest, which burst upon the combatants just before the battle was joined, and the Confederates fought under the disadvantage of the rain, which was swept by a violent wind directly into their faces. Two Federal Generals fell here, in front of Hill's division, Kearney and Stephens, and their death doubtless completed the discouragement of their troops. The next morning, the Federalists were within reach of their powerful works before Washington, and the pursuit was arrested. The Commander-in-Chief now purposed to transfer the strife to a new *arena*.

The total loss of the Confederate army in this series of battles was about seven thousand five hundred, of whom eleven hundred were killed upon the field. Of this loss, nearly five thousand fell upon the *corps* of Jackson; out of which number eight hundred and five officers and men were killed. The captures from him, in the whole of the long struggle, amounted to only thirty-five. The excessive loss in his command is explained by the fact that it was always the advance, and that the enemy continually directed the chief fury of his attacks upon him. The results of the battle of Manassas were the capture of seven thousand prisoners, in addition to two thousand wounded left in the hands of the Confederates; with twenty thousand small arms, thirty pieces of artillery, numerous colors, and a large amount of stores; and the deliverance of Northern Virginia from the footsteps of the invader, save where he still clung to a few miles along the Potomac included within his works. General Jackson closed his Report of the Campaign with these words:—

"For these great and signal victories our sincere and humble thanks are due unto Almighty God. We should in all things acknowledge the hand of Him who reigns in Heaven, and rules among the armies of men. In view of the arduous labors and great privations the troops were called to endure, and the isolated and perilous position which the command occupied, while engaged with greatly superior numbers of the enemy, we can but express the grateful conviction of our mind, that God was with us, and gave us the victory; and unto His holy name be the praise."

Few words are needed to point out the share which Jackson and his *corps* merited, in the glory of the second victory of Manassas. To the rapidity of his march, the promptitude and skill of his action in seizing and destroying the Junction, the wisdom which guided his selection of a position, and the heroic tenacity with which he held it against fearful odds until the arrival of General Lee, was the splendid result chiefly due. It was so ordered, as if to illustrate the superior prowess of the Confederate soldiery, that in this battle the positions of the combatants in July, 1861, were almost precisely reversed. The ground held by Jackson in the second battle, was that held by McDowell in the first; and the ground from which the Confederates drove Pope, at nightfall, the 30th of August, was that from which McDowell could not drive them, on the 21st of July; while the preponderance of numbers was still upon the Federal side.

The blunders of Pope in this short campaign, — which were almost as numerous as it was possible to make them, — are an instructive study to the commanders of armies. First, it was little short of lunacy to adopt, in Culpeper, a line of operations along the Orange Railroad, and even west of it, which was parallel to the Rapid Ann — the temporary base of the Confederates — in the presence of such masters of the art of war as Lee and Jackson. Instead of extending his right so far toward Madison, with the preposterous design of turning Gordonsville, upon the west, he should have directed the head of his column toward the lower course of the Rapid Ann, and perpendicular to it. He would thus have covered his own line of advance; and, if he succeeded in crossing that river, would have uncovered the communications of his adversary, which then would have been by the Central Railroad. Nothing but the delay of Lee's reserves in reaching Raccoon Ford, saved Pope here from a disaster far worse than that of Manassas. Second: after retiring across the Rappahannock, — which was a measure dictated by so stringent a necessity that a fool could not err therein, — he repeated the old, but seductive folly, of attempting to hold a river as a defensive line, by extending his whole force along its immediate bank, to watch and resist the passage of his opponent. Although a river is, to some extent, a barrier to the assailant attempting to cross it in the face of a force defending it; yet, if the latter consigns itself to the stationary defensive along its banks, the other is always enabled thereby to baffle his vigilance at some one point; or to mass at a single spot a preponderance of force, which will more than compensate him for the resistance of the natural obstruction, and break its way over it. Then the barrier, broken at one point, becomes useless, and must be forsaken at all. Such was the result here; the stream was passed above Pope's right, before he was in condition to prevent it. His next mistake was in the singular inefficiency of his cavalry, which seems to have been more busy in harrying the hen-roosts of the citizens, than in ascertaining whither the swift-footed Jackson was bent, when he disappeared to the northwest from his position before Warrenton Springs. Thus Pope was left in a shameful ignorance, even after his communications were cut at Bristoe Station, whether it was done by a serious force, or by an audacious incursion of horse. But on the evening of the 27th, at least, he was taught, in a bloody lesson by Ewell, that he had a formidable foe in his rear. The plainest deduction might have convinced him, that such a General as Lee would not have placed such a body of infantry and artillery, as he saw grimly confronting him across Broad Run at the close of that combat, so far from its base, without powerful supports.

From that moment the goal of safety for Pope should have been Centreville; and he should have lost no time in concentrating his whole army by forced marches, to strike the formidable obstruction from his rear, and secure his retreat thither. There he would have been front to front with his adversary once more, and within reach of the support of McClellan, by whose aid he might have advanced again, and quickly resumed his lost ground. But although it is but one march from Warrenton, where his headquarters were, to Manassas, two and a half precious days were wasted, between the 26th, when Jackson struck Bristoe, and the 29th, when Longstreet reached his right; and neither was Jackson crushed, nor Thoroughfare Gap effectually held, nor the army safely transferred to Centreville. At mid-day, on the 29th, the arrival of Longstreet rendered his fortunes difficult enough; but, as though he were intent to make them desperate, when his left was incommoded by the appearance of Longstreet's column behind it, instead of retiring squarely from his antagonists, keeping his right upon Bull Run, until his left met the support of the approaching column of Fitz-John Porter, from Aquia, he weakly sought to disengage his left, by manoeuvring to his right, and again confining his onset to the lines of Jackson. These were skilfully retracted, to lead him into the trap; and the result was, that on the third and decisive day, he was compelled to fight with the stream in his immediate rear, and with his whole army inclosed within the limits of the fatal fourchette. The Confederates might well pray that such leaders should ever command the armies of their enemies.

JOHN REUBEN THOMPSON

1823-1873

John Reuben Thompson, poet and editor, was born in Richmond, Virginia, on October 23, 1823. He attended the University of Virginia, was admitted to the bar, and practiced law for several years. When he was twenty-four his father purchased the *Southern Literary Messenger*. Thompson was editor from 1847 until 1860. He built up a wide literary acquaintance, both in the United States and abroad, and in 1856 he published a volume, *Across the Atlantic*, based upon his travels in Europe. During the Civil War he was an active writer for the Confederate cause and in 1864 he ran the blockade to England to help edit the pro-Confederate *Index*. After the war he contributed widely to British and American periodicals. He died on April 30, 1873. The collected *Poems of John R. Thompson* were edited with a biographical sketch by John S. Patton in 1920.

ASHBY

To the brave all homage render!
  Weep, ye skies of June!
With a radiance pure and tender,
  Shine, O saddened moon;
"Dead upon the field of glory!" —
Hero fit for song and story —
  Lies our bold dragoon!

Well they learned, whose hands have slain him,
  Braver, knightlier foe
Never fought 'gainst Moor nor Paynim —
  Rode at Templestowe:
With a mien how high and joyous,
'Gainst the hordes that would destroy us,
  Went he forth, we know.

Nevermore, alas! shall sabre
  Gleam around his crest —
Fought his fight, fulfilled his labor,
  Stilled his manly breast —
All unheard sweet Nature's cadence,
Trump of fame and voice of maidens,
  Now he takes his rest.

Earth, that all too soon hath bound him,
  Gently wrap his clay!
Linger lovingly around him,
  Light of dying day!
Softly fall the summer showers —
Birds and bees among the flowers
  Make the gloom seem gay!

John Reuben Thompson, 1823-1873

There, throughout the coming ages,
 When his sword is rust,
And his deeds in classic pages —
 Mindful of her trust,
Shall Virginia, bending lowly,
Still a ceaseless vigil holy
 Keep above his dust!

GEORGE WILLIAM BAGBY

1828-1883

George William Bagby was born in Buckingham County, Virginia, on August 13, 1828. He attended Delaware College and studied medicine at the University of Pennsylvania. Upon his graduation in 1849 he opened an office in Lynchburg, Virginia, but was less interested in medicine than in writing. He edited a daily newspaper in Lynchburg with another young Virginian, and when in 1855 he published an article in *Harper's Monthly Magazine* he had definitely given up medicine as a career. He wrote for newspapers and magazines, and in 1860 became editor of the *Southern Literary Messenger*. At the outbreak of the Civil War he joined the Confederate army. Upon a discharge for ill health, he resumed the editorship of the *Messenger* and served at the same time as a Richmond correspondent for newspapers throughout the South.

After the war he achieved a wide and enthusiastic following in Virginia as a humorous lecturer. He continued to write for newspapers and contributed to such magazines as *Lippincott's, Putnam's, Appleton's* and *Harper's*. A number of his lecturers were published in pamphlet form and shortly after his death, which occurred on November 29, 1883, there appeared a two-volume collection, *Selections from the Miscellaneous Writings of Dr. George W. Bagby*, with an introduction by Edward S. Gregory (1884-1885). A new edition of his work was edited by Thomas Nelson Page in 1910 under the title, *The Old Virginia Gentleman and Other Sketches*. A collection under the same title, edited by his daughter, Ellen M. Bagby, was published in 1938 and attracted enough interest to justify a new edition in 1943. Ellen Glasgow wrote of the volume: "These sketches have always been a part of my Virginia heritage. Long before I was old enough to understand them, I heard my father read them aloud to his elder children in the winter evenings by the fireside. The vital warmth and humanity of the writing will give this book a permanent place in the life and literature of Virginia." A biography of Dr. Bagby by Leonard J. King, Jr. was published by the Columbia University Press in 1927.

BACON AND GREENS: HOW TO MAKE A TRUE VIRGINIAN

We approach that strange variety of mankind which is compounded of bacon on the one hand, and cabbage or greens on the other hand. In the wildest flight of imagination, who would ever have supposed that the savage boar of the German forests and the ugly pot-herb of the sea-cliffs of England would come together in the same dish to produce the Virginian? So true it is that truth is stranger than fiction. I say, the Virginian; for while other people eat bacon and greens (and thereby become very decent people indeed), the only perfect bacon and the only perfect greens are found in Virginia; and hence it follows, as the night the day, not that the Virginians are the only perfect people, but that they are a peculiar and a very remarkable people.

In point of fact, the native Virginian is different from all other folks whatsoever, and the difference between him and other folks is precisely the difference between his bacon and greens and other folks' bacon and greens. How great this difference is, you are by no means aware. There is a theory in the books that the superiority of the Westphalia and Virginia bacon over all other bacon is due to the fact that our hogs are not penned up, but are allowed the free range of the fields and forests.

Nevertheless, you are not to infer that the Virginian is composed of equal parts of bacon and greens, and that he is, in point of fact, a saphead and a glutton. Such a conclusion would not only be unkind, but illogical. Drinking train-oil does not necessarily turn a man into an Eskimo, nor does the eating of curry compel one to become a coolie and worship Vishnu or Confucius. Still, there *is* a connection between diet and the ethnological characteristics of the human races; and I take it for granted, first, that a Virginian could not be a Virginian without bacon and greens; and, second, that in every Virginian traces of bacon and traces of greens are distinctly perceptible. How else are you to account for the Virginia love of good eating, the Virginia indifference to dress and household economy, and the incurable simplicity of the Virginia head? It has been affirmed by certain speculative philosophers that the Virginian persists in exhausting his soil with tobacco, because the cabbage he eats is itself an exhauster of the soil, and that, because the hog is fond of wallowing in mud-puddles, therefore the Virginian takes naturally to politics.

I am not prepared to dispute these points, but I am tolerably certain that a few other things besides bacon and greens are required to make a true Virginian. He must, of course, begin on pot-liquor, and keep it up until he sheds his milk-teeth. He must have fried chicken, stewed chicken, broiled chicken, and chicken pie; old hare, butter beans, new potatoes, squirrel, cymlings, snaps, barbecued shoat, roas'n ears, buttermilk, hoe-cake, ash-cake, pancake, fritters, pot-pie, tomatoes, sweet-potatoes, June apples, waffles, sweet milk, parsnips, artichokes, carrots, cracklin bread, hominy, bonny-clabber, scrambled eggs, gooba-peas, fried apples, pop-corn, persimmon beer, apple-bread, milk and peaches, mutton stew, dewberries, batter-cakes, mushmelons, hickory nuts, partridges, honey in the honey-comb, snappin'-turtle eggs, damson tarts, catfish, cider, hot light-bread, and cornfield peas all the time; but he must not intermit his bacon and greens.

He must butt heads with little negroes, get the worst of it, and run crying to his ma about it. Wear white yarn socks with green toes and yarn gallowses. Get the cow-itch, and live on milk and brimstone for a time. Make frog-houses over his feet in the wet sand, and find woodpecker nests. Meddle with the negro men at hog-killing time, and be in everybody's way generally. Upset beehives, bring big wasp-nests into the house, and get stung over the eye by a yellow-jacket. Watch setting turkeys, and own a bench-leg fice and a speckled shoat. Wade in the branch, eat too many black-heart cherries, try to tame a catbird, call doodle-bugs out of their holes — and keep on eating bacon and greens.

He must make partridge-traps out of tobacco-sticks; set gums for "Mollie-cotton-tails," mash-traps and deadfalls for minks; fish for minnows with a pin-hook, and carry his worms in a cymling; tie

George William Bagby, 1828-1883

Juney-bugs to strings, and sing 'em under people's noses; stump his toe and have it tied up in a rag; wear patched breeches, stick thorns in his heel, and split his thumb open slicing "hoss-cakes" with a dog knife sharpened, contrary to orders, on the grindstone.

At eight years old he must know how to spell *b a* ba, *b e* be, and so on; and be abused for not learning his multiplication table, and for riding the sorrel mare at a strain to the horse-pond, and for snoring regularly at family prayers. Still he must continue to eat bacon and greens. About this time of life, or a little later, he must get his first store clothes, and be sorely afflicted with freckles, stone-bruises, hang-nails, mumps, and warts, which last he delights in trimming with a Barlow-knife, obtained by dint of hard swapping. He must now go to old-field school, and carry his snack in a tin bucket, with a little bottle of molasses, stopped with a corn-cob stopper, and learn how to play marbles for good, and to tell stories about getting late to school — because he fell in the branch. Also to steal June apples and bury them, that they may ripen the sooner for his big sweetheart, who sits next to him. He must have a pop-gun, made of elder, with plenty of tow to "chaw" for wads; also plenty of india-rubber, and cut up his father's gum shoes, to make trap-balls, composed of equal parts of yarn and india-rubber. At the same time he must keep steadily eating bacon and greens. He must now learn to cut jackets, play hard-ball, choose partners for cat and chermany, be kept in, fight every other day, and be turned out for painting his face with pokeberry juice and grinning at the school-master.

After a good whipping from his father, who threatens to apprentice him to a carpenter, he enjoys his holiday by breaking colts and shooting field-larks in the daytime and by possum-hunting or listening to ghost-stories from the negroes in the night.

Returning to school, he studies pretty well for a time, but the love of mischief is so strong within him that, for his life, he can't refrain from putting crooked pins on the benches where the little boys sit, and even in the school-master's chair. The result is a severe battle with the school-master and his permanent dismissal.

Thrown upon the world, he consoles himself with bacon and greens, makes love to a number of pretty girls, and pretends to play

437

overseer. Failing at that, he tries to keep somebody's country store, but will close the doors whenever the weather is fine to "ketch chub" or play knucks.

Tired of store-keeping, he makes a trip, sometimes all the way on horseback, to the Far South, to look after his father's lands. Plays "poker" on the Mississippi, gets cheated, gets "strapped"; returns home, eats bacon and greens, and determines to be a better man. But the first thing he knows he is off on a frolic in Richmond, where he loses all his money at faro, borrows enough to carry him home and buy a suit to go courting in.

He next gets religion at a camp-meeting, and loses it at a barbecue or fish-fry. Then he thinks he will teach school, or ride deputy sheriff, or write in the clerk's office, and actually begins to study law; on the strength of which he becomes engaged to be married, and runs for the legislature. Gets beaten, gets drunk; reforms, all of a sudden; eats plenty of bacon and greens; marries — much to the satisfaction of his own, and greatly to the horror of his wife's family — and thus becomes a thorough-going Virginian.

JAMES BARRON HOPE

1829-1887

James Barron Hope wrote a number of occasional and commemorative poems upon Virginia themes. These occupied him from time to time over a quarter of a century — from a long work which he read at Jamestown in 1857 on the 250th anniversary of the founding of Virginia, to the "Metrical Address", *Arms and the Man,* which he prepared at the invitation of Congress in 1881 for the celebration of the 100th anniversary of the surrender of Cornwallis at Yorktown. But poets more abundantly endowed than Hope have found the role of laureate a difficult one, and his poetic skill is better exhibited in his simpler and less ambitious poems.

Hope was born in Norfolk, Virginia, on March 23, 1829. He grew up in Virginia and attended the College of William and Mary. He began the practice of law in Williamsburg, served for several years at sea as secretary to his uncle Commodore Samuel Barron, and was elected commonwealth's attorney of Hampton in 1856. When the Civil War broke out he joined the Confederate army, served throughout the war, and became a major under Joseph E. Johnston. After the war he worked for several Virginia newspapers, and in 1873 he established his own paper in Norfolk, which he edited until his death on September 15, 1887.

Hope's published poetry includes: *Leoni di Monote and Other Poems* (1857), *A Collection of Poems* (1859), *An Elegiac Ode* (1866) and *Arms and the Man: A Metrical Address* (1882). He was also the author of a novel, *Under the Empire,* and a collection of children's stories. A selection of his poems was edited by his daughter, Janey Hope Marr, in 1895 under the title, *A Wreath of Virginia Bay Leaves.*

VIRGINIA PASTORAL*

Over the farm is brooding silence now —
   No reaper's song — no raven's clangor harsh —
No bleat of sheep — no distant low of cow —
   No croak of frogs within the spreading marsh —
No bragging cock from litter'd farm-yard crows,
The scene is steep'd in silence and repose.

A trembling haze hangs over all the fields —
   The panting cattle in the river stand
Seeking the coolness which its wave scarce yields.
   It seems a Sabbath thro' the drowsy land:
So hush'd is all beneath the Summer's spell,
I pause and listen for some faint church bell.

The leaves are motionless — the song-bird's mute —
   The very air seems somnolent and sick:
The spreading branches with o'er-ripen'd fruit
   Show in the sunshine all their clusters thick,
While now and then a mellow apple falls
With a dull sound within the orchard's walls.

The sky has but one solitary cloud,
   Like a dark island in a sea of light;
The parching furrows 'twixt the corn-rows plough'd
   Seem fairly dancing in my dazzled sight,
While over yonder road a dusty haze
Grows reddish purple in the sultry blaze.

*Title supplied. From "Three Summer Studies" in *Leoni di Monota and Other Poems*, by James Barron Hope. J. B. Lippincott and Co., 1857.

JOHN ESTEN COOKE
1830-1886

John Esten Cooke wrote his best novel — the long, two-volume *The Virginia Comedians* — when he was twenty-four. Like his older brother, Philip Pendleton Cooke, and many another Virginia writer, he was torn between the practice of literature and the practice of law. But he re- solved the dilemma earlier than most. The year 1854 saw three historical romances by the young Virginia lawyer issued by New York publishers — *Leather Stocking and Silk* (Harper and Brothers), *The Virginia Comedians* (D. Appleton and Company) and *The Youth of Jefferson* (Redfield) — and with them John Esten Cooke turned his back finally upon the law.

Cooke had been writing as long as he could remember, and had been contributing to the *Southern Literary Messenger* since he was eighteen. He was born in Winchester, Virginia, on November 3, 1830, and spent his childhood at the family estate, "Glengary." When he was ten his family moved to Richmond — where his father had served a term in the legislature and had been a member of the Virginia Constitutional Convention of 1829 — and there young Cooke went to school. He hoped to enter the law school of the University of Virginia in 1847, but his father — there was a large family to support — was not able to provide the money. During the next two years he read law (and a great deal of what his father called "light reading," novels and poetry), but in 1849 the university still seemed as far away as ever. He was, however, admitted to the bar and practiced desultorily for a few years.

At twenty-four, Cooke was a literary success. He worked hard to make the most of it. He always wrote rapidly and before the Civil War he published three more books and contributed frequently to *Harper's*, *Putnam's* and other magazines. With the outbreak of the war, he entered the Confederate army as a private, became a captain under J. E. B. Stuart, and fought in most of the battles of the army of Northern Virginia. He wrote a wartime *Life of Stonewall Jackson*, published in Richmond in 1863, and in the years immediately following the war he found a ready audience for novels and sketches based on his experiences. His life of Jackson was enlarged and reissued; *Surry of Eagle's-Nest*, subtitled "Memoirs of a

441

Staff-Officer Serving in Virginia," appeared in 1866; *Wearing of the Gray* followed the next year; and in rapid succession came *Fairfax, Hilt to Hilt, Mohun, Hammer and Rapier* and *A Life of Gen. Robert E. Lee*. Even before the war, George W. Bagby had said that Cooke wrote as if he had "agreed to write a novel in twenty minutes by a stop-watch." Now Cooke seemed determined to justify the criticism. *Surry of Eagle's-Nest* was turned out in six weeks, and there was little of his work which did not exhibit the marks of hasty writing.

Cooke was married to Mary Frances Page in 1867. He established a home at "The Briars," was the father of three children, and spent his days in farming — and writing. In all, he published more than thirty volumes. Among his later books are *Stories of the Old Dominion, The Virginia Bohemians* and *Virginia: A History of the People*. He died on September 27, 1886, at the age of fifty-six.

Of all his books, *The Virginia Comedians* has stood up best over the years. A historical novel of pre-Revolutionary Virginia, it has a vigor which is absent from much of his subsequent work. In his preface to the novel Cooke wrote: "The author's wish was simply to depict some Virginia scenes and personages ten years before the Revolution." The selection which follows, "How the Man in the Red Cloak Threw His Net, and What He Caught," is a lively conversation piece on liberty and revolution. "The Man in the Red Cloak" is a portrait of Patrick Henry.

HOW THE MAN IN THE RED CLOAK THREW HIS NET, AND WHAT HE CAUGHT

The stranger was silent for some moments, then, drawing his old red cloak around him, he said:

"Liberty! Well, that is a great word; but, unfortunately, it is also one of those noble-sounding terms which fill the ears only, never conveying to the brain much more than a vague and doubtful meaning. What is liberty? True, I ask you to answer a hard question; but you have drawn it upon yourself, companion, by your anomalous and contradictory statements."

"How contradictory, sir?" said his companion, losing his absent-mindedness, and looking earnestly at the stranger.

"Why," replied the man in red cloak, coolly, "nothing could well be more paradoxical than your views. You agree that there are classes here, and elsewhere, separated by unreasonable distinctions, holding, as regards each other, unjust positions. You do not deny that we — we, the common people — are the mere hewers of wood and the drawers of water for our masters, and, when I chance to say what is perfectly reasonable and natural, namely, that we must hate and envy these dons, why, you answer, 'No, no; envy and hatred are not the elements of progress, the forerunners of liberty.' I say, they rule us! — the wealthy gentlemen, the house of burgesses, the English parliament — why not hate and envy, and, if necessary, match ourselves force for force against them, and see if we cannot achieve this noble end you speak of — liberty!"

"Because force — the blind force of envy and hatred, striking in the dark, and without thought — is the mere movement of the brute, who closes his eyes, and tears, without seeing, whatever comes beneath his paws. No, sir! before we can overturn parliaments, and dictate laws, we must mould public opinion."

"Public opinion? What is that?"

443

"It is the great unseen power which governs the world."

"Oh yes; the opinion of kings and autocrats. Now I understand."

"No, not of kings and autocrats — of common men, the masses! The calm, just judgment, formed in silence, and without prejudice, of those men and things which figure on the great stage of life. Not the mere impulses of envy and hatred, any more than the jealousy of rank, but the cool, deliberate weighing of events and personages in the scales of eternal justice."

"Fine words. Well, then, you would not overthrow the present state of things; or, perhaps, you are well content with the social organization of this colony. We must not hate, we must not envy — all is for the best!"

"No, sir, all is not for the best; far from it."

"It seems to me that we are wandering in our ideas, and liable to misunderstand each other. Let us see, now — explain. You are more or less dissatisfied with the present position of things; but you like the gentry, the Established Church, you admire the traditions of feudalism, and revere his gracious majesty King George. Eh? Come, let us know if you do not?"

"We must have misunderstood each other, indeed, sir. I would overthrow — or at least, materially change — all that you have mentioned."

"What, the gentry — the church — the king? Treason!"

"That cry does not daunt me, sir."

"Beware; I shall inform on you, and his majesty will send for you to come and visit his handsome residence, called the Tower."

"Let me explain, briefly, what I mean, and meant," said his companion, too gloomy to relish these pleasantries of the stranger. "You have misunderstood me wholly — you would say that I am an advocate of the present, with all its injustice, its wrong, its oppression; and, that, because I am not willing to go and turn out proprietors of great landed estates at the point of the bayonet; shatter those splendid mirrors, which reflect gold, and velvet, and embroidery, with a pistol's muzzle; organize the lower class, with bludgeons, hay-forks, cleavers, knives, and scythes, against the gentlemen, who roll in coaches, and eat from gold and silver plate — you would say, that because these revolutionary proceedings, the offspring of envy and hatred, are not to my taste, I am an advocate of those oppressions, those bitter wrongs, inflicted on the commons by the gentry. No, sir! I am not an advocate of them; I know them too well. I have studied, as far as possible, with a calm mind; an unbiassed judgment, this vestige of feudalism which curses us, and I have found, everywhere, as in the old feudal system, wrong, oppression, a haughty and unchristian pride of rank, and birth, and wealth —"

"Good, good," said the stranger, no longer interrupting his companion.

"An unjustifiable pride! an unchristian arrogance, scorning charity, humility, all that Christ inculcated, as so much weakness!" continued the thinker, in his noble and earnest voice; "I find it here, as I find it in the history of England, of France, of Germany, of the whole feudal world; among the gentry of to-day, as the nobles of the middle age! Go back to that middle age — see the great lord passing in his splendid armor, and surcoat of cloth of gold, on his glossy charger, followed by his squires, his men-at-arms, while the battlements of his great castle ring with trumpets, greeting his return; see the serf there in the shadow of the wall, with the ring around his neck, with his wooden shoes, his goatskin covering — swarthy, with his shaggy beard, his brow covered with perspiration, as becomes the villein, his cerebral conformation, as he takes off his greasy cap to lout low to his master, like the head of the wolf, the jackall, the hyena. That serf is no longer a man — he is a wild beast, with strong muscles and sinews like rope, who will fight well in the field, and be cut to pieces cheerfully, while his master reaps undying renown, covered by his proof armor of Milan — yes, he will fight and toil, and go home and kiss his children in their mud hovel — but he is not a man: his lord is a man — how can he be of the same race as that splendid and haughty chevalier, honored by kings and emperors for his deeds of chivalry, smiled on by fair ladies everywhere, like the noble dame who reigns in yonder castle with him. True, the serf has legs and arms, and his blood, strange to say, is much the color of the great seigneur's — but they do not belong to the same race of animals. They both feel it — are convinced of it. When my lord passes, see the back bent down; the eyes abased, as in the presence of the God of Day — the dog-like submission, when harsh words are uttered by the seigneur to his animal. The serf does not dream of there being any impropriety in all this — it is part of the order of things that he should be a wild beast, his lord a splendid, noble chevalier, glittering with stars, and clad in soft silk and velvet. He always submits: he is a part of the glebe, the stock — like the horse, the hound, the hawk. Does the seigneur wish some amusement for his noble guests? — the boor comes, and with another of his class cudgels away in the court-yard, until he is covered with bruises, and falls or conquers: and the noble lords and ladies, glittering like stars in the balcony, throw *largesse* to the knaves, who lout humbly, and go down to their proper place — the kitchen. "There is the past, sir — look at it!"

The stranger nodded.

"You don't like feudalism," he said.

"It makes me shudder, sir."

"How? why it's dead!"

"No: it is alive."

"Alive, say you?"

"To this very day and hour."

"What? in full force?"

"No, sir — not in full force: far from it. But in a degree, at least, it exists."

"Hum! you are a metaphysician."

"No, sir, I am practical."

"You are a dreamer!"

Waters sighed.

"I thought you dreamed as I did," he said.

"Perhaps I do — who knows?"

Waters was silent.

"Define your idea," said the stranger. "I understand you to say — and we won't discuss the subject — that this thing we call feudalism — which has come in for so much abuse from you, still exists in a degree? Come! let us see how it looks in Virginia."

"We have but the shadow — thank God, the edifice has crumbled in part: but the flanking towers remain, and that shadow still lies like gloom upon the land. See how human thought is still warped

446

and darkened by it — how rank and unwholesome weeds possess the earth!"

"Root out these weeds, then — begin! Hurl down these towers which shut out the sunlight, — your historical reading must have told you of the Jacquerie!"

"Yes, sir! and I have seen how that rising led to worse evils than before, for hatred was added to contempt. No, to attack this still vigorous remnant of feudalism, something besides hammers and pickaxes are necessary; gun-powder, even, will not blow it into atoms!"

"What, then?"

"The winds of Heaven! God will strike it; he has thrown down the donjon keep, where captives gnashed their teeth and cursed and blasphemed in darkness; he will also level with the ground what remains of the great blot upon the landscape!"

"Figures, figures!" said the stranger; "come, let us have ideas!"

"By the winds of Heaven — the breath of God — I mean those eternally progressive steps of mind, which go from doubt to certainty, from certainty to indignation, from indignation to revolution!"

"Very well; now we get on firm ground again. We meet and shake hands over that toast, 'Revolution!'"

"Understand me; revolution is not a slight thing. It levels many valuable things, as the hurricane and the tempest of rain sweeps away much more than the accumulated rubbish. Revolution, sir, is the last thing of all — the tornado which clears the poisonous atmosphere, cannot be loosed every day or year, for the land is strewed with ruins by it. The slow steps of public opinion must be hastened, the soil prepared for the seed, the distance made plain, the body armed — then, if it is necessary, the conflict."

"Ah, you come back to your ideas upon education, sir?"

"Yes; I would unfetter the mind."

"Enlighten it?"

"Yes, sir; I would teach the great mass of the people that God made this world, not man; that wrong and oppression is not the normal state of human things; I would point out all the falseness, I would point to the lash-marks on the back; I would, if necessary, pour brine into those bleeding furrows!"

"Yes, and drive to madness — to what you deprecate, mad violence!"

"No, for minds would be enlightened, men would see — and seeing, they would wait. I would have them know when to strike; I would organize in their minds an opposition, quiet, stubborn, unbending, never-sleeping; a confidence in time, faith in the ultimate intervention of God using them as his instruments."

"You generalize too much," said the stranger; "let us come now to Virginia, at this day and hour. Let us see what are the great abuses. Speak!"

"First, an established church, which dictates religious opinion — forces itself upon all the community, armed with the terrors of the law."

"Yes, that is just; and I promise you something will be said soon about the twopenny-act. Well, the church! What else?"

"The offspring of that feudalism I have spoken of — aristocracy!"

"Yes, 'power of the best;' that is, the wealthiest. What next?"

"Laws, without representation!" said his companion, compressing in these short words the great popular grievance of the age.

"Ah!" said the stranger, with a grim smile, "there is something in that, too. What more?"

"What more? Is it not enough, sir, for the Established Church to wring from you, whether you conform or not, support for its ministers — to stuff itself and its tenets down your throat? is it not bad enough for the house of burgesses to legislate for the great landed proprietors alone, who form the body, ignoring the very existence of the common man, who has no vote? is any thing more needed to make us slaves, than laws passed in the English parliament, crushing our trade, our very lives, without representatives of us there in council?"

"I confess that seems to me quite enough," said the stranger; "and this great, oppressive, intolerant church — this haughty arrogance of rank — lastly, that English lawlessness, seem to me to constitute a case of mortification — gangrene — to be burnt out by the hot iron of revolution!"

448

John Esten Cooke, 1830-1886

"No! it has not gone far enough yet; let us advance step by step. At present we contemplate that great, intolerant, bigoted establishment with respect and awe; we bow to the grand chariot, doffing our caps, we search in our minds for what will justify that oppression of Parliament; we are not convinced that this great triple wrong *is* a wrong. We doubt; let us scan the matter calmly — dispassionately investigate the nature of things; let us educate our minds, we common people, and with the calm, unobscured eyes of truth, test the error. We will not say to the parsons, 'Off with you, you are the vermin of a rotten system, you shall not tyrannize over us!' No, let us, with the Bible in our hands, and God in our hearts, say, 'We come to try you, we come to know whether you are false and bigoted, or true and Christlike —' "

"Yes," said the stranger, "and those worthy gentlemen, who procured benefices by marrying the cast-off mistresses of lords, will, with one voice, for about the space of two hours, cry, 'Great is Diana of the Ephesians! We are holy, pure, and immaculate!' What, then?"

"Reason! the light of education still! flooding the whole system, lighting up every hidden crypt!"

"Good! And you would apply these fine ideas to the aristocracy, too?"

"Yes. I would have men scan that system also; not strike it blindly; I would have them come with the law of nature in their hands, the evangel of truth and justice, and say, 'Show us what you are. Show us if you are really our natural and rightful superiors. Show us whether those titles you derive from kings, are like the authority of those kings, derived, as they say, from God, and so, just and right. Show us if you are really superior beings, because you descend from the knights of the middle age — w einferior to you, your born slaves, because we draw our blood from the serf who tilled the glebe below your grandsire's castle walls. Show us if this mysterious sentiment of awe we feel in your presence, is direct from the Deity, planted thus in us to make us keep our places; or, whether it is the mere tradition of the past, the echo of injustice, the shadow of that monstrous oppression of the dark ages, yet lying on our souls?"

"Very well — and what then?" said the stranger. "Why, these worthy gentlemen would reply, 'Friends, the distinction of classes

is absolutely necessary; some must rule, others obey; some wear
fustian, others velvet; some must ride in coaches, and eat from gold
plate, others jog along in the dust of the highway, eat their brown
bread and swill their muddy ale. Order is heaven's first law. Come,
now, and listen to this splendid passage from Shakespeare, about
degrees in a state; it is there, in that volume with a gilt back in the
Gothic book-case — don't muddy the carpet with your dirty brogues,
or stumble over that damask chair in reaching it. Very well. Now,
listen! Can any thing be more just than these views? Some must be
great, others small; one must vote, another be denied that privilege.
We are gentlemen, you commoners. Can any thing be plainer, than
that we should have the offices and honors, live easily, and sustain
our proper rank, while you till the glebe, and leave your interests in
our hands?' That is what they would say — what then?"

"Reason, again!" said his companion; "reason, turning away from
the dazzling pageant, stopping the ears to shut out the rumbling of
the coach and six, forgetting the past, and questioning that great
evangel of right open in their hands — reason, which should weigh
and test, and try the whole system by the rules of a stern, inexorable
logic."

"I admire your logic! and you think that it would apply to English
legislation on Virginia matters?"

"Yes; I would remonstrate, petition, debate with Parliament; I
would exhaust every means of testing and overthrowing this cruel
and bitter wrong; I would ask for light — ask nothing but that right
should be made manifest — I would go to the foot of the throne,
and say, 'Justice, justice, nothing but justice, as a British subject —
as one laboring under wrong!'"

The stranger's lip curled.

"Well, your system is now tolerably plain," he said. "You would
go and ask the parsons to tell you if they are, in truth, pure and immaculate — you would ask the gentry if they really are the distinguished gentlemen they pretend to be — you would fall at the feet
of King George, and sue for leave to argue the matter of taxation
with his gracious Majesty! Very well. Now, suppose — it is a very
extravagant supposition, I know, and springs, no doubt, from my
irreverent, incredulous, and obstinate prejudices — suppose, I say,

that the worthy parsons thus adjured, as to their purity, were to tell you that they were the salt of the earth, and that your question was an impertinence; suppose — if you can suppose such an incredible thing — that the wealthy gentleman tells you that he is your born lord, and that he will commit you in his quality of justice of the peace, for misdemeanor, should you intrude upon him again with your wretched folly; suppose his gracious Majesty were to remove your humble petition with his royal foot, bidding you begone, and learn that when money was wanted to support his splendor, you were to sweat and pay it, and be silent on pain of being whipped in by armed soldiers; suppose these disagreeable incidents greeted your philanthropic exertions — what then?"

"Then, revolution! revolution, if that revolution waded in blood!" cried his companion, carried away by his fiery thought, and losing all his calmness and self-control; "revolution, with God for our judge! history for our vindication! If, after all their sufferings, all their wrongs, all the injustice of long years, of centuries, the prayers of humanity were thus answered — revolution! A conflict, bitter, desperate, unyielding, to the death! A conflict which should root out these foul and monstrous wrongs, or exterminate us! A revolution, which should attack and overwhelm for ever, or be itself overwhelmed! That is the hurricane I spoke of, sir! If God decrees it, let it come!"

MONCURE DANIEL CONWAY

1832-1907

Moncure Daniel Conway, one of the most active men of letters of his day, was born in Stafford County, Virginia, on March 17, 1832. He studied at Fredericksburg Academy, Virginia, and was graduated at the age of seventeen from Dickinson College. His first publication appeared the following year. It was *Free Schools in Virginia,* a comprehensive and well-argued appeal for public education, addressed to the Virginia Convention of 1850. Conway briefly studied law, but under the influence of reading Emerson decided upon the ministry and served for a time as a Methodist circuit rider. Methodist doctrine did not satisfy his inquiring mind, and at the age of twenty-one he entered Harvard Divinity School. There he met Emerson, Thoreau, Lowell and most of the intellectual leaders of New England.

Upon his graduation he became pastor of the Unitarian Church in Washington, D. C. His vigorous sermons against slavery attracted wide attention and in 1856 he was forced to leave the pastorate. He accepted a call to the Congressional Church in Cincinnati, Ohio, and there continued his anti-slavery work. He contributed to many magazines, his sermons were distributed in pamphlet form, and in 1858 he published a 300-page volume, *Tracts for To-day.* In 1860 he founded *The Dial: A Monthly Magazine for Literature, Philosophy, and Religion* and the twelve issues which he edited included Emerson and William Dean Howells among the contributors. In 1861 he published an anti-slavery volume, *The Rejected Stone, by a Native of Virginia,* which had a wide circulation. It was followed in 1862 by *The Golden Hour.* The same year Conway moved to Massachusetts to edit an anti-slavery paper, *The Commonwealth.*

At thirty-one, author of several volumes and innumerable articles and pamphlets, a leader of the anti-slavery movement, he returned to Washington to deliver a sermon before the Senate. Some 2,000 persons crowded the galleries to hear the man who had six years before been dismissed from a Washington pulpit. That year he went to England to lecture for the anti-slavery cause. There he accepted the pastorate of the liberal South Place Chapel in London, published *Testimonies Concerning Slavery* in 1864, and decided to make his home in England.

Moncure Daniel Conway, 1832-1907

He traveled widely, made friends with many of the leading figures of the time, and devoted much of his energy to writing. His two-volume *Autobiography, Memories and Experiences,* published in 1904, gives a lively account of the intellectual life of the period. Among his many volumes were *A Necklace of Stories* (1880); two novels, *Pine and Palm* (1887) and *Prisons of Air* (1891); and studies of *Thomas Carlyle* (1881), *Emerson* (1883) and *Nathaniel Hawthorne* (1890). In 1892 he published his *Life of Thomas Paine,* for which he is perhaps best remembered today, and followed it with his comprehensive four-volume edition of *The Writings of Thomas Paine.* Other of his volumes included *Republican Superstitions* (1872), *The Earthward Pilgrimage* (1876), *Idols and Ideals* (1877) and *Demonology and Devil-Lore* (1879). A number of his South Place discourses were collected in 1883 under the title, *Lessons for the Day.* Several volumes dealing with Virginia were *Omitted Chapters of History: Disclosed in the Life and Papers of Edmund Randolph* (1888), *George Washington and Mount Vernon* (1889) and *Barons of the Potomac and the Rappahannock* (1892). He died in Paris on November 15, 1907. A selection of his work was published posthumously in 1909 under the title, *Addresses and Reprints: 1850-1907.* In that volume a bibliography lists the titles of more than seventy books and pamphlets by Conway. No bibliography has yet been undertaken of his voluminous work in periodicals.

EARLY RECOLLECTIONS*

The town of Falmouth, in Virginia, on the Rappahannock river, has been associated with important military events during the present war. Before the war, it was a village of about a thousand inhabitants, all of whom were very poor, with the exception of five or six families which were very rich. It is quite an ancient place, and was originally inhabited by some Scotchmen, — amongst others, an uncle of the poet Campbell, — who made it a centre of trade between the rich uplands of Virginia and Baltimore. It was once the exact head of navigation on the Rappahannock; but afterwards the river was so filled with bars, that the trade fell to Fredericksburg, about two miles lower. Falmouth has the advantage of being close to the falls which furnish the most magnificent water-power in Virginia; and if that State had been free, it must have been one of the chief manufacturing towns in America.

It was near this village that I was born, and in it that my parents resided during nearly all the early years that I can remember. There were a great many slaves and free Negroes in the neighbourhood. My father then owned fifty or sixty slaves, and many of my relatives a larger number. My parents were very kind to their slaves; and, indeed, I think that the marked contrast between the treatment of slaves to which I had been accustomed at home and that which I witnessed elsewhere, was the first occasion of my attention being drawn to what was going on around me. And yet no amount of benevolent intentions, or watchfulness, or religious observances on their part, was adequate to secure a quiet or happy home. Not long ago, in conversation with a strong defender of Negro Slavery, I found that the corner-stone of his theory was an impression that there was in the homestead of the South a simplicity, a patriarchal relationship between the servants and superiors, which contrasted favourably

*From *Testimonies Concerning Slavery*, by M. D. Conway, a native of Virginia. London: Chapman and Hall, 1864.

with the corresponding conditions in other communities, where, he maintained, the relation between servant and master being purely and at each moment mercenary, the ties must be galling to both parties. I can well believe that a scholar who had never come into personal contact with Slavery, might think of that system as wearing in America the Oriental costume of customs and relations which it wore in the early days when slaves belonged to and loved men who had ransomed them from death as captives, or with races and ages under less pressure than our own to turn every thing to gold. In Brazil, where Slavery exists in connection with a race and government far behind any that it can find in the United States, it is less out of place, and need not use much violence and coercion to exist at all; and hence there is much more simplicity and repose there with the institution. And so I was obliged to assure the gentleman alluded to that, however coarse and hard the relation between servants and employers in free communities might be, he was, in looking to the Southern States, appealing to an absolutely mythical Arcadia. Few are the really peaceful days that I remember as having smiled on my old Virginian home; the outbreaks of the Negroes among themselves, the disobediences which the necessary discipline can never suffer to be overlooked, the terrors of devoted parents at the opportunities for the display of evil tempers and the inception of nameless vices among their sons, I remember as the demons haunting those days. And for these most painful circumstances, giving to nearly every day its "scene," there is no compensation in the work accomplished. With two Irish girls for servants in Ohio, I am quite sure that I have had more work done, and infinitely better done, and with far less interruption of domestic quiet, than my father ever got from all his slaves. No doubt, if he had availed himself of the severe methods used by others around him, he might have got more work and money out of his slaves; for only perpetual violence and sleepless suspicion can really get any thing like the full amount of work out of men and women who know only the curse, and none of the rewards, of toil. I have often heard my parents say that the care of slaves had made them prematurely old.

The impression has gone around the world with ubiquitous sable minstrels that the slaves are a merry, singing, dancing population, far removed from the cares that gnaw the hearts of more civilised classes. In all the twenty-three years of my life in the land of Slavery, I never saw a Negro dance, though in those years I have heard of a few in our neighbourhood. The slaves of the Border States are almost invariably members of the Baptist and Methodist societies, which are particularly rigid in denying them such amusements. On the large plantations of the far South, dances are encouraged, and formerly were frequent; but of late years they have become infrequent, through the all-absorbing tendencies of the Negroes toward religious meetings. My observation confirms that of Dr. Russell when he visited the South as correspondent of the London *Times,* that the Negroes are a notably melancholy people. I have rarely known their enthusiasm enlisted in anything except prayer-and-experience meetings and funerals. Our own kitchen-fireside was nightly the scene of religious exercises and conversations which were very fascinating to me, and from which I had to be dragged with each returning bedtime. The dreams, visions, and ecstasies there related were as gorgeous as those of the *Pilgrim's Progress;* for these humble and ignorant souls, denied the reading of the Bible, had conceived a symbolism of their own, and burdens of prophecy, and had changed the fields on which they toiled into the pavements of the New Jerusalem, glorified with spirits arrayed in white. The cant phrases of the white preachers whom they listened to had become alive to them, and mingled strangely in their speech and hymns; they had, too, their own rudimental Swedenborgianism and Transcendentalism.

A boy was born on my father's estate, who was named Charles. His obvious parents were servants, whom my father had long owned; but they were both quite black, and the boy was nearly white, besides being embarrassingly like a pious gentleman who now and then visited us. This lad at an early age indicated a remarkable intelligence, and was also of a remarkable beauty according to the European type. As he grew older, he increased in vivacity, wit, and amiability; and at his sixteenth year I remember him as one of the handsomest and noblest specimens of Humanity. Wherever he went in the village, a group of admiring white boys was around him, listening to his bewitching songs or romances or mimicries. He seemed to us all a hero of romance, and such a thing as remembering his colour never entered our heads.

His occupation at this age was to attend my brother and myself to and from our school, which was two miles distant. The monotony of this daily journey he varied by his songs and stories, and to him we both looked with implicit reverence. He was active and brave too, proud of being our protector, and eager to pounce upon the biggest snake in our path, or encounter and subdue the fiercest dog.

The day came to him, as it had to come to millions before him, when he desired to learn what we were learning in school. But the laws forbid the teaching of a Negro to read under severest penalties; and no law relating to Negroes is so carefully and strictly enforced in the South as that which forbids their being taught. The long imprisonment of Mrs. Douglas at Norfolk, a few years ago, for teaching a Negro child to read is a familiar case. In Falmouth, two or three ladies whom I knew met on Sunday afternoon to teach some Negro children; they had not so met three times, before they were dispersed by the authorities, although it appeared that they only gave the children oral and religious instruction. I do not believe that my father approved these laws; but being a justice of the county, he of course must take care that the laws were observed in his own house. So Charles's thirst must go unslaked.

There is a cruel pang that comes to nearly every slave's life, which has been very little considered. It is customary in nearly all households in the South for the white and black children connected with each to play together. The trial I have referred to comes when the young Negroes who have hitherto been on this democratic footing with the young whites are presently deserted by their more fortunate companions, who enter upon school-life and the acquaintance of white boys, and, ceasing to associate with their swarthy comrades any longer, meet them in future with the air of the master. This is the dawn of the first bitter consciousness of being a slave; and nothing can be sadder than to see the poor little things wandering about companionless and comfortless. It is doubtful whether either my brother or myself had natural gifts equal to the slave boy Charles; nevertheless we were carried past him, and abandoned him.

457

His knowledge, which once seemed to us unlimited, we gradually discovered to be inferior to our own. We gained new (white) companions, and should have been ashamed to be seen playing at any game with Charles.

But meanwhile the power of intellect and temperament which Nature had lodged in that youth increased. Had there been about him a society able to enclose that power in a fit engine, and set it upon true grooves, he might have borne the burdens which such souls are sent into the world to bear. But as it was, this power was as so much steam without a valve: it was a danger. His temper, from being mild, became bitter; his bravery became fierceness; and by his recklessness the whole family was kept in perpetual panic. Punishment only made him defiant. He was to be a noted personage in one way or another; his daring and ingenious tricks became at first the town's talk and then the town's alarm. He signalised his nineteenth year by setting fire to a house; whereupon my father was forced by public opinion, or perhaps by a legal order, to sell him to the far South. So Charles is now buried, alive or dead, among the cotton plantations.

Although I have dwelt upon this case because it is that which represents, in my own experience, one of the most tragical forms in which Slavery outrages human nature, yet let none think of this as an incident in any respect peculiar. On the contrary, I have myself known many cases where minds of high gifts have been thus waylaid and robbed of their God-given treasures by Slavery. It perhaps requires powers higher than any ordinarily vouchsafed to the Anglo-Saxon to discern the rare quality of the purely Negro spirit and mind; but, were we to grant all that Cant and Sophistry say about the inferiority of the Negro, what shall be said of those millions of the Southern slaves who have Anglo-Saxon blood in them? Not one-third of the Southern slaves are purely African; and in at least a third of them the white blood predominates. Certainly these are not under the curse of Ham. At least we can be certain that the pride, the curiosity, the thirst for knowledge, which are inherent in the blood of the white race, must render Slavery to these a fearful crucifixion. Had Charles been born in the North, I know he would have been a noble and distinguished man. And I have known at least ten others in Virginia who, I am persuaded, would, by a few years' tuition of freedom, have been equal in character and influence to Douglass, Charles Remond, and others.

I know that there is an impression abroad that the people of mixed blood in the Southern States are a very low and vicious class,— an impression which naturally originated with the slaveholders, to whom coloured people are always odious and evil in proportion as they are hard to keep enslaved. My observation leads me to believe that, so far from being a poor or inferior set, we might, under proper training, have had from just that mixture of the Saxon mind with the African temperament some of the first men of the world. They are said to have bad health: it proves only the greater chafing of the yoke, and the intentional severity with which it is made to weigh upon them. They are driven to the lowest occupations.

But the laws of God are inviolable. The South has by its own passions forged, and given a Saxon temper to, the sword which is now suspended over it, and which must soon fall. For these are not the men who run off at once to the Union lines; they remain to strike the blow for their race, and share the fate of comrades. They are such as Denmark Vesey, who travelled through the world with his master, and might have had freedom a thousand times; but returned to South Carolina, to set on foot a gigantic plot for insurrection. A group of such I met from the cotton plantations early in this war; they had made their way to Ohio to consult with Abolitionists; having done so, they abandoned the free soil upon which they stood and went back to the far South, to abide their time with the rest. And there are thousands of these who have long lived in the North, and whose motto is now SOUTHWARD: in them are the fiery hearts of crusaders who march to rescue the holy places of Humanity from the road of the infidel. And for them wait the multitudes of starved intellects, beggared hearts, and famished souls, who have long lain under the altar, and cried day and night, "How long, O Lord; how long!"

VIRGINIUS DABNEY

1835-1894

Virginius Dabney was born at his father's plantation, "Elmington," in Gloucester County, Virginia, on February 15, 1835. He grew up in Virginia and Mississippi, went to school in Richmond, attended the University of Virginia, and traveled in Europe. He began the practice of law in Mississippi; but upon the death of his first wife, just before the Civil War, he returned to Virginia. He served in the Confederate army throughout the war and was mustered out with the rank of Captain.

After the war he remarried and abandoned law for teaching and writing. He founded the Loudoun School in Middleburg, Virginia, and conducted preparatory schools at Princeton and in New York City. He served as an editorial adviser to several publishing houses and was on the staff of the New York *Commercial Advertiser.*

In 1886 he published the novel, *The Story of Don Miff,* in which he wrote with charm and humor of the life of the slave-owning class in Virginia just before the war. The novel ran into four editions in six months, and in 1889 he published *Gold That Did Not Glitter.* He was engaged in other writing when he died on June 2, 1894.

LAGER BIER*

I think it will be allowed that, whatever else this story may be, it has been, so far, genteel. It is with regret, therefore, that, in the very opening of this eighth chapter, I find myself driven to the use of a word which hardly seems to comport with the previous dignity of our narrative. But, after turning the matter over in my mind again and again, I have found it impossible to discover any satisfactory synonym, or invent any delicately-phrased equivalent for the very plebeian vocable in question. With the reader's kind permission, therefore —

To a philosopher and a philanthropist (and I am somewhat of both, after a Bushwhackerish fashion) the word *Lager Bier* should undoubtedly be one of the most precious additions to a language already rich in such expressive linguistic combinations as Jersey Lightning, Gin Sling, Rum and Gum, Rye and Rock, Kill-Round-the-Corner, Santa Cruz Sour, Stone Fence, Forty-Rod, Dead Shot, etc., etc., etc., not to mention a host of such etymological simples as Juleps, Smashes, Straights, and Cobblers. For the introduction into this country of the mild tipple it indicates has unquestionably done more to arrest drunkenness than all the temperance societies that have been, are, or shall be. Still, the word itself, spell it how you will, has hardly a distinguished air; and hence I long sought, and should gladly have adopted, some such aristocratic expression as Brew of the Black Forest, Nectar of Gambrinus, Deutscher's Dew, Suevorum Gaudium (*i.e.* Schwabs' Bliss) — some genteel phrase, in a word — but that I was unwilling to sacrifice precision to elegance.

Now, the necessity that I am under of alluding to the Solace of Arminius at all, arises in the simplest way.

At the period of which I am writing, this beverage, newly intro-

*Title supplied. From *The Story of Don Miff*, by Virginius Dabney. J. B. Lippincott and Co., 1886.

duced, had great vogue in Richmond, notably among the young men. Especially did college-bred young fellows give in a prompt adhesion to the new faith; and if, in any party of such, assembled to discuss, in a double sense, this new ethereal mildness, there was found any man who had attended the German universities, that man was the lion of the evening. His it was to excite our wonder by reciting deeds of prowess that he had witnessed; his to tell us what had been done; his to show us how it could be done again. I wonder whether a young medical man whom I knew in those days (now a staid and solid doctor) remembers the laugh which greeted him when he essayed to explain, to an attentive class that he was coaching in the new knowledge, how the German students managed actually to pour their beer down their throats, — swallowed it without swallowing, that is.

"It is the simplest thing in the world," said he. "See here." And turning a glass upside down over his mouth, its entire contents disappeared without the slightest visible movement of his throat. "Didn't you see how it was done? The whole secret lies in the *voluntary suppression of the peristaltic action of the oesophagus.*"

"The deuce you say!" cried a pupil. "Then, if that be so, I for one say, Let's all suppress." And that became the word with our set for that season, and much beer perished.

Why is it that a man recalls with such pleasure the follies of his youth? And why is it that the wise things we do make so little impression on our minds? For my own part, I can remember, without an effort, scores of absurdities that I have been guilty of, while of acts of wisdom scarcely one occurs to me.

The favorite haunt of my beer-drinking friends at this period was a smallish room, — you could not have called it a saloon, — a regular nest of a place, situated, not to be too explicit, not very far from, say Fourth Street. Our little nook stood alone in that part of the city, and, being so isolated in an exceedingly quiet neighborhood, it met exactly the wants of the jovial though orderly set of young professional men who, with the honest Teutons of the vicinage, frequented it.

Well, on the occasion to which I have referred, half a dozen of us were grouped around a table, and were unusually merry and bright. Our doctor's new word had been hailed as a real acquisition, in honor of which there was some sparkling of wit, and more of beer, — a happy saying being as real a provocative of thirst as a pretzel, — and, moreover, there had arisen between him and a young and promising philologist, lately graduated at the university, and since become a distinguished professor in the land, a philologico-anatomical, serio-comical discussion, in which the philologian maintained that it was hopeless for American to emulate German youth in this matter of drinking beer, while at the same time maintaining a voluntary suppression of the peristaltic action of the oesophagus, for the very simple reason that the throat of the German, incessantly opened wide in pronouncing the gutturals of his language, and hardened by the passage of these rough sounds, becomes in process of time an open pipe, a clear, firm tube, — in a word, a regular rat-hole of a throat, such as no English-speaking youth might reasonably aspire to. The medical man, I remember, came back at him with the quick smile of one who knows, and asked him if he did not confound the larynx with the oesophagus.

"I do," broke in a young lawyer.

"You do what?"

"I confound the larynxes and the oesophagusses of both of you. Mine are growing thirsty. I say, boys, let's suppress 'em both. Here, funf bier!"

The mild Teuton behind the bar obeyed the order with a smile. He was never so well pleased as when a debate arose among us, sure that every flash of wit, every stroke of humor, would be followed by a call for beers all round. . . .

JOHN BANISTER TABB

1845-1909

John Banister Tabb was born on March 22, 1845, in Amelia County, near Richmond, Virginia, of a family which had long lived in the state. Because his eyes were weak from childhood, he was educated at home. During the Civil War he served as a blockade-runner until he was captured in 1864 and imprisoned at Point Lookout, Maryland. There he met Sidney Lanier, who was three years his senior, and the two young men became close friends.

Like Lanier, he was interested in music as well as poetry, and he planned to become a professional musician. As after the war he lacked funds to pursue a musical career, he took a position in a school for boys in Baltimore. In the years that followed he achieved considerable influence and popularity as a teacher. In 1872 he was received into the Catholic Church. In 1884 he was ordained a priest, but continued to devote himself to teaching and writing. He became totally blind in 1908 and died the following year. He was buried in Richmond.

Although he had issued a privately printed collection of verse in 1882, his first volume to attract wide attention was *Poems,* published in 1894. This was followed by *Lyrics* in 1897, *Child Verse* in 1899, *Later Lyrics* in 1902, and other volumes. A carefully prepared collected edition of his work, *The Poetry of Father Tabb,* was edited by Francis A. Litz and published by Dodd, Mead and Company in 1928.

POE'S PURGATORY*

All others rest; but I
Dream-haunted lie —
A distant roar,
As of tumultuous waters, evermore
About my brain.

E'en sleep, though fain
To soothe me, flies affrighted, and alone
I bear the incumbent stone
Of death
That stifles breath,
But not the hideous chorus crying "Shame!"
Upon my name.

Had I not Song?
Yea, and it lingers yet
The souls to fret
Of an ignoble throng,
Aflame with hate
Of the exulting fate
That hurls her idols from her temple fair
And shrines me there.

THOMAS NELSON PAGE

1853-1922

Thomas Nelson Page was born at Oakland Plantation in Hanover County, Virginia, on April 23, 1853. He was the great-grandson of two governors of Virginia, Thomas Nelson (1738-1789) and John Page (1744-1808). He attended Washington College (now Washington and Lee University) when Robert E. Lee was its president, and studied law at the University of Virginia. He began the practice of law in Virginia in 1874 and continued until 1893, when he moved to Washington, D. C. and devoted himself wholly to writing. He served as United States Ambassador to Italy from 1913 to 1918. He died in Virginia on November 1, 1922.

When Page was twenty-four he published a dialect poem in *Scribner's Monthly,* and continued to write both verse and prose as he found time during the practice of law. His first book, *In Ole Virginia,* a collection of six stories, was published by Scribner's in 1887. *"No Haid Pawn,"* which follows, is one of these six stories. The next year saw the publication of *Two Little Confederates,* a children's story, and *Befo' de War,* a volume of dialect verse written with Armistead C. Gordon. A second collection, *Elsket and Other Stories,* appeared in 1891.

Page's stories reached a wide audience, and with his growing popularity he turned all his energies to writing. His other fiction includes: *Pastime Stories, Red Rock, Bred in the Bone* and *John Marvel, Assistant.* He also wrote a number of volumes of non-fiction, among them, *The Old South, The Old Dominion: Her Making and Her Manners* and *Robert E. Lee: Man and Soldier.* The Plantation edition of his *Novels, Sketches, and Poems* was published in eighteen volumes by Scribner's in 1906-1912.

More than any other Virginia writer, Page built up the romantic legend of the ante-bellum South. His theme is stated explicitly by the Negro narrator of "Marse Chan," the first story in *In Ole Virginia:* "Dem wuz good ole times, marster — de bes' Sam ever see! Dey wuz, in fac'!" Unlike "Marse Chan," which has often been called the most representative example of Page's work, *"No Haid Pawn"* is not told in Negro dialect. It loses nothing by that fact. It is, perhaps, the best spectral story by a Virginia author — always, of course, excepting the work of Poe.

"NO HAID PAWN"*

It was a ghostly place in broad daylight, if the glimmer that stole in through the dense forest that surrounded it when the sun was directly overhead deserved this delusive name. At any other time it was — why, we were afraid even to talk about it! and as to venturing within its gloomy borders, it was currently believed among us that to do so was to bring upon the intruder certain death. I knew every foot of ground, wet and dry, within five miles of my father's house, except this plantation, for I had hunted by day and night every field, forest, and marsh within that radius; but the swamp and "ma'shes" that surrounded this place I had never invaded. The boldest hunter on the plantation would call off his dogs and go home if they struck a trail that crossed the sobby boundary-line of No Haid Pawn.

"Jack 'my lanterns" and "evil sperits" only infested those woods, and the earnest advice of those whom we children acknowledged to know most about them was, "Don't you never go nigh dyah, honey; hit's de evil-speritest place in dis wull."

Had not Big William and Cephas and Poliam followed their dogs in there one night, and cut down a tree in which they had with their own eyes seen the coon, and lo! when it fell "de warn no mo' coon dyah 'n a dog!" and the next tree they had "treed in" not only had no coon in it, but when it was cut down it had fallen on Poliam and broken his leg. So the very woods were haunted. From this time they were abandoned to the "jack 'my lanterns" and ghosts, and another shadow was added to No Haid Pawn.

The place was as much cut off from the rest of the country as if a sea had divided it. The river, with marshy banks, swept around it in a wide horseshoe on three sides, and when the hammocks dammed it up washed its way straight across and scoured out a new bed for itself, completely isolating the whole plantation.

*From *In Ole Virginia,* by Thomas Nelson Page. Copyright 1887 by Charles Scribner's Sons.

467

The owners of it, if there were any, which was doubtful, were aliens, and in my time it had not been occupied for forty years. The negroes declared that it was "gin up" to the "ha'nts an' evil sperits," and that no living being could live there. It had grown up in forest and had wholly reverted to original marsh. The road that once ran through the swamp had long since been choked up, and the trees were as thick and the jungle as dense now, in its track, as in the adjacent "ma'sh." Only one path remained. That, it was currently believed by the entire portion of the population who speculated on the subject, was kept open by the evil spirits. Certain it was that no human foot ever trod the narrow, tortuous line that ran through the brakes as deviously as the noiseless, stagnant ditches that curved through the jungle, where the musk-rats played and the moccasin slept unmolested. Yet there it lay, plain and well-defined, month after month and year after year, as No Haid Pawn itself stood, amid its surrounding swamps, all undisturbed and unchanging.

Even the runaway slaves who occasionally left their homes and took to the swamps and woods, impelled by the cruelty of their overseers, or by a desire for a vain counterfeit of freedom, never tried this swamp, but preferred to be caught and returned home to invading its awful shades.

We were brought up to believe in ghosts. Our fathers and mothers laughed at us, and endeavored to reason us out of such a superstition — the fathers with much of ridicule and satire, the mothers giving sweet religious reasons for their argument — but what could they avail against the actual testimony and the blood-curdling experiences of a score of witnesses, who recounted their personal observations with a degree of thrilling realism and a vividness that overbore any arguments our childish reason could grasp! The old mammies and uncles who were our companions and comrades believed in the existence of evil spirits as truly as in the existence of hell or heaven, as to which at that time no question had ever been raised, so far as was known, in that slumberous world. [The Bible was the standard, and all disputes were resolved into an appeal to that authority, the single question as to any point being simply, "Is it in the Bible?"] Had not Lazarus, and Mam' Celia, and William, and Twis'-foot-Bob, and Aunt Sukie Brown, and others *seen* with their own eyes the evil spirits, again and again, in the bodily shape of cats, headless dogs, white cows, and other less palpable forms! And was not their experience, who lived in remote cabins, or wandered night after night through the loneliest woods, stronger evidence than the cold reasoning of those who hardly ever stirred abroad except in daylight? It certainly was more conclusive to us; for no one could have listened to those narrators without being impressed with the fact that they were recounting what they had actually seen with their bodily eyes. The result of it all was, so far as we were concerned, the triumph of faith over reason, and the fixed belief, on our part, in the actual visible existence of the departed, in the sinister form of apparition known as "evil sperits." Every graveyard was tenanted by them; every old house and every peculiarly desolate spot was known to be their rendezvous; but all spots and places sank into insignificance compared with No Haid Pawn.

The very name was uncanny. Originally it had designated a long, stagnant pool of water lying in the centre of the tract, which marked the spot from which the soil had been dug to raise the elevation on which to set the house. More modernly the place, by reason of the filling up of ditches and the sinking of dikes, had become again simple swamp and jungle, or, to use the local expression, "had turned to ma'sh," and the name applied to the whole plantation.

The origin of the name? The pond had no source; but there was a better explanation than that. Anyhow, the very name inspired dread, and the place was our terror.

The house had been built many generations before by a stranger in this section, and the owners never made it their permanent home. Thus, no ties either of blood or friendship were formed with their neighbors, who were certainly open-hearted and open-doored enough to overcome anything but the most persistent unneighborliness. Why this spot was selected for a mansion was always a mystery, unless it was that the new-comer desired to isolate himself completely. Instead of following the custom of those who were native and to the manner born, who always chose some eminence for their seats, he had selected for his a spot in the middle of the wide

469

flat which lay in the horseshoe of the river. The low ground, probably owing to the abundance of land in that country, had never been "taken up," and up to the time of his occupation was in a condition of primeval swamp. He had to begin by making an artificial mound for his mansion. Even then, it was said, he dug so deep that he laid the corner-stone in water. The foundation was of stone, which was brought from a distance. Fabulous stories were told of it. The negroes declared that under the old house were solid rock chambers, which had been built for dungeons, and had served for purposes which were none the less awful because they were vague and indefinite. The huge structure itself was of wood, and was alleged to contain many mysterious rooms and underground passages. One of the latter was said to connect with the No Haid Pawn itself, whose dark waters, according to the negroes' traditions, were some day, by some process not wholly consistent with the laws of physics, to overwhelm the fated pile. An evil destiny had seemed to overshadow the place from the very beginning. One of the negro builders had been caught and decapitated between two of the immense foundation stones. The tradition was handed down that he was sacrificed in some awful and occult rite connected with the laying of the corner-stone. The scaffolding had given way and had precipitated several men to the ground, most of whom had been fatally hurt. This also was alleged to be by hideous design. Then the plantation, in the process of being reclaimed, had proved unhealthy beyond all experience, and the negroes employed in the work of diking and reclaiming the great swamp had sickened and died by dozens. The extension of the dangerous fever to the adjoining plantations had left a reputation for typhus malaria from which the whole section suffered for a time. But this did not prevent the colored population from recounting year after year the horrors of the pestilence of No Haid Pawn as a peculiar visitation, nor from relating with blood-curdling details the burial by scores, in a thicket just beside the pond, of the stricken "befo' dee *daid*, honey, befo' dee *daid!*" The bodies, it was said, used to float about in the guts of the swamp and on the haunted pond; and at night they might be seen if any one were so hardy as to venture there, rowing about in their coffins as if they were boats.

Thomas Nelson Page, 1853-1922

Thus the place from the beginning had an evil name, and when, year after year, the river rose and washed the levees away, or the musk-rats burrowed through and let the water in, and the strange masters cursed not only the elements but Heaven itself, the continued mortality of their negroes was not wholly unexpected nor unaccounted for by certain classes of their neighbors.

At length the property had fallen to one more gloomy, more strange, and more sinister than any who had gone before him — a man whose personal characteristics and habits were unique in that country. He was of gigantic stature and superhuman strength, and possessed appetites and vices in proportion to his size. He could fell an ox with a blow of his fist, or in a fit of anger could tear down the branch of a tree, or bend a bar of iron like a reed. He, either from caprice or ignorance, spoke only a *patois* not unlike the Creole French of the Louisiana parishes. But he was a West Indian. His brutal temper and habits cut him off from even the small measure of intercourse which had existed between his predecessors and their neighbors, and he lived at No Haid Pawn completely isolated. All the stories and traditions of the place at once centred on him, and fabulous tales were told of his prowess and of his life. It was said, among other things, that he preserved his wonderful strength by drinking human blood, a tale which in a certain sense I have never seen reason to question. Making all allowances, his life was a blot upon civilization. At length it culminated. A brutal temper inflamed by unbridled passions, after a long period of license and debauchery came to a climax in a final orgy of ferocity and fury, in which he was guilty of an act whose fiendishness surpassed belief, and he was brought to judgment.

In modern times the very inhumanity of the crime would probably have proved his security, and as he had destroyed his own property while he was perpetrating a crime of appalling and unparalleled horror, he might have found a defence in that standing refuge of extraordinary scoundrelism — insanity. This defence, indeed, was put in, and was pressed with much ability by his counsel, one of whom was my father, who had just then been admitted to the bar; but, fortunately for the cause of justice, neither courts nor juries were then so sentimental as they have become of late years, and the last occupant of No Haid Pawn paid under the law the full penalty of his hideous crime. It was one of the curious incidents of the trial that his negroes all lamented his death, and declared that he was a good master when he was not drunk. He was hanged just at the rear of his own house, within sight of the spot where his awful crime was committed.

At his execution, which, according to the custom of the country, was public, a horrible coincidence occurred which furnished the text of many a sermon on retributive justice among the negroes.

The body was interred near the pond, close by the thicket where the negroes were buried; but the negroes declared that it preferred one of the stone chambers under the mansion, where it made its home, and that it might be seen at any time of the day or night stalking headless about the place. They used to dwell with peculiar zest on the most agonizing details of this wretch's dreadful crime, the whole culminating in the final act of maniacal fury, when the gigantic monster dragged the hacked and headless corpse of his victim up the staircase and stood it up before the open window in his hall, in the full view of the terrified slaves. After these narrations, the continued reappearance of the murderer and his headless victim was as natural to us as it was to the negroes themselves; and, as night after night we would hurry up to the great house through the darkness, we were ever on the watch lest he should appear to our frighted vision from the shades of the shrubbery-filled yard.

Thus it was that of all ghostly places No Haid Pawn had the distinction of being invested, to us, with unparalleled horror; and thus to us, no less than because the dikes had given way and the overflowed flats had turned again to swamp and jungle, it was explicable that No Haid Pawn was abandoned, and was now untrodden by any foot but that of its ghostly tenants.

The time of my story was 185–. The spring previous continuous rains had kept the river full, and had flooded the low grounds, and this had been followed by an exceptionally dense growth in the summer. Then, public feeling was greatly excited at the time of which I write, over the discovery in the neighborhood of several emissaries of the underground railway, or — as they were universally considered in that country — of the devil. They had been run off or had disappeared suddenly, but had left behind them some little excitement on the part of the slaves, and a great deal on the part of their masters, and more than the usual number of negroes had run away. All, however, had been caught, or had returned home after a sufficient interval of freedom, except one who had escaped permanently, and who was supposed to have accompanied his instigators on their flight.

This man was a well-known character. He belonged to one of our neighbors, and had been bought and brought there from an estate on the Lower Mississippi. He was the most brutal negro I ever knew. He was of a type rarely found among our negroes, who, judging from their physiognomy and general characteristics, came principally from the coast of Africa. They are of moderate stature, with dull but amiable faces. This man, however, was of immense size, and he possessed the features and expression of a Congo desperado. In character also he differed essentially from all the other slaves in our country. He was alike without their amiability and their docility, and was as fearless as he was brutal. He was the only negro I ever knew who was without either superstition or reverence. Indeed, he differed so widely from the rest of the slaves in that section that there existed some feeling against him almost akin to a race feeling. At the same time that he exercised considerable influence over them they were dreadfully afraid of him, and were always in terror that he would trick them, to which awful power he laid well-known claim. His curses in his strange dialect used to terrify them beyond measure, and they would do anything to conciliate him. He had been a continual source of trouble and an object of suspicion in the neighborhood from the time of his first appearance; and more than one hog that the negroes declared had wandered into the marshes of No Haid Pawn, and had "cut his thote jes' swinin' aroun' an' aroun' in de ma'sh" had been suspected of finding its way to this man's cabin. His master had often been urged to get rid of him, but he was kept, I think, probably because he was valuable on the plantation. He was a fine butcher, a good work-hand, and a first-class boatman. Moreover, ours was a conservative population, in which every man minded his own business and let his neighbor's alone.

At the time of the visits of those secret agents to which I have referred, this negro was discovered to be the leader in the secret meetings held under their auspices, and he would doubtless have been taken up and shipped off at once; but when the intruders fled, as I have related, their convert disappeared also. It was a subject of general felicitation in the neighborhood that he was gotten rid of, and his master, instead of being commiserated on the loss of his slave, was congratulated that he had not cut his throat.

No idea can be given at this date of the excitement occasioned in a quiet neighborhood in old times by the discovery of the mere presence of such characters as Abolitionists. It was as if the foundations of the whole social fabric were undermined. It was the sudden darkening of a shadow that always hung in the horizon. The slaves were in a large majority, and had they risen, though the final issue could not be doubted, the lives of every white on the plantations must have paid the forfeit. Whatever the right and wrong of slavery might have been, its existence demanded that no outside interference with it should be tolerated. So much was certain; self-preservation required this.

I was, at the time of which I speak, a well-grown lad, and had been for two sessions to a boarding school, where I had gotten rid of some portion — I will not say of all — of the superstition of my boyhood. The spirit of adventure was beginning to assert itself in me, and I had begun to feel a sense of enjoyment in overcoming the fears which once mastered me, though, I must confess, I had not entirely shaken off my belief in the existence of ghosts — that is, I did not believe in them at all in the day-time, but when night came I was not so certain about it.

Duck-hunting was my favorite sport, and the marshes on the river were fine ground for them usually, but this season the weather had been so singularly warm that the sport had been poor, and though I had scoured every canal in the marsh and every bend in the river as far as No Haid Pawn Hammock, as the stretch of drifted timber and treacherous marsh was called that marked the boundary-line of that plantation, I had had bad luck. Beyond that point I had never penetrated, partly, no doubt, because of the training of my earlier years, and partly because the marsh on either side of the hammock would have mired a cat. Often, as I watched with envious eyes the wild duck rise up over the dense trees that surrounded the place and cut straight for the deserted marshes in the horseshoe, I had had a longing to invade the mysterious domain, and crawl to the edge of No Haid Pawn and get a shot at the fowl that floated on its black surface; but something had always deterred me, and the long reaches of No Haid Pawn were left to the wild-fowl and the ghostly rowers. Finally, however, after a spell whose high temperature was rather suited to August than April, in desperation at my ill-luck I determined to gratify my curiosity and try No Haid Pawn. So one afternoon, without telling any one of my intention, I crossed the mysterious boundary and struck through the swamp for the unknown land.

The marsh was far worse than I had anticipated, and no one but a duck-hunter as experienced and zealous as myself, and as indifferent to ditches, briers, mire, and all that make a swamp, could have penetrated it at all. Even I could never have gotten on if I had not followed the one path that led into the marsh, the reputed "parf" of the evil spirits, and, as it was, my progress was both tedious and dangerous.

The track was a mysterious one, for though I knew it had not been trodden by a human foot in many years, yet there, a veritable "parf," it lay. In some places it was almost completely lost, and I would fear I should have to turn back, but an overhanging branch or a vine swinging from one tree to another would furnish a way to some spot where the narrow trail began again. In other spots old logs thrown across the miry canals gave me an uncomfortable feeling as I reflected what feet had last crossed on them. On both sides of this trail the marsh was either an impenetrable jungle or a mire apparently bottomless.

I shall never forget my sensations as I finally emerged from the woods into the clearing, if that desolate waste of willows, cane, and swamp growth could be so termed. About me stretched the jungle, over which a greenish lurid atmosphere brooded, and straight ahead

towered the gaunt mansion, a rambling pile of sombre white, with
numberless vacant windows staring at me from the leafless trees
about it. Only one other clump of trees appeared above the canes
and brush, and that I knew by intuition was the graveyard.

I think I should have turned back had not shame impelled me
forward.

My progress from this point was even more difficult than it
had been hitherto, for the trail at the end of the wood terminated
abruptly in a gut of the swamp; however, I managed to keep on by
walking on hammocks, pushing through clumps of bushes, and wading as best I could. It was slow and hot work, though.

It never once struck me that it must be getting late. I had become
so accustomed to the gloom of the woods that the more open ground
appeared quite light to me, and I had not paid any attention to the
black cloud that had been for some time gathering overhead, or to
the darkening atmosphere.

I suddenly became sensible that it was going to rain. However, I
was so much engrossed in the endeavor to get on that even then I
took little note of it. The nearer I came to the house the more it arrested my attention, and the more weird and uncanny it looked.
Canes and bushes grew up to the very door; the window-shutters
hung from the hinges; the broken windows glared like eyeless sockets; the portico had fallen away from the wall, while the wide door
stood slightly ajar, giving to the place a singularly ghastly appearance, somewhat akin to the color which sometimes lingers on the
face of a corpse. In my progress wading through the swamp I had
gone around rather to the side of the house toward where I supposed the "pawn" itself to lie.

I was now quite near to it, and striking a little less miry ground,
as I pushed my way through the bushes and canes, which were
higher than my head, I became aware that I was very near the
thicket that marked the graveyard, just beyond which I knew the
pond itself lay. I was somewhat startled, for the cloud made it quite
dusky, and, stepping on a long piece of rotten timber lying on the
ground, I parted the bushes to look down the pond. As I did so the
rattle of a chain grated on me, and, glancing up through the cane,
before me appeared a heavy upright timber with an arm or cross-

beam stretching from it, from which dangled a long chain, almost rusted away. I knew by instinct that I stood under the gallows where the murderer of No Haid Pawn had expiated his dreadful crime. His corpse must have fallen just where I stood. I started back appalled.

Just then the black cloud above me was parted by a vivid flame, and a peal of thunder seemed to rive the earth.

I turned in terror, but before I had gone fifty yards the storm was upon me, and instinctively I made for the only refuge that was at hand. It was a dreadful alternative, but I did not hesitate. Outside I was not even sure that my life was safe. And with extraordinary swiftness I had made my way through the broken iron fence that lay rusting in the swamp, had traversed the yard, all grown up as it was to the very threshold, had ascended the sunken steps, crossed the rotted portico, and entered the open door.

A long dark hall stretched before me, extending, as well as I could judge in the gloom, entirely across the house. A number of doors, some shut, some ajar, opened on the hall on one side; and a broad, dark stairway ascended on the other to the upper story. The walls were black with mould. At the far end a large bow-window, with all the glass gone, looked out on the waste of swamp, unbroken save by the clump of trees in the graveyard, and just beside this window was a break where the dark staircase descended to the apartments below. The whole place was in a state of advanced decay; almost the entire plastering had fallen with the damp, and the hall presented a scene of desolation that beggars description.

I was at last in the haunted house!

The rain, driven by the wind, poured in at the broken windows in such a deluge that I was forced in self-defence to seek shelter in one of the rooms. I tried several, but the doors were swollen or fastened; I found one, however, on the leeward side of the house, and, pushing the door, which opened easily, I entered. Inside I found something like an old bed; and the great open fireplace had evidently been used at some earlier time, for the ashes were still banked up in the cavernous hearth, and the charred ends of the logs of wood were lying in the chimney corners. To see, still as fresh and natural as though the fire had but just died out, these remnants of domestic life that had survived all else of a similar period struck me as unspeakably ghastly. The bedstead, however, though rude, was convenient as a seat, and I utilized it accordingly, propping myself up against one of the rough posts. From my position I commanded through the open door the entire length of the vacant hall, and could look straight out of the great bow-window at the head of the stairs, through which appeared, against the dull sky, the black mass of the graveyard trees, and a stretch of one of the canals or guts of the swamp curving around it, which gleamed white in the glare of the lightning.

I had expected that the storm would, like most thunder-storms in the latitude, shortly exhaust itself, or, as we say, "blow over;" but I was mistaken, and as the time passed, its violence, instead of diminishing, increased. It grew darker and darker, and presently the startling truth dawned on me that the gloom which I had supposed simply the effect of the overshadowing cloud had been really nightfall. I was shut up alone in No Haid Pawn for the night!

I hastened to the door with the intention of braving the storm and getting away; but I was almost blown off my feet. A glance without showed me that the guts with which the swamp was traversed in every direction were now full to the brim, and to attempt to find my way home in the darkness would be sheer madness; so, after a wistful survey, I returned to my wretched perch. I thought I would try and light a fire, but to my consternation I had not a match, and I finally abandoned myself to my fate. It was a desolate, if not despairing, feeling that I experienced. My mind was filled, not only with my own unhappiness, but with the thought of the distress my absence would occasion them at home; and for a little while I had a fleeting hope that a party would be sent out to search for me. This, however, was untenable, for they would not know where I was. The last place in which they would ever think of looking for me was No Haid Pawn, and even if they knew I was there they could no more get to me in the darkness and storm than I could escape from it.

I accordingly propped myself up on my bed and gave myself up to my reflections. I said my prayers very fervently. I thought I would try and get to sleep, but sleep was far from my eyes.

Thomas Nelson Page, 1853-1922

My surroundings were too vivid to my apprehension. The awful traditions of the place, do what I might to banish them, would come to mind. The original building of the house, and its blood-stained foundation stones; the dead who had died of the pestilence that had raged afterward; the bodies carted by scores and buried in the sobby earth of the graveyard, whose trees loomed up through the broken window; the dreadful story of the dead paddling about the swamp in their coffins; and above all, the gigantic maniac whose ferocity even murder could not satiate, and who had added to murder awful mutilation: he had dragged the mangled corpse of his victim up those very steps and flung it out of the very window which gaped just beyond me in the glare of lightning. It all passed through my mind as I sat there in the darkness, and no effort of my will could keep my thoughts from dwelling on it. The terrific thunder, outcrashing a thousand batteries, at times engrossed my attention; but it always reverted to that scene of horror; and if I dozed, the slamming of the loose blinds, or the terrific fury of the storm, would suddenly startle me. Once, as the sounds subsided for a moment, or else I having become familiar with them, as I was sinking into a sleepy state, a door at the other end of the hall creaked and then slammed with violence, bringing me bolt upright on the bed, clutching my gun. I could have sworn that I heard footsteps; but the wind was blowing a hurricane, and, after another period of wakefulness and dreadful recollection, nature succumbed, and I fell asleep.

I do not know that I can be said to have lost consciousness even then, for my mind was still enchained by the horrors of my situation, and went on clinging to them and dwelling upon them even in my slumber.

I was, however, certainly asleep; for the storm must have died temporarily away about this hour without my knowing it, and I subsequently heard that it did.

I must have slept several hours, for I was quite stiff from my constrained posture when I became fully aroused.

I was awakened by a very peculiar sound; it was like a distant call or halloo. Although I had been fast asleep a moment before, it startled me into a state of the highest attention. In a second I was wide awake. There was not a sound except the rumble and roll of the thunder, as the storm once more began to renew itself, and in the segment of the circle that I could see along the hall through my door, and, indeed, out through the yawning window at the end, as far as the black clump of trees in the graveyard just at the bend of the canal, which I commanded from my seat whenever there was a flash of lightning, there was only the swaying of the bushes in the swamp and of the trees in the graveyard. Yet there I sat bolt upright on my bed, in the darkness, with every nerve strained to its utmost tension, and that unearthly cry still sounding in my ears. I was endeavoring to reason myself into the belief that I had dreamed it, when a flash of lightning lit up the whole field of my vision as if it had been in the focus of a sun-glass, and out on the canal, where it curved around the graveyard was a boat — a something — small, black, with square ends, and with a man in it, standing upright, and something lying in a lump or mass at the bow.

I knew I could not be mistaken, for the lightning by a process of its own, photographs everything on the retina in minutest detail, and I had a vivid impression of everything from the foot of the bed, on which I crouched, to the gaunt arms of those black trees in the graveyard just over that ghostly boatman and his dreadful freight. I was wide awake.

The story of the dead rowing in their coffins was verified!

I am unable to state what passed in the next few minutes.

The storm had burst again with renewed violence and was once more expending itself on the house; the thunder was again rolling overhead; the broken blinds were swinging and slamming madly; and the dreadful memories of the place were once more besetting me.

I shifted my position to relieve the cramp it had occasioned, still keeping my face toward that fatal window. As I did so, I heard above, or perhaps I should say under, the storm a sound more terrible to me — the repetition of that weird halloo, this time almost under the great window. Immediately succeeding this was the sound of something scraping under the wall, and I was sensible when a door on the ground-floor was struck with a heavy thud. It was pitch-dark, but I heard the door pushed wide open, and as a string of fierce oaths, part English and part Creole French, floated up the dark stairway, muffled as if sworn through clinched teeth, I held my breath. I recalled the unknown tongue the ghostly murderer employed; and I knew that the murderer of No Haid Pawn had left his grave, and that his ghost was coming up that stair. I heard his step as it fell on the first stair heavily yet almost noiselessly. It was an unearthly sound — dull, like the tread of a bared foot, accompanied by the scraping sound of a body dragging. Step by step he came up the black stairway in the pitch darkness as steadily as if it were daytime, and he knew every step, accompanied by that sickening sound of dragging. There was a final pull up the last step, and a dull, heavy thud, as, with a strange, wild laugh, he flung his burden on the floor.

For a moment there was not a sound, and then the awful silence and blackness were broken by a crash of thunder that seemed to tear the foundations asunder like a mighty earthquake, and the whole house, and the great swamp outside, were filled with a glare of vivid, blinding light. Directly in front of me, clutching in his upraised hand a long, keen, glittering knife, on whose blade a ball of fire seemed to play, stood a gigantic figure in the very flame of the lightning and stretched at his feet lay, ghastly and bloody, a black and headless trunk.

I staggered to the door and, tripping, fell prostrate over the sill.

When we could get there, nothing was left but the foundation. The haunted house, when struck, had literally burned to the water's edge. The changed current had washed its way close to the place, and in strange verification of the negroes' traditions. No Haid Pawn had reclaimed its own, and the spot with all its secrets lay buried under its dark waters.

WOODROW WILSON

1856-1924

Woodrow Wilson, President of the United States, was born at Staunton, Virginia, on December 28, 1856, and died in Washington, D. C., on February 3, 1924. He attended Davidson College and Princeton, studied law at the University of Virginia, practiced law for a year, and pursued graduate studies at Johns Hopkins. His dissertation for his doctorate, *Congressional Government, a Study in American Politics,* was published in 1885 and was the first of a number of able works on American history and politics.

He taught at Bryn Mawr and Wesleyan, and in 1890 became professor of jurisprudence and political economy at Princeton. During the next decade he achieved a wide reputation as an effective teacher and writer. Among his books during the period were *The State: Elements of Historical and Practical Politics* (1889), *Division and Reunion, 1829-1889* (1893), *An Old Master and Other Political Essays* (1893), *Mere Literature and Other Essays* (1893), *George Washington* (1897) and *A History of the American People* (1902).

Wilson became president of Princeton in 1902, and won national attention through his public speeches and articles and his vigorous attempt to democratize student life and raise educational standards at the university. In 1910 he received the Democratic nomination for governor of New Jersey and was elected with a plurality of nearly 50,000 votes. He immediately set about to fulfill the pledges of his liberal platform, to the surprise of some of his conservative supporters.

In 1912 Wilson had a nation-wide reputation as a liberal Democrat. When the Democratic National Convention that year became deadlocked among rival presidential candidates, Wilson received the presidential nomination on the 46th ballot. His speeches in the campaign which followed were of a quality quite extraordinary in contemporary American politics. They were collected under the title, *The New Freedom,* in 1913, and "Life Comes from the Soil," which follows, is from that volume.

Wilson benefitted from a three-way division of the vote among William Howard Taft on the Republican ticket, Theodore Roosevelt on the Progressive ticket and his own Democratic ticket. He won the impressive majority of 435 electoral votes, against 88 for Roosevelt and 8 for Taft, and his momentous years in the White House began.

LIFE COMES FROM THE SOIL*

When I look back on the processes of history, when I survey the genesis of America, I see this written over every page: that the nations are renewed from the bottom, not from the top; that the genius which springs up from the ranks of unknown men is the genius which renews the youth and energy of the people. Everything I know about history, every bit of experience and observation that has contributed to my thought, has confirmed me in the conviction that the real wisdom of human life is compounded out of the experiences of ordinary men. The utility, the vitality, the fruitage of life does not come from the top to the bottom; it comes, like the natural growth of a great tree, from the soil, up through the trunk into the branches to the foliage and the fruit. The great struggling unknown masses of the men who are at the base of everything are the dynamic force that is lifting the levels of society. A nation is as great, and only as great, as her rank and file.

So the first and chief need of this nation of ours today is to include in the partnership of government all those great bodies of unnamed men who are going to produce our future leaders and renew the future energies of America. And man who is swimming against the stream knows the strength of it. The man who is in the melee knows what blows are being struck and what blood is being drawn. The man who is on the make is the judge of what is happening in America, not the man who has made good; not the man who has emerged from the flood; not the man who is standing on the bank looking on, but the man who is struggling for his life and for the lives of those who are dearer to him than himself. That is the man whose judgment will tell you what is going on in America; that is the man by whose judgment I, for one, wish to be guided.

We have had the wrong jury; we have had the wrong group, — no, I will not say the wrong group, but too small a group, — in control of the policies of the United States. The average man has not been consulted, and his heart had begun to sink for fear he never would be consulted again. Therefore, we have got to organize a government whose sympathies will be open to the whole body of the people of the United States, a government which will consult as large a proportion of the people of the United States as possible before it acts. Because the great problem of government is to know what the average man is experiencing and is thinking about. Most of us are average men; very few of us rise, except by fortunate accident, above the general level of the community about us; and therefore the man who thinks common thoughts, the man who has had common experiences, is almost always the man who interprets America aright. Isn't that the reason that we are proud of such stories as the story of Abraham Lincoln, — a man who rose out of the ranks and interpreted America better than any man had interpreted it who had risen out of the privileged classes or the educated classes of America?

The hope of the United States in the present and in the future is the same that it has always been: it is the hope and confidence that out of unknown homes will come men who will constitute themselves the masters of industry and of politics. The average hopefulness, the average welfare, the average enterprise, the average initiative, of the United States are the only things that make it rich. We are not rich because a few gentlemen direct our industry; we are rich because of our own intelligence and our own industry. America does not consist of men who get their names into the newspapers; America does not consist politically of the men who set themselves up to be political leaders; she does not consist of the men who do most of her talking, — they are important only so far as they speak for that great voiceless multitude of men who constitute the great body and the saving force of the nation. Nobody who cannot speak the common thought, who does not move by the common impulse, is the man to speak for America, or for any of her future purposes. Only he is fit to speak who knows the thoughts of the great body of citizens, the men who go about their business every day, the men who toil from morning till night, the men who go home tired in the evenings, the men who are carrying on the things we are so proud of.

You know how it thrills our blood sometimes to think how all the nations of the earth wait to see what America is going to do with her power, her physical power, her enormous resources, her economic wealth. The nations hold their breath to see what this young country will do with her young unspoiled strength; we cannot help but be proud that we are strong. But what has made us strong? The toil of millions of men, the toil of men who do not boast, who are inconspicuous, but who live their lives humbly from day to day; it is the great body of toilers that constitutes the might of America. It is one of the glories of our land that nobody is able to predict from what family, from what region, from what race, even, the leaders of the country are going to come. The great leaders of this country have not come very often from the established, "successful" families.

I remember speaking at a school not long ago where I understood that almost all the young men were the sons of very rich people, and I told them I looked upon them with a great deal of pity, because, I said: "Most of you fellows are doomed to obscurity. You will not do anything. You will never try to do anything, and with all the great tasks of the country waiting to be done, probably you are the very men who will decline to do them. Some man who has been 'up against it,' some man who has come out of the crowd, somebody who has had the whip of necessity laid on his back, will emerge out of the crowd, will show that he understands the crowd, understands the interests of the nation, united and not separated, and will stand up and lead us."

If I may speak of my own experience, I have found audiences made up of the "common people" quicker to take a point, quicker to understand an argument, quicker to discern a tendency and to comprehend a principle, than many a college class that I have lectured to, — not because the college class lacked the intelligence, but because college boys are not in contact with the realities of life, while "common" citizens are in contact with the actual life of day by day; you do not have to explain to them what touches them to the quick.

There is one illustration of the value of the constant renewal of society from the bottom that has always interested me profoundly. The only reason why government did not suffer dry rot in the Middle Ages under the aristocratic system which then prevailed was that so many of the men who were efficient instruments of government were drawn from the church, — from that great religious body which was then the only church, that body which we now distinguish from other religious bodies as the Roman Catholic Church. The Roman Catholic Church was then, as it is now, a great democracy. There was no peasant so humble that he might not become a priest, and no priest so obscure that he might not become Pope of Christendom; and every chancellery in Europe, every court in Europe, was ruled by these learned, trained and accomplished men, — the priesthood of that great and dominant body. What kept government alive in the Middle Ages was this constant rise of the sap from the bottom, from the rank and file of the great body of the people through the open channels of the priesthood. That, it seems to me, is one of the most interesting and convincing illustrations that could possibly be adduced of the thing that I am talking about.

The only way that government is kept pure is by keeping these channels open, so that nobody may deem himself so humble as not to constitute a part of the body politic, so that there will constantly be coming new blood into the veins of the body politic; so that no man is so obscure that he may not break the crust of any class he may belong to, may not spring up to higher levels and be counted among the leaders of the state. Anything that depresses, anything that makes the organization greater than the man, anything that blocks, discourages, dismays the humble man, is against all the principles of progress. When I see alliances formed, as they are now being formed, by successful men of business with successful organizers of politics, I know that something has been done that checks the vitality and progress of society. Such an alliance, made at the top, is an alliance made to depress the levels, to hold them where they are, if not to sink them; and, therefore, it is the constant business of good politics to break up such partnerships, to re-establish and reopen the connections between the great body of the people and the offices of government.

486

Woodrow Wilson, 1856-1924

To-day, when our government has so far passed into the hands of special interests; to-day, when the doctrine is implicitly avowed that only select classes have the equipment necessary for carrying on government; to-day, when so many conscientious citizens, smitten with the scene of social wrong and suffering, have fallen victims to the fallacy that benevolent government can be meted out to the people by kind-hearted trustees of prosperity and guardians of the welfare of dutiful employees, — today, supremely, does it behoove this nation to remember that a people shall be saved by the power that sleeps in its own deep bosom, or by none; shall be renewed in hope, in conscience, in strength, by waters welling up from its own sweet, perennial springs. Not from above; not by patronage of its aristocrats. The flower does not bear the root, but the root the flower. Everything that blooms in beauty in the air of heaven draws its fairness, its vigor, from its roots. Nothing living can blossom into fruitage unless through nourishing stalks deep-planted in the common soil. The rose is merely the evidence of the vitality of the root; and the real source of its beauty, the very blush that it wears upon its tender cheek, comes from those silent sources of life that lie hidden in the chemistry of the soil. Up from that soil, up from the silent bosom of the earth, rise the currents of life and energy. Up from the common soil, up from the quiet heart of the people, rise joyously to-day streams of hope and determination bound to renew the face of the earth in glory.

I tell you, the so-called radicalism of our times is simply the effort of nature to release the generous energies of our people. This great American people is at bottom just, virtuous, and hopeful; the roots of its being are in the soil of what is lovely, pure, and of good report, and the need of the hour is just that radicalism that will clear a way for the realization of the aspirations of a sturdy race.

BOOKER T. WASHINGTON

1859-1915

Booker T. Washington, the foremost American advocate of industrial education for Negro youth, was born on a plantation in Franklin County, Virginia, shortly before the Civil War. His childhood under slavery in Virginia is described by Washington in the selection from his *Story of My Life and Work* which follows.

After the war Washington went to West Virginia, where he worked in a salt furnace and a coal mine and began his struggle for an education. He later attended the Normal and Agricultural Institute at Hampton, Virginia, where he worked as a janitor for his board, and was graduated in 1875. He returned to West Virginia to teach, attended the Wayland Seminary in Washington, D. C., and in 1879 returned to Hampton as an instructor.

In 1881 the state legislature of Alabama authorized an annual appropriation of $2,000 for a Negro normal school at Tuskegee, Alabama. Washington, still in his early twenties, was appointed principal of the new school. "When I reached Tuskegee," Washington later wrote, "the only thing that had been done toward the starting of a school was the securing of the $2,000. There was no land, building, or apparatus. I opened the school, however, on the 4th of July, 1881, in an old church and a little shanty that was almost ready to fall down from decay."

Under Washington's leadership, Tuskegee grew from these beginnings to a nationally famous center of Negro industrial education. By the turn of the century it was an institution housed in some forty buildings, most of which had been built by student labor. Washington was tireless as a teacher, organizer, writer and lecturer. He delivered hundreds of addresses throughout the United States in the promotion of interracial good will and the cause of Tuskegee. Among the many books which he published are *The Future of the American Negro* (1899), *Sowing and Reaping* (1900), *Character Building* (1902), *Working with the Hands* (1904), *Tuskegee and Its People* (1905), *Putting the Most into Life* (1906), *Life of Frederick Douglas* (1907), *The Negro in Business* (1907), *The Story of the Negro* (1909), *My Larger Education* (1911), and *The Man Farth-*

488

Booker T. Washington, 1859-1915

est Down: A Record of Observation and Study in Europe (1912). Washington died at Tuskegee on November 14, 1915.

Washington's story of his life, *Up From Slavery*, published in 1901, has been one of the most widely read of American autobiographies and has gone into more than forty editions. *The Story of My Life and Work*, from which the following selection is taken, is an earlier and less well-known autobiographical work.

CHILDHOOD AS A SLAVE IN VIRGINIA*

Many requests have been made of me to write something of the story of my life. Until recently I have never given much consideration to these requests, for the reason that I have never thought that I had done enough in the world to warrant anything in the way of an autobiography; and I hope that my life work, by reason of my present age, lies more in the future than in the past. My daughter, Portia, said to me, not long ago: "Papa, do you know that you have never told me much about your early life, and your children want to know more about you." Then it came upon me as never before that I ought to put something about my life in writing for the sake of my family, if for no other reason.

I will not trouble those who read these lines with any lengthy historical research concerning my ancestry, for I know nothing of my ancestry beyond my mother. My mother was a slave on a plantation near Hale's Ford, in Franklin County, Virginia, and she was, as I now remember it, the cook for her owners as well as for a large part of the slaves on the plantation. The first time that I got a knowledge of the fact that my mother and I were slaves, was by being awakened by my mother early one morning, while I was sleeping in a bed of rags, on a clay floor of our little cabin. She was kneeling over me, fervently praying as was her custom to do, that some day she and her children might be free. The name of my mother was Jane. She, to me, will always remain the noblest embodiment of womanhood with whom I have come in contact. She was wholly ignorant, as far as books were concerned, and, I presume, never had a book in her hands for two minutes at a time. But the lessons in virtue and thrift which she instilled into me during the short period of my life that she lived will never leave me. Some people blame the Negro for not being more honest, as judged by the Anglo-

*Title supplied. From *The Story of My Life and Work*, by Booker T. Washington. Copyright 1900 by Booker T. Washington.

Booker T. Washington, 1859-1915

Saxon's standard of honesty; but I can recall many times when, after all was dark and still, in the late hours of the night, when her children had been without sufficient food during the day, my mother would awaken us, and we would find that she had gotten from somewhere something in the way of eggs or chickens and had cooked them during the night for us. These eggs and chickens were gotten without my master's permission or knowledge. Perhaps, by some code of ethics, this would be classed as stealing, but deep down in my heart I can never decide that my mother, under such circumstances, was guilty of theft. Had she acted thus as a free woman she would have been a thief, but not so, in my opinion, as a slave. After our freedom no one was stricter than my mother in teaching and observing the highest rules of integrity.

Who my father was, or is, I have never been able to learn with any degree of certainty. I only know that he was a white man.

As nearly as I can get at the facts, I was born in the year 1858 or 1859. At the time I came into the world no careful registry of births of people of my complexion was kept. My birth place was near Hale's Ford, in Franklin County, Virginia. It was about as near to Nowhere as any locality gets to be, so far as I can learn. Hale's Ford, I think, was a town with one house and a postoffice, and my birth place was on a large plantation several miles distant from it.

I remember very distinctly the appearance of the cabin in which I was born and lived until freedom came. It was a small log cabin about 12 x 16 feet, and without windows. There was no floor, except a dirt one. There was a large opening in the center of the floor, where sweet potatoes were kept for my master's family during the winter. In this cabin my mother did the cooking, the greater part of the time, for my master's family. Our bed, or "pallet," as we called it, was made every night on the dirt floor. Our bed clothing consisted of a few rags gathered here and there.

One thing I remember more vividly than any other in connection with the days when I was a slave was my dress, or, rather, my lack of dress.

The years that the war was in progress between the States were especially trying to the slaves, so far as clothing were concerned. The Southern white people found it extremely hard to get clothing for themselves during that war, and, of course, the slaves underwent no little suffering in this respect. The only garment that I remember receiving from my owners during the war was a "tow shirt." When I did not wear this shirt I was positively without any garment. In Virginia, the tow shirt was quite an institution during slavery. This shirt was made of the refuse flax that grew in that part of Virginia, and it was a veritable instrument of torture. It was stiff and coarse. Until it had been worn for about six weeks it made one feel as if a thousand needle points were pricking his flesh. I suppose I was about six years old when I was given one of these shirts to wear. After repeated trials the torture was more than my childish flesh could endure and I gave it up in despair. To this day the sight of a new shirt revives the recollection of the torture of my first new shirt. In the midst of my despair, in connection with this garment, my brother John, who was about two years older than I, did me a kindness which I shall never forget. He volunteered to wear my new shirt for me until it was "broken in." After he had worn it for several weeks I ventured to wear it myself, but not without pain.

Soon after my shirt experience, when the winter had grown quite cold, I received my first pair of shoes. These shoes had wooden bottoms, and the tops consisted of a coarse kind of leather covering, and I have never felt so proud since of a pair of shoes.

As soon as I was old enough I performed what, to me, was important service, in holding the horses and riding behind the white women of the household on their long horseback rides, which were very common in those days. At one time, while holding the horses and assisting quite a party of visiting ladies to mount their horses, I remember that, just before the visitors rode away a tempting plate of ginger cakes was brought out and handed around to the visitors. This, I think, was the first time that I had ever seen any ginger cakes, and a very deep impression was made upon my childish mind. I remember I said to myself that if I could ever get to the point where I could eat ginger cakes as I saw those ladies eating them the height of my ambition would be reached.

When I grew to be still larger and stronger the duty of going to the mill was intrusted to me; that is, a large sack containing three or

Booker T. Washington, 1859-1915

four bushels of corn was thrown across the back of a horse and I would ride away to the mill, which was often three or four miles distant, wait at the mill until the corn was turned into meal, and then bring it home. More than once, while performing this service, the corn or meal got unevenly balanced on the back of the horse and fell off into the road, carrying me with it. This left me in a very awkward and unfortunate position. I, of course, was unable, with my small strength, to lift the corn or meal upon the horse's back, and, therefore would have to wait, often for hours, until someone happened to be passing along the road strong enough to replace the burden for me.

My owner's name was Jones Burroughs, and I am quite sure he was above the average in the treatment of his slaves. That is, except in a few cases they were not cruelly whipped. Although I was born a slave, I was too young to experience much of its hardships. The thing in connection with slavery that has left the deepest impression on me was the instance of seeing a grown man, my uncle, tied to a tree early one morning, stripped naked and someone whipping him with a cowhide. As each blow touched his back the cry, "Pray, master! Pray, master!" came from his lips, and made an impression upon my boyish heart that I shall carry with me to my grave.

When I was still quite a child, I could hear the slaves in our "quarters" whispering in subdued tones that something unusual — the war — was about to take place, and that it meant their freedom. These whispered conferences continued, especially at night, until the war actually began.

While there was not a single slave on our plantation that could read a line, in some way we were kept informed of the progress of the war almost as accurately as the most intelligent person. The "grapevine" telegraph was in constant use. When Lee surrendered all of the plantation people knew it, although all of them acted as if they were in ignorance of the fact that anything unusual had taken place.

Early one morning, just after the close of the war, word was sent around to the slave cabins that all the slaves must go to the "big house," the master's house; and in company with my mother and

493

a large number of other slaves, including my sister Amanda and brother John, I went to the "big house," and stood by the side of my mother, and listened to the reading of some papers and a little speech made by the one who read the papers. This was the first public address I had ever heard, and I need not add that it was the most effective one to which it had even been my privilege to listen. After the reading of the paper and the speech, my mother leaned over and whispered, "Now, my children, we are free." This act was hailed with joy by all the slaves, but it threw a tremendous responsibility upon my mother, as well as upon the other slaves. A large portion of the former slaves hired themselves to their owners, while other sought new employment; but, before the beginning of the new life, most of the ex-slaves left the plantation for a few days at least, so as to get the "hang" of the new life, and to be sure that they were free. My mother's husband, my stepfather, had in some way wandered into West Virginia during the war, and had secured employment in the salt furnace near Malden, in Kanawha county. Soon after freedom was declared he sought out my mother and sent a wagon to bring her and her children to West Virginia. After many days of slow, tiresome traveling over the mountains, during which we suffered much, we finally reached Malden, and my mother and her husband were united after a long enforced separation.

The trip from Franklin county to Malden, West Virginia, was the first one that had taken me out of the county where I was born, and, of course, it was quite an event, especially to the children of the family, although the parting from the old homestead was to my mother a very serious affair. All of our household and other goods were packed into a small wagon drawn by two horses or mules. I cannot recall how many days it took us to make this trip, but it seems to me, as I recall it now, that we were at least ten days. Of course we had to sleep in the wagon, or what was more often true, on the ground. The children walked a great portion of the distance.

ELLEN GLASGOW
1874-1945

Ellen Glasgow, one of the most distinguished of modern American novelists, was born in Richmond, Virginia, on April 22, 1874, of a family which had long lived in Virginia. She was educated privately, and from her earliest girlhood was determined to be a writer. She began her first published novel, *The Descendant,* when she was eighteen, and it appeared anonymously in 1897. The following year she published her second novel, *Phases of an Inferior Planet,* which also appeared anonymously.

With *The Voice of the People* in 1900, the first novel published under her name, Miss Glasgow began the remarkable series of novels to which she was to devote her next forty years and in which she was to trace a social history of her native state from the decade before the Civil War to the present. In them she attained, in her own modest phrase, a certain measure of achievement; and that estimate is excessively humble, except in terms of the achievement of the great figures of world literature.

Her novels have twice been brought together in collected editions, in *The Old Dominion Edition of the Works of Ellen Glasgow* in 1929-1933 and in *The Virginia Edition of the Works of Ellen Glasgow* in 1938. The twelve novels which make up the solid body of her work, in the chronological order of the time of their action as they stand in the "complete design" of *The Virginia Edition* (with the dates of their first publication) are: Novels of the Commonwealth, *The Battle-Ground* (1902), *The Deliverance* (1904), *The Voice of the People* (1900), *The Romance of a Plain Man* (1909), *Virginia* (1913), *Life and Gabriella* (1916); Novels of the Country, *The Miller of Old Church* (1911), *Barren Ground* (1925), *Vein of Iron* (1935); Novels of the City, *The Sheltered Life* (1932), *The Romantic Comedians* (1926) and *They Stooped to Folly* (1929).

In addition to these and her first two novels, Miss Glasgow was the author of five other volumes, including an early collection of poetry, which she did not care to include in the definitive edition of her work. And, although Miss Glasgow had resolved to bring her creative work to a close with *The Virginia Edition* of her writing, that edition was not in fact definitive. In 1941 she published *In This Our Life,* a novel of contemporary Virginia, which stands among her finest work.

495

Virginia Reader

Miss Glasgow was the recipient of many honors and awards. She received honorary degrees from the University of North Carolina, the University of Richmond, Duke University and the College of William and Mary. In 1940 she was awarded the quinquennial Howells medal for "eminence in creative literature as shown in the novel," and *In This Our Life* was awarded the Pulitzer Prize.

In 1943 she published *A Certain Measure: An Interpretation of Prose Fiction*, which brought together in one volume the stimulating prefaces to her novels which she prepared for *The Virginia Edition* of her work. The volume also includes a useful bibliography of the many critical essays on her work which have appeared in books and periodicals.

Miss Glasgow died in Richmond on November 21, 1945.

RETURN TO VIRGINIA*

As the train rushed through the familiar country, Dorinda counted the new patches of ploughed ground in the landscape. "James Ellgood must be trying to reclaim all his old fields," she thought.

The sun had not yet risen above the fretwork of trees on the horizon, but the broomsedge had felt the approach of day and was flying upward to meet it. Out of the east, she saw gradually emerge the serpent-like curves of Whippernock River; then the clouds of blown smoke, the irregular pattern of the farms, and the buildings of the station, which wore a startled and half-awake air in the dawn.

After more than two years how strange it felt to be back again! To be back again just as if nothing had happened! How small the station looked, and how desolate, stranded like a wrecked ship in the broomsedge. What isolation! What barrenness! In her memory the horizon had been so much wider, the road so much longer, the band of woods so much deeper. It seemed to her that the landscape must have diminished in an incredible way since she had left it. Even the untidy look of the station; the litter of shavings and tobacco stems; the shabbiness and crudeness of the country people meeting the train; the disreputable rags of Butcher, the lame negro, who lived in the freight car; the very fowls scratching in the dust of the cleared space; — all these characteristic details were uglier and more trivial than she had remembered them. A sense of loneliness swept her thoughts, as if the solitude had blown over her like smoke. She realized that the Pedlar's Mill of her mind and the Pedlar's Mill of actuality were two different places. She was returning home, and she felt as strange as she had felt in New York. Well, at least she had not crawled back. She had returned with her head held high, as she had resolved that she would.

*Title supplied. From *Barren Ground*, by Ellen Glasgow. Copyright 1925, 1933, by Ellen Glasgow. Reprinted by permission of Harcourt, Brace and Co., Inc.

The whistle was sounding again, and the brakeman was hastily gathering her bags. She followed him to the platform, where the conductor stood waiting, the same conductor who had helped her into the train the morning she had gone away. He did not recognize her, and for some obscure reason, she felt flattered because he had forgotten her.

The train was stopping slowly. The faces of the assembled farmers started out so close to the track that they gave her a shock. There was Jim Ellgood ready to leave for Richmond; there was Mr. Garlick meeting somebody, his daughter probably; there was Mr. Kettledrum, looking as stringy and run-to-seed, as if he had not moved out of his wheelrut since the morning he had picked her up in the rain. In the little group she saw Rufus, slender, handsome, sullen as ever. How black his eyes were, and how becoming the dark red was in his cheeks! Then, as the train reached the station, she saw Nathan Pedlar running down to the track with the mail bag in his hand. Just at the last minute, but always in time — how like Nathan that was!

The conductor, with one foot on the step, was swinging his free leg while he felt for the ground. She put up her hand, hurriedly arranging her small blue hat with the flowing chiffon veil. Then she lifted the folds of her skirt as the conductor, who was firmly planted now on the earth, helped her to alight. Her heart was sad for her father, but beneath the sadness her indomitable pride supported her. Yes, she had come back unashamed. She might not return as a conqueror, but she had returned undefeated. They were looking at her as she stepped to the ground, and she felt, with a thrill of satisfaction, that in her navy blue poplin with the chiffon veil framing her face (hanging veils were much worn in New York that year) she was worthy of the surprised glances they cast at her. A little thinner, a little paler, less girlish but more striking, than she was when she went away. Her height gave her dignity, and this dignity was reflected in her vivid blue eyes, with their unflinching and slightly arrogant gaze. Romantic eyes, Burch had called them, and she had wondered what he meant, for surely there was little romance left now in her mind. If experience had taught her nothing else, it had at least made her a realist. She had learned to take things as they are, and that, as Burch had once remarked whimsically, "in the long run fustian wears better than velvet." She had learned, too, she told herself in the first moments of her homecoming, that as long as she could rule her own mind she was not afraid of the forces without.

They had gathered round her. She was smiling and shaking the outstretched hands. "Well, it looked as if we'd about lost you for good." "You've been gone two years, ain't you?" "Hardly know Pedlar's Mill, I reckon, since Nathan's painted the store red?" "I saw her off," Mr. Kettledrum was saying over and over. "I saw her off. A good long visit, wasn't it?"

Moving out of the throng, she kissed Rufus, who looked dejected and resentful.

"How is Pa, Rufus?"

"There ain't any change. The doctor says he may drag on this way for several weeks, or he may go suddenly at any time."

"Well, we'd better start right on." Walking quickly up the slope to where the old buggy was standing, she put her arms round Dan's neck and laid her cheek against him. "He knows me," she said, "dear old Dan, he hasn't forgotten me. Is there anything you want for Ma at the store?"

"She gave me a list. I left it with Minnie May."

"Minnie May doesn't work in the store, does she? Who looks after the children?"

"She does. She does everything."

"Well, it's a shame. She oughtn't to, and only thirteen. I'll speak to Nathan about it."

At her commanding tone, Rufus grinned. "You've come back looking as if you could run the world, Dorinda," he observed with envy. "I wish I could go away. I'd start to-morrow, if it wasn't for Pa."

"Yes, that's why I came back. We can't leave Pa and Ma now. But it's hard on you, Rufus."

"You bet it is! It's my turn to get away next."

She assented. "I know it. If the time comes when Pa can do without you, I'll help you to go. You'll never make much of a farmer."

He stared moodily at the road, but she could see that her promise had encouraged him. "There's nothing in it," he answered, "I

499

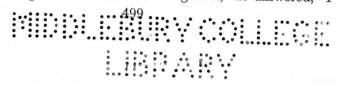

believe it is the meanest work ever made. You may slave till you drop, and there's never anything to show for it. Look at Pa."

"Pa never had a chance. He grew up at the wrong time. But all farming isn't bad. Suppose we had a dairy farm?"

He grinned again. "O Lord! with one cow! You're out of your head!"

"Perhaps. Anyway, I've come back to see what I can do."

Her glance wavered as Nathan, having dashed into the store with the mail bag, came toward them with the kind of lope that he used when he was in a hurry. "I didn't get a chance to speak to you at the train, Dorinda," he said, "but all the same I'm glad you're home again. The children want to get a peek at you in your city clothes. Minnie May's gone crazy about your veil."

In two years he had altered as little as the landscape. Lank, sand-coloured, with his loping stride, his hands that were all knuckles, and his kindly clown's face under hair that was as short as rubbed-off fur, he appeared to her, just as he used to do, as both efficient and negligible. Poor Nathan, how unattractive he was, but how good and faithful! Clean, too, notwithstanding the fact that he never stopped working. His face and neck looked well scrubbed, and his blue cotton shirt was still smelling of starch and ironing. The memory of the lunch he had given her when she went away was in her mind as she held out her hand to him and then stopped to kiss the children, one after one. How they must miss their mother, these children! She must do something for Minnie May, who had the stunted look of over-worked childhood. Nathan was well off for Pedlar's Mill, yet he let the little girl work like a servant. It was simply that he did not know, and she would make it her business, she told herself firmly, to instruct him. Minnie May was a nice, earnest child, with the look of her mother. She would be almost pretty, too, if she could get that driven expression out of her pinched little face. Her hair was really lovely, wheaten red like Rose Emily's, only it needed brushing, and she wore it dragged back from her forehead where, at thirteen, wrinkles were already forming. Yes, Dorinda decided, she would certainly speak to Nathan.

"You look fine, Dorinda," he was saying while he stared at her.

"She is like a paper doll in a book," Minnie May exclaimed. "One of those fashion books Miss Seena Snead has."

The three smaller children were staring with wide open eyes and mouths, and John Abner, the baby, she remembered, with the club-foot, was holding a slice of bread and butter in both hands. He limped badly when he walked, she noticed. What a job it must be keeping these children washed and dressed.

"Are you the nurse, too, Minnie May?" she inquired.

"Yes, I do everything," the little girl replied proudly, wrinkling her forehead. "We had a coloured girl, but the children didn't like her and wouldn't mind her."

Dorinda turned to Nathan. "It's too much, Nathan. You oughtn't to let her do it."

"I tell her not to slave so hard," he answered helplessly. "But it doesn't do any good. She promised her mother that she would take care of the children."

"But Rose Emily never meant this. It is making an old woman of the child before she grows up."

"I can't help it. She's as stubborn as a mule about it. Maybe you can do something."

Dorinda nodded with her capable air. "Well, I'll fix it." She looked cool, composed, and competent, the picture of dignified self-reliance, as she stepped between the muddy wheels of the dilapidated buggy.

"I hope you'll find your father better," Nathan said. "I'll come over later in the day and see if there is anything I can help about."

She smiled gratefully over her shoulder, and Rufus remarked, in his sullen, suppressed voice, as they drove off, "He's been over every single evening since Pa had his stroke."

"Nobody ever had a kinder heart," Dorinda responded absently, for she was not thinking of Nathan.

As the buggy jolted down the slope to the pine woods, a dogcart passed them on the way to the station, and she recognized Geneva Greylock. She was driving the dogcart with red wheels which she had used before her marriage; she was wearing the same jaunty clothes; but the change in her appearance made Dorinda turn to glance back at her. Though she was still in her early twenties, she looked like a middle-aged woman. Her sallow cheeks had fallen in, her long nose was bony and reddened at the tip, and her abundant flaxen hair was lustreless and untidy.

"How soon blondes break," Dorinda said aloud, and she thought, "Two years of marriage have made an old woman of her."

"Yes, she's lost what looks she ever had," returned Rufus. "She was always delicate, they say, and now her health has gone entirely. It's the life she leads, I reckon. Folks say he is beginning to follow in his father's footsteps. That's why the new doctor up by the Courthouse is getting all his practice." When he spoke of Jason he carefully refrained from calling his name.

"Are there any children?" Dorinda asked. Her spirits were drooping; but this depression, as far as she was aware, had no connection with Jason. Not her own regret, but the futility of things in general, oppressed her with a feeling of gloom.

"Not that I ever heard of," Rufus replied. "To tell the truth I never hear anybody mention his name. You can ask Nathan. He knows everything about everybody." He shut his sullen lips tight, and stared straight ahead of him.

"Oh, it doesn't matter. I was merely wondering why her health had failed."

They had come out of the woods, and the wheels were creaking over the dried mudholes. The sun had risen through a drift of cloud, and beneath the violent rim an iridescent light rained over the abandoned fields. While they drove on, it seemed to Dorinda that it was like moving within the heart of an opal. Every young green leaf, every dew-drenched weed, every silken cobweb, every brilliant bird, or gauze-winged insect; — all these things were illuminated and bedizened with colour. Only the immense black shadows of the horse and buggy raced sombrely over the broomsedge by the roadside.

"Nothing has changed," Dorinda thought. "Nothing has changed but myself."

Yes, it was all familiar, but it was different, and this difference existed only within herself. All that she had suffered was still with her. It was not an episode that she had left behind in the distance;

it was a living part of her nature. Even if she worked her unhappiness into the soil; even if she cut it down and burned it off with the broomsedge, it would still spring up again in the place where it had been. Already, before she had reached the house, the past was settling over her like grey dust.

They passed the Sneads' red brick house with white columns. The same flowers bloomed in the borders; the same shrubs grew on the lawn; the same clothes appeared to hang perpetually on the same clothes-line at the corner of the back porch. In the pasture the friendly faces of cows looked at her over the rail fence, and she remembered that two years ago, as she went by, she had seen them filing to the well trough. In a few minutes she would pass the burned cabin and the oak with the fading Gospel sign fastened to its bark. Her heart trembled. The racing shadow by the road appeared to stretch over the sunrise. She felt again the chill of despair, the involuntary shudder of her pulses. Then she lifted her eyes with a resolute gesture and confronted remembrance.

The place was unchanged. The deep wheelruts where the road forked; the flat rock on which the mare slipped; the cluster of dogwood which screened the spot where she had waited for Jason's return; the very branch she had pushed aside; not one of these things had altered. Only the fire in her heart had gone out. The scene was different to her because the eyes with which she looked on it had grown clearer. The stone was merely a stone; the road was nothing more than a road to her now. Over the gate she could see the willows of Gooseneck Creek. Beyond them the tall chimneys of Five Oaks lay like red smears on the changeable blue of the sky.

After they had left the fork, Dan quickened his pace.

"The fence has been mended, I see, Rufus."

"Yes, we had so much trouble with the cow straying. Pa was trying to get all the fences near the house patched before fall. We were using the rails that were left over from the timber he sold."

"Those weren't the woods Ma wrote me about?" She could never think of living trees as timber.

"No, he is holding on to that in hope of getting a better price."

They travelled the last quarter of a mile without speaking, and not until the buggy had turned in at the gate and driven up the rocky grade to the porch, did Dorinda ask if her father expected her.

"Yes, Ma told him, but she wasn't sure that he understood. He was awake before I left the place and Ma was seeing about breakfast."

"Haven't you had any yet?"

"Yes, I had a bite before I started. I'm no friend to an empty stomach, and I reckon I can manage a little something after I've turned Dan into the pasture. Pa was ploughing the tobacco field when he had his stroke, but he had decided not to plant tobacco there this year. We're going to try corn."

"I'm glad he's given up tobacco."

"He hasn't. Not entirely. But it takes more manure than he can spare this year. Well, we're here at last. Is that you, Ma?" he shouted, as the wheel scraped against the "rockery" by the steps.

At his second call, the door opened and Mrs. Oakley ran out on the porch.

"So you've come, daughter," she said, and stood wiping her hands on her apron while she waited for Dorinda to alight. How old she had grown, thought the girl, with a clutch at her heart. Only the visionary eyes looked out of the ravaged face through a film of despair as stars shine through a fog.

JAMES BRANCH CABELL

1879-

James Branch Cabell, most widely known contemporary Virginia man of letters, was born in Richmond on April 14, 1879. He was graduated in 1898 from William and Mary College, where he had served as instructor in French and Greek. In his early twenties he worked on newspapers in Richmond and New York. He published his first book, *The Eagle's Shadow*, when he was twenty-five. His subsequent biography is the record of his writing. With the announced purpose, "to write perfectly of beautiful happenings," he created the land of Poictesme and traced the "Biography of Dom Manuel" in eighteen volumes.

From the beginning he attracted a small and appreciative audience, but it was not until the publication of *Jurgen* in 1919, and its suppression, that Cabell became a national and international literary figure. When, two years later, the legal decision was handed down which lifted the ban on *Jurgen*, Cabell had become one of the most discussed writers in America. New editions of his earlier books were published and new titles appeared which ran into dozens of printings. A 73-page bibliography of the writings of Cabell appeared in 1924. Carl Van Doren published a study, *James Branch Cabell*, in 1925. H. L. Mencken added a brochure to the growing collection of work about Cabell in 1927. *Cabellian Harmonics*, by Warren A. McNeill, was published in 1928.

In 1927-1930 there appeared a definitive "Storisende" edition of the works of James Branch Cabell. The individual volumes, in the order in which they stand in the finished "Biography" (with the dates of their first publication), are: *Beyond Life* (1919), *Figures of Earth* (1921), *The Silver Stallion* (1926), *Domnei* (originally published in 1913 as *The Soul of Melicent), Chivalry* (1909), *Jurgen* (1919), *The Line of Love* (1905), *The High Place* (1923), *Gallantry* (1907), *Something About Eve* (1927), *The Certain Hour* (1916), *The Cords of Vanity* (1909), *From the Hidden Way* (1916), *The Rivet in Grandfather's Neck* (1915), *The Eagle's Shadow* (1904), *The Cream of the Jest* (1917), *Straws and Prayer-Books* (1924) and *Townsend of Lichfield* (1930).

With the conclusion of the "Biography," Mr. Cabell dropped the James from his name and as Branch Cabell has written a sizable body of work.

Among his later books are: *These Restless Heads* (1932), *Special Delivery* (1933), *Smirt* (1934), *Ladies and Gentlemen* (1934), *Smith* (1935), *Smire* (1937), *The King Was in His Counting House* (1938), *Hamlet Had an Uncle* (1940), *The First Gentleman of America* (1943) and *Let Me Lie* (1947). With the last title, Mr. Cabell resumed his full name.

The selection which follows, from *Straws and Prayer Books*, is a conversation piece between the youthful author of *The Eagle's Shadow* and the mature author of the finished "Biography."

THE AUTHOR OF THE EAGLE'S SHADOW*

1

"Would you advise me, sir," he was asking, "to become a regular writer — now?" For I had got just this far, and, as I have said, the clock behind me was just striking midnight, when I was interrupted by an unlooked-for visitor.

Most writers, for their sins, are used to the incursions of the literarily-inclined young man (with, as a rule, quite dreadful manuscripts hidden about his person) who wants advice as to his life-work. But that this especial young man should be calling upon me for that purpose, or for any other purpose, did, I confess, even on Walburga's Eve, astonish me. . . .

For he undeniably sat there. He was fat, remarkably fat for a lad of twenty-two or thereabouts; and he had, as I noticed first of all, most enviably thick hair, sleeked down, and parted "on the side" with some fanfaronade in the way of capillary flourishes. He was rather curiously dressed, too, I considered: the lapels of his coat were so abrupt and small and stiff that they must be held in place, I deduced, by a coat-spring, which would be to-day, I could have no doubt, the only coat-spring in existence. Then, too, he wore a fawn-colored waistcoat, and his rigorous collar towered, incredible in height, above a sky-blue "Ascot tie," which was resplendently secured with a largish sword-hilt asparkle everywhere with diamonds. And to describe the majestic rotundities of this boy's shoulders as due to "padding" would be, through understatement, to deceive you; since these coat-shoulders could have been designed and builded (I reflected), by no imaginable tailor, but only by an upholsterer. . . . It must have been, in fine, a good bit over twenty years since I had seen anybody appareled quite as he was. . . .

*From *Straws and Prayer-Books,* by James Branch Cabell. Published by Robert M. McBride & Co. Copyright 1924, 1930, by James Branch Cabell. Reprinted by permission of Farrar, Straus and Co.

"You see, I have just sold three stories to magazines," he continued, "and I was wondering, sir, if you would advise me to become a regular writer now."

To that I gave my customary, sage, and carefully considered reply. "Of course," I informed him, "there is a great deal to be said upon both sides."

"I wrote five, you see: and I mailed them all out together. And the *Smart Set* took one; and the *Argosy* took the one I sent them, too; and Mr. Alden wrote me a real nice letter about the one I sent *Harper's*, and said they would be very glad to use it if I would let them say 'paunch' where I had written 'belly' —"

"And so, already you are writing with offensive coarseness. But don't mind me. Go on."

"Well, but I was just going to say, and that's all right, of course, though you do sort of think of Falstaff as having one. But the other two came back, although I can't see why, when you look at the things those very magazines —!"

"You will see, by and by," I assured him: "and then you will wonder about the stories that did not come back."

"Anyhow, I got a hundred and five dollars for the lot of them. Yes, sir, not a cent less. And to have three out of five stick, the very first time, is pretty unusual, don't you think?"

To that I assented. "It is the bait in the trap, it is the stroke of doom, it is the tasted pomegranate of Persephone."

"Then I have the notion for a book, too. It's about a young man who is in love with a girl —"

"That now is a good idea. It is an idea that has possibilities."

"—Only, he can't ask her to marry him, because she has lots of money, and he is poor. Of course, though, it all comes out all right in the end. His uncle left another will, you see."

"Now was that will, by any chance," I wondered, "discovered some years afterward, in the secret drawer of an old desk? and did it transform your high-minded but impoverished hero into a multimillionaire?"

And the young man asked, "Why, how did you know?"

"It is not always possible to explain these divinations. Such flashes of imaginative clairvoyance just incommunicably come to me sometimes."

508

He considered this. He said, with a droll sort of awe,—

"Probably you do think of things quicker after you have been writing so long —"

I shook my head morosely. "Quite the contrary."

"And of course you have written so many books that — You see, I naturally wanted to read them, on account of our having the same names —"

"You liked them, I hope?"

Very rarely have I seen any young man counterfeit enthusiasm less convincingly. "Why, how can you ask that, I wonder! when everybody knows that your books, sir —!"

"Come, come!" I heartened him, "I have been reviewed a great deal, remember! the production of articles as to my plagiarisms and obscenities has, in my time, ranked as a national industry. Quite lately Judge Leonard Doughty exposed me to all Texas as a chancre-laden rat whose ancestry had mixed and simmered in the devil's cauldron of Middle Europe. And, besides, since Professor Fred L. Pattee let the news get out, in perfectly public print, that I am dead and my soul is already in hell, there does not seem much left for any moderately optimistic person to be afraid of."

"Well, but," the young man pointed out, "I'm not unbiased. There is so much about me in your books, you see, sir; and you do make me seem sort of funny. You sort of keep poking fun at me."

"I know. But I cannot help it. For you appear to me, I confess, the most ridiculous person save one that I have ever known. I am the other person."

"Well, I am afraid I don't entirely like your books, sir," he conceded.

And I sat looking at him, both amused and saddened. For never until to-night had it occurred to me how unutterably would this especial young man dislike my books if ever he could know of them. And he was trying so hard, too, to be polite about it.

2

"Why do you do it, sir?" the boy asked now, almost reproachfully. "You get a plenty of pleasure out of life, don't you? and what did you want, anyhow, that you never got?"

"Yes: and I don't know," I admitted, seriatim.

"Well, then, why don't you write some books that will make people see the world is a pretty good sort of place, after all?"

"Giséle —!" I answered. "But I forgot. You will not be meeting Miramon Lluagor's wife for some twenty years. . . . Meanwhile, as to the world's being, after all, a pretty good sort of place — Surely, it does not require two persons to point out such an obvious geographical feature? Cannot posterity rely upon you, by and by, to diffuse that truism single-handed?"

"I certainly do hope so," he replied. Now his voice changed. "For I would like to write the very nicest sort of books, — like Henry Harland's, and Justus Miles Forman's, and Anthony Hope's. They would be about beautiful fine girls and really splendid young men, and everything would come out all right in the end, so they could get married, and not be sort of bitter and smart-alecky and depress people the way" — he coughed, — "the way some people do."

"Young man," I started out severely, "it is quite evident you are not married —"

To which he countered, now I think of it, rather staggeringly. "But you, sir, are not in love. You never will be, sir, not ever any more."

I said: "Yes; that does make a difference. I remember." Then I said: "Stop talking bosh! and stop calling me 'sir'! I am not your grandfather. It is rather the other way round. And, besides, we were talking about books. Well, you may try, if you like, to write the blithering kind of novel you describe. But, somehow, I don't think you will ever succeed at it."

"You ought to know best, sir, of course, about my abilities. And so, if you would really and truly advise me — Still, I would certainly like to be a real author —"

He was looking at me now, across that remarkable blue tie and shiny sword-hilt, with very touching deference, and with, of all conceivable emotions, envy. I understood, with the most quaint of shocks, that I possessed every one of the things which this preposterous young fellow wanted. I had written and I had published, sometimes even with commercial extenuation, at least as many magazine stories and books as he hoped by and by to have to his credit:

510

James Branch Cabell, 1879-

I could imagine how my comfortable-looking large home, and my ownership of actual stocks and bonds, and my acquaintance with a number of more or less distinguished persons, would figure in his callow mild eyes: and I had tasted, too, if not of fame, most certainly of all the notoriety he ever aspired to. Why, but what does it not seem to this pathetic boy, I reflected, actually to have one's picture in the papers! For I could well remember certain ancient glancings toward that awesome pinnacle of being a celebrity.

I was, in fine, by this boy's standards, a success. I had to-day each one of the things he had ever consciously desired. That really was a rather terrible reflection. . . .

3

But he was speaking. "Then you would honestly advise me, sir, not to take up writing as a regular thing?"

"I don't see how I can advise you that, — not honestly, at least. For you will get out of the writing all — heaven help you! — that you hope to get."

"Why, then —" He was abeam.

"You simply wait until you have got it! You can attend to your grinning then, if you feel like it. For you will get every one of the things you think you want. Only, you will get them by the, upon the whole, most philanthropic process of not ever writing any of the mush which you now plan to write."

"But I don't understand —"

"Nor do I, either, quite. But from the start will be tugging at your pen a pig-headed imp that will be guiding it his way instead of the way you intended. And with each book he will be growing stronger and more importunate and more cunning, and he will be stealing the pen away from you for longer and longer intervals. And by and by that imp, full grown now and the very devil of a taskmaster, will be dictating your books from beginning to end, — not to speak here of his making you sweat blood when you revise, at his orders, all the earlier ones, and then after that, still at his orders, give over every day of three whole years to revising the entire lot, all over again, for what will be called the Storisende Edition —"

511

"Come, now," — and the young fellow was looking at me rather like a troubled cow, — "come, now, sir, but you don't really mean I am going to be possessed by a devil?"

"Some people will put it that way, only a bit less politely. But I would say, by a daemon. Socrates had one, you may remember."

"Yes, but this one —?"

"You," I replied, "will call him the desire to write perfectly of beautiful happenings. Other persons will call him quite different things. Anyhow, with time, you will fall into a sort of bedrugging daemon-worship, and you will go the way he commands you, without resisting any longer. It will be most deplorable. So Professor Henry A. Beers will have, after all, to dismiss your literary claims from the pale of serious consideration, because you are not of Colonial stock —"

The boy viewed this as urgent. "But, sir, my father's people came in 1727, and my mother's in 1619 —"

"That will not matter. Facts are but reeds in the wind of moral indignation. And Maurice Hewlett must become very cuttingly sarcastic about your being a Jew brought up on the Talmud —"

"Me, sir?"

"Most certainly, you. And a transfigured Richard Le Gallienne, purified by his intellectual death and descent into the helotage of reviewing, will be compelled to unmask you as a moral and spiritual hooligan with a diminutive and unkempt and unsavory ego. And an enterprising young person named Bierstadt will, on the strength of having twice had luncheon with you, write out for the *Bookman* a remarkably intimate account of how partial you are to provoking tragedies and throwing flesh-pots at people's heads. And there will be others — oh, quite a number of others. . . . So that, altogether, you perceive, you will get, through this daemon-worship, into some trouble."

Very rarely have I seen any young man more unaffectedly appalled. "But look here, sir! I don't want to get into any trouble. I simply want to contribute to the best magazines, and write some wholesome and nice, entertaining books, that will sell, like *The Cardinal's Snuff-Box* and *The Prisoner of Zenda.*"

"I know. It is rather funny that you should begin with just those goals in view. You will not ever attain them. That will not matter so much — after a while. But what will very vitally matter — to you, anyhow, — is that, having once meddled with the desire to write perfectly of beautiful happenings, you will not ever be able to forswear your daemon. And such folly is, of course, enough to set every really well-thought-of person in America braying. So that in time — who knows — you too may come to be a chancre-laden rat, and a German Jew with a soul in hell and simmered ancestors and a notoriously unkempt ego, and may otherwise help out with the week's literary gossip."

Whereon the young man rose; and he remarked, with a perhaps not wholly unwarranted uncertainty, "Then you advise me, sir —?"

"I cannot advise you the one way or the other, I am merely forewarning you that, if you insist upon writing books, you will get what you wanted."

He smiled now, brightly, intimately, strangely. "I see: but isn't that also in the one way which matters," he demanded of me, "true?"

And I smiled back at him, "Yes," I admitted, "it seems true in the one way which matters, also."

"Why, then," said he, "I reckon I had better keep right on with *The Eagle's Shadow.*"

After that he went quite suddenly away. He returned, I imagine, to 1902 or thereabouts.

I hope he did, for his sake. There was a rather nice girl awaiting him, back there in 1902. Then, in addition to her, he would have the facile, false inspirations of *The Eagle's Shadow* to play with, I reflected, as I went back, a little saddened somehow, to concocting the needed epilogue for the long Biography of Dom Manuel's life. . . .

4

But that queer boy's brief visit had quite broken my train of thought. His passing seemed, indeed, to have disproved my train of thought. For the instant I had proved, to my own satisfaction, that what I, in common with all creative writers, got out of writing was, exactly, nothing,—at that same moment he had appeared with his mild, bleated, so respectful question,—

"Would you advise me, sir, to become a writer — now?"

And I had answered his question. I had failed, at least, to advise him not to become "a regular writer." I had, virtually, admitted that were my youth restored to me, as Jurgen's was, and had I my life to muddle through all over again, I would, still somewhat in the Jurgenic manner, repeat that life's so unprofitable dedication. I could not deny to this pathetic boy, I could not truthfully deny to anybody, that, in the one way which really seemed to count, I had in the end got what I wanted.

5

No doubt it had been intermixed with a great deal which nobody could conceivably enjoy. From the beginning, my books had been strong irritants to many of their readers,— and indeed it well might be that their manner, as Dr. Canby put it, was "annoying to all warm-hearted people." In any event there were my scrapbooks bulging with "reviews" by persons who appeared to have written in seizures of incoherent rage, without ever having discovered precisely what they were angry about. These chattered denunciations had begun with *The Eagle's Shadow:* and no book by me had since failed to evoke them in respectable volume. . . . *The Cords of Vanity,* in fact, had seemed to unhinge all power of self-control and self-expression in well-nigh everybody who wrote about it: the scrapbooks which contained the press clippings relative to this novel suggested just the corybantics and mowings of a madhouse. The people who had at most length and most bitterly denounced "such a book as *Jurgen*" did at least base upon understandable ground their claims to be heard with respect,— this ground, of course, being that their judgment had been kept healthily uncontaminated by their abstention from reading *Jurgen*.

Nor was time outmoding this frenzy. *The High Place* appeared, just then, to have aroused in sundry quarters much the same quality of inexplicable or, in any event, of unexplained fury. There was no doubt about it: the instinctive reaction of many, many persons everywhere to each of my books — even, as it seemed, without reading one line in any of my books,— had been the instant, unreasoning response of a reputable business-man, or of a bull, to the Soviet flag. . . . And that had not been pleasant.

Apart from those who went about thus incommunicatively raging, had been the pitilessly explicit. These had, indeed, been tirelessly explicit in their exposure of my auctorial crimes and defects. Nobody could pretend to remember all the literary vices which I had practised, nor all the contagions in which I had been detected, but every one of these infamies had, as I recalled it, been competently exposed, over and over again. I was both knave and imbecile, whose "mannered" writing was mere kleptomania; I had, indeed, no sort of natural endowments once you excepted the singular nastiness of my feeble mind: such were the facts that had been quite regularly deplored, now I thought of it, for the fifth part of a whole century. And when the press clippings came in next week, somebody would, I knew, still be regretting these facts. I could have little doubt that for the rest of my life I would be continually encountering these envenomed regrets. . . . And that, too, was not pleasant.

What the reviewers had said did not, of course, especially and eventually, matter. They were, in fact, to-day united in their abuse nowhere except in my scrapbooks. I alone had — now for some twenty years, and rather charitably, I thought,— been at pains to preserve their utterances. Otherwise, all of yesterday's Olympians had loosed their thunderbolts and had passed sonorously; and each demolishing of me was to-day as little remembered as was any other of that year's thunderstorms. To-day — if with a lessened frequency, from even loftier altitudes, — still now and then descended peltingly the onslaughts of young godlings. Yet to-day I still clung, somehow, to the belief that my intelligence and my morals were not so markedly below the average as I was constantly assured. And, in the manner of those elder tempests, so likewise, I knew, must pass away the reverberant condescensions of the young, who were condemned as yet to appraise my book, and to appraise all books, in the light of their contrast with that masterpiece which youth is immemorially about to dash off on some vacant Saturday afternoon. For presently

515

these godlings too would turn from the serious work of reviewing creative literature to the diversion of writing it. . . .

And whatever any other formally empowered or free-lance commentator might futurely say, whether in print or conversation, about my stupidity and my crass plagiarisms and my self-conceit and my futile pruriencies, would not, I knew, matter either, in itself. The one trouble was that all this maintained a clouded and sulphuric atmosphere in which I dubiously moved, so far as went the thoughts of so many dear, dull persons. . . . Meanwhile I had got the hearing which throughout eighteen years of unreason I had hoped to get, and had always believed to be imminent; and the book which I had written, in the Biography of Dom Manuel's perpetuated life, was finished, more or less, and would for its allotted season remain. With the length, or, if you will, with the extreme brevity of that season, I had no concern: it was enough to know that the Biography was finished, and would outlast me.

6

For that infernal boy had drawn from me the truth: I really had got out of life what I most wanted: I had wanted to make the Biography of the life of Manuel: and I had made it, in just the way which seemed good to me. To do that had been, no doubt, my play and my diversion, in the corridors where men must find diversion, whether in trifling with bank notes or women, whether in clutching at straws or prayer-books, or else go mad: and my enlinked deductions held as far as the chain stretched.

But one link more was needed. For it seemed to me, too, that I had somehow fulfilled, without unduly shirking, an obligation which had been laid upon me to make the Biography. I was not, heaven knew, claiming for myself any heavenly inspiration or even any heavenly countenance. Rather, it seemed to me that the ability and the body and the life which transiently were at my disposal had been really used: with these lent implements which, properly speaking, were not ever mine, and which before long would be taken away from me, I had made something which was actually mine. That something was the Biography of Dom Manuel's life, an ended and perfected labor, at last. . . .

7

And still, —with all the bright day gone, and with the deepest gloom of midnight also an affair of the past,— still, I seem not quite to have found that final link, not wholly to have completed my epilogue. Some word, as yet unthought of, stays needed to round off all. . . .

Here then, upon this shelf, in these green volumes which contain the entire Life of Manuel in its final form, I can lay hand and eye upon just what precisely my own life has amounted to: the upshot of my existence is here before me, a tangible and visible and entirely complete summing up, within humiliatingly few inches. And yet, as I consider these inadequate green volumes, I suspect that the word I am looking for is "gratitude." It most certainly is not "pride"; and, as I hastily admit, nobody else is called on to share in my suspicion.

But I at least, who have found human living and this world not wholly admirable, and who have here and there made formal admission of the fact, feel that in honor one ought to acknowledge all courtesies too. With life, then, I, upon the whole, have no personal quarrel: she has mauled, scratched, and banged, she has in all ways damaged me: but she has permitted me to do that which I most wanted. So that I must be, I suppose, grateful.

— With which decision I very lightly pass my finger-tips across these eighteen book-backs; and touch in this small gesture, so didactically small, the whole of that to which, for good or ill, I have amounted. And thereafter (with a continuing sense of wholesome allegory) I go quietly to bed.

ANNE SPENCER

1882-

Anne Spencer is a poet of authentic talent whose work is less well known than it deserves to be, because she has never published a volume. Many years ago James Weldon Johnson, on a visit to Lynchburg, read a group of her poems with growing enthusiasm and urged her to "put a back and front to these sheets and send them to a publisher." It was advice which she has never taken, and her poems are known only through their scattered appearance in anthologies. Johnson himself published a selection of her work in 1922 in his *Book of American Negro Poetry*. Five years later a larger selection was published by Countee Cullen in his anthology, *Caroling Dusk*. More recently a selection of her poetry has appeared in *The Negro Caravan*, edited by Sterling A. Brown, Arthur P. Davis and Ulysses Lee. But neither publication by such editors nor the praise of such critics as Louis Untermeyer (in his *American Poetry since 1900*) has provoked her to the making of a book.

The poet was born on February 6, 1882, at Bramwell, West Virginia, and moved to Lynchburg, Virginia, when she was eleven. She was educated at the Virginia Seminary in Lynchburg, and has served for many years as librarian of the Dunbar High School there.

LIFE-LONG, POOR BROWNING . . .

Life-long, poor Browning never knew Virginia,
Or he'd not grieved in Florence for April sallies
Back to English gardens after Euclid's linear:
Clipt yews, Pomander Walks, and pleachéd alleys;

Primroses, prim indeed, in quiet ordered hedges,
Waterways, soberly, sedately enchanneled,
No thin riotous blade even among the sedges,
All the wild country-side tamely impaneled . . .

Dead, now, dear Browning lives on in heaven, —
(Heaven's Virginia when the year's at its Spring)
He's haunting the byways of wine-aired leaven
And throating the notes of the wildings on wing;

Here canopied reaches of dogwood and hazel,
Beech tree and redbud fine-laced in vines,
Fleet clapping rills by lush fern and basil,
Drain blue hills to lowlands scented with pines . . .

Think you he meets in this tender green sweetness
Shade that was Elizabeth . . . immortal completeness!

AT EASTER, FOR JIM

If ever a garden was Gethsemane,
with old tombs set high against
the crumpled olive tree — and lichen,
this, my garden, has been to me.
For such as I none other is so sweet:
Lacking old tombs, here stands my grief,
and certainly its ancient tree.
Peace is here and in every season
a quite beauty.
The sky falling about me
evenly to the compass . . .
What is sorrow but tenderness now
in this earth-close frame of land and sky
falling constantly into horizons
of east and west, north and south;
What is pain but happiness here
amid these green and wordless patterns, —
indefinite texture of blade and leaf:

Beauty of an old, old tree,
last comfort in Gethsemane

DOUGLAS SOUTHALL FREEMAN

1886-

Douglas Southall Freeman, biographer of Robert E. Lee and of George Washington, was born in Lynchburg, Virginia on May 16, 1886. He was graduated from Richmond College in 1904, and continued his studies at Johns Hopkins where he received his Ph.D. in 1908. Dr. Freeman was for a time a member of the staff of the Richmond *Times-Dispatch* and in 1913 he became associate editor of the Richmond *News Leader*. He has been editor of the *News Leader* since 1915.

Dr. Freeman's monumental four-volume biography, *R. E. Lee,* appeared in 1934 and was awarded the Pulitzer Prize that year. It was followed by the three-volume companion study, *Lee's Lieutenants,* in 1942-1944. The first two volumes of his *George Washington,* a biography projected upon an equally comprehensive scale, were published in 1948.

He is also the author of *The South to Posterity* (1939) and other studies in Southern history. Dr. Freeman's distinguished career has brought him many honors. He has received degrees from more than a score of colleges and universities and he holds a number of positions of trust and responsibility.

"The Last Parade," which follows, was first published in the *News Leader* on June 24, 1932, the last day of the forty-second annual reunion of the United Confederate Veterans. It was reprinted in book form the same year.

THE LAST PARADE*

They thronged the streets of this old town when Bonham brought his volunteers with their Palmetto flag in 1861. They cheered the lads who took up arms when first Virginia called. With doubtful glance they looked upon the men who hailed from New Orleans, the "Tigers" of the bayou state.

When Longstreet led his veterans from Centreville to hold the Yorktown line, all Richmond brought out food and flowers and draped the bayonets. When first the city heard the distant growl of Union guns, each regiment that came to strengthen Lee was welcomed as the savior of the South. The long procession of the carts that brought a groaning load across the Chickahominy from Gaines' Mill was watched with aching hearts.

Another year and solemn strains and mourning drums received the train that had the silent form of him who was the "right arm" of his famous chief. That was the darkest day, save one, that Richmond ever knew, for when the "stonewall" fell, the stoutest bulwark of the South was down. With Jackson dead, where was another such?

When Pickett's soldiers came, a shattered fragment of defiant wrath, to tell how hell itself had opened on that hill at Gettysburg, the townsfolk gazed as if on men who had upturned their graves. The months that followed saw a steady flow into the mills of death. Each night the sleeping street was wakened by the tread of veterans who hurried on to meet the sullen Meade or hastened back to check the wily Sheridan. The clatter of the horses' hoofs, the rumble of the trains, the drum at dawn, the bugle on the midnight air — all these the leaguered city heard till children's talk was all of arms, and every chat across the garden wall was punctuated by the sound of fratricidal strife.

*Reprinted with the permission of Dr. Douglas Southall Freeman.

Douglas Southall Freeman, 1886-

Ten months of thunder and of ceaseless march and then the end. Brave Custis Lee led out the last defenders of the town, and limping Ewell rode away while flames leaped up and bridges burned and Trojan women waited death. The next parade was set to fastest time, as up the hill and past St. Paul's and in the gates the Federals rode and tore with wildest cheers the still-defiant flag from off the capitol. Dark orgy in the underworld and brutish plunder of the stores, a wider stretch of fire, the mad rejoicing of the slaves, the sly emergence of the spies; and after that the slow return of one gray rider through the wreck of fanes and dreams, a solitary horseman on a weary steed, with only youth and age to pay him homage as he stopped before his door and bowed to all and climbed the steps and went within and put aside his blade to work for peace.

Excited days of preparation then, and pontoons thrown across the James. The army of the victor, Grant, the gossips said, was soon to march through Richmond and to see the ashes of the pinnacles on which its distant gaze had long been fixed. They came. In endless lines, all day they moved, all night, until the city's tearful folk became bewildered in their count and asked, How could the "thin, gray line" have stood so long against that host?

At last the blue-coats left and civil rule returned, in poverty and pain, but with a memory that made the humblest rich. The fallen walls were raised again, the peaceful smoke of busy trade rose where the battle-fumes had hung. For twenty years, the soldiers of the South remained behind the counter or the plow, until the day when Johnston led them out to lay the cornerstone of what the South designed to be a fit memorial to the matchless Lee. A few years more, and when the figure stood upon the pedestal, the word went out that every man who wore the gray should muster in the ranks again and pass before the chieftain on old Traveller. A day that was when love became the meat of life!

Reunions multiplied. A grateful city gladly threw its portals wide each time the aged survivors of Homeric strife returned to view the scenes of youth. A deep emotion rose as Forrest's troopers galloped past and Texans raised the "rebel yell." Today the city has its last review. The armies of the South will march our streets no more. It is the rear guard, engaged with death, that passes now. Who that remembers other days can face that truth and still withhold his tears? The dreams of youth have faded in the twilight of the years. The deeds that shook a continent belong to history. Farewell; sound taps! And then a generation new must face its battles in its turn, forever heartened by that heritage.

EMILY CLARK

1892-

Emily Clark was born in Richmond, Virginia on September 8, 1892, of a family which has long lived in the state. She grew up in Richmond, and during her childhood spent part of each year at her grandparents' home in southern Virginia. She prepared for Bryn Mawr in Richmond, but after passing the entrance examinations refused at the last moment to go to college. In February, 1921, she started the literary magazine, *The Reviewer,* in Richmond, and edited it until its issue of January, 1925, after which, under the editorship of Paul Green, the magazine was published at Chapel Hill, North Carolina. She contributed to the *Virginia Quarterly Review,* the *American Mercury,* the *Smart Set* and other magazines, and wrote book reviews for newspapers in Richmond, Baltimore, Philadelphia and New York. In 1927 she published *Stuffed Peacocks,* a collection of sketches from which "The Shade of Distinction" is taken. This was followed in 1931 by *Innocence Abroad,* which discusses a number of literary figures, including Amelie Rives, Ellen Glasgow and James Branch Cabell. In 1924 Miss Clark was married to Edwin Swift Balch of Philadelphia, in which city she now makes her home.

THE SHADE OF DISTINCTION*

When Miss Wilder heard that there was a really notable Gilbert
Stuart in the most improbable surroundings in the State, her pleasure was as vivid as her astonishment. For there seemed no doubt that
it could easily be removed by her to a background completely suitable. She had sometimes found it difficult, since coming South, to
carry out her irreproachable plans, because of an unaccountable
stubbornness in the fibre of the native population. Miss Wilder had
already spent the six most uncomfortable weeks of her life — her
superlatively effortless, luxurious life — in the most ancient commonwealth, with results which had, in a measure, repaid her. On the
whole, however, these results were not overwhelming. Relaxed in
the warm peace of her hotel sitting-room — a hotel which Palm
Beach and Aiken visitors were able to endure with serenity on their
way to and from the North — she contemplated her late experiences
in a number of the counties with the curious satisfaction that mortification of the flesh, safely past, can sometimes produce. She had
traversed the flat, yellow, sandy roads of Tidewater, and jolted over
the hilly, terra-cotta roads of Piedmont, in Fords. Most primitively
exciting of all her adventures, she had covered at least a part of
the gorgeous, lusciously sticky red mud of the Southside in a buggy,
with an elderly roan horse named General B. Gordon and a diminutive brown driver named Buster. It had been difficult for Miss
Wilder to address her courier so informally. She had asked him on
their first pilgrimage for his correct name, but if he possessed any
other, he was unaware of it, and she was forced to use the only name
available. It annoyed her, because it made her feel that a liberty
was being taken. Whether this liberty was being taken by herself
or Buster she could not precisely decide. Perhaps by both. Certainly
it placed her on an undesirably familiar basis, and at the same time

*From *Stuffed Peacocks*, by Emily Clark. Copyright 1927 by Alfred A.
Knopf, Inc. Reprinted by permission of Alfred A. Knopf, Inc.

detracted from the dignity of Buster's race. A dignity which she had been brought up to respect, but which did not, apparently, in the least disturb the people among whom she found herself at present.

Miss Wilder, through the possession of one of the largest fortunes in America, not exactly a new one either, because it was now two generations old, had been born in a position whose security was unquestioned in her own mind or the minds of her friends. The fact that her grandfather had created a remarkably successful soap in no way detracted from her distinction of appearance and manner. It did not, indeed, detract from an innate distinction of personality. No one who met her could possibly doubt that Miss Wilder was a lady, in every sense of that Victorian, justly scorned, but indubitably indispensable word. In spite of a New York house which faced the Park and a far more impressive establishment at Mount Desert, with, best of all, the knowledge that she could have as many other houses in as many other places as she chose, she had never been drawn into any of the more vulgar diverisons of the excessively rich. She was more conservative in mind and manner than some of those whose ancestors had made New York, long before Miss Wilder's grandfather had made soap. Her clothes were so triumphantly inconspicuous that only the close inspection of a trained eye could completely compass their expensive perfection. She was, in brief, unnoticeable in every way, and even, at times, wore her hat just a shade too far back on her well-brushed, uncurled head. And this, as all the world knows, is the final test of assurance and unshakable belief in oneself and one's position.

She had travelled, naturally, very widely, and spoke several languages quite beautifully in an exquisitely cultivated voice. Pictures were her deepest interest in life, and portraits and miniatures of early Americans her special branch of picture-collecting. An entirely sensible and estimable collecting fad, which saved many historic examples of excellent early America for lamentable later America, examples that, in this poverty-stricken section, might otherwise be scattered Heaven knew whither. Of course in New England it was different. Things were, in the main, well preserved there, perhaps because there had been so little in the beginning. All of which shows that Miss Wilder was by no means a mere rich, flamboyant New Yorker, come down to jeer at the nakedness of the land and the shiftlessness of its inheritors and inhabitants, but a right-thinking, well-bred person who could not only meet the most unyielding, native old lady, but meet with the approval of the same old lady. She was completely prepared for genteel poverty, for the special sort of pride which conceals or ignores it, expecting others to do likewise, and to treat this pride with tenderness and delicacy. She had encountered its like in Boston and Philadelphia, and even occasionally in New York. But in the counties her ideas had been a trifle upset. There was pride enough, to be sure, but of the sort which speaks carelessly and openly of deplorable conditions rather than attempts to veil them.

Moreover, these people did not know how to get the best results from the few desirable things they possessed. They clung, in many cases, to their pictures with peculiar tenacity, although now and then they had parted with them in order to make necessary repairs in their houses. But they had usually failed to dispose of them to the best advantage, and the owners of the pictures had sometimes been deceived as to their real worth. In spite of all ill-fortune some really good paintings, Copleys, St. Memins, Peales, Gilbert Stuarts, and Sullys, still remained in the State. The inhabitants were more inclined to part with books than with pictures. In its present era the commonwealth could, by no stretch of the imagination, be called literary. Miss Wilder had heard that in an early golden age — say, the forties — it had been so. But in the back of her exceedingly well-trained mind Miss Wilder permitted herself a small doubt concerning the authenticity of this legend. True, there were "gentlemen's libraries" scattered about, but it scarcely seemed that these libraries had been the important preoccupation of their owners. Planting, fighting, law-making, and attending to the majestic affairs of the Church had filled the larger portions of their existence. In one house, notably, already draped with a blanket of mortgages, whose nice, steep old steps were beginning to tumble down, there had been a rather fine eighteenth- and early-nineteenth-century library in the best classical tradition. Unpardonably, this library had never been appraised, but had been sold piecemeal, whenever a stray purchaser desired a book, or perhaps two or three books at a time. The proceeds of these casual sales were thrust into a pigeon-hole of the shabby secretary, and when a member of the family needed immediate cash, a bill was extracted.

Certainly the progenitors of this breed were even less occupied with painting pictures than with writing books, but pictures represented the family in a more direct way than books could ever do. Therefore pictures were harder to buy. Miss Wilder could well understand that a portrait removed from a colonial wall, or even a miniature from a colonial desk or mantelpiece, might leave an unpleasant, yes, a reproachful, vacancy. But in the affair of the rumoured Stuart she was hopeful, positively buoyant, for she had heard that its home was almost squalid, and that its owners were persons who had so far degenerated that they could not possibly be appreciative of its artistic, or its particularly historic, value. Miss Wilder knew what degeneration could mean. In some of the counties she had encountered specimens of it in people whose ancestors had governed and made laws for the American people generations before her grandfather was born to cleanse them with his superior soap. And Miss Wilder, without abnormal conceit, could not help knowing that she, the product of only two generations, was thoroughly adequate in every obligation of her existence. These specimens had, it appeared, been happily ignorant of almost everything worth knowing, but had managed to maintain, somehow, an unaccountable superiority to circumstances. This superiority may, it is true, have been attributable solely to complacency, in which quality they were without peers. Who were they, she wondered, what had they done, what, indeed, had their ancestors done, to make their descendants so sure that all was well with them, and equally sure that much was wrong with the outside world?

But in the matter of the historic Stuart there was no estate as a background, nor, Miss Wilder had heard, a single servant to support the assumption to which she had now become accustomed. And she knew the household was desperately in need of money, consisting as it did of an old woman and her unmarried daughter. The only son had married as badly as he might have been expected to marry, and had moved to another city.

The hour arrived for Miss Wilder's appointment at this house, and with it her car, which had waited for her here at her headquarters while she spiritedly roamed the country-side in hired Fords. In an extremely short time she stood in the dark, narrow hallway of the incongruous shrine of the Stuart, conversing with the daughter of its owner. Miss Wilder's manner was, as always, perfection, as she asked if she might see, immediately, the picture. The girl, whose colouring, figure, and voice left a blurred impression of vagueness, took her into a room which was all that Miss Wilder had anticipated from the hall. A musty room, furnished sparsely with drab horrors. A withered little woman rose to receive them. Could it be possible, thought Miss Wilder, that these were authentic descendants of the celebrated soldier whose beautiful wife had been painted, in admiration, by Stuart? Did they themselves fully realize the connexion? For they had long since lost all claim to social position, even in the State which their family had helped to make. And how much comfort could be bought with the price which she was willing to pay! She would not dream of using their probable ignorance for her own profit. They were, obviously, ignorant of much. That was clear from their conversation and their ideas of decoration. After a suitable period — Miss Wilder never did anything unsuitably — of desultory conversation she asked to see the Stuart. The little old woman, whose wraith-like appeal was not shared by her daughter, moved across the room and with her claw-like, small fingers indicated the strip of wall next the window. From its shabby surface shone a face of rose and blue and gold. It was the wife of the great American, and all her radiance rightfully belonged to the two shadowy women. This was what a period of unendurable poverty had robbed them of. And this was what an equal period of ease and beauty had done for Miss Wilder. Miss Wilder, who was, beyond all doubt, a lady.

That dead, smiling lady of gold and blue and rose would unquestionably be more at home in the setting which awaited her with Miss Wilder. How lightly detached she seemed here.

"Yes," the little old woman was saying, with a voice and enunciation that proved the length and completeness of her separation from her own kind, "people often come to look at her. She's such a pretty thing, and the General's wife besides."

"Have you ever had a price fixed for the picture?" hesitatingly asked Miss Wilder.

The two amazing descendants of the loveliest of ladies looked blankly puzzled.

"Why, no," replied the daughter, "why should we?"

Miss Wilder put up her hand to touch the smooth, rose ivory face of the ancestress who had been almost as conspicuous as her husband in Virginia, in Washington, in Philadelphia, while her own thoroughly commendable forbear was dealing competently with fate, weather, and Indians in her staunch log-cabin, and thought how miraculously the laws of evolution and decadence were bringing this colourful and distinguished shade to her ultimate and proper haven on Fifth Avenue. She delicately mentioned a sum which sounded large even to her. "That is what the picture is worth," she said, "and I will pay it."

"You will pay it," echoed the mother. "What does she mean, Annie?"

"I don't know mother, she only said she wanted to see the picture. Lots of people do."

"I mean," patiently explained Miss Wilder, "that I want to buy the portrait."

"Buy the portrait," repeated the little old woman again, parrot-like. "But you can't buy the portrait, you know. It's not for sale. It's a member of the family."

LEIGH HANES

1894-

Leigh Hanes was born at Montvale, Bedford County, Virginia, on December 24, 1894. He grew up in Virginia, attended public school there, and was graduated from Hampden-Sydney College in 1916. He entered the law school of Washington and Lee University, received his LL.B. in 1920, and was admitted to the Virginia Bar the same year. He has been a practicing attorney in Roanoke, Virginia, since 1920.

In September, 1929, he became editor of *The Lyric,* a Virginia quarterly of verse established in 1921, and has edited it continuously since then. He has lectured extensively on poetry, and has taught courses on English and American poetry at Hollins College and for the Extension Division of the University of Virginia. He was awarded a Litt.D. degree by Hampden-Sydney College in 1936, and in 1938 received an M.A. from Washington and Lee University and was elected to Phi Beta Kappa.

His first collection of poetry, *Song of the New Hercules and Other Poems,* was published in 1930, and a new edition appeared in 1933. A second collection, *Green Girdle,* was published in 1939, and has gone through four printings. A third collection, tentatively entitled *The Star That I See,* is now in preparation.

SCREECH OWLS*

Once every summer, in an emerald light,
I watch the little screech owls try their wings
For the first time, between the dusk and night
   Eerie with quaverings.

But whence they come I never yet have known,
Save that the woods seem full of owlet doors,
And come they do, ubiquitously blown
   In two's and three's and four's,

Till suddenly I have become aware
Of wizened faces, cowled heads awry,
And eyes that stare as only owlets stare
   Before they tilt and fly:

Leaving me there in darkness to surmise
How well it goes with owlets in their flight,
And silent wings, and fixed nocturnal eyes
   Needing no outer light.

*From *Green Girdle*, by Leigh Hanes. Copyright 1939 by The Lyric Press. Reprinted by permission.

STRINGFELLOW BARR

1897-

Stringfellow Barr was born at Suffolk, Virginia, on January 15, 1897. He attended the University of Virginia, was awarded a Rhodes Scholarship and attended Balliol College, Oxford, and later studied at the Sorbonne and the University of Ghent. He taught history at the University of Virginia from 1924 to 1936, and was editor of the *Virginia Quarterly Review* from 1930 to 1934. In 1936 he left the University of Virginia to become visiting professor of liberal arts at the University of Chicago. The following year he became president of St. John's College at Annapolis, where he instituted a new curriculum, which became widely known as the St. John's Program, based upon the study of some 100 great books. He has lectured widely throughout the country on the problems of liberal education, and as a member of the adult education board of the Columbia Broadcasting System he originated the radio program, *Invitation to Learning*, based on the books of the St. John's curriculum. In 1947 he resigned as president of St. John's College to establish a college along similar lines in Massachusetts.

Mr. Barr is the author of *Mazzini: The Portrait of an Exile*, and he has been a frequent contributor to periodicals. "The Pig," which follows, is from *Three Fables*, which was issued by the Madison Lane Press at the University of Virginia in 1932.

THE PIG*

I have a friend down near Smithfield, a pig, who lives in a pigpen built for his special use. There is not another animal on the farm where he lives who receives half his attention now that the fattening season is on. I had occasion to visit him recently at the hour when he was being fed. A bucketful of shelled corn had been poured into his pen, and the bright golden grains lay in his trough, in the mud beside it, and even in the long bristles of his neck behind his ears. He seemed bathed in plenty. He was eating with that enormous chuffling noise with which not only pigs, but people too, eat Indian corn.

At this hour most of his friends avoid him, but I frankly prefer it for visiting, since it is when he is buried in corn that he comes nearest to ecstasy, and I like to share his simple joys. Moreover I do not mind him when he chuffles; it is when he sloshes that I hate him. This occurs when he is being slopped. I was therefore glad to find him on this occasion at his cereal. While he chuffled and snorted and crunched and grunted, I greeted him in my accustomed vein.

"Hello, you *are* looking well!" I cried. "What shoulders you are getting! As the time for cutting throats draws near, I declare one can scarcely dissociate you from your mountain of acquired flesh. Yet it becomes you too. What have you been up to since I left?"

"It is very kind of you," he snorted out between mouthfuls, "to remind me of fall killing. After all it is a fate that awaits everyone alike and had best be forgotten. One must make the best of things as they are. As for what I have been doing, I have not been making clever remarks. I have lived simply, feeding thrice daily — and plentifully enough too, I thank God, though lately the slops have seemed a trifle rich—"

"You infuriate me," I said simply. "I can keep my temper, for-

*From *Three Fables*, by Stringfellow Barr. Copyright 1932 by The Madison Lane Press. Reprinted by permission.

tunately, by looking at your absurd shoulders. But underneath I am angry. Each time I visit you, I shudder afresh. I then try to laugh it off with a little sarcasm, but it won't work. You are gross, you are impervious, you are preposterous.

"I am sure, my dear fellow, that you are not lying when you say you have made no clever remarks. I am sorry your slops grow too rich. No doubt your habit of living simply and bathing in your food thrice daily, as you put it, has the ultimate effect of changing your standard of simplicity. In that case refuse that before seemed juicy would then seem too heavy for you. I am not a dietitian and anyhow I should not choose to tamper with your diet for fear of defeating the very purpose of your existence."

"And what," he asked, sucking out of the mud about him one or two stray yellow grains, "what do you consider that purpose to be?"

I detest him when he picks his words and discriminates in his meanings; so I replied brutally: "Why, to be born, to get fat, and die with as few heart-rending, ear-splitting screams as possible. Dying under the knife, I think they call it. Surely that *is* your destiny, if I grasp the full significance of this pen. Then let's not be sentimental about it."

"I do not wish to be sentimental," he answered plaintively. "I am grateful for this chance of discussing my destiny with you. I have often wondered lately what would be your comment on my present life." He stopped, braced himself on all four legs, and leaning against a sharp corner of his trough, swayed backward and forward chafing his hide voluptuously.

"Fleas," he grunted parenthetically, "if anything, worse this week than last. Or perhaps those rich slops are irritating my skin. . . . Now, about my destiny, there is a good three hours' time for discussing it before my slops are brought out. Let us be frank with one another and perhaps we can be of mutual service. Service! Now that's what I wanted to discuss with you. That is my idea of life: to serve others — to eat my slops without grumbling, to put up with those fleas I can't rub off, and if I must die, to do it willingly with the knowledge that by me others may live and dine as I have dined."

"I see: to be slopped regularly and to serve others — including fleas. I begin to grasp your problem: unlike your ancestors, you do not have to bother about food and shelter; like them, fleas suck your blood hourly; unlike them, your death by violence in the prime of life is certain. Do you know, I think I should have preferred your ancestors to you."

"My mother once told me," he replied with what he evidently intended for quiet dignity, "that they were not happy; and that civilization, whatever clever people might say about it, had at least brought us pigs security."

"Your mother must have been a clever sow," I replied.

"On the contrary," he said stiffly, "she was like me, simple, unable or unwilling to make epigrams, and ready to do her duty."

"In short, an anti-intellectual. No, my good chap, it is no use. I hate you, too much even to discuss philosophy with you. You are the flea-bitten, filthy, over-fed son of a flea-bitten, filthy, over-fed mother. I hate you both. For you are not only flea-bitten, filthy, and over-fed; you like fleas and filth and food. You have no soul. I once liked you, because of the way your tail wiggled nervously. I took it as a sign of some small buried discontent —"

"Oh, I *am* discontented. Often, at night, when I have eaten rather heavily, and I ache all through the center of my body I lie awake and wonder what it is all for, what can be the immutable purpose that condemns me to fleas, why my slops should suddenly become too rich for me, and whether I am really serving others to the best of my ability. And then—"

"And then you nod off, I suppose.'

"Yes," he admitted, "but not without great agony of soul. For I *have* got a soul, truly. Nobody without a soul could possibly suffer as I have suffered. Ah, I can see that your heart is softened. Let us talk about the verities, about what It all means, about—"

And suddenly he raised his snout sharply, wrinkled his nose, and sniffed. Incredulity spread itself all over his foolish face. A sudden fierce joy seized him, and a wild light came into his eyes. "Slops!" he said tensely. "At first I couldn't believe it. But it is; it really is my slops. Oh, I *am* happy. Perhaps," and he inclined his head gallantly, "they are in your honor. They are fully three hours ahead of time. I am sure they are in your honor."

MURRELL EDMUNDS

1898-

Murrell Edmunds was born at Halifax, Virginia, on March 23, 1898, of a family which has long lived in Virginia. His grandfather, Paul Carrington Edmunds, was a member of Congress from Virginia, and his family includes a member of the first Supreme Court of Virginia and a member of the first Congress of the United States from Virginia. He grew up in Lynchburg, went to public school there, and attended the College and the Law School of the University of Virginia. He taught and coached at the Episcopal High School in Alexandria for a year and entered the practice of law in Lynchburg in 1922. He now lives in New Orleans and devotes his time wholly to writing. His first book, *Poems,* was published in Richmond in 1923. *The Music-Makers,* a novel, appeared in 1927; *Earthenware,* a collection of short stories, in 1930; and *Sojourn among Shadows,* a novella, in 1936. In his later work he has been increasingly concerned with themes of freedom and human brotherhood in the South. *Between the Devil,* a novel about Virginia, was published in 1939; *Red, White and Black: Twelve Stories of the South* in 1945; and *Time's Laughter in Their Ears,* a novel, in 1946. A Danish translation of *Time's Laughter in Their Ears* was published by Skandinavisk Bogforlag of Odense, Denmark, in 1947, and an edition for distribution in Czechoslovakia is now in preparation. A new book, a short novel entitled *Behold, Thy Brother,* is scheduled for publication in 1949. "Prelude," which follows, is from *Red, White and Black;* when it was originally published it was placed on the Honor Roll of the American Short Story by the late Edward J. O'Brien.

PRELUDE*

As soon as he come into the house, I knew he had done it. I knew his mind was made up. My heart near stopped beating. His face was all lit-up and shining and he didn't look worried no more, and everything he done was kind of free and easy, like somebody had done lifted a heavy burden from off his chest.

I hadn't even took off my clothes, I had been setting there in front of the stove all night long waiting for him, and the sight of his face skeered me a little. So I says, "Son, here 'tis almost morning, and you didn't come home for your supper again tonight. I don't know what's got into you lately, never coming to your meals and staying out half the night with God knows what sort of people."

Now he ain't had a job for six months, but he says, "I been busy here lately, ma, there's a powerful heap of work for a man to do these days."

And then he throwed back his head, like he was laughing, but the sound what come from his mouth didn't sound like nothing funny to me. I noticed how white he looked in the light from the lamp and how old and wrinkled-up his face was for just a boy. It made me feel sick all over. I knew who he had been going with and I knew what sort of doings he had been up to without him telling me.

So I says, "Them Reds is agoing to get you into trouble, son. You better 'tend to your own business and obey the law and let them Reds alone."

But he just keep on laughing, like he was doing before without nothing funny or happy in it, and says, "You better not talk about them Reds like that no more, ma, you liable to hurt my feelings. Yes," he says, "you liable to hurt your own son's feelings. *Us* Reds," he says, "*us* Reds is got aplenty to do without no bad advice, and we

*From *Red, White and Black: Twelve Stories of the South,* by Murrell Edmunds. Published by Bernard Ackerman, Inc. Copyright 1945 by Murrell Edmunds. Reprinted by permission.

aims to do it." That's what he says, and he thinks I don't know what's on his mind, and he keeps right on: "And when I ain't here for supper," he says, "just wash up the dishes and put 'em away, ma, because I'll be busy."

And he laughed some more. "And when I stays out late at night, you just rest easy in your bed, ma, because I'm in good company with a lot of other people. They's a hunderd millyun of us, ma," he says, "scattered here and there about the world if you'd only stop to count us. Us workers is more numerous like the sands of the sea, ain't we?" he says, "and we is just beginning to find it out, and we ain't got no time for sleeping even in the night time."

Well, I knew where he had got all that kind of talk from, and I didn't like it. Not that I ain't had my full share of misery from the mills, girl and woman, wife and mother, God knows I have! I give a husband to 'em, and three sons before Jim, and I hate 'em and them what owns 'em, God knows I do!

But I been around here a long time, and I know what comes from fighting 'em. I seen plenty of men try before. And when I hear my boy, Jim, which is just a kid and the only thing I got left in the world, running his lip off about standing up against the bosses, about collecting all the workers together to fight 'em, I got memories that come to me and send cold chills up my back, and I ain't got no more strength or reason than a baby.

So I says, fighting for time, "Look here, son, I ain't young no more and I ain't strong, and I ain't got nothing in this world left but you. Now I can't make no kind of argument with you since you is too smart for me. But I got this thing all figured out in my own way setting in front of this stove all night long waiting for you, and I ask you to set here a minute and listen to me."

'Twas getting on toward daylight. Through the window I see a little yellow creeping up behind the mountains and I know it ain't long before the sun comes popping up like it was shot from a cannon. I ain't got much time I know, so I pulls up a chair beside the stove for Jim and tells him to set down.

"All right," he says, hesitating a minute and then setting down, "spill it, ma," he says, "but make it fast, because I ain't got but a few minutes and then I got to be leaving here."

540

Murrel Edmunds, 1898-

Now I been here a long time and I keep my ears open and I knew where he was going and what he was going for. Today was the day the bosses was going to start putting everybody outa mill houses what hadn't paid their rent, and I had heard all the talk that had been going around in Milltown, since the Reds come, about not standing for it no more, about all the mill people joining together to keep themselves and their wives and children from being thrown out into the streets by the bosses.

So I says, "Look here, son, you better think twice before you go to fighting with the bosses." He lifts his head kind of surprised, but I didn't give him a chance to say nothing. "The bosses," I says, "will get the best of you in the end, no matter what you do. You only got one chance with 'em — if you act meek and humble and keep your mouth shut and work your heart out for 'em, they'll give you enough to keep living so you can keep on making money for them. That's your only chance, son, the way things are between you and the bosses. But if you act foolish, if you go around talking too much, if you try to fight 'em, they'll hate you and spy against you and — and kill you. Now . . ."

But Jim had done jumped to his feet. "Look here, ma," he hollers, "you don't mean nothing like that. You is just so skeered for me, you done stopped thinking sense. I won't listen to that kinda talk from you, ma, or nobody else," he hollers, "I done already made up my mind, and it ain't no use for you to try to fool me. I ain't got time to argue with you, but they's a hundred millyun of us, ain't they? and we is more numerous like the sands of the sea, ain't we, ma? And if we just stick together, if we stand by each other and fight for each other and don't take nothing more off of the bosses, we is bound to win in the end, ain't we? even if some of us does get killed?"

Well, he looked so serious standing there by the stove with the yellow sky behind him that I couldn't say nothing, not a word. He grabs me by the shoulders, his eyes shining, "They been killing us all the time, ma, that's what you got to understand. Look at pa," he says, his voice calmer; he had done stopped shouting, "and Ed and Joe and Sam," he says, naming his brothers what died from the mills in one way or another, direct or indirect; "the ground around

541

here is red with the blood of us workers now, ain't it, ma? And ain't nobody gonta stop it, but ourselves, us workers," he says. "Yes," he says, "they got guns and they got cops and they got money and they got power, but, ma, they's a hunderd millyun of us, ain't they? and we is more numerous like the sands of the sea."

I couldn't say a word. I just set there in front of the stove. I knew I had lost him, I had knowed it all the time, but he was my only son left and I got to be excused for fighting for him a little.

But I didn't say nothing — I knew there wan't nothing I could do, nothing wan't gonta stop him now, not cops, not soldiers, not bosses, not mothers, not nothing. My boy had done fell in love with something you couldn't put your hand on like a woman and love her up for a night or two and then forget her. My boy had done give himself away to something men don't never grow tired of, and there wan't nothing I could do about it.

So I didn't say a word. When he finished talking and goes into his room and I see him through the door taking down the old rifle his pa used to shoot squirrels with in the mountains before we ever come to these God forsaken mills, I don't open my mouth. He come back into the room and stands there with the risen sun behind him, holding that gun in his two hands and looking at me. And I don't say a word, I don't open my mouth.

"So long, ma," he says, his voice a little shaky, "I got to be leaving here."

"All right, son," I manages to say, and can't move outa my chair to save my life, I got such a sudden pain across my chest.

"So long, ma," he says again, like he had forgot he said it once already, "don't you fret none, they ain't got nothing to be skeered of."

"All right, son," I says, "take keer of yourself wherever you goes."

I set paralyzed in my chair by the stove and watch him go down the street, half running, with that old squirrel rifle of his pa's crooked over his right arm. When he come to the corner and I can't see him no more, I jumps up and run after him. I says to myself all of a sudden, "Wherever Jim goes, I gotta go, too!"

I can't keep back the tears no more, and as I run after him I hear my own breath coming and going like it was somebody else running along beside me. When I reach the corner, I see him way down the street.

"Son," I yell, "Jim, you wait for me!"

But he don't hear me. I hadn't slept none and I'm getting weaker and weaker all the time, and the heavy panting is tearing the guts out of me. My head starts going round and round and I can't see which way to go. Pretty soon somebody grabs me and I collapses.

"What's wrong here?" I hear somebody holler, way off, and then somebody hollers again, "what's wrong with her?"

"Us workers," I says, "us Reds . . ."

"What's that?" somebody asks closer to me, "who's dead?"

"We're a hunderd millyun, ain't we?" I yell. "We is more numerous like the sands of the sea, ain't we?"

CRADDOCK EDMUNDS
1899-

Craddock Edmunds was born at Halifax, Virginia, on August 5, 1899. He is the brother of Murrell Edmunds. He went to school in Lynchburg, received his A. B. degree at Randolph-Macon College and his M. A. at the University of Virginia. He enlisted in the army during the first World War and was taking officers training at Camp Lee, Virginia, when the armistice was signed. His first book, *Ulysses and Other Poems,* was published in 1923. It was followed by *Mass* (1927), *Geese Are Swan* (1929), *Poems* (1931), *The Renaissance* (1932) and *Five Men* (1937). *Twenty Nine Poems,* his collected work to that date, was published in 1940. As its prefatory note, Edmunds wrote: "In addition to its new poems, this book contains all of the published work that I care to save." He lives at Halifax, Virginia.

❦

MARCH*

For seven days a bird has throttled his song
As if afraid winter was still in our lands
And might creep back to strangle it with icy hands.

Now he knows that winter has gone;
And with a long-drawn note,
He sends the beauty of all dead springs out of his throat.

*March and Nocturne are from Twenty Nine Poems, by Craddock Edmunds. Copyright 1940 by Craddock Edmunds. Reprinted by permission.

NOCTURNE

I have watched night, like some calm benediction
Pronounced by nature at the close of day,
Walk with drowsy feet up this steep way;
Then while the strident friction
Of iron and steel becomes a muffled sound,
Have seen her put her long, black fingers down
As if to heal all living.

                  This is not so,
    for though content has a quieter face,
    and joy grows lithe with a quicker grace,
    there is no pain or secret woe
    but night makes sharp and deeper.
    There is no fear but night makes grow
    to broader girth.
    And there is no crime but night—
    a giant midwife—
    broods by the bedside and gives it birth.

I have watched night, like some calm benediction
Pronounced by nature at the close of day,
Walk with drowsy feet up this steep way
As if to heal all living.

545

VIRGINIUS DABNEY

1901-

Virginius Dabney was born on February 8, 1901, at the University of Virginia, where his father, Richard Heath Dabney, was professor of history. He is the grandson of Virginius Dabney (1835-1894), author of *The Story of Don Miff*. He grew up in Virginia and attended the University of Virginia. He taught for a year, but in 1922 left teaching for journalism and served as a reporter for the Richmond *News Leader* until 1928. In 1928 he joined the editorial staff of the Richmond *Times-Dispatch* and became chief editorial writer in 1934. He has been editor of the *Times-Dispatch* since 1936. He is the author of *Liberalism in the South* (1932) and *Below the Potomac* (1942), and has contributed to a number of magazines. He was awarded the Pulitzer Prize in 1948 for distinguished editorial writing.

AN APPROACH TO VIRGINIA*

We Virginians modestly admit our superiority to citizens of all other American states, just as any Southerner will readily concede that he can handle a Northerner without half trying, whether it be inside the squared circle, at the brass rail, or with derringers at ten paces. The only other Southerners who are equally adept with us at looking down their noses at outsiders are the South Carolinians, who, in fact, have been known to look down theirs at Virginians. It will be seen, therefore, that an encounter between a Charlestonian and a Richmonder suffers not at all by comparison with the proverbial and justly-famed *rencontre* between Greek and Greek.

There is also that little matter of Virginia's relationship to North Carolina. In other days, denizens of Tarheelia were more restrained in their behavior, which led me to remark to my friend, Jonathan Daniels, not long ago: "Perhaps one of the best reasons for the change is that for some twenty years, we Virginians have been try-ing not to slide gradually into that "valley of humiliation" which, we naively imagined, had been reserved exclusively for our neighbors to the South. First we were startled at finding ourselves taunted in the middle 1920's with the fact that North Carolina was building her highway system much more rapidly than we. Then almost simul-taneously the University of North Carolina entered a *resorgimento* which has lasted until the present day, and little Trinity College nearby was left some $40,000,000 by James B. Duke, on condition that it change its name to Duke University. I do not pretend to speak for South Carolina, the other "mountain of conceit" flanking the "valley of humiliation" in the ancient and apocryphal saying, but certainly these two states are being put on their mettle by the progress, both material and spiritual, which North Carolina has ex-hibited in the past two decades.

*A review of Virginia Moore's *Virginia Is a State of Mind*. From the special Southern issue of *The Saturday Review of Literature*, January 23, 1943. Copy-right, 1943. Reprinted by permission.

Virginia Reader

It is noteworthy, however, that such matters are largely outside the field of interest of Miss Virginia Moore, in her lately published book, "Virginia Is a State of Mind." The commonwealth which she examines is primarily the Virginia of history and legend. Miss Moore does not treat of the state as it is today, except in certain limited spheres. She is concerned, for example, with contemporary Virginia batterbread, and Virginia literature, Virginia watermelon and Virginia sunsets, but not at all with the state's industry, agriculture, economics, or politics. She is fully conscious of Jamestown and Williamsburg, of George Washington and Patrick Henry, but such mundane matters as the rise of industrialism, the Negro problem, the poll tax, and the price of tobacco, are not within her ken.

However, Miss Moore obviously did not set out to write a sociological treatise. Her avowed purpose was to discover and to adumbrate the "quintessence of Virginia." She felt that this could best be done by considering the Old Dominion under five general headings: "Her Body," Her Mind," "Her Suffering," "Her Appetite," and "Her Literature."

It is indicative of Miss Moore's approach that the author from whom she quotes most frequently in this volume is George William Bagby, who died in 1883. Bagby wrote perceptively and humorously of the antebellum and postbellum Virginians, and his writings are enjoying something of a vogue in the state at this time, but the fact that he is her most-cited source concerning the foibles, characteristics, and attitudes of Virginians is not without significance. Many of the things which Bagby said about Virginians and their *mores* sixty or seventy years ago, are as true today as they were then, but the fact remains that important aspects of latter-day Virginia civilization necessarily are not touched upon in his writings.

It is questionable, moreover, whether the "quintessence of Virginia" can be pinned to paper without a rather careful and thorough scrutiny of the state as it is in this fifth decade of the twentieth century. There is more to the Old Dominion in this year of our Lord than blackeyed peas and cider, trumpet vines and mockingbirds, plus a quick glance at Ellen Glasgow and James Branch Cabell. Miss Moore's remarkable, and largely unsupported, declaration that "no state in the Union could challenge Virginia's supremacy in higher education," does little to remedy these deficiencies. If her concern with the contemporary scene is somewhat broader than I have indicated, whole areas of interest are not touched by her at all.

However, "Virginia Is a State of Mind" captures the spirit of seventeenth, eighteenth, and nineteenth century Virginia in adequate fashion. Miss Moore has put together material of considerable variety and piquancy, and has gathered numerous lively anecdotes and pungent quotations, with the result that much of the atmosphere of old Virginia emerges. If the greater part of this material is familiar to informed citizens of the state, it is considerably less so outside Virginia's borders, and it is to be found nowhere else within the pages of a single volume.

Most of Miss Moore's writing is good, but some of it is bad. Her judgments concerning persons and places are provocative. For instance, she has a kind word to say for that pious old fraud, "Parson" Weems, who wrote the "life" of Washington, and embalmed therein for posterity the cherry tree yarn, with its immortal "I cannot tell a lie, Pa." She doubts if Weems invented this story, and considers the lingo which the parson attributes to Augustine Washington, George's father, "not un-Virginian." It will be remembered that George's "I cannot tell a lie, Pa," brought the following pearl from his pater: "Run to my arms! Glad am I, George, that you killed my tree, for you have paid me for it a thousandfold! Such an act of heroism in my son is worth more than a thousand trees of silver, with fruits of purest gold!" All I can say is, if that stilted piece of fustian is "not un-Virginian," then I'm going to tell everybody hereafter that I'm from Kansas.

Then there is Miss Moore's startling pronouncement that "the only real city in Virginia, Norfolk, is unavoidably so by reason of its fine harbor." The Norfolk Chamber of Commerce ought to appreciate this judgment, but when did the possession of a good harbor become the determining factor in such matters? By the same token, Marseilles is more important than Paris, Southampton more significant among municipalities than London. It is a novel concept, to say the least.

Miss Moore presents a quantity of Virginia lore in her book, most of it accurate, but she trespasses, at times, upon the historical verities. She accepts the familiar story of how Pocahontas saved Captain John Smith, although there is much uncertainty as to its authenticity. She declares that the father of George Mason, author of the Virginia Bill of Rights, fought in the army of Charles I. This first George Mason to come to Virginia was the great-grandfather, not the father, of George Mason of Gunston Hall. Four errors having to do with the Civil War were noted: (1) It is stated that "Stonewall" Jackson often raised his arm in prayer on the battlefield, but this is not accepted by historians. At First Manassas Jackson was wounded in the hand, and held the injured member up to stop the bleeding. When he raised it aloft on other fields, he is believed to have done so because of a delusion that this was necessary to exercise the limb. (2) The Bloody Angle is placed at Gettysburg, when it should have been put at Spotsylvania. (3) The McLeans, in whose home the terms of surrender were drafted at Appomattox, moved there from Manassas, to get away from the fighting, not from Gettysburg. (4) The Virginian who fired the first shot against Fort Sumpter was Edmund Ruffin, not Edmund Rufus. And finally, the celebrated teacher of law at the University of Virginia, John B. Minor, was known as "John B. Minor" or "old John B." — seldom, if ever, as "old John Minor," although Miss Moore says he is "always" called that in Virginia.

The only other major quarrel I have with Miss Moore is for her statement that Virginians are "raised on grits," and that they have it for breakfast and also for lunch. As a native of Miss Moore's County of Albemarle, I can testify that this is a grievous slander. Let her go to South Carolina or Georgia, and try to avoid having grits thrown at her in restaurants almost daily, along with pork, "turnip greens," and collards, but let her be more careful hereafter as to her dicta in the field of Virginia dietetics. I am surprised, too, that her book contains no apostrophe to the old Virginia mint julep. This is so startling an omission that it may even be seized upon by Kentuckians as evidence that their brummagen claims to primacy in the creation of the julep are justified.

CARLETON DREWRY

1901-

Carleton Drewry was born in Stevensburg, Culpeper County, Virginia on May 21, 1901. He grew up in Virginia, and first studied in a one-room school in the village of Gum Spring, in Louisa County, which was conducted by his father, a minister in the Methodist Conference of Virginia. He worked at a number of jobs from the time he was eighteen. He now lives in Roanoke, Virginia, where he is doing work in statistics for the Norfolk and Western Railway.

In his early twenties he began to contribute poetry to such leading periodicals as the *Dial*, the *Nation* and the *New Republic*. His first volume of poetry, *Proud Horns*, was published by the Macmillan Company in 1933. His second volume, *The Sounding Summer*, was published by E. P. Dutton and Company in 1948. He is also the author of much poetry and prose which he does not feel is sufficiently finished for publication.

THIS TREE*

At the last utterly
To earth's own end
Let the bole of this tree
Break when its boughs bend.

Let every branch blow bare,
All fallen leaves lie mute:
The mind was of the air,
The heart is with the root.

Now let the season claim
Another to the past
Who, naked of a name,
Enters the earth at last.

Forever be forgot
These boughs with blooms they bore
Where dead winds tremble not,
Trouble this tree no more.

*First published in *Poetry: A Magazine of Verse*, September 1945. Reprinted by permission.

LAWRENCE LEE

1903-

Lawrence Lee, well known as a Virginia poet, was born in Gadsden, Alabama, on January 3, 1903. He attended the public schools of Alabama and entered the University of Virginia in 1920. He edited the student magazine at the University in 1923-1924. When the *Virginia Quarterly Review* was established in 1925 a group of his poems appeared in the second issue, and he continued as a frequent contributor. He taught at the University of Virginia from 1930 to 1942. His first collection of verse, *This Was Her Country,* was published at the University in 1932. A larger collection, *Summer Goes On,* was published the following year by Scribner's and received considerable critical attention. He contributed poetry to the principal American and British literary magazines, and his volumes, *Monticello and Other Poems* (1937) and *The Tomb of Thomas Jefferson* (1940), added to a growing reputation. In 1939 he became editor of the *Virginia Quarterly Review* and served as editor for two years. During World War II he was a Naval officer in the European theatre. After the war he served as literary editor of *Reader's Scope* and as chairman of the editorial board of *'48 — The Magazine of the Year.* He is now completing a novel scheduled for publication in 1949.

THE TOMB OF THOMAS JEFFERSON*

Slowly the night gives way
And the great solemn woods
Grow wide with day.
The stars are gone,
But early morning broods
Upon the stone.

Once flesh and spirit woke
At such an hour as this,
And spirit spoke;
So we have set
This needle lest man miss
True north or else forget.

After the fallen leaf
So strict a form will show
Not all is brief,
Not all unsure
Of what man's mind may know,
His heart make pure.

If history falters now,
With vision a thin disk
Beyond a pitching bough,
We have the sky,
This obelisk
To travel by.

Look toward it as a sun
By which the brave must work;
For half undone

Lawrence Lee, 1903-

Is all he wrought,
And some, in deepening dark,
Would make it naught.

This is an ignorant year
Within a cruel time.
If he were here
We might rebuild
The firm wall raised by him,
The column felled.

In his creative grip,
As symbols of man's thought
Plain clay took shape.
Leaves, hawks in wind,
By inner sight were caught,
Their grace confined.

Mute marble or the word
Both one clean will expressed.
The line unblurred,
Proportioned stone,
Sang that the simple just
Had found their own.

Yet, he had enemies;
Allies who were but men.
We are of these,
Walkers of mud
Whose sweat shall keep earth green —
Or else whose blood.

In the long evening light,
To men returning home
This sign shows white.
Seeing afar,
Believe that good will come
As the first star.

JULIAN R. MEADE

1909-1940

Julian R. Meade was born in Danville, Virginia, on February 4, 1909, of a family which have been Virginians since the colonial period. His brother, Robert Douthat Meade, is the author of the biography, *Judah P. Benjamin: Confederate Statesman.* He grew up in Virginia and attended the University of Virginia. He early began to write and received the encouragement of Ellen Glasgow. In 1935 he published his first book, *I Live in Virginia,* a highly readable volume about his native state. It was followed the next year by *Adam's Profession and Its Conquest by Eve.* His novel, *The Back Door,* appeared in 1938 and *Bouquets and Bitters* in 1940. These busy years also saw the publication of three books for children: *Teeny and the Tall Man* (1936), *Miss Couch and the Scamps* (1938) and *Peter by the Sea* (1940).

Julian Meade died on July 9, 1940, at the age of thirty-one. He was just approaching his full powers as a writer, but he was already an author of substantial achievement.

Mary Lou, which follows, is the opening scene of *The Back Door,* a perceptive novel of Negro and white relationships in Virginia.

MARY LOU*

Mary Lou glanced at the clock on top of the kitchen cabinet. It was twenty minutes past four. Soon the meeting in Mrs. Pugh's living-room would be over and the ladies would be ready for their refreshments. Everything was in order: damp cloths covered the platters of sandwiches; the devil's-food cake and all the little silver bowles of almonds and mints and lemon slices stuck with cloves were lined up so there would be no mistake; gas was flaming under a kettle of water for the tea. Just for safety's sake (Mrs. Pugh would dog the life out of her if anything went wrong), she checked once more: napkins, cups and saucers, the best spoons . . .

"I be dawg!" she said to herself and the empty kitchen. "Lord ha' mercy, wouldn't I be puttin' my foot in a sweet mess of trouble if I forgot the tongs for that lump sugar?"

She pushed the swinging door to the dining room and tiptoed toward the sideboard; for once the silver drawer opened quietly and the tongs were in their place. She stood still and listened to the ladies in the living room. The door was not shut tight, so she could hear and see a little without being seen. There was a side view of one thin, long-faced lady standing and talking to all the other ladies who sat on the sofa and the crowded chairs. The thin lady wore a plain black hat and a black dress with a white lace collar and the glasses on her nose were chained to some sort of pin on her flat bosom.

"There's just one more announcement," whined the voice. "You've heard it before but I want to impress it on you so *nobody* will forget. Let's every one of us draw a ring on our calendars around the fifth of April — which isn't even a month off now. I want every man, woman, and child in our church to hear Reverend Hobart Miles

*Title supplied. From *The Back Door*, by Julian R. Meade. Published by Longmans, Green and Co. Copyright 1938 by Julian R. Meade. Reprinted by permission.

speak on 'Our Cross in Japan.' I believe we've got a rich experience ahead of us and I don't want anybody to miss it. I know we're going to hear a Message that will inspire us and make us *proud* that we've done our bit to further God's work on foreign soil. Reverend Miles is reported by all who've heard him as being a delightful speaker — as well as a consecrated Christian who has fought the good fight to save the world for Jesus. Everybody remember the fifth of April. As I said at our last get-together, the meeting will be at night in the church auditorium and afterward there will be a social hour so all of us can meet Reverend Miles. And, now, I *know* we'd like to have one more hymn before we hear from Mrs. Tucker about the sale of window cleaners. Mrs. Clayton, I wonder if we couldn't have Hymn 255. I'm sure it's dear to all of us — and it's in keeping with our thoughts this afternoon."

Mary Lou could not see the corner occupied by the piano. But she heard Mrs. Clayton playing the hymn through while the other ladies stood up, ready to burst into song. She hoped the vase of pussy willows would not fall off the piano.

> From Greenland's icy mountains,
> From India's coral strand,
> Where Afric's sunny fountains
> Roll down their golden sand.

Suddenly Mary Lou remembered the bathroom; Willie Pugh was just dumb enough to have gone in there and dirtied the wash-stand when his mother wanted everything as clean as a new pin. That morning, while she was stirring the cake batter, Mrs. Pugh had said, "Now, Mary Lou, *don't you fail* to have my bathroom so's I can take anybody in it." Then she had said to Mrs. Patrick from next-door who made the pink and green mints, "You know, Empsie, it just makes me sick to put out my best bath mat and my best company face towels. But that nosey Mrs. C. S. Jennings — why it's just like her to ask to go to the bathroom so she can see how I keep it."

Just to be on the safe side, Mary Lou tiptoed out of the dining room and across the dark hall by the hatrack. She turned the knob of the bathroom door and looked around; thank heavens, the bowl was just like it was when she finished scrubbing it and there were no signs of Willie Pugh. She closed the door and went back to the dining room to get the sugar tongs off the sideboard. The ladies were still singing.

> Can we whose souls are lighted
> With wisdom from on high,
> Can we to men benighted
> The lamp of life deny?

Although she did not understand some of those words, Mary Lou thought the tune of the hymn was pretty and when she reached the kitchen she could not keep from patting her feet in time with the music.

While she listened she got her small hand-mirror out of one of the cabinet drawers and looked at herself to see if she had the maid's cap fixed right. Mrs. Pugh wanted everything to be so stylish for company. When there were guests for dinner she used the butter spreaders which were folded in chamois skin the rest of the time; although Mr. Pugh complained and said he wanted a full cup of coffee with his meals just like he was used to having it, Mrs. Pugh took the tiny blue cups out of the corner cupboard and served coffee in the living room. Mary Lou hated all that as much as Mr. Pugh did, because it kept her on till nearly nine o'clock and Junie got tired of waiting out on the sidewalk . . . The cap looked nice, if she did say so herself. She wished Junie could see her now but maybe he wouldn't like it; he never stopped saying he hated for her to be in service. Junie thought nothing was good enough for her. She believed he *really meant it* when he said she was the prettiest girl in God's world. Was she really pretty? Well, Junie wasn't the only one who said it. Other boys tried to sweet-talk her; she knew how to put them off with a laugh but still she could not help wondering, even as she did now while she gazed into the mirror. She looked at her clear bright skin and her black eyes (that made Junie think of such fancy words) and her white teeth (that she brushed hard with salt and soda). Well, she *hoped* she was pretty because she *knew* Junie was a fine-looking boy. If another girl made any time with him she could not bear it. Even the slightest notion of losing him made a pain in her heart.

Footsteps on the back porch startled her and she looked up to see Willie Pugh at the kitchen door.

"Loafin' as usual?" he said. He was fifteen now but he still had the goslings; sometimes his voice was so funny Mary Lou had to bite her lip to keep from laughing. He was the most hateful white boy she knew. He never stopped stuffing his big flabby body; the kitchen, especially when his mother was away, was his favorite spot. He ate enough for six people and was lazier than the shiftiest Negro on Stoke Alley; ask him to help around the house a little and he sulked like a baby. "Listen, you, who's all those old ladies in yonder?"

"Missionary Circle," Mary Lou replied.

The boy approached the table and lifted the towel from one of the platters. She wished she could slap his cheeks. Whoever saw anybody with such shifty cat eyes in a big fat face? Why did people talk about "nigger lips" when Willie Pugh's mouth stuck forth like a pig's snout? He naturally had thick rubberish lips and, from the way he was always pouting, anybody would wonder if he were ready to suck an egg or if that was what came from spoiling babies with sugar tits and pacifiers.

"Mr. Willie, *please* don't bother them sandwiches."

"Go sit on a tack," the boy replied. He crammed one of the round sandwiches between his teeth and then he spoke with his mouth full. "I know durn well *you* hook a plenty on the sly."

She was hot inside but she made no answer. She knew some cooks stole but she had never stolen anything in her life and it made her sick with shame to be accused of roguishness. Mrs. Pugh counted eggs and oranges and was always saying, "I wonder what happens to the sugar" or "It beats me the way butter goes in this house." Sometimes Mary Lou was too tired at night to eat her supper and for a while she had taken home some rolls with meat between them or whatever she would have eaten at the kitchen table. But when Mrs. Pugh asked her not to "carry off" all the paper bags she knew what that meant and she stopped taking anything home. Well, Mrs.

Julian R. Meade, 1909-1940

Pugh would do better to watch Willie, who prowled around the refrigerator and bread box between meals like a starved rat. But, oh no, Willie would never bother anything. Never in this world.

"Mr. Willie, *please* keep out of that cake —"

He turned around and poked out his tongue at her. Why, who would think he was fifteen years old, going to high school? Let him be as ugly as he pleased; it did not hurt her and, anyhow, there was nothing she could do. But she would hate for Junie to hear him. Sweet Jesus, now that *would* be something.

He was opening the refrigerator door. There! She knew he would find that pitcher.

"That boiled custard is for supper, Mr. Willie —"

He picked up the white pitcher and, tilting it high, drank a mouthful. The thick yellow stuff dripped on his chin. She could hardly stand any more. She knew how his mother would be hounding her about the way things disappeared.

His fat hands were investigating every tray . . . There! He had found the three apple dumplings she was saving for tomorrow's lunch. Mrs. Pugh had said to warm them over and make some more hard sauce. There were only three and Mrs. Pugh would be mad as a hornet if one was missing.

"Look here, boy. Leave them dumplin's alone —"

" '*Mis*-ter Willie,' if you please," he said while he removed the bowl. "Good thing Mama didn't hear you call me 'boy.' "

He slammed the refrigerator door. Holding the bowl in one hand, he went to the table drawer for a spoon and then he began to gobble the cold dumpling. It made Mary Lou sick as well as mad to watch him.

"I'm certain'y gonna tell Mrs. Pugh," she said. "I'm not —"

"Up your fat yellow legs, you frizzle-headed coon!"

Mary Lou went to the window and looked out at the bare maple tree against the gray sky. Tears of rage filled her eyes; it was all she could do to be still; she wanted to fight back or to run away from this house where she was less than nothing to everybody except Mr. Pugh, and he was away most of the time. Dear Jesus, she thought, what a hateful white boy this is, what a dirty tongue he has!

She heard Mrs. Pugh coming through the dining room. Willie was quick to put the bowl with the other two dumplings back into the refrigerator. When his mother pushed through the swinging door his hands were on the water bottle and he was meek as a lamb.

"Thirsty, son? After Mama's meeting is over you can have some goodies. Now, make 'aste, Mary Lou! We're ready now. Turn up the gas under the kettle! I *told* you to put a parsley leaf on top of each sandwich. Didn't I show you that picture in Good Housekeeping Magazine? I know good and well I did. Well, come on now, make 'aste!"

That low-down boy had made her boiling mad but she made up her mind to forget him until she was through serving the ladies. If she got nervous and spilled or dropped anything it would only make matters worse.

As she went into the living room with the tray-load of steaming cups her ear-drums felt as though they would burst. Never had she heard such a racket in one room! The ladies sat together in groups and all of them seemed to be screaming at the same time.

She held the tray in front of the thin lady in black and white. The lady had her tea napkin spread out on her lap, all ready for her refreshments, but for the moment she was too lost in her own words to pay attention. So Mary Lou just stood there waiting.

"Oh, no, Mrs. Tucker, you don't understand my viewpoint. I *certainly do* think we need the sanatorium but we *don't* have to put it over at River View. You may call it prejudice if you like —"

Mrs. Pugh came up behind Mary Lou and interrupted the high voice.

"Tea, Miss Agnes?"

"Oh, please excuse me," piped Miss Agnes while she reached out a bony hand for the gold-banded cup. "I was so absorbed in what I was saying to Mrs. Tucker —"

Mary Lou passed on to the sofa where three ladies sat in a row. One of them, a plump-faced lady, whispered, "I hope it's not too strong for me. I wonder why some people want it strong as lye." Mary Lou did not know whether she was supposed to hear that but she said, "Could I bring you some hot water, ma'am?"

Julian R. Meade, 1909-1940

"Oh, no," said the plump-faced lady, looking a little surprised, "I was just running on. This will be perfectly all right."

As she moved along to the other side of the room Mary Lou heard one of the ladies on the sofa say, "Did you ever! Honestly, they're all ears. That's the reason I said just now Mrs. Tucker might be a little more careful about discussing this sanatorium business. But for all we know *she* discusses it *with them* —"

"Will you please tell me what this Circle has to do with a T. B. sanatorium for —"

One conversation was lost in another. All of a sudden Mary Lou nearly tilted the tray; after that she kept her mind strictly on her business and did not listen to the white ladies' words. She must be certain that everyone was served. Tea first, sandwiches next, then cake, last the almonds and mints. Mrs. Pugh was close behind her to see that nothing went wrong.

"Oh, now, Mrs. Clayton, you've got to try my devil's-food. I made it myself. Oh, go 'long, you're not fat. Why, the very *i*-dea. That's right, dear, take that corner piece with lots of icing."

Back in the kitchen again, she sat by the window and looked outside where starlings were scratching under the maple. It was getting darker every minute and the black clouds above the bare trees made her think of another cold March rain. Oh, Lord, she hoped not, for Stoke Alley was so muddy now she had to pick her way slowly step by step, trying to find firm places between deep puddles and slippery ruts and gullies. And, if the heavens poured much more water, the plank that served as foot-bridge across Minnow Branch would be covered as it was last October.

Once more she thought of the dumplings. She would be glad to be done with the matter one way or the other. Maybe Mrs. Pugh would be feeling good on account of the Missionary Circle; but there had been exactly enough dumplings for tomorrow's lunch and they never failed to make scraps do after any kind of party. Well, why worry? This job wasn't worth a hoot; even if she had to wait a while for something else, it would be mighty nice not to have Mrs. Pugh sniffing and snooping after her like the Law in skirt-tails.

Anyway, she and Junie and Miss Ada would get along; she and Junie always said they had each other while Miss Ada had the Lord.

"How come them Missionary ladies don't quit chewin' the rag an' go on home!" she said to herself while she got up to fill the kettle again. If she had hot water ready for the dishes she might get through a little sooner, so she lit the gas jet under the vessel and went back to her seat by the window; long ago Miss Ada told her that a watched pot takes longer to boil and she had never forgotten.

There was a mist on the window pane. Yes, it was beginning to drizzle.

"Mary Lou!"

She reached for her tray and hurried through the swinging door. Mrs. Pugh was bending over the dining-room table, seeing which tea napkins could be used again.

"Everybody's gone. Everything passed off real nice. Well, now, let's get busy. You can start right in on these dishes. Please be extra careful with my cups and saucers — they're my best, you know. We won't cook any supper. Mr. Pugh's away and I think Willie can do with sandwiches and cake. If he wants it, we can cook him some eggs —"

Mary Lou loaded her tray with china and returned to the kitchen. Mrs. Pugh, carrying the silver cream pitcher and the left-over lemon slices, came behind and went straight to the refrigerator. Mary Lou felt her heart pumping hard under her ribs but she tried to be hopeful. Oh, Lord, maybe Mrs. Pugh wouldn't say anything! She ought to be in a good humor when she had had her hair fixed by the beauty parlor and was all dressed up in her purple silk. But there! She couldn't set the cream pitcher down without seeing. Yes, Jesus, she was picking up the bowl.

Mary Lou stood right still and waited. Mrs. Pugh, holding the bowl in one hand, shut the refrigerator door. She turned around and her big face flushed crimson; her watery blue eyes were snappish and she pursed her full lips.

"What happened to the other dumpling?"

"I didn't bother it, Mrs. Pugh," Mary Lou replied, her voice quivering.

Julian R. Meade, 1909-1940

"It's getting to be so I *never* know what I've got. I was counting on dumplings for tomorrow's lunch. If you didn't bother them, who did? They couldn't walk away by themselves —"

"I didn't touch the dumplin's, Mrs. Pugh —"

"If you didn't, *who* did? Well, say something!"

"I rather not say, ma'am. But maybe Mr. Willie thought you didn't care if he was to eat it —"

Mrs. Pugh set the bowl on the table and hurried into the house. "Willie Pugh!" she screamed. "Willie Pugh!"

Mary Lou waited there by the kitchen table for a long, long minute. Then Mrs. Pugh came back, breathing hard under her purple silk because she was too fat and too angry. Willie came behind, shifty-eyed, sulking, and somehow like a snake ready to hiss.

"Willie, did you eat a dumpling out of that bowl?"

"No, ma'am, *I did not*. Who said I did?"

"Mary Lou says —"

The boy stuck out his mouth and glared for a second.

"She's a stinkin' liar. I haven't even been in this kitchen —"

Mary Lou could swallow no more.

"That's *not* so, Mr. Willie. Mrs. Pugh, *you* know it ain't so. You spoke to him yourse'f when he was gettin' water —"

"You forgot that, son —"

Willie was at a loss, but only for a moment.

"Oh, I forgot. Yeah, I did come in once to get a drink. But, long as she remembers so good, I remember something, too. She was eating something when I came in, because —"

"Why, Mr. Willie, you oughter be 'shamed!"

"You *were* eating, too! And, listen, Mama! She calls me 'boy' whenever you can't hear her —"

"What about them ugly words you called me?"

Mrs. Pugh held up her hand with the diamond ring so fine and glittering.

"Not another word! Willie, run on back in the house—"

"But, Mama, I'm not going to have her 'cusin me of what I didn't do!"

He could sound very meek and humble when he wanted to and he could beg like a baby. Mary Lou was mad now, more mad than frightened.

"We don't need to discuss this any more," Mrs. Pugh said. "I won't need you any more, Mary Lou. I'm sorry but I just can't have anybody in my house when —"

"I'll leave, Mrs. Pugh. It's O.K. about that. But what Mr. Willie said wasn't so."

"Don't you *dare* to say that again. I never knew a more truthful boy —" Mrs. Pugh was puffing and blowing. "You finish washing the dishes and I'll pay you for the two days I owe you for. At $5.00 a week I'll owe you — well, I'll figure it out and have the money ready —"

Mary Lou crossed the room and reached down in the corner by the cabinet for her things: the old slippers she used when she did heavy cleaning or scrubbing and the umbrella with the broken spoke. She got her mirror from the drawer and took her hat and coat off the hook. That was all.

"As long as I'm goin', Mrs. Pugh, I'd heap rather go right now —"

"I'm not going to pay your wages till you're through your work."

"That's all right, Mrs. Pugh. Maybe that money can he'p pay for them things you say I stolen."

Mrs. Pugh's big face was redder every second and her full lips twitched as her rage mounted higher. Mary Lou wanted to go quickly before she said something really bad, before back-talk led her into serious trouble.

"Suit yourself, Mary Lou. But my advice to you is to change your ways. You'll never get along the way you're going."

Mary Lou shut the door and went down the back steps into the rainy dusk.

BEN BELITT

1911-

Ben Belitt was born on May 2, 1911, in New York City. He came to Virginia when he was ten years old, attended public school there, and entered the University of Virginia in 1928. He received his A.B. degree in 1932, edited the student magazine in 1932-1933, held a service fellowship in English, received his M.A. degree in 1934, and worked toward his doctorate.

While at the university Belitt published poetry, short stories and reviews in a number of magazines. In January, 1936, he left the university to become assistant literary editor of *The Nation,* and later that year was co-winner of the Shelley Memorial Award for poetry. His first book of poems, *The Five-Fold Mesh,* was published in 1938. He resigned from *The Nation* in 1938 to join the faculty of Bennington College, Vermont, where he was a member of the Literature and Humanities faculty until 1942, when he entered the army.

During the war he served as an Infantry private, and later was employed at the U. S. Signal Corps Photographic Center, wrote a technical manual on motion picture cameras, and edited a film for the War Department archives on the action of the Seventh Army.

He was awarded a Guggenheim Fellowship in 1946. In 1947 he published a group of translations from Rimbaud. At present he is preparing a second book of poems.

NIGHTPIECE

Rise, cleanly trust, divided star,
And spend that delicate fraud upon the night—
A lover's instance, moving mindful air
To make its peace in dedicated light

Whose look is charnel. Lustres, intent and blind,
Give darkness downward with a glow, like sheaves,
A gleaner's pittance, withered in the bind,
That keeps the summer godhead of the leaves:

And bends tremendous evening under it,
Doubles its theft within a lonely course,
Till eye and eye repeat the counterfeit
And shape the replenishing mercy of its source.

All else were ravage: a demon-gaze of terror,
The emblem blackened in the living head,
The eye, the image, and the image-bearer
Struck to an awe with smiling on the dead.

Therefore that bounty which, however false,
Tenders survival, and is purely given,
. And lends the viewless prisms at its pulse
To make an easy legendry in heaven.

Restore that grace. Indeed, the look is grace
That deals this desert providence in air
And lifts a death's head, burning, into place
To serve a lover's faith.
                                    Rise, carrion star.

PRESTON NEWMAN
1913-

Preston Newman was born in Blacksburg, Virginia, on June 2, 1913. He grew up in Virginia, attended public school there, and entered the Virginia Polytechnic Institute in 1931. He did his undergraduate work in biology, receiving a B. S. degree in 1935, and graduate work in wildlife conservation. After leaving college he worked for the Virginia Wildlife Federation and for two Virginia newspapers. In 1939 he returned to the Virginia Polytechnic Institute as a member of the Department of English, where he is now Assistant Professor. His poems, marked by originality and an ironic temper, have appeared in *Poetry: A Magazine of Verse*, the *Nation* and the *New Republic*.

THE INDIANS IN THE MOVIES SAY "UGH!"*

The Indians in the movies say "Ugh!"
The Indians in the novels say "Me Chief Thundercloud. Me kill
    white man"
The Indians on the reservations say "Okay, so I owe you the two
    bucks"
But the Indians in the movies aren't real and the Indians in the nov-
    els aren't real and the Indians on the reservations aren't
    real either anymore

I wonder what the Indians really did say? How did they act? What
    did they do with their hands?

Hey there, Big Chiefs, what was it like to be an Indian?
    Powhatan? The British crowned me King of Virginia
    Little Turtle? I caught that elegant white man's disease —
        gout
    Seattle? They named a city for me and by the laws of my
        religion I must writhe in death each time the name
        is spoken
    Tecumseh? I was elevated in rank from Chief of the
        Shawnees to Brigadier-General in the British Army
    Black Hawk? They dug me up and put my head on exhibi-
        tion
    Crazy Horse? I remember only a bayonet in the belly
    Sitting Bull? They say I was a graduate of West Point and
        the author of French and Latin poems, I don't
        know, maybe I was
    Keokuk? My declining years were spent dead drunk
    Geronimo? I joined the Dutch Reformed Church and pa-
        raded at Teddy Roosevelt's first inauguration

*First published in *Poetry: A Magazine of Verse*, December, 1944. Reprinted by permission.

Preston Newman, 1913-

Hm-m-m...Had we better call in a white man. What about Kit
    Carson? He saw more redskins than any man who ever
    lived, he ought to know. Hey there, Kit, what were the
    Indians like?

There was an Arapaho girl named Grass Singing
and she was young and clean and high-breasted
Alice, I called her
And there was a Cheyenne girl, Making-Out-The-Road
and she burned bright and slow, like a pine-knot
They were good girls, those two
but I don't know how I felt about the Indians
Once at a camp above the Sacramento
the Tlamaths came war-whooping down at night
and leading them in was a frail old chief
When our bullets struck he fell at our feet
and the arrows in the fancy quiver on his back
rattled out across his shoulders
and his feathered bonnet fluttered to earth
like a bird dying
After we drove the Tlamaths back to the woods
I laid a blanket over their dead chief
At dawn I woke up, carefully removed the blanket
and with a hand-axe beat that brown old head
until the brains splashed out
and the blood spilled over the tangled feathers
I don't know how I felt about the Indians

Thank you, Kit. Goodnight. You must be tired, you once had a coun-
    try on your hands

But wasn't there someone somewhere who knew a plain ordinary
    Indian — no chief, no mystic, no warrior? Wasn't there
    a Blackfoot or a Cherokee who married the fat little girl
    from a neighboring tribe and built her a wigwam by the
    river? Weren't there cold winters when deer were scarce
    and buffalo moved their range and the hungry papooses

571

wailed on the sled? Wasn't there sickness? Good days and bad? Didn't this Indian like the smell of pinewoods after rain? Didn't he maybe grow old and live in the lodge of his tall sons? Didn't he maybe die a gentle death, remembering mountains, the feel of bearskins, fires at night?

Hey back there . . . Who knows? Who'll step forward and tell us now?

KARL SHAPIRO

1913-

Karl Shapiro was born in Baltimore, Maryland, on November 10, 1913. His family moved to Virginia, where he attended public school in Norfolk and entered the University of Virginia in 1932. He found the university uncongenial and left before the end of his first year. He spent the next years reading and writing. A privately printed volume of *Poems* appeared in 1935. He entered the library school of the Enoch Pratt Library in Baltimore and was working there when he was drafted into the army in March, 1941.

His first poems to attract attention were a group collected while he was at Camp Lee, Virginia, for the volume, *Five Young American Poets,* published in January, 1942. Later that year, while he was serving in the southwest Pacific area, his book, *Person, Place and Thing,* was published and received wide and enthusiastic critical acclaim. He was awarded a post-service Guggenheim Fellowship and a special award of the American Academy of Arts and Letters. *The Place of Love* was published in 1943 in Australia, but was not issued in the United States. *V-Letter and Other Poems* was published in 1944 and Shapiro was awarded the Pulitzer Prize for poetry. *Essay on Rime,* a 2,000-line verse-essay, was published in 1945 shortly after his return to the United States. For the most part, it was written, as was *V-Letter and Other Poems,* while he was on active duty in the southwest Pacific. In 1946 he was appointed Poetry Consultant at the Library of Congress in Washington, D. C., and made his home in near-by Arlington County, Virginia. In 1947 he published his fourth major volume, *The Trial of a Poet.*

JEFFERSON*

If vision can dilate, my noble lord,
Farther than porticos, Italian cells,
Newtonian gardens, Haydn, and cuisine,
Tell us, most serious of all our poets,
Why is the clock so low?

I see the tender gradient of your will;
Virginia is the Florence of your soul,
Yes, ours. The architecture of your hands
Quiets ambition and revives our skill
And buys our faithlessness.

So temperate, so remote, so sure of phrase,
Your music sweeps a continent, a sphere,
Fashions a modern language for a war
And by its cadence makes responsible
Our million names to you.

When you were old the god of government
Seemed to recede a pace, and you were glad.
You watched the masons through your telescope
Finish your school of freedom. Death itself
Stood thoughtful at your bed.

And now the surfaces of mind are rubbed
Our essence starts like serum from our eyes.
How can you not assume the deities
That move behind the bloodshot look and lean
Like saints and Salem devils?

ISRAFEL*

Picture the grave in his diabolical dream
Where death would come with clues and scenery,
The bulbous forehead and the crooked mouth
Leaking a poison, the translucent hands.

Perhaps like Juliet he could come alive
To hate Longfellow and to outrage life,
But dare not from his wretched rusty stone,
Landmark for girls developing in slums.

Here he is local color, another crank;
Pawnshops and whores and sour little bars
Accept him. Neither alarming nor prophetic,
He pleases like a wop or a jack-o-lantern.

Others up town forgive his nasty eyes
Because he was sick and had a mind to err;
But he was never dirty like Hawthorne,
But boyish with his spooks and funerals

And clammy virgins. What else were his codes
But diagrams of hideouts of the mind
Plugged up with corpses and expensive junk,
Prosopopoeia to keep himself at bay?

Think of him as a cicerone with data
False as a waxworks and that understood
Ask pitifully for pain. Or think that now
Four cities claim him as France recommended.

INDEX OF AUTHORS

576